Baedeker

Spain

Contents

Principal Sights of Tourist Interest

Note: The places listed above are merely a selection of the principal places of interest in themselves or for attractions in the surrounding area. There are of course innumerable other places worth visiting throughout Spain, to which attention is drawn by one or more stars.

Preface

This guide to Spain is one of the new generation of Baedeker guides.

These guides, illustrated throughout in colour, are designed to meet the needs of the modern traveller. They are quick and easy to consult, with the principal places of interest described in alphabetical order, and the information is presented in a format that is both attractive and easy to follow.

The present guide covers the whole of Spain, including the Balearics and the Canary Islands, and also takes in Spain's African possessions of Ceuta and Melilla as well as Andorra and Gibraltar.

The guide is in three parts. The first part gives a general account of the country, its topography, climate, flora and fauna, population, government and society, economy, history, art and culture. A number of suggested routes for visitors provide a lead-in to the second part, in which places and features of tourist interest – cities and towns, the different regions and islands – are described. The third part contains a variety of practical information. Both the sights and the practical information are listed in alphabetical order.

The new Baedeker guides are noted for their concentration on essentials and their convenience of use. They contain numerous specially drawn plans and colour illustrations; and at the end of the book is a large map making it easy to locate the various places described in the "A to Z" section of the guide with the help of the co-ordinates given at the head of each entry.

How to use this book

Following the tradition established by Karl Baedeker in 1844, sights of particular interest and hotels and restaurants of particular quality are distinguished by either one★ or two★★ stars.

To make it easier to locate the various sights listed in the "A to Z" section of the Guide, their co-ordinates on the large city map are shown in red at the head of each entry, e.g. ★ Barcelona P 3 .

Only a selection of hotels and restaurants can be given; no reflection is implied, therefore, on establishments not included.

The symbol ⓘ on a town plan indicates the local tourist office from which further information can be obtained. The post-horn symbol indicates a post office.

In a time of rapid change it is difficult to ensure that all the information given is entirely accurate and up to date, and the possibility of error can never be completely eliminated. Although the publishers can accept no responsibility for inaccuracies and omissions, they are always grateful for corrections and suggestions for improvement.

5

Facts and Figures

Spain is one of the world's great holiday countries; but it has much more to offer than its endless beaches and its southern sun. Its attractions lie not only along its coasts but inland: not only world-famous sights like the Alhambra in Granada, Seville Cathedral and the monastery of Montserrat but a variety of beautiful scenery, numbers of picturesque villages and towns and a profusion of splendid churches and castles, many of them awaiting discovery well away from the beaten tourist track. This guide covers not only the Spanish mainland but also the outlying islands as well as the neighbouring territories of Andorra and Gibraltar.

General

Situation and territory

The kingdom of Spain (Reino de España or Estado Español) lies in the extreme south-west of Europe, between latitude 36° and 44° north and between longitude 9° west and 5° east. It is bounded on the north by France and the tiny state of Andorra, on the west and north-west by Portugal and on the south by the British territory of Gibraltar, which is claimed by Spain. The Atlantic washes the Spanish coasts on the north (Bay of Biscay), north-west and south-west (Gulf of Cádiz), to the west of the Straits of Gibraltar, only 14km/9 miles wide, which separate Europe from Africa. Within the straits the whole of eastern and south-eastern Spain is bounded by the Mediterranean. Also part of Spain are the Balearic Islands (Majorca, Minorca, Ibiza, Formentera and various smaller islands), which lie off the Mediterranean coast, and the Canary Islands (the largest of which are Gran Canaria and Tenerife) off the north-west coast of Africa. The towns of Ceuta and Melilla on the North African mainland and the three small islands of Peñón de Vélez, Alhucemas and Chafarinas off the Moroccan coast also belong to Spain (*presidios* or *plazas de soberanía*), but are claimed by Morocco.

Spain

© Baedeker

The Straits of Gibraltar serve rather to link Spain with Africa than to separate the one from the other; but the almost continuous bastion of the Pyrenees in the north has been, both geographically and historically, a barrier between Spain and the rest of Europe.

Area

Spain, including the Balearics, the Canaries and the North African enclaves, has a total area of 504,782 sq.km/194,897 sq.miles. Of this total 492,463 sq.km/190,140 sq.miles are accounted for by mainland Spain – roughly four-fifths of the total area (595,000 sq.km/230,000 sq.miles) of the Iberian peninsula – 7242 sq.km/2796 sq.miles by the Canaries and 5014 sq.km/1954 sq.miles by the Balearics. The Atlantic coast of Spain is 711km/442 miles long, with a further 770km/478 miles on the Bay of Biscay; the Mediterranean coast is 1663km/1033 miles long, giving Spain a total coastline of 3144km/1954 miles.

◀ On the Costa Brava

Topography

Natural Regions

From the morphological point of view three topographical forms can be distinguished in mainland Spain: the central plateau (Meseta), the inner ring of mountains surrounding this plateau and the mountains and basins on the outer fringes.

Central plateau
(Meseta)

The vast plateau of the Meseta extends over an area of more than 200,000 sq.km/77,000 sq.miles at altitudes of between 600 and 1000m (2000 and 3300ft). The Cordillera Central or Central Range, consisting of the Sierra de Gredos to the south-west of Madrid, which rises to 2592m/9504ft in the Pico de Almanzor, and the Sierra Guadarrama (highest point Pico Peñalara, 2430m/7973ft) north-west of the capital, divides the Meseta into a northern half, the Meseta Septentrional, and a southern half, the Meseta Meridional. The smaller Northern Meseta takes in the historical provinces of Old Castile and León and is

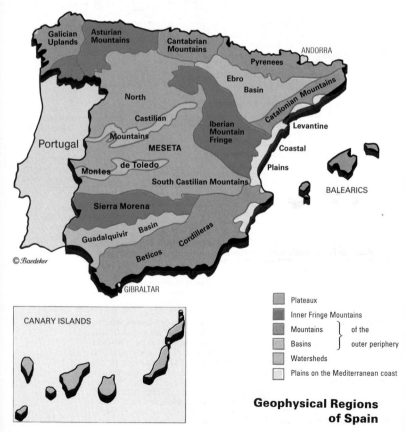

	Plateaux
	Inner Fringe Mountains
	Mountains } of the
	Basins } outer periphery
	Watersheds
	Plains on the Mediterranean coast

**Geophysical Regions
of Spain**

8

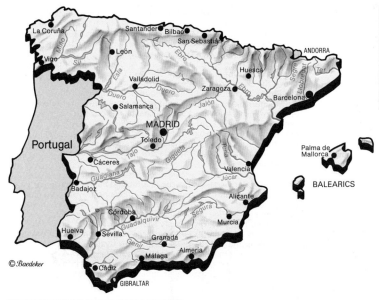

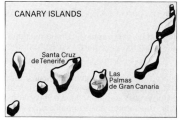

**Rivers,
Lakes and
Reservoirs
in Spain**

traversed by the River Duero. The Southern Meseta corresponds to the provinces of New Castile and Extremadura, which slopes down on the south-east to between 300 and 150m (1000 and 500ft). The southern plateau is drained by the Tagus (Tajo) and the Guadiana, with the Montes de Toledo separating the Tagus basin from the Guadiana basin.

To the north are the Asturian Mountains, whose highest point, in the Picos de Europa, is the Torre de Cerredo (2648m/8688ft). The Iberic Mountains, partly plateau-like and partly mountainous (Sierra de Moncayo, 2313m/7589ft), form the northern, north-eastern and eastern border of the central plateau, reaching towards the Mediterranean coast and falling steeply down to the Ebro basin. The Southern Meseta is separated from the Guadalquivir basin by the relatively low (up to 1300m/4265ft) but barren Sierra Morena.

Inner ring
of mountains

In the extreme north-west of Spain are the Galician Uplands, with a coastline indented by numerous rías (drowned river estuaries), giving the landscape the character of the Norwegian fjords. To the north the

Fringe regions

9

Cantabrian Mountains, rising to 1700m/5600ft, link the Asturian Mountains (part of the inner mountain ring) with the Pyrenees, which reach their highest point in the Pico de Aneto (3404m/11,169ft). To the southwest are the Catalonian Mountains, rising to 1700m/5600ft. These last two ranges enclose the basin of the Ebro, which cuts its way through the Catalonian Mountains to the Mediterranean.

In the south the Cordillera Bética or Andalusian Mountains extend from the Strait of Gibraltar to Cabo de la Nao, with Spain's highest peaks, the Cerro de Mulhacén (3481m/11,421ft) and the Pico de Veleta (3428m/11,247ft), in the Sierra Nevada. The range falls down towards the Mediterranean, affording a link at a relatively low level between the Southern Meseta and the Valencia coastal region. The Balearics are a continuation of the Cordillera Bética. Between the Cordillera and the Sierra Morena lies the basin of the Guadalquivir, which flows into the Atlantic in an extensive delta. The Mediterranean coastal plains around Barcelona, Valencia and Murcia are frequently referred to as the Levante.

Rivers and lakes

The main watershed between the Atlantic and the Mediterranean runs from the Pyrenean river Ariège, which flows northward into France, along the main ridge of the Pyrenees and the ridge of the Cantabrian Mountains to the Pico de los Tres Mares at the east end of the Asturian Mountains. There it turns sharply south-east and then, before the Río Jalón, bears south, after which it turns west again in the Cordillera Bética. Thus the only large Spanish river system flowing into the Mediterranean is that of the Ebro. All the other large rivers – the Duero, the Tagus, the Guadiana and the Guadalquivir – flow into the Atlantic.

Spain has no large inland lakes, though there are numerous artificial lakes formed by dams.

Historical Regions

In addition to these regions defined by geographical conditions there are a series of historical regions conditioned partly by natural and partly by political factors.

Catalonia

Catalonia (Catalunya in Catalan, Cataluña in Spanish) is the most northerly of the Spanish Mediterranean regions, which as a result of their natural conditions and historical development have a very different character from inland Castile. The Catalonian Mountains run parallel to the coast, linking the eastern Pyrenees with the hills bordering the Meseta on the north-east. Originally a continuous range, they were later broken up by tectonic disturbances into isolated massifs – Montseny (1745m/5725ft) in the north, Montserrat (1241m/4072ft) with its famous monastery and Montsant (1071m/3513ft) in the south.

Catalonian Longitudinal Valley

Between the main mountain range and a lower coastal chain extends the Catalonian Longitudinal Valley, a syncline filled with Late Tertiary deposits. This is the heart of the region, densely populated and covered with olive-groves, vineyards, market gardens and plantations of cork-oaks, particularly round Gerona. The rivers flowing down from the Pyrenees, in particular the Llobregat, cut through the hills in narrow gorges; their abundant flow of water, used for irrigation from early times, is now also harnessed to provide electric power for industry. In the west Catalonia extends also into the Ebro basin.

Pyrenees

Catalonia also includes a region of sparse population and rugged mountain scenery in the Pyrenees. In the mountains, near the source of the Río Segre, is the remote little republic of Andorra, which has maintained its separate existence since the 9th century. In the east the

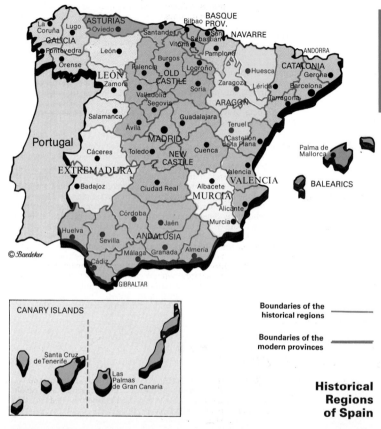

Boundaries of the
historical regions

Boundaries of the
modern provinces

**Historical
Regions
of Spain**

Pyrenees fall down in a number of separate ridges to the Ampurdán uplands, where olive-groves, vineyards and woods of cork-oak fringe the base of the hills.

As Hispania Tarraconensis, Catalonia was the first nucleus of Roman Spain. After periods of Visigothic and Moorish rule it became the Spanish March of the Frankish kingdom, until Wilfred the Hairy broke free of Frankish control in 874 and established the Condado de Barcelona. In the middle of the 12th century it was united with Aragon by marriage, and in 1469, together with Aragon, it was joined to Castile, losing political and economic importance but preserving its constitutional freedom and many special rights and privileges (*fueros*). In 1640, when Philip IV levied troops for war with France and demanded oppressive taxes, the Catalans resisted, and with French help held out for some time against Spanish forces. The surrender of Barcelona in 1652, however, was followed by the re-establishment of Spanish authority, though the Catalan *fueros* were renewed. Not until the wars of liberation against Napoleon was Catalonia finally united with Spain. The flowering of Catalan literature, however, demonstrated that

History

11

Catalonia's separate political and cultural consciousness was still very much alive.

Economy

The densely populated region of Catalonia has become the economic centre and the most progressive part of Spain. A leading place is occupied by the textile industry, in Barcelona, Sabadell and Tarrasa; part of the Spanish automobile industry has developed around Barcelona; and other important branches of industry are leatherworking, papermaking, the manufacture of soap from olive oil, the production of ironmongery and cork processing.

The Costa Brava, with its beautiful hinterland, is one of the great Meccas of mass tourism.

Aragon and Navarre

The old kingdoms of Aragon and Navarre fall mainly within the Ebro basin, a depression formed by Late Tertiary limestones, clays and marls lying between the Pyrenees in the north and the scarplands bordering the Meseta in the south-west, forming an acute angle in the north-west and cut off from the Mediterranean by the Catalonian Mountains. The Ebro, flowing down from the Catalonian Mountains, enters the basin through the Conchas de Haro, continues with a fairly gentle gradient and carves a narrow passage through the Catalonian Mountains to the sea. In contrast to the busy activity of Catalonia and the almost Central European character of the Basque provinces, the featureless uplands of Aragon have an austerity and isolation reminiscent of Castile. Enclosed by hills, they have a continental climate like that of the Meseta, with arid summers during which an oppressive heat haze (*calina*) hangs over the whitish-grey plain. With a high salt and gypsum content, the soil is infertile, nourishing only a steppeland of esparto grass and meagre grazing for sheep. The growing of corn, vegetables and other crops is confined to the land bordering the rivers,

The Irati valley in the Pyrenees

particularly the Ebro and the Segre. Almost the only source of irrigation is the Canal Imperial, which runs along the right bank of the Ebro for some 90km/55 miles. The few settlements of any size in this sparsely populated land are to be found in these oases straggling along the rivers, the *huertas*. The capital of Aragon, Zaragoza, lies in one of these huertas, in which almonds, olives, figs and vines all flourish.

To the north Aragon and Navarre extend to the main ridge of the Pyrenees. At the west end, where they adjoin the Cantabrian Mountains, they are still of medium height, rising to not much over 1500m/4900ft and passable at many points without difficulty. In this region, where the Basques are settled on both sides of the mountains, the little kingdom of Navarre developed, strategically situated in command of the passes. Its capital, Pamplona, lies in a treeless basin between the main Pyrenean ridge and the sierra zone. To the east of the Somport pass (1631m/5351ft) the Pyrenees form a mighty mountain barrier, with few passes, which reaches its highest point in the Pico de Aneto (3404m/11,169ft), in the Maladeta group, a granite massif on the Spanish side of the range. The central ridge, made up of metamorphic and magmatic rocks, shows signs of considerable glaciation in the form of small mountain lakes and valleys. The gentler scarps on the south side, contrasting with the steep rock faces on the French side, consist mainly of much folded Cretaceous and Tertiary rocks, as does Monte Perdido (Mont Perdu; 3352m/10,998ft). The Spanish side of the Pyrenees has little rain and therefore lacks the green mantle of forest found on the northern slopes, the flanks of the valleys being clad only with meagre mountain pastures and scrub.

Pyrenees

The Basque provinces of Guipúzcoa, Vizcaya and Alava occupy the eastern part of the Cantabrian Mountains, between the valley of the Nervión, which reaches the sea at Bilbao, and the Pyrenees. This is an upland region of medium height, with only a few peaks rising higher, like the Peña de Gorbea (1475m/4839ft). The coastal hills are separated from the main ridge of the Cantabrian Mountains by longitudinal valleys through which east–west traffic passes. Under the influence of the moist north and north-west winds this coastal tract produces a rich growth of vegetation. At the higher altitudes there are forests of oak, beech and chestnut or, where these have been destroyed, a dense growth of bracken or plantations of pines and eucalyptus. The hills and valleys are covered with meadows, fields of maize and groves of walnuts and fruit-trees. In certain favoured areas a light country wine (Chacolí) is produced, but the usual drink is cider (Basque *sagardüa*, Spanish *sidra*). The northern slopes of the Cantabrian Mountains are a pleasant region, with a climate which is agreeable even in summer and a landscape of lush green fields and picturesque Basque farms (*caseríos*). The coast is particularly attractive, with cliffs frequently rising to over 300m/1000ft and little fishing towns, many of which have developed into popular seaside resorts.

Basque country
(Basque Euskadi; Spanish País Vasco)

The southern slopes of the Cantabrian Mountains differ in landscape and economy from the coastal regions. Wide open valleys alternate with larger basins; the rainfall is considerably lower, and wheat rather than maize is grown. In the open landscapes of Álava province the pattern of settlement takes the form of compact villages rather than the separate farmsteads of the coast.

Interior

The economic life of the Basque provinces is closely bound up with the products of their soil. In addition to agriculture – still to some extent carried on by simple techniques – there is a well developed metalworking industry based on the iron ores of Bilbao, and the abundance of timber provides the raw material for a furniture-making industry which has a national reputation. A plentiful supply of water favours papermaking, particularly in Guipúzcoa, and the mountain streams have been harnessed to supply electric power.

Economy

Topography

Asturias

The former principality of Asturias, now a province named after its capital, Oviedo, is a mountainous region extending along the Bay of Biscay to the west of Santander province, almost completely occupied by the Cantabrian Mountains, here rising to Alpine altitudes and reaching a height of 2642m/8668ft in the Picos de Europa. In the west they are wild and rugged, offering unexpectedly romantic mountain scenery. High passes run south through the range, but only the Puerto de Pajares (1364m/4475ft), which is followed by the road from Oviedo to León, links Asturias with central Spain.

Oviedo basin

In the centre of Asturias – covered, thanks to its oceanic climate, with a green mantle of vegetation – is the Oviedo basin, a fertile upland region extending to the coast. Asturias has few towns, the only one of any size apart from Oviedo being the port of Gijón. Along the picturesque coast, with its sheer cliffs, are many small fishing settlements which have in most cases developed in recent years into lively little seaside resorts.

Economy

The economy of Asturias is based on the growing of maize and fruit and on stock-farming (particularly pigs: the ham of Asturias is renowned). The agricultural population live in small villages, individual farms and, most commonly, in straggling hamlets. The coal-mines of Asturias are also of major economic importance, supplying half Spain's total output of coal. Other minerals are fluorspar, zinc and iron, which have promoted the industrial development of the region. The lowlands yield peat and amber.

Galicia

Galicia (Galician form Galizia) occupies the north-western corner of the Iberian peninsula, extending south to the frontier with Portugal. The mountain chains which dominate so much of Spain are lacking here. The extensive areas of granite and other crystalline rocks have

A Galician hórreo (maize store)

militated against the development of any particular line of folding, so that the river systems have played a more important part in determining the topography of the region than in the Cantabrian Mountains. Here wooded valleys (pine, oak, eucalyptus), in the form of elongated basins like that of the Miño, are enclosed by ridges of hills, between which are plateaux traversed by numerous rivers flowing through steep narrow valleys.

A particular feature of Galicia is the series of long fjord-like inlets at the mouths of the rivers, known as *rías* (the Rías Altas on the north coast, the Rías Bajas on the west coast). These arms of the sea, often with beautiful sandy beaches, provide safe havens on the storm-swept coast, and some of them contain important Atlantic ports like Vigo and La Coruña.

Rías

By Spanish standards Galicia is an economically underdeveloped region. Industry is found only round the large towns of La Coruña and Vigo, and accordingly fishing, particularly for sardines, plays an important part in the Galician economy. The low ridges of hills along the rías are covered with forests and a variety of crops. In the interior the tenant farmers gain a modest subsistence on their small and heavily burdened holdings, growing maize, corn and, in the south-west, grapes. The mild damp climate also favours stock-farming. The extraction of tin and tungsten also makes an important contribution to the economy.

Economy

All over Galicia are found the *hórreos* – granaries for the storage of maize – which are characteristic of the region. These temple-like structures, raised high above the ground on stone supports to provide protection from vermin and splashing rain, have side walls of stone slabs or wooden laths set closely together, leaving only narrow slits which allow the wind to enter but not birds or large insects. Between the main structure and the supports is a projecting slab of stone which denies access to mice. The maize cobs are stored whole and are taken out and threshed as required. In Asturias the hórreos are larger and are square in form, built of wood and roofed with straw.

Hórreos

Castile (Spanish form Castilla), the heartland of Spain, is an inland region, the Meseta (the "large table"), bordered by ranges of hills, with most of its area lying far from the sea. The plateau, formerly defended by a string of castles, is divided by the Central Castilian Range, consisting of the Sierra de Guadarrama, the Sierra de Gredos and the Sierra de Gata, into Old Castile (Castilla la Vieja) to the north and New Castile (Castilla la Nueva) to the south-east. The two parts of the plateau, in which the basement rock is covered by more recent deposits, slope down towards the west and are traversed by large but non-navigable rivers, which cut through the western rim in rocky gorges. The northern scarp, in the province of Santander, a region of oceanic climate, is formed by the Cantabrian Mountains.

Castile

The considerable altitude of the Meseta (900m/2950ft and over in Old Castile, 600–700m/2000–2300ft in New Castile) gives the climate a continental character, with hot summers and severe winters. Most of the land was formerly left unused as a result of the low rainfall (400mm/15¾in.), lack of trees and scanty population, but more recently has been brought under cultivation (wheat, etc.) following the construction of reservoirs to provide irrigation and afforestation with quickly growing eucalyptus trees. The spring and autumn rains produce grazing for the merino sheep from Extremadura which are brought here in summer. On the large expanses of fertile steppeland in León, around Palencia, Valladolid and Zamora, and on the Mesa de Ocaña in New Castile (with artificial irrigation in some areas), corn is grown, as well as the popular *garbanzos* (chick peas), an essential

Meseta

ingredient of the national dish, *cocido.* Along the eastern and northern edges of the Meseta are the bleak and empty *páramos* or *parameras,* high and arid limestone plateaux, lashed by wind in winter, formed of rocks which are older than those in the lower-lying areas, and thus older than the dusty limestone expanses of Don Quixote's La Mancha.

Monotonous and colourless as the central Spanish plateau may be, it has its moments of scenic grandeur when the sun sinks down in the west and the red colouring of the soil merges into the varying hues of the sunset sky.

León

The three provinces of León, Zamora and Salamanca which make up the old historical region of León are now regarded, geographically and administratively, as belonging to Castile–León. They take in the greater part of the northern Meseta, which is bounded on the north by the Cantabrian Mountains and on the south by the Sierra de Gredos. The central part of the region is occupied by the Duero basin, which is dissected in varying degree by the Río Duero and its tributaries.

At higher altitudes poor soils and unfavourable weather conditions allow only modest arable farming and stock-farming (cattle, including fighting bulls, and sheep) on pastures (*dehesas*) with a loose scatter of cork-oaks. In the valleys of the rivers, which are increasingly being dammed to provide water for irrigation and the production of electric power, wheat (in Zamora) and rye (in León) are grown. The character of the people matches the unyielding nature of the landscape. The older generation are strongly attached to their traditional way of life, while the young emigrate to the towns or to other parts of Spain.

History

León has a glorious history going back to Visigothic times, which have left some relics of art and architecture. After the foundation of the kingdom of Asturias by Pelayo following his victory over the Moors Alfonso III (866–919) pushed its frontiers southward to the Duero and moved its capital from Oviedo to León, which then gave its name to the kingdom. After its union with Aragon and Navarre the kingdom of León enjoyed a period of prosperity, but was repeatedly weakened by conflicts with Castile, whose power had been increased by the Reconquista. In the reign of Alfonso VI (1065–1109), whose vassal Rodrigo Díaz de Vivar is celebrated in the Spanish epic as the Cid, Castile itself became subject to the crown of León, and the king claimed the title of emperor. León's independence was finally lost, however, in 1230, during the reign of Ferdinand III, son of Alfonso IX of León and of a daughter of Alfonso VIII of Castile.

Valencia

Valencia occupies a narrow coastal strip extending from the Ebro delta to the mouth of the Río Segura – though the province of Alicante, south of Cabo de la Nao, belongs geographically to Murcia. Here the treeless reddish-grey limestone and sandstone plateaux of the Meseta approach the sea and terminate in steep and rugged coastal cliffs slashed by narrow river gorges. The rivers flowing down from the interior, like the Guadalaviar and the Júcar, which surge down in great spates (*avenidas*) after thunder showers or when the snow melts, depositing fertile alluvial soil along the coast, provide water for the irrigation of the thirsty lands lying in the rain shadow of the hills. The irrigation system, first constructed by the Romans and later developed by the Moors, makes Valencia the most fertile part of Spain. An ancient code of regulations provides for the equitable distribution of the precious water, which is carried far and wide throughout the region in a network of countless canals and smaller channels and stored up during the winter in reservoirs (*pantanos*) against the summer drought.

Huertas

The irrigated areas (the *campo de regadío*) form the *huertas,* in which crops grow and ripen so rapidly that several harvests can be taken in a year. In addition to fields of wheat, maize, lucerne and vegetables there

A windmill in Murcia

are also, particularly around the marshy Albufera lagoon to the south of Valencia, extensive rice-fields, which must lie under water for many weeks. In the shade of the orange-, apricot-, almond- and fig-trees melons, tomatoes and other vegetables are grown. More attractive than the huertas, on which the fruit-trees are frequently set out in regular geometric formation, are the areas where the fruit orchards are planted on terraces, with clumps of slender palms and cypresses adding variety to the scene. On the non-irrigated land, the *campo secano,* olives, vines and carobs flourish. The little white houses of the peasants (*hortulanos*) are scattered about at regular intervals in the green of the huertas. The creaking water-wheels (*norias*) of the Moors, powered by donkeys, are increasingly giving way to electric pumps and are now only rarely to be seen.

In addition to agriculture and tourism the Valencia area has considerable industry – silk and wool weaving, papermaking, the winning of salt from the coastal lagoons, fishing and the processing, canning and export of agricultural produce.

    The capital, Valencia, is one of the most attractive towns in Spain. Its port, Grao, ships the produce of the huertas.

Economy

Adjoining Valencia on the south is Murcia, where the Andalusian Mountains reach the sea. The northern ranges run parallel to the coast, ending in the limestone promontory of Cabo de la Nao; much of the southern range has sunk, and only isolated fragments like the Sierra de Cartagena still rise out of the coastal plain, formed of soil deposited by the rivers, which with the exception of the Río Segura are short and have a poor flow.

Murcia

The climate is extremely hot and dry. From the end of July until the end of September the heat haze (*calina*) blankets the countryside: the sky

Summer heat

appears bluish-grey, and the rising sun and moon gleam redly through the brownish haze on the horizon. Thinly populated except in the oases along the river valleys, the region is a desert-like salt steppe on which only esparto grass and a meagre covering of scrub can grow. Some cultivation is made possible by irrigation, but this is limited by the shortage of water. In the huertas of Murcia, Totana and Lorca oranges, lemons, mulberries and dates are grown, and Elche is famous for its forest of date-palms, originally planted by the Arabs.

Economy

A major contribution to the economy of Murcia is made by the mining of lead, zinc and iron, particularly in the Sierra de Cartagena.

As a result of the levelling influence of tourism along the coasts the people of both Valencia and Murcia have lost much of their distinctive individuality, little of which survives even in folk events put on for the benefit of tourists.

Extremadura

Extremadura is the western continuation of the Meseta, but in this region the tableland is more deeply slashed by the trough valleys of the Tagus (Tajo) and Guadiana and their tributaries. On the north it is separated from León and Old Castile by the Sierra de Gata (1735m/5693ft), the Sierra de Béjar and the Sierra de Gredos (2592m/8504ft). It falls away towards Andalusia in the gently sloping Sierra Morena, and is divided by the Sierra de Guadalupe (1736m/5696ft) into Extremadura Alta (Upper Extremadura: Tagus valley, Cáceres province) and Extremadura Baja (Lower Extremadura: Guadiana valley, Badajoz province).

Agriculture

The region is dry, and much of it is covered with stony moorland (*jarales* or *tomillares*), particularly at the foot of the Sierra de Gata (the area known as Las Hurdes, where wheat-growing has been developed on a considerable scale). The growing of corn and pulses is confined to the Cáceres area and Extremadura Baja, frequently exposed to the hazards of inundation by the rivers and devastation by swarms of migratory locusts (*langostas*) from the moorland regions. Vines, olives, figs and almonds grow in the valleys, mulberries only in the Plasencia area, where the hillsides are terraced to form orchards. Pig-farming flourishes in the oak forests of Extremadura, and the hams produced there are reckoned to be the best in Spain.

Sheep-farming

From time immemorial Extremadura has been traversed in the winter months by flocks of transhumant merino sheep, which come down from the Meseta in autumn to seek fresh grazing, under the system known as the Mesta. In order to avoid conflicts between the settled peasant farmers and the owners of the sheep a special court, the Consejo de la Mesta, was set up in 1526; and in 1834 it was laid down by statute that a strip of grazing land 90 yards wide (the *cañada real*) must be left on either side of main roads for the use of the sheep-drovers.

Andalusia

For many people Andalusia (Spanish form Andalucía) is the Spain of their imagination. It is a land of fascinating contrasts – of snow-capped mountains and massive coastal dunes, of sun-scorched plateaux and lush green huertas along the rivers, of palm-groves and heaths covered with rock roses. To all this it adds the monuments of a glorious past, culminating in the Mosque in Córdoba with its forest of columns and the gleaming red towers and beautiful patios of the Alhambra in Granada.

Andalusian
Mountains

The southern part of Andalusia is dominated by the Andalusian Mountains or Cordillera Bética. This range of folded mountains running from the south towards the main Iberian land-mass consists of an inner zone

Andalusian landscape, Medina Azahara

of crystalline schists and an outer zone of Mesozoic and Tertiary sediments, which begins at the limestone rock of Gibraltar and extends north to the Jaén uplands. Later tectonic disturbances have produced collapse basins such as the fertile vega of Granada and formed a sheer scarp to the Mediterranean. Although the range includes Spain's highest peak, Mulhacén (3481m/11,421ft), it consists mainly of rounded hills of medium height. The higher altitudes, with large areas of scree, are covered with steppe vegetation, grazing suitable only for goats and macchia-like scrub. At lower levels are forests of cork-oaks and chestnuts. The region is thinly populated, and the high valley of the Alpujarras has afforded refuge to a population which still shows strong Moorish traits.

Very different is the more densely populated coastal strip to the south, which is subject to the influence of the moist sea winds and has become a Mecca of international tourism. This is a region of fruit orchards, plantations of sugar-cane and bananas, vineyards and cotton fields laid out on terraces. Málaga has considerable industry and its port handles a large export trade, particularly in its famous wine. Algeciras and Cádiz are also busy industrial towns.

The coast

Between the Andalusian Mountains and the Sierra Morena are the Andalusian Lowlands, a former arm of the sea filled with Tertiary and alluvial deposits and watered by the River Guadalquivir. The eastern part of the Guadalquivir basin is a much dissected upland region: only below Seville is it a genuine lowland area. In this area are the *marismas,* great expanses of fenland occupied by waterfowl and herds of bulls. The hot dry uplands are still largely covered with steppeland and areas of grazing for fighting bulls and Andalusian horses. Wheat and vegetables, vines and citrus fruits are grown only in those areas where irrigation is available. Andalusia's capital, Seville, lies in a fertile garden landscape of this kind. The province of Cádiz, turned towards the

Andalusian Lowlands

Topography

sea, is a region of large landowners and sharp contrasts in the social structure.

Economy

Together with agriculture and tourism mining plays a major part in the economy of Andalusia. The Sierra Morena produces copper (Río Tinto) and zinc (Linares), the Andalusian Mountains lead, silver and iron (Almería). Stock-farming (horses, mules, cattle, fighting bulls) also makes an important contribution.

Balearics

The Balearic Islands (Illes Balears in Catalan, Islas Baleares in Spanish) lying off the south-east coast of Spain in the western Mediterranean, between latitude 38° and 40° north and between longitude 1° and 4° east, consist of the Balearics proper (the two main islands of Majorca, with an area of 3640 sq.km/1405 sq.miles, and Minorca, with an area of 700 sq.km/270 sq.miles) and the smaller group of the Islas Pityusas, made up of Ibiza (in the local dialect Eivissa; 572 sq.km/221 sq.miles) and Formentera (100 sq.km/39 sq.miles), together with some 150 smaller islands, including Cabrera (17 sq.km/6½ sq.miles), to the south of Majorca, and numbers of rocky islets, some used for military or nautical purposes, others totally unoccupied.

The name of the Balearics is derived from the Latin *balearii* ("sling-throwers"), which may come either from the Greek *ballein* ("throw") or the Semitic *ba'al yarah* ("skilled in using the sling"). The name of the Pityusas comes from the Greek *Pityoussai* ("islands of pines").

All these islands together form the Comunidad Autónoma de las Islas Baleares, the autonomous region of the Balearics, which has a total area of 5014 sq.km/1936 sq.miles, with Palma de Mallorca as its capital.

The autonomous Balearic region has a population of some 720,000, almost exclusively Roman Catholics – 582,000 on Majorca, 62,000 on Minorca and 76,000 on Ibiza and Formentera. The most densely populated area is the Palma de Mallorca conurbation, the most thinly populated the island of Formentera, whose inhabitants have the highest life expectancy of all Spaniards.

Origins

The Balearics are the continuation, broken off from the main mass, of the Andalusian Mountains, which extend on the mainland of Spain from Gibraltar by way of the Sierra Nevada to Cabo de la Nao. In the Late Tertiary era the islands were cut off from the Iberian peninsula by tectonic movements which resulted in massive collapses of the land and marine transgression. The archipelago is now separated from the mainland by a trough up to 1500m/4900ft deep. The Balearics and the Pityusas each have their own continental shelf.

Canary Islands

The Canary Islands (Islas Canarias, "Dog Islands"), also known as the Islas Afortunadas, the Fortunate Islands, are a group of seven islands and six smaller islets in the Atlantic, some 100 to 300km (60 to 180 miles) off the north-west coast of Africa (Morocco/Western Sahara) and 1100km/680 miles from the Spanish mainland (Cádiz). They extend between longitude 13° and 18° east and between latitude 27° and 29° north. The whole archipelago extends for 500km/300 miles from east to west and 200km/125 miles from north to south.

The westerly islands of Tenerife (area 2047 sq.km/790 sq.miles; pop. 600,000), La Palma (728 sq.km/281 sq.miles; pop. 72,000), Gomera (378 sq.km/146 sq.miles; pop. 20,000) and Hierro or Ferro (277 sq.km/107 sq.miles; pop. 6000) form the province of Santa Cruz de Tenerife (chief town Santa Cruz); the eastern islands of Gran Canaria (1532 sq.km/592 sq.miles; pop. 660,000), Fuerteventura (1731 sq.km/668 sq.miles; pop. 30,000), Lanzarote (795 sq.km/307 sq.miles; pop. 54,000) and five small subsidiary islands (Alegranza, Graciosa, etc.) the province of Las Palmas de Gran Canaria (chief town Las Palmas). Since 1982 the two provinces have had administrative self-government as the Comunidad

Pico de Teide, Tenerife

Autónoma de Canarias, the autonomous community of the Canaries, with Las Palmas and Santa Cruz alternating as capital of the region.

The Canaries are of volcanic origin. Above the lowest formations, which frequently outcrop, particularly on Fuerteventura, are layers of slag and lava deposited by a long series of eruptions which have taken place since the Miocene period, leaving huge calderas (cauldron-like cavities) on Palma and Tenerife and also on Hierro and Gran Canaria. Later eruptions of stones, ash and lava have almost completely filled the huge cavity on Tenerife known as the Cañadas and built up the Pico de Teide, a volcanic cone rising to 3718m/12,199ft above sea level. Major eruptions devastated Palma in 1677, Lanzarote in 1730–36 and 1824 and the north-west coast of Tenerife in 1705, 1706, 1796 and 1798. The last eruption in the Canaries was on La Palma in 1971. The effects of erosion are everywhere to be seen in the wide humus-rich valleys and deeply indented gorges (*barrancos*), particularly on the islands to the west, which everywhere rise steeply out of the sea, with hardly any natural harbours.

Origins

Climate

Spain lies predominantly within the zone of Mediterranean climate, which is characterised by hot, dry summers and mild, wet winters: a seasonal alternation resulting from the fact that the climate is influenced in summer by the subtropical zone of high pressure and drought and in winter by the temperate zone of west winds, which are displaced over the year along with the position of the sun.

The pattern of Spain's Mediterranean climate is determined by the size of the country, with considerable distances between the central

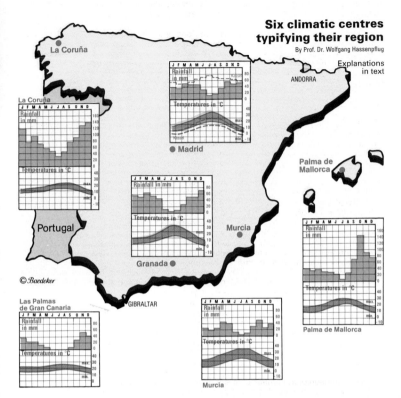

Six climatic centres typifying their region
By Prof. Dr. Wolfgang Hassenpflug

area and the peripheral areas, which are under stronger maritime influence, and variations in height above sea level (with 60% of the country lying at altitudes of 600m/2000ft or over), which produce corresponding climatic variations.

In this chapter the climates of different regions are described with the help of climatic diagrams for typical weather stations. On this basis it is possible to estimate the climate of particular areas, using the following guidelines:

Other things being equal, temperatures increase from north to south by about 0.53°C/0.95°F per degree of latitude, and rainfall (precipitation) decreases.

Temperature variations decrease from the interior of the peninsula towards the periphery (reflecting the transition from a continental to an oceanic climate), and rainfall increases, particularly to the west and north.

Temperatures decrease by about 0.7°C/1.26°F for every 100m/300ft above sea level, while rainfall increases.

On the lee side of hills rainfall decreases. Under the influence of the föhn low-lying basins become drier and temperatures rise.

The interplay of these climatic factors produces the two extremes between which local climates in Spain vary: the north-west, which is always wet, with relatively low temperatures and moderate temperature ranges, and the south-east, which is almost always dry, with relatively high temperatures and an almost African climatic pattern.

The climatic characteristics of particular regions and islands are displayed in the climatic diagrams on page 22, which show temperatures and rainfall over the year as recorded at weather stations in those areas. The blue columns show average monthly precipitation (rainfall) in millimetres. Temperatures (in degrees Celsius) are represented as an orange band, the upper edge of the band showing average maximum day temperatures and the lower edge average minimum night temperatures.

Weather stations

Central Spain, lying high above sea level at some distance from the sea, and for the most part separated from it by mountains, shows a distinctly continental modification of the Mediterranean climate. Summers are hotter and winters colder than on the coast. The high summer temperatures, resulting from anticyclones from the Azores, cloudless skies and high solar irradiation, reach their peak in August with average maximum day temperatures of around 30°C/86°F. Absolute maximum temperatures are higher than in the tropics, and, with correspondingly low minimum night temperatures, produce wide temperature variations. The decrease in temperature with height is completely outweighed by the summer increase.

Central Spain (Madrid weather station)

During the summer months there hangs over central Spain, particularly in the south, a dry dusty haze (*calina*) formed from dust particles drawn up from the dry ground by rising currents of heated air. Rain falls mainly in spring and autumn; in July and August there are only two or three days with any rain. The average annual rainfall in the central region ranges between 400mm/16in. and 700mm/28in.; there are, however, considerable variations from year to year.

In the mountains which rear above the plateau the winter precipitation falls mainly in the form of snow, offering facilities for winter sports. The frequency of snowfalls and the duration of snow cover increase with height and from south to north. In the north snow can be expected every year at heights above 300m/1000ft, in the Madrid area above 600m/2000ft; the Sierra de Guadarrama, at 1350m/4430ft, has snow falling on 56 days in the year.

As a comparison of its climatic diagram with that of Madrid will show, this region, lying between the Atlantic and the Bay of Biscay, has a very different climate from the rest of Spain, belonging as it does to the oceanic and cool temperate zone. Daily and annual temperature variations are slight. Rainfall is high, and occurs throughout the year. The rainiest place in Spain, Santiago de Compostela, with annual rainfall of over 1600mm/63in., lies in this region. Even in July and August there are likely to be eight or nine days with rain.

Northern fringe regions from Pyrenees to Galicia (La Coruña weather station)

The climate of the Catalonian and Valencian Mediterranean coast is more equable than that of the interior. Compared with the Atlantic coast of the Iberian peninsula, summer air temperatures here are some 6–7°C/11–12.5°F higher, water temperatures 4–6°C/7–11°F higher. During fine weather in summer there are strong offshore and onshore winds everywhere on the coasts. The onshore winds blowing throughout the day can reach up to 50km/30 miles inland, tempering the heat of the day.

Eastern fringes of the Balearics (Palma de Mallorca weather station)

Rainfall on the coast decreases perceptibly towards the south. Barcelona has an annual rainfall of 593mm/23in., Valencia 422m/17in. Maximum rainfall is in October, with a second maximum in May; the months of lowest rainfall are July and August.

Temperatures, on the other hand, increase towards the south. The maximum day temperature at Valencia in July and August is 29°C/84°F, 1.3°C/2.3°F higher than at Barcelona.

Climate

In winter the north is influenced by the tramontana, a cold, dry north-north-west wind.

Surface temperatures of the sea on the Costa Brava and Costa Blanca are: April 14–15°C/57–59°F, May 17°C/63°F, June 20°C/68°F, July 23–24°C/73–75°F, August 25°C/77°F, September 23–24°C/73–75°F, October 21°C/70°F.

Balearics

The climate of the Balearics is still more equable than on the coast of the mainland. The maximum rainfall in October is more marked. Rainfall decreases from north to south, though much influenced by the local topography. Thus the Cordillera Norte (1445m/4740ft) on Majorca has up to 1400mm/55in., but the depression to the south, on the lee side of the hills and subject to the föhn, is considerably drier; the western part of the Sierra de Levante is so dry that salt can be recovered from seawater in the salt-pans here. Annual rainfall on Minorca is 580mm/23in., on Majorca 450mm/18in., on Ibiza 350mm/14in. and on Formentera under 200mm/8in.

Northerly winds (the tramontana) are more frequent on Minorca (165 days annually) and on Majorca, reaching storm force mainly in winter.

In the maritime climate of the islands frost and snow are almost completely absent.

South-eastern fringe region (Murcia weather station)

The coast from Alicante to Almería, sheltered by the Cordillera Bética, ranks with smaller areas round Valladolid and Zaragoza as the driest part of Spain. In climate, vegetation and landscape it already has an African character. Annual rainfall is below 400mm/16in. almost everywhere, sometimes well below (Murcia 304mm/12in., Almería 232mm/9in.), particularly on promontories projecting into the sea: Cabo de Gata has the lowest rainfall in Europe (128mm/5in.). The rain falls irregularly during the winter half-year in the form of cloudbursts, on no more than 4–6 days in a month. At other times the sky is always blue, and a blazing hot parching wind, the *leveche,* often blows in summer. Westerly winds of föhn type blow over the hills inland from the coast, bringing no rain. Six to eight months of the year are arid: that is, they bring less rain than would be lost by evaporation. The flourishing date-palms of Elche are a reflection of these climatic conditions.

Southern fringe region (Granada weather station)

The Costa del Sol is a stretch of coast which is particularly favoured climatically as well as scenically. The average annual temperature at Málaga (28.6°C/83.5°F) is 0.6°C/1.1°F higher than at Murcia and Almería; rainfall (470mm/18½in.) is considerably higher (Murcia 304mm/12in., Almería 232mm/9in.).

The climate of Granada (alt. 690m/2265ft) differs in summer from that of the coast in its greater daily temperature variations (17–34°C/63–93°F as against 21–29°C/70–84°F) and in winter in its lower minimum night temperatures (2–3°C/36–37°F).

The narrow coastal strip is completely snow-free; Granada has an average of 3 days with snow in the year.

The Sierra Nevada (the "Snowy Mountains") has snow cover for 110 days on the north side at 2000m/7560ft, 77 days on the south side and 200 days on the summit ridge. The remnants of a small glacier have disappeared only in the last few decades.

The coast itself has the warmest winter temperatures on the European mainland – with high snow-capped mountains as backdrop. To the west, towards the Atlantic, temperatures fall slightly and rainfall increases; this applies also to Gibraltar and the Atlantic coast of Andalusia. In inland Andalusia temperatures increase again and rainfall decreases (average annual temperature at Seville 18.8°C/65.8°F, minimum and maximum temperatures for July and August 19°C/66°F and 36°C/97°F).

The climate of the Canaries, thanks to their insular situation in lower latitudes, differs considerably from that of mainland Spain. It is warmer at sea level and, under oceanic influence, more equable.

Within the Canary Islands there are considerable climatic variations, depending on the degree of exposure to the north-east trade winds and on altitude. The prevalence of the north-east trades, interrupted only during the winter months, leads to a sharp division between the humid weather side to the north and east and the dry – indeed desert-like – lee side of the mountainous islands. Rain falls only during the winter months, brought on by areas of low pressure from more northerly latitudes.

The weather side is itself divided into several climatic zones according to altitude. Up to about 500–600m/1650–1950ft there is a dry, hot zone with average temperatures of 20–21°C/68–70°F (January 17–18°C/63–64°F, August 23–24°C/73–75°F). Annual rainfall nowhere exceeds 500mm/20in. and in many places is considerably lower (Las Palmas 233mm/9in., Santa Cruz 290mm/11in.). Water temperatures range between about 18°C/64°F and 24°C/75°F over the year.

Between about 600m/2000ft and 1500m/4900ft is a middle zone with lower temperatures (average annual temperature 16°C/61°F), heavy mist and cloud formation on the slopes of the hills and higher rainfall (about 600–800mm/24–31in. of rain, plus condensation of mist). Occasional inflows of hot air from the Sahara (carrying dust from the desert) during the summer may bring maximum temperatures of 40°C/104°F in both the lower and the middle zone; and conversely inflows of cold air in winter can bring frost in the middle zone. Above the middle zone on Tenerife and Palma, after a layer of drier and warmer air (the result of temperature inversion), is a zone of dry, cold mountain climate on both the weather and the lee side, with rainfall of around 300mm/12in. In winter the snowline comes down to 2000m/6560ft, so that the Pico de Teide (3718m/12,199ft) has a winter cap of snow.

Canary Islands
(Las Palmas de
Gran Canaria
weather station)

Flora and Fauna

The flora of Spain has reached its present form through the influence of man. Once large areas of the Iberian peninsula were covered by pine and oak forests, which from prehistoric times were largely destroyed by felling for metal-smelting and by clearance from Roman to medieval times to provide land for cultivation and pasture. Now only 5% of Spain's total area is covered by forest. In the cooler and wetter northwest deciduous trees like oaks, beeches and chestnuts predominate; in the Pyrenees conifers. Towards the south, with its dry summers, there are forests of holm oaks and cork-oaks, scanty growths of shrubs (broom, thyme, lavender, rosemary) and sclerophyllous (hard-leaved) evergreens. In central and south-eastern Spain a dense macchia (Spanish *monte bajo*) of evergreen scrub (tree heaths, carobs, arbutus, wild olive-trees) has developed out of the undergrowth of the vanished forests. In very dry areas used for grazing the macchia has become a garrigue in which the bushes are lower and farther apart, the ground between them being frequently bare or covered with grass and thistles.

Flora

Wild plants

The olive-tree, the characteristic element in the flora of the Mediterranean, extends in inland Spain as far north as Madrid; on the Mediterranean coast it reaches right up to the Pyrenees and into southern France. Other plants of cultivation, or plants associated with cultivation, are the cork-oak, the sweet chestnut, the fig-tree, the vine, various species of palms and the widely distributed prickly pear. In the irrigated huertas (from Latin *hortus*, "garden") on the Mediterranean coast citrus fruits, peaches, almonds, dates and figs are grown. In

Cultivated plants

Andalusia there are large areas devoted to the growing of rice and cotton.

On the Mediterranean coast, mainly in private gardens and public parks, the whole range of Mediterranean flora can be seen – bougain-villeas, oleanders, hibiscus, palms and agaves.

Reafforestation·

Since the Franco period efforts have been made to halt the erosion and drying-out of the soil by reafforestation programmes, which are also designed to provide the raw material for papermaking. Often, how-ever, the areas of forest lost by the annual forest fires are as great as the newly planted areas.

Canaries

The flora of the Canary Islands occupies a special position. Here, within a small area, are found plants from almost all the world's vegetation zones; and here, too, there is an unusually high proportion of endemic species (plants found nowhere else). The most striking of these is the dragon tree, which is closely related to the yucca and can reach a height of 20m/65ft. The Canary date-palm has spread from the Can-aries all over the Mediterranean. The Canary pine, which grows at heights of between 1000 and 2000m (3300 and 6600ft), causes mois-ture in the clouds brought by the trade winds to condense in its branches. During the winter months the red poinsettias are a ubiqui-tous feature of the landscape. Since the end of the 19th century the banana has been the most important food crop on the islands; it is rather smaller than the Central American species, and in recent years has had difficulty in finding markets.

Fauna

Both the numbers and the numbers of species of Spanish fauna have been much reduced by deforestation. The number of species is now very low, as it is in the rest of the Mediterranean area and in Central Europe. In the mountain regions there are still chamois, the Spanish ibex (*Capra pyrenaica* or *hispanica*) and even, very occasionally, wolves and bears. There are also foxes, lynxes, wild cats, wild pigs, the Spanish red deer (*Cervus elaphus hispanicus*), birds of prey (including the imperial eagle) and owls. In wetlands waterfowl and waders (her-ons, bitterns, flamingoes, grebes, ducks and geese) may be encoun-tered; and there are also snakes and lizards. Curiosities of the Spanish fauna are the genet and the Egyptian mongoose. Gibraltar has the last monkeys living wild in Europe, the Barbary apes.

The variety of species in the marine life of the Mediterranean coasts is also falling. The large groupers and cephalopods which were not uncommon in the early fifties are now rarely to be seen. This is the result of increasing pollution of coastal waters and uncontrolled under-water fishing. Fortunately, however, fishing with an aqualung is now prohibited. The Atlantic coastal waters are still well stocked with fish, crustaceans and shellfish, which are of considerable economic importance.

Nature reserves

Animals which have now become rare can sometimes be seen in the nine National Parks established in mainland Spain and on the islands and the nature parks in the various autonomous regions. These nature reserves also contain numerous species of plants requiring protection.

Population

Density of
population

Spain has a total population of 39.5 million or 78 inhabitants per sq.km/199 per sq.mile. This population is very unevenly distributed among the regions. 79% of all Spaniards live in just over 600 towns with more than 10,000 inhabitants. The most densely populated areas are the province of Barcelona, with 608 inhabitants to the sq.km/1575 to the sq.mile, and the Madrid region, with 613 to the sq.km/1588 to the

On a breeding farm for fighting bulls

sq.mile. There are other large concentrations of population in the provinces of Vizcaya (545 to the sq.km/1412 to the sq.mile) and Guipúzcoa (353 to the sq.km/914 to the sq.mile). The most thinly populated areas are the provinces of Soria (10 to the sq.km/26 to the sq.mile), Teruel (11 to the sq.km/28 to the sq.mile) and Guadalajara (12 to the sq.km/31 to the sq.mile). The most populous cities are Madrid (3 million, conurbation 4.95 million), Barcelona (1.65 million, conurbation 4.65 million), Valencia (765,000), Seville (674,000) and Zaragoza (593,000).

The figures show that the main concentrations of population apart from Madrid lie mainly on or near the coast. During the 1960s and 1970s in particular there was a great flow of immigrants from disadvantaged rural areas to Madrid, Barcelona, the towns of the Basque country and, to a lesser extent, Valencia, where there were prospects of employment in industry, commerce and tourism and the climate – at least on the coast – was more agreeable. The unattractive blocks of flats on the outskirts of the cities are evidence of these movements of population, which still continue, though in recent years on a smaller scale.   Urbanisation

More than 4 million Spaniards now live abroad.

The overwhelming majority of the population (96.7%) profess the Roman Catholic religion, though since 1978 this is no longer the state religion. Spain also has some 250,000 other Christians, 300,000 Muslims including the North African enclaves and 15,000 Jews.   Religion

According to the statistics Spain has a working population of 15.2 million people (38% of the total adult population). The actual number of Spaniards in work, however, either on their own account or as employees, is around 11 million, of whom 5.9 million are in the services sector, 2.3 million in productive industry (including 1.1 million in   Employment the construction industry) and 1.2 million in agriculture, forestry and fishing. The number engaged in the service industries is increasing, while the numbers in productive industry are falling. The agricultural population is an ageing one: 60% of agricultural workers are between 40 and 65 years old and only 35% are under 40.

Unemployment

Some 3.4 million Spaniards, or about 22.3% of the working population, are at present registered as unemployed. The transformation of a basically agricultural country into an industrial nation has reduced the number of jobs by a fifth since 1976, and for all practical purposes new jobs are available only in the services sector. Roughly a quarter of all workers have only a short-term contract of employment, rarely with a term exceeding six months. Adolescents and young adults are particularly hard hit: some 37.9% of the 16–25 age group are without work. Although membership of the state social insurance system is obligatory only about half the unemployed satisfy the conditions for the payment of an unemployment allowance. Many regions have begun to pay a "social wage" to those without any unemployment assistance. Among the consequences of high unemployment have been the development of a considerable "grey" economy and the increasing numbers of beggars, hawkers and lottery-ticket sellers on the streets, and unfortunately also an increase in crimes of theft – the dark side of an economy which has been for years steadily booming. 4 million Spaniards live below subsistence level, 8 million are regarded as poor.

Ethnic Groups and Linguistic Areas

Spain is a country of very varied ethnic composition, whose various ethnic groups differ from one another in ways of life, dress and above all language. The 1978 constitution recognises the independent existence of these groups and declares the Catalan, Basque and Galician languages to be official languages which are taught in the schools of these regions alongside Castilian Spanish.

In the course of the political reforms of recent years many place-names, street names and names of buildings and institutions have been changed, particularly in Catalonia, the Basque country and Galicia. In this guide the Spanish names which up till now have been in general use are given first, followed where appropriate by the form of the name in the regional language.

Castilian (castellano)

The largest language family, spoken by 28.9 million, is Castilian, which developed into classical Spanish. Spanish is the official language of 19 states, and is spoken worldwide, with dialectal variations, by some 250 million people. Within Spain, in addition to Castilian itself, Asturian, Leonese, Aragonese, Andalusian, Murcian and Canarian belong to the Castilian language family. In the course of time the linguistic differences have been reduced, though the ethnic differences between the various groups are still very marked.

Catalan (català)

Catalan is an independent Romance language spoken by some 6 million people in north-eastern Spain, Andora and parts of southern France. Since the end of the Franco era it has increased steadily in importance and has far outstripped Castilian in everyday use. It differs considerably from Castilian and shows Provençal influence in vocabulary (e.g. "table" is *taula* in Catalan, *mesa* in Castilian, and "corn" is *blat* in Catalan, *trigo* in Castilian). Catalan does not diphthongise Latin root vowels as Castilian does, and drops terminal vowels (Latin *portus,* Castilian *puerto,* Catalan *port;* Latin *bonus,* Castilian *bueno,* Catalan *bo*). Related to Catalan are Valencian and Balearic.

Galician (galego, gallego)

The Galician language (Galician *galego,* Spanish *gallego*) is spoken by some 2.4 million people. It is so closely related to Portuguese that no sharp linguistic boundary can be drawn. The political frontier, however, does not coincide with the linguistic boundary.

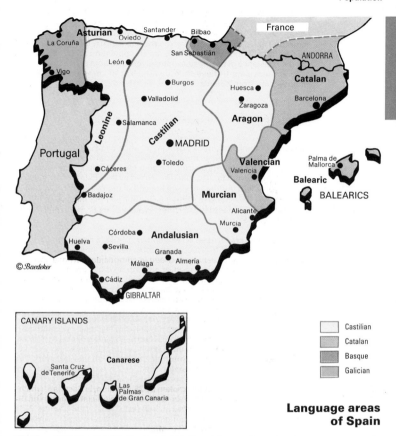

**Language areas
of Spain**

Castilian
Catalan
Basque
Galician

The Basque language (Basque *euskarra*, Spanish *vasco*), spoken by around 600,000 people in the Spanish and French Basque country, stands quite by itself. This very ancient tongue bears no relationship to any other European language, but is the only surviving representative of a pre-Indo-European language. With its recognition as an official language there is the prospect that it may enjoy a fresh lease of life.

Basque
(euskarra, vasco)

The Sinti and Roma (Spanish *gitanos*) originally came from north-western India, which they left in medieval times, spreading first over Europe and going on in the 19th century to North America. The Spanish gipsies came by way of North Africa into Andalusia with the Moors. They speak *caló,* a language of their own which includes in addition to Spanish elements borrowings from other European languages and from Sanskrit.

There are now around 500,000 Sinti and Roma in Spain, living socially as well as geographically on the fringes of society. This people, which has made significant contributions to the culture and folk traditions of Spain, suffers from high unemployment, lack of vocational training, widespread illiteracy, poor life expectancy and high infantile

Sinti and Roma

29

mortality. Something like half the Spanish gipsies live in wretched shanty towns on the outskirts of cities, struggling to make a living as scrap dealers, hawkers, beggars and sometimes thieves. Their integration into society is hindered on the one hand by inherited feelings of resentment on the part of the Spanish population and on the other by the resistance of the gipsies themselves, who hold to their traditions and are unwilling to have their own feeling of community upset by intervention from outside.

Government and Society

Flag and coat of arms

The flag of the kingdom of Spain is red and yellow, which have been the Spanish colours since medieval times. The coat of arms consists of a shield of four quarters bearing the emblems of Castile, León, Aragon, Navarre and Granada. The shield is flanked by the "Pillars of Hercules", which in ancient tradition marked the end of the world and are usually identified as the Straits of Gibraltar. Along with the motto "Plus ultra" on an encircling ribbon they symbolise the history of Spain as a world and maritime power.

Spain since the death of Franco

When General Franco died on November 20th 1975 King Juan Carlos I, long designated as his successor, took over as head of state; but Spain's future course at first remained unclear. Arias Navarro, Franco's prime minister, continued in office, making no move towards a democratic system of government. Political forces representing all shades of opinion in favour of the democratisation of the country joined together in the Platajunta and, with the support of public opinion, brought such strong pressure to bear that at the beginning of 1976 the king called for Arias's resignation. His successor was Adolfo Suárez, secretary general of the Movimiento Nacional, the only political party permitted by the Franco regime. To the surprise of many, he gave a decisive impetus to the process of democratisation. Political parties were now permitted, though not at first the Communist Party; but shortly before the election which had been fixed for June 1977 it too was allowed. The election reduced the party spectrum essentially to Suárez's middle-class Unión de Centro Democrática (UCD), which won most votes, the right-wing Alianza Popular, the Socialists (PSOE), the Communists (PCE), the Basque and Catalan nationalist parties and a number of smaller parties, including the Fuerza Nueva ("New Force"), which in spite of its name consisted of the old hard-line Franco supporters. The most urgent task of the new Parliament – the first freely elected Parliament since 1936 – was to work out a new constitution, following the pattern of the western democracies, which was promulgated after a referendum in December 1978.

In subsequent years the political balance of power changed fundamentally. In an election in October 1982 the Socialist Party, led by Felipe González, won an absolute majority in both houses of the Cortes, and this success was repeated in the 1986 election; but in a further election in 1989, called before the completion of the normal four-year term, the González government lost its absolute majority.

Attempted coups

On February 23rd 1981 the old forces made an attempt to turn the clock back. A company of the Guardia Civil under the command of Lt-Col. Tejero occupied Parliament, and television pictures of Tejero brandishing a pistol on the speakers' rostrum went round the world. That night Juan Carlos I acted vigorously in defence of democracy, condemning the coup in a television address to the nation and calling on the armed forces to remain in barracks, thus depriving Tejero of the support he had hoped to get from the military.

A further coup planned by an army colonel for October 1982 was discovered in time and frustrated.

The constitution which came into force in December 1978 makes Spain (Reino de España, the Kingdom of Spain) a parliamentary monarchy committed to the principles of a democratic social state founded on law. The king as head of state has the duties of watching over the course of government business as "arbiter and guide" and representing Spain in its relations with other countries. He is also supreme commander of the armed forces. For the ordinary citizen the constitution contains major advances over the Franco regime – a code of basic rights, the establishment of the social state, the assurance of security under the law, the recognition of the role of the parties in developing an informed political opinion, the right to refuse military service, the abolition of the death penalty (except under military law) and the end of Roman Catholicism as the state religion.

Spain a parliamentary monarchy

The Spanish Parliament is the Cortes Generales, with two houses, the Congreso de los Diputados (Congress of Deputies) and the Senate. The Congress is elected every four years and has a minimum of 300 members and a maximum of 400. The electoral system is a mixture of direct election and proportional representation. The deputies elect the prime minister, who is then appointed by the king. An important feature of the parliamentary system is the "constructive vote of no confidence": the prime minister can be voted out of office by the Congress only if they elect a successor at the same time.

Parliament

The Senate represents the Autonomous Communities (regions), which consist of one or more provinces. Each province elects four senators, and in addition the parliaments of the autonomous communities elect one senator each, plus additional senators for each million inhabitants. The Senate has a right of veto on the government.

The movements seeking regional independence originated in those regions which have a language and culture differing markedly from those of the Castilian Spaniards – Galicia, the Basque country and Catalonia. Under the Second Republic (1931–36) Catalonia and the Basque provinces were granted autonomous status, and similar provision for Galicia was in preparation. Under the Franco regime, however, all strivings for autonomy were repressed, Castilian was declared the only official language and traditional local customs were forbidden. The 1978 constitution guarantees the right to administrative self-government for nationalities and regions, and Catalan, Basque and Galician are recognised as official languages and taught in schools in the regions concerned.

Regionalism

The most important change, however, has been the establishment between 1979 and 1983 of seventeen Autonomous Communities (Comunidades Autónomas: see map on page 32), consisting of one or more provinces. Each community has its own parliament and is responsible for a variety of services (public works, culture, social security, police, health services, protection of the environment). The communities differ widely in size, population density and economic strength, with highly developed regions like Catalonia at one extreme and backward regions like Extremadura at the other. The territories of the communities do not always coincide with the historical regions (see map on page 32). The former province of Santander, in the north of Old Castile, has become the autonomous region of Cantabria; the old province of Logroño, to the north-east, is now the autonomous province of Rioja; and the other provinces of Old Castile have been combined with the provinces of the kingdom of León to form the autonomous region of Castile–León. To the south, New Castile, with the addition of the province of Albacete (part of the historical region of

Autonomous Communities

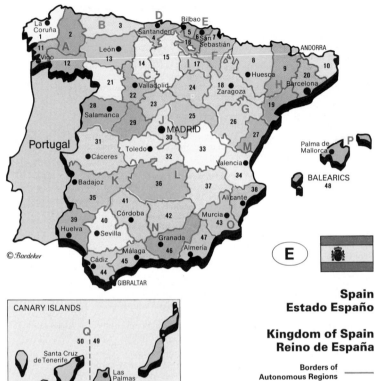

Spain
Estado Españo

Kingdom of Spain
Reino de España

Borders of
Autonomous Regions ———

Borders of
Provinces ———

Autonomous Communities (Comunidades Autónomas)	Area in sq.km	Area in sq. miles	Population
A **Galicia**	29,434	11,364	2,871,000
B **Asturias**	10,565	4,079	1,140,000
C **Castile–León** (Castilla y León)	94,147	36,350	2,602,000
D **Cantabria**	5,289	2,042	527,000
E **Basque Country** (País Vasco, Euzkadi)	7,261	2,803	2,177,000
F **Navarre** (Navarra)	10,421	4,024	522,000
G **Aragon** (Aragón)	47,669	18,405	1,216,000
H **Catalonia** (Cataluña, Catalunya)	31,930	12,328	6,057,000
I **La Rioja**	5,034	1,944	263,000
J **Madrid**	7,995	3,087	4,907,000
K **Extremadura**	41,602	16,063	1,084,000
L **Castile–La Mancha** (Castilla–La Mancha)	79,226	30,589	1,670,000
M **Valencia**	23,305	8,998	3,790,000
N **Andalusia** (Andalucía)	87,260	33,691	6,736,000
O **Murcia**	11,317	4,370	1,007,000
P **Balearics** (Islas Baleares)	5,014	1,936	720,000
Q **Canary Islands** (Canarias)	7,273	2,808	1,442,000

Provinces (Provincias)	Area in sq.km	Area in sq. miles	Population
1 La Coruña	7,876	3,041	1,115,900
2 Lugo	9,803	3,785	414,000
3 Asturias	10,565	4,079	1,140,000
4 Cantabria	5,298	2,046	527,000
5 Vizcaya	2,217	856	1,209,000
6 Guipúzcoa	1,997	771	706,000
7 Navarra	10,421	4,024	522,000
8 Huesca	15,613	6,028	218,000
9 Lérida	12,028	4,644	359,000
10 Gerona	5,886	2,273	476,000
11 Pontevedra	4,477	1,729	902,000
12 Orense	7,778	3,003	439,000
13 León	15,468	5,972	527,000
14 Palencia	8,035	3,102	190,000
15 Burgos	14,309	5,525	366,000
16 Alava	3,047	1,176	262,000
17 La Rioja	5,034	1,944	263,000
18 Zaragoza	17,252	6,661	842,000
19 Tarragona	6,283	2,426	522,000
20 Barcelona	7,733	2,986	4,702,000
21 Zamora	10,559	4,077	230,000
22 Valladolid	8,202	3,167	485,000
23 Segovia	6,949	2,683	150,000
24 Soria	10,287	3,972	101,000
25 Guadalajara	12,190	4,707	145,000
26 Teruel	14,785	5,708	156,000
27 Castellón	6,679	2,579	449,000
28 Salamanca	12,336	4,763	367,000
29 Avila	8,048	3,107	185,000
30 Madrid	7,995	3,087	4,907,000
31 Cáceres	19,945	7,701	429,000
32 Toledo	15,368	5,934	481,000
33 Cuenca	17,061	6,587	219,000
34 Valencia	10,763	4,156	2,147,000
35 Badajoz	21,657	8,362	655,000
36 Ciudad Real	19,749	7,625	481,000
37 Albacete	14,862	5,738	344,000
38 Alicante	5,863	2,264	1,194,000
39 Huelva	10,085	3,894	438,000
40 Sevilla	14,001	5,406	1,546,000
41 Córdoba	13,718	5,297	754,000
42 Jaén	13,498	5,212	669,000
43 Murcia	11,317	4,370	1,007,000
44 Cádiz	7,385	2,851	1,034,000
45 Málaga	7,276	2,809	1,072,000
46 Granada	12,531	4,838	793,000
47 Almería	8,774	3,388	430,000
48 Baleares	5,014	1,936	720,000
49 Las Palmas de Gran Canaria	4,072	1,572	745,500
50 Santa Cruz de Tenerife	3,170	1,224	695,000
SPAIN	504,751	194,885	38,830,000
Spanish territories in Africa			
Ceuta	19	7.3	72,000
Melilla	12	4.6	58,000
Andorra	462	178	42,000
Gibraltar	6.5	2.5	31,000

Murcia) has become the autonomous region of Castile–La Mancha. The capital, Madrid, is an autonomous region on its own. The North African towns of Ceuta and Melilla, which have belonged to Spain since the 15th/16th century and are claimed by Morocco, belong to the provinces of Cádiz and Málaga respectively.

The first regions to be granted autonomy were the Basque country (Euzkadi, País Vasco) and Catalonia (Catalunya, Cataluña), where the urge to break away completely from the Spanish state was particularly strong. While it has been possible to satisfy to some extent the aspirations of the separatist movements in Catalonia, however, the efforts to achieve independence for the Basque country, and in particular the terrorist activities of the militant underground movement ETA, have continued unabated.

ETA (Euzkadi Ta Azkatasuna, "The Basque Country and its Freedom"), founded in 1959, pursues a radical left-wing nationalist policy and seeks to achieve its aims by violence and terrorist attacks. In the closing years of the Franco regime ETA attracted much sympathy and support from the Basque population, for under Franco all expressions of regional culture were repressed and ETA was ruthlessly pursued, giving its members the status of heroes. In 1974 ETA split into a military wing, ETA Militar, and a politico-military wing, ETA Politico-militar; and after Franco's death increasing democratisation allowed the Basques to establish political organisations, in particular the moderate Basque Nationalist Party (the governing party in the autonomous region) and Herri Batasuna, often seen as the political arm of ETA Militar. In spite of a general amnesty proclaimed in 1976, however, ETA Militar continued with its terrorist activities, which became increasingly pointless and finally were directed against "deviants" and compromisers. Sympathy for ETA has declined considerably in the Basque country, but many Basques still show marked reluctance to talk when the subject of ETA comes up.

Spain has been a member of the United Nations since 1955, of NATO since 1982 and of the European Community since 1986. Its entry to the Community was repeatedly delayed because other Community countries which were exporters of agricultural produce, particularly the wine-producing countries France and Italy, were reluctant to face Spanish competition. Spanish membership of NATO and the presence of American military bases in Spain have continued to be the subject of violent controversy, although a referendum in 1986 produced a majority in favour of remaining in NATO.

On the basis of its history as a colonial power Spain maintains close relations with many Latin American states and is a permanent observer member of the Organisation of American States (OAS).

Economy

From the Colonial State to the European Partner

Within no more than three decades Spain has developed from a predominantly agricultural land into an industrial country of importance to Europe. Particularly since Franco's death in 1975 this change has been reflected in a changed economic system.

For centuries Spain had turned its back on Europe, its attention almost exclusively directed on its colonies. In the 20th century this was bound to change; but the particular political development of Spain had by the end of the 1950s given it a more markedly peripheral situation within Europe – a result of the Civil War, Spain's neutrality in the Second World War and its political isolation and striving for self-sufficiency during the first two decades of the Franco dictatorship. As a result of the gradual economic and political liberalisation of the country the early sixties saw the beginnings of a social change which after Franco's death finally led to a process of increasing democratisation. Within a very few years Spain set out on the road to a modern industrial and consumer society, which brought with it major changes in the country's political structure.

The most difficult time was during the years of change after Franco's death. After the 1973 oil crisis Spain, like many other countries, became a victim of the worldwide recession. The sudden increase in expenditure hit an economy based on an outdated and largely backward agricultural structure and an antiquated industry in the towns. Attempts at modernisation by looking outside Spain were blocked by the sheltered internal market, for in order to protect the domestic economy the state had erected high customs barriers which hampered development projects. The transition to a parliamentary monarchy, too, had originally produced an inflation rate of almost 30% and stimulated the outflow of capital. In order to streamline the economy, therefore, the government embarked on a policy of *reconverción*. As a result fully 1.5 million jobs were lost from 1978 onwards and some 200,000 firms went out of existence and this process is still not completed.

Spain and Portugal's entry into the European Community (now the European Union) on January 1st 1986 sealed the process of European integration for the countries of the Iberian peninsula. Spain itself experienced economic growth during the first five years of membership which made other countries envious of Madrid. With a growth rate of 23% (EC average 16%) Spain ranked fifth place among the EC countries with the most dynamic economy, after the "big four" Germany, Great Britain, France and Italy. Hundreds of thousands of new jobs were created, the income per capita rose considerably and for the first time in years the unemployment figures fell below 15%. The climax of this rapid development was to be 1992 when Spain, as host to the 25th Summer Olympics in Barcelona and the EXPO '92 exhibition in Seville, wanted to present itself as a competitive and technologically advanced country.

EC membership: boom and recession

By mid-1991, however, the economy was showing signs of overheating. The rapid growth which had been urgently encouraged to reach EC levels compounded the economic problems. The inflation rate could easily be reduced but the trade deficit was growing at such an alarming rate that in 1992 Spain had the second largest balance of trade deficit (36 billion US dollars) among the industrial nations after the USA. The main reason – together with the effect of the general European economic crisis – was seen to be the falling level of competitiveness of the Spanish economy, caused by wages and salaries which had been continually rising since 1985 and the strength of the peseta on the currency market. Consequently the euphoria of the Eighties resulted in a decline in the gross national product and private consumption, lack of investment and a drop in industrial production.

A further worrying indicator for the state of the Spanish economy was the sharp increase again in the number of unemployed: 22.3% (= 3.4 million) of the working population were unemployed in mid-1993 and with 37.9% of 16 to 25 year olds unemployed the country was well above the EC average of 19 per cent.

The optimism of 1992, which for a time outshone the clouds on the horizon, was followed by bitter disillusionment, even though it was thought at the beginning of 1994 that the first signs of improvement could be detected. The González government, having lost its absolute majority in the 1993 elections, is following a hard course involving savings in the public sector, particularly on wages and social expenditure, a more flexible structuring of the employment market, measures

Outlook

to create jobs such as restrictions on wage increases and the possible privatisation of nationalised industries. In so doing it is definitely tackling the economy but alienating its supporters, the trade unions, and the general strike on January 27th 1994 demonstrated that the workers were not prepared to meet the cost of economic recovery alone – not when in mid-1993 profits were still rising.

Agriculture and Fisheries

Agricultural structure

Spain's geographical situation and topography give it a wide range of climates and landscapes – areas with a hot climate and dry summers (the south-east), others with only short periods of drought (the central regions), or with a perpetually wet climate (the north and north-east of the Iberian peninsula). The variations related to changes in altitude range from the Mediterranean coastal regions, with their mild winters, by way of the upland regions of peripheral Iberia, with a warm temperate climate, to the high plains of Castile with their cold winters and abundance of snow. The sequence of different climatic zones between the centre and the periphery is reflected in the different patterns of agriculture. Thus the Levante ranks as one of the most fertile regions in Spain, producing large crops of fruit (almonds, apricots, oranges, figs) and vegetables in the irrigated *huertas* and *vegas*. The principal crops on the irrigated coastal plains on the Mediterranean are rice, sugarcane and sugar-beet. Lower Andalusia, in the south of Spain, produces more than half the Spanish olive crop: in the province of Granada, for example, a third of the agricultural land is devoted to olives, with cotton and wine as other important crops. The agricultural pattern is very different in Extremadura, north-west of the Sierra Morena: this region of large landholdings is mainly devoted to pastoral farming. To the east of Extremadura, in New Castile, is the La Mancha plain, the granary of Spain, situated at an altitude of 800m/2600ft.

Patterns of land ownership

The uneven distribution of land ownership has long been one of the main problems of Spanish agriculture. In spite of several attempts at land reform there has up till now been very little change in the situation. Tiny peasant landholdings predominate particularly in Galicia, Navarre and the Basque country, large estates in Andalusia and Extremadura. At the last agricultural census (1972) 2.5% of landholdings (over 100 hectares/250 acres) had more than 59% of the total area, while 77% of landholdings (under 10 hectares/25 acres) had barely 12% of the total. Almost 20% of all holdings were under a hectare (2½ acres). Up to the present, efforts to remedy the situation have been confined mainly to measures for the reparcelling of land. Under the auspices of the Instituto Nacional de Colonización (INC), which was established in 1949, 1.8 million hectares/4.4 million acres were redistributed between 1954 and 1967, but some 8 million hectares/20 million acres remain to be dealt with. Although a new law passed in 1979 provides for the expropriation of land on large estates which is not being used for agriculture, the pattern of agricultural land ownership has up to the present barely changed. The establishment of the European single market, however, is likely to bring pressure for change.

Agricultural produce

In the output of agricultural produce Spain continues to enjoy a leading place within Europe. This is true particularly of the production of citrus fruits and olives. Other important crops are barley, wheat, maize, rice, potatoes and sugar-beet. As a producer of wine-grapes Spain takes fourth place in Europe; in the production of wine it takes third place. The government has promoted stock-farming on marginal land, and Spain now has some 5 million head of cattle. This development has its drawbacks, since in some areas over-grazing has led to increased erosion of the soil – already a problem in southern Spain as a result of the fall in the water table caused by the heavy demands on water for irrigation.

Spain falls far short of meeting the demand for timber from its own resources. Over-felling in the past has largely destroyed the forests of the Iberian peninsula, and reafforestation has failed to keep pace with the destruction caused every year by forest and bush fires. Fast-growing species of eucalyptus and poplar help to meet the rapidly growing demand for papermaking. Traditional branches of forestry in Spain are the harvesting of resin and turpentine from pine-trees and of cork from the bark of cork-oaks.

Forestry

In recent years the importance of the Spanish fisheries has been much reduced, partly as a result of restrictions on fishing imposed by the European Union and by Morocco. Most of the fish landed comes from the central Atlantic fishing grounds. The principal Spanish fishing ports are on the Galician coast, where shellfish farming is also an important activity. Other good fishing grounds are around the Canary Islands and in the southern Atlantic. Up to half the sardines and tunny caught are canned for export. Catches of crustaceans and molluscs are becoming increasingly important.

Fisheries

Mining and power production

Spain possesses a wide range of minerals, some of them in consid-erable quantity, although low prices in world markets and relatively high production costs have led to reductions in extraction and in revenue. As a result the output of minerals such as copper, tin, lead and energy-producing minerals including coal has fallen. Many small or

Minerals

Shellfish culture on the Galician coast

badly situated mines are no longer economic to work. Thus the working of manganese, bismuth and titanium has been abandoned. For some minerals, however, Spain occupies a leading place in the world market, for example pyrites, mercury and potassium salt. Spain also produces significant amounts of copper, tin, lead, iron ore, zinc, tungsten and fluorspar. Mining only comprises a very small percentage of the gross domestic product.

Power production

Among sources of energy Spain has large supplies only of coal – sufficient to meet 88% of demand. The coal is not, however, of high quality, so that for smelting in particular it is necessary to import supplies of better-quality coal. Spain has only enough oil to meet less than 3% of demand, and it has no significant resources of natural gas. Its resources of hydraulic power are sufficient to supply 17% of installed power station capacity. Electricity is mainly supplied from oil, gas and coal power stations and 36% from nuclear power stations. Wind and solar energy is harnessed chiefly in the south.

Industry

Until the beginning of the 1950s Spain was mainly an agricultural country. Only in the Basque country and Navarre were there old-established shipbuilding and metalworking industries, in particular the construction of heavy machinery. The basis for this development was provided by the large deposits of iron ore and coal in Asturias. The textile industry was established at an early stage in Catalonia, particularly in and around Barcelona.

Industrial areas

Industry is still very unevenly distributed over Spain. In the interior of the country there is little, except for the Madrid industrial area. There is a high level of industrialisation in most areas along the Mediterranean coast, particularly between Tarragona and Murcia. The coast to the east and west of Gibraltar also has a good deal of industry: the most recent developments in this area have been along the coast from Algeciras to Cádiz and Huelva, where steelworks, shipyards and large chemical plants have been established. There are also industrial concentrations in the southern cities of Seville, Córdoba and Granada.

Industrial products

Since the beginning of the 1960s industrial output has increased at a rate above the international average, and now accounts for 36% of the gross domestic product. A distinction must be made between traditional branches of industry such as leather goods, boots and shoes, textiles and food-processing, which are mainly dependent on home-produced raw materials, and the new forward-looking industries.

The day has long gone when Spain's only export trade was in agricultural produce. In recent years exports of agricultural products has been declining, in spite of large harvests, and now take second place among Spain's exports. The first place is now occupied by car manufacture and the vehicle supply industry; engineering comes third. Apart from tourism, cars are the largest earners of foreign currency, contributing over 6.5 billion dollars in 1992 to Spain's total revenue from exports of 52.9 billion dollars. The Italian car manufacturer Fiat was brought to Spain by the state-owned holding company INI as early as 1950, and thereafter the small cars marketed under the name of SEAT laid the foundation for the motorisation of Spain. In 1980 SEAT finally achieved inclusion in the list of the 200 largest car firms in the world. A year later, however, the second world energy crisis led to the break-up of the link with Fiat, which was now replaced by Volkswagen. Through Volkswagen's involvement Spain is now the third largest producer of cars in Europe after Renault and Opel with an annual output of 1.8 million vehicles.

Car manufacturing plant, Barcelona

Among Spain's industrial exports machinery and equipment take second place to cars. Third place is occupied by iron and steel products, badly hit by the international recession.

Tourism

Tourism in Spain makes a larger contribution to total earnings of foreign currency than in any other European country. Since the beginning of the Fifties tourism in Spain has become a major branch of the economy. In 1975 total earnings from tourism amounted to 3.4 billion dollars and by 1990 this had reached 18.4 billion dollars with 52 million visitors, they provided employment for at least 7% of Spain's total work force. Fully half the visitors travel by car or bus. After 1988, however, in spite of an increase in the number of beds available, the number of visitors stopped rising, apparently because of Spain's 7% inflation rate and the consequent *de facto* increase in the value of the peseta. Spain is no longer the cheap holiday country it was – at any rate not in the popular tourist centres.

In recent years there has been heavy investment in the tourist trade. In 1987 and 1988 alone hotel development added another 100,000 beds to the country's stock, and Spain now has more than 3500 hotels in the first three categories, with a total of 625,000 beds.

The tourist boom and its problems

The building and tourist boom has had unattractive consequences especially on the Mediterranean coast with mile upon mile of concrete tower blocks. Increasing complaints about poor service, high prices and dirty beaches led to a decline in the number of tourists coming to Spain at the end of the Eighties and early Nineties so that nervous tour operators together with the Spanish government had to take action. Image campaigns, tighter building regulations, construction of sewage plants and staff training were aimed at attracting more tourists back to Spain's beaches. The initiatives were successful, the tourists returned, partly because Turkey had become too risky and former Yugoslavia no longer was an option. In 1993 57.2 million visitors came to Spain, 3.5% more than in the previous year, a significant increase which gives the tourist industry cause to be optimistic about the future.

The growth of tourism has also led to a considerable increase in population in the coastal areas. At the beginning of the century the 478 Spanish communes on the coasts (accounting for 7% of the country's total area) had 12% of the Spanish population, a proportion which has now risen to 35%. All this, combined with the fact that more than 60% of Spain's industrial capacity lies near the coast, has led to fierce competition for the available land. The great increase in traffic in the coastal areas on the mainland is an increasing threat to the landscape and the environment. Over 80% of all holidaymakers in the Iberian peninsula, both natives and foreigners, make for the beaches.

Tourist centres

The tourist trade is heavily concentrated on the Balearics (particularly Majorca and Ibiza), the Canary Islands, the Mediterranean coast and the Atlantic coast of northern Spain. Every year 60% of all visitors choose the Spanish islands for their holiday. Thanks to the mild Mediterranean climate the tourist trade is now an all-the-year-round business, particularly on the islands. Older people from less favoured parts of Europe now spend the winter there; and Majorca's capital Palma in particular draws large numbers of pensioners in winter, mainly from Britain and Germany. Palma now has the second largest airport in Spain, handling more than 12 million passengers annually. In mainland Spain the leading holiday areas are the Costa Brava, north of Barcelona, and the Costa del Sol, around Málaga. The Sierra Nevada, the mountain area near Granada which rises to a height of 3000m/10,000 feet, has developed into a new centre for winter sports and summer holidays.

History

From Prehistory to the Moorish Conquest (c. 10,000 B.C. to A.D. 711)

The territory of Spain was already populated in the Palaeolithic period. The earliest attested inhabitants are the Ligurians on the north-east coast and the Iberians, probably immigrants from North Africa, in the east and south. The Basques, in the western Pyrenean region, are thought to be the remnant of a pre-Indo-European population.

Late Palaeolithic: notable cave paintings (Altamira, El Castillo, etc.).	c. 10,000 B.C.
Neolithic: cave paintings (scenes of war and hunting) in eastern Spain.	5000–2000
Megalithic culture (Copper Age): monumental tombs and cult structures.	2000–1600
The Phoenicians establish trading posts on the south coast – Gadri (Cádiz), Malaka (Málaga), Tartessos, etc.	about 1100
The Celts, who in subsequent centuries mingle with the Iberians to become Celtiberians, thrust into the interior of the country.	after 1000
A number of ports – Emporion (Ampurias), Mainake (at Torre del Mar, 30km/20 miles east of Málaga), etc. – are established by the Greeks, mainly Ionians from the Phocaean colony of Massalia (Marseilles).	from 700
The Carthaginians drive out the Greeks.	from 600
After the First Punic War the Carthaginians under Hamilcar Barca, Hasdrubal and Hannibal extend their colonial power from the Tagus to the Ebro.	236–206
Foundation of Carthago Nova (Cartagena).	about 225
At the beginning of the Second Punic War Hannibal destroys Saguntum, an ally of Rome.	219
Under a peace treaty with Rome Carthage gives up its Spanish possessions.	201
Establishment of the Roman provinces of Hispania Citerior in the north-east and Hispania Ulterior in the south-west. A series of risings – by the Lusitanians under the leadership of Viriathus (154–139), the Celtiberians (143–133), the Asturians, Cantabrians and other tribes (25–19), etc. – hamper the complete subjection of the peninsula but not the rapid linguistic and cultural Romanisation of the country (with the exception of the Basque territories).	197
The Roman praetor Sertorius, a supporter of Marius, tries to establish an independent Celtiberian state.	81–72
Julius Caesar defeats Pompey's sons and supporters at Munda (south-west of Córdoba) and becomes dictator. His veterans are settled on the properties of his defeated rivals.	45
Spain is divided into the provinces of Hispania Tarraconensis (in the north and east), Lusitania (in the west, between the Duero/Douro and the Guadiana) and Baetica (the original Hispania Ulterior).	27

19	The Iberian peninsula is fully incorporated into the Roman Empire by Augustus. The Romanised population of Spain produces writers like Seneca, Lucan and Martial and the Emperors Trajan, Hadrian and Theodosius (the Great).
A.D. 74	Vespasian grants the principal towns the *ius Latii* (municipal charters).
from 100	Beginning of the Christianisation of the Iberian peninsula.
after 400	During the Great Migrations the Alans (a tribe from the Iranian steppe) settle in what is now Portugal, the Vandals (an East Germanic people) in southern Spain, the Suevi (from southern Germany) in the north-west.
414	The Visigoths (West Goths), led by King Athaulf, advance into Catalonia (Gotalonia).
429	The Vandals move on into Africa.
466–84	King Eurich, ruler of the Visigothic kingdom of Tolosa, defeats the Suevi and establishes Visigothic rule throughout Spain (except the north-west). The oldest Germanic code of law, the Codex Euricianus, written in Latin, is compiled during his reign.
507–711	After the fall of the kingdom of Tolosa the Visigoths continue to rule Spain, with their capital at Toledo.
551	Under Justinian the Byzantines conquer the south coast of Spain, but lose it again by 624.
587	The conversion of the Arian Visigoths to orthodox Catholicism is followed by their rapid amalgamation with the Romanised population.
711	The Arab general Tarik defeats a Visigothic army led by Roderick at Jerez de la Frontera.

Spain under the Moors (711–1492)

	During the period of Arab rule the peninsula enjoys an economic and cultural flowering. Eastern and Hellenistic learning is transmitted through Spain to the Christian West.
from 714	Spain (with the exception of the upland regions of Asturias, Galicia and the Basque country) is a province of the Umayyad Caliphate of Damascus.
732	Through his victory at Tours and Poitiers Charles Martel drives the Arabs out of Gaul.
756	The Umayyad Abderrahman I flees to Spain and founds the Emirate of Córdoba, which extends over the whole of the peninsula. The introduction of new crops (rice, sugar, etc.), irrigation and the growing output of silk and weapons make possible a period of great economic prosperity and high cultural achievement. The Arabs show religious tolerance to Christians and Jews. Many Christians become converts to Islam and adopt the Arabic language and Arab customs (the Mozarabs).
778	Charlemagne loses his Spanish conquests after the defeat of his rearguard in the pass of Roncesvalles, in which Roland (hero of the "Chanson de Roland") is killed.

Caliphate of Córdoba. Abderrahman III assumes the title of Caliph in 929. This was the heyday of Moorish culture in Spain (mosques, terraced gardens adjoining the Alhambra, large library, new palace at Medina Azahara, etc.).	929–1031
The Caliph conquers Toledo, and in the following year north-western Africa to beyond Tahert (lost in 979).	930
Almansor ("the Victorious"), grand vizier of Caliph Hisham II, conquers Barcelona (985), León (987) and Santiago de Compostela (997) – the farthest expansion of Moorish military power in Spain.	985–97
Fall of the last Umayyad Caliph, Hisham III. The Caliphate of Córdoba is split up into more than 20 independent petty states (taifas), later to be reunited by the Almoravids.	1031
Alfonso VI of Castile takes Toledo after a five years' siege.	1085
The Almoravids, a Berber sect from North Africa, responding to a call for help from the Moorish Emirs, defend the Moorish states against Christian attacks under the leadership of Yusuf ibn Tashfin and unite the Muslim south of Spain with their kingdom in North Africa.	from 1086
The Almoravid kingdom in North Africa is conquered by the Almohads, a fanatical Berber sect, who maintain their position in Spain from 1195 to 1225, continually at war with the Christian kingdoms.	1146
Caliph Mohammed en-Nasir suffers a heavy defeat at Las Navas de Tolosa at the hands of the combined army of Castile, Aragon and Navarre. A number of petty Muslim states are established, but cannot prevent the decline of the Almohad empire. The Moors lose Córdoba (1236), Seville (1248), Cádiz (1263) and other towns.	1212
The Emirate of Granada, under the Nasrid dynasty.	1238–1492
Mohammed ibn al-Ahmar, of the Beni Nasr tribe, establishes the Emirate of Granada (incorporating Málaga and Almería). Granada becomes the wealthiest town in the peninsula and its cultural centre.	1238
Granada is required to pay tribute to the king of Castile.	1246
Mohammed II, with the help of Sultan Abu Yusuf of Morocco, defeats the Castilians at Ecija and Martos.	1275
The Emirate loses Tarifa to Castile, followed by Gibraltar in 1309 and Algeciras in 1344.	1292
Granada's brilliant cultural heyday (construction of the Alhambra).	1300–1400
Recovery of Gibraltar (until 1462).	1333
Yusuf I, allied with the Sultan of Morocco, suffers a heavy defeat on the Río Salado.	1340
Beginning of the war between Granada and Castile, which gradually conquers the whole of Granadan territory.	1481
After the fall of Málaga (1487) and Granada (1492) Emir Abdallah Mohammed XIII, known to the Spaniards as Boabdil, withdraws to North Africa. This is followed by the expulsion of the Moors and the Jews, seriously hampering the further economic development of Spain.	1492

43

The Rise of the Christian States until the Union of the two Leading Kingdoms, Castile and Aragon (c. 718–1516)

The Reconquista (recovery by the Christian kingdoms) of the Iberian peninsula, starting in the north, ends in the final expulsion of the Moors and the formation of a Spanish national state. The medieval culture of Spain bears the mark of its contact with Islam as well as with the Christian West.

722	Pelayo, a Goth, defeats the Moors at Covadonga and founds the kingdom of Asturias in the Asturian hills.
about 750	Alfonso I unites Asturias with Cantabria and acquires León, Old Castile and Galicia. Under Alfonso III León becomes capital of the kingdom.
after 778	The Counties of Catalonia (capital Barcelona) and Navarre are formed out of Charlemagne's Spanish March.
about 900	The County of Castile (named after the castles built for defence against the Moors) comes into being.
after 910	Alfonso III's sons divide the kingdom into Galicia, Asturias and León.
1029	King Sancho III of Navarre inherits the County of Castile. The division of his kingdom between his three sons leads to the formation of the kingdoms of Castile, Navarre and Aragon.
1037	Ferdinand (Fernando) I, the Great, of Castile wins León.
1072	Alfonso VI of Castile reunites the kingdom (which had again been split up), enlarges it by the addition of part of Navarre and in 1085 conquers New Castile and Toledo. Rodrigo Díaz, the Cid (from Arabic *sayyid,* "lord"), later to become the Spanish national hero, briefly enters the service of the Moors and conquers Valencia (1094).
1109	Portugal becomes an independent County (from 1139 a kingdom).
1118	Alfonso I of Aragon extends his kingdom during his wars with the Moors and conquers Zaragoza (which becomes his capital). Failure of attempts to unite Castile and Aragon.
1130	Alfonso VII of Castile becomes emperor, with authority over all the Christian states in Spain, but his empire is divided up again by the laws of succession into Castile and León.
1137	Union of Aragon and Catalonia.
1212	In the battle of Las Navas de Tolosa the combined knightly armies of Castile, Aragon and Navarre win a decisive victory over the Almohad Caliph.
1229–38	Jaime I of Aragon victorious over the Moors. Conquest of the Balearics (1229–35) and Valencia (1238).
1230	Ferdinand III of Castile finally unites Castile and León, and conquers Córdoba (1236), Murcia (1241) and Seville (1248).
1234–1441	Navarre under French rule.
1263	Alfonso X of Castile (from 1257 also king of Germany) conquers Cádiz and Cartagena.
1282	Pedro III of Aragon gains possession of Sicily.

Under the peace of Anagni Jaime II of Aragon gives up Sicily, and in return receives Sardinia and Corsica from the Pope. — 1295

The Cortes (the estates representing the church, the nobility and the towns) of Aragon, Catalonia and Valencia meet together. — from 1307

Aragon acquires the kingdom of Naples. — 1443

Juan II, king of Navarre since 1425, becomes king of Aragon on the death of his brother Alfonso VI. — 1458

The marriage of Ferdinand II of Aragon (1479–1516) and Isabella of Castile (1474–1504) unites the two kingdoms. Under the Catholic Monarchs the transition to an absolute monarchy takes place. — 1469

Reorganisation of the Inquisition in Aragon and Castile by Jiménez de Cisneros (from 1495 archbishop of Toledo). — 1486–88

The conquest of Granada ends the Reconquista. Thereafter the fanatical expulsion of Moors and Jews begins.
  Isabella gives her support to Christopher Columbus (Cristóbal Colón), whose voyages of exploration prepare the way for the establishment of the Spanish colonial empire in America. — 1492

The treaty of Tordesillas lays down a demarcation line between Spanish and Portuguese colonial interests in America. — 1494

Ferdinand II recovers Naples and Sicily after the fall of the royal house (a collateral line of the Aragonese kings). — 1504

Navarre up to the Pyrenees falls to Spain. — 1515

Spain as a World Power – to the Peninsular War (1516–1813)

Spain rises to international importance in the 16th century through the enormous expansion of its territories in Europe and the colonies and as a centre of the Counter-Reformation. After the death of Philip II it loses its dominating position, since the numerous wars it fights to maintain the Catholic faith ruin the country economically and financially.

Charles I, a Habsburg, becomes king of Castile and Aragon. After the death of his grandfather Maximilian I he inherits the Habsburg territories and in 1519 becomes Holy Roman Emperor as Charles V (coronation in Rome 1530). He is now ruler of Spain, the Netherlands, Sardinia, Naples, Sicily, Milan, Franche-Comté and numerous American colonies. He hands over the Habsburg possessions in Germany to his brother Ferdinand in 1521. — 1516

Establishment of colonial rule in America. The Spanish conquistadors Cortes and Pizarro conquer Mexico (1519–21), Peru (1531–34) and Chile (from 1535). Vast quantities of gold and silver are brought back to Spain. — 1519–35

The rising of the Comuneros (the towns of Castile) is repressed, and absolutism prevails; the Cortes lose their importance. — 1520–21

Charles V fights five wars against France in order to maintain Spanish hegemony in Italy and Burgundy. — 1521–56

Ignacio de Loyola founds the Jesuit order (the Society of Jesus). — 1534

Charles V's forces occupy Tunis and Algiers. — 1535–41

45

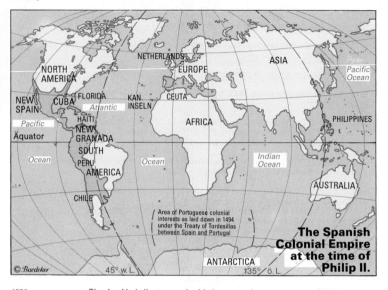

Area of Portuguese colonial interests as laid down in 1494 under the Treaty of Tordesillas between Spain and Portugal

The Spanish Colonial Empire at the time of Philip II.

© Baedeker

1556	Charles V abdicates and withdraws to the monastery of Yuste.
1556–98	Philip II, Charles's son, assumes the leadership of the Counter-Reformation in Europe. With the help of the Inquisition he fights heresy in Spain and has the Christianised Moors (Moriscos) in Andalusia almost completely exterminated.
1559	The treaty of Câteau-Cambrésis ends the war with France for supremacy in Italy and Burgundy.
1563–84	Building of the Escorial.
1565–72	Conquest of the Philippines.
1571	In the naval battle of Lepanto the Turkish fleet is annihilated by Spanish warships.
1580	Spain is united with Portugal in a personal union (which lasts until 1640). The acquisition of the Portuguese colonial possessions brings the Spanish empire to its greatest extent.
1581	The fanatical severity with which Philip II and his general the Duke of Alba seek to repress the Protestant and patriotic rising in the Netherlands leads to the secession of the northern Netherlands under William of Orange.
1588	With the destruction of the Armada in the Channel Spain loses the fight with Britain for command of the sea.
1609–10	Expulsion of the last Moriscos and Jews (about 600,000) from southern Spain in the reign of Philip III.
1618–48	Spain takes part in the Thirty Years' War on the side of the Austrian Habsburgs.

The destruction of the Armada

Resumption of the fight against the free Netherlands (whose independence Spain has later to recognise under the treaty of Westphalia).	1621
Portugal dissolves its union with Spain.	1640
A Catalan rising (which had begun in 1640) is repressed.	1652
Under the Peace of the Pyrenees Spain cedes Roussillon, Cerdaña (Cerdagne) and part of Flanders to France.	1659
Spain finally cedes Franche-Comté to France.	1678
In the War of the Spanish Succession the Bourbon claimant, Philip of Anjou, a grandson of Louis XIV, fights for recognition against the Austrian Habsburgs, Britain and the Netherlands.	1701–13
Under the treaty of Utrecht Philip V cedes Spanish territory in the Netherlands, Milan and Naples to Austria, Sicily to Savoy, Minorca and Gibraltar to Britain, but retains the Spanish colonies.	1713
Unsuccessful conflicts with Austria for Sardinia and Sicily.	1717–30
The kingdom of Naples and Sicily passes to a collateral line of the Spanish Bourbons, as does the Duchy of Parma and Piacenza in 1748.	1735
The Bourbon Charles III (Duke of Parma 1731–35, King of Naples and Sicily 1723–59) rules in the spirit of enlightened absolutism.	1759–88
At the end of the Seven Years' War Spain loses Florida to Britain but acquires western Louisiana from France.	1763
Expulsion of the Jesuits.	1767

1783	Under the treaty of Versailles at the end of the War of American Independence Spain recovers Florida and Minorca from Britain.
1788–1808	Advised by his favourite Manuel de Godoy, Charles IV leads Spain into total dependence on Napoleon.
1801	Return of Louisiana to France.
1805	Destruction of the French and Spanish fleet by Nelson at Trafalgar.
1808	A rising in Aranjuez overthrows the Francophile Godoy and compels Charles IV to abdicate in favour of his son Ferdinand (Fernando) in March. Seeing his interests in the Iberian peninsula in jeopardy, Napoleon occupies Spain and compels both Charles and Ferdinand VII to abdicate. Napoleon's brother Joseph becomes king of Spain, his brother-in-law Marshal Murat king of Naples.
	A revolt by the people of Madrid against Murat's troops on May 2nd marks the beginning of a Spanish national rising. Juntas (committees) are formed to organise a guerrilla war against French rule. A French army surrenders at Bailén in July, and Joseph flees from Madrid. A British army commanded by General Wellesley (later Duke of Wellington) supports the Spanish war of liberation, and Napoleon then intervenes personally in the war.
1808–09	Napoleon occupies Madrid, takes Zaragoza and enables Joseph to return. Spain is almost completely occupied.
1810–25	The Spanish colonies in South America declare their independence.
1812	The Cortes, meeting in Cádiz, adopt the first Spanish constitution.
1813	Wellington's victory in the decisive battle of Vitoria frees Spain from foreign rule.

From the Restoration to the Establishment of the Second Republic
(1813–1931)

	The history of Spain in the 19th century is marked by a series of civil wars, caused by the reactionary policies of the restored monarchy, the country's economic backwardness and a number of misadventures in foreign policy. Although Spain remains neutral in the First World War and prospers economically, the country's internal conflicts become more acute for lack of the necessary economic and social reforms.
1814	Ferdinand VII returns to the throne, rejects the liberal constitution of 1812 and rules as an absolute monarch.
1820	Liberal revolution in Cádiz, led by Colonel Rafael del Riego Núñez. The king thereupon recognises the 1812 constitution. The Liberals soon fall into two schools of thought, the Moderados and the Exaltados (radicals), who are constantly at odds.
1823	On behalf of the Holy Alliance France represses the revolution by military intervention. Absolutism is restored.
1830	In the "Pragmatic Sanction" Ferdinand VII provides for his daughter Isabella to succeed him on the throne.
1834	Introduction of a moderately liberal constitution.
1834–39	First Carlist War. Don Carlos, Ferdinand VII's brother, declares himself king (Charles V) in opposition to the regency of the Queen Mother,

María Cristina of Naples, during the minority of Isabella II. He is supported by the Basque provinces, Aragon and Catalonia, but the enterprise fails and he flees to France (1839).

Isabella comes of age.	1843
Reactionary constitutional reform.	1845
The Second Carlist War and republican risings aggravate internal conflicts.	1847–49
Concordat with the Pope confirming the exclusive status of the Roman Catholic religion in Spain.	1851
War with Morocco: Spain's only gain is Tetuán.	1859–60
Spain participates in the unsuccessful French expedition to Mexico.	1861–62
Revolt led by General Prim and Marshal Serrano: Isabella is deposed and flees to France.	1868
The Cortes appoint Serrano Regent pending the choice of a new king. The candidature of Prince Leopold of Hohenzollern fails because of French resistance.	1869
Amadeo I, a son of Victor Emmanuel II of Italy, abdicates because of opposition by the left. First Republic established by the Cortes.	1871–73
The Third Carlist War, initiated by Don Carlos's grandson, is directed against Amadeo I and the First Republic. Mass socialist risings.	1872–76
Serrano becomes Dictator; end of the First Republic. Restoration of the Bourbons following a military coup led by General Martínez de Campos.	1874
Alfonso XI, son of Isabella II, makes possible a quieter course of internal development.	1874–85
A new constitution provides for freedom of association and freedom of the press, but does away with jury trial and civil marriage. End of the Carlist War.	1876
Foundation of the Spanish Socialist Workers Party and the General Workers' Union.	1879–88
Regency (until 1902) of the Queen Mother, María Cristina of Austria, during the minority of Alfonso XIII.	1885
Introduction of universal suffrage.	1890
Autonomist movements in Catalonia, the Basque country and Galicia.	from 1890
Spanish–American War. Spain loses its last large colonies (Cuba, the Philippines, Puerto Rico). Its only foreign possessions are now in North Africa.	1898
Spain sells the Mariana, Caroline and Pelew Islands to Germany.	1899
Agreement on Morocco between Spain and France.	1904
Beginning of campaign in Morocco against the Rif rising, which is not quelled until 1926.	1909

Anarcho-syndicalist (from *sindicato,* trade union) rising in Barcelona.

1910–12 Prime Minister Canalejas develops a liberal cultural policy, but fails to undertake economic or social reform. Increasing emigration to America.

1914–18 Spain remains neutral in the First World War.

1923 General Primo de Rivera establishes a military dictatorship, with Alfonso XIII's approval. Dissolution of the Cortes.

1925 Primo de Rivera transforms his military dictatorship into a civil dictatorship. Reform of financial and tax system; attempted land reform. Increasing opposition in the country.

1926 Spain leaves the League of Nations (re-admitted 1928).

1930 Revolutionary and republican disturbances lead to Primo de Rivera's resignation; he dies in Paris in March.

1931 After a Republican victory in local government elections Alfonso XIII leaves the country. Beginning of the Second Republic.

From the Second Republic to the Death of Franco (1931–75)

Since the European democracies do nothing to help the new Spanish republic, and even the Soviet Union believes that the time is not ripe for a social revolution in Spain, the Republican forces are defeated by the Fascist dictatorship of General Franco, with support from Hitler and Mussolini. After the Second World War the Franco regime is unable to lead Spain out of its political and economic isolation; only after Franco's death is the way clear for the liberalisation and democratisation of the country.

1931 Spain receives a new constitution, liberal and progressive in its provisions: separation of church and state, a unified state, regional self-government for Catalonia (1932) and the Basque country (1936), a limited degree of land reform.

1932–33 Foundation of the Confederation of the Autonomous Right (CEDA) and the fascist Falange.

1933 Election victory for Monarchists and Fascists. During the next three years there are a succession of government crises and serious disturbances, which lead to the dissolution of Parliament.

1936 After the victory of the Popular Front (Republicans, Socialists, Syndicalists and Communists) there is much social unrest (breaking up of large estates, occupation of factories).

1936–39 The Spanish Civil War breaks out after the murder of a monarchist member of Parliament, Calvo Sotelo (July 13th), and a military rising (July 17th) led by General Francisco Franco y Bahamonde (1892–1975) in Spanish Morocco. Franco and other generals set up a government in Burgos, and the Junta de Defensa Nacional (Committee of National Defence) appoint him as their leader (Caudillo) and supreme commander of the rebel forces (September 30th). As leader of the Falange he is supported by the Monarchists and the conservative clergy.

While Franco's forces receive military support from Germany, Italy and Portugal the Republican government receives help only from Mexico and the Soviet Union and from the volunteers of the International Brigade. Germany and Italy recognise the Franco government (November 18th 1936).

Amalgamation of the Falange Española and the Traditionalists to form the Falange Española Tradicionalista, led by Franco.   1937

Recognition of Franco's regime by France, Britain (February 27th) and the United States (April 1st). With the entry of Fascist troops into Madrid (March 28th) the Civil War comes to an end. Spain joins the Anti-Comintern Pact (April 7th) and leaves the League of Nations (May 8th).   1939

During the Second World War Spain remains neutral in spite of its links with the Berlin–Rome axis. At Hitler's request, however, Franco sends the "Blue Division" (some 18,000 volunteers) to the eastern front.   1939–45

Spain occupies the International Zone of Tangier (November 3rd). The Trade Union Law (December 6th) prohibits strikes and free trade unions, which are replaced by paternalistic corporative organisations. Wage freeze, leading to an upturn in the economy.   1940

Spain is obliged to restore the International Zone of Tangier (October 11th).   1945

Spain is politically and economically isolated as a result of Franco's authoritarian regime. It is not a founding member of the United Nations and receives no aid under the Marshall Plan.   from 1945

A national referendum approves Franco's plan to restore the monarchy at a later date.   1947

The economic and diplomatic sanctions imposed on Spain by the United Nations in 1946 are lifted on the initiative of the United States; Spain grants the United States military bases.   1950

Opposition to Franco's dictatorship grows. Major strikes, largely promoted by separatist movements (Aragon, Basque provinces, Asturias), and student revolts, and from 1962 battles over pay, directed against lack of political freedom and social abuses.   from 1951

Agreement on US bases: Spain receives economic and military aid worth a billion dollars which promotes economic development.   1953

Spain becomes a member of the United Nations.   1955

Loss of Spain's North African possessions (except the ports of Ceuta and Melilla) to Morocco.   1956

Ifni, Spanish Guinea and the Spanish Sahara are declared to be Spanish overseas provinces.   1958

Spain becomes a member of the OEEC and OECD.   1959–60

Spain enjoys a considerable economic upsurge thanks to mass tourism, much foreign investment and remittances from Spanish workers in western Europe.   from 1960

Spain applies for association with the EC.   1962

Miners' strikes in Asturias.   1962–63

A new Organic Law of the State is promulgated as a substitute for a new constitution.   1966

History

1966–68	Demonstrations by students and priests calling for liberalisation.
1968	Spain closes the frontier with Gibraltar at La Linea after the introduction of a new constitution in Gibraltar.
1969–73	The Roman Catholic organisation Opus Dei gains important posts in the government and economy and prevents any moves towards liberalisation.
1969	Juan Carlos (b. 1938 in Rome), grandson of the last king, Alfonso XIII, is nominated as successor (and from 1971 deputy) to Franco and as the country's future king.
	Spain cedes Ifni to Morocco.
1970	Military agreement with France and renewal of the agreement on US bases. Basque rising (led by ETA, a militant separatist movement) against political repression. The Falange, whose influence had been steadily reduced by Franco since the 1950s, is renamed the Movimiento Nacional.
1972–73	Strikes in Asturias and Catalonia.
1973	Carrero Blanco, appointed prime minister in June, is murdered by ETA (December).
1974	The new prime minister, Arias Navarro, introduces minor political reforms. Spain (which is not a member of NATO) signs a "NATO parallel declaration".
from 1974	The effects of the worldwide energy crisis and the economic recession aggravate Spain's internal difficulties: increased unemployment, high inflation, budgetary and balance of payments deficits. Increased terrorist activity by extremist organisations of left and right, harsh anti-terrorist laws and wildcat strikes reflect the country's political and social insecurity.
1975	State visit by US President Ford (June); renewal of agreement on US bases (October).
	On Franco's death (November 20th) Prince Juan Carlos becomes king of Spain as Juan Carlos I. Basque, Catalan and Galician are recognised as teaching and official languages.

Democratic Spain (from 1975)

	After Franco's death King Juan Carlos I begins the process of democratisation, which continues in spite of attempted coups. Spain becomes a full member of the democratic community of states.
1975	Arias Navarro, Franco's last prime minister, at first remains in office, but resigns at the beginning of 1976 under the pressure of public opinion, which demands a return to democracy, and at the king's request.
1976	Arias is succeeded as prime minister by Adolfo Suárez, secretary general of the Movimiento Nacional. In spite of this background he gives a decisive impulse to democratisation.
	The withdrawal of the last troops from the former province of Spanish Sahara marks the end of Spanish colonial rule (January 12th). Treaty of friendship with the United States: Spain is now in practice integrated into the NATO defence system (June).
	Two-thirds of the country's political prisoners are freed under an amnesty (August 2nd).

Resumption of diplomatic relations with the Soviet Union (February   1977
9th). Dissolution of the Movimiento Nacional and legalisation of the
Communist Party (PCE; April). The first democratic election since 1936
is held on June 15th. The new Cabinet, headed by Suárez, consists
almost exclusively of members of the UCD (Unión del Centro Demo-
crático; July 4th).

    Spain applies formally for membership of the European Community
(July). In order to stimulate the economy and reduce unemployment
the peseta is devalued by 20% against the US dollar; price controls and
measures to promote employment are introduced at the same time
(July 24th).

Spain joins the Council of Europe (February 24th).   1978
    Amalgamation of the socialist parties (April 30th).
    There is a further wave of violence by Basque separatists.
    After a plebiscite on December 6th–7th a new democratic constitu-
tion comes into force: constitutional monarchy, abolition of the death
penalty, reintroduction of civil marriage (with the possibility of
divorce).

In the second parliamentary election since the liberalisation of the   1979
country (March 2nd) the UCD, led by Prime Minister Suárez, maintain
their lead over the Socialists. The Basque provinces elect members
associated with the extreme separatists, leading high military officers
to express alarm and utter threats.

    Free local government elections are held for the first time since the
Civil War.

    In referendums held in October Basques and Catalans approve mea-
sures giving them wide powers of regional self-government. In
November Parliament, by a majority, adopts charters of autonomy for
the Basque country (charter of Guernica) and Catalonia (charter of
Sau).

Regional parliaments are elected in the Basque country and Catalonia.   1980
Other regions seek charters of autonomy.

    A law on freedom of religion comes into force: Catholicism is no
longer the state religion.

Prime Minister Suárez resigns (January 29th).   1981
    During voting on the appointment of Leopoldo Calvo Sotelo (UCD)
as prime minister over 200 soldiers of the Guardia Civil force their way
into Parliament and hold members prisoner for ten hours (February
23rd). In a radio address King Juan Carlos condemns this attempted
coup. Calvo Sotelo is elected as head of government (February 25th).

    Further terrorist attacks by ETA, aimed at securing the complete
independence of the Basque region.

    The two largest Spanish parties, UCD (the Union of the Democratic
Centre) and PSOE (the Spanish Socialist Workers Party), join in the
"Autonomy Pact", a plan to make Spain a largely decentralised state
(August 2nd).

Spain becomes the 16th member of NATO (May 30th).   1982
A "law on the harmonisation of the autonomy process", agreed between UCD and PSOE, is passed (June 30th).

    Parliament is dissolved in August; the Socialists win the subsequent
election (October 28th).

    Pope John Paul II visits Spain (November).

    The Socialist leader Felipe González becomes prime minister
(December 1st).

Dissolution of the UCD.   1983
    State visit by Prime Minister González to the United States, seeking
economic aid for Spain (June).

Regional elections on May 8th, which confirm the Socialist party's increased support, mark the formal conclusion of the move towards autonomy. There are now seventeen "autonomous communities", each with a regional constitution and an elected representative body.

1984

Demonstration against Spain's membership of NATO and the US military bases on Spanish soil (February 19th).

Differences of view in Brussels between the EC countries and Spain over Spanish membership of the Community.

Call for the union of the Basque provinces of Spain, southern France and the Spanish region of Navarre (June).

1985

The frontier crossing between Spain and Gibraltar is reopened after being closed for sixteen years (February 5th).

A law treating the Muslim inhabitants of Melilla and Ceuta, the Spanish enclaves in North Africa, as foreigners, who may be expelled to Morocco, comes into force and gives rise to demonstrations.

1986

Spain joins the European Community on January 1st.

An agreement between the Spanish government and the towns of Melilla and Ceuta makes provision for the more rapid grant of Spanish citizenship to the Muslim inhabitants of these places (February).

A national referendum shows a majority in favour of continued Spanish membership of NATO (March 12th).

In parliamentary elections on June 22nd the Spanish Socialist Workers Party (PSOE) again wins a majority; Felipe González is re-elected prime minister for a further four-year term.

1987

In local government and regional elections in June the PSOE, which since 1982 has had an absolute majority in most regions, suffers significant losses.

An ETA bomb attack on a department store in Barcelona kills eighteen people (June 19th).

Spain signs the treaty banning nuclear weapons (November 5th).

A further ETA attack on a Guardia Civil barracks in Zaragoza leaves eleven dead (December 11th). All parties in Parliament except the radical Basque parties Herri Batasuna and Eusko Alkartasuna sign a "State Pact against Terrorism and Violence" which excludes any negotiation with ETA.

1988

The withdrawal of American fighter planes from the Torrejón air force base is seen as a success for Spanish policy.

Mrs Thatcher becomes the first British prime minister to visit Spain (September).

At the turn of the year the conflict between the socialist government and UGT, a trade union which has been closely associated with the PSOE for more than a hundred years, becomes more acute. UGT accuses Prime Minister González of abandoning socialist ideals and calls for measures of social justice and action to reduce high unemployment. In December UGT and the communist workers' committees call a general strike.

1989

Spain takes over the presidency of the European Community.

Negotiations between the trade unions and the government to settle the conflict make no progress.

Discussions, in progress since January, between ETA leaders and the government in Algiers, to which the ETA representatives have been expelled from France, end without result. ETA calls off the ceasefire to which it had agreed, and this is followed by several bomb attacks on railway lines. The government, with the support of almost all parties, declares that it is no longer prepared to negotiate with ETA.

Camilo José Cela is awarded the Nobel Prize for literature (October).

In a parliamentary election in October the González government loses its absolute majority, but Felipe González remains prime minister. The main gainer in the election is the Izquierda Unida (United Left), which increases its representation from seven to eighteen seats, while the conservatives stagnate (PP) or lose seats (CDS).

The Basque Regional Parliament passes a resolution stressing the right of self-determination of the Basques and of freedom of power. 1990

In country-wide local and regional elections the PSOE records modest success but loses a number of strongholds. The Conservatives make considerable gains at the expense of the centre parties. 1991

The ETA carries out several attacks during the run-up to the Olympic Games and the International Exhibition. In one bombing attack in May on the Guardia-Civil barracks near Barcelona nine people are killed.

Spain celebrates the 500th anniversary of the voyage of discovery of Columbus. From April 20th until October 12th EXPO '92 is held in Seville, the last world exhibition in the 20th c. To mark the occasion Spain's first high speed train "AVE" comes into operation on the route between Seville and Madrid. 1992

On July 25th the 25th Summer Olympic Games of modern times are opened in Barcelona.

In February a bomb attack by ETA claims five lives in Madrid. In March the French police arrest the three ETA leaders.

A tanker runs aground in December off the coast of La Coruña spilling 70,000t of oil which pollute the Galician coastline.

The continuous economic crisis causes Felipe González to call early elections in which his party, the PSOE, loses its absolute majority. He forms a minority government with the support of the moderate Catalan and Basque regional parties. 1993

Another ETA attack in May kills seven people.

In January the trade unions call a general strike in protest at the restructuring of the employment market and the economic policy. Several cases of corruption bring about a governmental crisis in May. 1994

Art and Culture

Prehistory and Antiquity

Stone Age

The earliest forms of artistic expression in Spain date from the Late Palaeolithic (40,000–10,000 B.C.). They are the cave paintings of the Franco-Cantabrian area which have been found in more than a hundred caves in France and north-western Spain. For the most part they depict animals, which were of central importance in the life of the Stone Age hunters and gatherers – as the hunters' quarry, as divinities, animal ancestors, protective spirits or fertility symbols, or in other cult functions. These paintings and engravings, which often use the surface of the cave walls to achieve an effect of relief, have great expressive force and often show a stylisation reminiscent of contemporary art. The colours were applied either directly by rubbing with the pigmented substances (various minerals, including manganese) or – ground down and diluted with water – by a stick or brush. This art reached its peak in the Magdalenian period (16,000–10,000 B.C.). To this period belong the paintings in the Altamira Caves, near Santillana del Mar, which rank among the finest so far discovered. In addition to many other caves in Cantabria Stone Age cave paintings have also been found near Málaga in Andalusia. Other cave paintings, found mainly on the Mediterranean coast between Barcelona and Valencia, are dated to the Mesolithic and Neolithic. Mostly occurring in the open on the walls of gorges or on overhanging rock faces, they also represent hunting scenes.

These rock paintings are not the only evidence of artistic activity in the Neolithic period (6000–4000 B.C.). Numerous fragments of the pottery known as impressed ware, decorated with impressions of shells, have been found on the Mediterranean coast from Gibraltar to the Pyrenees, for example at El Pany in Catalonia and near Valencia. From the 4th century B.C. incised patterns are found; particularly well preserved examples have been recovered at Alhama de Granada in Andalusia. On the threshold of the Metal Ages was the Almerian culture in south-eastern Spain (El Garcel, Tres Cabezos), where remains of an agricultural people who were already using some metal tools have been found (round and oval huts, undecorated pottery).

Copper and Bronze Ages

During the Copper Age (3000–1800 B.C.) settlements resembling towns begin to appear in Spain. Characteristic of this period are large tombs, either with corbelled vaulting (southern Spain) or more commonly of megalithic construction (Cueva de Menga, Andalusia; Majorca). The settlements already show defensive features. In pottery the bell beaker is found all over the Iberian peninsula. The Bronze Age (c. 2000–1600 B.C.) produced finely worked metal tools, including some of gold and silver. Typical structures of this period are the round towers (talayots), table-shaped stone formations (taulas) and chamber tombs in the form of an upturned boat (navetas) found in the Balearics.

Phoenicians, Greeks, Carthaginians

The various peoples who founded colonies in the Iberian peninsula in antiquity have also left their traces. The Phoenicians, who established trading posts on the south coast from about 1100 B.C., later to be succeeded by the towns of Cádiz (Gadri) and Málaga (Malaka), are represented mainly by grave goods. They were followed from about

An Iberian sphinx

The "Lady of Elche"

700 B.C. by the Greeks, whose principal settlement was Emporion (Ampurias, Catalan Empúries), the remains of which can still be seen. The Carthaginians left evidence of their skill in the form of terracotta figures and other pottery, mainly on the Balearic island of Ibiza.

Of the original inhabitants of Spain the Iberians living on the Mediterranean coast have left the most striking evidence of their artistic skills, shown mainly in the form of pottery and sculpture. Among the finest examples of their sculpture are the "Lady of Elche", a bust of the 3rd or 4th century B.C. found in 1897 in the Iberian settlement of Illici, the "Goddess of Baza" and a number of statuettes found at Cerro de los Santos (all in the Archaeological Museum, Madrid). Iberian sculpture shows clear Greek influence. A good example of Iberian urban layout is the large settlement of Ullastret in the province of Gerona.

Iberian art

There are considerable remains of Roman buildings of the colonial period at Mérida (theatre), Segovia (aqueduct, town walls), La Coruña (lighthouse), Tarragona and other places, together with many smaller objects, e.g. from Mérida and Itálica (near Seville) in the Roman province of Baetica. So firmly was Roman culture established in Spain that in A.D. 74 the population, already completely Romanised, was granted Roman civil rights.

Roman art

Visigothic and Moorish Art

The Visigoths, who drove the Romans out of Spain, incorporated elements of both Roman and Byzantine architecture in their aisled basilicas with timber roofs, decorated with vine tendrils and grapes. Germanic decorative features were the rope frieze, the rosette and the circle. A notable feature is the use of horseshoe arches before the

Visigothic art

coming of the Moors. The finest surviving church is San Juan Bautista at Baños de Cerrato (near Palencia), which dates from 661. Many examples of Visigothic jewellery and ornaments, including crowns, have been found at Toledo, once the Visigothic capital.

Asturian art

The Visigoths, withdrawing before the advancing Arabs, left a type of architecture in Asturias which is also categorised as pre-Romanesque. It is characterised by stilted round-headed arches, round columns with the appearance of having been turned on a lathe or decorated with herringbone patterns, and capitals with double cord decoration. Some churches are on a Greek cross plan. The finest examples of this style are at Naranco, near Oviedo – the church of Santa Maria de Naranco, originally built about 845 as the royal hall of King Ramiro I, and the palace chapel of San Miguel de Lillo, which dates from the same period.

Moorish–Arab art

After their victory at Jerez de la Frontera in 711 the Moors established a number of caliphates in Spain which, particularly in the south of the country, enjoyed a great flowering of intellectual life, accompanied by a splendid development of architecture. Many features of later Spanish art are derived from this earlier Islamic art.

The essential features of Islamic architecture are the horseshoe arch, often richly decorated, stalactitic vaulting in domes, arches and niches, made up of four elements (rectangles, parallelograms, equilateral and right-angled triangles), projecting eaves (*aleros*) with carved ornament, double windows with horseshoe arches (*ajimeces*), coffered ceilings (*artesonados*) and glazed tiles (*azulejos*). Since Islam prohibits the representation of human figures (though this prohibition is strictly observed only in religious art), mosques were decorated only with majolica tiles in floral patterns and friezes in Kufic script of verses from the Koran, in which the artists displayed abundant fantasy and delight

Moorish ornament in the Alhambra, Granada

in colour. The structure of mosques, with their outer court and prayer hall, was modelled on that of the Prophet's house, which consisted of a courtyard with a covered ambulatory borne on palm stems – a feature reflected in the forests of columns in mosques. The Spanish mosques were often designed in the form of four-aisled halls with transepts. Many churches and synagogues were converted into mosques, or the Muslims might move into an existing church or synagogue, tolerating its use also by other faiths (e.g. the Bib Mardum mosque in Toledo, originally a Visigothic chapel and now the church of Cristo de la Luz). In addition to mosques the Moors left behind them a number of mighty castles and the most magnificent achievement of Moorish secular architecture, the Alhambra palace in Granada.

Moorish–Arab faience bears witness to the consummate skill of their craftsmen. World-famed, too, were the damascene blades of Toledo and the finely wrought articles in filigree openwork.

In the Moorish regions of Spain there developed among the Mozarabs (Christians under Moorish rule) a hybrid Christian/Moorish style, which took over Moorish features such as the horseshoe-arched window. Mozarabic art flowered with particular splendour in the book illumination of the 10th century.

More important, however, was the Mudéjar style, named after the Moors who remained in the territories recovered during the Reconquista. Between the 12th and the 16th centuries Mudéjar architects erected both sacred and secular buildings for their Christian masters which combined numerous Moorish stylistic elements – glazed bricks, tiles, horseshoe arches, stellar vaulting, coffered ceilings and even Kufic inscriptions – with Romanesque, Gothic and Renaissance features. The Mozarabic style also influenced Christian architects. Its finest achievements were in artistic and decorative craftwork.

Mozarabic and Mudéjar art

The old Caliphal capital of Córdoba still betrays the original Moorish layout, and many of its houses show Eastern architectural features. The finest monument of Moorish art and architecture in Córdoba, however, is the gigantic Mezquita (785–999), the principal mosque of the western Islamic world, with its seemingly endless rows of red and white double horseshoe arches stretching away in the dim light of the interior, borne on 856 columns and forming nineteen aisles. After the Reconquista it was converted into a cathedral.

Important Moorish buildings in Andalusia

Córdoba

Seville has two magnificent examples of Islamic architecture in the Giralda, the 93m/305ft high tower of the cathedral (c. 1190), originally a minaret of the principal Moorish mosque, and the old courtyard of the mosque, the Patio de los Naranjos (Court of Orange-Trees), adjoining the cathedral. The old Alcázar of Seville, the Moorish stronghold, was rebuilt in Mudéjar style after the Reconquista, but its beautiful gardens and courtyards still display the creative power of Moorish masters. In its present form the Alcázar dates from the second half of the 14th century.

Seville

The finest achievement of Moorish secular architecture in Spain is the Alhambra ("the Red"), begun under Yusuf I in the mid 14th century, which towers over Granada on a rocky crag. Externally unimpressive, like all Moorish secular buildings, its inner courtyards (Court of Myrtles, Court of Lions) are of magical beauty, with charming fountains and ornamental pools. The interior decoration is mainly of wood and stucco, with colourful azulejos and rich arabesque ornament. All the wall surfaces are framed in Arabic inscriptions, mostly in praise of Allah. The palace was much dilapidated by the 18th century but was restored in the 19th.

Granada

Art

Romanesque

Churches

The step-by-step advance of the Reconquista, beginning around A.D. 1000 in northern Spain and continuing for almost 500 years, was accompanied by the conversion of Moorish buildings to Christian uses and the gradual displacement of the Moorish style. The beginnings of a distinctive Spanish art can be dated roughly to the 11th century. Under French and Lombard influence the Romanesque style now established itself in Spain. Spain's finest Romanesque building is the Cathedral of Santiago de Compostela, Europe's greatest medieval pilgrimage centre, built between 1060 and 1096, which shows southern French influence. Particularly beautiful is the south doorway, the Puerta de las Platerías (12th–13th c.). The west front, the Obradoiro, was remodelled in lavish Baroque style in the 18th century. Under the high altar is a crypt containing the tomb of the Apostle St James (Santiago), whose name the town bears.

In Catalonia Lombard influence was introduced by the Benedictines in their famous monastery of Santa María de Ripoll (874). Most churches built in northern Spain during this period are modest in size and decoration.

Sculpture

Romanesque sculpture achieved in this period a great flowering, particularly in the decoration of doorways (Santa María de Ripoll; San Vicente, Avila; Pórtico de la Gloria, Santiago de Compostela, begun by Master Mateo in 1168; reliefs in the cloister of Santo Domingo de Silos).

Painting

Splendid frescoes, mainly of the 12th century, have been preserved in towns and villages lying off the main through roads.

Catalan painting, showing an austerity reminiscent of Byzantine art, set a pattern which was much imitated. Less rigid and other-worldly are the frescoes in the Panteón Real in San Isidoro, León.

The book illumination of the period is also of splendid quality; among the finest examples are the Apocalypse manuscripts of the 10th and 11th centuries.

Gothic

Churches

In Spain as in other countries the displacement of Romanesque by Gothic was a gradual process. The Burgundian form of Gothic was brought to Spain by the Cistercians, a fine example of this style being the monastery of Las Huelgas, Burgos. For long a transitional style prevailed, producing charming buildings in a blending of Romanesque and Gothic, in which for the first time a typically Spanish spirit comes to the fore, as in the Old Cathedral of Salamanca.

The buildings of this period still have a plain earth-bound solidity, combined with an impressive spatial effect; but the Gothic striving towards greater height and an opening up of the wall surfaces to produce quite new effects of light became steadily more evident. The three cathedrals of Burgos, Toledo and León show the complete assimilation of the French style of cathedral architecture which had been brought in by foreign masters. Burgos Cathedral (1221), with its twin Norman towers, was followed in 1227 by Toledo Cathedral, seen as a "protest against Moorish architecture". The masterpiece of this French style was León Cathedral (c. 1250), with an over-abundance of tracery and, on the model of Burgos, double lateral aisles.

After the Reconquista cathedrals of hall-church type were built on the site of Moorish mosques at Zaragoza (begun 1188) and Seville (begun 1402). Seville Cathedral, with its huge nave and double aisles, is one of the largest Gothic churches ever built.

Other outstanding examples of 14th and 15th century church architecture are Avila Cathedral with its rich girdle of chapels, the churches

The Gothic tomb of the Constable of Castile, Burgos

of Santa María la Antigua and San Benito in Valladolid and the cathedrals of Astorga, Segovia, Pamplona and Barcelona. In Catalonia a special type was developed under southern French influence, the aisleless hall church (Gerona Cathedral).

The moving of the choir (*coro*) into the nave (*trascoro*) is a feature, found in many Spanish churches, which detracts seriously from the spatial effect of the interior – a fault which is not redeemed by the rich sculptural adornment of the choir walls. Sometimes, too, the wide windows and openwork walls are concealed behind masonry, severely reducing the amount of light admitted (Avila Cathedral).

The Mudéjar style, enriched by the incorporation of Late Gothic and ancient classical forms, developed into the Plateresque, a highly charged decorative style in which the façades of buildings are covered with a riot of variegated and intricate details. The earliest example is the Colegio de Santa Cruz in Valladolid (1480–92), by the silversmith (*platero*) Pedro Díez. The cathedrals of Salamanca (1513) and Segovia (1525), built by the brothers Juan and Rodrigo Gil de Hontañón in sumptuous style, with a superabundance of decoration, are the last great creations of Gothic architecture in Spain, already giving expression to a sense of national pride enhanced by the successful completion of the Reconquista and reflecting also the rising national prosperity due to the shipments of gold and silver from the newly discovered territories in America.

Plateresque

Spain's Gothic sculpture, like the architecture, was strongly influenced by France. Monumental sculpture is seen at its finest in the cathedrals of Vitoria, León and Burgos, the Apostles' Doorway of Valencia Cathedral and in Tarragona. Leading figures of the period were Master Bartolomé (active 1278) and Castalys (1375). The beautiful Gothic statues of the Virgin usually show particularly strong French influence, if indeed they are not actually of French origin (Seville, Toledo).

Sculpture

Catalonia, where the rich flowering of art continued – here too showing strong French influence – is notable for its large retablos (reredoses), made up of numerous separate carved scenes (fine examples in Barcelona, Vich and Lérida museums; high altar of Tarragona Cathedral, by Johan de Valfogona, *c.* 1430) and fine tombs (tomb of Archbishop Lope Fernández de Luna, Zaragoza Cathedral, after 1382).

In sculpture as in architecture the 15th century brought a trend towards a luxuriant proliferation of forms, promoted by the example of Dutch and German masters – Gil de Siloé (an architect and sculptor from Nuremberg), Anequin de Egas, Juan Alemán, Enrique and Juan Guas, Rodrigo Alemán. The huge retablo in Toledo Cathedral (1504) was the work of seventeen foreign masters.

Gothic painting too was subject to French influence; later it was also influenced by Italy, and in the 15th century by Dutch artists. Many Italian painters worked in Spain, including Gherardo Starnina and Nicolás Fiorentino, and the Sienese school was particularly influential. The Barcelona school of painters, which developed in the 15th century under Dutch influence, nevertheless achieved vigorous characteristics of its own, a marked realism and great splendour (Luis Dalmau, Bartolomeo Vermejo, Jaime Huguet). In the later 15th century schools of painting also developed in Valencia and Castile, the latter school showing strong North German influence (Fernando Gallegos). A number of artists from the Netherlands also worked in Spain, among them Francisco de Amberes (= Antwerp), Juan de Flandes, Juan de Holanda and Juan de Borgoña (= Burgundy). In Seville there were Juan Sánchez de Castro and a German artist, Alejo Fernández; while Pedro Berruguete was the first artist in whom distinctively Spanish characteristics can be detected. The emerging national spirit in painting, however, was to suffer a setback as a result of the powerful impulses sent out by the Italian Renaissance.

Painting

Renaissance

In architecture the forms of the Renaissance were at first applied to purely decorative purposes, the buildings themselves being still informed by the Gothic spirit. Extraordinary minglings of styles – Plateresque (Late Gothic), Moorish, Renaissance – are found, for example in the cloister at Santiago de Compostela (1521–86), the largest in Spain; the Casa de Pilatos, Seville; and the courtyard of the University and the Casa de las Conchas (1514) in Salamanca. The summer palace, built for Charles V by Pedro Machuca on the Alhambra hill in Granada, (1526) is the finest example of High Renaissance architecture in Spain, already radiating imperial greatness. Burgos became a centre of the new architectural style under the leadership of Diego de Siloé, son of Gil. More attuned to the Spanish national character than the uncluttered forms of the Roman Renaissance, however, were the Mannerist and early Baroque grotesqueries of the "Estile monstruoso". Only under the influence of the Counter-Reformation, which was opposed to an excessive proliferation of ornament, was it possible for a new style of imposing austerity and rigour to come to the fore. The masterpiece of this new severe style is the huge Escorial (completed by Juan de Herrera in 1584), a convent, a fortress and a palace all in one, which already shows the influence of the early Baroque. Valladolid Cathedral (begun 1580), also by Herrera, was planned on such a gigantic scale that it was never completed.

Architecture

In sculpture too the Renaissance style displaced Gothic only very gradually. A particularly fine example of the free-standing tombs with

Sculpture

◄ *The Isabelline façade of Santa María la Real, Aranda de Duero*

Juan de Juni: "Entombment"

recumbent figures is the monument of Ferdinand and Isabella, the Catholic Monarchs, in the Capilla Real in Granada. The leading names in 16th century sculpture are Alonso Berruguete, Felipe Vigarní (also known as Felipe de Borgoña, Philip of Burgundy) and Damián Forment. Like Berruguete, Forment developed a Renaissance style of wholly Italian stamp (altar of Nuestra Señora del Pilar, Zaragoza). With Berruguete was associated Juan de Juni, who was probably of French origin. The "Romanist" reaction which reflected the severity and austerity of the Counter-Reformation toned down the fervid emotionalism of the previous style in favour of lofty grandeur and rigidity (as in the retablos of northern Spain, which sometimes cover the whole of the choir wall up to the vaulting: retablo in Astorga Cathedral by Gaspar Becerra, *c.* 1560). The Arfe family of sculptors created mainly works of small sculpture and liturgical utensils.

Painting

Many painters, including Juan de Juanes, Juan Fernández Navarrete (surnamed el Mudo, the Dumb), Bartolomé González and Luis de Morales, modelled themselves on the great masters of the Italian Renaissance.

Baroque and Neo-Classicism

Architecture

The Spanish Baroque introduced into the vocabulary of architectural form created by Borromini the elaborately decorative style known as Churrigueresque after its originator José de Churriguera – a riot of fanciful ornament, often totally uncontrolled, which catered for the Spanish penchant for unrestrained richness of decoration and was frequently carried to the pitch of extravagance. Fine examples of Churrigueresque are the sacristy of the Cartuja (Charterhouse) in Granada (1727–64) and the Plaza Mayor in Salamanca.

In the second half of the 18th century, under the Bourbons, a reaction set in, and the sober lines of Neo-Classicism came into fashion. An early masterpiece in this style is the Royal Palace in Madrid, designed by an Italian, Filippo Juvara, and built by another Italian, Giovanni Battista Sacchetti. The most celebrated pioneer of Neo-Classicism in Spain, however, was Francisco Sabatini, also an Italian. Charles III's court architect, Ventura Rodríguez, continued work on Nuestra Señora del Pilar in Zaragoza, while Juan de Villanueva built the finest example of the Neo-Classical style in Spain, the Prado in Madrid (1785–1819).

Spanish Baroque sculpture is almost exclusively confined to religious themes, which are treated with great realism, and sometimes in an exaggeratedly naturalistic manner, in order to achieve a dramatic – often, indeed, disturbing – effect: the statues are clad in fabric garments and wigs, and have artificial eyes, artificial tears and realistically depicted wounds. Gregorio Fernández or Hernández worked in Castile, Martínez Montañés in Seville. Celebrated examples of the sculpture of this period are the *pasos* (figures associated with Christ's Passion) which are carried in the great religious processions, such as the Cristo del Gran Poder in San Lorenzo.

Sculpture

Alonso Cano and Pedro de Mena were talented successors to Martínez Montañés.

Spanish painting of the Baroque period ranks among the supreme achievements of European art. In his visionary pictures the great Mannerist painter El Greco ("the Greek": born in Crete as Domenikos Theotokopoulos) gives expression to the religious experience with tremendous intensity and a very personal style ("Burial of Count Orgaz", in Santo Tomé, Toledo). Although closely attuned to the Spanish character, El Greco did not form a school. More typical of Spanish Baroque painting were Francisco Ribalta and Jusepe de Ribera (Velázquez's teacher), Zurbarán and Murillo. Francisco Zurbarán is mainly known for his portraits of monks and his sharp chiaroscuro effects in the manner of Caravaggio.

Painting

El Greco

Diego Velázquez (1599–1660) was the outstanding painter of the Spanish Baroque, a great realist who, as court painter to Philip IV, painted unflattering portraits of court society, notable for their expressiveness and acute delineation of character, as well as charming portraits of children, such as the Infante Baltasar Carlos on horseback and the little Infanta Margarita Teresa, but produced practically no religious pictures.

Velázquez

Perhaps Spain's most popular painter is Bartolomé Esteban Murillo, the best collections of whose works are in Seville and in the Prado in Madrid. He painted religious visions and ecstasies, but also charming genre pictures, appealing little street-boys and sorrowful figures of Christ ("Purísima", Prado; "St Anthony", baptistery of Seville Cathedral).

Murillo

After the flowering of Baroque painting in the 17th century, the 18th century produced no artists of any real consequence. The German painter Anton Raphael Mengs attempted, as court painter, to develop the Neo-Classical style in painting, but without much success. Nor did the Italian master Giovanni Battista Tiepolo, who lived in Madrid from 1761 to 1770, have any great effect on Spanish painting.

It was not until the turn of the 18th and 19th centuries that the painter and graphic artist Francisco Goya (1746–1828), standing alone at the beginning of a new development, broke out of the stagnation of the 18th century and gave a powerful new impetus to European art. A man of profound humanity, with a sharp eye for the seamy sides and

Goya

Velázquez: "The Infanta Margarita of Austria"

cruelties of life, he produced works of great emotional effect, among them several series of etchings ("Desastres de la Guerra", "Proverbios", "Caprichos"). His great skill as a portrait painter found ample scope in the corrupt world of Charles IV's court ("Charles IV and his Family"). His masterpieces (over 120 pictures) are in the Prado in Madrid ("Maja Nude" and "Maja Clothed", "The Shooting of the Rebels of 2nd May").

19th and 20th centuries

Architecture

The architecture of the 19th century in Spain, as in other European countries, shows a mingling of the most diverse historical styles, in the manner practised by the exponents of Historicism. A good example of this trend is the Almudena Cathedral in Madrid, designed by the Marqués de Cubas (begun 1895). The Catalan architects Luis Doménech i Montaner and Antoni Gaudí, representatives of the Neo-Catalan style, went their own ways. Gaudí's Templo de la Sagrada Familia in Barcelona, begun in 1882 and still under construction, is a monumental cathedral in a fantastic style which owes something to Art Nouveau, with forms reminiscent of Gothic and others of almost organic effect based on vegetable forms.

Purely functional buildings have made their appearance in Spain only during the economic upswing of the last few decades, particularly in the cities of Madrid and Barcelona. The mushroom development of the resorts on the Mediterranean coasts of Spain has led to a building boom of extraordinary dimensions and to the building-up of whole stretches of the coast which become real ghost towns during the off-season. Often of poor architectural quality, these new developments represent an assault on the landscape, the full effects of which cannot yet be measured.

The sculpture of the 19th century was influenced by the ideas of Historicism (Dos de Mayo monument, Madrid, 1840), but the old traditions of Catalan sculpture were carried on by the Vallmitjana brothers in Barcelona, Julio Antonio and José Llimona. The first half of the 20th century produced the remarkable metal sculpture of Julio González and Eduardo Chillida. Pablo Picasso initiated a radical break with tradition in the field of sculpture. The dependence of Cubist sculpture on painting is very evident. Instead of the traditional materials the artists of this period preferred montages of papier-mâché, plywood and miscellaneous objects of all kinds.

Notable successors to Goya in the field of portrait painting were Vicente López, Federico Madrazo, Leonardo Alenza and José de Madrazo. There were also some excellent painters of historical scenes.

In the first half of the 20th century Ignacio Zuloaga developed a very personal style. José María Sert achieved international reputation as a fresco painter.

Pablo Picasso (1881–1973), living in Paris, became the leading exponent of a new artistic trend. After the earlier phases of his long artistic development (the Blue period, the Rose period) he was associated with Georges Braque in creating the Cubist style, in which the objects and persons represented are reduced to the basic forms of the cube, the cone and the sphere and the many possible ways of regarding the subject are given expression. Picasso developed into the most important painter of our century, a great experimenter with a profound concern for human values, as in his famous painting "Guernica", commemorating the destruction of the little Basque town of Guernica by a Fascist air attack during the Civil War (now in El Casón, an annexe of the Prado, Madrid).

Juan Gris was another exponent of Cubism, while Joan Miró went in for Surrealism, which developed in Paris in the 1920s. His lively and subtly elegant pictures are among the most attractive creations of modern art. Salvador Dalí, who was influenced by the Italian "Pittura metafisica" and by Freudian psychoanalysis, was the most celebrated representative of Surrealism ("The Burning Giraffe"), a painter who repeatedly enlivened the art scene with his penchant for the eccentric.

The impoverishment of Spanish artistic life which resulted from the Civil War has gradually been overcome since the end of the Franco regime. The young Spanish avantgarde, led by Antonio Tapiés (co-founder in 1948 of the "Dau al Set" group), developed a radically modern school of painting of specifically Spanish stamp. While preserving the freedom of the various individual styles, this group has been concerned to explore the dramatic effects which can be derived from the material. Centred in Madrid and Barcelona, it forms one of the most interesting schools of painting of the present day, with such artists as M. Cuixart, J. J. Tharrats, Antonio Saura, Luis Feito, Rafael Canogar and the still younger generation of E. Alcoy, F. de Echevarría, G. Rueda, J. M. de Vidales, Eduardo Arroyo and others.

Literature

Spain can look back with pride on a literature going back almost 2000 years. The first literary works produced on Spanish soil were written by Romans, in a Latin noted for its purity. Among them were Seneca the Elder (54 B.C.–A.D. 39), his son Seneca the Stoic (4 B.C.–A.D. 65), the epic poet Lucan (A.D. 39–65) and the epigrammatist Martial (A.D. 42–104).

Literature

Christian literature in Latin, which began to develop in the 4th century, was cut off before reaching its full flowering by the Moorish conquest (battle of Jerez de la Frontera, 711). Its principal representatives were Juvencus (c. 330), Prudentius (348–410), St Damasus (Pope from 367 to 384), Paulus Orosius, a disciple of St Augustine and a universal historian, and St Isidore of Seville (c. 570–636), who compiled the first encyclopaedia in his "Etimologías". Under the very tolerant regime there were also Christian theologians, including the Biblical commentator Juan Hispalense (c. 839) and Alvare de Córdoba, known as the "Indiculus Luminosus", the most learned of the Mozarabs. The Christians not under Moorish rule produced only the "Cronicones", which are of very limited literary value.

Of greater importance were the writings of Arabs living in Spain, since the Moorish kingdoms in the Iberian peninsula achieved a considerable flowering of learning and literature. Scholars and writers at the Arab universities preserved and extended the heritage of antiquity which the Christian scholars of the early Middle Ages rejected. Early thinkers influenced by Plato, such as Aben Masarra (883–931) and Aben Hazam (994–1064), were followed by an Aristotelian school whose principal representative Ibn Rushd, known in Latin as Averroes (1126–98), wrote commentaries on Aristotle which transmitted and developed much scientific knowledge. The most important historians of the period were Abdelmelic ben Habib (d. about 853) and Ahmed Arrazi (887–955). Leading geographers were El Becri ("The Roads and the Province", one of the earliest geographical works) and El Idrisi (1100–69), known as the Arab Strabo.

Jewish writers include Abraham ibn Ezra (1092–1167) and the great Moses ben Maimon, known as Maimonides (1135–1204), who wrote both in Hebrew and in Arabic.

Even before Castilian had developed into a written language Galician had become the language of poetry (Alfonso the Wise's "Cantigas de Santa María"), used even at the Castilian court.

Catalan became a literary language when the Majorcan philosopher, poet and missionary Ramón Llull (Raimundus Lullus, 1234–1314) wrote his copious works not only in Latin and Arabic but also in the vernacular. Earlier, in the 12th and 13th centuries, the Catalan troubadours had used the related Provençal language.

Spanish National Literature

Castilian achieved its predominant position only with the development of epic poetry. The earliest work of this kind which has come down to us in written form is the "Cantar de Mio Cid", written about 1140, which recounts the life and exploits of Ruy Díaz de Vivar, known as the Cid, and became the prototype of the Spanish heroic epic. Other anonymous heroic poems, surviving only in incomplete form, are "The Seven Infantes of Lara" and "The Deeds of Sancho II of Castile", together with fragments of the epic of Roncesvalles, an early form of the "Chanson of Roland".

The minstrel poetry of the *mester de juglaría*, mostly transmitted only in oral form, was followed in the 13th century by the learned genre of the *mester de clerecía*, which is recorded in writing. At first it was mainly concerned with Christian themes (poems on the life of the Virgin by Gonzalo de Berceo); then came subjects taken from antiquity ("Libro de Alexandre") and from Spanish history ("Poema de Fernán González"). Didactic poetry culminated in the works, notable both for their quantity and their content, of Alfonso X of Castile, the Wise (reigned 1252–84). They comprised works of Spanish and universal history, collections of laws and voluminous translations of Arabic scientific and didactic works, and provided the basis for the further development of Spanish prose. Alfonso's nephew the Infante Juan Manuel wrote "El Conde Lucanor", a collection of tales of great stylistic perfection. His contemporary Juan Ruiz, Archpriest of Hita, mingled secular themes with mystical ideas in his "Libro del Buen Amor" ("Book of True Love").

The Spanish drama developed out of plays on religious themes, the *autos sacramentales*. On the threshold of modern times it reached a first peak in the "Tragicomedy of Calisto and Melibea", usually known as "La Celestina" after its principal character, the bawd Celestina, which is attributed to Fernando de Rojas (*c.* 1500).

Early dramas

The Golden Age (Siglo de Oro)

The Spanish theatre rose to universal significance, however, only in the Siglo de Oro, the Golden Age, the beginning of which can be set about the middle of the 16th century.

After a period of Italian influence, brought back by Spanish noblemen from the campaigns in the kingdom of Naples (Juan Boscán, *c.* 1490–1542), and his friend Garcilaso de la Vega, 1503–36), two main schools came to the fore in a great flowering of drama, the Salamanca school (Fray Luis de León, 1527–91) and the Seville school (Fernando de Herrera, 1534–97), the former full of mystical and pantheistic exuberance, the latter notable for its fine simplicity. A controversial figure in his day was Luis de Góngora (1561–1627), the most typical representative of Baroque poetry, who used complicated metres and affected Latinised diction, founding the school known as *cultismo*.

During this period, too, more popular genres came into vogue – the romance of chivalry ("Amadís de Gaula", 1508), pastoral poetry ("Diana", 1559?) and the more realistic picaresque novel ("Lazarillo de Tormes", 1554), which were all followed by numerous continuations, imitations and translations.

The world-famous novel "Don Quixote" ("Don Quijote de la Mancha") was directed in the first place against the excesses and fashionable follies of the romances of chivalry; but thanks to the genius and literary skill of its author, Miguel de Cervantes Saavedra (*c.* 1547–1616), it developed into a work of high stylistic quality and profound human significance in which Don Quixote incarnates head-in-the-clouds idealism and his squire Sancho Panza down-to-earth reality. Cervantes' other works – short stories ("Novelas Ejemplares", 1613), plays and poems – are also of considerable quality, but tend to be overshadowed by this masterpiece of world literature.

Cervantes

The drama of the Siglo de Oro reached its peak in Lope de Vega (1562–1635), the real creator of the Spanish national theatre and one of the world's most prolific playwrights, the author of more than a thousand plays. In addition to his *comedias,* in which comedy and tragedy are mingled in a fashion characteristic of his work, he wrote fine lyric poems. His best known followers were the Mexican Ruiz de Alarcón y Mendoza (*c.* 1580–1639) and Tirso de Molina (*c.* 1571–1648), whose "Burlador de Sevilla" ("The Seducer of Seville") was the prototype of all later treatments of the Don Juan theme.

Lope de Vega

The greatest dramatist after Lope de Vega, however, was Calderón de la Barca (1600–81), a typical representative of Baroque drama. His best known play is the profound "La vida es sueño" ("Life is a Dream").

Calderón

Literature

Mysticism

The religious literature of the Golden Age is notable for its passionate mysticism. In addition to the Dominican Fray Luis de Granada (1504–88) and the Augustinian Fray Luis de León, already mentioned as a dramatist, Spain's two greatest mystics belong to this period – St Theresa of Avila (1515–82) and her disciple St John of the Cross (San Juan de la Cruz, 1542–91), both members of the Carmelite order.

Satire

Worlds apart from the fervid piety of the mystics are the worldly wisdom and shrewd satire of Francisco de Quevedo (1580–1645: "La Vida del Buscón") and Baltasar de Gracián (1601–58: "El Criticón"), whose works, in both content and style, were directed against the symptoms of decadence in the society and the literature of their day.

18th and 19th centuries

18th century

This decadence is reflected in a sharp decline in creative force which began in the second half of the 17th century and marked the end of the Golden Age. The country's intellectual life was wholly determined by the French influence which became increasingly strong under the Bourbons (Nicolás Fernández de Moratín, 1737–80) and a harking back to the Spanish national tradition. A leader of this latter trend was Gaspar Melchior de Jovellanos (1744–1811), poet, philosopher, economist and statesman, who suffered much persecution for his fierce resistance to French oppression.

19th century

At the beginning of the 19th century the Romantic movement came to Spain. Of enduring value is the lyric poetry – post-Romantic rather than Romantic – of Gustavo Adolfo Bécquer (1836–70), whose life overlapped into the second half of the century, the period of Realism, marked in Spain by descriptions of the scenery and way of life of the various regions and the frequent use of dialect and occupational jargons. Outstanding among the Realists, who were mostly novelists, were Pedro de Alarcón (1833–91: "The Three-Cornered Hat"), Juan Valera (1824–1905: "Pepita Jiménez"), Benito Pérez Galdós (1843–1920: "Angel Guerra"), Leopoldo Alas (1852–1901), who wrote under the pseudonym Clarín ("La Regenta"), and Vicente Blasco Ibáñez (1869–1928), an author widely known beyond the bounds of Spain. Compelled to flee from Spain on account of his Republican views, he later became a member of the Cortes of the First Republic. In his novels he describes the life of country people, particularly in his native province of Valencia ("The Cabin", "Blood and Sand").

20th century

Modernism

At the beginning of the 20th century the Modernist school came to the fore, at first very much under French influence. Its real founder was the Nicaraguan Rubén Darío (1867–1916: "Cantos de vida y esperanza"), who, like his followers, preferred lyric poetry as a means of expression. By looking back to Spanish folk poetry for inspiration the members of this school soon broke away from their foreign models and found a distinctive voice. Their leading representatives were Juan Ramón Jiménez (1881–1958; Nobel Prize 1956), Manuel Machado (1874–1947) and his brother Antonio Machado (1875–1939), Rafael Alberti (b. 1902) and Vicente Aleixandre (b. 1900; Nobel Prize 1977). In prose Ramón del Valle Inclán (1866–1936) followed a similar line.

Generación del 98

Simultaneously with the emergence of the Modernist school a group of writers, all about the same age, were striving to reintegrate the intellectual life of Spain, rigidly fixed in its isolation, into the mainstream of European thinking and to overcome the inferiority complex in relation to Europe which many Spaniards had felt since the end of the 17th century. After the salutary shock of defeat in the Cuban War of 1898 they sought to return to the true spiritual values of Spain and to link them up again with the main trends of European thought. The members of this group – very different from one another as they were – called themselves the "Generation of '98". They showed a common preference for the essay and the novel.

The intellectual leader of the group was Miguel de Unamuno (1864–1936), a Basque of strong opinions who taught at Salamanca University but was exiled to the Canaries in 1924 for his opposition to the dictatorship and later lived in voluntary exile in France. In his works (essays, interpretations of "Don Quixote", novels, plays) he gave expression to a tragic view of life, making him one of the forerunners of Existentialism, and argued not only for the europeanisation of Spain but for the hispanisation of Europe. Other representatives of the Generation of '98 were José Martínez Ruiz (1873–1967), author, under the pseudonym of Azorín, of essays and novels depicting life in Castile, who also lived in voluntary exile from 1936 to 1939; the deeply pessimistic novelist Pío Baroja (1873–1956), who describes interesting aspects of his Basque homeland; and Ramón Menéndez Pidal (1869–1968), a scholar who made major contributions in the fields of literary history and Romance philology until his premature retirement in 1939.

Miguel de Unamuno

Outstanding among prose writers of a rather later generation are José Ortega y Gasset (1883–1955), who developed the essay into a distinctive art form and in works like "The Revolt of the Masses" and "The Modern Theme" had a considerable influence on European thinking; the witty Salvador de Madariaga (1886–1978), who won the city of Aachen's Charlemagne Prize in 1973; and the Catholic essayist, lyric poet and dramatist José Bergamín (1897–1983), who lived in exile for many years.

Ortega y Gasset

In the period before the Civil War lyric poetry was given fresh stimulus, particularly in the choice of a new system of metaphors, by the movement called Ultraísmo which was initiated by the Chilean Vicente Huidobro (1893–1948). To this school belonged Gerardo Diego (1896–1987) and Federico García Lorca (1898–1936). Soon, however, Lorca broke free from attachment to any particular school and found a distinctive voice of his own. His intricately contrived lyric poetry has its roots in the folk poetry of Andalusia ("Romancero Gitano") and the improvised songs of the flamenco dancers ("Poema del cante jondo" – cante jondo being the most melancholy form of flamenco), but in dealing with modern themes he employs bold and surrealist forms of expression ("Poeta en Nueva York"). He was director of the student theatre, La Barraca, and wrote psychologically subtle plays of social criticism in lofty poetical language full of surprising metaphors, employing music, singing, dancing and sometimes puppets to create the total effect. His most important plays are "Bodas de Sangre" ("Blood Marriage"), "Yerma" ("Waste Land") and "La Casa de Bernarda Alba" ("The House of Bernarda Alba"). He had perhaps not reached the peak of his achievement when he was murdered by fanatical Francoists.

Lyric poetry

Lorca

A lyric poet more interested in "poésie pure" was Jorge Guillén (1893–1984), who lived in exile in the United States from the time of the Civil War until 1977. Luis Cernuda (1902–63), who was influenced by the English Romantic school, died in exile in Mexico. The Neo-Classicist Miguel Hernández (1910–42), another Republican, died in prison.

Spain also lost a number of excellent prose writers as a result of the Civil War, such as Román Pérez de Ayala (1881–1962), until 1936 ambassador of the Spanish Republic in London, who lived in Argentina until 1954, when he returned to Spain. Ramón Gómez de la Serna (1888–1963), the author of novels and striking epigrams (greguerías),

Prose writing

lived in Buenos Aires. Ramón José Sender (1902–82) spent some time in Guatemala and Mexico before moving to the United States (San Diego, California), where he died.

Drama

Alejandro Casona (1903–65), a dramatist influenced by Lorca ("The Trees Die Erect", "The Woman at Break of Day"), also spent many years in exile.

Contemporary writers

After the Civil War a new generation of writers came forward, mainly novelists. Among them was José Antonio de Zunzunegui (b. 1901), who showed a preference for the "roman objectif".

Cela

Camilo José Cela (b. 1916) was the originator of Tremendismo, a school of harsh realism based on the theories of Existentialism. For his leading role in the renewal of Spanish literature after the Civil War he was awarded the Nobel Prize for literature in 1989. Perhaps his best known work is "The Beehive". José María Gironella (b. 1917) wrote a trilogy of novels on the Civil War. The novels of Carmen Laforet (b. 1921) and Ana María Matute (b. 1926) are concerned with contemporary themes. The prose writing of Rafael Sánchez Ferlosio (b. 1927) uses a modern "montage" technique taken over from the cinema.

Goytisolo

The journalist and novelist Juan Goytisolo (b. 1931) paints realistic and critical pictures of Spanish society. The dramatist Fernando Arrabal (b. 1932), who lives in Paris, sets out in his surrealist plays to destroy bourgeois taboos.

Folk Traditions

Folk Dances and Music

Flamenco

The manifestation of Spanish folk art best known abroad is the Andalusian flamenco; but what is offered to tourists under that name, particularly outside Andalusia, is often no more than a colourful dance show to Andalusian rhythms. In the genuine *tablao* (from *tablado*, "stage") the virtuoso playing of the *tocadores* (guitarists) and the improvised words and melodies of the *cantaores* (singers) are more important than the dancing of the *bailaores,* which rises out of the elaborate rhythms of the music, accompanied by the cries of the participants and the spectators. The oldest and most authentic form of the flamenco is the *cante jondo* ("deep" or fervent singing), which shows evident Arab influence in its complicated rhythms and melodies (pentatonic chords). The *cante chico* ("small" song) seems lighter, more dance-like and more familiar to European ears. Two melancholy types of song are the *soleá* (from *soledad,* "loneliness"), usually singing of unhappy love, and the *saeta,* formerly improvised by spectators of the great Holy Week processions commemorating Christ's Passion.

Catalonia

The national dance of Catalonia is the *sardana,* a sedate round dance which is very probably of Greek origin. It is accompanied by the rather nasal sounds produced by the *cobla,* an orchestra whose characteristic instruments are the oboe-like *tenora* and the *fluviol,* a flute played with only one hand. In the *xiquets de valls* tall human pyramids are built up to the music of the *gralla,* a tapered oboe.

Basque country

The folk music of the Basque country is quite different from anything found in the rest of Spain. The *aurresku* is a war dance performed by men, which ends with the turbulent *arin-arin,* accompanied by the piercing cries (*irrinchis*) of the dancers. The *zorzico* is a quiet and

The Romería de Rocio (Huelva province)

sedate dance. Another popular dance is the *ezpata dantza,* a sword dance. All these dances are accompanied by the *silbotia,* a large flute, and the smaller *chistuak,* which is played with only one hand while the other beats the *tiun-tiunak,* a small drum hanging from the player's sleeve, and by the *atabal,* a high-pitched drum.

In Galicia, still bearing the marks of Celtic culture, the sword dance is performed by men. More popular is the *muneira* (dance of the millers' wives). The characteristic Galician instrument, in addition to the percussion instruments, is the *gaita,* a small bagpipe (which is also played in Asturias). Galicia

Bullfighting

Although increasingly critical voices are raised, even in Spain itself, against the bloody spectacle of the bullfight (*corrida de toros*), a visit to the bullring is still one of the favourite Spanish recreations. Newspapers devote several pages to reports on bullfights, with detailed assessments of the bullfighters and the bulls. During the bullfighting season fights in the leading Spanish bullrings are shown live on television, with passionate running commentaries by sports reporters, and the television sets in bars often attract a bigger audience for a bullfight than for a football match. Visitors will decide for themselves whether they want to go to a bullfight.

Until the 16th century bullfights were held as a form of weapon training or on the occasion of fiestas in noble circles, the mounted *caballeros* being pitted against the bulls with their lances. From the beginning of the 17th century the riders increasingly gave place to men challenging the bull on foot. The present bullfighting rules are essentially those devised by Francisco Romero, who was born about 1700 in Ronda. The building of the first large *plaza de toros* in Madrid in 1749 finally made bullfighting a public spectacle, in which only professional *toreros* now take part. (Torero is the correct name of the bullfighter – not the traditional English "toreador".)

In central and southern Spain and in Barcelona bullfights are held on almost every Sunday and public holiday from Easter to November, and sometimes also on weekdays (particularly Thursdays). They take place, weather permitting, between 4 and 6 or between 5 and 7 in the afternoon. During the period of great heat at the end of July and beginning of August and from mid October onwards only the lesser forms of bullfight known as *novilladas* are held, with less experienced bullfighters (*novilleros* and young bulls (*novillos*). In northern Spain and Catalonia bullfights are usually held only on great feast-days and during the summer fair.

The bullring is exactly circular, with the dearer seats on the shady side (*sombra*) and the cheaper ones in the sun (*sol*). The black or brownish-red bulls, which must not be more than six years old and weigh around 500 kilograms (about half a ton), come mainly from breeding farms in Andalusia.

The bullfight (*lidia*) has three main parts (*suertes*). After a brief prologue during which the *capeadores* tease the bull by playing it with their brightly coloured capes (*capas*) there follows the *suerte de picar* or *suerte de varas*, in which the mounted *picadores* provoke the bull to attack them, plunge their lances (*garrochas*) into its neck and withstand the charges of the infuriated beast as best they can. When the bull has been sufficiently weakened (*castigado*) by his wounds (*varas*) the second stage, the *suerte de banderillas*, begins. The *banderilleros* run towards the bull carrying several *banderillas* and, skilfully eluding its charge at the last moment, plant them in its neck. The normal banderillas are 75cm/30in. long, with barbed points and paper streamers; the *banderillas a cuarta* are only about 15cm/6in. long. Bulls which are too quiet or are vicious are stimulated or distracted by plays with a cloak (*floreos*). When three pairs of banderillas have been planted in the bull's neck the *suerte suprema* or *suerte de matar* begins. The *espada* or *matador,* armed with a red cloth (*muleta*) and a sword (*estoque*), begins by teasing the bull with the cloth and seeks to manoeuvre it into a position in which he can give it the death stroke (*estocada*), after which the coup de grâce is administered by a *punterillo,* who thrusts a dagger into the back of its neck. If the bull has shown itself courageous and aggressive it will be loudly applauded. Unskilled bullfighters are the subject of vociferous criticism and whistles from the crowd.

Games

Basque country

The Basques have their own characteristic sports. The national game is *pelota* (*frontón, jai alai*), a fast ball game in which a small hard ball is directed against a high blank wall, the *frontón*, either with a curved basketwork racket, a net or the bare hand. Other characteristic Basque sports are wood-chopping contests, in which the *aizkolaris* have to cut through a thick tree-trunk, lifting heavy stones, tugs of war (*soka-tira*) and stone-pulling by oxen. On the coast there are rowing regattas, in which old fishing boats manned by thirteen oarsmen and a coxswain race in the open sea on a course.

Suggested Routes

The following suggested routes are designed to help visitors travelling by car to plan their itineraries, while leaving plenty of scope for variation and individual choice.

The routes suggested take in all the principal tourist attractions. Not all the places of interest described in this guide, however, are on or near one of the routes, and the individual entries in the "A to Z" section of the guide contain numerous suggestions for excursions and side trips which can be fitted into visitors' programmes according to their interests and the time available.

The routes suggested here can be followed on the map accompanying this guide, which will help with detailed planning.

Places for which there is an entry in the A to Z section are shown in these routes in **bold** type. Most of the places, regions and archaeological sites described in the guide are included in the Index at the end of the book, making it easy to find full information about features of interest.

Most of the routes described follow national highways (identified by the letter N and a number) or major regional roads (identified by the letter C and a number). The distances (in kilometres and miles) shown for each route are rounded figures for the main route only; distances for detours or alternative routes of any length are given separately.

1. Through the Basque Country and the Pyrenees to the Costa Brava
(about 900km/560 miles)

This route enters Spain from the French Atlantic coast at the Hendaye–Irún frontier crossing. A short distance beyond the frontier on the A 1 motorway is **San Sebastián** (Basque Donostia), the fashionable resort on the Basque coast. From here either the motorway or the coast road can be taken to **Bilbao** (Basque Bilbo), an industrial town and capital of the province of Vizcaya (Basque Vizkaia). From Bilbao the route turns south on A 68, but soon leaves this to head east on C 6210 to **Vitoria-Gasteiz**, capital of the province of Alava. From here N I runs west to rejoin the motorway, which runs south-east via Haro to **Logroño**, in the centre of the Rioja wine country. From Logroño N 111 leads north-east by way of **Estella** to **Pamplona**, famous for the "running of the bulls" on the fiesta of San Fermín. The route continues from there on N 240 along the foot of the Pyrenees and through the Sierra de la Peña to **Jaca**, which is a good centre for excursions into the Pyrenees. N 240 continues to **Huesca** and **Lérida** (Catalan Lleida), another good base for trips into the hills, for example to **Seo de Urgel** (Catalan La Seu d'Urgell) and on to **Andorra** (160km/100 miles). From Andorra it is a short distance into France. Those who want to stay in Spain should take N II from Lérida to the **Costa Brava**, passing the monastery of **Montserrat** and continuing to the Catalan capital, **Barcelona**. From there the best plan is to turn north along the coast road to see the beauties of the Costa Brava (still there in spite of the over-development for tourism), re-entering France at Port-Bou. (Those who are pressed for time can return to France on the A 7 motorway, crossing the frontier at La Junquera.)

2. From Madrid to Galicia and Asturias (about 2500km/1550 miles)

The starting-point of this long trip to north-western Spain ("Green Spain"), which also takes in some of the most interesting towns on the central plateau, is **Madrid**. From Madrid N VI runs past one of Spain's principal sights, the monastery/palace of **El Escorial**. From the Escorial C 505 runs along the Sierra de Guadarrama to **Avila**, one of Spain's oldest towns, still surrounded by its medieval walls. Farther west on N 501 is the old university town of **Salamanca**, from which we turn north on N 630, driving via **Zamora** and **Benavente** to **León**, which has one of Spain's most beautiful Gothic cathedrals. From León the route runs west, following the ancient **Way of St James** (N 120, then N VI). This passes through **Astorga** and comes to the mining area round Ponferrada, from which the road climbs to the Puerto de Piedrafita, the gateway to Galicia. From here N VI continues to the handsome city of **Lugo**, still surrounded by a complete circuit of Roman walls. Leaving Lugo on N 640 and going south-west, we turn west on C 547 to **Santiago de Compostela**, the great pilgrimage centre with the tomb of the Apostle St James, housed in a magnificent cathedral with a richly decorated Baroque façade and a Romanesque interior.

Detour

From Santiago de Compostela an attractive round trip of about 290km/180 miles can be made to the Rías Bajas, to the south. The route runs via **Pontevedra** to **Vigo**, where it turns inland for **Orense** (Galician Ourense), and so back to Santiago.

The main route leads north to the port of **La Coruña** (Galician A Coruña), at the extreme north-western tip of the Iberian peninsula, and then turns east on E 50 by way of **Betanzos** to reach the north coast of Galicia. N 632 then skirts the coast to **Avilés**, from which the A 8 and A 66 motorways run south to **Oviedo**. From here a short detour can be made to see the Visigothic churches of Santa María de Naranco and San Miguel de Lillo. The main route continues on E 50 (N 634), which runs north of the **Picos de Europa** through fine scenery to the pictur-esque Asturian coast, with the beautiful little town of **Santillana del Mar**. A short distance away are the **Altamira Caves** and the port of **Santander**, capital of Asturias. From here N 623 cuts through the Cantabrian Mountains to **Burgos** with its magnificent cathedral, from which N 620 runs south-west via **Palencia** to **Valladolid**, where the National Museum of Sculpture is a "must". Finally N 403 and N VI (with a possible detour to **Segovia**) bring us back to **Madrid**.

3. From Madrid via Zaragoza to Valencia (about 1200km/745 miles)

From **Madrid** N II runs north-east by way of **Alcalá de Henares, Guada-lajara, Sigüenza** and **Calatayud** to the capital of Aragón, the fine city of **Zaragoza**. N 232 then heads south-east, passing through **Alcañiz**, to reach the Mediterranean on the Costa del Azahar. From here the A 7 motorway leads south to **Castellón de la Plana**, the chief town on this stretch of coast, and continues down the coast by way of **Sagunto**, originally a Carthaginian foundation, and **Valencia**, Spain's third largest city. The route then turns inland, through **Játiva** into La Man-cha, continuing through **Albacete** and the picturesque town of **Cuenca** to return to **Madrid**.

4. Around Madrid (about 370km/230 miles)

Within easy reach of **Madrid** are some of the most important and beautiful towns in Spain. Leaving the capital on N IV, we come to **Aranjuez**, famous for its gardens, and from there turn south-west, following the Tagus, to the uniquely beautiful city of **Toledo**, once capital of Spain. From Toledo N 403 runs through the **Sierra de Gredos** to **Avila**, from which a detour (about 198km/123 miles there and back) can be made to **Salamanca**. Some 60km/40 miles north-east of Avila is the fascinating town of **Segovia**, from which we turn south to return via **El Escorial** to **Madrid**.

5. From Madrid to Extremadura (about 820km/510 miles)

From **Madrid** we take N 401, which runs south to **Toledo**, and from there turn north-west on N 403 to the junction with E 90 (N V), which we then follow south-west to **Talavera de la Reina**. The route then continues by way of **Béjar** to **Trujillo**, birthplace of Pizarro, the conqueror of Peru, and from there to **Mérida**, with the finest Roman remains in Spain. The farthest point on the route is reached at **Badajoz**, on the frontier with Portugal, where we turn north-east on N 523 to the medieval town of **Cáceres**. From Cáceres the route continues on N 630 and later N 110, passing through **Plasencia** and **Avila**, to return to **Madrid**.

6. Circuit of Andalusia (about 1000km/620 miles)

This tour, starting in **Córdoba**, with its famous mosque, includes among much else the magnificent remains of Arab culture in Spain. From Córdoba N IV runs west by way of Ecija to the Andalusian capital, **Seville**. From here a detour (182km/113 miles there and back) can be made to **Huelva**, on the **Costa de la Luz**. The main route continues south from Seville on the A 4 motorway to **Jerez de la Frontera**, the home of sherry. A few miles beyond this is **Cádiz**, from which we continue along the southern section of the Costa de la Luz by way of **Algeciras** to **Gibraltar**. Beyond this is the **Costa del Sol** with its internationally renowned seaside resorts. A short distance inland from **Marbella** is **Ronda**. The main route continues along the coast to **Málaga** and **Nerja**. Some distance beyond Nerja N 323 runs north to the majestic city of **Granada**, with the world-famed Alhambra. N 323 then continues through the **Sierra Nevada** to the "silver town" of **Jaén**. From here we go on to the beautiful Renaissance towns of **Baeza** and **Ubeda**, and from there turn west to return to **Córdoba**. Alternatively it is possible to turn off at Bailén into N IV, which runs north to **Madrid** (about 300km/185 miles).

Spain from A to Z

Since the end of the Franco regime many place-names and street names, as well as the names of various buildings and institutions, in certain parts of the country, particularly in Catalonia, the Basque country and Galicia, have been changed. In this guide the Spanish forms of names are given first, followed where appropriate by the names in the regional language.

Aguilar de Campóo G 2

Province: Palencia (P). Telephone dialling code: 988
Altitude: 870m/2854ft. Population: 8000

The ancient little town of Aguilar de Campóo, on the Río Pisuerga, is believed to have been the Roman settlement of Vellica. It flourished particularly between the 13th and 15th centuries, when the town and surrounding area formed a marquisate.

The castle of Aguilar de Campóo

Sights

Aguilar de Campóo has preserved six gates in the old town walls, including the 14th century Puerta de Reinosa, with a Hebrew inscription which is all   Town walls and castle

◄ *Almansa Castle (Albacete province)*

that remains of the old Jewish quarter. The 12th century castle which looms over the town is now in ruins.

Town houses

There are a number of old palaces and mansions ranging in date from the Middle Ages to the Baroque period.

San Miguel

The Early Gothic church of San Miguel, in the Plaza de España, contains many tombs of the 12th–16th centuries. Particularly fine are the tombs of the Conde de Aguilar and his wife and Archpriest García González.

Other churches worth seeing are Santa Cecilia (Romanesque) and Santa Clara (Gothic).

Albacete   K 6

Province: Albacete (AB). Telephone dialling code: 967
Altitude: 686m/2251ft. Population: 125,000

Albacete (from Arabic Al-Basita, the Plain), chief town of its province and the see of a bishop, lies in a fertile wine-producing area in La Mancha. Now largely a modern town, it has an old-established reputation as a centre of cutlery manufacture, and the knives (*navajas*) and daggers (*puñales*) made here are popular souvenirs.

Sights

San Juan
Bautista

The most important building in the old upper town (el Alto de la Villa) is the cathedral of San Juan Bautista (16th c.), a Gothic church originally designed by Diego de Siloé and continued in Renaissance style. It has a fine Churrigueresque high altar (1726). In the sacristy are five grisaille wall paintings of Biblical scenes (1550).

★Museo
Arqueológico

In the newer lower part of the town, housed in the modern provincial government offices (Diputación Provincial) in the Parque de Abelardo Sánchez, is the Archaeological Museum, which has been declared a national monument in virtue of the importance of its collections. It has two sections, a department of archaeology and a department of modern art. Among the treasures of the department of archaeology are objects from archaeological sites in the province, including Iberian sculpture from Cerro de los Santos (75km/47 miles south-east), Roman articulated dolls of ivory and amber from Ontur (80km/50 miles south-east), Roman mosaics from Balazote and Gothic religious objects. The department of modern art has pictures by Benjamín Palencia and other local artists.

Other features of interest in the lower town are La Sartén (the Pan), an 18th century banqueting hall, and the turn-of-the century shops in the glass-roofed Pasaje de Lodares.

Surroundings of Albacete

Chinchilla de
Monte Aragón

13km/8 miles south-east of Albacete, on a steep-sided crag, is the old Moorish stronghold of Chinchilla de Monte Aragón (alt. 896m/2940ft), which was chief town of the province until 1833. Over the town looms the Castillo, built by Don Juan de Villena in the 15th century, which was for a time the residence of Cesare Borgia. The narrow lanes running up from the Plaza Mayor towards the castle are lined by Gothic houses and palaces in Mudéjar style.

Santa María
del Salvador

In the Plaza Mayor is the important Gothic church of Santa María del Salvador (15th–16th c.), which is notable particularly for its richly decorated Plateresque apse. The Capilla Mayor has a superb retablo. The Museo Parroquial displays a variety of sacred objects.

Opposite the apse of the church is the Baroque Town Hall, which has a Renaissance façade with a bust of Charles II. On the castle hill (200m/650ft) is the 14th century monastery of Santo Domingo, with a beautiful cloister. The hill is riddled with old cave dwellings, some of them now occupied by potters' workshops. The National Museum of Ceramics displays a wide range of Spanish ceramic products.

Town Hall

Santo Domingo
Cave dwellings

64km/40 miles from Chinchilla on the road to Almansa (N 430) a side road goes off to Alpera, a few kilometres from which are the Cuevas de la Vieja, with Stone Age rock paintings of hunting and fighting scenes. To see them, apply to the mayor's office in Alpera.

Cuevas de
la Vieja

Charmingly situated on a rocky hillside above the Río Jucar, to the north of Alpera, is the village of Alcalá de Jucar, dominated by its tower.

★Alcalá
de Jucar

Prominently situated on a limestone crag above the town of Almansa (alt. 712m/2336ft), 74km/46 miles from Albacete, is a massive Moorish castle. In the level country round the castle was fought the last battle in the War of the Spanish Succession (April 25th 1707), between Philip V's troops under the command of the Duke of Berwick and the army of Archduke Charles of Austria. The 15th century church of the Asunción below the castle has a fine doorway and contains pictures by the Colombian painter Carlos Sosa and chapels with stellar vaulting. The palace of the Conde de Cirat, known as the Casa Grande, also dates from the 15th century. Notable features are the Baroque doorway and the patio, with a double gallery. The Convento de las Agustinas (1564) has a Baroque/Renaissance façade.

Almansa

La Asunción

Casa Grande
Las Agustinas

The little town of Hellín (alt. 566m/1857ft), 61km/38 miles from Albacete on N 301, has many typical old houses with Baroque façades. The magnificent *camarín* (niche for an image) in the church of the Conventos Franciscanos also dates from the Baroque period. In the surrounding area are sulphur mines which were already being worked in Roman times.

Hellín

8km/5 miles east of Hellín are the Cuevas de Minateda, with Stone Age representations of men and animals. To see them, apply to the mayor's office in Hellín.

Cuevas de
Minateda

From Albacete N 322 runs south-west to Balazote, where the Iberian sculpture known as the Bicha de Balazote (Hind of Balazote), dating from the 5th century B.C., was found in 1898. It then continues through lonely country to Alcaraz (alt. 798m/2618ft), 79km/49 miles from Albacete. Over this picturesque little medieval town, on a nearby hill, stands a Moorish castle. Alcaraz was the birthplace in 1509 of the 16th century architect Andrés de Vandelvira.

Alcaraz

The beautiful Plaza Mayor, surrounded by arcades, has been declared a national monument. Around it are the principal buildings of the town.

Plaza Mayor

The square is entered from the Calle Mayor through the Puerta de la Aduana. The town's finest church is La Trinidad (1486), with a fine tower, a beautiful doorway and wood statues by Salzillo and Roque López. It contains a museum of sacred art. Adjoining the church is the Lonja del Corregidor, the old market hall and commercial exchange. Built in 1518 and renovated in 1718, it has a large tower, the Torre de Tardón (1568). The Neo-Classical façade of the Ayuntamiento (Town Hall), opposite the church, dates from 1588.

From Alcaraz a road runs south by way of Fábricas de Riopar to Siles in the Sierra de Alcaraz, near which is the Cueva de Chorro. An impressive sight here is the source of the Río Mundo emerging from a cave.

Source of the
Río Mundo

From Albacete N 301 runs north-west, crosses the Canal de María Cristina and continues via La Gineta to La Roda (alt. 716m/2349ft), 36km/22 miles from Albacete, a little market town in a fertile agricultural area.

La Roda

The church of El Salvador (16th c.), with a dome of dark-blue azulejos, has a fine Churrigueresque retablo of 1721. The Museo de Antonio Martínez has a collection of material on the history of the town.

Alba de Tormes   F 4

Province: Salamanca (SA). Telephone dialling code: 923
Altitude: 821m/2694ft. Population: 4200

The old-world little town of Alba de Tormes, 22km/14 miles south-east of Salamanca on a hill on the right bank of the Río Tormes, is one of the most important pilgrimage centres in Spain, in which Santa Teresa of Ávila, who died here in 1582, is revered. In the 16th century Alba de Tormes had eighteen churches, of which only four survive. In the Golden Age the town, as the seat of the Dukes of Alba, was an intellectual and political centre which in its heyday had a population of more than 22,000; but when the Dukes moved their residence to Piedrahita in the 18th century Alba de Tormes declined.

Sights

★ Tomb of
Santa Teresa

The town has many memories of the great mystic Santa Teresa of Ávila. Her tomb is in the richly furnished church of the Carmelite convent of the Anunciación, which she founded in 1570. The convent, which has a handsome Renaissance doorway, lies below the beautiful Plaza Mayor; the way to it, along a narrow lane, is signposted. The saint's remains (her heart and one arm) are preserved in a reliquary above the altar, a gift of the Infanta Isabel Clara Eugenia, daughter of Philip II.

La Anunciación

Tomb of Santa Teresa

In an adjoining building is a small museum with other relics of the saint and of St John of the Cross.

All that remains of the palace of the Dukes of Alba is a massive tower, the Torre de la Armería, which looms darkly over the town.

Castillo de los
Duques de \lba

In the Plaza Mayor is the brick-built church of San Juan (12th c.), in Romanesque/Byzantine style, with a Churrigueresque retablo of 1771 and a Romanesque group of the Apostles in the apse.

San Juan

The church of Santiago Apóstol is the town's oldest church. San Miguel has fine tombs and recumbent figures of the 13th–15th centuries.

Other churches

On the outskirts of the town stands the monastery of San Jerónimo, now housing a small archaeological museum (Roman material from the surrounding area).

Museo
Arqueológico
de San Jerónimo

Alcalá de Henares

H 4

Province: Madrid (M). Telephone dialling code: 91
Altitude: 587m/1926ft. Population: 142,000

The old town of Alcalá de Henares, rebuilt after severe destruction during the Civil War, lies some 30km/20 miles east of Madrid on the left bank of the Río Henares. It was the Roman Complutum and the Moorish al-Kal'a.

The town was the birthplace of Cervantes and the Emperor Ferdinand I. It had a famous university, founded by Cardinal Jiménez de Cisneros in 1498, where the first polyglot Bible in Europe was published in 1517. The university was moved to Madrid in 1836, and thereafter the town lost much of its importance. Alcalá de Henares suffered severe devastation during the Civil War.

History

Sights

Of the Colegio de San Ildefonso in the Plaza de San Diego, built between 1498 and 1508 to house the University, only the Great Hall survived the Civil War. The Plateresque main front (1543) in the Plaza de San Diego is one of the finest in Spain. The first courtyard, the Patio de Santo Tomás y Villanueva, is surrounded by a double gallery and contains a fountain decorated with swans (the heraldic emblem of Cardinal Cisneros) and a statue of the founder (1670). This courtyard leads into a museum on the history of the University (on first floor). Beyond this is the Patio de Filósofos, and this in turn goes into the Patio Trilingüe (named after the three classical languages – Greek, Hebrew and Latin). In this courtyard is the Great Hall, the Paraninfo, one of the few parts of the building which have remained unchanged since the original foundation.

Colegio de
San Ildefonso
★Main front

Adjoining the University is the church of San Ildefonso, the finest thing in which is the early 16th century tomb of Cardinal Cisneros (by Domenico Fancelli and Bartolomé Ordóñez).

★Tomb of
Cardinal Cisneros

Within the town are other buildings belonging to the University, notably the Colegio de Málaga (a little way south in Calle de los Colegios), with fine brick masonry and beautiful inner courtyards.

Colegios

From the Colegio de San Ildefonso the Calle Mayor runs west to the Plaza del Palacio. On the way there, on right (at the corner of Calle Imagen), is the Museo Casa de Cervantes. This is not the writer's actual birthplace but a 20th century reproduction of a 16th century house built on what is believed

Museo Casa
de Cervantes

to be the site of the house in which he was born. The house, furnished in the style of the period, contains mementoes of the author of "Don Quixote".

Plaza del Palacio

In the Plaza del Palacio is the fortress-like Archbishop's Palace, begun in the 13th century but considerably altered in the 14th and 16th. The side fronts are Gothic, the main front Plateresque. From the massive Torreón de Tenorio the defensive walls run to the Puerta de Madrid, one of the town gates, and from there to the Puerta de Burgos.

Here, adjoining the palace, is the Convento de San Bernardo, founded in 1617. Notable features are the statue of St Bernard over the doorway, the oval church with its six chapels and Capilla Mayor, which has paintings by Angelo Nardi.

The group of sacral buildings around the plaza is completed by the brick buildings of the Convento de la Madre de Dios to the east and the Oratorio de San Felipe Neri. Not far south is the Iglesia Magistral with its soaring bell tower.

Alcañiz   M 4

Province: Teruel (TE). Telephone dialling code: 974
Altitude: 338m/1109ft. Population: 10,000

The ancient little town of Alcañiz, situated in a bend on the Río Guadalope, is the centre of one of the most characteristic parts of Lower Aragón, noted for the production of olive oil. The town stands on a steeply sloping eminence, surrounded by hills. It is noted for the sweets produced here.

A Roman army was annihilated by the Carthaginians here in 212 B.C. In the 12th century Alfonso I conquered the area and built a castle on Pui Pinos ("Pine Hill") which became the headquarters of the Order of Calatrava in Aragon. Alcañiz was the favourite residence of Jaime I.

Sights

Castillo de
los Calatravos

The origins of the Castillo de los Calatravos, on Pui Pinos, go back to 1179. The only features that have survived from that period are the cloister and the chapel, over which towers the keep. In the chapel is the tomb (by Damián Forment, 1537) of Juan de Lanuza, Viceroy of Aragon. The ground floor of the keep (in which is the entrance to the chapel) and the great hall have 14th century wall paintings, mostly depicting scenes of chivalry. The keep was considerably altered in the 18th century, and the southern half is now occupied by the Palacio de los Comendadores, flanked by twin towers, with a gallery of typically Aragonese type. The palace now houses a parador.

Ayuntamiento
and Lonja

In the Plaza de España, forming a harmonious group, are the 16th century Ayuntamiento (Town Hall), in severe style, and the richly decorated 15th century Lonja. The Town Hall has the town's coat of arms in the centre of the façade, and within it are preserved fragments of Juan de Lanuza's tomb and other remains. With its pointed arches the Lonja has a rather Italian air; once the market hall, it is now the House of Culture.

Santa María
la Mayor

Near the Town Hall stands the church of Santa María la Mayor (1736), a massive and imposing structure of cathedral-like dimensions. The richly decorated doorway leads into the magnificent interior, the most striking features of which are the great high altar and the domed chapels.

Alcántara   D 5

Province: Cáceres (CC). Telephone dialling code: 927.
Altitude: 240m/787ft. Population: 4100.

The old-world little frontier town of Alcántara lies above the south bank of the Tagus, which is dammed here to supply a hydro-electric power station (capacity 950,000 kW). The town, originally founded about A.D. 106, was the place of origin of the knightly Order of Alcántara and the birthplace of San Pedro de Alcántara.

Sights

The town's most important monument is the famous Roman bridge (Arabic *al-kantara*) built over the Tagus in A.D. 105. Constructed entirely of granite blocks, without the use of mortar, it is 194m/637ft long and 8m/26ft wide, spanning the river with six arches up to 58m/190ft high. Half-way across the bridge is a triumphal arch in honour of Trajan, on which in later times the arms of the Habsburgs and Bourbons were mounted. On the left bank of the river is a small Roman temple dedicated to the builder of the bridge, Gaius Julius Lacer.

★ Roman bridge

In the main square, opposite the Town Hall, is the Gothic church of Santa María de la Amocóbar, built in the 13th century on the site of a mosque, with a handsome flight of steps leading up to it. Notable features of the interior are the fine choir-stalls and a number of tombs of Grand Masters of the Order of Alcántara.

Santa María de la Amocóbar

Diagonally opposite, at the entrance into the square, can be found the Neo-Classical church of San Pedro de Alcántara, built on the site of the saint's birthplace. The beautiful Baroque retablo was brought here from the chapel of La Soledad, in a lane behind Santa María de la Amocóbar. It was originally a synagogue.

San Pedro de Alcántara

The monastery of San Benito (1550), on the outskirts of the town, was the seat of the Portuguese Order of Alcántara, which succeeded the Order of

San Benito

Alcántara's Roman bridge

San Julián de Pereiro, founded in 1170, when that order moved to Alcántara in 1218. Of the Order's castle only ruins remain. The monastery of San
Benito is also partly ruined, but the Gothic tower and the two-storey Gothic
cloister are still well preserved. Opposite it is a modern auditorium with
seating for an audience of 2000 in which classical Spanish plays are performed. In the Plateresque church of San Benito are splendidly decorated
chapels commemorating the Order's Grand Master Antonio Bravo de Jerez
and Nicolás de Ovando, governor of the West Indian colonies.

Algeciras F 9

Province: Cádiz (CA). Telephone dialling code: 956
Altitude: sea level. Population: 100,000

The port of Algeciras lies near the southern tip of the Iberian peninsula on
the west side of Algeciras Bay, opposite Gibraltar. It is an important ferry
port, with services to Ceuta and Tangier in North Africa.
  The Roman Portus Albo was re-founded by the Moors in 713 under the
name of al-Gezira al-Khadra ("green island"). It was captured by Alfonso XI
of Castile in 1344 and destroyed by Mohammed V of Granada in 1368, so
that it has preserved only scanty remains from that period. After 1704,
when Gibraltar became a British possession, Algeciras was resettled by
Spaniards from Gibraltar.

Sights

Casa Consistorial The only building of any note is the Casa Consistorial (Town Hall) in Calle
Regio Martínez, built in 1897, in which the international Conference of
Algeciras was held in 1906. The conference met after the first Moroccan
crisis of 1905–06 which was sparked off by the German Emperor Wilhelm
II's provocative visit to Tangier. Germany was seeking to counter French
policy in North Africa and win influence in Morocco, but at the Algeciras
conference these aspirations were rejected and France and Spain were
recognised as having control over Morocco.

Alicante M 7

Province: Alicante (A). Telephone dialling code: 965
Altitude: sea level. Population: 248,000

Alicante, chief town of its province, lies in a picturesque bay on the south-
east coast of Spain, at the foot of Mt Benacantil, which is crowned by the
Castillo de Santa Bárbara. With its many hotels and tower blocks Alicante,
known to the Romans as Lucentum (the "place of light") and to the Moors
as Lecant or al-Lucant, is a town of modern aspect.

Alicante, the chief place on the Costa Blanca, is both a summer and a winter
resort. In recent years new parks and gardens have been laid out and many
streets and boulevards have been widened. The town also has a variety of
industry (chemicals, aluminium), and it is an important port for the shipping of wine, raisins, southern fruits, oil, liquorice and esparto grass.

Sights

Harbour
★ Explanada
de España

The central feature of the town is the Plaza de Sotelo, from which the
Avenida del Doctor Gadea leads down to the spacious harbour, protected
by large breakwaters. Along the front runs the palm-shaded Explanada de

Alicante
300 m

España, almost 600m/660yd long, paved in colourful mosaic patterns.
From the breakwater, and particularly from the lighthouse at its east end,
there are beautiful views. The line of the Explanada de España is continued
beyond the Plaza Puerta del Mar by the Paseo de Gómiz, which runs along
the Playa del Postiguet to the suburban district of Roig and the Playa de San
Juan.

A short distance beyond the Plaza Puerta del Mar, on the left, is the park-like
Plaza del Teniente Luciáñez, to the north of which is the old Santa Cruz
quarter, with the church of Santa María, which was built by the Catholic
Monarchs. It was remodelled in the 18th century, with a Rococo doorway,
and has a richly decorated Baroque interior. In the Plaza Santa María (No. 3)
is the Asegurada Museum, with a collection of 20th century art.

Santa María

South-west of Santa María is the fine Ayuntamiento (Town Hall), built
between 1696 and 1760, with two square towers 35m/115ft high and a
beautiful Churrigueresque façade. On the steps leading up to it is the "zero
point" by reference to which all heights above sea level in Spain are
measured. The Salón Azul (Blue Room) of the Town Hall is particularly
worth seeing.

Ayuntamiento

North-west of the Town Hall is the 17th century church of San Nicolás de
Bari (also known as the Concatedral or Co-Cathedral), dedicated to the
town's patron saint. The interior is impressive, with a number of notable
retablos and a fine cloister.

San Nicolás
de Bari

The best way to reach the Castillo de Santa Bárbara, on Mt Benacantil
(209m/686ft), is to take the lift from the east end of the Paseo de Gómiz.
From the castle there are magnificent views of the town, the coast and the
huerta and of the hills to the north. The Castillo itself is the successor to a
Carthaginian stronghold built by Hamilcar Barca.

★ Castillo de
Santa Bárbara

In the north-west of the town, housed in the massive building occupied by
the Diputación Provincial in Avenida General Mola, is the Archaeological
Museum, which has an interesting collection of Greek, Roman and Iberian

Museo
Arqueológico

material, including a figure of the goddess Tanit, as well as a picture gallery and a coin collection.

Castillo de
San Fernando

A counterpart to the Castillo de Santa Bárbara is the 19th century Castillo de San Fernando, situated on a low hill.

Almería   K 8

Province: Almería (AL). Telephone dialling code: 951
Altitude: sea level. Population: 150,000

Almería, chief town of the province of that name in southern Spain, was already an important Mediterranean port in Roman times (Portus Magnus), and was known to the Arabs as Al-Mariyya ("mirror of the sea"). It lies in the Gulf of Almería, which is enclosed on the west by the Sierra de Gádor (1443m/4734ft), on the north-east by the Sierra Alhamilla (1359m/4459ft) and on the south-east by Sierra de Gata (513m/1683ft) and the cape of the same name. Above the town are two picturesque castles. The port handles a considerable export trade in fresh grapes, southern fruits and esparto grass, as well as iron ore and other minerals from mines in the hinterland. This trim town of whitewashed houses nestling amid subtropical vegetation is one of the leading centres on the stretch of coast, so popular with holidaymakers, whose bountiful climate (with an average of 320 days of sun in the year) has earned it the name of Costa del Sol, the Sunshine Coast.

Sights

Santiago
el Viejo

The central feature of the town, which is reminiscent of an eastern city with its Moorish-style houses, is the Puerta de Purchena, from which Calle de las Tiendas runs south-west to the 16th century church of Santiago el Viejo, with a 55m/180ft high Romanesque tower. The church, which was destroyed during the Civil War, is now a national monument.

Plaza Vieja

Calle Lope de Vega leads to the Plaza Vieja, with the Ayuntamiento (Town Hall), which preserves a banner presented to the town by the Catholic Monarchs.

Cathedral

To the south of the Town Hall is the Plaza de la Catedral, in which are the Bishop's Palace (Palacio Episcopal) and the Seminary.
   On the south side of the square is the cathedral, a fortress-like structure with four massive corner towers, a tower-like apse and battlements, rebuilt by Diego de Siloé between 1524 and 1543 after destruction in an earthquake. It has fine carved walnut choir-stalls by Juan de Orea (1558) and a statue of San Indalecio, the town's patron saint, by Salcillo. In the Capilla del Cristo de la Escucha is the tomb of the founder, Bishop Villalán.

★ Alcazaba

On a hill to the west, dominating the town, is the Alcazaba, a Moorish fortress which was built in the reign of Caliph Abderrahman III of Córdoba, enlarged by Almansor and completed by Hairan, and later extended by the Emperor Charles V. Particularly impressive is the massive 15th century keep, the Torre del Homenaje (Tower of Homage), with a Gothic doorway and the arms of the Catholic Monarchs. Concerts and dramatic performances are given here during the August fiesta.

Castillo de
San Cristóbal

On the adjoining hill, to the north, are the ruins of the Castillo de San Cristóbal, which is linked with the Alcazaba by a defensive wall.

Santuario de
Santo Domingo

Between the cathedral and the Paseo de Almería, in the Plaza de la Virgen, is the 17th century Santuario de Santo Domingo (restored), with a fine Baroque altar and an image of the Virgen del Mar, patroness of the town, which is said to have been found on the beach at Torre García in 1502.

North of Santo Domingo, on the Glorieta de Sartorius, is the church of San Pedro, founded in 1494 on the site of a mosque. The present church, which dates from 1795, has frescoes by Fray Juan García in the dome.

San Pedro

On the far side of the Paseo de Almería, in Calle Javier Sanz, is the Archaeological Museum, with four rooms displaying prehistoric material from the caves in the surrounding area and Iberian, Greek, Roman and Moorish antiquities.

Museo Arqueológico

Surroundings of Almería

North-east of Almería, reached by way of Carboneras, is the picturesque village of Mojácar (alt. 175m/574ft), known in Arabic as Murgis-akra, which still preserves Moorish traditions in its architecture and way of life. 5km/3 miles north are the Castillo de Garrucha and a lighthouse, and in the surrounding area are several old watch-towers. Near Mojácar is the Playazo de Vera, one of the last unspoiled stretches of coast, a "leisure town" is in course of development; with an area of 70 hectares/175 acres, it will have four hotels, blocks of flats, shopping centres and an archaeological museum.

★ Mojácar

Altamira Caves

G 1

Province: Cantabria (S)

In a hill some 35km/22 miles east of Santander (see entry) and 2km/1½ miles from Santillana del Mar (see entry) on C 6316 are the famous Altamira Caves (Cuevas de Altamira), with 15,000-year-old Stone Age rock paintings which are without parallel for their representational skill, vivid colouring and excellent state of preservation.

Admission to the caves is restricted in view of the danger of destruction of the paintings by visitors' breath. Written application to visit must therefore be made at least four months (during the summer at least six months) in advance to the Centro de Investigaciones y Museo de Altamira, E-39330 Santillana del Mar. Depending on the time of year, the number of visitors is limited to between ten and forty per day.

Note

High-quality reproductions of the paintings in the Sala de Pinturas can be bought in the National Archaeological Museum in Madrid.

The Museum, housed in three pavilions near the caves, can be visited without prior application. It contains a variety of Stone Age material and has displays illustrating the life of Stone Age man. Particularly interesting is the third pavilion, which shows a video film on the paintings and illustrates Stone Age burial practices; one remarkable exhibit is the remains of a Palaeolithic man enclosed in a block of transparent plastic. The Museum is open on weekdays (except Mondays) from 10am to 1pm and 4 to 6pm (in winter to 5pm), Sundays 10am to 1pm.

Museum

To the left of the Museum a narrow path leads through a fence to a stalactitic cave discovered some years ago which has some very fine stalagmites. The cave, like the Museum, can be visited without prior reservation.

Stalactitic cave

★★Cave paintings

The caves were accidentally discovered by a hunter in 1869. They were first explored by an archaeologist, Marcellino Sanz de Sautuola, in 1875, and four years later he discovered the underground chambers containing the

History

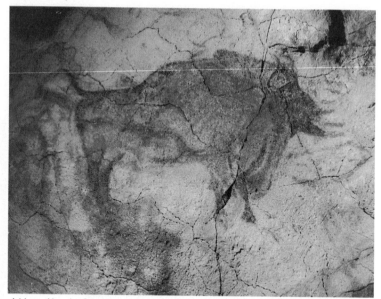

A bison, Altamira Caves

paintings. His belief that the paintings were prehistoric was not shared by the learned world of the day, and it was only after the discovery of similar paintings at Font-de-Gaume in southern France in 1901–02 that the authenticity of the Altamira paintings was generally accepted. Most of them are dated to the late Magdalenian period (c. 15,000–10,000 B.C.), though some more primitive paintings are around 10,000 years older.

★★ Sala de Pinturas

Visitors follow the course of an underground river to reach the Sala de Pinturas (Hall of Paintings), the beauty and vivid colouring of which have earned it the style of the "Sistine Chapel of cave art". The ceiling of the chamber, which measures 9 by 18m (30 by 60ft), is covered with paintings of animals, including several bison (one of them over 2m/6½ft high), a red wild horse, a wild boar and a hind. The Stone Age artists used the structure of the rock and the areas of shadow to achieve spatial effect and movement. The predominant colours are red, ochre and brown, obtained by the use of minerals mixed with water. The pigments were applied with a finger or a stick, or directly by rubbing the minerals on the rock. The outlines of the animals are drawn in charcoal. Some of the paintings have been damaged by the cracking or erosion of the rock.

Ampurias/Empúries

Q 2

Province: Gerona (GE). Altitude: sea level

The excavations of the ancient Greek town of Emporion, now Ampurias (Catalan Empúries), lie just above the sea on the Costa Brava, 35km/ 22 miles north-west of Gerona (see entry), with extensive views of the promontories to north and south. The nearby village bears the name of San Martín de Ampurias (Catalan Sant Martí de Empúries).

*Mosaic floors in a
Roman villa, Ampurias*

In the 6th century B.C. a Greek settlement, probably called Kypsela but known to archaeologists as Palaiopolis, was established on an island at the mouth of the Río Fluviá. Soon, however, the increasing numbers of settlers made it necessary to establish a new settlement on the mainland to the south. This was called Emporion (in Greek, "market"), and now, under the name of Neapolis ("new city"), constitutes the greater part of the excavation site. Between the two settlements was the harbour, now silted up. The Romans captured the Greek colony in the 3rd century B.C., and during the Second Punic War the first Roman troops, led by Scipio Africanus, landed here to establish a diversionary front against Hannibal. In 195 B.C. the town was Cato the Elder's base in his campaign to subdue the Iberians. Finally Caesar established a colony of veterans which flourished particularly in the 1st and 2nd centuries A.D. The decline of the city, which in early Christian times became the see of a bishop, began with the Frankish and Alemannic incursions. When the town of La Escala (see Costa Brava) was founded nearby in the 17th century the ruins of Emporion became a quarry of building material. The first excavations were carried out by the Spanish archaeologist Emilio Gandía y Ortega.

History

The ★ Site

The lower town is entered through the remains of a once massive town gate. Beyond this is a small square, to the left of which are the remains of a temple dedicated to the god of healing Asklepios (Aesculapius), with a cast of a statue which was found here. Adjoining are the foundations of another temple, probably dedicated to Hygeia, Asklepios's consort. On the far side of the square was a large temple of Zeus Serapis (seen as a fusion of Zeus and Asklepios). From here the broad main street leads to the Agora (market place), near which is an Early Christian basilica. Farther on are remains of mosaic pavements in geometric designs.

Neapolis
(lower town)

91

Museum

The tour of the lower town ends at the Museum, housed in the church of a former Servite monastery. In addition to the original of the statue from the temple of Asklepios the Museum displays models and finds from the site illustrating the life of an ancient Greek and Roman town.

Upper town

Beyond the Museum the ground rises to the site of the Roman town. The first house entered is House I, a model of which, based on the work of the Roman architectural writer Vitruvius (1st c. B.C.), can be seen in the Museum. Remains of pavement mosaics have been left in situ. The decoration of the rather smaller House II is similar. Beyond this is the Forum, with the main street, the cardo maximus, running into it on the south. This leads to the main gate, on the stone threshold of which are the marks left by wheeled traffic.

Andorra   O 2

State: Principality of Andorra (Catalan Principat d'Andorra, Spanish Principado de Andorra, French Principauté d'Andorre)
Capital: Andorra la Vella
Area: 468 sq.km/181 sq.miles

State flag

Altitude: 900–3000m/2850–9850ft. Population: 64,000

International Car Registration

The little principality of Andorra lies in the eastern Pyrenees between Spain and France. The main settlements are scattered about in the high valleys of the river Valira and its two source streams, the Valira d'Orient and the Valira del Nord. Andorra became accessible from Spain only in 1913, when a pass road was opened up. It is reached from France by the road over the Port d'Envalira (2408m/7901ft), built in 1931. The construction of an airport on the plateau surrounding the village of Sant Julià is under consideration.

Like other small states, Andorra is famed as a tax haven. It also attracts increasing numbers of visitors (13 million in 1984) as a duty-free area under its customs union with France. Stock-farming, once Andorra's principal source of revenue, now takes second place to tourism. Other contributions are made to the country's economy by its two radio stations, the export of electricity to France and the sale of Andorran stamps to collectors.

Some 12,000 of the inhabitants are Catalan Andorrans, about 30,000 come from Spain, 5000 from France and a few from Portugal. The language of Andorra is Catalan, but most Andorrans also speak French and/or Spanish. There is no independent Andorran currency, and both French francs and Spanish pesetas are in circulation.

Many farmers have built supermarkets, hotels and restaurants on their fields so that, over the last thirty years, the road which now runs through the once idyllic mountains and valleys, which were once cut off from the world, is a noisy conglomerate of tower blocks, car parks and a few old buildings with the tourist buses queueing bumper to bumper in the high season.

Sport

Andorra offers magnificent scope for hill walking and climbing. The mountain streams and lakes are well stocked with trout. Popular winter sports resorts are Pas de la Casa–Grau Roig, Soldeu–El Tarter, Arinsal, Pal and Arcalis.

History and Constitution

Archaeological finds in Andorra show that the high valleys were inhabited in the Bronze and Iron Ages. Legend has it that Andorra was founded by Charlemagne. It is first mentioned in a document of 839 recording the consecration of the cathedral in the Spanish town of Seo de Urgel (Catalan La Seu d'Urgell) as belonging to the County of Urgel. In 1133 the territory

Map labels:

F r a n c e

El Serrat
Pic de l'Estanyo △ 2915 m
Pic de les Fonts △ 2748 m
Pic de Casamanya 2740 m △
Arinsal
La Cortinada
El Tarter
Soldeu
Canillo
Valira d'Orient
Ordino
Meritxell
Coll de la Botella 2069 m
Pal
Les Bons
Encamp
Port d'Envalira 2408 m
Pas de la Casa 2096 m
Anyós
Valira del Nord
Pic de Carroi △ 2334 m
Grau-Roig
Coll Blanc 2528 m
ANDORRA la Vella
Sant Miguel d'Engolasters
Les Escaldes
Pic dels Pessons 2858 m
Santa Coloma
Nagol
Pic de la Portelleta 2905 m △
St. Julià de Lòria
Gran Valira
Torre dels Soldats 2761 m

Andorra
5 km
© Baedeker

S p a i n

came into the hands of the bishop of Urgel, who granted it as a fief to the Caboet family. When Andorra passed by marriage to the Counts of Foix this gave rise to a dispute over sovereignty with the bishop of Urgel, which was eventually settled by an agreement (*pareatge*) signed in 1278 and a further agreement ten years later. Under these agreements, which have remained in force to the present day, Andorra is under the joint protection of the Count of Foix and the Bishop of Urgel as representative of the Pope. It is thus, legally, still a medieval feudal state, though in practice sovereign. In 1419 the Andorrans were granted the right to establish a council (the Consell de la Terra) to deliberate on their own affairs, and this still operates under the name of Consell General. Universal suffrage was introduced only in 1970.

Arms of the Principality

The original six communes (valleys) of the principality were increased in 1978 to seven – Canillo, Encamp, Ordino, La Massana, Andorra la Vella, Sant Julià de Lòria and Escaldes–Engordany. Each commune elects four representatives (Consellers General) to the Consell General. Under a constitutional and administrative reform in 1981 the Consell General was given the right to elect the head of government (President of the Executive Council), who forms a government of between four and six members and in many fields also acts as head of state.

Constitution

In March 1993 the Andorrans finally voted with a three-quarters majority in a referendum in favour of a new constitution which changed the small

Sovereign state

93

state with medieval feudal practices into a modern state: sovereignity is transferred from the two representative heads of state, the French president and the Bishop of Seo de Urgel, who, for the sake of tradition, remain as "Co-princeps" to the Andorran people. Parties are admitted and a single chamber parliament is elected. Since May 4th 1993 Andorra has been a sovereign state. From July 28th 1993 it became a member of the United Nations and from November 1994 a member of the Council of Europe.

Andorra la Vella

The capital of the principality, Andorra la Vella (alt. 1029m/3376ft), is finely situated on the Gran Valira river under the east side of the Pic d'Enclar (2317m/7602ft).

★ Casa de la Vall

In the centre of the town is a plain building of undressed stone, built about 1580, which originally belonged to a noble Andorran family and is now the seat of government, with the courtroom and the meeting-place of the Consell General. Over the entrance are the arms of the principality, set up here in 1761, with the mitre and crosier of the bishop of Urgel, the four pales of Catalonia, the three pales of the Counts of Foix and the two oxen of the Counts of Béarn in its four quarters. The reception room on the first floor has 16th century wall paintings. In the council chamber (Sala de Sessiones) is the "cupboard of the seven keys", to which each of the seven communes has a key. It contains the archives of the principality, including documents which are said to date from the time of Charlemagne and Louis the Pious. The courtroom has magnificent wood panelling. Before every meeting of the Council the councillors attend a service in the Capilla Sant Ermengol. The large kitchen with its old utensils gives an impression of domestic life in the 16th century.

Until 1992 the second floor housed the Postal Museum. This space is now an assembly hall and was the setting of the drafting of the Andorran

Casa de la Vall

Constitution in 1993. (Open for guided tours: Tues.–Sat. 10am–1pm and 3–6pm, Sun. 10am–1pm; subject to meetings and functions.)

Sant Esteve, the town's principal church, dates from the 12th century; it was enlarged in 1969. It has fine carved woodwork.

Sant Esteve

The main street of Andorra la Vella is lined with shops selling hi-fi equipment, cameras, tobacco goods, spirits and perfume in which visitors (mostly day-trippers) can stock up with duty-free goods.

Duty-free shops

Valira d'Orient Valley

From Les Escaldes (alt. 1105m/3626ft), north of Andorra la Vella on the road to the French frontier, a narrow and winding road leads up to the Capilla de Sant Miquel d'Engolasters, a typical example of a Pyrenean church in Lombard Romanesque style, probably dating from the 11th century. From here there is a pleasant walk to the Estany d'Engolasters, an artificial lake created by a dam.

Les Escaldes

Les Escaldes was the home of the Catalan sculptor Josep Villadomat, many of whose works are displayed in the Salita Park.

Other features of interest in the village are the ruined chapel of Sant Romà and an old bridge, the Pont dels Escalls.

Les Escaldes is also a popular spa (sulphurous water).

In 1994 the thermal baths opened at Caldea, worth visiting for the bizarre architecture, with 25,000sq.m. of bathing facilities.

The village of Encamp (1238m/4062ft) has a Romanesque church.

Encamp

The National Automobile Museum (Museu Nacional de l'Automòbil) displays 250 old cars, motorcycles and bicycles from 1898 to 1950, and also has a collection of miniature china cars. (Open for guided tours: Tues.–Sat. 10am–1pm and 4–7pm; Sun. 10am–1pm.)

Near Encamp, huddled round a ruined castle, is the village of Les Bons, with the chapel of Sant Romà de Les Bons (consecrated 1163).

Les Bons

North of Encamp, on a hill to the right of the road, is the chapel of Our Lady of Meritxell. The old pilgrimage chapel was burned down in 1972, and in its place was built a modern chapel designed by Ricardo Bofill (consecrated 1976). In the new chapel each of the seven Andorran communes is represented by an image of its patron saint, and there is a reproduction of the original image of the Virgin of Meritxell, patroness of Andorra since 1873.

Meritxell chapel

A little way north of the old-world little village of Canillo, which has Andorra's tallest church tower, can be found the chapel of Sant Joan des Caselles, one of the finest Romanesque chapels in the principality, dating from the 12th century. Notable features of the interior, which is decorated with frescoes, are a retablo of 1525 ("St John and the Apocalypse"), the choir grille and a Romanesque stucco figure of Christ on the Cross, surrounded by polychrome painting.

Sant Joan des Caselles

Valira del Nord Valley

A road passing through the valley of the Valira del Nord ends in the mountains in the north-west of the principality.

After passing a medieval bridge, the Pont de Sant Antoni, the road comes to the picturesque village of Anyòs, with the chapel of Sant Cristofor.

Anyòs

The chief place in the valley is Ordino (alt. 1305m/4282ft), the most interesting feature in which is the Casa Plairal d'Areny de Plandolit. The

Ordino

house, originally started inn 1613 but mostly built after 1633, was rebuilt in the mid 19th century by its then owner, the Baron de Senaller, initiator of the "New Reform" of 1866, which gave heads of households, for the first time, a limited right of election to the Consell General. The house, which has a magnificent wrought-iron balcony of 1849, is now open to the public (Tues.–Sat. 10am–1pm and 3–6pm; Sun. 10am–1pm). The tour begins in the hall, which contains a reproduction of the original "cupboard of the six keys". On the ground floor are store-rooms for wine, oil and meat and a blacksmith's shop. On the upper floor are the old armoury (now the principal room in the house, with a large barrel-organ), the kitchen and the dining room, in which the baron's Limoges and Sèvres dinner services (the latter a gift from the Austrian Emperor), bearing the family arms, are displayed. Other interesting rooms are the library (with the coats of arms of related families), the music room (with a copy of the original version of the Andorran national anthem), the private chapel and a bakery. In the garden are displayed old stone blacksmith's hammers.

La Cortinada

In La Cortinada, a village surrounded by fields of tobacco, stands the church of Sant Martí de la Cortinada, with Romanesque frescoes, a charnel-house and a beautiful old dovecot.

El Serrat

At the end of the road is the magnificently situated mountain village of El Serrat (alt. 1540m/5053ft).

Gran Valira Valley

Between Andorra la Vella and Les Escaldes the Valira d'Orient and Valira del Nord join to form the Gran Valira river, which flows south towards the Spanish frontier.

Santa Coloma

To the right of the main road to Spain, in the little village of Santa Coloma, is a fine Romanesque church with a three-storied round tower very different from others in the principality. It contains a much venerated 12th century statue of the Virgin of El Remei. On the arched entrance are Mozarabic frescoes. The church has a notable medieval font.

Sant Vicenç

Above the village is the 12th century castle of Sant Vicenç, built by Roger Bernat, Count of Foix.

San Julia de Lòria

The road continues past another medieval bridge, the Pont de la Margineda, to Sant Julià de Lòria (alt. 939m/3081ft), from which a narrow road winds its way up to the church of Sant Cerní de Nagol, with fine Romanesque frescoes.

The church of Sant Julià de Lòria has a Romanesque bell-tower, a figure of the Virgin of the same period and a 17th century crucifix.

Aranjuez   H 5

Province: Madrid (M). Telephone dialling code: 91
Altitude: 492m/1614ft. Population: 36,000

Aranjuez, formerly a royal summer residence, lies on the Tagus 47km/ 29 miles south of Madrid. Its regularly planned streets, its avenues radiating from the central square and its gardens and palaces follow the course of the river, which has made the surrounding area a lush garden-like landscape and the main source of fruit and vegetables for Madrid.

300m
© Baedeker

Madrid

Aranjuez

Tajo ←Tajo

Jardín de la Isla

Casa de Marinos

Pradera

Casita del Labrador

Tajo

Colmenar de Oreja

Jardín del Príncipe

Reina

Reina

Estación

Plaza de Armas

1

Plaza de S. Rusiñol

Príncipe

Alpages

Toledo

Toledo

Palacio Real

Plaza de las Parejas

Plaza de San Antonio

2

Infantas

Moreras

San Antonio

Teatro

Real

Mercado

Paseo

Ayuntamiento

Florida

Andalucía

Capitán

Palacio de Medinaceli

Convento de San Pascual

Plaza de Toros

Toledo

1 Parterre, Jardín de las Estatuas
2 Jardín de Isabel II.

*Royal Palace

The Royal Palace (Palacio Real) was begun in 1560 at the behest of Philip II. The original architect was Juan Bautista de Toledo, who was also the first architect of the Escorial. The work was continued by Juan de Herrera, who gave the palace the classical austerity characteristic of his style. The palace was twice destroyed by fire, in 1660 and again in 1665, but each time Philip had it rebuilt. In the reign of the Bourbon king Charles III, who enlarged and planned the town on the rationalist principles of the Enlightenment, Francesco Sabatini added two projecting side wings to the palace, forming a spacious parade ground. The main front is in Herrera's Renaissance style, but the Baroque influences of his successors are very evident.

Opening times
Summer: Wed.–Mon. 10am–1pm and 3–6.30pm
Winter: Wed.–Mon. 10am–1pm and 3–5.30pm

Conducted tours
English, French, Spanish

The rooms of the palace are decorated and furnished in a style befitting the rank of its occupants, with valuable tapestries, furniture, porcelain, clocks, pictures and objets d'art. Particularly notable features are the magnificent staircase designed by Giacomo Bonavia, the Chapel Royal (by Sabatini), the velvet-clad Throne Room and above all the Porcelain Room (Sala de China), lavishly decorated with plaques of Buen Retiro porcelain depicting Chinese scenes. Other fine rooms are the Arab Saloon, modelled on the Hall of the Two Sisters in the Alhambra in Granada, and the Saloon of the Infantas or Sala de Papeles Chinos, decorated with delicate paintings on rice paper. The decoration of the palace was the work of the painters Luca Giordano, Anton Mengs, Francisco Bayeu and Mariano Maella.

Interior

**Porcelain Room

*Gardens

The gardens of Aranjuez are justly famed. They surround the palace and border the Tagus with their ancient trees.

Jardín de Isabel II	On the south side of the Plaza de San Rusiñol is the Jardín de Isabel II, a favourite resort of the Bourbon queen of that name.
Parterre	On the east side of the palace is the Parterre, a garden in the French style laid out by Philip V in 1726. In the Parterre is the Jardín de las Estatuas, which dates from the reign of Philip II, with busts of Roman Emperors and statues of gods and heroes.
Jardín de la Isla	The Jardín de la Isla, on an artificial island in the Tagus, is the oldest of the islands of Aranjuez. Isabella the Catholic caused a huerta to be converted into a garden, which was extended in the reign of Philip II. A beautiful avenue of plane-trees runs along the banks of the Tagus.
Jardín del Príncipe ★ Casa del Labrador	The largest and most beautiful of the gardens is the Jardín del Príncipe, laid out for Charles III in 1763 by the French landscape gardener Etienne Boutelou, who had previously designed the Parterre. In addition to a number of fountains and the many exotic plants the most notable feature is the Casa del Labrador (Peasant's House), at the end of Calle de la Reina, at the eastern tip of the garden. This charming little palace, consisting of a main block and two side wings, was built for Charles IV in 1803 by Isidro González Velázquez. The façade is decorated with statues of ancient heroes. The principal features of the sumptuous interior, decorated in Louis XVI and Empire style, are the grand staircase, the billiard room, the Sculpture Gallery, the Great Saloon, the Sala de María Luisa and the Gabinete de Platina.
★ Casa de Marinos	The Casa de Marinos (Seamen's House), in a bend on the Tagus within the Jardín del Príncipe, is a boathouse containing six royal barges, the most magnificent of which are Charles IV's barge, with painted decoration by Maella, Alfonso XII's mahogany boat and Philip V's felucca, presented to him by a Venetian noble.
The Town	The town was laid out on a strictly geometrical plan during the reign of Ferdinand VI and has a number of interesting Baroque and Rococo palaces. The Tagus is spanned here by the elegant Puente Largo, built in 1761.

Arévalo   G 4

Province: Ávila (AV). Telephone dialling code: 918
Altitude: 826m/2710ft. Population: 7000

The little town of Arévalo lies in the north of Ávila province at the junction of the Río Arevalillo with the Río Adaja. A number of churches and convents bear witness to its former importance as one of the keys of Castile. The old town has been declared a national monument.

Sights

Plaza de la Villa	This spacious square, paved with light-coloured stone and surrounded by old houses, the upper floors of which are supported on timber or stone columns, creating shady arcades, will leave visitors with a lasting impression of the way of life of the people of Castile.
San Martín	On the east side of the Plaza de la Villa stands the church of San Martín (13th–14th c.), with two large Mudéjar towers. There are remains of Romanesque frescoes in the porch.
Santa María	On the west side of the square the church of Santa María (12th c.) is built in Romanesque/Mudéjar style, with Romanesque wall paintings of the Catalan school in the apse. The street runs through an arched gateway under the massive tower.

Castillo de Arévalo

In the 14th century castle, with an imposing keep, which stands above the Río Adaja, on the north-western outskirts of the town, Isabella the Catholic spent her early years.

Castillo

In Plaza del Real, to the south of Plaza de la Villa, are a number of noble mansions. The Arco de Alcocer, on the south side of the square, was originally the main gate in the town walls.

Plaza del Real

On a hill 2km/1½ miles south of the town is the church of La Lugareja, one of the finest examples of Mudéjar architecture, though only the apse and the transepts are preserved. The church belonged to a Visigothic monastery which was rebuilt in the 13th century.

La Lugareja

In the west of the town stands the church of San Miguel, which has a beautiful retablo; south of this, just inside the old town walls, is the 14th century church of San Juan; and in the Plaza de Arrabal is Santo Domingo, which has a Byzantine apse.

Other churches

Astorga

E 2

Province: León (LE). Telephone dialling code: 987
Altitude: 869m/2851ft. Population: 12,600

Astorga, still partly surrounded by walls dating from the late Roman period, is an old-world episcopal city beautifully situated on an outlier of the Manzanal range. Described by Pliny in Roman times as a "splendid city" (*"urbs magnifica"*), it rose to prosperity and power in the 9th century and became an important staging point on the pilgrim road to Santiago de

Compostela. The Roman walls are best seen from the main road (N VI) on the west side of the town.

Sights

Cathedral

The town's finest building is the cathedral (15th–16th c.), which has three Plateresque doorways with sculptured scenes from the life of Christ on the west front and two 17th century towers.

★Interior

The high altar has a retablo (1562) by Gaspar de Hoyos and Gaspar de Palencia, with fine carving by Gaspar Becerra. The choir-stalls, with a riot of carved decoration, date from 1551. The Gothic cloister was rebuilt in 1780.

★Museo Diocesano

The Diocesan Museum displays the valuable cathedral treasury, including a silver gilt casket presented by Alfonso III (866–910), a reliquary containing a fragment of the True Cross and an 11th century chalice.

Palacio Episcopal ★Museo de los Caminos

Adjoining the cathedral is the Bishop's Palace, a Neo-Gothic building by Antoni Gaudí (1893). It now houses the Museo de los Caminos (Museum of the Pilgrim Way), with a variety of material on the history of the pilgrim road to Santiago de Compostela (see entry), and also collections of Roman antiquities and Maragato costumes.

Casa Consistorial

In the arcaded Plaza Mayor can be found the 17th century Casa Consistorial (Town Hall). A notable feature is the clock, with two figures in Maragato costume which strike the hour (at present removed during the restoration of the clock).

Ergástula Romana

In the basement of the building to the left of the Town Hall is the Ergástula Romana, an underground room 60m/200ft long, 10m/35ft wide and

The Archbishop's Palace, Astorga, by Gaudí

8.5m/28ft high which is said to have been a prison for Roman slaves. On the Plaza Romana are the remains of a 3rd c. mansion with fine mosaic floors.

Ávila

Province: Ávila (AV). Telephone dialling code: 918
Altitude: 1130m/3708ft. Population: 43,000

Ávila, chief town of the province of that name in Old Castile and the see of a bishop, is situated on a ridge of high ground, falling steeply down on three sides, in a treeless plateau watered by the Río Adaja. It is enclosed by high hills except on the north, and accordingly has a very harsh climate. Ávila is the highest provincial capital in Spain.

Ávila's wealth of medieval buildings (particularly its well preserved Roma- **★★ Townscape**
nesque churches and Gothic palaces) and the ancient walls which still enclose the heart of the old town make it one of the most interesting cities in Spain. As the birthplace of Spain's national saint, Terese of Ávila, it is also a much frequented pilgrimage centre.

Originating as the legendary Roman town of Avela, Ávila alternated be- History
tween Arab and Christian rule for more than three centuries after the Moorish invasion in 714, but was finally won for the Christians by Alfonso VI in 1085. Thereafter many noble families settled in the town, earning it the

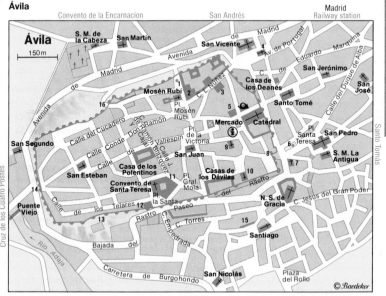

1 Fuente del Sol	7 La Magdalena	12 Casa de Núñez Vela
2 Casa de Aguila	8 Puerta del Alcázar	13 Puerta de la
3 Casa de Verdugo	9 Las Nieves	Mala Dicha
4 Humilladero	10 Santo Tomé	14 Puerta del Puente
5 Casa de Velada	11 Torréon	15 Paneras del Rey
6 Santa Teresa	de los Guzmanes	16 Puerta del Carmen

Medieval Ávila, seen from the Cruz de los Cuatro Postes

name of Ávila de los Caballeros ("Ávila of the Nobles") – as its numerous noble palaces still testify. Ávila's heyday was in the 16th century, when its life was dominated by the presence of Santa Teresa de Jesús (1515–82). After the expulsion of the Moors in 1607–10, during the reign of Philip III, the town fell into decline. It is still a quiet little town with much of the atmosphere of medieval Castile.

★★ Town Walls

★ Viewpoint

After the final reconquest of the town Ávila became an important element in a defensive line against the Moors. Raimundo de Borgoña, son-in-law of Alfonso VI, built the massive circuit of walls, the best preserved in Spain, which still completely enclose the town, between 1090 and 1099. The walls, battlemented throughout their length and incorporating stone from Roman buildings, are 2557m/2797yd long, 12m/40ft high on average and 3m/10ft thick. The 88 semicircular towers, set at intervals of 20m/65ft, give the defences an imposing aspect, particularly when seen from the Cruz de los Cuatro Postes, west of the town on the Salamanca road. There are nine gates in the walls, the most massive of which are the Puerta de San Vicente and the Puerta del Alcázar (in which re-used Roman stones can be seen), on the east side of the town. Between the two is the apse of the cathedral, known as the Ciborro, which, as the highest tower in the circuit of walls, forms part of the town's defences. Beside the Puerta del Carmen, on the north side of the town, is a slender tower, topped by one of the storks' nests which are to be seen all over Castile. Near this gate are steps leading up to the wall-walk, which is open to visitors.

★ Cathedral

On the east side of the old town, just inside the walls, is the massive Cathedral of San Salvador, begun in 1091 but not completed until the 14th

century. Built of granite, it has a fortress-like aspect, and the apse forms part of the town's circuit of walls. Of the two towers on the west front, with the main entrance, only the northern one (14th c.) is complete. The doorway (15th c.) was the work of Juan Guas but was altered in 1779. The figural decoration on the north doorway, the Apostles' Doorway (*c.* 1200), dates from the 15th century and was originally on the west doorway. The sculpture, which has suffered badly from air pollution, is at present in course of restoration.

A striking feature of the interior, with aisles flanking the nave, is the red and white granite stonework of the walls, which dates from the early building phase. From the crossing there are fine views of the dome and the stained glass in the transepts. The richly carved choir-stalls (1544) in the *coro* were the work of Cornelis de Holanda and Isidro Villoldo, who took as their model the stalls by Diego de Siloé in the church of San Diego in Valladolid (see entry). The outer walls of the *coro* are richly decorated with reliefs in Plateresque style.

Interior

The retablo in the Capilla Mayor was begun in 1499, largely finished by 1508 and finally completed in 1522. Leading artists like Pedro Berruguete, Juan de Borgoña and Santa Cruz took part in the decoration of the church with paintings and sculpture. In the *trassagrario,* to the rear of the high altar, is the alabaster tomb of Bishop Alfonso de Madrigal (d. 1455), in Italian Renaissance style (1518). The bishop was known as El Tostado (the "burnt one") because, as a great reader, he frequently burned himself with his candle; he is shown seated, reading.

There are nine side chapels containing some very handsome tombs; the finest are the Capilla de San Antolín in the north transept, with a magnificent retablo, and the Capilla de Nuestra Señora de Gracia in the ambulatory, with the tomb of Bishop Sancho (d. 1181), the first bishop to be buried in the cathedral.

Ávila

★ Museo de la Catedral/ ★ Sacristy	In the south transept is the entrance to the Cathedral Museum, which has five rooms. The finest room, following an anteroom, is the Sacristy (Sacristía), notable particularly for its ribbed vaulting and an alabaster group by Isidro Villoldo and Pedro de Salamanca. In the adjoining room, which mostly contains liturgical utensils and sculpture, the items of most interest are a very beautiful Isabelline screen and (behind, to the right) an El Greco portrait. In other rooms are silver articles, vestments, paintings, large music-books and sculpture, including works by Berruguete and Juan de Frías. The last room contains only one thing – a magnificent silver monstrance by Juan de Arfe (1571), 1.7m/5ft 7in. high.
★ Monstrance	
Cloister	On the south side of the cathedral, entered through a Romanesque doorway, is the 14th century cloister.
Plaza de la Catedral	At the north-west corner of the Plaza de la Catedral is the large palace of the Velada family, now a restaurant. Opposite the north doorway is the former Bishop's Palace (Palacio Episcopal), now occupied by the Post Office. Another old noble mansion, the Casa de Valderrábanos (15th c.), in the part of the square outside the west front, is now a hotel.

Within the Town Walls

Jewish quarter	The Jewish community of Ávila lived in two areas within the walls, in the north-east corner of the town, round the Puerta de San Vicente, and in the south-west corner, between the Puerta de la Mala Dicha and the Puerta del Puente.
Plaza Mayor	The central feature of the old town of Ávila is the Plaza de la Victoria or Plaza Mayor, a small enclosed square to the west of the cathedral, surrounded by arcades which now house shops and bars. On the north side is the handsome Town Hall, on the south side the church of San Juan, with the font at which Santa Teresa was baptised. The church has balconies from which the nobles of the town once watched bullfights in the square. Around the square are Ávila's main shopping streets, and to the north-east, towards the cathedral, is the two-storey market hall.
Convento de Santa Teresa	On the south side of the old town, opposite the gate now known as the Puerta de la Santa, there formerly stood the house in which Santa Teresa was born. The site is now occupied by the church (1638) of the Convento de Santa Teresa de Jesús, a convent of Discalced Carmelite nuns. Over the doorway in the relatively plain Baroque façade is a statue of the saint. The main feature of the interior, reached from the north transept, is the room in which Santa Teresa was born, now converted into a lavishly decorated Baroque chapel. On the altar is a statue (by Gregorio Fernández) of the saint at the moment of her vision of the Cross, richly ornamented and decked with jewellery and precious fabrics.
Casa de los Dávila	Built against the town walls a little way east of the convent, beyond Plaza General Mola, is one of Ávila's many noble mansions, the huge Casa de los Dávila (13th–15th c.).
Torreón de los Guzmanes	The most striking feature of the palace of the Guzmán and Oñate families, which was built on to the convent in the 16th century, is the massive battlemented tower.
Casa de Núñez Vela	Diagonally opposite the convent church is another noble mansion, the Casa de Núñez Vela, built in 1540 for Blasco Núñez Vela, first Viceroy of Peru. It is now occupied by legal offices; the beautiful inner courtyard can be seen during office hours.
Casa de los Polentinos	North-west of the convent is yet another mansion, the Casa de los Polentinos, now occupied by the military authorities.

Convento de Santa Teresa, Ávila

To the north of the Plaza Mayor, between the Puerta del Carmen and the Puerta de San Vicente, is a less crowded part of the old town. Here in 1516 Mosén Rubí, a converted Jew belonging to a noble family of Ávila, built a burial chapel for his aunt María Herrera and her husband. The alabaster tomb was carved by Vázquez Dávila. The chapel, which now belongs to a Dominican nunnery, contains a 17th century polychrome figure of Christ, the Cristo de las Batallas.

Capilla de
Mosén Rubí
de Bracamonte

Opposite the chapel is the Casa de los Aguila, a 16th century noble mansion.

Casa de
los Aguila

In Calle López Núñez, which runs north-east to the Puerta de San Vicente, is the fortress-like Casa de los Verdugos, with four corner towers. The doorway is decorated with the girdle of the Franciscan order.

Casa de
los Verdugos

Outside the Town Walls

San Vicente, Ávila's most important church after the cathedral, stands just outside the Puerta de San Vicente, on the spot where San Vicente and his sisters Sabina and Cristeta are believed to have been martyred in A.D. 300. Begun in the early 12th century (the apses, transepts and part of the nave were apparently built by 1109), it was not completed until the 14th, and the towers were left unfinished. On the south side of the church is a portico added in the 14th century which is said to have been a place of judgment. The south doorway, which dates from the earliest building period, has a very fine Romanesque Annunciation. The west doorway, with a porch, has one of the finest groups of Romanesque sculpture, with column figures of Apostles and, on the central column, Christ with two other Apostles.

★ San Vicente

★ West doorway

Interior

The interior, with an aisled nave, is dominated by the saints' magnificent shrine under the crossing. The late 12th century shrine, under a 16th century canopy, is decorated with reliefs of outstanding quality. On the ends are Christ Pantokrator and the Adoration of the Kings; on the front are seven panels relating the story of San Vicente and his sisters. In the crypt of the church is the rock on which the saints are said to have been martyred. The crypt also contains several figures of the Virgin, the most notable of which is the Romanesque Virgen de la Soterraña.

Casa de los Deanes/ Museo Provincial

The 16th century Casa de los Deanes (Deanery), a two-storey building, stands to the south of San Vicente in Plaza Naivillos. It now houses the Provincial Museum, which displays in three rooms a collection of sacred sculpture from the Romanesque period to the Renaissance, tapestries, a triptych attributed to Hans Memling, pictures, weapons and ceramics.

Santo Tomé

Immediately adjoining the Museum is the little 12th century church of San Tomé, now a lapidarium (at present closed).

San José

Farther east is the convent of San José or Las Madres, the first house founded by Santa Teresa (1562). It contains a fine retablo by Alonso Cano.

Plaza de Santa Teresa

Just outside the Puerta del Alcázar is the spacious Plaza de Santa Teresa, another important shopping area, with many cafés and bars. Not to be missed is the El Grande café with its long bar and wide range of *tapas* and drinks of all kinds.

★ San Pedro

Dominating the east side of the square is the church of San Pedro with its large rose window. This aisled church with a plain but impressive west doorway was built in the 12th and 13th centuries. The most notable items in the interior are a painting by Morán ("St Peter in Chains", 1673) in the north aisle and the high altar by Juan de Borgoña.

★ Santo Tomás

From San Pedro the Paseo de Santo Tomás runs south-east to the Dominican convent of Santo Tomás, founded in 1483 by María Dávila and Tomás de Torquemada following his appointment as the first Grand Inquisitor of Spain. The Catholic Monarchs also used it as a summer residence. From the outside the church looks austere and cold; the only decoration on the façade is provided by ball friezes and the emblem of the Catholic Monarchs (a yoke and sheaf of arrows).

Interior

The interior of the church is dark. A striking feature is that the high altar and choir are opposite each other on two galleries accessible only from the cloisters: that is, only for the monks, who looked down from the high altar on the choir with its richly carved stalls. The tribunals of the Inquisition met in the choir, and from the choir the Catholic Monarchs followed the mass. The retablo of the high altar, the masterpiece of Pedro de Berruguete (c. 1499), depicts scenes from the life of St Thomas Aquinas. Under the dome over the crossing is the magnificent tomb of the Infante Don Juan, only son of the Catholic Monarchs, who died in 1497; the recumbent alabaster figure of the young prince and the scene of his burial were the work of the Florentine sculptor Domenico Fancelli (1510–13). In one of the side chapels are the tombs, by Vasco de la Zarza, of Núñez Arnalte, treasurer to the Catholic Monarchs, and his wife.

Cloisters

There are three cloisters. The simplest is the Claustro del Noviciado (Cloister of the Novices), which leads into the Claustro del Silencio (Cloister of Silence), from which a flight of steps leads into the choir. On the first floor is a doorway leading to the high altar, with Berruguete's retablo. Opening off the two-storey Claustro de los Reyes (Royal Cloister) are a number of rooms housing a museum of Eastern art.

Under the south-east corner of the town walls is the Convento de Nuestra Señora de Gracia, in which the future St Teresa was brought up.

Nuestra Señora de Gracia

This little 12th century church on the Río Adaja, below the south side of the town walls, contains the tomb (by Juan de Juni, 1573) of St Secundus, first bishop of Ávila.

San Segundo

Teresa of Ávila spent 29 years of her life in the convent of the Encarnación (north-west of the walled town), of which she was prioress. A chapel was built over her cell in 1630 and there is a museum containing relics of the saint.

La Encarnación

Badajoz

D 6

Province: Badajoz (BA). Telephone dialling code: 924
Altitude: 183m/600ft. Population: 114,000

Badajoz, the "key of Portugal", lies on a low ridge of hills on the left bank of the Río Guadiana, near the Portuguese frontier. It is the chief town of its province and the see of a bishop. The three most important towns of Estremadura are Badajoz, Cáceres (see entry) and Trujillo (see entry).

The town was known to the Romans as Colonia Pacensis, to the Moors as Badaljóz. After the fall of the Caliphate of Córdoba the Aftasids established a small Moorish kingdom here. In 1229 the town was captured by Alfonso IX of León. Down to the 20th century Badajoz was frequently the scene of military conflict and was occupied by many different armies. In 1385, 1396 and 1542 it was taken by the Portuguese; in 1580 it was Philip II's headquarters during the conquest of Portugal; in 1660 it was retaken by the

History

View of Badajoz

Portuguese; in 1701, during the War of the Spanish Succession, it was besieged by the Allies; in 1810 the French were driven out of Badajoz by British forces; and the town was also the scene of bitter fighting in 1936, during the Civil War.

Sights

★ Alcazaba

On a hill to the north-east of the town is the Alcazaba, once the seat of its Moorish rulers, with remains of the Mudéjar-style palace of the Dukes of Fería, now in a public park. A striking feature is the octagonal Torre de Espantaperros or Torre del Apéndiz, a massive battlemented keep built by the Almohads, from which there are extensive views of the Río Guadiana and Extremadura. A former mosque houses the Archaeological Museum.

San Juan

In the centre of the old town is the Plaza de España, with the Palacio Municipal (Town Hall). Opposite it is the Cathedral of San Juan, a fortress-like structure built between 1232 and 1284 with a sturdy square tower and a later Renaissance façade and doorway (1619). The interior is aisled, with a large Renaissance choir (by Jerónimo de Valencia) and fine choir-stalls. There are twelve chapels, the most notable of which are the Capilla de Santa Ana and the Capilla de los Duques, with pictures by Luis de Morales (1509–86), a native of Badajoz. There are six Flemish tapestries in the Sacristy.

Museo Capitular

The diocesan museum in the chapterhouse also has pictures by Luis de Morales as well as by other artists.

Museo Provincial de Bellas Artes

From the Plaza de España Calle Sarna runs north-west to the Palacio de la Diputación Provincial which houses the Provincial Museum of Art, mainly containing works by contemporary Extremadura artists but also pictures by Morales and Zurbarán.

Puente de Palmas

From the Museum Calle M. Evora leads to the battlemented Puerta de Palmas, a late 16th century town gate. Beyond this is the Puente de Palmas, a granite bridge built in 1596 on Roman foundations; 582m/637yd long, it spans the Guadiana with 32 arches.

Other sacred buildings

Other sacred buildings of interest are the churches of the Concepción and San Agustín, both containing fine tombs, and the Convento de Santa Ana.

Surroundings of Badajoz

Alburquerque

C 530 runs north from Badajoz and over the Puerto de los Conejeros to Alburquerque (alt. 750m/2460ft), 44km/27 miles away. This is an old-world little town situated on a hill, still preserving remains of its walls. Over the town loom the ruins of a mighty castle, built in 1276 by Alonso Sánchez, an illegitimate son of the king of Portugal.

The Gothic church of Santa María del Mercado, with its fortified tower, similarly reflects the history of Alburquerque as a much fought-over frontier town.

Through Southern Extremadura

Olivenza

26km/16 miles south of Badajoz on C 436 is Olivenza (alt. 160m/525ft), a little walled town with handsome town gates. It belonged to Portugal until 1801, when it finally passed to Spain as a result of the "Orange War". Its long allegiance to Portugal is reflected in the predominance of the Manueline style (named after Manuel I of Portugal, who reigned 1495–1521), otherwise rarely found in Spain. The Manueline style combines Moorish and Late Gothic elements with early Renaissance features, and incorporates a variety of decorative forms derived from the Portuguese conquests in America and Asia (exotic plants, corals, shells) and seafaring symbols like ropes and knots.

A good example of the Manueline style is the 16th century church of Santa María Magdalena, with ribbed vaulting borne on columns resembling ships' ropes. The sumptuous high altar is Baroque.

Santa María Magdalena

The church of Santa María del Castillo, near the castle, has a Gothic winged altar depicting the genealogy of the Virgin in the left-hand apse. The right-hand side altar is in Manueline style.

Santa María del Castillo

Close by the church is the massive keep (1488) of the castle, the origins of which go back to 1306. It now houses the Museo Municipal, the only museum on the ethnography of Extremadura.

Castillo

This old hospital, just outside the town walls at the Puerta de los Angeles, is notable for its chapel, lavishly decorated with azulejos (glazed tiles).

Santa Casa de Misericordia

The doorway of the Municipal Library is another good example of the Manueline style, with two carved stone armillary spheres, symbolising Portugal's status as a seafaring nation and a world power.

Municipal Library

From Olivenza C 436 continues by way of Villanueva del Fresno, with a ruined castle and the Convento de la Luz, to Oliva de la Frontera, where the palace of the Dukes of Gandía is worth a visit.

Oliva de la Frontera

The route continues to Jerez de los Caballeros, which gets its name (*caballeros* = "knights") from the Knights of the Temple who captured the town from the Moors in 1229. When the dissolution of the Order was proclaimed in a papal bull the knights of Jerez put up a fierce resistance to Ferdinand IV's troops.
   Jerez de los Caballeros was the birthplace of Vasco Núñez de Balboa, the first European to cross the Isthmus of Panama and reach the Pacific Ocean, and Hernán de Soto, one of the conquistadors of Florida and the Mississippi delta.

Jerez de los Caballeros

The Templar castle stands on a hill on the south-eastern outskirts of the town. The site is now a park. A striking feature is the Torre Sangriente (Bloody Tower), in which the surviving Templars were executed after the capture of their castle.

Castillo de los Templarios

The church of Santa María, below the castle, is the oldest foundation in Extremadura, going back to a Visigothic church consecrated on Christmas Eve in the year 559. In the 17th century the church, already much altered, was remodelled in Baroque style.

Santa María

A prominent landmark in the town centre is the tower of the church of San Miguel (1749). Above the brick-built base are several storeys with rich sculptural ornament.

San Miguel

The counterpart to the tower of San Miguel in the upper town is the tower of San Bartolomé, a church begun in the 16th century which is more gaily decorated than San Miguel, with blue and yellow glass and blue azulejos.

San Bartolomé

East of Jerez de los Caballeros by way of Burguillos de Cerro is Zafra (alt. 509m/1670ft), a town which has an Andalusian air. It was the Iberian settlement of Segida, the Roman Julia Restituta and the Moorish Zafar.

Zafra

The most imposing building in Zafra, in the centre of the town, is the Gothic Alcázar (15th–16th c.) of the Dukes of Fería, dominated by a battlemented

★ Alcázar

round tower – a good example of an old Spanish palace of Arab origin. It is now a Parador Nacional, a high-class hotel, boasting a marble patio attributed to Juan de Herrera.

Colegiata de
la Candelaria

To the north of the Alcázar is the collegiate church of La Candelaria, begun in 1546, which has a retablo (1644) painted by Francisco de Zurbarán. There is a small museum of sacred art.

Convento de
Santa Clara

The Convento de Santa Clara, founded in 1428 by the first Duke of Fería, contains a number of fine tombs, including those of the founder and his wife.

Plaza Grande
Plaza Chica

Zafra has two picturesque and attractive squares, the palm-shaded Plaza Grande, surrounded by 18th and 19th century houses, and the sleepy, arcaded Plaza Chica, on which the market used to be held.

From Zafra there is a choice of routes back to Badajoz – either the direct road on N 432 (E 102) or on N 630 via Mérida (see entry).

Baeza   H 7

Province: Jaén (J). Telephone dialling code: 953
Altitude: 760m/2495ft. Population: 15,000

The old-world town of Baeza, the Roman Vivatia, lies in the upper valley of the Guadalquivir, among the foothills of the Loma de Ubeda, surrounded by olive-groves, fields of corn and vineyards. The see of a bishop in Visigothic times, it was conquered by the Moors and finally became Christian again in the 13th century. In the 16th century a university was founded in the town. As a trading town on the border between La Mancha and Andalusia Baeza prospered particularly in the 16th century: a prosperity which found expression in the building of many handsome town houses and noble mansions.

★ Townscape

Sights

Paseo de la
Constitución

The spacious Paseo de la Constitución in the centre of the town is surrounded by handsome 17th century houses. The two most striking buildings, at the east end, are the clock-tower known, after a Moorish family, as Los Aliatares and the old Cornmarket with its triple arched gallery. In the little street behind the Cornmarket is the old granary, from which grain was conveyed direct into the market.

★ Plaza de
los Leones

The little Plaza de los Leones at the west end of the Paseo owes its name to the fountain in the centre of the square, which incorporates four figures of lions from the Roman site of Cástulo and an Ibero-Roman female figure traditionally identified as Hannibal's wife Imilce. Around the square are several handsome buildings: the 16th century Antigua Carnicería (butcher's shop), which in spite of its humble function has a gallery and a magnificent coat-of-arms of Charles V; the Casa del Pópulo, with an extraordinary Plateresque façade; the Puerta de Jaén; and the Arco de Villalar, a triumphal arch erected in 1521 to commemorate the repression of the Comunero rising.

Plaza
Santa María

The first thing to strike the eye in the Plaza Santa María, south-east of the Plaza de los Leones, is a fountain in the form of a triumphal arch bearing the arms of Philip II.

Cathedral

On the south side of the square stands the Gothic Cathedral of Santa María, originally built on the foundations of a mosque and rebuilt between 1567 and 1593. The Puerta de la Luna is in Moorish style; the Puerta del Perdón,

Plaza de los Leones, Baeza

spanning a street, is Gothic. Notable features of the interior (designed by Andrés de Vandelvira) are the Capilla Mayor, with stellar vaulting, and the Capilla del Sagrario, which has a richly decorated choir screen by Bartolomé de Jaén. The six-sided wrought-iron pulpit dates from 1580. The cloister still preserves a few arches from the former mosque.

Facing the Cathedral is the doorway of the Seminary of San Felipe Neri.

From the Plaza Santa María the Cuesta de San Felipe Neri leads to the little Plaza de Santa Cruz, with the church of Santa Cruz. Opposite it is the imposing Palacio Jabalquinto, the palace of the Counts of Benavente, which has a late 15th century Isabelline façade by Juan Guas with faceted stonework and Moorish buttresses.

★Palacio Jabalquinto

A narrow street separates the Palacio Jabalquinto from the Old University, which was founded in 1542 and converted into a school in 1875. At the beginning of this century the poet Antonio Machado taught French here (commemorative plaque in courtyard).

Old University

The street between the palace and the University leads back to the Plaza de los Leones.

The most important building to the north of the Paseo de la Constitución is the Ayuntamiento (Town Hall), on the Paseo Cardinal Benavides. It has a charming façade with very beautiful balconies and fine coats of arms, including that of Philip II.

Ayuntamiento

Close by are the ruins of the Convento de San Francisco and the former Hospital de la Concepción, which has a beautiful south doorway.

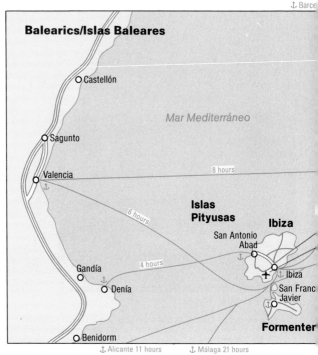

⊥ Barce

Balearics/Islas Baleares

O Castellón

Mar Mediterráneo

O Sagunto

Valencia

8 hours

Islas Pityusas

Ibiza

6 hours

San Antonio
Abad

Gandía
O

4 hours

O Denía

Ibiza

San Franc
Javier

O Benidorm

Formenter

⊥ Alicante 11 hours   ⊥ Málaga 21 hours

Balearics   O–R 5/6

Autonomous Community
Organ of government: Consell General de les Illes Balears
Province: Baleares (Balearics)
Telephone dialling code: 971 (all islands). Population: 720,000

The description of the Balearics in this guide is abridged, since there are
detailed AA/Baedeker guides to Majorca/Minorca and Ibiza/Formentera.

Shipping services — There are car ferries from Barcelona, Tarragona, Valencia, Denia, Alicante
and Málaga in mainland Spain, from Marseilles and Sète in France and
from Genoa in Italy. There are also ferry services between the islands (see
Practical Information, Car Ferries).

Air services — Majorca and Ibiza are served by both scheduled services and charter flights
throughout the year. Minorca has scheduled services from Madrid and
Barcelona and charter flights from other European airports during the
summer months; in winter it is not easy to get a flight to Minorca.

The islands — The island group known as the Balearics (Islas Baleares), lying in the
western Mediterranean off the south-eastern coast of Spain, consists of the
Balearic islands proper of Majorca (Mallorca) and Minorca (Menorca),
together with Ibiza and Formentera, which are also known as the Islas
Pityusas ("Pine Islands"), and about 150 smaller islands, including

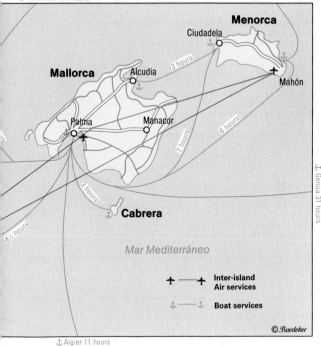

Cabrera, to the south of Majorca, some of which are used for military or nautical purposes, while others are totally unoccupied.

The languages spoken in the islands are Majorcan (Mallorquí), Minorcan (Menorquí) and Ibizan (Ibicenco), which are all dialects of Catalan. The language of business is Spanish.

Language

Until the advent of mass tourism the main source of revenue was agriculture. Nowadays – particularly during the summer months – the islands no longer produce enough to meet their own needs. One traditional crop in the Balearics is almonds, which are grown on a large scale on Majorca, producing great masses of blossom in January and February. Other crops are figs, apricots, citrus fruits and vegetables. On Minorca and Ibiza dry farming methods predominate. The production of wine is declining. Stock-farming is practised only on a small scale, though there is a fair amount of dairy farming on Minorca. The fisheries have declined and can no longer meet the islands' needs.

Economy
Agriculture

A major export from Ibiza and Formentera is salt, which is harvested from large marine salt-pans and exported, predominantly to Scandinavia, as table salt.

Salt

The most important non-agricultural source of revenue is the leather industry of Majorca and Minorca which manufactures shoes, handbags, etc. There is also some textile production, particularly on Ibiza.

Crafts

Pottery and ceramics are old-established traditional crafts. Faience, originally introduced by the Moors, was already being exported in medieval times from Majorca to Italy, where it became known as majolica (a name derived from Majorca).

Other products of the islands are glass, silver and artificial pearls.

Tourism

With their mild climate, beautiful scenery and good bathing, the Balearics attract visitors throughout the year, and tourism – mainly on the coasts – now contributes more than half the total tax revenue of the Autonomous Community of the Balearics. The tourist boom, however, has severely damaged the established economic structures of the islands, and it is now being questioned whether the development of the last three decades has brought only benefits to the islanders. It is increasingly being suggested that a brake should be put on the further expansion of tourism.

History

Naveta d'es Tudóns

There are abundant remains of the prehistoric and early historical periods in the Balearics, often excellently preserved. They belong predominantly to the Talayot culture (from Arabic *atalaya*, "lookout"), a megalithic culture which flourished between 1500 B.C. and the Roman conquest, erecting the characteristic Balearic *talayots* (towers built of massive blocks of stone). From the same period date the *taulas* (Catalan *taula*, "table"), which are found only on Minorca – table-like structures with a large stone slab resting horizontally on a vertical monolith. Other monuments of this period are the *navetas* ("boats"), which have the form of an upturned boat.

In the 3rd century B.C. the early inhabitants of the islands were subjugated by the Carthaginians, and their great leader Hannibal is believed to have been born on Ibiza or a nearby islet. In 123 B.C. the Romans, led by Quintus Caecilius Metellus (Balearicus), established themselves in the Balearics, to be succeeded in the 5th century A.D. by the Vandals, who in turn were driven out by the Byzantines. Finally in 798 the islands were conquered by the Moors. After the disintegration of the Caliphate of Córdoba the islands became the haunt of pirates, who harried shipping off the coasts of Catalonia, Provence and Italy. In 1229 Jaime I of Aragon ("el Conquistador") launched a punitive expedition against the corsairs and conquered Majorca. This later developed into an independent kingdom, but in the 14th century was reincorporated in Aragon. Thereafter it became an important centre of Mediterranean trade. After the discovery of America and the shift of European interest to the Atlantic the Mediterranean trade, and with it the Balearics, declined. Under the treaty of Utrecht after the War of the Spanish Succession Minorca was assigned to Britain, which had already occupied the island in 1708. During the 18th century it was successively occupied by Britain, France and Spain, finally becoming Spanish in 1808. During the Spanish Civil War Majorca and Ibiza were controlled by the Nationalists, Minorca by the Popular Front. After the Second World War, from the 1950s onwards, mass tourism came to the Balearics on a rapidly increasing scale. This sparked off an uncontrolled building boom, particularly on Majorca, which radically changed the life of the islands.

On February 22nd 1983 the Balearics became an Autonomous Community.

★★Majorca

P/Q 5/6

Area: 3650 sq.km/1410 sq.miles. Population: 582,000

Topography

Majorca (Mallorca in Spanish), the largest and most visited of the Balearics, is made up of three markedly different parts. Running parallel to the north-west coast is the Sierra del Norte, a range of wooded hills which includes the highest point on the islands, the Puig Mayor (1443m/4734ft). The hills fall steeply down to the sea in much-indented cliffs which form picturesque little coves and creeks (*calas).* In the south-east of the island is the much lower Sierra de Levante (San Salvador, 509m/1670ft), in which are a number of stalactitic caves. Here too there are innumerable *calas.* Between these two ranges of hills the bays of Alcudia and Pollensa to the north-east and Palma to the south-west cut deep into the Llanura del Centro, a fertile plain given up to intensive agriculture.

Palma de Mallorca/Ciutat P 5

Altitude: sea level. Population: 315,000

Palma de Mallorca (Majorcan Ciutat), capital of Majorca and of the Autonomous Community of the Balearics, is picturesquely situated on the Bahía de Palma, which reaches inland for some 20km/12½ miles on the south-west coast of the island. This lively city is an important Mediterranean port, the economic and cultural centre of the islands and the see of a bishop. It

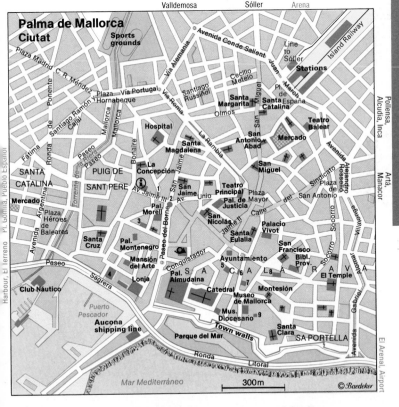

1 Fuente del Sepulcro	3 Casa Belloto	7 Casa Oleza
2 Fuente de la Princesa	4 Consulado del Mar	8 Casa del Marqués de Palmer
	5 Casa Oleo	9 Baños Árabes
	6 Almudaina-Bogen	(Casa Font y Roig)

was the birthplace in 1235 of the famous mystic, philosopher and writer Ramón Llull (Raimundus Lullus).

With its busy central area, its historic old town and the extensive beaches surrounding the whole of the bay, Palma is one of the most popular holiday resorts in Spain and a good base from which to explore the rest of the island, since Majorca's whole road network is centred on the town.

Sights

★ Cathedral

Above the Old Harbour rises the cathedral (La Seo), a massive sandstone structure begun about 1230 in Early Gothic style but not completed until the 16th and 17th centuries, with three doorways, a beautiful south front (14th c.), two 19th century towers and a bell-tower of 1270. From the terrace on the south side of the cathedral there is a magnificent view of the bay.

Museum

A doorway on the north side leads into the Cathedral Museum, with three rooms displaying manuscript books of plainsong, altarpieces, a Late Gothic monstrance, sculpture and a variety of other sacred objects.

Interior

The interior of the cathedral, which is entered from the Museum, was remodelled by Antoni Gaudí in the early 20th century. With its aisled nave rising to a height of 44m/144ft, it covers an area of 6600 sq.m/71,050 sq.ft. It is lit by stained glass windows and no fewer than seven rose windows, the largest of which, in the apse, dates from 1370. In the Capilla Real (Chapel Royal) is the high altar, over which is suspended a gigantic baldachin by Gaudí in the form of a crown of thorns. On the side walls are the tombs of Bishops Berenguer Batle and Guillem de Villanova, who made major contributions to the construction of the cathedral in the 14th century. Behind the Capilla Real are the bishop's throne and, in the Capilla de la Trinidad, the sarcophagi of Kings Jaime II and III.

Palma Cathedral

Directly opposite the choir of the Cathedral is the Bishop's Palace, which now houses the Diocesan Museum (Museo Diocesano), with liturgical utensils, incunabula, ceramics, etc.

Diocesan Museum

Opposite the west doorway of the cathedral is the Palacio de la Almudaina, once the residence of the Moorish viziers and from 1230 a royal stronghold. It is now occupied by military offices and by the Museo Nacional (National Museum). In the courtyard is the Gothic Capilla de Santa Ana.

Palacio de la Almudai .a

Below the cathedral is the modern Parque del Mar, on the south wall of which is a tiled panel with a picture by Joan Miró. This leads into the palm-shaded Paseo Sagrera, which runs alongside the harbour. On the right is the Lonja (originally the Commercial Exchange), built in the 15th century in Gothic style by the Majorcan architect Guillem Sagrera.

Lonja

Adjoining the Lonja is the Consulado del Mar, the old Admiralty Court, with a beautiful Renaissance gallery around the upper floor. It is now occupied by the government of the Autonomous Community.

Consulado del Mar

In Calle de los Apuntadores, a little way north, is the Mansión del Arte, with all Goya's etchings in original copies and works by Picasso.

Mansión del Arte

From the Old Harbour the Avenida Rey Jaime III runs north by way of the Plaza de la Reina to the Paseo del Borne, Palma's principal promenade. On its west side is the large Palacio Morell (Palacio Sollerich; 1763); the interior, with its valuable furniture, is open to the public.

Paseo del Borne

From the north end of the Paseo a street leads east past the Law Courts (Palacio Berga) and the Theatre (Teatro Principal) to the Rambla (Via Roma), the city's second promenade. The flower market is held under the plane-trees here. From the near end of the avenue a large flight of steps leads up to the Plaza Mayor, the central feature of the old town. From here Calle San Miguel runs north to the church of San Miguel, which was originally a mosque.

Rambla

Plaza Mayor

Between the Plaza Mayor and the cathedral lies the old town of Palma, with its narrow lanes and its picturesque nooks and crannies.

★ **Old town**

In Plaza Cort stands the handsome three-storey Ayuntamiento (Town Hall). North-east of this is the High Gothic church of Santa Eulalia, with a fine but dark interior. In Calle Almudaina, which is spanned by the Moorish Arco de Almudaina, is the Case Oleo, with an interesting art collection. Nearby in Calle Morey is the Casa Oleza, a Renaissance mansion containing a fine collection of tapestries. Both of these houses have beautiful patios.

To the east of Santa Eulalia, in Plaza de San Francisco, is the church of San Francisco, built between 1281 and 1317, with a Plateresque/Baroque doorway. The second chapel on the left contains the alabaster tomb of Ramón Llull. The Late Gothic cloister is surrounded by slender columns.

San Francisco

At Calle Portella 5, to the south of the Town Hall, is the Palacio Ayamans, which now houses the Museo de Mallorca, with collections of Moorish, medieval and 18th/19th century art. On the east side of the Museum, at Calle Serra 7, is the Casa Font y Roig, in the garden of which are the remains of a 10th century Arab bath-house.

★ Museo de Mallorca

On higher ground to the west of the town centre is the Pueblo Español (Spanish Village), with reproductions of important and characteristic old buildings from all parts of Spain. Many of them are occupied by craftsmen's workshops.

★ Pueblo Español/ Poble Espanyol

Above the city to the west, at a height of 113m/370ft above sea level, is the Castillo de Bellver, once a royal stronghold (13th c.). Its circular plan points to the influence of Eastern models. A bridge leads into the courtyard of the

★ Castillo de Bellver

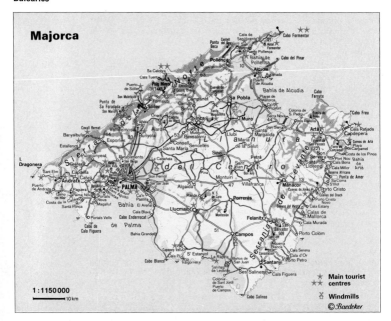

castle, which is surrounded by Romanesque and Gothic arcades. The well in the centre of the courtyard draws water from a cistern occupying almost the whole area under the courtyard. On the lower floor of the castle is the Museo Municipal, with prehistoric and archaeological material. A number of rooms on the first floor are open to the public.

★ Fundación Pilar y Joan Miró   The former house of Joan Miró (C. Saridakis 29) has been recently opened as a museum and gallery with paintings, graphics and sculptures by the Catalan artist.

Surroundings of Palma de Mallorca

Huerta de Palma   The fertile Huerta de Palma, to the west of the city, is dotted with numerous villages, estates and country houses (Majorcan *son*). The best known of these houses are Son Vida (5km/3 miles west), once the seat of the Marqués de la Torre, and Son Berga (6km/4 miles north), which dates from 1776. Near the artists' colony of Genova (5km/3 miles west) can be found an interesting little stalactitic cave. There are still large numbers of the characteristic Majorcan windmills in the Huerta.

Bahía de Palma   From Palma C 719 runs west to Cala d'en Blanes, where the main attraction is Marineland, with a dolphinarium, an aquarium and a tropicarium. The road continues by way of Magalluf, an unfortunate example of the excesses of the tourist boom, to the village of Portals Vells, at the southern tip of the peninsula, with an old cave church in the bay.

Above the coast road runs the motorway, which passes close to the Castillo de Bendinat (13th c.). At Palma Nova it comes to the Coll de sa Batalla (Battle Pass), where Jaime I's army defeated the Moors.

The motorway runs east from Palma to the airport of Son San Juan (10km/ 6 miles). The parallel coast road runs through a number of old fishing villages and past the extensive sandy beaches of the Playas de Palma to El Arenal, one of the great centres of mass tourism. This stretch of coast is now an almost continuous tourist resort, well provided with hotels, restaurants, shops and places of entertainment.

Around the Island

The routes suggested below can as a rule be covered in one day, but for the trip through the hills to Cabo Formentor two days should be allowed. The starting-point in each case is Palma, from which the main roads of the island radiate.

☆ Circuit via Andraitx and Sóller

From Palma take either the motorway or the coast road (C 719), going west. The two roads join just beyond Palma Nova and continue to the turn-off (20km/12½ miles) for the holiday centre of Santa Ponsa. 2km/1¼ mile west of the town, on the rocky promontory of Sa Caleta, stands a cross commemorating the landing of Christian forces in 1229.

Santa Ponsa

The route continues by way of the lively holiday resort of Paguera to Andraitx (Majorcan Andratx), a beautifully situated little country town in a fertile agricultural area. Son Mas, an old country house, is now a local museum. The fortress-like church of Santa María dates from the 13th century.

Andraitx/ Andratx

From here C 719 runs 5km/3 miles south-west to the little port of Puerto de Andraitx (Majorcan Port d'Andratx), beautifully situated at the mouth of the Torrent de Saluet, which here opens out into a narrow bay forming an excellent natural harbour. The little town still preserves something of an old-world aspect.

Puerto de Andraitx/ Port d'Andratx

From Andraitx C 710 runs along the impressive north-west coast of Majorca, with numerous viewpoints. One of the finest is the Mirador de Ricardo Roca, 6km/4 miles south-west of the picturesque village of Estellencs (Majorcan Estallenchs). Around both here and the next village of Bañalbufar (Majorcan Banyalbufar) vegetables are grown on the terraced fields characteristic of Majorca.

☆ North-west coast

Beyond Bañalbufar C 710 turns inland and in a few kilometres comes to a junction where a road goes off on the right to Esporlas (Majorcan Esporles). 1km/¾ mile along this road is the old country house of La Granja (the "Grange"). There was a house here in Moorish times which was later occupied by Cistercian monks. The present owners have left it largely unrestored, so that it conveys an impression of unspoiled authenticity, with its sheds for farming equipment, living rooms, kitchen, bakery, domestic chapel, store-rooms and various workshops, still containing their implements and equipment, and walls faced with majolica tiles.

La Granja

C 710 then continues north to another junction, where a road branches off on the right to Valldemosa. The great feature of interest here is the old Carthusian monastery (Cartuja, Charterhouse), originally established in 1399 on the site of a Moorish alcázar and rebuilt in the 17th and 18th centuries, in which Frédéric Chopin and George Sand spent the winter of 1838–39. The rooms they occupied are now open to the public. Here Chopin composed his "Raindrop Prelude" and other works, and George Sand gathered impressions for her book "A Winter on Majorca". Visitors can also see the monastic church and the former monks' cells; of particular interest, too, are the 18th century pharmacy, with its beautiful majolica drug jars, and the library. The monastery also houses the Municipal

☆ Cartuja de Valldemosa

Valldemosa

Museum, which has a collection of material on the life and work of Archduke Ludwig Salvator (see below).

Adjoining the monastery is the sumptuous Palace of King Sancho, a building redolent of the atmosphere of the past.

Miramar
Son Morroig

Continuing on the coast road, we come to the country house and estate of Miramar, once the property of the Austrian Archduke Ludwig Salvator (1847–1915), second son of Grand Duke Leopold of Tuscany. A great amateur of the natural sciences, he pursued his researches during extensive travels in the Near East and the Mediterranean area. Between 1860 and 1913 he lived mostly on Majorca, in his country house of Son Morroig (2km/1¼ miles north-east of Miramar), which is now preserved as a memorial to him. There he wrote his seven-volume opus on the Balearics, which is still a standard work.

Sóller

The road continues through the charming artists' village of Deya (Majorcan Deiá), for many years the home of the poet Robert Graves, and then via Lluch Alcari, once a Moorish country estate, to Sóller, nestling in the fertile Valle de los Naranjos in the shelter of high hills, with plantations of citrus fruits reaching almost into the heart of the town. Features of interest are the parish church of San Bartolomé and a number of handsome 17th and 18th century patrician houses. 5km/3 miles north is Puerto de Sóller, the most important port on the north coast.

Sóller can also be reached from Palma by rail (five or six services daily); this trip should not be missed by railway enthusiasts. Sóller and Puerto de Sóller are linked by an old-world tram.

★ Gardens of
Alfabia

From Sóller C 711, heading for Palma, climbs to the Coll de Sóller. On the far side of the pass are the gardens of Alfabia, once the country residence of the Moorish Viziers, who, with their skill in irrigation techniques, created these very beautiful gardens, in which date-palms, bamboos, lemons and oranges flourish. The house, in Late Baroque style, contains valuable furniture and paintings.

C 711 continues past the little market town of Buñola (Majorcan Bunyola) and comes in another 2km/1½ miles (off the road to the right) to the country house of Raixa (Majorcan Raxa), once a Moorish estate, which has beautiful Italian-style terraced gardens with fountains.
   From here the road continues due south to Palma.

Raixa/Raxa

An alternative for the return route is to turn off at Buñola into a hill road on the left which runs up, through beautiful scenery, to the Coll de Hono, passes through Orient and comes to the Castillo de Alaró, the origins of which probably go back to Roman times. The road continues south through Alaró to join C 713 at Consell, from which it is 19km/12 miles back to Palma.

Alternative route

Through the Hills to Cabo Formentor

This route begins by following C 711 to Sóller, and a short distance beyond the town turns right into a magnificent hill road (C 710) which follows a winding course, passing the picturesque old mountain village of Fornalutx and the viewpoint of Ses Barques, to the foot of Majorca's highest peak, Puig Mayor (1443 m/4734ft). Here the road passes through the Gorch Blau ("Blue Ridge"), a rocky gorge 500m/550yd long and up to 110m/330ft deep. The mountain stream which has carved out the gorge has now been dammed higher up to make a reservoir, the Barranco del Gorch Blau. Above this, to the east, is the Puig de Massanella (1348m/4423ft), famed for the magnificent panoramic views to be had from the top; it can be climbed from Lluch monastery (see below) in around eight hours.

★ Gorch Blau

A little to the east of Gorch Blau the road known as La Calobra (the "Snake") goes off on the left and descends through wild and romantic scenery, with many bends, to the coast far below. It is well engineered but testing for the driver. Near the top, in what is known as the Nus de la Corbeta ("knot in the tie"), it turns through an angle of 270 degrees and passes under itself. It then continues down past labyrinthine rock formations and great monolithic pinnacles to the Cala de Calobra, a little cove enclosed by steep cliffs. From here it is a few minutes' walk to the narrow gorge of the Torrent de Pareis, which reaches the sea in a wide rock basin.

★ La Calobra
Torrent de Pareis

From the turn-off for La Calobra C 710 continues north-east. At the hamlet of Escorca a country road goes off on the left to the monastery of Nuestra Señora de Lluch, Majorca's principal pilgrimage centre, where, according to legend, a shepherd boy found a black wooden figure of the Virgin in the forest. The present monastic buildings date from the 17th and 18th centuries. On the first floor of the monastery is a museum. In the aisled Baroque church, on the wall facing the high altar, is the much venerated image of the Virgin known as La Moreneta (the "Dark-Skinned One"). Adjoining the monastery is a Way of the Cross.

Monasterio de Lluch

The road now runs down through a karstic landscape to the plain below and comes to Pollensa (Majorcan Pollença), a centre of the Majorcan textile and shoemaking industries. From the parish church of Nuestra Señora de los Angeles a flight of 365 steps, flanked by cypresses, leads up the Puig del Calvari to a Baroque pilgrimage chapel.

Pollensa/
Pollença

From Puerto de Pollensa, an old fishing village, a very beautiful road runs 21km/13 miles north-east to Cabo Formentor (Majorcan Cap Formentor), at the end of a long, narrow peninsula. It first climbs to a saddle in the hills, with the Mirador de Mal Pas (magnificent views), and then runs down, with many bends, passing a side road leading to the luxury Hotel Formentor, beautifully situated above a bay on the south side of the peninsula, and continues to Cabo Formentor with its lighthouse, the most northerly point on Majorca (panoramic views).

Cabo Formentor/
Cap Formentor

Cabo Formentor

Palma to Alcudia

Inca

From Palma C 713 runs north-east over the Huerta de Palma and after passing through Santa María del Camí comes to Inca (29km/18 miles), where most of Majorca's leather factories are based.

Cuevas de Campanet

8km/5 miles beyond Inca a road goes off on the left to the village of Campanet, near which is a cave system discovered in 1945. The caves, which are now open to visitors for a total length of 1300m/1425yd, contain interesting sinter formations.

Alcudia

After passing a side road (on the left) to Pollensa C 713 continues to Alcudia, a Phoenician foundation which during the Roman period became capital of the island under the name of Pollentia (not to be confused with Pollensa: see above). The old town is surrounded by an almost complete circuit of excellently preserved 14th century walls, incorporated in which, at the south-west corner, is the parish church of Sant Jaume. To the south of the church are the excavations of Roman Pollentia. In the old town there are a number of handsome burghers' houses and an archaeological museum (beside the Town Hall). Outside the town, on the road to Puerto de Alcudia, are the remains of a small Roman amphitheatre.

Puerto de Alcudia itself is very much a tourist resort, with numerous hotels, bars and discothèques.

To the Caves on the East Coast

Algaida

From Palma C 715 runs east to Algaida. A few kilometres before the town, at Son Gual, is a Prehistoric Park, with lifesize reproductions of prehistoric animals.

2km/1½ miles before Algaida are the Gordiola glassworks, where visitors can watch glass-blowers at work, and where there is a small but interesting museum of glassware.

The most attractive excursion from Algaida, and one of the most rewarding excursions on the whole island, is to the Puig de Randa (542m/1778ft), with three monasteries which are much frequented places of pilgrimage. It is reached by taking the Lluchmayor road as far as Randa (5km/3 miles), from which a minor road ascends to the monasteries through beautiful scenery.

Half way up the hill a track goes off on the right and passes through a gateway into the monastery of Nuestra Señora de Gracia (15th c.), magnificently situated under a sheer rock face in which large numbers of birds have made their nests.

Soon afterwards a majolica panel on the main road indicates the way to the 14th century monastery of Sant Honorat, the forecourt of which is planted with pines and carob-trees. Within the monastery, in front of the church, is a majolica figure of the Virgin and Child, flanked by Ramón Llull and Arnau Desbrull, founder of the monastery.

On the summit of the Puig de Randa is the hermitage of Nuestra Señora de la Cura. Ramón Llull (1235–1316), who lived here for some time, made the hermitage an important centre of intellectual and spiritual life. In the loggia to the right of the church are a series of fine majolica panels. In the church is a "Bethlehem Grotto" of the type common on Majorca.

The main route continues on C 715 and after passing Montuiri, a picturesque little town off the beaten tourist track, comes, soon after Villafranca de Bonany, to the turn-off for Petrá. This was the birthplace of the Franciscan friar Junípero Serra (1713–84), who was active as a missionary in the Mexican peninsula of Baja California and the American states of California and Texas. He founded a number of mission stations, including two which developed into the cities of San Francisco and Los Angeles. He is commemorated in Petrá by a series of majolica panels which can be found in a narrow street beside the church of San Bernardino, in the Museo Serra, and in the house nearby where he was born.

Manacor, the island's second-largest town, lies on C 715 50km/31 miles from Palma. It is known far beyond the bounds of Spain for its artificial pearls, which non-experts cannot distinguish from the real thing. The oldest and best-known factory is the Firma Majórica, founded in 1890, which has a showroom and shop at the west end of the town, on C 715; visitors who want to see the process of manufacture will be guided to the factory in the town centre.

C 715 continues to Artá. Here, on a hill surrounded by battlements from which there are good views, is the Baroque Santuario de San Salvador. In a wooded area to the south of the town are the remains, known as Ses Paises, of a megalithic settlement (c. 1000–800 B.C.) surrounded by a double ring of walls.

Beyond Artá on C 715 is Capdepera, an old-world little town with a prominently situated 14th century castle, the chapel of which (1323) still survives.

From Capdepera a detour can be made to Cala Ratjada, once a fishing village and now a holiday resort. From here it is a 2km/1½ mile walk to the lighthouse on Cabo Capdepera, the most easterly point on Majorca.

Minor roads run south-east from Artá and south-west from Capdepera to a crossroads from which a road continues south-east, passing a 13th century watch-tower, to the Cuevas de Artá, on the coast. The entrance to this cave system, which has a total length of 450m/500yd, is 40m/130ft above sea level. The caves contain impressive stalactites and stalagmites.

Balearics

Reserva Africana

From the crossroads just mentioned the road running south-west comes to Son Servera, from which a road goes down to Cala Millor. To the south of this resort is the Reserva Africana, an area of some 40 hectares/100 acres in which large African mammals (but no big cats) live in natural conditions. Visitors can drive through the reserve in their cars.

★★ Cuevas del Drach

The road continues to the attractive little port of Porto Cristo. 1.5km/1 mile south of the village are the Cuevas del Drach ("Dragon Caves"), one of Majorca's major tourist attractions. There are four chambers containing a variety of fantastically shaped stalactites and stalagmites and a large underground lake. The Lago Martel, named after the French speleologist Edouard Martel, who explored the caves, lies 39m/128ft under the surface and is 177m/194yd long and 29m/95ft deep.

★ Cuevas dels Hams

2km/1½ miles west of Porto Cristo on the road to Manacor are the Cuevas dels Hams ("Caves of the Fish-Hooks"). The caves get their name from the shape of some of the stalactitic formations, particularly in the chamber known as the Angel's Dream, which grow in all directions and curve into the shape of fish-hooks. In these caves too there is an underground lake, known as the "Venetian Lake".

To the South and South-East Coasts

Lluchmayor/ Llucmajor

From Palma the route follows the fine new road to the airport and then continues through the resorts on the Playa de Palma. At El Arenal the road turns inland and comes to the market town of Lluchmayor (Majorcan Llucmajor), which owes its prosperity to the shoemaking industry. North-east of the town in 1349 was fought the battle in which the Majorcan king Jaime III was defeated by his cousin Pedro IV of Aragon; Jaime lost his life and Majorca lost its independence.

From Lluchmayor an excursion can be made to the Puig de Randa (see page 122).

Campos del Puerto

From Lluchmayor C 717 runs south-east to Campos del Puerto, which preserves something of its medieval atmosphere. The parish church of San Julián, on the main road, has a painting by Murillo.

Ses Salines

Beyond Lluchmayor, still on C 717, is Santañy (Majorcan Santanyi). From here a road runs south-west to Ses Salines, which takes its name from the large salt-pans to the west of the town. Round the village are numerous prehistoric remains.

Calas

From Santañy the route turns north-east. From this road there are many little side roads running down to picturesque *calas* on the south-east coast which have been developed in varying degree for tourism.

Felanitx

Soon after the side road running down to the little port of Porto Colom another road turns inland and goes north-west to Felanitx. The most notable feature of the town, which is built on four hills, is the handsome parish church of San Miguel, which was begun in the 13th century and rebuilt in the 16th and 17th. Felanitx is also noted for its sausages.

★ Ermita de San Salvador

2km/1½ miles before Felanitx a road of great scenic beauty, particularly in the second half, goes off on the left to the Ermita de San Salvador, an important Majorcan pilgrimage centre. At the sanctuary stands a 7m/23ft high figure of Christ, from the base of which there are magnificent views of the coast. The church (18th c.) contains one of the "Bethlehem grottoes" commonly found in Majorcan churches.

★ Castillo de Santueri

6km/4 miles south-east of Felanitx, on the main ridge of the Serranía de Levante, is the Castillo de Santueri, one of the best preserved medieval castles on the island.

Instead of taking the direct road from El Arenal to Lluchmayor it is possible to follow the coast road, which at Cabo Blanco turns inland and comes to Capicorp Vey (Majorcan Capocorp Vell), a site of the Pre-Talayot period (1000–800 B.C.), with remains which include five talayots.

Alternative route Capicorp Vey/ Capocorp Vell

The road now returns to the coast at Cala Pí, a fjord-like inlet with crystal-clear water. From here it is possible either to continue to Ses Salines or to turn back to Lluchmayor.

★Cala Pí

Cabrera

The barren little island of Cabrera (Goat Island) lies off the south coast of Majorca. It can be reached by ferry from Palma, but it has little to offer visitors – except those with a boat of their own, who will find attractive anchorages for diving and swimming.

★Minorca

Q/R 5

Area: 711 sq.km/275 sq. miles. Population: 62,000

Minorca (Spanish form Menorca) is a relatively quiet holiday island, which in addition to good beaches and excellent facilities for water sports has much of historical and artistic interest to offer, including in particular its megalithic monuments – though some of these can be reached only on rough and unsignposted paths. In recent years tourism has increased considerably in importance, but the example of tourist development on Majorca, some aspects of which are distressing, has led to second thoughts on Minorca, and some large-scale development projects have not been carried out. A pleasant feature of the new Minorcan holiday resorts is the relative absence of high-rise hotels. Agriculture continues to be the islanders' main source of income.

North-western Minorca is a region of gentle upland country rising to a height of 357m/1171ft in Monte Toro and falling down to a coast slashed by fjord-like inlets. The south-west of the island is an extensive lowland area with a cliff-fringed coast which lacks such inlets.

Topography

Mahón/Maó

Altitude: sea level. Population: 23,000

Mahón (Minorcan Maó), chief town and principal port of Minorca, lies on a cliff-edged site at the east end of the island. Strategically situated at the head of a long inlet, sheltered from wind and weather, it is perhaps the best natural harbour in the Mediterranean. It was occupied in turn by the Carthaginians, the Romans and the Moors, until in 1287 Alfonso III of Aragon began the reconquest of the island. During the War of the Spanish Succession, in 1708, Minorca was occupied by British forces, and in 1713, under the treaty of Utrecht, it became a British possession; and British influence can still be detected in the island's architecture and way of life. The French occupation of 1756–63 has left no traces. Mahón is still a military base.

Sights

Although Minorca has good air connections with Spain and the rest of Europe, the approach by sea – for visitors coming from one of the other Balearic islands – is an experience which will leave a lasting impression, as the boat makes its way up the 5km/3 mile long fjord-like inlet, passing a series of old forts, islands and *calas*.

★Approach by sea

Balearics

The town Plaza España	The life of Mahón centres on six squares. From the harbour the Rampa de Abundancia leads up to the Plaza de España, with the Iglesia del Carmen and the stalls of the market set out under the arcades of the former Carmelite friary.
Plaza Miranda	A narrow stepped lane going off the Rampa on the left leads to the Plaza Miranda, from which there is a good view of the inner harbour.
Plaza de la Constitución	From the Plaza de España Calle de Cristo runs into a pedestrian zone, to the right of which is the Plaza de la Constitución. In this square are the Ayuntamiento (Town Hall) and the church of Santa María, founded in 1287 and rebuilt in Neo-Classical style in the 18th century.
Plaza de la Conquista	A street to the right of the Town Hall leads to the Plaza de la Conquista, with a monument to Alfonso III. On the left side of the square is the Public Library, which also houses a Museum.
Plaza Bastión	From the Town Hall Calle de San Roque runs west to Plaza Bastión, in which is the Puerta de San Roque, a relic of the old town walls.
Plaza Explanada	The Plaza Explanada, on the west side of the town, is the starting-point of the buses which ply between Mahón and the interior of the island. At the north-east corner of the square is the Ateneo Científico, with a museum of natural history, archaeology and art.

Surroundings of Mahón

Golden Farm	4km/2½ miles north-east of Mahón, on the road to Punto Espero, on Cap La Mola, which bounds the harbour inlet on the north, is the fine colonial-style mansion of San Antonio (Minorcan Sant Antoni), known as the Golden Farm, where Nelson stayed with Lady Hamilton in 1799 and 1800. The estate is not open to the public.
Punta Espero	Punta Espero, the easternmost tip of Minorca, is a military area closed to the public, but it is worth while driving along the road to the point for the sake of the views it affords of the harbour inlet.
North-east coast	A road of great scenic beauty runs along the north-east coast of the island from Mahón to Fornells, with numerous side roads leading down to holiday resorts on the coast.
Faro de Favaritx	One of the most striking points is the lighthouse of Favaritx. 10km/6 miles from Mahón a side road goes off on the right to the promontory on which the lighthouse stands. This too is a military area closed to the public, but the road to it offers a view of a barren rocky landscape uncharacteristic of the Mediterranean.
★Son Parc	12km/7½ miles farther on another side road goes off on the right to the modern development of Son Parc. This is a well planned and beautifully maintained holiday resort, built around a golf course.
Fornells	Fornells, which can be reached from Mahón either on the coast road or via Mercadal on C 723, is a long straggling town of whitewashed houses with a good harbour on the Bahía de Fornells. Many of the inhabitants still live by fishing. Around the bay are a number of attractive holiday settlements. From Fornells there is a rewarding boat trip to the caves in the peninsula on the east side of the Bahía de Fornells. The most striking of these is the Cova Na Polida (accessible only by sea), with stalactites.
★Talati de d'Alt	A little way south of the Mahón–Alayor road (C 721), 5km/3 miles west of Mahón, in farming country, is the megalithic *taula* of Talati de d'Alt, perhaps the most beautifully situated monument of the kind on Minorca. There is also a hypostyle chamber, roofed by a thick stone slab supported on a central monolith.

The road which runs south-west from Mahón to the airport continues through San Clemente (Minorcan Sant Climent) and comes in 9.5km/ 6 miles to a side road on the left leading to the charming little bay of Cala Coves, with numerous cave dwellings (*cuevas trogloditas*) which are believed to date from prehistoric times.

★Cala Coves

The main road continues to the holiday settlement of Cala'n Porter, on the south coast. In the cliffs beyond it is the Cueva d'en Xoroi, a fantastically situated cave which is now occupied by a bar and discothèque.

Cueva d'en Xoroi

A road runs south from Mahón through San Luis (Minorcan Sant Lluis) and then turns west into a secondary road leading to Binibeca Vell. This imaginatively planned holiday resort is designed in the image of an old fishing village and creates a striking impression, with dark stained wood standing out against the dazzling white of its walls and roofs.

★Binibeca Vell

Above the harbour inlet, east of Mahón, is Villa Carlos, a settlement established by the British in the 18th century under the name of Georgetown which still preserves something of a British air.

Villa Carlos

South-west of Villa Carlos, on the road to San Luis, are the remains of the prehistoric settlement of Trepucó, with the largest and best preserved *taula* in the Balearics.

★Trepucó

Around the little country town of Alayor (Minorcan Alaiort), 23km/14 miles north-west of Mahón on C 721, are several prehistoric sites, now forming part of Alayor's open-air archaeological museum (Museo Arqueológico al Aire Libre).

Alayor/Alaiort

5km/3 miles south-west of Alayor is the remarkable prehistoric site of Torre d'en Gaumés, with the remains of three massive round towers, *taulas* and a unique hypostyle chamber.

★Torre d'en Gaumés

View from Monte Toro

Ibiza Harbour

Son Bou	The hotel and holiday colony of Son Bou, on the south coast 8km/5 miles from Alayor, has one of the longest sandy beaches on Minorca.
★Monte Toro	From the centre of Mercadal, 9km/5½ miles north-west of Alayor, a winding road climbs up Monte Toro (357m/1171ft). From the outlook terraces on the summit there are extensive views over the whole island, in clear weather as far as the east coast of Majorca. On the hill is the Santuario de Nuestra Señora de El Toro which draws numerous pilgrims throughout the year. It was built by Augustinian monks in the 17th century and consists of a picturesque group of buildings set around a courtyard.

Ciudadela de Menorca/Ciutadella

Altitude: sea level. Population: 19,500

Ciudadela (Minorcan Ciutadella), once capital of Minorca, is picturesquely situated above its fjord-like harbour inlet at the western tip of the island. In 1558 an army of 15,000 Turkish corsairs captured the town, destroyed it, slaughtered the inhabitants and carried off the survivors to Istanbul as slaves.

Sights

Plaza del Borne	The central feature of the town is the Plaza del Borne, in which stands an obelisk commemorating the events of 1558. On the west side of the square is the Town Hall. From here there is a good view of the harbour inlet.
Palacio Salort	The east side of the square is dominated by the Palacio Salort, a mansion in early Neo-Classical style, with a richly furnished interior (open to visitors).

A short distance from the Plaza del Borne is the Plaza Pio XII, on the left of which stands the cathedral (1287–1362), a hall church without transepts.

Cathedral

Just south of the cathedral, in Plazuela del Rosario, is the Capilla del Rosario, with a fine Plateresque façade.

Capilla del Rosario

Surroundings of Ciudadela

6km/4 miles east of the town, a little way south of C 721, is the Naveta d'es Tudóns, the best known and best preserved *naveta* on the island and the oldest man-made structure in Spain (about 15th c. B.C.). Built of massive cyclopean blocks, it stands in open country near the old Roman road, here clearly traceable. This was a place of burial; among those buried here were several clan chieftains.

★Naveta d'es Tudóns

From Ferrerías, 24km/15 miles west of Mahón on C 721, a road leads south (7km/4½ miles) to the holiday resort of Santa Galdana, picturesquely situated in a bay enclosed by almost vertical rock walls, with a small stream running into it; good bathing.

★Cala Santa Galdana

★Ibiza

O 6

Area: 541 sq.km/209 sq.miles. Population: 71,000

Two gently rounded ranges of hills with generally smooth contours traverse the north and south of Ibiza, the largest of the Islas Pityusas, with a maximum length of 48km/30 miles and a maximum breadth of 24km/15 miles. The southern range, with Atalayasa de San José (476m/1562ft) as its highest point, is higher than the northern range, which is broken up by a number of depressions. The two ranges are separated by a swathe of lower land extending across the island from west to north-east. The southern tip of the island is occupied by a wide alluvial plain.

Topography

Ciudad de Ibiza/Eivissa

Altitude: 0–100m/0–330ft. Population: 31,000

The island's capital, Ibiza (Ibizan Eivissa), lies in the south of the island in a sheltered harbour inlet open only to the south-east. It is now a popular holiday resort, particularly in summer, attracting visitors from all over the world, who come here to enjoy a relaxed, unconstrained holiday away from the conventions of everyday life.

Sights

★Townscape

Visitors arriving by sea enjoy an excellent view of the town, with its houses rising above the harbour and the massive bastions of the upper town, with the church of Santo Domingo and the cathedral.

Lower town
La Marina

To the south of the harbour is the lower town, now Ibiza's busy commercial and shopping quarter. The streets in its western part, La Marina, are lined with shops, boutiques, bars and restaurants. The street leading to the upper town runs past the fruit and vegetable market and the meat and fish market.

Sa Penya

The eastern district of Sa Penya, the former fishing quarter, is the oldest part of the town outside the walls. With its whitewashed houses and its

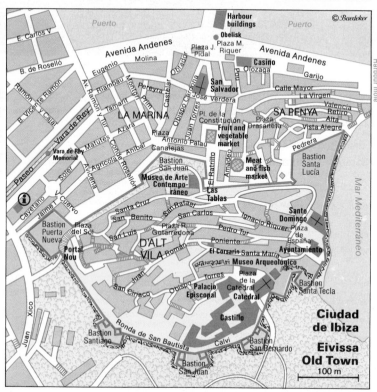

picturesque nooks and corners it still preserves something of the atmosphere of the past in spite of its numerous cafés and boutiques.

Above the lower town rise the massive walls of the fortress, built on the remains of the Arab walls between 1554 and 1585 by an Italian architect, Calvi, at the behest of the Emperor Charles V. The circuit of walls, with seven corner bastions and three gates, encloses the upper town (Ibizan D'Alt Vila) with its winding stepped lanes and old patrician houses. The upper town is entered through the main gate, the Puerta de las Tablas (with the arms of Philip II), the gatehouse of which is now occupied by a museum of contemporary art.

★ **Upper town**

The upper town is crowned by the Cathedral of Nuestra Señora de las Nieves (Our Lady of the Snows), built in the 13th and 14th centuries. Of the original Gothic building there remain only the tower and the sacristy doorway. The sacristy contains a small museum displaying handsome vestments and liturgical utensils.

Cathedral

North of the cathedral, in the underground casemates of the fortress, is the Archaeological Museum, with Phoenician, Punic and Roman antiquities found on the island.

Museo Arqueológico

North-east of the cathedral and much lower down, just inside the outer walls, is the 16th century church of Santo Domingo, with tiled walls and floors and frescoes.

Santo Domingo

From the west gate of the fortress, the Portal Nou, the Via Romana leads to the Puig des Molins (Mill Hill), on which the largest known Punic necropolis, with some 4000 tomb chambers, has been excavated.

Puig des Molins

Finds from the tombs, including many terracottas and a number of sarcophagi, are displayed in the Museo Monográfico, immediately adjoining the site. Some of the tombs in the necropolis can also be visited.

Museo Monográfico

North-east of the town is the semicircular Cala Talamanca, where the hotel settlements of Talamanca and Ses Figueres have been built. The beaches are of fine sand, but are frequently littered with rubbish from the harbour. On the Isla Grossa is a lighthouse, the Faro de Botafoch.

Talamanca

Excursions from Ibiza Town

The southern tip of the island, a few kilometres from Ibiza Town, is occupied by the area known as Las Salinas (Ibizan Ses Salines), where salt is produced in extensive salt-pans.

Las Salinas/ Ses Salines

From Ibiza Town a beautiful road runs 12km/7½ miles west to San José (Ibizan Sant Josep), chief place in the commune of that name. The picturesque cliff scenery on the west coast and the broad beaches of fine sand to the south have encouraged the large-scale development of tourist facilities in this area. The town's whitewashed church, on the main road, has on the right-hand side of the porch a feature characteristic of many Ibizan churches, a stylised symbol of Golgotha consisting only of three crosses.

San José/ Sant Josep

South-west of San José is the holiday resort of Cala Vedella, to the south of which is Cabo Jue, the south-western tip of the island, with an old watchtower, the Torre del Pirata.

Cala Vedella

Half way between Ibiza Town and San Antonio Abad is San Rafael (Ibizan Sant Rafel), an attractive little place with many potters' workshops.

San Rafael

Once a small fishing village, San Antonio Abad (Ibizan Sant Antoni de Portmany), 15km/9 miles north-west of Ibiza Town, has developed into a lively and noisy tourist resort and the island's second largest town. The

San Antonio Abad/ Sant Antoni de Portmany

whitewashed parish church, on a low hill, dates from the 14th century. A fortress-like structure, it retained a battery of cannon into the 19th century.

Santa Inés/
Santa Agnes

Near the north-west coast is Santa Inés (Ibizan Santa Agnes), with the Cueva de Santa Inés, a cave in which a a catacomb-like chapel was discovered in 1907, together with fragments of pottery and Arab weapons. According to a local legend a wooden image of Santa Inés was found here in the 16th century.

San Miguel/
Sant Miquel

San Miguel (Ibizan Sant Miquel), 20km/12½ miles north of Ibiza Town, takes its name from the fortified medieval church of San Miguel on a hill above the village, which attracts many visitors with its presentations of folk-dancing and singing. There is good bathing in a cove north of the village.

★Balafí

On C 733, which runs north from Ibiza Town, is the fortified hamlet of Balafí, which has preserved its old-world aspect. The houses huddle round an old watch-tower to which the inhabitants used to withdraw for safety during Turkish raids.

★Cala Portinatx/
Portinaitx

On the northern tip of the island, 30km/19 miles from Ibiza Town, is Cala Portinatx (Ibizan Portinaitx), which offers many attractions for holiday-makers, with its beaches and its sailing and surfing schools. The bay is sheltered from the open sea by a much eroded rock barrier, usually lashed by heavy surf, which ends at Punta Galera.

Cala San Vicente/
Cala de
Sant Vincent

Around the Cala San Vicente (Ibizan Cala de Sant Vincent), at the north-eastern corner of the island, lies an attractive holiday development. 2km/1½ miles north is the cave of Es Cuyeram, in which a sanctuary of the Carthaginian fertility goddess Tanit, remains of Neolithic pottery and a bronze plaque with inscriptions of the 4th and 2nd centuries B.C. were found. Finds from the cave are now displayed in the New Museum in Ibiza Town.

Santa Eulalia
del Río/
Santa Eulária
del Riu

Santa Eulalia del Río (Ibizan Santa Eulária del Riu) lies 15km/9 miles north-east of Ibiza Town on the only river on the island with a reasonably regular flow – though in recent years it has increasingly been running dry as a result of the rise in consumption of water. The simple cube-shaped houses of the old town cluster picturesquely round the hill crowned by the fortified church of Santa Eulalia. On the south-west side of the town is a Roman viaduct spanning the Río Santa Eulalia.

The surrounding beaches and villages were a favourite haunt of hippies during the 1960s, but Santa Eulalia is now a well ordered and well-equipped holiday resort.

Formentera

O 6

Area: 82 sq.km/32 sq.miles. Population: 5000

Formentera, with a length of 23km/14 miles and a breadth ranging between 1.7km/1 mile and 17km/10 miles, lies to the south of Ibiza, separated from it by Es Freus, a channel only 4km/2½ miles wide. The islanders live in four loosely settled communes, with agriculture as their main source of income. In recent years, however, tourism has made an increasing contribution to the island's revenues.

During the Middle Ages the island was constantly harassed by the bloody raids of the Barbary pirates, which in about 1400 led to its total depopulation. It began to be resettled only in the late 17th century.

Topography

Two low ranges of hills, the Meseta de la Mola in the east and the Puig Guillén in the west, form the main structure of the island. They are linked by a narrow spit of land 5km/3 miles long flanked by dunes. On the south side of the island is a beautiful sheltered sandy beach; the north coast is fringed by cliffs.

The Island

Formentera offers only limited variety. It is an ideal holiday place for those who like unspoiled nature, quiet beaches and clear water and are quite happy to accept simpler standards of accommodation (mainly to be found on the south coast).

In La Sabina, which has the island's only harbour, there is little to be found apart from the harbour buildings, car hire firms and bars.

La Sabina

East of La Sabina is the Estanque Pudent (Ibizan Estany Pudent, "Stinking Pool"), a brackish lagoon separated from the sea by a 5km/3 mile long ridge of dunes with a beautiful sandy beach and linked with it by a narrow channel. At the north end of the lagoon are extensive salt-pans.

Estanque Pudent/ Estany Pudent

San Francisco Javier (Ibizan Sant Francesc Xavier) is the chief place on the island and its administrative centre. In the central square is the plain parish church (1738). To the south of the town is an ancient fig-tree, its branches supported by numerous timber props; it is said to be the oldest in the Balearics.

San Francisco Javier/ Sant Francesc Xavier

A little way east of San Francisco Javier, at San Fernando (Ibizan Sant Fernan), is a recently discovered stalactitic cave, now open to visitors.

San Fernando

On the south coast of the island is the extensive holiday development of Maryland, equipped with every conceivable facility for holidaymakers. The name Maryland has nothing to do with the American state of that name, but is an artificial compound made up of the Spanish "mar y" ("sea and") and the English "land".

Maryland

At the eastern tip of Formentera is the village of Nuestra Señora del Pilar, with an attractive white fortified church. From here it is a short distance to the Punta de sa Ruda, the island's most easterly point. Just north of the lighthouse is a stone (erected 1978) with a bronze plaque commemorating Jules Verne, whose novel "A Journey through the Solar System" refers to the island of Formentera.

Nuestra Señora del Pilar

Barcelona

Province: Barcelona (B). Telephone dialling code: 93
Altitude: sea level to 512m/1680ft (Tibidabo)
Population: 1.8 million (Greater Barcelona about 4 million)

The description of Barcelona in this guide is abridged, since there is a detailed description in the Baedeker guide "Barcelona".

Barcelona lies on the Costa Dorada (Catalan Costa Daurada), between the mouths of the Riu Besós and the Riu Llobregat. The ancient and the modern capital of Catalonia, a university town and the see of a bishop, it is Spain's largest city after Madrid, its principal industrial and commercial town and the third largest seaport (in terms of traffic volume) in the Mediterranean, with an important international airport.

The city has a favoured situation in a wide coastal plain which rises gradually from the sea to the ridge of Tibidabo and is bounded on the north-east by the Montaña Pelada and on the south-west by Montjuïc

Barcelona

Barcelona

200 m

© Baedeker

—————O———— Metro

(Spanish Montjuich). Beyond the Montaña Pelada is the valley which the Riu Besós has carved through the hills; to the south of Montjuïc the Riu Llobregat reaches the sea after flowing through a wide and fertile valley which provides Barcelona with its vegetables and fruit.

The old town of Barcelona is bounded by the harbour and by the wide ring roads (*ramblas*) which have replaced the old town walls. On the highest point in the town centre, Monte Tabor (12m/40ft), stands the cathedral, surrounded by medieval streets. The main street is the broad tree-shaded Rambla, which divides the old town into two parts. The newer parts of the city *(ensanches)*, with their avenues of plane-trees and handsome houses, are for the most part laid out in accordance with a regular plan. Round the city, from Montjuïc to the Montaña Pelada, are a series of attractive modern residential areas; industry and commerce are concentrated in the north-east. The Olympic Summer Games of 1992 have indelibly changed the face of Barcelona, not only through the new building and upgrading of the Olympic sites but also in the town itself where avant-garde artists and designers have left their mark on the new harbour promenade and in many of the modern bars and restaurants.

History

According to local tradition Barcelona was founded by the Carthaginian general Hamilcar Barca in 218 B.C. It is first recorded under the Iberian name of Barcino, and in the time of Augustus it became a Roman colony under the name of Julia Faventia, to which the designations Augusta and Pia were later added. In 414 the Visigoths took the town, calling it Barcinona, and in 531 made it their capital. Under the Moors, who captured it in 716, it was called Barshaluna. Louis the Pious recovered it in 801 and made it the capital of the Spanish March which had been established by Charlemagne in 778.

In 874 the Counts of Barcelona achieved independence, and under their rule and during the later period when Catalonia was united with Aragon Barcelona ranked with Genoa and Venice as one of the leading commercial cities of the Mediterranean. Its power was shattered, however, by the union with Castile in the 15th century, and still more by the exclusion of Catalonia from trade with the New World. During the War of the Spanish Succession (1701–13) it supported the cause of Archduke Charles of Austria, from whom it hoped to secure increased privileges, and much of the town was destroyed when it was stormed by the French in the autumn of 1714. In the reign of Charles III, who granted the right to trade with America, Barcelona began to prosper again, and in the course of the 19th century it recovered its former importance in the Mediterranean area. Major international exhibitions were held in the city in 1888 and 1929.

After the proclamation of the Republic in 1931 Catalonia was granted autonomy in 1932 (a status which it retained until 1939) and became the seat of the regional government. During the Civil War, in the course of which many old churches in the city were destroyed by fire, Barcelona was held by the Republicans until 1939. (From about 1880 until the 1930s it was a stronghold of the Spanish anarchist movement.)

In 1975 Catalan was recognised as an official language and the language of teaching. In a referendum held in October 1979 the people of Catalonia voted in favour of far-reaching proposals for self-government; soon afterwards the Spanish Congress of Deputies passed a law granting Catalonia autonomy; and in the following year a regional parliament was elected.

The year 1992 was doubly important for Barcelona. It hosted the 25th Summer Olympics with great success and also witnessed celebrations for the 500th anniversary of Columbus' first voyage of discovery.

Sightseeing programme

This great international city has so much to offer the visitor that it is not possible to include everything in a single itinerary. In the following description, therefore, the main features of interest are grouped together in convenient sections.

In planning a sightseeing programme it should be borne particularly in mind that Barcelona was the great centre of Modernismo, the Spanish version of Art Nouveau, and has many examples of this style, in particular the buildings of Antoni Gaudí.

In view of the density of traffic and the shortage of parking space, particularly in the city centre – and also because of the break-ins to cars – it is not a good idea to do your sightseeing by car. The excellent public transport system, in particular the underground (Metro) with its frequent services, brings all the sights of Barcelona within easy reach.

In the following description place-names are given first in their Catalan form, followed by the Spanish form.

Harbour Area

The Harbour (Catalan Port, Spanish Puerto), with an area of around 300 hectares/750 acres including the outer harbour, ranks with those of Gijón and Bilbao as one of the largest and most modern in Spain, handling some 40 million tons of goods annually. The main imports are coal, corn and cotton, the main exports wine, olive oil and cork. There are car ferry services linking Barcelona with the Balearics: Majorca, Minorca and the Islas Pityusas (Ibiza). The attractive north-east part of the harbour is of most interest to the visitor having been partly rebuilt for the Olympic Games.

Harbour

Metro station
Drassanes (Line 3)
Barceloneta (Line 4)

Columbus Monument

In Plaça del Portal de la Pau (Spanish Plaza Puerta de la Paz) is the 60m/200ft high Columbus Monument (Monumento a Cristóbal Colón), erected in 1888. On a base decorated with reliefs of scenes from Columbus's life and expeditions stands an iron column covered with allegorical figures, which

Location
Plaça del Portal de la Pau

Barcelona Harbour from Montjuïc

in turn bears an 8m/26ft high bronze statue of Columbus. Within the column is a lift to a viewing platform at the top, affording panoramic views of the city and harbour; the entrance is on the harbour side, down a few steps. Opening times: from June to late Sept. daily 9am–9pm. Rest of year: Tues.–Sat. 10am–2pm and 3.30–7pm, 8pm Mar. to May, Sun. and pub. hols. 10am–7pm, 8pm late Mar. to May.

"Santa Maria"

At the quayside a short way north of the Columbus Monument there used to lie a reproduction (1951) of the "Santa Maria", the flagship of Columbus on his first voyage to America. In 1990 the ship was destroyed by fire, but there are hopes that it can be rebuilt.

★★ Maritime Museum

Location
Plaça del Portal de la Pau

Opening times
Tues. and Sat.
9.30am–1pm
and 4–7pm;
Wed.–Fri.
9.30am–2pm and
4–8pm;
Sun. and pub. hols.
10am–2pm

Beyond the Passeig de Colom (Spanish Paseo de Colón), which separates the harbour from the city centre, is the extensive complex of arched, aisled halls of the old Royal Shipyard (Reales Atarazanas), in an area once occupied by docks (Catalan *drassanes,* Spanish *dársenas*). The yards now house the Maritime Museum (Catalan Museu Marítim, Spanish Museo Marítimo) which is presently undergoing refurbishment so that a detailed description of the collection is not possible as many of the exhibits are not on show at present and may be subject to alteration.

The shipyard was originally established in the mid 13th century and was enlarged in later centuries, until by the 18th century it had twelve halls. Here the galleys of the Crown of Aragon were built, maintained and repaired. When the bulk of maritime trade moved to the Atlantic after the discovery of America, however, the shipyard rapidly declined in importance and began to be used as warehouses, a powder magazine and barracks. In 1936 it was decided to establish a museum in the shipyard. On the south side are some remains of the old town walls.

The Museum, which is continually being expanded, illustrates all aspects of the sea and seafaring, with ships and ship models, nautical equipment, implements and arms, diagrams and illustrations. A route round the museum is signposted.

The Great Hall is dominated by an excellent full-scale reproduction of the galley "Real", flagship of the fleet commanded by Don John of Austria which defeated the Turks in the battle of Lepanto (Greek Naupaktos) on October 7th 1571 and established Spanish predominance in the Mediterranean. The "Christ of Lepanto", which is believed to be the figurehead of the original vessel, is in Barcelona Cathedral (see page 142). The reproduction was built from 1960 onwards for the 400th anniversary of the battle in 1971.

Other interesting exhibits include two reproductions of large wooden submarines, one of which was launched in Barcelona in 1859 and carried out 54 dives down to depths of 20m/66ft.

★★ Port Vell

The old port is currently being developed in one the most ambitious port remodelling projects in the world, covering an area of 55 hectares/ 136 acres and at a cost of over 50,000 million pesetas. The plan is to open up the port to the city with visitors drawn by numerous and varied attractions. The project covers three basic areas:

Moll Barcelona

The Moll Barcelona is dominated by a new International Trade Centre due to be completed in 1996, with offices, convention facilities and restaurants. There are also shops and the new Museum of the History of Catalonia (Catalan Museu d'Història de Catalunya, Spanish Museo de Història de Cataluna).

Mol de la Fusta

The section of the harbour between Portal de la Pau and Plaça d'Antoni López is the Moll de la Fusta, a seafront promenade with benches, restau-

The galleon "Real", flagship of the Don Juan of Austria ▶

rants and bars. Nearby is the departure point for short harbour cruises aboard a "Golondrina" (every 30 minutes).

Moll d'España

The Moll d'España, joined to La Rambla by a new bridge, abounds with shops, eateries, bars, an eight-hall cinema and an aquarium.

Mundo Submarino

Opening times
Mon.–Fri.
10am–9pm,
Sat. and Sun.
10am–10pm

The largest aquarium in Europe – Mundo Submarino (Underwater World) – opened on the Moll d'España in 1995. Around 8000 examples of 300 different species, including 30 sharks, are displayed in 20 vast themed tanks. An enormous central tank (the "Oceanario") with an 80m/262ft-long walk through a glass corridor enables visitors to inspect the sea creatures at close quarters.

Vila Olympíca/Vila Olympico
Port Olímpic/
Puerta Olimpíco

A promenade known as Rambla del Mar leads from the Columbus Monument along the shore to the Olympic Village (Catalan Vila Olympíca, Spanish Vila Olympíco) which now provides living accommodation, and onto the Olympic Port (Catalan Port Olímpic, Spanish Puerta Olimpíco), with a yacht harbour and lively open-air restaurants and bars. There are plans to extend the promenade well beyond the outskirts of the city alongside 3km/5 miles of cleaned-up sandy beaches.

Harbour Cableway

Promenade

The whole of the main harbour is spanned by a cableway (Catalan Transbordador Aeri, Spanish Funicular Aéreo). The outer station is the Torre de San Sebastián, a 96m/315ft high steel pylon on the New Mole; the intermediate station is the 158m/518ft high Torre de Jaime I. The cableway ends on the slopes of Montjuïc. Open: Generally Tues.–Sat. noon–5.45pm; Sun., pub. hols. noon–7pm, but enquire locally as hours vary.

Passeig de Colom/Paseo de Colón

From the Columbus Monument the Passeig de Colom (Spanish Paseo de Colón), a palm-lined avenue 42m/138ft wide, runs north-east to the Head Post Office. It is flanked by many ships' chandlers' shops, which also sell attractive little brass articles.

La Merced

To the left of the avenue, in Carrer de la Mercé (Spanish Calle de la Merced), is the handsome domed church of La Merced, built in the middle of the 18th century. On the high altar is a much revered 13th century statue of the Virgen de la Merced, patroness of Barcelona.

Lonja

The street ends at the Head Post Office (1928) and, just beyond this, the Lonja (Exchange), founded in 1382, with a very fine dealing hall (Sala de Contrataciones). Around the square on the north side of the Exchange, the Plaça del Palau (Spanish Plaza del Palacio), the hub of Barcelona's maritime trade, are numbers of business and commercial houses and administrative offices, including the Govern Civil (Gobierno Civil, government administration).

Estació de França

Further north on the Passeig Isabel II is the historic station of Estació de França (Spanish: Estacion de Francia) recently renovated and an interesting technological monument.

To the west, in the cramped old town, are the church of Santa María del Mar (see page 148) and the Picasso Museum (page 148).

Nova Icària

To the right of the station the Avinguda de Icària (Spanish Avenida de Icària) leads to Nova Icària, the earlier Olympic village and Olympic Harbour. Dominated by the Olympic towers and the new tower of the Ritz Carlton Hotel (Arts de Barcelona), an up-market and therefore expensive, architecturally prestigious residential and shopping centre.

Parc de la Ciutadella/Parque de la Ciudadela

The Parc de la Ciutadella (Spanish Parque de la Ciudadela) is a large park of 30 hectares/75 acres on the north-east side of the old town, laid out on the site of the old Citadel, with pleasant avenues, flowerbeds, ornamental ponds and monuments. Also in the park are the Zoo, a number of museums and the Catalonian Parliament.

Metro stations
Barceloneta,
Ciutadella (Line 4)

At the west end of the park is the Zoological Museum (Museu de Zoologia; Spanish Museo de Zoología), housed in a curious building in a hybrid pseudo-Moorish style which was erected for the Universal Exposition of 1888 and is popularly known as the Castell dels Tres Dragons ("Castle of the Three Dragons").

On the ground floor are a large collection of insects, skeletons of a whale and a mammoth, and displays of shellfish, snails and preserved specimens of birds. There are also periodic special exhibitions. A staircase leads up to the first floor, where the main permanent collections are displayed. They include a collection of birds' eggs, specimens of mammals (many of them having a skeleton of the same species beside them), as well as molluscs, fishes, reptiles and amphibians preserved in oil. At the end of the main hall, beyond a glass door, is a collection of shellfish and snail shells. All the collections are used for research and teaching. They are excellently arranged and well looked after; the methods of display are old-fashioned, but have great nostalgic charm. It is presently undergoing large-scale extensions.

Zoological Museum

Location
Passeig de
Picasso/Passeig
dels Til-lers

Opening times
Tues.–Sun.
10am–2pm

The Geological Museum (Museu de Geologia; Spanish Museo de Geología), also known as the Museu Martorell after its founder, is run by the Scientific Institute. It occupies a building in Neo-Classical style, with the entrance in the pedimented central section of the park front. In the rooms to the left of the entrance lobby are displayed minerals, mainly precious and semi-precious stones (including copies, in rock crystal, of the best known of the great diamonds), and exhibits illustrating the use of precious and non-ferrous metals in technology. The minerals are arranged according to their chemical structure. At the end of the room, with agate sheets giving borrowed light, is a darkened room showing minerals under long- or short-wave ultraviolet rays, with interesting light effects.

In the room to the right of the vestibule is a collection of fossils.

Geological Museum

Location
Passeig
de Picasso/
Passeig dels
Til-lers

Opening times
Tues.–Sun.
10am–2pm

Immediately adjoining the Geological Museum is the Palm House, with a display of exotic flora.

Palm House

The Zoo, which occupies the eastern half of the park, contrives, with great skill and imagination, to house an extraordinary variety of animals in a small space. Particularly notable among the anthropoid apes is a large white gorilla, a very rare light-coloured variant form of this species. There is a very fine reptile house and a remarkable dolphinarium, whose inhabitants also include a killer whale *(Orcinus orca)*. The pool is surrounded by the two-storey Aquarium (seawater on the upper floor, fresh water on the lower floor), with armoured glass through which visitors can look into the dolphinarium. The bird house, with a special section for nocturnal birds, is also attractive and well designed.

Zoo

Opening times
daily
9.30am–7.30pm

The Museum of Modern Art (Museu d'Art Modern; Spanish Museo de Arte Moderno) has been housed since 1945 in the extreme left wing of the Palau de la Ciutadella (Spanish Palacio de la Ciudadela), which also accommodates the regional parliament, the Parlament de Catalunya. The palace was built in the 18th century as an arsenal; the museum wing was added about the turn of the 19th–20th century.

The name Museum of Modern Art is something of a misnomer, for the collections reach back from our own day by way of Historicism to the

Museum of Modern Art

Location
Plaça d'Armes

Opening times
daily 10am–9pm

Romantic period. As a result, although the arrangement of the museum is mainly chronological, in the earlier sections the pictures are conventionally arranged by subject (portraits, genre scenes, landscapes, large historical paintings). There is an important Art Nouveau section (furniture, pictures, sculpture), and other fields well represented are Expressionism, the early modern school and the sculpture of the first third of the 20th century.

Temporary exhibitions are shown on the upper floor from time to time.

★Ramblas

The Ramblas are the succession of main streets, lined with plane-trees, which run north-west through the old town from the Columbus Monument (see page 137) in the Plaça del Portal de la Pau for a total distance of 1180m/1290yd, linking the harbour area with the Plaça de Catalunya (Spanish Plaza de Cataluña), the largest and busiest square in Barcelona, and continuing to the Avinguda de la Diagonal (Spanish Avenida de la Diagonal), the wide main avenue of the new town, which cuts diagonally through the rectangular grid of the streets.

To the east of the Ramblas is the heart of the old town, the Barri Gotic (Gothic Quarter: see page 145).

On the Ramblas are the flower and bird markets, numbers of book and newspaper stands and many restaurants and cafés with tables set out in the open air. Pavement artists, impromptu acrobats and street musicians add to the colour of this avenue. The Ramblas are also a popular haunt of pickpockets in the main tourist season.

Rambla de Santa Mónica

The first section of the Ramblas, starting from the Columbus Monument, is the Rambla de Santa Mónica. At the near end, on the left, is the Naval Command Headquarters. Farther on, on the right, set back from the street, is the Museu de Cera (Spanish: Museo de Cera), or Wax Museum (open: Summer daily 10am–8pm; Winter Mon.–Fri. 10am–2pm and 4–8pm; Sun. and pub. hols. 10am–8pm).

Rambla dels Caputxins/Rambla de los Capuchinos

Palau Güell/ Palacio Güell

Museu de les Arts de l'Espectacle/ Museo de Arte Escénico

In the Carrer Nou de la Rambla, a little way west of the Rambla dels Caputxins, which continues the line of the Rambla de Santa Mónica, is the Palau Güell (1885–89), an imposing building by Antoni Gaudí in his very individual style. It is now occupied by the Museum of the Theatre (Museu de les Arts de l'Espectacle; open: Tues.–Fri. 11am–2pm and 5–8pm), with sketches of stage settings and costumes, a section on ballet, a library, etc.; it is expected to be closed until 1996 for refurbishment.

Plaça Reial/ Plaza Real

On the opposite side of the Rambla is a street leading to the Plaça Reial, a beautiful enclosed square surrounded by Neo-Classical houses with arcades on the ground floor.

Gran Teatre del Liceu/Gran Teatro del Liceo

Farther along the Rambla, on the left, is the façade of the Gran Teatre del Liceu, built in 1844 and opened in 1847, the biggest opera house in Spain and second largest traditional theatre after the Scala opera house in Milan. The building was burned to the ground in January 1994 caused by a spark from welding work but should be rebuilt by 1997.

Sant Pau del Camp/San Pablo del Campo

From here the Carrer de Sant Pau leads to the Romanesque church of Sant Pau del Camp (Spanish San Pablo del Campo), built in 1117 on a site which was then outside the town – hence its name of St Paul in the Fields – with a very fine doorway. On the south side of the church is a charming little 13th century cloister.

Rambla dels Flors/Rambla de las Flores

From the Plaça de la Boqueria the Rambla de Sant Josep (Spanish Rambla de San José) continues north-west. A colourful flower market is held here in the morning: hence its alternative name of Rambla dels Flors, the Rambla of Flowers. On the left is the Mercat (Market Hall), where a great range of wares are offered for sale. In the centre is the fish market, with fascinating displays of every variety of fish, shellfish, crustaceans and other seafood.

Mercat/Mercado

A few paces from the Market is the former Palace of the Vicereine, recognisable by the two bronze equestrian statues flanking the entrance. The palace was built between 1772 and 1777 as the residence of the Viceroy of Peru and after his death was occupied by his widow until 1791. The façade is Neo-Classical, the interior Baroque. The palace is currently being renovated so that the established museums (art and craft museum and the numismatics cabinet) have been relocated.

Palau de la Virreina/ Palacio de la Virreina

Rambla dels Estudies/Rambla de los Estudios
Rambla Canaletes/Rambla Canaletas

Beyond this is the Rambla dels Estudies, where the bird and ornamental fish market is held in the morning. Together with the Rambla Canaletes, it leads to the Plaça de Catalunya (Spanish Plaza de Cataluña).

Plaça de Catalunya/Plaza de Cataluña

The Ramblas, and with them the old town of Barcelona, come to an end in the busy Plaça de Catalunya, a spacious square with gardens and ornamental ponds. Around the square are many of the leading banks, with the Banco Español de Crédito occupying a dominant position on the north-west side. On the east side is the massive Telefónica building, with the offices of the Telephone Corporation.

Under the square is a Metro station, the busiest junction in the system.

To the east of the Plaça de Catalunya, in Carrer Sant Pere Més Alt (Spanish: Calle Alta de San Pedro), stands the Palace of Catalan Music, in a building designed by Domènech i Montaner which is a prime example of the Spanish version of Art Nouveau, Modernismo. The lavish and excellently preserved decoration, particularly in the concert hall, ranks among the finest examples of the art of the period. (Open for visits by arrangement; closed Aug.)

★ Palau de la Música Catalana/ Palacio de la Música Catalana

From the south corner of the Plaça de Catalunya the Carrer de Pelai (Spanish: Calle de Pelayo), lined with shops, runs west to the Plaça de la Universitat (Spanish: Plaza de la Universidad). Barcelona University, founded in 1450, is now housed in buildings erected between 1863 and 1873, with two handsome courtyards. The University Library is also here.

University

Passeig de Gràcia/Paseo de Gràcia

The Passeig de Gràcia is a magnificent avenue 61.50m/202ft wide, forming the main axis of the Quadrat d'Or (Golden Square), a quarter with numerous examples of modern architecture.

★ Quadrat d'Or

In Carrer d'Aragó, which branches off the avenue to the right, is the church of Nuestra Señora de la Concepción (on the left), with a 14th century cloister; the church was brought here from the Old Town in 1869.

Barcelona

Casa Battló   At No. 43 in the Passeig de Gràcia can be seen the Casa Battló (1904–06), a fantastic creation by Antoni Gaudí which was inspired by the legend of St George. (Open by arrangement; tel. 2 04 52 50.)

Casa Milá   At No. 92 (on the right) is the Casa Milá (1905–10), another building by Gaudí, popularly called "La Pedrera" (the stone quarry).
The freely curving forms and the plant-like wrought-iron work of the balustrade show how strongly Gaudí was influenced by Art Nouveau (open for guided tours of the roof garden only Tues.–Sat. 10, 11am, noon, and 1pm).

Fundació Antoni Tápies   The building of a former publishing house (Casa Montaner i Simón) at the intersection with the Carrer d'Aragó houses the Fundació Antoni Tápies where in addition to works by the artist there are also temporary exhibitions of contemporary art (open: Tues.–Sun. 11am–8pm).

Avinguda de la Diagonal/Avenida de la Diagonal

At the north end of the Passeig de Gràcia is the Plaça de Joan Carles I (Plaza de Juan Carlos I), at the junction with the Avinguda de la Diagonal (Avenida de la Diagonal), the main traffic artery of the new town, over 10km/6 miles long.

Museu de la Música/Museo de la Música   A little way east of the Plaça de Joan Carles I, at No. 373, is the Music Museum (Tues.–Sun. 10am–2pm, Wed. also 5–8pm except late Jun. to late Sept.). The collection consists mainly of musical instruments from the 16th–20th centuries, including one of the largest collections of guitars in Europe.

Camp Nou   Near the west end of the Avinguda de la Diagonal, on the left, is the Camp Nou Stadium, one of the largest football grounds in the world, which can accommodate 125,000 spectators. This is the home of F.C. Barcelona, a famous team who have several times been champions of Spain and winners of the European Cup. Their fame is celebrated in the Museu del Futbol Club Barcelona in the stadium (Open: Apr. to Oct. Mon.–Sat. 10am–1pm and 3–6pm, pub. hols. 10am–2pm; Nov. to Mar. Tues.–Fri. 10am–1pm and 3–6pm, Sat., Sun. and pub. hols. 10am–2pm).

Pedralbes

Zona Universitaria   In the adjoining district of Pedralbes are the buildings of the University (Zona Universitaria).

Monestir de Pedralbes/ Monesterio de Pedralbes   The convent of St Clare in Pedralbes was founded in 1326. The single-aisled convent church, the cloister and the museum are all of interest (open Tues., Fri. and Sun. 10am–2pm, Sat. 10am–5pm).

Fundació Colección Thyssen-Bornemisza   In Baixada del Monestir (No. 9), is the recently installed Fundació Colección Thyssen-Bornemisza, an exhibition of 72 paintings and eight sculptures from the famous Thyssen-Bornemisza collection. It includes Italian and German works and traces the history of art from the 13th to 17th century (open: Tues.–Fri. and Sun. 10am–2pm, Sat. 10am–5pm).

Museu d'Art Contemporáni de Barcelona (Barcelona's Museum of Contemporary Art)   The recently completed building (designed by Richard Meier), a work of art in itself, opened from November 1995. It is located in the cultural belt of the Old City, parallel to the Ramblas, and it adjoins the Centre de Cultura Contemporánia de Barcelona (Casa de Caritat, Montalegre 5) – a new cultural centre with the city of Barcelona as its theme. For details of the Museum – Fax: 00 34 34 12 46 02.

The Palau de Pedralbes now houses the Ceramics Museum which was moved here from the Palau Nacional. It possesses a magnificent collection of historical and contemporary ceramics, including Arab and Catalan pieces, azulejos and two large tile-paintings of 1710 (open: Tues.–Sun. 9am–2pm).

★Museu de Cerámica/ Museo de Ceràmica

The Palau de Pedralbes also houses the Museum of Decorative Arts (moved here from the Palau de la Virreina). A collection of Catalan artefacts from the 17th–20th centuries (open: Mon.–Fri. 10am–1pm by prior arrangement; free entry).

Museu d'Arts Decoratives/ Museo d'Artes Decorativas

Old Town

★Barri Gòtic/Barrio Gótico

North-east of the Ramblas extends the Barri Gòtic (Spanish Barrio Gótico) or Gothic Quarter, the principal surviving part of the medieval town. This maze of narrow streets is now mostly a pedestrian zone, with many shops (jewellery, textiles, leather goods, souvenirs), small bars, restaurants.

Metro stations
Liceu (Line 3),
Jaume I (Line 4)

From the Rambla dels Caputxins Carrer Ferran Jaume I leads north-east to the Plaça de Sant Jaume (Plaza de San Jaime). On the south-east side of this square (to right) is the imposing Casa de la Ciutat (City Hall), which goes back to the 14th century. The sides of the building retain some Gothic work; the main front dates from 1847. Notable features of the interior are

Casa de la Ciutat/ Case de la Ciudad

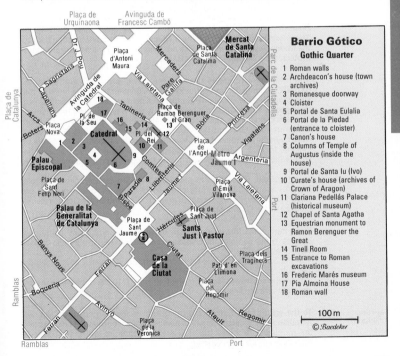

Barrio Gótico
Gothic Quarter

1 Roman walls
2 Archdeacon's house (town archives)
3 Romanesque doorway
4 Cloister
5 Portal de Santa Eulalia
6 Portal de la Piedad (entrance to cloister)
7 Canon's house
8 Columns of Temple of Augustus (inside the house)
9 Portal de Santa Iu (Ivo)
10 Curate's house (archives of Crown of Aragon)
11 Clariana Pedellás Palace (historical museum)
12 Chapel of Santa Agatha
13 Equestrian monument to Ramon Berenguer the Great
14 Tinell Room
15 Entrance to Roman excavations
16 Frederic Marés museum
17 Pia Almoina House
18 Roman wall

100 m
© Baedeker

the large 14th century Council Chamber (Saló de Cent/Salón de Ciento) and the Saló de Cróniques/Salón de las Crónicas, murals by José María Sert.

Palau de la Generalitat

Opposite the Town Hall stands the Palau de la Generalitat, originally the Casa de la Diputación, built in the 15th century to house the Estates of Catalonia. It is now occupied by the offices of the Generalitat de Catalunya, the provincial government. It has a magnificent patio (inner courtyard) in Gothic style, and on the first floor is the Gothic St George's Chapel. In the rear part of the building is the charming Patio de los Naranjos (Court of Orange-Trees). To the north is the Audiencia, the old courtroom. Carrer del Bisbe Irrurita (Calle del Obispo Irrurita), which runs from here to the Cathedral, is spanned by a graceful Gothic "bridge" providing a link with the Canons' Lodgings.

★ Cathedral

Opening times
daily 8am–1.30pm
and 4–7.30pm

On Monte Tabor, the highest point in the old town (alt. 12m/40ft), stands the cathedral (Santa Cruz or Santa Eulalia), begun in 1298 on the site of an earlier Romanesque building (some carving from which survives on the north-east doorway) and completed by 1448 apart from the main façade and the domed tower, which were added in 1898 and 1913 respectively.

Cloister

The street coming from the Plaça de Sant Jaume passes the very beautiful cloister, planted with magnolias and palms, which is entered by the Puerta de Santa Eulalia. The cloister, built between 1380 and 1451, is surrounded by numerous chapels with altars dedicated to various saints. At the south-west corner is the Capilla de Santa Lucía (1270), and adjoining this, in the Chapterhouse (Sala Capitular), is the Cathedral Museum, with pictures by Spanish masters of the 14th and 15th centuries (open: daily 11am–1pm). The geese in the cloisters are the continuation of a tradition dating back to the Middle Ages. The noisy birds are there to guard the cathedral as they protected the Capitol in Ancient Rome.

Interior

The interior, with aisles flanking the nave, is in High Gothic style, 83.3m/273ft long, 37.2m/122ft wide and 25.5m/84ft high. The finest of the side chapels is the Capilla del Santísimo Cristo or Capilla del Santo Cristo de Lepanto, to the left of the high altar, which was originally the chapterhouse. It contains the alabaster tomb (15th–16th c.) of the sainted Bishop Olegarius (d. 1136) and the "Christ of Lepanto", which is believed to have been the figurehead of Don John of Austria's flagship at the battle of Lepanto in 1571. In the last side chapel before the north transept can be seen a black Virgin very similar to the famous Virgin of Montserrat (see entry).

The stained glass dates in part from the 15th century. Other notable features are the 15th century choir-stalls in the nave, surrounded on three sides by walls; the beautiful pulpit (1403); and a Late Gothic retablo (16th c.) in the Capilla Mayor.

From the Capilla Mayor steps lead down to the Crypt, lit by numerous candles, which contains the alabaster sarcophagus of Santa Eulalia (Italian work of about 1330).

In the Sacristy is the fine Cathedral Treasury (Catalan Tresor, Spanish Tesoro).

From the south-west tower of the Cathedral (210 steps; entrance inside church) there are fine views.

Casa del Arcediano

To the west of the Cathedral's main front is the 15th century Casa del Arcediano (Archdeaconry), with a beautiful inner courtyard. It now houses the Municipal Archives (Catalan Arxiu Històric de la Ciutad, Spanish Archivo Histórico de la Ciudad).

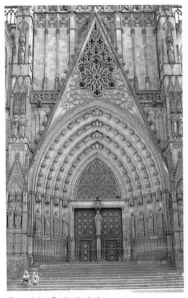

Barcelona Cathedral, doorway . . .   *. . . and tower*

Immediately opposite the cathedral, across Carrer del Bisbe Irrurita, is the Bishop's Palace (Palau Episcopal), which is first mentioned in the records in the year 926 and has several times been rebuilt since then.

Palau Episcopal

Museu Frederic Marès/Museo Federico Marès

In a little square immediately east of the cathedral, on the far side of Carrer dels Comtes de Barcelona (Calle de los Condes de Barcelona), is the Museu Frederic Marès (founded 1946), in a building which was once the residence of the Counts of Barcelona and the kings of Catalonia and Aragon. It contains a rich collection of Classical, Romanesque, Gothic, Baroque and 19th century sculpture, mainly from Spain, and a separate collection of jewellery, fashion accessories and luxury articles. There are also smaller sections on the history of tobacco and photography.

Location
Carrer dels
Comtes de
Barcelona 10

Opening times
Tues.–Sat.
10am–5pm,
Sun. and pub. hols.
10am–2pm

Museu d'Història de la Ciutat/Museo de Historia de la Ciudad

In the Plaça del Rei, south-east of the Cathedral, is the 15th century Casa Padellàs, a typical town mansion of the late medieval period, which was rebuilt here in 1931. During the preparation of the site considerable Roman remains were found. The Historical Museum is now housed in the mansion and in the former church of Santa Agata, which stands slightly higher up, and the Salón de Tinell (1370), a large hall belonging to the former royal palace, in which Columbus was received by the Catholic Monarchs after his return from his first voyage to America.

Most of the exhibits are in the Casa Padellàs. They include objects dating from the pre-Roman period, Moorish times, the Middle Ages and the period of Catalan naval power, as well as items of folk interest.

Location
Veguer 2,
Plaça del Rei

Opening times
Tues.–Sat.
10am–2pm and
4–8pm (Jul.–Sept.
10am–8pm),
Sun. and pub. hols.
10am–2pm

147

Items of particular interest in the church of Santa Agata (which has a fine painted timber ceiling) include a large Gothic painted altar, two Gothic tombs and various priestly vestments. In the sacristy is the iron mechanism of a tower clock of 1576. The old stained glass in the choir and clerestory displays a variety of coats of arms.

★★Museu Picasso/Museo Picasso

Location
Carrer Montcada
15–19

Opening times
Tues.–Sat.
10am–8pm,
Sun. and pub. hols.
10am–3pm

From the Plaça de l'Angel Carrer de la Princesa runs east. Off this street on the right is Carrer Montcada; between numbers 15–19 are the handsome Gothic mansions of Palau Berenguer Aguilar, Palau Baró de Castellet and Palau Meca, now occupied by the Picasso Museum.

Following extensive reorganisation the collection consists of paintings, drawings, lithographs and etchings from the early period of Picasso's work.

Museu Tèxtil i
de la
Indumentària/
Museo de
Indumentaria

On the opposite side of the street (No. 12–14), in a 13th century palace, is the Textile Museum (Museu Tèxtil i de la Indumentària, Spanish Museo de Indumentaria, open: Tues.–Sat. 9am–2pm and 4.30–7pm, Sun. and pub. hols. 9am–2pm), with fabrics and clothing from the 4th century A.D. onwards (Coptic, Spanish/Moorish, the Christian West).

Santa María del Mar

Location
Plaça Santa María

Opening times
Daily 8am–1pm and
5–8pm

A little way south is the church of Santa María del Mar (1329–83), Barcelona's most important church after the cathedral. An aisled Gothic building without transepts, it occupies the site of a Late Roman necropolis where Santa Eulalia is believed to have been buried. Over the richly decorated main doorway is a large rose window. The stained glass mostly dates from the 15th–17th centuries. In the chapel beside the left-hand side doorway is a black Virgin, and on the high altar is a Gothic statue of the Virgin, with a model of an old merchant ship in front of it.

★Montjuïc/Montjuich

On the south side of the city is the 213m/699ft high hill of Montjuïc (Spanish Montjuich, pronounced Monchúik), falling steeply down to the sea. The name means "Hill of the Jews", after a large Jewish cemetery which once occupied the site. There are a few gravestones from the cemetery in the Archaeological Museum.

Access

From the harbour there is a cableway (Transbordador Aeri/Funicular Aéreo) to the Parc de Miramar on the north-east slope of the hill (see page 140). From the Avinguda del Paral-lel (Metro station Paral-lel, Line 3) there is a funicular (operating noon–2.50pm and 4.30–9.15pm; first section underground) to Montjuïc, from which a cableway goes up to the castle.

Castell de Montjuïc/Castillo de Montjuich

On top of the hill is the castle, where the cableway ends. From here, particularly from the bastions at the corners, there are magnificent views of the cities. On the west side is a bombastic memorial to General Franco, and within the castle grounds are a number of modern heavy guns. From the flat roof of the citadel there are fine panoramic views of the sea, the harbour, the city and the surrounding hills.

Military Museum

In the central part of the Castillo, which is usually open until 9pm, is the Military Museum (open: Tues.–Sat. 9.30am–2pm and 3.30–8pm, Sun. and pub. hols. 10am–7pm; closes 8pm Apr.–Sept.). In the courtyard can be seen 19th and early 20th century guns. The Museum's fifteen rooms, in the old casemates, display arms and armour from all over the world, models of fortifications, dioramas with tin soldiers and modern handguns.

★★ Olympic Sites

The sports sites on Montjuïc were the principal venues of the 25th Summer Olympics in 1992. Even without any sporting events a visit to this ensemble of modern architecture with its avant-garde buildings anticipating the 21st century is worth a visit.

Modern architecture

The Olympic stadium is not new: it was built for the Universal Exposition in 1929. The Italian architect Vittorio Gregoti and his four Catalan colleagues enlarged the old building to accommodate a capacity of 70,000 spectators by lowering the level of the playing field by 11m/36ft and creating additional rows of seats (open: Mon.–Thur. 10am–8pm, Fri.–Sun. 10am–11pm).

Olympic stadium

The Sports Palace, named after the Catalan national saint Sant Jordi, was designed by the Japanese Arata Isozaki and can house 17,000 spectators under its dome.

Sports Palace

Between the Olympic Stadium and the Sports Palace (Palau Sant Jordi) is a uniquely designed area by the Japanese artist Aiko Migawaki consisting of a "wood" of stone columns with wires growing out of them. Above this space towers the most spectacular and controversial construction on Montjuïc: the Telefónica radio mast which according to the statistics is a masterpiece. Architect Santiago Calatrava conceived this tower which is unlike any other, and reminds some people of a floating gramophone needle.

Radio mast

The Catalan architect Ricard Bofill designed the present Sports College INEFC where competitions were held during the Olympics. Bofill's design is inspired by Classical Greek architecture.

Sports College

Parc de Atraccions/Parque de Atracciones

Montjuïc is famed particularly for the amusement park on its north-eastern slopes. There are large car parks near the entrances. The park is like a large permanent fair, with a Ferris wheel, sideshows, a variety theatre and restaurants.

Amusement park

Below the Parc de Atraccions lies the Mirador del Alcalde, a viewpoint laid out with fountains and an unusual form of paving, with concrete pipes, the necks and bases of bottles, transmission chains and other odds and ends laid in ornamental patterns.

Mirador del Alcalde

West of the amusement park are the descending water terraces of the Jardins de Mossèn Verdaguer. On the seaward slope of Montjuïc are the Jardins de Mossèn Costa i Llobera, famous for succulents, cactii and euphorbia.

Parks and Gardens

Nestled into the north slope of Montjuïc is the original modern group of buildings of the Fundació Joan Miró. Instigated by Joan Miró the foundation has numerous works by the artist and his contemporaries, including a mercury fountain by Alexander Calder (Tue., Wed., Fri., Sat. 11am–7pm, Thur. 11am–9.30pm, Sun. and pub. hols. 10.30am–2.30pm).

★ Fundació Joan Miró

★★ Museu Nacional d'Art de Catalunya/Museo Nacional de Arte de Cataluña

Location
Mirador del Palau

Metro station
Plaça d'Espanya
(Lines 1 and 3)

Some distance from the Plaça d'Espanya, situated on high ground and approached by a broad flight of steps, is the Palau Nacional (Spanish Palacio Nacional), a huge domed building in a rather overcharged architectural style which has been occupied since 1934 by the National Museum of Catalan Art. This great collection, covering all periods of Catalan art, is one of Barcelona's principal tourist attractions.

The building has undergone radical alteration under the direction of the Italian architect Gae Aulenti and after five years of closure re-opens in December 1995.

Romanesque art

The Museum's outstanding collection of Romanesque art (11th–13th c.) is internationally famed. Particularly remarkable are the beautiful frescoes from churches in the Catalan Pyrenees, which have been set up here in exact reproductions of the vaulting and apses from which they came.

Gothic art

The collections of Gothic art (14th and 15th c.) include wood and stone sculpture, pictures and altarpieces both from Catalonia and from other parts of Spain.

Jardí Botànic/Jardín Botánico

Opening times
Closed temporarily

Behind the Palau Nacional is the Botanic Garden (Catalan Jardí Botànic, Spanish Jardín Botánico), with a wide range of beautiful flowers and plants. It was laid out immediately after the Universal Exposition of 1929 on land which included a number of disused quarries, and as a result offers a variety of micro-climates. It is currently being reorganised and extended and so is closed for the foreseeable future.

Nearby is the Institut Botànic (Spanish: Instituto Bótancio), the Botanic Institute (open only to specialists), is associated with the Botanic Garden. A road runs past the Institute and various sports grounds to the Poble Espanyol (see below).

Museu Etnològic/Museo Etnológico

Location
Passeig de
Santa Madrona

The Ethnological Museum, housed since 1973 in a new building on a hexagonal plan, displays costumes, domestic equipment, furniture and crafts, mainly from Africa, America, Asia and Oceania (open: daily 10am–5pm, Tues. and Thur. until 7pm).

The Spanish and Catalan section of the Museum (Museu d'Arts, Indústries i Tradicions Populars) is in the Poble Espanyol.

Museu Arqueològic/Museo Arqueológico

Location
Passeig de
Santa Madrona

The collections of the Archaeological Museum, housed in one of the pavilions built for the Universal Exposition of 1929, are concerned mainly with the archaeology of Spanish territory. There are sections devoted to prehistory, the Balearic culture, finds from the Greek and Roman settlement of Ampurias (Catalan Empúries) and classical archaeology. In the vestibule is a collection of Etruscan antiquities. (Open: Tues.–Sat. 9.30am–1pm and 3.30–7pm, Sun. and pub. hols. 10am–2pm.)

Teatre Grec/Teatro
Grec

Directly beyond the road leading up to Montjuïc is the Teatre Grec (Spanish: Teatro Grec), a Greek Theatre situated in an abandoned quarry on the slope of the hill. It was designed for the 1929 Universal Exposition using Epidauros as a model.

★Poble Espanyol/Pueblo Español

On the west side of the Montjuïc park is the "Spanish Village" (Catalan Poble Espanyol, Spanish Pueblo Español), originally built for the 1929 Universal Exposition, with reproductions of typical buildings from different parts of Spain. Well known artists, including Maurice Utrillo, were involved in the selection of the buildings and the planning of the village. As in most Spanish country towns, the houses are grouped around the Plaça Major, where there is an information office, book and souvenir shop. Open air events occasionally take place here.

In the square are a restaurant and the Spanish and Catalan section of the Ethnological Museum.

A number of picturesque little streets and lanes run west from the Plaça Major, affording glimpses of attractive little patios. The buildings house a surprising variety of craft studios where traditional art and crafts are practised and the products sold.

Two museums, the Folk Art and Crafts Museum and the Museum of Books and Printing, are situated here.

Location
Avinguda Marquès de Comillas

Opening times
Sun. 9am–10pm, Mon. 9am–8pm, Tues.–Sat. until late evening

Museums

The Trade Fair Grounds on Montjuïc

The area between the Palau Nacional and the Plaça de Espanya is occupied by the extensive complex of buildings and grounds of the Barcelona Trade Fair (Fira de Barcelona). The Avinguda de la Reina María Cristina, which extends between the foot of the flight of steps and the Plaça de Espanya, is a wide boulevard (frequently illuminated at night) flanked by a series of fountains.

Shortly before the Avinguda de la Reina María Cristina, coming from the Poble Espanyol, reaches the Trade Fair grounds it passes the Mies van der Rohe Pavilion (Pavelló Mies van der Rohe). Ludwig Mies van der Rohe, born in Aachen in 1886, was the last director of the famous Bauhaus in Dessau and designed the German pavilion for the 1929 Universal Exposition in Barcelona. This exact reproduction of the original was built to mark the 100th anniversary of his birth. The building is notable for the austerity and clarity of its lines and the aesthetic effect of the materials used (glass, steel, polished natural stone). Associated with it is a documentation centre, which co-operates closely with the Mies van der Rohe Archives in New York's Museum of Modern Art.

★Mies van der Rohe Pavilion

Opening times
Daily 8am to 8pm (winter), midnight (summer)

The busy roundabout of the Plaça de Espanya (Spanish Plaza de España) is the most important traffic intersection of the city. In the centre of the square is an elaborate memorial fountain representing "España ofrecida a Dios" ("Spain dedicated to God"). On the north side of the square is the Bullring (Arenas de Barcelona).

Plaça de Espanya/ Plaza de España

Sights in the North of the City

★Temple Expiatori de la Sagrada Família

In the north of the city, beyond the Avinguda de la Diagonal, is the conspicuous and very striking Temple Expiatori de la Sagrada Família (Church of the Atonement of the Holy Family), a monumental unfinished church in Neo-Catalan style which ranks as the principal work of the Catalan architect Antoni Gaudí (1852–1926). Work on the church had begun in 1882, but when Gaudí took it over in the following year he completely altered the original plan and continued the building in accordance with his own ideas.

Location
Carrer de Mallorca

Metro station
Sagrada Família (Line 5)

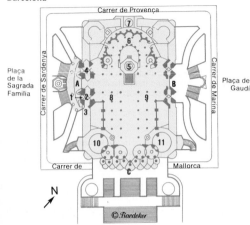

Temple Expiatori de la Sagrada Família

A Doorway of the Passion
B Doorway of the Nativity
  (above two towers)
C Doorway of majesty

1 Entrance
2 Ante-room
3 Gaudi Multivision
4 Sales kiosk
5 Altar (crypt below)
6 Apse
7 Chapel of Resurrection of the Virgin
8 Gaudi Museum
9 Model workshop
10 Baptistry
11 Chapel of the Sacrament

Opening times
Daily from 9am to 9pm Jun.–Aug., 8pm May and Sept., 7pm Mar., Apr. and Oct., 6pm Nov.–Feb.

The cost of constructing this "church of the poor", as Gaudí called it, was met from offerings and donations.

The church is planned to have a total length of 110m/360ft and a height of 45m/150ft, with the main dome rising to 160m/525ft and the twelve towers symbolising the Apostles to 115m/375ft. All that is built so far, however, is the east doorway (the Christmas Doorway) with its four towers (representing the four Evangelists), the outer walls of the apse, the crypt (in which Gaudí was buried in 1926), part of the west doorway, also with four towers, and the walls of the nave. Recently four granite capitals upon which the arches of the eastern wings will eventually be built, have been installed, also three massive ornately decorated windows in the façade have been completed. Work is proceeding only very slowly, and there is no saying whether or when the gigantic building will be completed.

Architecturally the Temple Expiatori de la Sagrada Família is a highly unconventional mingling of stylistic borrowings and new creations. The ground-plan, the spatial proportions and the general lines of the building are very much in the spirit of Gothic and Neo-Gothic, but with these features are combined flowing patterns of organic, plant-like ornament as found in Art Nouveau architecture.

Interior

At the intersection of the transepts and the apse is the high altar, with a baldachin, and below this is the main crypt (which is usually closed). The two subsidiary crypts, however, are open to the public. In the right-hand one is a large model of the completed church on a scale of 1:25; here too is the modelling workshop. In the left-hand crypt is the Gaudí Museum (Museu Gaudí), which displays a model showing a cross-section of the nave and documentation on other buildings by Gaudí.

Towers

The towers of the east doorway can be climbed, though the ascent of the spiral staircases within the openwork towers is not recommended for those liable to vertigo, an easier option is by way of the recently installed lift. From the towers there are good views of the interior of the church and the mosaic decoration of the spires, and also extensive views of the city.

★ Parc Güell/Parque Güell

Location
Carrer Olot

On a hillside in the north-west of the city, in the outlying district of Vallcarca, lies the Parc Güell, which was laid out between 1900 and 1914 to the design of Gaudí. In the park is Gaudí's house, now a museum (Casa-Museu Gaudí).

Sagrada Familia   *Parc Güell*

On the south-east wall of the park, in Carrer Olot, are brightly coloured majolica medallions giving the park's name. At the entrance is a porter's lodge in flowing architectural forms with a tower, much of it clad in coloured majolica tiles. From here a double, symmetrical staircase leads up to a columned hall, divided into two by a fountain which has a brightly coloured ceramic salamander-like animal as its main feature. Between the capitals of the dark-coloured archaic-style columns is a rich polychrome decoration of ceramic and glass mosaics.

Metro stations
Plaça de Lesseps,
Vallcarca (Line 3)

On the roof of the hall is a spacious open area enclosed by walls shaped in the form of long undulating stone benches covered with an unusual decoration of ceramic fragments in every shade of colour. From the terrace there are far-ranging views over the city and the sea.

There are a variety of other details designed by Gaudí in the park – colonnades, viaducts, grottoes, etc.

Antoni Gaudí lived from 1906 to 1926 in the park. He moved into a house designed by Francesc Bereguer which is now a museum and furnished with original pieces by Gaudí.

Casa-Museu Gaudí

★Tibidabo

North-west of the city centre is Mt Tibidabo (512m/1680ft), one of the most popular excursions in the immediate area of Barcelona. Its name is taken from Matthew 4,9: "Haec omnia tibi dabo" ("All these things will I give thee").

From Plaça de Catalunya an underground railway (Ferrocarril de la Generalitat) runs to the Avinguda del Tibidabo station, terminus of the line. From there an old-fashioned tram (known from its dark blue livery as the Tramvia Blau in Catalan, Tranvía Azul in Spanish) takes passengers to the funicular which continues up to the summit of Tibidabo. Times of service relate to

Access

the opening hours of the amusement park: Muntanya Màgica (see below), so check locally.

Museu de la Ciència/ Museo de la Ciencia	Near the Tramvia Blau, at Carrer Teodor Roviralta 55, is the Science Museum, founded by the Catalonian Social Fund (Caixa). It displays permanent collections in the fields of optics, mechanics and space research, and has associated with it a meteorological station, a planetarium and an observatory (open: Tues.–Sun. 10am–8pm).
Sagrat Cor	On the summit of Tibidabo, above the funicular station, is the huge church of the Sagrado Corazón de Jesús (1961), with a large statue of Christ on the roof. From the foot of the statue there is a good view of Barcelona and the surrounding area.
TV and radio tower	The view from Sagrat Cor is now superceded by that from the platform of the radio and TV tower Torre de Collserola, built for the occasion of the Olympic Games. The spindle-like tower designed by Norman Foster is 288m/944ft above sea level. There are views of the whole city and, in fine weather, as far as the Balearics. Inland the view takes in Monserrat, Montseny and to the north the Pyrenees. The tower can be reached by a cable railway.
Muntanya Màgica	The great attraction on Tibidabo is the amusement park (Muntanya Màgica) extends down the steep hillside on several levels. Recently renovated, the park combines the most modern rides with traditional fairground attractions.
	The Museum of Automata, housed in a former theatre, displays mechanical dolls, games and vehicles. The park – best visited on a half-day trip from Barcelona – is a particular attraction for families with children.

Surroundings of Barcelona

Sabadell	From Barcelona the A 18 motorway and N 150 run 21km/13 miles north-west to the industrial town (textiles) of Sabadell (alt. 190m/623ft), on the Río Ripoll. There is an interesting museum with material of the prehistoric and early historical periods and exhibits on the history of the town.
	From Sabadell N 150 continues to Tarrasa (Catalan Terrassa: see entry).
San Cugat de Vallés/ Sant Cugat del Vallès	A secondary road leads 12km/7½ miles north-west via Tibidabo to San Cugat de Vallés (Catalan Sant Cugat del Vallès; alt. 180m/590ft), a residential town in a wooded setting with a Dominican monastery which is first mentioned in the records in 897.
	The present buildings, dating from the 11th–17th century, are Romanesque and Gothic, with later alterations. The church (aisled) has a beautiful altar of All Saints (1375) and contains the 14th century tomb of Abbot Odo. To the left of the church is the entrance to the cloister, which has 150 figural capitals.

Along the Costa Dorada to the Costa Brava

Badalona	From Barcelona (Plaça de les Glòries) the A 19 motorway crosses the Río Besós (Catalan Riu Besos) and runs north-east to Badalona, a long straggling industrial town, with an oil refinery and steelworks, which has now almost completely joined up with Barcelona.
Costa Dorada/ Costa Daurada	From Badalona N II continues north-east: a beautiful stretch of road running close to the beaches of the Costa Dorada (Catalan Costa Daurada;

"Golden Coast"), from which it is separated by the railway. The coast is lined with seaside resorts, hotels and camping sites which attract many thousands of sun-seekers every year.

After passing through the little resort of Vilasar de Mar (Catalan Vilassar de Mar) the road comes to Mataró (alt. 26m/85ft). From this modest little commercial and industrial town the first railway in Spain ran to Barcelona in 1848.

Mataró

10km/6 miles beyond Mataró is Arenys de Mar, with the interesting Museu Marés de la Punta (Lace Museum), which has a large collection of pillow lace. The parish church (16th–17th c.) has one of the finest Baroque altars in Catalonia.

Arenys de Mar

The road continues, with many bends, along the cliff-fringed coast of the promontories of La Serp and Las Rosas and, passing through Canet de Mar and San Pol de Mar (Catalan Sant Pol de Mar) with the battlemented tower of its castle, follows the rocky coast to Calella. Once a quiet little place, this is now a busy resort much favoured by German holidaymakers.

Calella

Beyond Pineda N II comes to a junction where a secondary road goes off on the right to Malgrat de Mar, where the great tourist attraction is Marineland (performances by dolphins and sealions), situated outside the town on the road to Palafolls (reached from the coast road signposted to Blanes).

Malgrat de Mar

The coast road continues from Malgrat de Mar to the Costa Brava (see entry); N II runs inland to Gerona (see entry).

To Puigcerdá in the Pyrenees

Starting from the Plaça de les Glòries, the route follows the A 17 motorway, heading north for Gerona (Catalan Girona), turns into N 152 (E 9) and then takes a minor road on the right to Granollers (alt. 145m/475ft), a busy little town with a well known livestock market. It was largely destroyed during the Carlist wars and as a result has preserved few old buildings apart from the 14th century Gothic church of San Esteban. There is an interesting archaeological museum.

Granollers

From Granollers a detour can be made to the north-east by way of San Celoni (Catalan Sant Celoni) to the wooded hills of the Sierra de Montseny, with the highest peak in the Catalonian Mountains, Turó del Home (1712m/5617ft). From San Celoni a scenic road winds its way, with many bends but beautiful views, to Santa Fe del Montseny (alt. 1100m/3610ft), on the Estanque de Santa Fe. The village, which originally grew up around an abbey, is a good base for hill-walkers and climbers.

★ Sierra de Montseny

N 152 continues from Granollers up a rocky valley to La Garriga (alt. 260m/855ft) and then winds its way up to Ayguafreda (Catalan Aiguafreda) and Tona, which is dominated by a large ruined castle. It then crosses the plain to the old episcopal city of Vich (Catalan Vic: see entry). Thereafter it continues via Montesquíu, with the Castillo de Besora, and through the valley of the Río Ter to the boundary between the provinces of Barcelona and Gerona. Just over the border is the little town of Ripoll (see entry).

From Ripoll a beautiful stretch of road (waterfalls) continues by way of Aguas de Ribas to Ribas de Freser (Catalan Ribes de Freser; alt. 926m/3038ft), a spa in a wooded setting on the Río Freser which is also a popular summer resort. 8km/5 miles north is the winter sports resort of

Nuna (alt. 2000m/6560ft), which can also be reached by rack railway. N 152 continues, climbing between Puigmal (2912m/9554ft) on the right and the Sierra del Cadi on the left, to the Puerto de Tosas (1800m/5906ft). From the pass it runs high up on the hillside, with many bends, to the little village of Urtg (alt. 1190m/3905ft), from which a side road leads to the magnificent winter sports area of La Molina (1600–2500m/5250–8200ft). A few kilometres beyond this C 1313 branches off on the left to Seo de Urgel (Catalan La Seu d'Urgell).

Puigcerdá

N 152 then continues to the old fortified frontier town of Puigcerdá (alt. 1147m/3763ft), charmingly situated on a hill at the junction of the Río Segre and Río Carol. Thanks to this beautiful situation amid the Pyrenees it is a much frequented resort both in summer and in winter. It has a monastery founded in the 12th century and the 14th century church of Santa María (destroyed in 1938).

Llivia

5km/3 miles north-east is the littlle medieval town of Llivia (protected as a national monument), which has since 1659 been a Spanish enclave in French territory. The Municipal Museum contains the oldest pharmacy in Europe (15th c.).

5km/3 miles north, at Ur, N 152 comes to the frontier crossing into France.

Béjar

E 4

Province: Salamanca (SA). Telephone dialling code: 923
Altitude: 950m/3115ft. Population: 17,500

Béjar, an important centre of cloth manufacture, is attractively situated on a hill above a valley in the western foothills of the Sierra de Gredos. Its agreeable climate makes it a popular summer resort.

Palacio Ducal, Béjar

Sights

The town's most notable building is the fortress-like Palacio Ducal, the 16th century palace of the Dukes of Béjar, in the walled old town, which has a beautiful Renaissance courtyard and a magnificent staircase.

Palacio Ducal

The brick-built church of Santa María, built in the 13th century and rebuilt in the 16th, has a fine sculpture of Nuestra Señora de las Angustias by Luis Salvador Carmona.

Santa María

The Museo Mateo Hernández, in the church of San Gil, has sculpture and pictures of the Flemish and Spanish schools, enamels, porcelain, ivories and miniatures.

Museo
Mateo Hernández

Above the town is the Santuario del Castañar (alt. 1050m/3445ft), from which there are fine views. The chapel, built in the 17th and 18th centuries, with a Baroque interior, is situated on the spot where the Virgin is said to have appeared to some monks in 1447. Since then the Virgen del Castañar, of whom there is a much venerated 15th century image in the chapel, has been the patroness of Béjar.

Santuario del
Castañar

Belmonte   G 5

Province: Cuenca (CU). Telephone dialling code: 967
Altitude: 79m/259ft.Population: 3000

The whole of the ancient little fortified town of Belmonte, 158km/98 miles south-east of Madrid, has been declared a monument of tourist interest. It was the birthplace of the religious writer and poet Fray Luis de León (1527–91)

Sights

The mid-15th century castle of Belmonte, now declared a national monument, looms over the town on a gently rising hill in the barren plain of La Mancha. This star-shaped stronghold has six round towers and a double circuit of battlemented walls. There are three gates, the most remarkable of which is the Pilgrim Gate, with a carved cross and scallop-shell, emblem of the pilgrimage to the shrine of St James at Santiago de Compostela. The triangular courtyard is surrounded by a double gallery with fine relief decoration. The rooms in the interior of the castle are mostly empty, but have fine coffered ceilings, foreplaces and windows. From the wall-walk there are extensive views over the countryside of La Mancha.

★Castillo

Notable features of the former collegiate church (also a national monument) are the magnificent choir-stalls from Cuenca Cathedral (see entry), the Gothic retablos and the font at which Luis de León was baptised.

Church

Benidorm   M 6

Province: Alicante (A). Telephone dialling code: 965
Altitude: 4m/13ft. Population: 28,000

Once a small fishing village, Benidorm has now become an internationally known resort, one of the most popular holiday centres on the Costa Blanca ("White Coast").

The long beaches of fine sand and the warm climate (345 days with sunshine in the average year) attract three million visitors annually to Benidorm. In recent decades the town, which now has 250,000 beds for visitors,

Resort

has completely changed its aspect. The seafront promenade is lined with hotels and high-rise apartment blocks, and entertainments of all kinds are available by day and by night. A rocky promontory crowned by a castle divides the beach into an eastern (Playa de Levante) and a western part (Playa de Poniente). On the promontory is the old fishing village, with picturesque narrow streets. From a terrace in the Parque Castillo, in the grounds of the castle, there are fine views of the bay.

North of the town is Aqualand, one of the largest water parks in Europe, with facilities for all kinds of water sports.

Into the Sierra de Aitana

★ Guadalest

C 3318 runs north through an agricultural region in which citrus fruits and medlars are grown. At Callosa de Ensarría C 3313 goes off on the left and traverses the Sierra de Aitana to Alcoy. On this road, 18km/11 miles from Benidorm, is the fascinating little village of Guadalest, built into the rock and accessible only through a tunnel driven through the hill. In 1609 this was the last refuge of the Muslim Moriscos before their final expulsion from Spain. An earthquake in 1744 almost completely destroyed the old Moorish castle, but the extraordinary situation and the views from the top make it well worth while to climb the crag on which it stood.

Tárbena

From Callosa de Ensarría C 3318 continues to Tárbena, which was refounded in the 17th century by Majorcans, whose descendants have preserved something of the Majorcan dialect.

Along the Coast to the North

Altea

The coast road runs north-east to the tourist resort of Altea, beautifully situated on the hillside to the left of the road, with fortifications built in the reign of Philip II. The village church is charming, with its white walls, pink roof tiles and blue domes.

Calpe

The road continues above the coastal cliffs, with magnificent views of the Peñón de Ifach (see below) and the sea; then through two tunnels and into a side road on the right to reach the little fishing town of Calpe (alt. 20m/65ft), on a site which was already occupied in Phoenician times. The town has old walls and a little church in Mudéjar style. Salt is still won from the sea in salt-pans. The principal landmark of the town and of the Costa Blanca is the great crag of the Peñón de Ifach (383m/1257ft), rising out of the sea like a lesser Gibraltar. It can be climbed on a good path in about 1½ hours, and the climb is well worth the effort for the sake of the superb views of the coast, reaching east as far as Cabo de la Nao (see Denia, Surroundings), and the coastal hills. Below the Peñón, to the left, is the beach of Playa de la Fosa.

Along the Coast to the South

Villajoyosa

The coast road, running at some distance from the sea, comes in 10km/ 6 miles to Villajoyosa, a little port town beautifully situated above the sea. The old fishing quarter, with its brightly painted houses, has been preserved intact. Of the old fortifications there survive imposing remains of walls and towers and the fortress-like Gothic church, with a Renaissance doorway, which was incorporated in the town walls. There is an ethnographic museum in the Casa de Cultura. Worth seeing is the daily fish market in the harbour when the day's catches are sold.

From here the coast road continues to Alicante (see entry).

Peñón de Ifach

Betanzos

C 1

Province: La Coruña (C). Telephone dialling code: 981
Altitude: 25m/82ft. Population: 11,500

Betanzos, the old Roman port of Brigantium Flavium, lies on the Ría de Betanzos, an inlet reaching far inland. It is an attractive little town surrounded by vineyards and fields, with remains of its medieval walls, town gates, noble mansions, narrow streets and picturesque nooks and corners.

Sights

The Plaza o Campo is the focal point of Betanzos with a monument to two citizens who emigrated to America, and a fountain with a statue of Diana. The plaza is surrounded by typically Galician houses with glass fronts.

Plaza o Campo

The monastic church of San Francisco, built at the end of the 14th century at the behest of Count Fernán Pérez de Andrade, is one of the finest Gothic churches in Galicia, with large windows in its three apses and rich sculptural decoration on its doorways. It also contains fine sculpture and tombs, notably that of Count Pérez de Andrade (1387): the count is depicted, with his hunting dogs at his feet, lying on his sarcophagus, which is decorated with reliefs of hunting scenes and supported by a wild boar and a bear.

★San Francisco

The most notable feature of the church of Santa María del Azogue (14th–15th c.) is the façade with its large Gothic rose window. In niches on either side of the doorway are figures of the Virgin and the Archangel Gabriel. This church also has a number of noble tombs, as well as a medieval retablo of Flemish origin.

Santa María del Azogue

Santiago The parish church of Santiago (15th c.) is the mother church of the town. Originally dating from the 11th century, it was renovated in the 15th century by the tailors' guild of Betanzos. In the tympanum is a figure of St James (Santiago) on horseback. The chapel of San Pedro and San Pablo (SS. Peter and Paul) has a Plateresque altar by Cornelis de Holanda.

El Pasatiempo "Pasatiempo" means pastime or amusement; and this was what Juan Carcá Naveira had in mind when, at the end of the 19th century, he laid out on the banks of the Río Mandeo a fantastic garden with fountains, grottoes and all kinds of exotic plants. During the 1920s the gardens attracted large numbers of visitors.

Bilbao/Bilbo G 1

Province: Vizcaya (BI). Telephone dialling code: 94
Altitude: 19m/62ft. Population: 433,000

Bilbao (Basque Bilbo), lying 14km/9 miles from the sea on the Río Nervión (Basque Nerbioi), is chief town of the Basque province of Vizcaya (Basque Bizkaia) and the see of a bishop. It is also Spain's leading port in terms of revenue from goods handled, and the centre of a gigantic industrial conurbation.

History From its foundation in 1300 by Don Diego López de Haro, feudal lord of Vizcaya, Bilbao played an important part in the maritime trade on the north coast of Spain. Iron ore was exported from here to England, and the town's pre-industrial iron and steel industry brought it prosperity. Its rise to become one of Spain's leading industrial centres began in the mid 19th century with the development of industrial smelting of iron ore from the mines in the hinterland. During this period, particularly in the sixties and seventies, large numbers of people came to Bilbao from the poorer country regions in search of work. Heavy rainfall in 1983 led to floods which caused severe damage in the industrial areas.

Bilbao industrial region The industrial region round Bilbao now extends for some 18km/11 miles from Galdácano (Basque Galdakao), to the east of the city, along both banks of the Río Nervión down to its mouth. Within this region there are 28 independent communes, including Barracaldo (Basque Barakaldo), Portugalete, Sestao and Las Arenas (Basque Areeta) which have developed into industrial towns and grown together into a conurbation with a population approaching the million mark. The left bank of the river is traditionally dominated by iron and steel, shipbuilding and engineering, to which in recent years the chemical industry and an oil refinery have been added. In this area the blocks of flats in which the workers live are frequently sited next door to the industrial installations. The right bank is less heavily industrialised, with small and medium-sized establishments, residential areas and a number of small seaside resorts. Bilbao has become an administrative and banking centre.

Harbour The starting-point of Bilbao's industrial development was the harbour. Ocean-going vessels of up to 4000 tons can sail inland on the Río Nervión; at the end of the 19th century a deeper outer harbour was constructed at El Abra, in the estuary of the river; and in recent years huge port installations capable of handling vessels of up to 500,000 tons have been built at Punta Lucero and Punta la Galea, far out in the estuary.

Industrial pollution As a result of escalating industrial growth the Bilbao region has the highest level of air pollution in Spain and one of the highest levels in Europe. The Río Nervión is heavily laden with harmful substances, and other rivers on the Basque coast suffer, sometimes severely, from pollution.

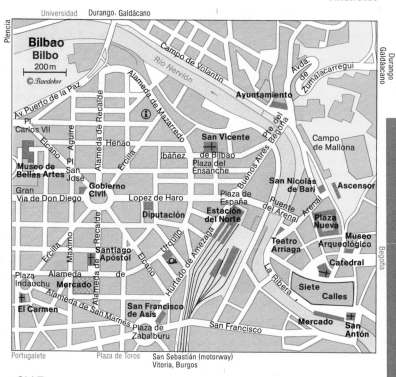

Universidad   Durango, Galdácano

Bilbao
Bilbo
├── 200 m ──┤
© *Baedeker*

Plencia

Av. Puerto de la Paz

Pl.
Carlos VII

Eicano

Aguirre

Alameda de Recalde

Henao

Ercilla

Ibáñez

Alameda de Mazarredo

Río Nervión

Campo de Volantín

Avda. de Zumalacarregui

Ayuntamiento

San Vicente
de Bilbao
Plaza del
Ensanche

Pie de Begoña

Buenos Aires

Campo
de Mallona

**Museo de
Bellas Artes**

Pl.
San
José

Gran
Via de Don Diego

**Gobierno
Civil**

Lopez de Haro

Plaza de
España

**San Nicolás
de Bari**

Ascensor

Diputación

**Estación
del Norte**

Puente
del Arenal

Arenal

**Plaza
Nueva**

Ercilla

Maximo

Recalde

Eicano

Urquijo

Hurtado de Amezaga

**Teatro
Arriaga**

La Ribera

**Museo
Arqueológico**

Catedral

**Santiago
Apóstol**

Alameda

de

Plaza
Indauchu

Mercado

Alameda de San Mamés

El Carmen

**San Francisco
de Asis**

Plaza de
Zabalburu

San Francisco

**Siete
Calles**

Mercado

**San
Antón**

Begoña

Durango
Galdácano

Portugalete

Plaza de Toros

San Sebastián (motorway)
Vitoria, Burgos

Old Town

On the right bank of the Río Nervión, between the Puente de San Antón and
the church of San Nicolás, extends the old town of Bilbao, linked by five
bridges with the new town (the Ensanche). The core of the old town lies
around the "Siete Calles" ("seven streets") – Somera, Artecalle, Tendería,
Belosticalle, Carnicería Vieja, Barrencalle and Barrencalle Barena – with
numbers of enticing shops, bars and cafés.

Visitors approaching the old town from the north by way of the Puente del
Arenal find themselves in the Paseo del Arenal, the main artery of this part
of the town. To the right, in Plaza de Arriaga, can be seen the Teatro Arriaga,
built in 1890 and now renovated, the cultural hub of the city.

Teatro Arriaga

To the left of the bridge the Paseo leads to the church of San Nicolás de Bari,
on an octagonal plan, which dates from the 14th century but which was
completely rebuilt in 1756. The beautiful carved altar was the work of Juan
de Mena, who was also responsible for some of the paintings in the church.

San Nicolás
de Bari

The district of Begoña lies on a higher level and is not part of the old town.
Its pilgrimage church is most easily reached by taking the lift from behind
the church of San Nicolás. There is also a footpath (20 minutes' walk) to
the top of the hill, from which there is a good view of the city. The church
(16th c.) has an image of the Virgin of Begoña, patroness of the city,
and an interesting painting of "The Pilgrimage of Begoña".

Basílica de
Begoña

Bilbao: the old town and the Río Nervión

Plaza Nueva

The Plaza Nueva, to the south of San Nicolás, is enclosed by three-storey buildings with arcades on the ground floor. It is the scene of popular fairs and colourful markets selling a great variety of local produce.

★Museo
Arqueológico,
Etnográfico e
Histórico Vasco

The former Jesuit college of Santos Joanes is now occupied by the Museum of Basque Archaeology, Ethnography and History (Museo Arqueológico, Etnográfico e Histórico Vasco; in Basque Euskal Arkeoloja, Etnografia eta Kondaira Museoa), with three departments documenting the history and way of life of the Basques.

The archaeological section, on the ground floor, displays prehistoric finds from burials in Basque territory. The cloister houses various tombs, memorial stones and pieces of sculpture, with the mysterious idol of Mikeldi in the centre.

The ethnographic section displays selected objects illustrating the fisheries, agriculture, folk art and crafts of the Basque country. In a separate room is a large relief model of the Basque provinces.

The historical section includes examples of woodcarving and weapons, but is mainly devoted to the history of the Consulate of Bilbao, which regulated shipping and commerce in Bilbao from 1511 to 1829.

Cathedral

South-west of the Museum in Plaza de Santiago, in the centre of the old town, is the Catedral de Santiago, built in the early 14th century on one of the pilgrim routes to Santiago de Compostela (see entry). The original building was badly damaged by fire in 1571 and was then rebuilt in its present form, with a Renaissance porch on the south side and a Gothic cloister. The Neo-Gothic façade and tower date from the 19th century.

San Antón

From the cathedral one of the "seven streets" leads down to the bank of the river. Along this on the left are the fine Market Hall and, at the end of the Puente de San Antón, the church of San Antón, which was built by Guillot de Beaugrant in the 15th century on the site of an earlier castle. The tower dates in its present form from the 18th century. There is a beautiful retablo by Beaugrant in one of the chapels.

New Town

The new town of Bilbao, the Ensanche, occupies the left bank of the Río Nervión. Its main artery is the 1.5km/1 mile long Gran Vía de Don Diego López de Haro (whose statue stands in the Plaza de España at the near end of the street, just over the river). Farther along the street to the west is the Palacio de la Diputación Provincial (by Luis Aladrén, 1897), seat of the provincial government. Beyond this the Gran Vía cuts across the spacious Plaza Federico Moyúa to end at the tall memorial in honour of the Sagrado Corazón de Jesús (1927).

Gran Vía

To the right of the western section of the Gran Vía, one street away, is the Parque Doña Casilda de Iturizza (named after a benefactress of the city), at the north-east end of which are the two buildings of the Museum of Art, with a collection of outstanding quality.

★Museo de Bellas Artes

The older building displays work by many great European masters. Dutch and Flemish painting of the 15th–17th centuries is well represented, with such masterpieces as Quentin Matsys' "Money-Changers" and Dirk Bouts' "Virgin and Child" and works by van Dyck and Vos of the 17th century Flemish school. Spanish painting of the 14th and 15th centuries is represented by Jaime Huguet, Bartolomé Bermejo and Pedro Serra, the 16th and 17th centuries by El Greco ("Annunciation"), Zurbarán ("Virgin and Child with St John", his last dated work), Velázquez and Jusepe de Ribera. There are three extraordinary portraits by Goya, the most remarkable of which is that of the poet Fernández de Moratín. Other rooms are devoted to Italian painting of the 16th and 17th centuries, 19th century French painting (Gauguin's "Washerwomen of Arles") and Romanesque and Gothic sculpture. On the first floor are works by Basque artists, including 22 pictures by the landscape painter Darió de Regoyos (the largest collection of his works in any museum).

The modern building is devoted mainly to work by contemporary Spanish artists.

Surroundings of Bilbao

Along the Estuary of the Río Nervión

After passing through the industrial districts of Deusto and Erandio the road down the right bank comes to the residential suburbs of Las Arenas (Basque Areeta), Neguri and Algorta, with beaches which are much frequented by the people of Bilbao.

Right bank

From Guecho (Basque Getxo), which still preserves a few handsome 19th century villas, there is a good general view of the estuary of Bilbao and its industrial installations. To the north lies Punta Galea, where new port facilities have been established for huge ocean-going vessels.

Guecho/ Getxo

C 6320 continues by way of Sopelana (Basque Sopela) to the former fishing village of Plencia (Basque Plentzia), which, like the neighbouring village of Gorliz (Basque Gorlitz), has beautiful beaches.

From here a road follows the coast to Bermeo (see below).

Plencia/ Plentzia

The road down the left bank also passes through industrial suburbs, with iron and steelworks, including the Altos Hornos de Vizcaya rolling mill, the second largest in Spain.

Left bank

Beyond this is Portugalete, which has developed from a quiet little fishing village into an industrial centre, though the old town still has some char-

Portugalete

Bilbao/Bilbo

★ Puente Colgante

ming nooks and corners. A sight of technological interest is the Puente Colgante, the transporter bridge which links Portugalete with Las Arenas on the other side of the estuary. This consists of two 63m/207ft high pylons linked at a great height by a lattice structure, from which the cabin carrying passengers across the river is suspended on steel cables.

From the end of the harbour quay extends a 1km/¾ mile long breakwater with a lighthouse at its tip from which there are good views of the estuary.

Santurce/
Santurtzi

The culinary specialty of Santurce (Basque Santurtzi), the next place on the road, is fried sardines – a reminder of the town's former importance as a fishing port, now increasingly being swallowed up in industrial development.

★ Castro
Urdiales

From Santurce a road runs along the coast, affording fine views, to the little port of Ciérvana (Basque Zierbena) and then follows the right bank of the Río Barbadún to San Juan de Somorrostro, on the borders of the province of Cantabria. From here N 634 continues to Castro Urdiales (the Roman town of Flaviobriga), in Cantabria. This picturesque little port town, now a popular seaside resort, is probably the oldest settlement on the Cantabrian coast. It is dominated by the fine Gothic church (14th–15th c.) of Nuestra Señora de la Asunción, which has a beautiful doorway, the Puerta del Perdón, and by the Castillo de Santa Ana, on a rocky outcrop above the harbour. The castle, once held by the Templars, now serves as a lighthouse. The fiesta of Coso Blanco is celebrated annually on the first Friday in July with fireworks and a battle of flowers.

To Ondárroa by the Coast Road

★ Bermeo

From the old town of Bilbao C 6313 runs north via Begoña to Munguía. From here it climbs, with many bends, to the ridge of Monte Acherre, from

The church and castle of Castro Urdiales

which there is a picturesque view of Bermeo; to the right is the hill of Sollube (684m/2244ft), with a television transmitter on the summit. The road then descends to Bermeo, beautifully situated on the slopes of the hill, its harbour crowded with colourful fishing boats.

Bermeo, originally a Roman foundation, is the most important fishing port on the Cantabrian coast. The Fisheries Museum (Museo del Pescador) has an interesting collection which includes models, fishing equipment and fittings from fishing boats. It is housed in the Torre Ercilla (now a protected monument), which was once occupied by the adventurer and poet Alonso de Ercilla (1533–94). The church of Santa Eufemia, a short distance away, dates from the 13th century.

A narrow road leads out from Bermeo to Cabo Machichaco (Basque Matxitxako), from which there are extensive views. To the west are the romantic rocky peninsula of San Juan de Gaztelugache (Basque Gaztelu-gatxe) and the bathing beach of Baquino (Basque Bakino).

From Bermeo C 6315 goes south-east to Mundaca (Basque Mundaka), at the mouth of the broad Ría de Guernica, and continues to Guernica y Luno (Basque Gernika-Luno: see entry), from which the route continues on C 6212, heading north.

C 6212 runs via Ereño to Lequitio (Basque Lekeitio), a little seaside resort and port (tunny fishing) beautifully situated in a bay sheltered by the rocky wooded island of San Nicolás. On the harbour is the church of Santa María de la Asunción (14th–15th c.), with filigree Gothic buttresses and a finely sculptured doorway; notable features of the interior are the extraordinary high altar and a Gothic retablo in the third chapel on the right. In a Baroque side chapel can be seen a simple 12th century wooden figure of Nuestra Señora de la Antigua, venerated as patroness of the town. | Lequeitio/ Lekeitio

The road follows the coast to the little fishing port of Ondárroa, charmingly situated in a bay on the borders of the province of Guipúzcoa. Its main features of interest are the fortress-like Gothic church of Santa María (1492) and a bridge of Roman origin. | Ondárroa

El Burgo de Osma　　　　　　　　　　　　　　　　　　　　G 3

Province: Soria (SO). Telephone dialling code: 975
Altitude: 850m/2790ft. Population: 5000

The old episcopal city of El Burgo de Osma, originally founded by the Visigoths, lies south-west of Soria on the Río Ucero, in the valley of the Duero. Its heyday was in the 16th century.

★Cathedral

The town's finest building is the Gothic Cathedral, begun in the 12th century in Romanesque style and continued from 1232 onwards in Gothic; the 72m/236ft high tower, a notable landmark, was completed in the 18th century. Facing on to the square is the south doorway, with rich 13th century sculptural decoration. The cloister dates from 1512.

The Capilla Mayor has a beautiful retablo (1552–56) by Juan de Juni and his pupil Picardo. The wrought-iron choir screen (16th c.) was the work of Juan Francés. In the north aisle is the painted limestone tomb of San Pedro de Osma (13th c.). The finest of the chapels is the Baroque Capilla de Palafox, by Juan de Villanueva, who also designed the 18th century New Sacristy. The Old Sacristy has remains of Romanesque wall paintings. | Interior

The Cathedral Museum has a large collection of vestments and liturgical utensils; but it is surpassed by the valuable collection of miniatures in the | Museum

Library. Here the greatest treasure is a copy (1086) of a commentary on the Apocalypse by a monk named Beatus of Liébana.

Universidad de Santa Catalina

The Universidad de Santa Catalina, founded by Bishop Acosta in 1551, has a Plateresque façade.

Palacio Episcopal

In the Plaza Mayor are a number of handsome buildings, including the 17th century Bishop's Palace, with a curious doorway.

Hospital San Agustín

The finest building in the Plaza Mayor, however, is the Hospital San Agustín (17th c.), with two Baroque towers bearing coats of arms.

Surroundings of El Burgo de Osma

★ Berlanga de Duero

24km/15 miles from El Burgo de Osma (most easily reached by taking C 116 and then turning off on the right) is the little town of Berlanga de Duero, still surrounded by its old walls. It has an imposing 15th century castle with a massive keep, surrounded by a double circuit of walls. The beautiful church, La Colegiata (1530), has a magnificent retablo. The Palacio de los Marqueses de Berlanga is in Plateresque style.

Burgos   H 2

Province: Burgos (BU). Telephone dialling code: 947
Altitude: 860m/2820ft. Population: 156,000

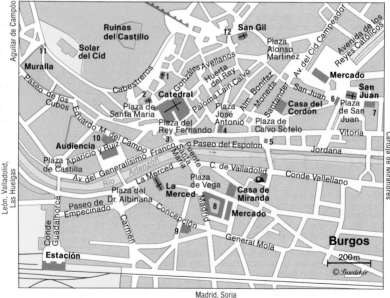

1 San Esteban
2 San Nicolás
3 Arco de Santa María
4 Ayuntamiento
5 Monumento del Cid
6 Arco de San Juan
7 Museo Marceliano Santa María
8 Estación de Autobuses
9 San Cosme y San Damián
10 Palacio Arzobispol
11 Arco de San Martín
12 Arco de San Gil

Burgos, famous for its magnificent cathedral, was capital of Old Castile in the 10th and 11th centuries and is now chief town of Burgos province and the see of an archbishop. It lies on both banks of the Río Arlanzón in the centre of the fertile North Castilian plain, under a hill (100m/330ft) crowned by the remains of an old castle. Although Burgos is a busy town with a good deal of industry, a visitor strolling along the banks of the Arlanzón, where frogs croak in the dense beds of reeds, might imagine himself in the heart of the country rather than the centre of a city. The promenades along both sides of the river, with their cafés, offer the chance of relaxation after sightseeing in a city which has so many treasures of art and architecture to see.

The climate of Burgos, with its long winters and torrid summers, has earned it the description (also applied to the climate of Madrid), "nine months of winter, three months of hell".

The origins of the town go back to a castle built in 884 by Count Diego Porcelos. In 951 it became chief town of the County of Castile and in 1037 capital of the united kingdoms of Castile and León – a status which it retained until the completion of the Reconquista in 1492. In those days Burgos was already a centre of the arts and of commerce, playing a leading part, until the end of the 16th century, in the Castilian wool trade. The town was occupied in 1808 by French troops, who were only driven out by Wellington's army in 1813. During the Spanish Civil War, from 1936 to 1939, Burgos was the seat of Franco's Nationalist government.

History

Burgos is associated with the story of Rodrigo Díaz de Vivar, better known as the Cid (1026–99), who was born in the village of Vivar, 9km/5½ miles north. His remains were deposited in the cathedral in 1921.

★★ Cathedral

Prominently situated on a terrace at the foot of the castle hill is the Cathedral of Santa María, in its general structure and its profusion of sculpture one of the most impressive of Gothic cathedrals. Built of white limestone with some of the quality of marble, it was begun in 1221, when Ferdinand II laid the foundation stone. The nave and aisles, together with the doorways, were completed by the middle of the 13th century, and the towers were built in the 15th century, but work on the completion of the building

Catedral de Burgos

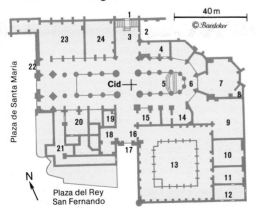

40 m
© Baedeker

Plaza de Santa María

Cid

N

Plaza del Rey
San Fernando

1 Puerta de la Coronería
2 Puerta de la Pellejería
3 Escalera Dorada
4 Capilla de la Natividad
5 Capilla Mayor
6 Trassagrario
7 Capilla del Condestable
8 Sacristía (Souvenirladen)
9 Capilla de Santiago
10 Capilla de Santa Catalina
11 Capila del Corpus Christi
12 Sala Capitular
13 Claustro
14 Sacristía Nueva
15 Capilla de San Enrique
16 Puerta del Claustro
17 Puerta del Sarmental
18 Capilla de la Visitación
19 Relicario
20 Capilla de la Presentación
21 Capilla del Santísimi Cristo
22 Puerta Principal
23 Capilla de Santa Tecla
24 Capilla de Santa Ana

Burgos: a peaceful scene in the heart of the city

dragged on into the 16th century. The founder, Bishop Mauricio, employed Spanish architects, but his 15th century successor Alonso de Cartagena brought in master builders from northern Europe – Felipe Vigarny (Felipe de Borgoña) from Burgundy, Gil de Siloé from Flanders and Juan de Colonia (Hans of Cologne) from Germany.

★ West front

The west front of the cathedral, which was originally white but has suffered badly from air pollution, is dominated by the two magnificent openwork spires, 84m/276ft high, built by Juan de Colonia in 1458. Above the main doorway (Puerta Principal), which was altered in the 18th century and lost much of its sculptural decoration, is the beautiful rose window (*estrellón*), and above this again are eight statues of kings.

Doorways

The other doorways are also very fine: at the end of the north transept the richly decorated Puerta de la Coronería (*c.* 1250), also known as the Puerta de los Apóstoles from the magnificent figures of Apostles; also on the north side but facing east, the Puerta de la Pellejería (1516), a lively example of Plateresque by Francisco de Colonia, grandson of Juan de Colonia; and at the end of the south transept the Puerta del Sarmental (*c.* 1230), also richly decorated with sculpture (Christ as teacher of the Apostles).

Interior

★ Cimborio

The interior of the cathedral (excluding the Capilla del Condestable) is 84m/276ft long and of impressive height. In the centre of the nave, borne on four massive piers, is the 59m/194ft high Cimborio (Lantern), a masterpiece of Plateresque art, richly decorated with sculpture and coats of arms; it was erected by Juan de Vallejo in 1568 after the collapse of an earlier dome by Simón de Colonia (son of Juan de Colonia). A plain copper plate under the dome marks the spot where the remains of the Cid and his wife Jimena were deposited in 1921.

At the end of the north transept a double staircase, the Escalera Dorada ("Golden Staircase") leads up to the Puerta de la Coronería, 8m/26ft above the floor level of the cathedral. This magnificent example of Plateresque, with its gilded balustrade and superb reliefs, was the work of Diego de Siloé, son of Gil de Siloé.

The choir and Capilla Mayor are separated from the rest of the church by high wrought-iron screens. The double rows of richly carved walnut stalls in the choir (1521) are mostly by Felipe Vigarny. In the centre of the choir is the tomb of Bishop Mauricio (d. 1240), whose recumbent figure is covered with enamelled sheet copper.

Choir

In the centre of the Capilla Mayor is the richly gilded high altar (by Rodrigo and Martín de la Haya, 1580). In front of it are the tombs of several members of the royal house of Castile and León. The reliefs in the *trascoro* (retrochoir) are mainly by Felipe Vigarny.

Capilla Mayor

Behind the ambulatory is the entrance to the Capilla del Condestable (Constable's Chapel), in the richest Plateresque style, which was built between 1482 and 1494 by Simón de Colonia, to the design of his father Juan, for Pedro Hernández de Velasco, Constable of Castile. In the centre of the chapel are the tombs of the Constable and his wife Doña Mencia de Mendoza, with lifelike recumbent figures in Carrara marble (illustration, page 64). To the right is the carved wooden altar of St Anne. The rest of the decoration of the chapel (reliefs, sculpture, coats of arms) was the work of Simón de Colonia and Gil de Siloé. The adjoining Sacristy is now a souvenir shop; in a wall cupboard above the counter is a fine painting of Mary Magdalene by Gian Petrino, a pupil of Leonardo da Vinci.

★★ Capilla del Condestable

The first chapel in the south aisle is the Capilla del Santísimo Cristo, with the famous Cristo de Burgos, a figure of Christ covered with buffalo hide. In the third chapel on the right, the Relicario or Reliquary Chapel, is the much revered Virgen de Oca, probably dating from the 16th century.
  The first chapel in the north aisle is the Capilla de Santa Tecla, built by Churriguera in 1736, with over-ornate coloured Rococo decoration and a very large altar; it also contains a Romanesque font. High up on the outside wall of this chapel can be seen the Papamoscas ("Flycatcher") clock, with a figure which opens its mouth every hour on the hour. In the adjoining Capilla de Santa Ana is a gilded Gothic retablo by Gil de Siloé and Diego de la Cruz.
  The other chapels all contain fine examples of religious art of the 13th–16th centuries, and in some of them there are also sumptuous tombs.

Side chapels

From the vestibule of the New Sacristy (Sacristía Nueva), richly decorated in Baroque style, a handsome doorway leads into the two-storey 13th century Cloister (Claustro), which contains a number of notable tombs, including that of Ferdinand III and his wife Beatrice of Swabia. In the Capilla del Corpus Cristi is preserved the Cofre del Cid, an iron-bound chest which the Cid left with some Jewish merchants as security for a loan of 600 silver marks – though it is said that the chest was filled with sand and stones instead of the silverware it was supposed to contain. A better side of the Cid's character is shown by his signature on his marriage contract, which can be seen, with other old documents, in the Capilla de Santa Catalina. The Capilla de Santiago contains the valuable cathedral treasury.
  On the first floor of the cloister, in the old chapterhouse, is the Diocesan Museum, with valuable 16th and 17th century tapestries and fine gold and silverware.

★ Cloister

Around the Cathedral

Outside the west front of the cathedral is a small square with a fountain, the Plaza de Santa María. On the far side of the square is Calle Santa Agueda, with the Early Gothic church of Santa Agueda, in which Alfonso VI swore in presence of the Cid that he had not murdered his brother Sancho II.

Santa Agueda

San Nicolás | From the Plaza de Santa María a flight of steps leads up to the 15th century church of San Nicolás (completely restored in 1911), facing the west corner of the cathedral. This has fine vaulting and some notable tombs, but its principal treasure is the sumptuous high altar by Francisco de Colonia (1505), with polychrome alabaster reliefs of Old and New Testament scenes involving no fewer than 465 figures.

San Esteban | North-east of San Nicolás is the Gothic church of San Esteban (1280–1350), with a richly sculptured west doorway, a beautiful rose window and an Early Gothic cloister.

Remains of Fortifications

Castillo | Going north from San Esteban, through the Mudéjar-style Arco de San Esteban, and turning left along the old town walls (begun 1276), we come to the Castillo (destroyed by fire in 1736), from the ramparts of which there are fine views.

Solar del Cid | Below the south side of the castle ruins, at the west end of Calle Fernán González, are three stone pillars marking the site of the Solar del Cid, the ancestral home of his family. Close by is the 14th century Arco de San Martín, a gate in the old town walls running south-west from the Castillo. Continuing down the wall towards the south and turning left, we come into the Paseo de los Cubos, named after the semicircular towers (*cubos*) set at intervals along the walls – a fine example of Castilian military engineering.

Palacio de la Isla | In the park opposite the Paseo is the Palacio de la Isla, which was the seat of the Nationalist government during the Civil War.

★Paseo del Espolón

The Paseo del Espolón, the favourite promenade of the people of Burgos, extends along the Río Arlanzón from the Puente de Santa María to the Puente de San Pablo, shaded by plane-trees and lined with cafés and shops. It is rather quieter in the gardens parallel with the Paseo on the banks of the river. Here visitors will see sights unusual in a city – the river flowing quietly by between meadowland and banks of reeds, frogs croaking their noisy concert, perhaps even a shepherd driving his sheep along the meadows.

★Arco de Santa María | At the near end of the Paseo, opposite the Puente de Santa María, is the Arco de Santa María (originally 14th century, rebuilt in 1552), a massive town gate flanked by two semicircular towers, best seen from the bridge over the Arlanzón. The entrance to the town is guarded by statues of Castilian heroes and kings: in the centre of the lower row is Diego Porcelos, the town's founder, flanked by Nuño Rasura and Lain Calvo, the first judges of Castile, and in the upper row (from right to left) the Cid, the Emperor Charles V and Count Fernán González. Through the arch is the Plaza del Rey San Fernando, on the south side of the cathedral.

Puente de San Pablo | The Paseo ends at the Puente de San Pablo, which is decorated with statues of Castilian heroes. Opposite the north end of the bridge is the Plaza Primo de Rivera, dominated by a heroic equestrian statue of the Cid.

Around the Plaza Mayor

Plaza Mayor | A little way east of the cathedral and just off the Paseo del Espolón can be found the arcaded Plaza José Antonio or Plaza Mayor, which ranks with the cathedral as one of the main centres of the city's life. On the south side of

Doorway of the Casa del Cordón, Burgos   *Arco de Santa María*

the square is the Ayuntamiento (Town Hall), built in 1791, which also houses the Municipal Archives.

North of the Plaza Mayor, reached through narrow lanes, is the 14th century church of San Gil, with stellar vaulting. It has a 15th century Pietà, several fine tombs and, in the Capilla de la Natividad, a retablo by Felipe Vigarny.

San Gil

In Plaza Calvo Sotelo, to the east of the Plaza Mayor, is the Casa del Cordón, a house built in 1482–92 for the Constable of Castile. The name comes from the *cordón*, the girdle worn by Franciscan friars, which features in the decoration over the doorway. In this house Columbus was received by the Catholic Monarchs in 1497 after his return from his second voyage to the New World; here too Philip I died in 1506; and here the French king Francis I was held prisoner after the battle of Pavia in 1525.

Casa del Cordón

Farther east, in the Plaza San Juan, is the church of San Lesmes (14th–15th c.), which has a number of Late Gothic tombs and altars.

San Lesmes

In a former Benedictine abbey opposite San Lesmes can be seen a collection of pictures by the Burgos-born Impressionist painter Marceliano Santa María (1866–1952).

Museo Marceliano Santa María

★ Monasterio de las Huelgas

The Monasterio de las Huelgas was originally a country residence of the kings of Castile (*huelga* = "repose, relaxation"), which Alfonso VIII converted into a Cistercian convent for ladies of the highest rank in 1187 at the request of his wife Eleanor, daughter of Henry II of England. The convent was also to be the place of burial of the kings of Castile.

Location
1.5km/1 mile
SW of town centre

Church

The Gothic church, built in the undecorated style of the Cistercians in 1248, contains in the Coro de los Capillanos, in the centre of the nave, the tomb of Alfonso and Eleanor, with kneeling figures of the king and queen. In the south transept, in which the infantes were buried, is the tomb of Alfonso X's eldest son Fernando de la Cerda. The gilded pulpit could be turned to face either the choir or the nave, which were separated by the rood screen, so that either the nuns or the ordinary faithful, according to circumstances, could hear mass. The transept contains fine Beauvais tapestries.

Sala Capitular

In the chapterhouse, which opens off one of the Romanesque cloisters, are a banner captured from the Moors in the battle of Las Navas de Tolosa (1212) and four Turkish standards taken in the battle of Lepanto (1571), as well as tapestries and various sacred objects.

★ Museo de Ricas Telas

This Museum of Fabrics displays a unique collection of garments and fabrics found in sarcophagi in the church.

Capilla de Santiago

In Alfonso VIII's palace, reached by way of another Romanesque cloister with plant capitals, is the Capilla de Santiago (St James's Chapel), which has a figure of the saint with a movable arm holding a sword. This is said to have been used for the knighting of royal personages, including the future king Edward I of England.

Hospital del Rey

Some 2km/1¼ miles north-west of Las Huelgas is the Hospital del Rey, a hospice for pilgrims travelling on the Way of St James (see entry) founded by Alfonso VIII. It has a fine Plateresque doorway of 1526.

★ Cartuja de Miraflores

Location
4km/2½ miles E of town centre

The Cartuja de Miraflores, situated on a wooded hill to the east of Burgos, was a Carthusian house founded by King John II and intended as a burial place for himself and his wife Isabella of Portugal. After being destroyed by fire in 1452 it was rebuilt by Juan de Colonia and his son Simón. The plain Gothic exterior of the church contrasts with the sumptuous furnishings of the interior, notably the large gilded high altar by Gil de Siloé and Diego de la Cruz and the alabaster tomb of John and Isabella (also by Gil de Siloé), one of the richest of its kind in Spain. In a recess in the north wall is the alabaster tomb of the Infante Alfonso (d. 1468), decorated with luxuriant arabesques. The Capilla de San Bruno has a statue of the saint by Manuel Pereira.

Surroundings of Burgos

Covarrubias

Leave Burgos on N I and turn left into the Soria road (N 234), which runs south-east by way of Cuevas de San Clemente to Hortigüela, where a road branches off on the right to Covarrubias (40km/25 miles from Burgos). This was the capital of a principality which under Fernán González rose to become the kingdom of Castile and played the decisive role in the Reconquista. The fine collegiate church (12th c.) contains a triptych of the Three Kings, probably by Gil de Siloé, and numerous tombs of infantes and abbots, including those of Fernán González and his wife, and Princess Cristina of Norway, daughter of Haakon IV, who married the Infante Felipe in 1258. In the sacristy is the parish museum, with fine sculpture, goldsmith's work and pictures by Metsys, Jan van Eyck, Berruguete, El Greco and Zurbarán. There are remains of the town's old fortifications, notably the massive Torreón de Doña Urraca (10th c.).

★ **Santo Domingo de Silos**

From Covarrubias BU 902 runs south to join BU 903, which leads east to the monastery of Santo Domingo de Silos. The monastery, believed to have been founded in 593 by the Visigothic king Reccared, was destroyed by the Moors but was rebuilt by Santo Domingo, who was abbot from 1047 to 1073. The two-storey cloister has magnificent carved capitals decorated with fabulous beasts, lions, stags, eagles and other birds and rich arabesques. At each corner of the cloister are two reliefs on New Testament themes. The Mudéjar ceiling of the lower cloister has paintings of scenes from medieval life, depicting a variety of musical instruments. In the north gallery is the tomb of Santo Domingo.

Among the principal treasures displayed in the museum are a Romanesque sculpture group, manuscripts, Mozarabic music books, filigree work, including a 12th century chalice, and ivories. The 18th century pharmacy displays a fine collection of drug jars in Talavera faience and the pharmacy library of 387 volumes. The main monastery library has 40,000 volumes.

Museum

At Quintanilla de las Viñas, 36km/22 miles south-east of Burgos, just off N 234, is the Visigothic hermitage church of Santa María de Lara (7th–8th c.), with an unusual triple frieze of bas-reliefs on the outer walls.

Quintanilla de las Viñas

35km/22 miles from Burgos on the Madrid road (N I) is the ancient little town of Lerma (alt. 752m/2467ft), which was founded in the 8th century. The old town with its circuit of walls and collegiate church, situated on a hill above the Río Arlanza, can be seen from a long way off. Lerma owed its prosperity to Philip III's favourite the Duke of Lerma, who embellished it in the 17th century. The old town is entered through a massive gate flanked by two round towers, from which there is a steep climb to the large square on the far side of which is the imposing palace of the Dukes of Lerma, built in 1614 by Fray Alberto de la Madre de Dios. To the left, past the Town Hall, are steps leading up to the wall-walk, from which there are extensive views of the countryside of Castile, with the Río Arlanzón flowing through it. At the western tip of the old town stands the collegiate church (1616), in which can be found the bronze tomb of Bishop Cristóbal de Rojas of Seville.

Lerma

Cáceres

E 5

Province: Cáceres (CC). Telephone dialling code: 927
Altitude: 493m/1618ft. Population: 68,000

The busy commercial town of Cáceres, chief town of Cáceres province in western Spain and the see of a bishop, lies near the Portuguese frontier in a fertile agricultural area. A walk through the old walled town takes visitors back to the Middle Ages.

The town was originally founded in the 1st century A.D., probably on the site of an Iberian settlement, by the Roman consul Caecilius Metellus under the name of Norba Caesarina or Castra Caecilii and became one of the five most important colonies in the province of Lusitania. During the period of Visigothic rule the town was abandoned, but it was rebuilt by the Moors, who called it Quazri. It passed to León in 1227.

History

★★Old Town

The old town of Cáceres (Ciudad or Barrio Monumental) lies on a hill, separated from the modern town by a medieval (originally Moorish) circuit of walls with twelve towers and five gates. It preserves many old aristocratic mansions. They originally had tall towers, but these were demolished on the orders of Isabella the Catholic in 1477.

The starting-point is the Plaza Mayor (Plaza del General Mola), outside the walls. The finest of the towers which can be seen from this point is the Torre

Tour of the old town

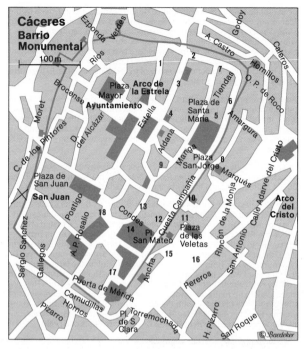

1 Torre de Bujaco
2 Palacio de Toledo Moctezuma
3 Palacio de Mayoralgo
4 Palacio Episcopal
5 Santa María la Mayor
6 Palacio de Carvajal
7 Torre de los Espaderos
8 Palacio de los Golfines de Abajo
9 Casa del Mono
10 San Francisco Javier
11 Casa de las Cigüeñas
12 San Mateo
13 Torre de la Plata
14 Casa del Sol
15 San Pablo
16 Casa de las Veletas
17 Casa del Comendador de Alcuéscar
18 Casa de los Golfines de Arriba

del Bujaco or Torre del Reloj (Clock-Tower), to the left, near the north-east corner of the old town. A remnant of the old Roman walls, it is topped by a statue of Ceres.

To the left of the Torre del Bujaco is the Arco de la Estrella (by Churriguera, 1723), crowned by a statue of the Virgin, through which we enter the picturesque old town. From here Avenida Estrella leads into the Plaza de Santa María, the heart of the old town.

★Plaza de Santa María

Around the Plaza de Santa María are several old noble mansions, including (opposite the church) the Bishop's Palace (Palacio Episcopal; 1567), with a handsome doorway over which is a medallion representing the Old and the New World.

Adjoining the Bishop's Palace is the Palacio de Mayoralgo, with a Gothic façade (16th c.).

Palacio de Toledo Moctezuma

From the north side of the square Calle Canilleros leads to the Palacio de Toledo Moctezuma, at the north-east corner of the walls. This mansion, with a domed tower, was the residence of Juan de Cano Moctezuma, son of a daughter of the Aztec ruler Moctezuma II.

On the east side of the square stands the Late Gothic Cathedral of Santa María la Mayor (16th c.). The Renaissance door of the sacristy was the work of Alonso Torralba (1527). The high altar has a remarkable retablo of 1551.

Facing the apse of the church is the Palacio Carvajal, which is open to the public (fine patio; rooms with 16th–19th c. furniture and pictures). Near here, in Calle de la Tiendas, is the Torre de los Espaderos, with a large projecting gallery from which missiles could be dropped.

Near the cathedral, in Plaza San Jorge, is the Palacio de los Golfines Abajo (late 15th c.), in which the Catholic Monarchs were frequently guests. The façade combines Gothic, Mudéjar and Plateresque elements; the most striking features are the family's coat of arms and the frieze of griffins along the edge of the roof.

A little way south of the palace is the church of San Francisco Javier (18th c.), a large Baroque structure in the Jesuit style. Just beyond this, on the highest point in the town, is the 15th century church of San Mateo, on the site of an earlier mosque. The main doorway, facing the Plaza San Mateo, is in Plateresque style (16th c.). The church has an impressive Baroque retablo and contains a number of fine tombs.

The Calle de la Monja, behind the church, leads to the 15th century Casa del Mono, now occupied by the Museo de Bellas Artes (pictures, costumes, weapons).

Immediately south-east of the Plaza San Mateo is the Plaza de las Veletas, at the north corner of which is the Casa de las Cigüeñas ("House of the Storks"), with a slender battlemented tower in Florentine Renaissance style – the only tower in the town to escape demolition in accordance with Queen Isabella's orders.

Plaza San Jorge, Cáceres

Palacio de los Golfines Abajo

Cádiz

Casa de las
Veletas
(Museo Provincial)

At the opposite corner of the square stands the Casa de las Veletas ("House of the Weather-Vanes"), now occupied by the Provincial Museum. The house was built on the foundations of the old Moorish Alcázar, and still preserves a relic of it in the Aljibe, an 11th century cistern. The museum contains prehistoric and Roman antiquities (particularly notable being a number of decorated stelae), a collection of coins, traditional local costumes and craft products. There is also a collection of pictures, including works by Luca Giordano, Ribera and Esquivel.

From the Plaza San Mateo Calle Ancha, on the left, descends to the Casa del Comendador de Alcuéscar, which has a well preserved defensive tower. Straight ahead is Calle Condes, which leads to the Palacio de los Golfines de Arriba, just inside the town walls. On the way there, immediately north of San Mateo, are two tall tower houses, the Torre de la Plata and the Casa del Sol.

Cádiz   D 9

Province: Cádiz (CA). Telephone dialling code: 956
Altitude: 5m/16ft. Population: 158,000

★Situation

The Andalusian port of Cádiz, chief town of Cádiz province and the see of a bishop, is splendidly situated on a isolated limestone rock rearing out of the sea at the end of a 9km/6 mile long promontory which projects into the Atlantic in the Gulf of Cádiz and is linked to the mainland by a bridge.
Stout walls up to 15m/50ft in height protect the town from the violence of the waves, with tides which have a rise and fall of almost 2m/6½ft (3m/10ft at the spring tides). The tall white flat-roofed houses with their balconies and characteristic little outlook towers (*miradores*), as well as the many parks and gardens with their palms and their extensive sea views, give Cádiz the particular charm which has earned it the name of a *taza de plata,* a "silver bowl" – though it must be said that at first sight the town makes a rather unattractive impression, more particularly since successive wars have left it with few monuments of its great past. Today Cádiz is one of Spain's leading ports, with a considerable shipbuilding industry and oil refineries in the surrounding area. Major contributions are also made to the town's economy by fishing and fish-canning. Rota, on the north side of the bay, is an American air and nuclear submarine base.

History

Cádiz is probably the oldest town on the Iberian peninsula. Founded by the Phoenicians about 11th c. B.C. under the name of Gadir (the "Fortress") as an entrepot for the trade in tin and silver, it was occupied about 500 B.C. by the Carthaginians, who advanced from here into southern Spain. During the Second Punic War the town, now known as Gades, was taken by the Romans, under whom it rose to great prosperity, with the name of Julia Augusta Gaditana, as a port shipping silver, copper and salt. Greek scientists came here to study the movement of the tides, to them a new phenomenon; and the cuisine of Cádiz was also renowned during this period.

During the Middle Ages the town, known to the Arabs as Jeziret Kadis, sank into insignificance. After its conquest by Alfonso the Wise in 1262 it began to be repopulated, and after the discovery of America it became an anchorage for the Spanish silver fleet. Later wars, pirate raids (including Sir Francis Drake's "singeing of the king of Spain's beard") and above all the loss of Spain's American colonies brought a further period of decline.

During the Spanish war of independence Cádiz held out against French attempts to capture it. The Cortes met in the town in 1810, and in 1812 promulgated a constitution, which was withdrawn in 1814 by Ferdinand VII. Eight years later Ferdinand was taken prisoner by patriots in Cádiz, and was freed only after the intervention of French troops on behalf of the Holy Alliance in the "battle of Trocadero".

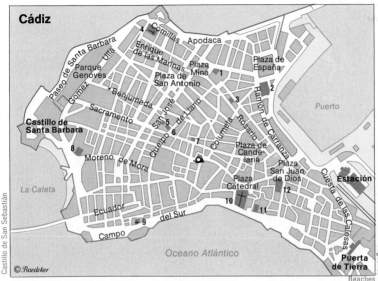

Cádiz

1 Museo Provincial de Bellas
  Artes
2 Diputación Provincial
  (Provincial administration)
3 Santa Cueva

4 Nuestra Señora del
  Carmen
5 San Felipe Neri
6 Museo Histórico
7 Torre del Vigía

8 Hospital de Mora
9 Santa Catalina
10 New Cathedral
11 El Sagrario
12 Ayuntamiento (Town hall)

Sights

The town is reached from the mainland either by the toll bridge (Puente de Peaje) or on the expressway which begins at San Fernando in the old part of the town. Both roads join a main road leading to the Plaza de la Constitución. From here we enter the town through the Puerta de Tierra (1755) and continue north-west by way of the Plaza Santa Elena and along Calle de las Calesas, passing close to the railway station, to the harbour. Immediately on the left is the Plaza San Juan de Dios, an attractive square in which is the handsome Ayuntamiento (Town Hall) of 1816. From here a beautiful palm-shaded boulevard, the Avenida Ramón de Carranza, extends along the harbour to the Diputación Provincial (1773), the offices of the provincial administration.

Harbour area

Ayuntamiento

Beyond this, in the spacious Plaza de España, is a massive monument commemorating the meeting of the Cortes in Cádiz in 1810–12 – Spain's first representative national assembly, which enacted the constitution of 1812.

Plaza de España

To the north of the Plaza de España are two seafront promenades on the Atlantic coast, the Alameda de Apodaca and its westward continuation the Alamada Marqués de Comillas, from which there are very fine views of the north side of the bay. At the end of the Alameda Marqués de Comillas, on the left, is the twin-towered Baroque church of Nuestra Señora del Carmen (1737–64), which has a beautiful inner courtyard and an altarpiece by El Greco. On the north-west side of the rock on which the town stands, close to the sea, is the Parque Genovés, with a theatre (used in summer) and a beautiful palm garden. From the platform of a grotto there is an extensive view. Farther south, beyond the balustrade in front of the Castillo

Seafront promenades

Nuestra Señora del Carmen

Parque Genovés

177

Seafront, Cádiz

de Santa Catalina, is the little bay of La Caleta, with the Playa de la Palma. To the left are the provincial hospital, the Hospital de Mora (1904), and the Hospicio Provincial, an orphanage and poorhouse. On the south side of La Caleta, on a promontory reaching far out into the ocean, are the Castillo de San Sebastián and a lighthouse.

South side of the town

Along the town's southern sea-wall extends a long avenue, the Campo del Sur. A little way along this, on the left, is a former Capuchin convent, now a psychiatric hospital. In the conventual church of Santa Catalina (begun 1639; entrance through courtyard), on the high altar, is Murillo's last work, the "Mystic Marriage of St Catherine". While painting this he fell from the scaffolding and died of his injuries in Seville on April 3rd 1682. The church also has an early work of his.

New Cathedral

Continuing along the Campo del Sur, with views of the towering silhouette of the town, we reach the New Cathedral (Catedral Nueva), the main front of which faces the south side of the Plaza de Pio XII. Building began in 1722 by Vincente de Acero but was not completed until 1838. The interior, with lateral aisles, is 85m/279ft long and 60m/197ft wide, with massive pillars and a magnificent dome over the crossing, 52m/171ft high. The choir has fine 18th c. stalls by Pedro Duque Cornejo; the crypt contains the tombs of various bishops and of the composer Manuel de Falla (1876–1946), a native of Cádiz. There is an interesting museum containing the cathedral treasury, including a silver monstrance 4m/13ft high, the *custodia del millón*, which is said to be set with a million precious stones. There are also a number of valuable pictures, including works by Alonso Cano and Murillo.

El Segrario

Adjoining the cathedral is the church of El Segrario, the Old Cathedral, which was originally built in the 13th c. but after its destruction in 1596 was rebuilt in 1602 in Renaissance style. It contains wall paintings and has a richly decorated high altar by Saavedra (c. 1650).

The centre of Cádiz is an area of narrow streets with a number of handsome squares, including the palm-shaded Plaza de Candelaria, north of the New Cathedral. The Calle del Sacramento cuts diagonally across the old town, and in this street, on the highest point in the town, stands the Torre del Vigía, 34m/112ft high.

A little way south, in the chapel of the Hospital del Carmen de Mujeres, can be seen El Greco's "Ecstasy of St Francis".

North-west of the Torre del Vigía, in Calle Santa Inés, is the chapel of San Felipe Neri, an oval structure built in 1671, in which the Cortes met in 1812; there is a commemorative plaque on the west side of the chapel. On the high altar is an "Immaculate Conception" by Murillo.

On the south side of the chapel is the Municipal Historical Museum. In addition to much material on the period of the Spanish war of independence it contains a number of interesting models, including one of 18th century Cádiz in ivory and mahogany.

Calle San José runs north, passing the Plaza de San Antonio (on the left), to the Plaza de Mina. At the east corner of this square are the buildings of the Museo de Cádiz which is in three sections. On the ground floor is the archaeological section, which displays grave goods from the Phoenician necropolis of Cádiz, including a unique marble sarcophagus of the 5th century B.C., and other Greek, Roman, Visigothic and Arab antiquities. The picture gallery on the first floor has 21 works by Zurbarán, including his "Ecstasy of St Bruno", "Vision of St Francis of Assisi" and "Pentecost". Some of the pictures come from the Cartuja (Charterhouse) of Jerez. Other important artists represented are Murillo ("Ecstasy of St Francis", "Ecce Homo"), Ribera, Rubens ("Holy Family"), Alonso Cano, van Eyck and Rogier van der Weyden. On the top floor is a museum of the Andalusian puppet theatre, with many puppets and a video show of puppet plays.

In Calle Rosario, which runs south-east from the Plaza de Mina, can be found the oval church of Santa Cueva (1783), which has wall paintings by Goya (1795).

Within the city area there are bathing beaches in the bay of La Caleta and, south-east of this, at Playa de Santa María, Playa la Victoria and Playa de Cortadura – though these are less attractive than they were as a result of industrial development and the increasing numbers of high-rise blocks.

Surroundings of Cádiz

The North of the Province

At the mouth of the Río Guadalete, 18km/11 miles north of Cádiz, is El Puerto de Santa María, originally a Greek foundation and later a Roman port (Portus Menesthei). The town retained its importance into the 15th and 16th centuries, when Columbus, Juan de la Costa, one of his helmsmen, and Amerigo Vespucci lived there. Its main sources of income are now fishing and the wine and brandy made in the surrounding area.

The church of Nuestra Señora de los Milagros has preserved its 13th century façade and has a very beautiful Plateresque doorway. It takes its name from its 13th century figure of the Virgin, patroness of the town. The palm-shaded Avenida Aramburu de Mora leads to the Castillo San Marcos, built by the Moors in the 13th century, which later became the seat of the Dukes of Medinaceli. Some of the town's celebrated wine-cellars can be visited.

Beyond the commercial port a marina was recently constructed, with 1800 moorings, making it the second largest in Spain. It is equipped in the most modern style and has numerous quays.

Seaside resorts on the Costa de la Luz	To the west of El Puerto de Santa María, on the Costa de la Luz (see entry), are a number of seaside resorts with beautiful beaches, often fringed by pinewoods. Among them are Fuentebravia, its neighbour Rota, a walled town with the largest American military base in Spain, and Chipiona on Punta Camerón, 2km/1¼ miles south of which is the tile-decorated chapel of the Virgen de la Regla, with an image of the Virgin much revered by seamen. This resort, which is mostly frequented by Spaniards, has a fine square in which stands the attractive church of Nuestra Señora de la O.
Sanlúcar de Barrameda	From Chipiona C 441 runs north-east to Sanlúcar de Barrameda (alt. 30m/100ft). From this town, beautifully situated on the Guadalquivir, Columbus sailed on his third voyage to the New World in 1498 and Magellan set out on his first circumnavigation of the globe in 1519. Sanlúcar is now a fishing port, but its particular fame rests on Manzanilla, the very dry, light sherry which is matured in the bodegas of the lower town (El Bajo).
Nuestra Señora de la O	The 16th century parish church of Nuestra Señora de la O has a richly decorated Mudéjar doorway, a fine Renaissance panelled ceiling and a notable Baroque retablo.
Castillo Santiago	On the highest point in the town is the Castillo Santiago, from which there are wide panoramic views.
Noble mansions	The finest of the town's noble mansions is the palace of the Dukes of Medina Sidonia, which contains the archives of the Medina Sidonia family and has pictures by El Greco, Dürer, Murillo and Goya. The Casa de la Cilla now houses a small wine museum.
★Arcos de la Frontera	From Sanlúcar C 440 runs 24km/15 miles south-east to Jerez de la Frontera (see entry), from which N 342 continues 25km/15 miles east to Arcos de la Frontera (alt. 187m/614ft). The beautiful old town, ranged in a semicircle high above the Río Guadalete, has been declared a national monument. It has a number of fortified mansions and two fine churches. Santa María, in the Plaza de España and San Pedro, situated above a steep drop, which preserves two Arab banners, relics of the days when the town was on the frontier between Christian Spain and the territories still held by the Moors.
Medina Sidonia	36km/22 miles south of Arcos de la Frontera, situated on a hill (300m/985ft), is Medina Sidonia, a Phoenician foundation which later became the seat of the Dukes of Medina Sidonia. Its main features of interest are the Gothic church of Santa María de la Coronada, which has a Plateresque retablo; the Town Hall, with a tiled staircase; the Torre de Doña Blanca in the ruins of the castle; and remains of town walls.
Alcalá de los Gazules	Around Alcalá de los Gazules, 25km/15 miles east of Medina Sidonia, are a number of caves with prehistoric drawings and paintings.

Along the Costa de la Luz to Tarifa

San Fernando	The long straggling port town of San Fernando (alt. 20m/65ft), the chief place in the Isla de León, 18km/11 miles south of Cádiz, was established in the 18th century on a kind of rocky island in the salt marshes from which salt was already being won in Roman times. During the Spanish war of liberation San Fernando was the last refuge of the Cortes. It now has a considerable shipbuilding industry. In the Panteón de los Marinos Ilustres are 52 monuments commemorating famous seamen.
Chiclana de la Frontera	The Puente Zuazo, a bridge which is probably of Roman origin, crosses the salt-pans of Caño de la Carraca, linking San Fernando with Chiclana de la Frontera (alt. 17m/56ft), which with its light-coloured houses and mosque-like church of San Juan Bautista has an almost Moorish aspect. The town is

noted for its sherry and for the manufacture of dolls. On the Canal de Sancti Petri is the popular beach of La Barrosa.

Offshore is the island of Sancti Petri, with the remains of a famous Greek temple of Hercules, thought to have been the successor to a Phoenician temple of Melkart.

Sancti Petri

A short distance south is Conil de la Frontera, with a beautiful beach and a ruined Arab castle, the Torre de Guzmán, built on Roman foundations.

Conil de la Frontera

Picturesquely situated high above the Río Barbates is the old fortified town of Vejer de la Frontera (alt. 218m/715ft), one of the most beautiful of the "white villages" of Andalusia. Six centuries of Arab rule have left their mark on the town, whose charm is enhanced by the large numbers of storks which nest here.

★Vejer de la Frontera

14km/9 miles south-west of Vejer de la Frontera is Cape Trafalgar, known to the Romans as Promontorium Junonis and to the Moors as Tarif al-Ghar ("Cape of the Caves"), off which Nelson won his famous victory over a French and Spanish fleet commanded by Admirals Villeneuve and Gravina on October 21st 1805. Although Nelson was killed in the battle, Villeneuve was also fatally wounded and Gravina was taken prisoner.

Cabo Trafalgar

2km/1¼ miles east of the lighthouse on Cape Trafalgar is the village of Los Caños, with a long sandy beach.

Los Caños

After crossing the Río Barbates the road (N 340) passes through the Sierra del Niño and 50km/31 miles from Vejer de la Frontera reaches Tarifa (alt. 8m/25ft), the most southerly town in Spain. Thanks to the town's strategic situation on the Straits of Gibraltar, its possession was often hotly contested in the course of its history. There was a settlement here in Iberian and Phoenician times, and the town was known to the Romans as Julia Traducta. The Visigoths embarked here in A.D. 429 for the conquest of the Roman province of Africa. Possession of the town was particularly important to the Arabs and it was fortified by Tarif ben Malik. Tarifa is now a fishing port with a considerable foodstuffs industry. Europe's largest wind power station (250 towers 30MW capacity) has been operational here since 1993).

Tarifa

Tarifa's old Moorish castle, the Castillo de Guzmán el Bueno, was built in the 10th century and rebuilt in the 13th. Its name commemorates Alonso Pérez de Guzmán, commandant of the fortress after its capture by Christian forces in 1292. The Moors at once laid siege to the castle and took the commandant's nine-year-old son as a hostage, threatening to murder him unless Guzmán surrendered the castle. Legend has it that Guzmán threw his dagger to the Moors, saying that if they had no other weapon they should use it to kill his son. The niche in the walls where this is supposed to have taken place is still shown to visitors. From the castle there is a a fine view of the Straits of Gibraltar.

Castillo de Guzmán el Bueno

With its favourable wind conditions at this meeting-place of the Atlantic and the Mediterranean, the sea off Tarifa is one of the best wind-surfing areas in Europe.

A surfer's paradise

Tarifa lies just north of the most southerly point on the European mainland, Punta Marroquí or Punta de Tarifa. From here, at the narrowest point on the Straits of Gibraltar, it is possible, in clear weather, to see the African coast and the Moroccan coastal hills, 13.4km/8½ miles away.

★Punta Marroquí

15km/9 miles north-west of Tarifa on N 340 a side road on the left (signposted to Playa de Bolonia) leads to Bolonia, where the remains of the Roman settlement of Belonia Claudia, founded in 171 B.C., were discovered

Bolonia

and excavated by French archaeologists in 1917–22. The town, which remained in existence for 700 years, was surrounded by a 4m/13ft high wall and gained its subsistence from fishing. Excavation has brought to light the forum, with a semicircular fountain and three temples of the 1st century A.D., and remains of baths and a theatre of the same period.

Puerto del Cabrito
★★ View of
Africa

From Tarifa N 340 climbs, with gradients of up to 12%, to the Puerto del Cabrito (340m/1116ft), in the rocky Sierra del Algarrobo. From the pass there is a magnificent view over the straits to Africa.

The road then continues over the Puerto del Bujeo (320m/1050ft) to Algeciras (see entry).

Calatayud   K 3

Province: Zaragoza (Z). Telephone dialling code: 976
Altitude: 522m/1713ft. Population: 18,000

Calatayud, situated in the valley of the Río Jalón 90km/55 miles south-west of Zaragoza, is an old Aragonese frontier town. It takes its name from the Moorish stronghold of Kalat Ayub ("Ayub's Castle"), built in the 8th century near the remains of Roman Bilbilis.
    The Infante Ferdinand, later Ferdinand II, was proclaimed here in 1461 as heir to the throne.

Sights

Moorish quarter

The Moorish quarter, with its narrow winding streets, still retains something of its Moorish character. Above it rear the ruins of the castle built by Ayub, founder of the town.

The Moorish stronghold of Calatayud

The octagonal Mudéjar tower of the church of Santa María la Mayor is a prominent landmark in the old town. It was originally the minaret of a mosque, which was converted into a church after the conquest of the town by Alfonso I in 1120. The church has an alabaster doorway in Plateresque style (1526, by Juan de Talavera and Esteban de Obray). The oldest parts of the church are the chapterhouse and a brick-built cloister walk which dates from Moorish times. The Gothic cloister has 15th century wall paintings.

Santa María
la Mayor

A short distance away is the church of San Andrés, which also has an elegant Mudéjar tower.

San Andrés

In Calle Sancho Gil is the 12th century Templar church of San Sepulcro, once the mother church of the Order in Spain. It was rebuilt in the 17th century but has retained the Gothic cloister of the earlier church.

San Sepulcro

Surroundings of Calatayud

3km/2 miles north-east of the town, on the left bank of the Río Jalón, are the remains of Bilbilis, a Celtiberian foundation which was taken over by the Romans. It was the birthplace of the satirical poet and epigrammatist Martial (A.D. 40–100). Only a few fragments of buildings remain.

Bilbilis

From Calatayud C 202 runs 27km/17 miles south-west to the village of Nuévalos, near which is the Cistercian Monasterio de Piedra, founded in the 12th century and mostly built during the 13th, using the local reddish limestone to fit in with its surroundings. From this period date the keep, the chapterhouse, the refectory and the apse of the old church. Part of the monastery is now a hotel.

**Monasterio
de Piedra**

An unexpected feature of the monastery is the nature park which surrounds it – an area of lush green country in an otherwise barren landscape, watered by the Río Pedra, with grottoes, lakes and waterfalls. The park – the first of its kind in Spain – was laid out in the 19th century by Juan Federico Muntadas. Particularly picturesque is the Cola de Caballo ("Horse's Tail") waterfall, over 50m/165ft high, with the Grotto of Iris concealed behind the veil of water.

★Nature park

Canary Islands

Autonomous Community
Organ of government: Junta de Canarias
Provinces: Las Palmas de Gran Canaria, Santa Cruz de Tenerife
Telephone dialling code for Las Palmas de Gran Canaria: 928
Telephone dialling code for Santa Cruz de Tenerife: 922
Population: 1.5 million.

The description of the Canaries in this guide is abridged, since there are detailed AA/Baedeker guides to Gran Canaria/Fuerteventura/Lanzarote and Tenerife/La Palma/Gomera/Hierro.

The Canary Islands (Islas Canarias) are a group of seven large and six smaller islands in the Atlantic, 100–300km/60–180 miles off the north-west coast of Africa (Morocco, Western Sahara) and around 1100km/680 miles from mainland Spain (Cádiz). They lie between latitude 27°38' and 29°35' north and between longitude 13°20' and 18°14' west. The archipelago extends for some 500km/310 miles from east to west and 200km/125 miles from north to south and has a total land area of around 7550 sq.km/2915 sq.miles.

Situation

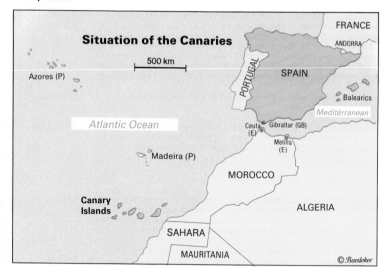

The eastern islands of Gran Canaria (area 1532 sq.km/592 sq.miles), Fuerteventura (1731 sq.km/668 sq.miles), Lanzarote (795 sq.km/307 sq.miles), Graciosa (27 sq.km/10½ sq.miles), Alegranza (10 sq.km/4 sq.miles), Lobos (6 sq.km/2½ sq.miles) and Montaña Clara (1 sq.km/½ sq.mile), together with the reefs of Roque del Oeste and Roque del Este, form the province of Las Palmas de Gran Canaria (chief town Las Palmas). The province of Santa Cruz de Tenerife (chief town Santa Cruz) consists of the western islands of Tenerife (2057 sq.km/794 sq.miles), La Palma (728 sq.km/281 sq.miles), Gomera (378 sq.km/146 sq.miles) and Hierro (277 sq.km/107 sq.miles).

Origin of name

It is not known for certain how the Canaries got their name. The designation "Isla Canaria" appears for the first time on a Spanish chart of 1339. In antiquity the group was known as the Blessed or Fortunate Islands; later the name Canaria was applied by Pliny the Elder (A.D. 23–79) to the island now known as Gran Canaria. Pliny related the name (*canis* = "dog") to the large dogs which lived on the island. There were certainly dogs in the Canaries in Pliny's time, though they were not unusually large. The Romans associated the islands with the kingdom of the dead which lay in the west; and it is possible that this had something to do with the name, for in ancient mythological conceptions the dead were conducted into the underworld by dogs. It has also been suggested that the bird known to the Romans as *canora* (singing bird) may have lived on the islands. Still another possibility is that the name may have come from the cape of Canauria (probably Cape Bojador) on the African coast.

Flora and fauna

The flora of the Canaries is unique in two respects. On the one hand there are found here within a relatively small area species of plants from almost every vegetation zone in the world; on the other there is a strikingly high proportion of endemic species (plants which are found only here). Altogether the flora of the Canaries comprises almost 2000 species, fully 30% of which are endemic.

The fauna shows a much narrower range of species than the flora, though here too endemic species are relatively numerous. There are no large mammals – only rabbits, hedgehogs and bats. It is reassuring for visitors that there are no scorpions or poisonous snakes.

Prominent in the landscape of the Canaries are the extensive banana plantations. Bananas are grown predominantly on the north side of the islands at height of up to 400m/1300ft. At higher levels and on the south side of the islands the main crops are tomatoes and potatoes, together with corn, maize, fruit, vegetables and fodder plants for domestic use. Wine grapes are of lesser importance. Since the Canaries have a relatively low rainfall, agriculture depends on extensive irrigation schemes or on the use of special dry-farming methods.

Stock-farming is of secondary importance. In many areas goats are reared; cattle and sheep farming meets only part of the islands' requirements. Fishing (particularly tunny-fishing) is practised off all the islands.

In general agriculture, once the main means of subsistence, is declining, accounting for barely 10% of the gross domestic product. The production of foodstuffs covers only 25% of local consumption.

Agriculture

Industry contributes about 25% of the gross domestic product. It concentrates mainly on food-processing, but there are also a number of medium-sized woodworking, papermaking and fish-canning plants and factories producing building materials and fertilisers. Craft goods (embroidery, etc.) are produced in small (sometimes very small) establishments.

Industry

Since 1852 the Canaries have been a free trade (duty-free) zone, and this has given a great boost to trade. Shortage of water, raw materials and power, however, put a brake on economic development, and as a result the balance of trade has long been in deficit. Imports, principally from mainland Spain, are increasing.

Commerce

The hotel business may only constitute 15% of the total economic income of the islands but 60% of the gross domestic product is generated either directly or indirectly through tourism. Tenerife alone attracts 2.5 million visitors annually. Despite concern for the environment tourist development continues to expand with the smaller islands also wanting their share of the "tourist cake".

Tourism

The Canaries are believed to have been settled from around 3000 B.C. onwards by at least two waves of incomers. The history of these first inhabitants (often called Guanches, though that name should properly be applied only to the people of Tenerife), living almost totally isolated from the rest of the world, is obscure. There are no written records – apart from some rock inscriptions which have not been deciphered – until the Spanish conquest.

From 1402 onwards Castile made serious attempts to take over the islands, and this process was completed by the conquest of Tenerife in 1496. Those of the original inhabitants who were not sold as slaves gradually became assimilated into the Spanish population.

The economy of the islands began to develop in the 19th century with the establishment of free ports, and from the mid 20th century tourism took possession of the archipelago.

History

There are weekly ferry services by the Spanish company Trasmediterránea from Genoa to Palma de Mallorca, Málaga, Cádiz, Santa Cruz de Tenerife, Las Palmas de Gran Canaria and Arrecife (Lanzarote). The voyage from Genoa to Gran Canaria takes six days. There are regular ferry services between the various islands.

Shipping services

There are frequent scheduled flights by the Spanish national airline Iberia from London Heathrow to Gran Canaria (Las Palmas) and Tenerife (Santa Cruz), usually with an intermediate stop at Madrid or Barcelona, and less frequent services to Lanzarote (Arrecife), with an intermediate stop at Las Palmas. It is also possible to fly from airports around the world to Madrid and get a connecting flight from there. In addition there are numerous charter flights from London and other European cities, usually as part of a package which includes accommodation.

Air services

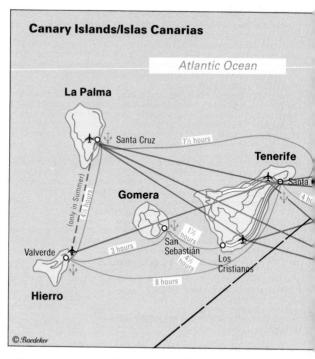

Canary Islands/Islas Canarias

Atlantic Ocean

La Palma

Santa Cruz 7½ hours

Tenerife

Santa

(only in Summer) 4½ hours

Gomera

San Sebastián 1¼ hours

Valverde 3 hours Los Cristianos 4½ hours

8 hours

Hierro

© Baedeker

There are regular scheduled services between the various islands (except Gomera which as yet has no airport, planned for 1995).

Gran Canaria

Area: 1532 sq.km/592 sq.miles. Population: 660,000

Gran Canaria draws larger numbers of holidaymakers than any of the other islands. Although its scenery is less spectacular than that of Tenerife, it has the great attraction of the beautiful sandy beaches in the south of the island and is well equipped with sport and entertainment facilities.

Topography

The centre of Gran Canaria, which is almost exactly circular in form, is occupied by a range of mountains which reach their highest point in the Pozo de las Nieves (1949m/6395ft). This central mountain massif, also known as the Cumbre ("Summit"), divides the island into two very different landscape zones. While the hill slopes in the north are covered with a luxuriant growth of vegetation, the south side, with the exception of a few fertile valleys, is desert-like in character. From the Cumbre deep wedge-shaped valleys *(barrancos)* run down to the coast. The largest of these gorges are on the west and south sides of the island; the barrancos of Agaete, Aldea, Mogán and Fataga are particularly impressive.

On the west side of the island the mountains fall steeply down to the coast; on the north side they merge into an upland region of medium height with a fringe of coastal cliffs. Only at the mouths of the barrancos are there narrow

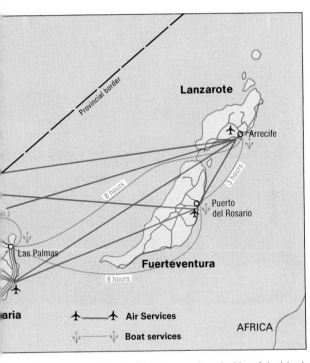

Lanzarote

8 hours

3 hours

Arrecife

Puerto
del Rosario

Las Palmas

8 hours

Fuerteventura

8 hours

aria

✈━━━✈ **Air Services**

⚓━━━⚓ **Boat services**

AFRICA

beaches of sand and stones. On the east and south sides of the island
there are coastal plains bordered by sandy beaches, some of them of
considerable size. The longest and most beautiful sandy beaches are at
Maspalomas/Playa del Inglés.

Las Palmas de Gran Canaria

Province: Las Palmas de Gran Canaria
Altitude: 0–210m/0–690ft. Population: 366,000

Las Palmas de Gran Canaria, chief town of the province of that name and
of the island of Gran Canaria, lies at the north-eastern tip of the island,
extending along the coast for a distance of some 14km/9 miles.

Situation and
characteristics

With its population of 366,000 Las Palmas is by far the largest town in the
Canary archipelago and the eighth largest in the whole of Spain. It has long
been a major centre of industry, commerce and communications, much of
its economic importance being due to its harbour (Puerto de la Luz). Its
favourable situation at the intersection of shipping routes between Europe,
Africa and South America has enabled it to become one of the world's
largest Atlantic ports.

The many thousands of visitors who come to Las Palmas from all over
the world, whether as seamen or as tourists, have given it something of an
international air. It has some 200 hotels; but many foreign visitors prefer to
see the sights of this rather noisy and hectically busy city on a day trip and
spend the rest of their holiday in the south of the island with its more
reliable sunshine.

Las Palmas and the Isleta

Sights

In this section the features of interest in Las Palmas are described from north to south. Although there is a distance of some 5.5km/3½ miles between the Castillo de la Luz, on the harbour, and the Plaza de Santa Ana, it is preferable, given the constant traffic chaos in the city, to tour the town on foot.

Puerto de la Luz

In terms of freight handled (6.9 million tons annually) Puerto de la Luz takes sixth place among Spanish ports, but in terms of shipping movements it does considerably better, with some 14,000 vessels putting in every year.

Castillo de la Luz

On the west side of the harbour is the Castillo de la Luz, built in the 16th century to protect the town from pirate raids.

Playa de las Canteras

The Playa de las Canteras, one of the longest city beaches in the world, extends for some 2.6km/1½ miles to the north-west of Las Palmas. Alongside the beach runs the Paseo de las Canteras, a seafront promenade with innumerable hotels, cafés and restaurants.

Parque Doramas

Farther south, in the Ciudad Jardín (Garden City) district, lies the Parque Doramas. It is planted with typical Canarian flora, including several fine specimens of dragon trees. On the edge of the park is the Pueblo Canario (Canarian Village), established in 1939 as an example of traditional Canarian architecture. In the village is the Museo Néstor, with works by the Canarian painter Néstor Martín Fernández de la Torre (1887–1938), together with furniture and other items from the artist's studio.

Catedral de Santa Ana

In the Vegueta quarter, the oldest part of the town, stands the Cathedral of Santa Ana. Construction began in 1498, but work stopped in 1570, and the main front, in Neo-Classical style, was completed only in the late 18th and

early 19th centuries. The Diocesan Museum of Sacred Art (Museo Diocesano de Arte Sacro) is housed in one of the aisles; among its treasures are statues of saints and a small collection of pictures, including works by 16th century Flemish painters and 17th and 18th century Canarian artists.

Beyond the east end of the Cathedral is the Casa de Colón (House of Columbus). The house, rebuilt in typical Canarian style in 1777, was once the residence of the governor of the island. Columbus is believed to have lived here during a brief stay on Gran Canaria.

Casa de Colón

The Casa de Colón now houses an exhibition on the theme "Columbus and his Times" and a collection of pictures.

South-west of the Cathedral, at Calle Doctor Verneau 2, is the Museo Canario, the finest museum in the archipelago. The most important section of the museum is its collection of pre-Hispanic antiquities. Of particular interest are the mummies, skeletons and skulls of the ancient Canarians and the objects illustrating their culture and way of life.

★Museo Canario

Tours on Gran Canaria

Since the two hotel towns of Playa del Inglés and Maspalomas, now fused into one, form by far the largest tourist centre on the island, the tours suggested in this section all start from there.

Circuit of the Island

From Playa del Inglés the coast road runs west and comes in 17km/11 miles to Puerto Rico, with a small sandy beach which has been artificially built up.

Puerto Rico

The dunes of Maspalomas

Puerto de Mogán	Puerto de Mogán is the most westerly outpost of the great tourist centres in the southern half of Gran Canaria. It is worth having a look at this high-class holiday development, complete with boating marina.
	The coast road ends here, and the route continues north on C 810, running up the fertile Barranco de Mogán. Beyond the little town of Mogán the road turns north-west and then returns to the coast soon after San Nicolás de Tolentino. On this stretch of coast the cliffs fall steeply down to the sea, so that it is necessary to negotiate an endless series of bends before reaching Agaete, 40km/25 miles from San Nicolás de Tolentino.
Barranco de Agaete	This pleasant little town lies near the mouth of the Barranco de Agaete, the most fertile valley on the island. 8km/5 miles up the valley, through luxuriant tropical and subtropical vegetation, is Los Berrazales, formerly a spa.
Puerto de las Nieves	From the centre of Agaete a road leads 1km/¾ mile west to Puerto de las Nieves, from which there is an excellent view of the bizarrely shaped rock known as the Dedo de Deus ("Finger of God"). Here too are numerous fish restaurants where visitors can sample seafood fresh from the sea.
Gáldar	C 810 runs north-east from Agaete and comes in 10km/6 miles to Gáldar, a typical little Canarian town. Its main feature is the Cueva Pintada (Painted Cave), the walls of which are covered with coloured geometric patterns. Nothing comparable has been found in any other cave in the Canaries.
★Cenobio de Valerón	Some 4km/2½ miles beyond Gáldar we leave C 810 and continue on the old winding coast road. A signpost points the way to the Cenobio de Valerón, a complex of 298 caves under a natural basalt arch which is one of the most interesting relics of the ancient Canarians – and one of the most puzzling, since it is not known what function it served.
Arucas	The old coast road pursues its winding course along the slopes of the hill and then, at San Felipe, joins the modern expressway. At Bañaderos a road

goes off on the right to Arucas, with a huge church built of dark-coloured volcanic stone which is visible from a long way off. This Neo-Gothic church of San Juan Bautista was begun in 1909, but the last of its four towers was completed only in the late sixties.

The route continues by way of Tamaraceite and San Lorenzo to the little town of Tafira, near which is the Jardín Canario. In this "Canarian Garden" only plants are grown which are native to the Canaries or the Macaronesian (Middle Atlantic) islands.
    From Tafira the road continues to Marzagán, from which the motorway provides a fast route back to the south of the island.

Tafira/
★Jardín Canario

Interior of the Island

From Playa del Inglés a road signposted to San Bartolomé de Tirajana goes due north. Soon the last houses are left behind and the road enters the mountain world in the centre of the island, with magnificent views of the bizarre and barren landscape. In 24km/15 miles it comes to San Bartolomé de Tirajana, the administrative centre of southern Gran Canaria.

San Bartolomé
de Tirajana

10km/6 miles beyond San Bartolomé de Tirajana, in the village of Ayacata, a road branches off on the right to the Pozo de las Nieves, the island's highest peak, from which, in clear weather, there are fantastic views of the whole of Gran Canaria.

★Pozo de
las Nieves

There are also grandiose views from the main road as it continue towards Tejeda. Particularly imposing is the Roque Nublo ("Cloud Rock"), which is seen on the right soon after Ayacata. This bizarrely shaped rock is a landmark and emblem of the island.

★Roque Nublo

After many curves and sharp bends the road comes, 7km/4½ miles beyond the mountain village of Tejeda, to the Cruz de Tejeda, on the highest point of the pass (1490m/4890ft). Here there is a constant bustle of commercial activity (souvenirs, refreshments, etc.). Nearby is a parador.

Cruz de Tejeda

Just after the Cruz de Tejeda a road goes off on the left to Artenara, in a region of beautiful and still almost entirely unspoiled scenery. In Artenara itself there are cave dwellings and a cave church. Beyond Artenara a narrow road continues to the Pinar de Tamadaba, a beautiful pine forest which offers good walking or, for the less energetic, a place for rest and relaxation. (From the Cruz de Tejeda to the Pinar de Tamadaba and back is something over 50km/30 miles.)

Artenara

From the Cruz de Tejeda the main road continues east to Vega de San Mateo, from which C 814 leads to Valsequillo. This area is particularly beautiful in December and January, when the almond-trees are in blossom. From Valsequillo it is 11km/7 miles to Telde, the second largest town on the island. The church of San Juan Bautista is worth a visit, but otherwise there is little to detain the tourist in this rather noisy little town.

Telde

From Telde C 812 runs south to Ingenio, with the Museo de Piedras y Artesanía Canaria (Museum of Rocks and Canarian Handicrafts), which is mainly a showroom for the sale of Canarian handicrafts. The road then continues via Agüimes to join the motorway at the Vecindario/Arinaga junction, from which it is 20km/12½ miles back to Playa del Inglés.

Ingenio

North of the Island

The quickest way to get to the north of the island from Playa del Inglés is to take the Las Palmas motorway, leave it at the Marzagán exit and continue

Tafira

north-west from there to Tafira Alta. The opportunity of seeing the Jardín Canario, below Tafira Alta, should not be missed (see above, Circuit of the Island).

★Pico de Bandama

From here the route continues west on C 811 and at Monte Coello turns left into a road to the Pico de Bandama. From the viewpoint on the summit of the hill there are fine views into the Caldera de Bandama and northward towards Las Palmas.

La Atalaya

From the foot of the Pico de Bandama a road runs south to La Atalaya, which is included in almost every organised tour of the island. Here pottery is still made in the traditional way without the use of a wheel – though now the ware is mass-produced.

A minor road runs north from La Atalaya to rejoin the main road (C 811) 2km/1¼ miles south on this road is Santa Brigida, an attractive little residential town, and beyond this the next place of any size is Vega de San Mateo, which attracts many visitors, particularly to the cattle market on Sundays.

★Teror

From Vega de San Mateo C 814 goes off on the right to Teror, which many people consider to be the prettiest place on Gran Canaria. The town still has many handsome old houses with elaborately carved balconies.

Firgas

The next place on the route, north of Teror, is Arucas (see above, Circuit of the Island). From here C 814 runs west and then south to Firgas, which has mineral springs. More interesting than the place itself is the vegetation in this region: thanks to the abundance of water there are flowers and greenery everywhere.

Santa María de Guía

From Firgas we return on the same road to Buenlugar and from there take a road which runs west by way of Moya to Santa María de Guía. This was the birthplace of Luján Pérez, the Canarian sculptor whose statues of saints are to be seen in all the major churches in the archipelago. Visitors who have not already seen the Cenobio de Valerón (see Circuit of the Island) can make a detour from here to visit it.

The return route is on the fine new road to Las Palmas. Since there is no bypass it is necessary to drive through the town to reach the motorway to the south.

★Lanzarote

Area: 795 sq.km/307 sq.miles. Population: 54,000

Lanzarote is the most easterly of the Canaries, separated from Africa by 115km/71 miles of sea. Off its northern tip are the three small islands of Graciosa, Montaña Clara and Alegranza.
  Like Gran Canaria, Lanzarote has been invaded in recent years by mass tourism, but it has developed in a rather different way. The holiday settlements are smaller and less brash, and the extraordinary lava landscape with its gleaming white towns exerts a powerful charm.

Topography

The island's greatest length from north to south is 60km/37 miles, from east to west 20km/12½ miles. There is more evidence of volcanic activity on Lanzarote than on the other islands in the Canaries: it has about 300 volcanic cones, varying in height but mostly between 400m/1300ft and 600m/2000ft, which create a kind of lunar landscape in the interior of the island. At the north end of the island the hills fall steeply down to the strait between Lanzarote and Graciosa, El Río; in the south they merge gradually into the coastal plain, El Rubicón.

Sights

The island's capital and port, on the east coast, owes its name *(arrecife =* "reef") to the many small ridges of rock off the coast. Arrecife is not only important as the base of the Canarian deep-sea fisheries: it also has several canning factories and is the centre of the island's commercial life. So far it has remained largely untouched by tourism.

Arrecife

On a tiny offshore island is the Castillo de San Gabriel (1590), which now houses a small historical museum. The Castillo de San José, at the north end of the town, was built in 1779 on the orders of King Charles III; it is now occupied by the Museo Internacional de Arte Contemporáneo (International Museum of Contemporary Art).

The Montañas del Fuego (Mountains of Fire), on the west side of Lanzarote, are the central feature of the Timanfaya National Park (area 5107 hectares/20 sq.miles), which was established in 1974. The road into the mountains ends at the Islote de Hilario, a crater with the highest surface temperatures in the whole region: only a few metres below the surface temperatures up to 400°C/750°F have been recorded.
    The most interesting of the natural phenomena in the park can be seen on the 14km/9 mile long Ruta de los Volcanes (Volcano Route). A convoy of cars, led by a motorcyclist, sets out from the Islote de Hilario several times a day.

★★Parque Nacional de Timanfaya

On the plateau of La Geria visitors can see the methods of dry-farming used on the island, involving the addition of volcanic lapilli and pumice to the soil to hold moisture. El Golfo, on the west coast, is a semicircular crater now filled by a small lake. Teguise, once the chief town of Lanzarote, has some interesting old buildings. Other great tourist attractions are the Cueva de los Verdes, a 6100m/6700yd long cave system, and the Jameos del Agua, a cave with an attractive garden laid out by the local artist and architect César Manrique.

Other sights

Fuerteventura

Area: 1731 sq.km/668 sq.miles. Population: 30,000

Fuerteventura differs from the other islands in possessing many miles of sandy beaches, still almost empty. It is an ideal place for holidaymakers who want to spend as much time as possible on the beach and are content with the facilities for water sports and the entertainments available in the hotels.

Fuerteventura is the largest of the Canary Islands after Tenerife, extending for more than 110km/68 miles from south-west to north-east and measuring 30km/19 miles across at its widest point. The centre of the island is occupied by a plateau averaging 300m/1000ft in height, bounded on its east and west sides by low ranges of hills. The hilly terrain has a barren and almost desolate air, the only variety being provided by the colouring of the rocks, which shimmer in various shades of brown and grey. Few visitors would be attracted to Fuerteventura were it not for the beautiful long sandy beaches in the north and south of the island. The beaches in between are smaller, with black sand.

Topography

The most attractive place on the island is undoubtedly Betancuria, named after Jean de Béthencourt, who founded it in 1405. It has two small museums and a church of some interest.

Sights

The chief town is Puerto del Rosario, which has borne that name only since 1957; before that it was known, more prosaically, as Puerto de Cabras (Goats' Harbour). It has no attractions for tourists, who prefer to stay at

Corralejo in the north of the island or Morro del Jable and Jandia in the south.

★Tenerife

Area: 2057 sq.km/794 sq.miles. Population: 600,000

Tenerife, the highest of all the Atlantic islands, with the Pico de Teide (3718m/12,199ft), is regarded by many as the most beautiful of the Canary Islands. None of the other islands has scenery of such overwhelming grandeur – the bizarre stony desert of the Caldera de las Cañadas, the great expanses of pine forest, the fertile valleys in which bougainvilleas, poinsettias and hibiscus flourish. Its disadvantage is that it has no long sandy beaches. Only in the south of the island are there a few small coves; elsewhere bathers and sunbathers are dependent on beautifully laid out artificial lidos.

Topography

Tenerife, the largest of the Canaries, is shaped like an isosceles triangle pointing north-east, with the Pico de Teide in its centre. Encircling the peak is the Caldera de las Cañadas, a gigantic collapsed crater. To the north-east extends the Cumbre Dorsal, which slopes gradually down from 2200m/7200ft to 1700m/5600ft and then falls sharply to the plateau of La Laguna (550–600m/1800–2000ft). The north-eastern tip of the island is occupied by the rugged Montañas de Anaga.

These ranges of hills divide the island into two totally different landscape zones. While the hill slopes in the north are covered with a luxuriant growth of vegetation the country to the south is desert-like in character.

The hills are broken up by *barrancos* (gorges), which with one exception (the Barranco del Infierno) are no longer traversed by watercourses. In spite of this the lower reaches frequently offer favourable conditions for agriculture. On the flanks of the hills extend a number of wide and fertile valleys like the Valle de la Orotava in the north and the Valle de Güimar in the south.

Santa Cruz de Tenerife

Province: Santa Cruz de Tenerife
Altitude: 0–200m/0–650ft. Population: 210,000

Santa Cruz de Tenerife, chief town of the Spanish province of that name and of the island of Tenerife, lies in a sheltered bay at the foot of the Montañas de Anaga in the north-east of the island. The town owes its economic importance to the steady development of its harbour since the mid 18th century, making it one of Spain's largest ports. Major contributions are also made to the city's economy by an oil refinery, chemical plants, fish-processing and cigar factories.
    Visitors are attracted to Santa Cruz by its excellent shopping facilities, by far the best on the island.

Sights

Plaza de España

The flower-decked Plaza de España, near the harbour, is the hub of the city's life. In the centre of the square rises the Monumento de los Caídos, commemorating the dead of the Spanish Civil War.

Museo
Arqueológico

On the south side of the Plaza de España is the Palacio Insular, a huge complex housing the island administration, the National Tourist Office and the Archaeological Museum (Museo Arqueológico), which has the largest collection of material on the history and culture of the ancient Canarians after the Museo Canario in Las Palmas (Gran Canaria).

North-west of the Plaza de España a former Franciscan friary houses the Municipal Museum of Art (Museo Municipal de Bellas Artes), with a collection which includes works by Dutch and Italian masters as well as pictures and sculpture by contemporary Canarian artists.

Museo Municipal de Bellas Artes

Some 300m/330yd south of the Plaza de España is the city's oldest and most important church, the Iglesia de Nuestra Señora de la Concepción. Originally built in 1502, it was much altered in the 17th and 18th centuries after a fire. It contains valuable Baroque works of art.

Nuestra Señora de la Concepción

Farther south, reached by way of the Puente Serrador, is the city's principal market, the Mercado de Nuestra Señora de Africa. An arched gateway gives access to the central courtyard with its innumerable stalls selling fruit, vegetables, flowers, meat, fish and even live animals.

Mercado de Nuestra Señora de Africa

★★Parque Nacional del Teide

The Pico de Teide (3718m/12,199ft), or Teide for short, and the Caldera de las Cañadas, a gigantic volcanic crater, together form the Parque Nacional del Teide (Teide National Park), which occupies the centre of the island. Established in 1954, it was Spain's third National Park. The whole area of the park (14,500 hectares/33,300 acres) lies above 2000m/6560ft.
 Further information about the park can be obtained at the visitor centre (Centro de Visitantes) at El Portillo.

Almost everywhere on Tenerife the Pico de Teide dominates the horizon, provided always that it is not shrouded in cloud. The north side of Teide falls steeply down to the coast; on the south-western and eastern slopes are two outlying spurs – to the south-west the Pico Viejo (3135m/10,286ft), to the east the Montaña Blanca, so called from its covering of light-coloured lapilli.
 The last volcanic eruption in this area was in 1798. Teide is now in the solfatara stage, with only residual volcanic activity in the form of the sulphurous vapours at a temperature of 86°C/189°F which issue from various vents.
 There are four good roads leading to the cableway station at the foot of Teide. It takes eight minutes to reach the Rambleta, an old crater at a height of 3555m/11,664ft, from which it is a 25 minutes' walk to the summit.
 It is also possible, even for those without mountaineering experience, to ascend Teide on foot from the Montaña Blanca, where a large plan is displayed showing the route to the summit. The climb can be made in one day, but it is possible to spend the night in the Altavista hut.

Teide

The Caldera de las Cañadas has a diameter of 16km/10 miles and a circumference of around 45km/28 miles. It is bounded on the north by Teide and on the east, south and west by high rock walls rising to a height of 500m/1650ft above the plain. Within the crater are great expanses of scoriae, and other masses of scoriae rear up over smaller volcanoes and overlie earlier lava flows. The rocks show a wide range of colouring, from almost black to shades of red. Bizarre rock formations like Los Roques give this grandiose landscape an almost unreal character.

Caldera de las Cañadas

Circuit of the Island

Puerto de la Cruz lies in northern Tenerife, at the mouth of the famous Orotava valley. Within a few decades it has passed through a lightning

Puerto de la Cruz

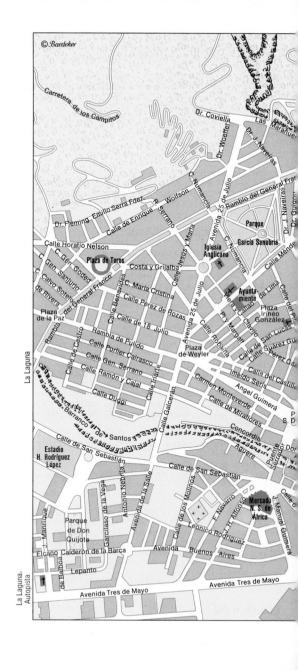

© Baedeker

Carretera de los Campitos

Dr. Coviella

Las Marañue

Dr. Waetter

Dr. J. Naveiras

Dr. Gorgon

Dr. Fleming

Emilio Serra Fdez.

Wolfson

P. Serrano

Calle de Enrique

C. Numancia

Avenida 25 de Julio

Ramblo del General Fran

Parque

Dr. J. Naveiras

Calle Horatio Nelson

García Sanabria

C. Gen. Goded

Calle Jesús y María

Iglesia Anglicana

C. Numancia

Calle Ménde

C. Gen. Sanjurjo

Plaza de Toros

Costa y Grijalba

C. Calvo Sotelo

del General Franco

Ayunta-miento

Calle de Lima

Calle del Pila

de Rivera

C. María Cristina

Méndez Nuñez

Pi y Margall

Claudio

Plaza Irineo González

Plaza de la Paz

Calle Pérez de Rozas

Calle de San Lucas

Rambla

Calle de Castro

Calle de 18 Julio

Avenida 25 de Julio

Calle Robaina

Calle Suárez Gu

Calle Pérez Ga

Rambla de Pulido

Plaza de Weyler

Calle del Castillo

Calle Porlier Cairasco

Calle Gen. Serrano

Calle Triana

Imeldo Seris

Calle Ramón y Cajal

Carmen Monteverde

Angel Guimerá

Calle Duggi

Calle Galcerán

Calle de Miraflores

La Laguna

Barranco de

Santos

Concordia

P. S. D

Calle de San Sebastián

Aguere

P. Dor

Estadio H. Rodríguez López

Calle de San Sebastián

Mercado N. S. de África

Antonio Nebrija

Calle de los Molinos

F. Navarro

F. Afonso

Calle

Manuel Guimerá

J. Manrique

Garcilaso de la Vega

Avenida de la Salle

Parque de Don Quijote

Leonico Rodríguez

Elcano

Calderón de la Barca

de Balboa

Avenida

Buenos Aires

Lepanto

La Laguna, Autopista

Avenida Tres de Mayo

Avenida Tres de Mayo

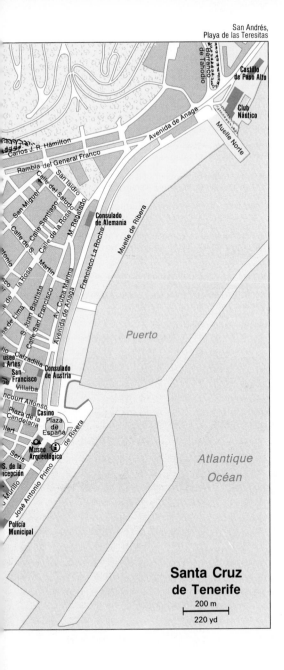

Castillo
de Paso Alto

Club
Náutico

Barranco
de Tahodio

Avenida de Anaga

Muelle Norte

Carlos J. R. Hamilton

Rambla del General Franco

San Isidro

Calle del Saludo

San Miguel

Calle de S

Calle Santiago

Calle de la Rosa

M. Regalado

Consulado
de Alemania

Muelle de Ribera

Francisco La Roche

ntonio

a Rosa

Martín

Juan Bautista

Calle San Francisco

AV. Cuba Marina

Avenida de Anaga

sco

de Lima

S

io

Calzadilla

useo
Artes

San
Francisco

Villalba

Consulado
de Austria

Puerto

ncourt Alfonso

Plaza de la
Candelaria

Casino

Plaza
de
España

de Rivera

llart

Museo
Arqueológico

Seris

S. de la
cepción

Murillo

José Antonio Primo

*Atlantique
Océan*

Policía
Municipal

Santa Cruz
de Tenerife

200 m

220 yd

course of development from a small fishing town into an internationally known tourist resort, the largest on Tenerife.

The main attractions for holidaymakers are undoubtedly the bathing centre designed by the Lanzarote architect and artist César Manrique and the seafront promenade on the Avenida de Colón. The Jardín Botánico has a marvellous display of over 200 species of plants and trees from all over the world in an area of no more than 2.5 hectares/6 acres. In the Loro Parque (Parrot Park) visitors can see more than 200 out of the world's 335 known species of parrots.

★ La Orotava

The road running east from Puerto de la Cruz joins N 820 in 4km/2½ miles, and 1km/¾ mile along this to the west is a side road signposted to La Orotava. One of the most attractive and most typical of Canarian towns, La Orotava enjoys a climatically favoured situation which makes possible a highly productive agriculture. Its central feature is the flower-decked Plaza de la Constitución, from which there is a superb view over the roofs of the town to the coast which has earned the square the name of the "balcony of La Orotava". Some 300m/330yd west of the square is the church of Nuestra Señora de la Concepción (1768–88). With its high dome and two small towers, it is a masterpiece of Baroque architecture, with some Rococo features. A little way south of the church are the Casas de los Balcones, two houses with beautifully decorated balconies of traditional Canarian type.

Icod

From the centre of La Ortava a minor road runs through La Perdoma to Los Realejos, a long straggling little town, at the far end of which, in Realejo Alto, it joins N 820, which continues west, parallel with the coast, to San Juan de la Rambla and Icod. The main sight of Icod, which is included in almost every organised trip around the island, is its famous dragon tree, one of the oldest and finest on Teneriffe.

★★ Dragon tree

3km/2 miles north is the little fishing port of San Marcos, with a beach of black sand.

Dragon tree, Icod

The coast road continues for another 6km/4 miles to Garachico, with its
beautiful old town centre. Its finest building is the Castillo de San Miguel, a
16th century stronghold belonging to the Counts of Gomera which survived a volcanic eruption in 1700 unscathed.

Garachico

From the far end of Garachico a road winds its way up to Tanque and soon
after this joins N 820. For the next part of the route plenty of time must be
allowed, as the road pursues a tortuous course, with innumerable curves
and bends, through the lonely mountain world. The next place of any size is
Santiago del Teide, a good base for walks in the rugged Teno Hills to the
west; the place which attracts most visitors is the hill village of Masca.

Macizo de Teno
(Teno Hills)

5km/3 miles beyond Santiago, at Tamaimo, a road branches off on the right
to Puerto de Santiago, opening up a magnificent view of the imposing cliffs
of Los Gigantes.

Los Gigantes

The coast road continues south, passing through Alcalá and San Juan, and
then turns inland to Adeje, 30km/19 miles from Tamaimo. Immediately
north-east of the town is the canyon-like Barranco del Infierno (Gorge of
Hell), through which a narrow path runs down along a little stream. At the
end of the gorge are cliffs over 1000m/3300ft high, with a waterfall plunging
down from a height of 80m/260ft.

Adeje

From the unspoiled little town of Adeje it is only a short distance on N 822 to
the great tourist centres on the south coast, Playa de las Américas and Los
Cristianos. While Playa de las Américas is a totally new resort, Los Cristianos has grown up around an old fishing village, which has preserved much
of its original character. It has no buildings of particular consequence, but
the pedestrian zone with its shops and restaurants and the square by the
harbour have a character of their own.

Playa de las
Américas,
Los Cristianos

A short way beyond Los Cristianos is the beginning of a four-lane motorway, the Autopista del Sur. 60km/37 miles along this is the exit for Candelaria, with the most important pilgrimage centre in the Canaries, the church
of Nuestra Señora de la Candelaria, which dominates the little town.

Candelaria

From Candelaria it is 18km/11 miles to Santa Cruz, from which the route
continues north-east past the extensive port installations to the fishing
village of San Andrés, with the palm-shaded beach of Las Teresitas. There a
road goes off on the left, signposted to El Bailadero. It winds its way uphill,
with many bends, through scenery which becomes steadily greener, and at
last reaches the crest of the hills and the viewpoint of El Bailadero, 11km/
7 miles from San Andrés. It then continues west along the crest of the
Anaga range and crosses the Bosque de las Mercedes, a dense forest of
laurel-trees, with frequent views of the imposing Montañas de Anaga, the
best all-round view being from the Pico del Inglés mirador. The laurel forest
continues to the village of Las Mercedes.

★Montañas
de Anaga

From Las Mercedes there are two roads to La Laguna, the largest town on
the island after Santa Cruz, with the only university in the Canaries. Often
thought to be the most Spanish town in the islands, La Laguna has preserved its original chequerboard plan, with many handsome burghers'
houses and noble mansions and a number of interesting churches. The
most notable of these are the Cathedral (founded 1515, rebuilt at the
beginning of the 20th century) and the church of Nuestra Señora de la
Concepción, the oldest church in the town.

★La Laguna

★Gomera

Area: 378 sq.km/146 sq.miles. Population: 20,000

Gomera, lying 30km/19 miles west of Tenerife, is the second smallest of the
Canary Islands (after Hierro). It has long been a favourite haunt of devotees

of the "alternative" culture, but many holidaymakers on Tenerife also take a day trip from there to see something of Gomera.

Topography
The island is ringed by bare cliffs up to 900m/2950ft high, with only a few coves and beaches of black sand to vary the scenery. The lush interior of the island is cut by deep gorges *(barrancos)* many of which open up into wider valleys in their lower reaches. Here and in the higher regions of the island, which rises to 1487m/4879ft in Mt Garajonay, are scattered villages and hamlets.

Sights

San Sebastián de la Gomera
The island's chief town and port, San Sebastián de la Gomera, is a place that most visitors merely pass through, partly because there is nothing of outstanding interest in the town itself but also because the bathing facilities are unattractive.

The most important old building in the town is the Torre del Conde, built in Castilian style in 1447 as part of the town's defences. It is now a museum.

Hermigua
The second largest place on the island, Hermigua, is surrounded by terraced banana plantations. Its houses extend down the gorge to the Playa de Hermigua. It has an interesting 16th century monastic church and a small ethnological museum.

Los Organos
This imposing stretch of cliffs, 200m/220yd long and over 80m/260ft high, is made up of large numbers of basalt columns resembling organ-pipes. It can be seen only from the sea.

★ Valle Gran Rey
With its profusion of palms, its large banana plantations and its scatter of little houses, the Valle Gran Rey (Valley of the Great King) has a thoroughly exotic aspect. Many devotees of the alternative society have settled here in recent years.

★ Parque Nacional de Garajonay
Gomera's central massif of hills has been declared a National Park, the Parque Nacional de Garajonay. Here tree heaths and laurels grow, sometimes reaching a height of 20m/65ft. The lichens, up to a metre long, which hang from the trees give the area something of the aspect of a primeval forest.

★La Palma

Area: 728 sq.km/281 sq.miles. Population: 72,000

An international body has designated La Palma as one of the three most beautiful islands in the world, and it is easy to see why. The magnificent scenery and fascinating vegetation make an immediate appeal to all who explore the island, either on foot or by car. And because it lacks any large beaches it has remained largely unspoiled by mass tourism.

Topography
This heart-shaped island has a maximum length from north to south of 47km/29 miles and a maximum breadth from east to west of 30km/19 miles. Hills encircle the island, falling steeply down to the coast, with only a few coves with beaches of black sand to break the line of rugged cliffs. In the centre of La Palma is the Caldera de Taburiente, with the island's highest peak, the Roque de los Muchachos (2426m/7960ft).

Sights

Santa Cruz de la Palma
Santa Cruz de la Palma, the island's chief town, lies on the east coast, on the rim of a volcanic crater, La Caldereta. The life of the town is centred on its

two main streets running parallel to the coast, the Avenida Maritima and Calle O'Daly (or Calle Real), which have preserved a number of old houses with finely decorated wooden balconies alongside imposing modern buildings.

Calle O'Daly runs into the Plaza de España, in which are the Town Hall (16th c.) and a number of 18th century noble mansions. A broad flight of steps leads up to the church of El Salvador (second half of 16th c.), with a beautiful Mudéjar coffered ceiling and Gothic vaulting in the sacristy.

Calle O'Daly and its continuation go north to the Maritime Museum (Museo Naval), housed in a reproduction of the "Santa María", in which Columbus sailed to America in 1492.

The Caldera de Taburiente, in the centre of the island, was declared a National Park in 1954. With a circumference of 28km/17 miles and a maximum diameter of almost 9km/5½ miles, it is one of the largest volcanic craters in the world. There is a magnificent view into the crater from the Cumbrecita viewpoint (1833m/6014ft), which can be reached by car on a narrow asphalted road.

★★ Caldera de Taburiente

Another good viewpoint is the Mirador de Las Chozas, reached from the Cumbrecita on a forest track negotiable by cars.

Puerto Naos, on the west coast, has developed into the island's most popular tourist centre thanks to its beach, the longest on the island (though still only a few hundred metres long). It has some fairly modest tourist facilities, a seafront promenade and a number of restaurants.

Puerto Naos

The most recent volcanic eruption on La Palma occurred at the southern tip of the island in 1971, after a series of preliminary seismic movements, and the masses of ash and lava ejected formed the Volcán de Teneguia (439m/1440ft). It is no longer active, but there are still emissions of vapour from fissures in the valley bottom.

Volcán de Teneguia

Caldera de Taburiente

Hierro

Area: 277 sq.km/107 sq.miles. Population: 6000

Hierro, the most westerly of the Canaries, lies 130km/80 miles from Tenerife. As a holiday place it is still the preserve of a few individualists.

Topography

At first sight Hierro, surrounded by cliffs up to 1000m/3300ft high, with only a few small beaches, looks distinctly inhospitable. The centre of the island is occupied by an upland region with Mt Malpaso (1500m/4920ft) as its highest peak. This area and the lower country on the north side of the island offer the most favourable conditions for settlement and agriculture.

Sights

Valverde

Valverde, the chief place on Hierro, still justifies its name ("Green Valley"), being surrounded by numbers of small fruit orchards, fields of vegetables and flower gardens. It has an 18th century church and two small museums.

★El Golfo

From the Mirador de la Peña there is an extensive view over the bay of El Golfo on the north-west coast. Below the sheer rock faces is a fertile plain.

Puerto Estaca

A few kilometres south-east of Valverde is the island's port, Puerto Estaca. Until the beginning of the 20th century passengers and goods had to be brought to land in small boats: hence the name of the town, from the mooring-pole *(estaca)* to which the fishermen tied the boats. It was only after King Alfonso suffered an involuntary ducking during transhipment in 1906 that it was resolved to build a pier.

On the way to Valverde is an access road to the Parador Nacional El Hierro.

Cartagena   L 7

Province: Murcia (MU). Telephone dialling code: 968
Altitude: sea level. Population: 174,000

Cartagena, one of Spain's most important commercial and naval ports, lies in a deeply indented bay on the Mediterranean which is guarded by two forts, Las Galerias and San Julián, situated on steep rocky promontories.

Minerals were already being mined in the hinterland in Carthaginian times, and iron, tin and lead smelting still makes a major contribution to the town's economy. It also has large shipyards, mainly building naval vessels. At Escombreras, south of Cartagena, are a gigantic oil refinery and, associated with it, a thermal power station.

History

An Iberian settlement on this site named Mastia was captured in 223 B.C. by the Carthaginian leader Hasdrubal, who became the real founder of the town. As Nova Carthago it was for many years the most important Roman establishment on the Iberian peninsula. During the period of Moorish rule it formed the independent emirate of Cartajana, which in 1242 was conquered by Ferdinand III of Castile. The Arabs established Cartagena's fame as a dockyard for the building of warships and greatly improved its agriculture. In 1588 the surviving vessels of the Spanish Armada sought refuge in Cartagena, but were pursued by an English fleet under the command of Sir Francis Drake, who sacked the town. In 1936, at the outset of the Civil War, the Spanish navy, which had declared in favour of the Popular Front government, was unable to prevent Franco's troops from landing in Cartagena, and the town suffered severe destruction.

Sights

Harbour

At the west end of the promenade flanking the harbour is the Monumento de los Heroes de Cavite, which commemorates the dead of the Spanish–

American War of 1898. At the quay just south of this is one of the oldest submarines in the world, the "Peral", built in 1888 by Isaac Peral of Cartagena. North of the monument is the Plaza del Ayuntamiento, with the Town Hall (1907). To the east of this can be seen the ruins of the Cathedral of Santa María la Vieja, which was destroyed during the Civil War.

From the Cathedral a flight of steps leads up to the 11th century Castillo de la Concepción, 70m/230ft above sea level, which is now a public park, the Parque Torres. From here there is a fine view of the harbour and, prominent to the south, the Escombreras refinery.

Castillo de la Concepción

The most interesting museums in Cartagena are all outside the central area. The Museo Naval (Maritime Museum) is in Calle Real, near the Plaza de España. On the far side of the harbour basin, adjoining the Faro (lighthouse) de Navidad, is the Museo Nacional de Arqueológia Submarina (Museum of Underwater Archaeology), which displays antiquities recovered from the sea.

Museums

The most important museum is the Museo Arqueológico Municipal (Archaeological Museum) in Calle Ramón y Cajal, in the north-east of the city. Housed in an old 19th century market hall, it has a collection of Carthaginian, Roman, Visigothic and Arab antiquities, including a Roman copy of a Greek statue of Hermes.

Surroundings of Cartagena

La Unión, 12km/7½ miles east of Cartagena, is the centre of the largest ore-mining area in Europe. The town developed as a result of the increasingly intensive mining activity of the last hundred years or so, and its prosperity during this period is reflected in a number of handsome Art Nouveau buildings.

La Unión

★ Costa Cálida

The 250km/150 mile long Costa Cálida ("Hot Coast") which extends southwest and north-east of Cartagena is frequented in summer by countless thousands of holidaymakers, who come here to enjoy the spacious beaches, most of them relatively quiet, which are interrupted here and there by rocky sections of coast. Along the coast are holiday villages, hotels, bathing beaches and a variety of other tourist facilities – all of which are largely deserted in winter.

The main centre of tourist activities is the Mar Menor ("Little Sea") north-east of Cartagena. This is a large lagoon (area 180 sq.km/70 sq.miles), with water of high salt and iodine content, which is cut off from the sea by a narrow spit of land, La Manga, 22km/14 mile long and between 50m/55yd and 150m/165yd wide, which is traversed by several channels. The water of the lagoon, which has an average depth of 7m/23ft, is so warm that bathing is possible almost all year round. La Manga and the strip of coast on the mainland side of the lagoon are lined with facilities for bathers, hotels and tourist centres. The most important of these on the mainland are San Pedro de Pinatar, San Javier (which is also a military air base), Los Alcázares, Los Urrutias and Los Belones. The last of these has one of the longest and most beautiful 18-hole golf courses in Spain, the Campo de Golf La Manga. The most important tourist resort on La Manga itself is La Manga del Mar, with houses built on piles over the water and high apartment blocks. At the south end of La Manga Cabo de Palos falls steeply down to the sea.

★ Mar Menor

The coast of the Golfo de Mazarrón, to the south of Cartagena, is rather quieter. Here N 332 runs some distance inland, only occasionally coming down to the coast but linked with the coastal resorts by numerous side

Golfo de Mazarrón

roads. After passing through the seaside resort of Puerto de Mazarrón the road comes in 37km/23 miles to the little town of Mazarrón (alt. 99m/325ft), an old mining village with a ruined castle which belonged to the Velez family. It then continues, skirting the Sierra de Almenara, to Aguilas, the most southerly town on the Costa Cálida, with the Castillo de San Juan de las Aguilas looming over it. On the seaward side the town is defended by a stretch of medieval walls with a 12m/40ft high tower built in 1414.

Castellón de la Plana/Castelló de la Plana   M 5

Province: Castellón (CS). Telephone dialling code: 964
Altitude: 28m/92ft. Population: 125,000

The attractive town of Castellón de la Plana (Catalan Castelló de la Plana), chief town of its province, lies in a fertile plain, the Huerta de la Plana, and is a centre of the trade in oranges, large quantities of which are shipped from the port of El Grao de Castellón, to the east of the town on the beautiful Costa del Azahar ("Orange-Blossom Coast").

Castellón was one of the last strongholds of the Republicans in the Spanish Civil War and as a result was largely destroyed, so that it has preserved very few old buildings and presents a predominantly modern aspect.

Sights

Santa María Mayor

The church of Santa María Mayor, which was originally Gothic, was rebuilt after its destruction in 1936. Its free-standing octagonal bell-tower of 1604, El Fadri, 46m/151ft high, is a prominent landmark. It contains a number of pictures by the Castellón-born painter Francisco Ribalta (1551–1628), who is commemorated by a monument on the Paseo de Ribalta.

Ayuntamiento/ Museo Provincial de Bellas Artes

The Ayuntamiento (Town Hall) opposite the church was built about 1700. In the provincial government offices (Diputación Provincial) in Calle Caballeros is the fine Provincial Museum of Art, which has pictures by Ribalta, Ribera and Osona.

★ Costa del Azahar

The southern continuation of the Costa Dorada (see entry) is the Costa del Azahar ("Orange-Blossom Coast"), the beautiful stretch of coast which extends in a wide arc along the shores of the provinces of Castellón and Valencia. The longest and flattest stretch of coast in Spain, it gets its name from the countless lemon- and orange-trees which grow all along the coast. The orange-blossom pervades the whole region with its delicate fragrance, and the mild climate makes this stretch of coast ideal for both summer and winter holidays.

Coast Road to Tarragona

There are a number of roads running north from Castellón – the A 7 motorway, the N 340, which is described here, and a secondary road from El Grao de Castellón which joins N 340.

Benicasim

N 340 leads through orange-groves and plantations of olives, passing the rugged limestone crags of the Peña Golosa (1831m/6009ft), and comes, 21km/13 miles from Castellón, to Benicasim (alt. 15m/50ft), a tourist resort set amid plantations of palms, with a very clean beach. From the Desierto de las Palmas above the town there are extensive views of the coast.

Tourist development, Benicasim

8km/5 miles beyond this is Oropesa del Mar (alt. 33m/108ft), picturesquely situated on a rocky hill crowned by a ruined castle which dates from Moorish times. The Cid took the castle in 1090 but was obliged soon afterwards to give it up. The quiet little town now earns its living from agriculture and tourism. Near the town, on a crag above the sea, is the Torre del Rey, a 15th century watch-tower which now houses a small museum of the sea (objects found along the coast, fishes and other marine fauna).

Oropesa del Mar

N 340 now runs through arable country to Torreblanca, with the seaside resort of Torrenostra, crosses a (usually dry) river-bed, the Rambla de las Cuevas, and comes to Alcalá de Chivert. Just outside the town the ruins of the Castillo de Chivert can be seen on the right in the Sierra de Irta. The town's Baroque parish church has a striking tower which tapers towards the top.

Alcalá de Chivert

12km/7½ miles from Alcalá de Chivert a side road branches off N 340 on the right to Peñiscola (73km/45 miles from Castellón), on a rocky peninsula reaching out into the Mediterranean. The picturesque little town huddles within its stout walls in the shadow of its castle. The Phoenicians and the Greeks, followed later by the Carthaginians, established a stronghold on the promontory, as did the Moors, from whom King Jaime I captured it in 1223. He then handed the castle over to the Knights Templar, who gave it roughly its present form. In 1319 it passed to the Order of Montesa. Its later history is closely bound up with the fate of the Aragonese Cardinal Pedro de Luna, who, as the Antipope Benedict XIII, contested possession of the Holy See with Popes Urban VI and Boniface VII. After losing all support he withdrew in 1415 from Avignon to Peñiscola, where he maintained his claim to be the rightful Pope and held a modest court in the castle. The chapel, library and other apartments used by the Pope, together with the meeting-place of the conclave of cardinals, are among the rooms shown to visitors. Benedict XIII died in the castle in 1424. The treasury of the Baroque parish church in the old town preserves some mementoes of him.

★**Peñiscola**

Castillo

205

Ceuta

<table>
<tr><td>Virgen de
la Ermitana</td><td>Near the castle is the church of the Virgen de la Ermitana, where the Moros y Cristianos dance is performed annually in September – a commemoration of the fighting between Moors and Christians. The church contains an image of the Virgin said to have belonged to the Apostle St James.

The old town of Peñíscola is crowded with visitors in summer; the newer part of the town is a district of hotels and apartment blocks just off the beaches.</td></tr>
<tr><td>Benicarló</td><td>A few kilometres beyond Peñíscola is Benicarló (alt. 11m/36ft), situated amid orange-groves and vineyards. The parish church (1743) has an octagonal tower with an azulejo-clad dome and a magnificent doorway. The 18th century Casa del Marqués de Benicarló now houses a small "kitchen museum" with a variety of old domestic equipment.</td></tr>
<tr><td>Vinaroz</td><td>The road continues through vine-growing country and comes, 75km/47 miles from Castellón, to the fishing port of Vinaroz (alt. 6m/20ft), the last place on the Costa del Azahar, which is famed for its king prawns, freshly caught here and appetisingly served.</td></tr>
</table>

Ceuta F 9

Province: Cádiz (CA). Status: *plaza de soberanía*
Telephone dialling code: 956
Altitude: sea level. Population: 71,000

<table>
<tr><td>Ferry services</td><td>The Trasmediterránea company runs five or six ferries a day between Algeciras and Ceuta; the crossing takes about 45 minutes. From Ceuta there are several ferries a day to Tangier and Melilla, and there are also regular connections with Cádiz, Barcelona and the Canaries. The landing-stage for the ferries is on the Muelle España in the harbour.</td></tr>
<tr><td>Situation</td><td>Ceuta (Arabic Sebta), the African port nearest to Europe, situated at the eastern entrance to the Straits of Gibraltar, is an enclave under Spanish sovereignty *(plaza de soberanía)* on the Moroccan coast, 75km/47 miles east of Tangier and 38km/24 miles north of Tetuan. It has an area of only 19.4 sq.km/7½ sq.miles. Also under Spanish sovereignty is the peninsula of El Hacho, which extends 8km/5 miles north-east into the Mediterranean, flanked by long beaches and terminating in Punta Almina (lighthouse). The old town of Ceuta is built on the isthmus, only 350m/380yd across, leading to the point. The town and the peninsula form part of the Spanish province of Cádiz. There are passport and customs controls on the frontier with Morocco.

Some 85% of the inhabitants are Spanish citizens; only 8% are Muslims.

Ceuta has the air of an Andalusian town and shows very little North African influence. It consists of two parts: the walled old town, with a citadel (17th–18th c.), and the new town, laid out on a regular grid plan, with taller buildings. The development of the new town began only in 1912, when northern Morocco became a Spanish protectorate and Ceuta acquired a hinterland which it had not previously possessed and enjoyed a great economic boom. After Morocco became independent in 1956 the town went into a decline and the population fell from 120,000 to 65,000. In recent years, thanks to the development of tourism and the popularity of excursions from Spain, there has been a slight rise in population.

The port is still of importance as a fishing centre, with fish-processing industries and small shipyards, and a ferry port. In spite of tax concessions and its status as a free port the town has lost much of its industry and has long been overshadowed by Tangier. With its strategic situation, however, Ceuta is still an important military town.</td></tr>
<tr><td>Drugs</td><td>Ceuta is an active market for the hashish produced in the Rif mountains, which is widely offered for sale in the town. Visitors should beware of</td></tr>
</table>

patronising the drug-dealers, since there are severe penalties, both in Spain and Morocco, for the possession of hashish.

Ceuta is likely to have been an important Phoenician settlement, though there are no traces of occupation earlier than the Romans, who called the town Septem Fratres – from which the Arabic name Sebta and the Spanish name Ceuta are derived. The Roman name ("Seven Brothers") came from the seven hills of the Jebel Musa range, on the slopes of which the town was built. Monte Hacho features in Greek and Roman mythology, under the name of Mount Abyla, as one of the Pillars of Hercules. The town was captured by the Vandals in A.D. 429 and held by them until 534, when it was retaken by the East Roman Emperor Justinian. In 618 the Visigoths occupied the town, but were unable to hold on to it. In 711, after heavy fighting, Ceuta was taken by the Arabs, who thereafter beat off repeated Spanish attacks on the town, which became a place of great military importance with the Arab invasion of Spain. Thereafter, until 1415, Ceuta belonged to various Arab kingdoms in Morocco and mainland Spain. From the 12th century onwards Ceuta developed into an important port carrying on a lively trade with Italy, France and Spain. In the 13th and 14th centuries it enjoyed a period of prosperity as a customs station and the largest commercial town and port in Morocco.

History

In 1415 Ceuta was captured by King John I of Portugal, with 50,000 men and 200 ships. As a result of the union of Spain and Portugal in 1580 under Philip II Ceuta became Spanish, and since then it has remained continuously in Spanish hands, in spite of repeated Arab attacks, including a 27-year siege (1674–1701) by the troops of Moulay Ismail; the last attack, also unsuccessful, was in 1860. In the 19th and early 20th centuries it was a Spanish penal colony with a sinister reputation. From 1912 onwards it was developed to become the principal port in the Spanish protectorate of northern Morocco and enjoyed a great economic boom. The Spanish war against the Kabyles of the Rif mountains was largely directed from Ceuta, and it was here that Franco made plans for his seizure of power in 1936.

Sights

The central feature of Ceuta is the palm-shaded Plaza de Africa. Around the square are the town's most important and finest buildings, which replaced earlier Moorish buildings in the 18th century.

Plaza de Africa

The church of Nuestra Señora de Africa, with its slender tower, was built between 1704 and 1726 on the site of a mosque. The interior is in Spanish Baroque style. The most notable features are the high altar, with a 16th century statue of the Virgin, patroness of the town, which is probably of Portuguese origin, and the church treasury, in a side room.

Nuestra Señora de Africa

At the south end of the square is the twin-towered Cathedral (1729), with a Neo-Classical façade and a black marble doorway. This occupies the site of the former Great Mosque, which was converted to Christian use in 1432. The interior has wall paintings of New Testament scenes. In the nave, under handsome grave slabs, are the tombs of bishops of Ceuta.

Cathedral

Also in the Plaza de Africa is the Palacio Municipal (Town Hall) of 1929, with murals by Mariano Bertuchi, a noted painter of the colonial period.

Palacio Municipal

A little way west of the Plaza de Africa are the remains of the fortress of El Canderlo, built by the Portuguese in 1530 and strengthened in the 17th and 18th centuries: a reminder of the time when Ceuta was a hotly contested garrison town. The remains consist of a massive stretch of wall and two bastions. The deep moat of San Felipe on the west side of the wall, which protected the town on the landward side at the narrowest point of the peninsula, dates from the same period.

El Canderlo

Ceuta

Plaza de África, Ceuta

Ferry port

From El Canderlo a road goes off on the right to the Muelle España and, to the left of this, the Muelle Cañonero Dato, the quays used by the ferries.

Museo Municipal de Arqueológia

In the Jardines de la República Argentina, above the harbour to the left, is the small Archaeological Museum, with pottery, weapons and other objects of the Neolithic, Carthaginian and Roman periods. In other cases are objects of European and Arab/Berber origin from medieval and modern times. Under the museum is the entrance to a 2.5km/1½ miles long system of underground passages *(galerías subterráneas)* of the 16th and 17th centuries designed to secure military control of the ground in front of the town and the water supply.

Museo de la Legión

In the Paseo de Colón, south-east of the Plaza de Africa, is another small museum, the Museo de la Legión, which was founded by General Millán Astray in 1920. It is devoted to the history of the Spanish Foreign Legion, which maintains a garrison in Ceuta.

Monte Hacho

An attractive trip from Ceuta is to Monte Hacho (194m/637ft), 4km/2½ miles away. From the summit of the hill, on which are the Ermita de San Antonio (1593) and an old fort, there are extensive views from the town and harbour, the Moroccan coast and, in clear weather, Gibraltar (see entry). Monte Hacho is probably the legendary Mount Abyla, in Greek and Roman mythology one of the Pillars of Hercules which marked the end of the known world. Its counterpart in Europe is the Rock of Gibraltar.

Monte Hacho is reached by taking the coast road (the Recinto Sur) which runs east along the south side of the peninsula. This leads to the lighthouse on Punta Almina, from which there are magnificent views of Gibraltar to the north and the Rif mountains to the south-east.

El Desnarigado

Soon after this a road goes off on the right to the summit of Monte Hacho, crowned by the fortress of El Desnarigado. This now houses a Military

Museum, with five rooms of objects illustrating the history of Spanish forces in Ceuta.

Beyond this is the Ermita de San Antonio, where there is a lively fiesta in honour of the saint on June 13th, with folk dancing and other traditional events.

Ermita de San Antonio

Ciudad Real   H 6

Province: Ciudad Real (CR). Telephone dialling code: 926
Altitude: 632m/2074ft. Population: 51,000

Ciudad Real, the "Royal City", lies between the rivers Guadiana and Jaba-lón in a fertile region which produces the wines of Valdepeñas. It preserves few remains from its glorious and warlike past. Now chief town of its province, it lies in the centre of La Mancha, the home of Don Quixote, the "knight of the rueful countenance".

In 1252 Alfonso X, the Wise, established the fortress of Villareal on the site of the town of Alarcos, which had been destroyed by the Moors, in order to assert his authority against the over-mighty power of the Order of Cala-trava and the Knights Templar in this frontier region facing Moorish terri-tory. In 1420, during the reign of John II, the place was chartered as a town and given its present name.

History

Sights

The 14th century Puerta de Toledo is the only relic of the town's once mighty walls. The gate, in Mudéjar style. flanked by two square towers, is now a national monument.

Puerta de Toledo

The massive Gothic Cathedral (1531) is dedicated to the Virgen del Prado, whose image shows her seated on a silver throne. Notable features of the church are the 12th century west doorway, the retablo by Giraldo de Merlo (1616) and a painting by Eugenio Caxés, "The Beheading of St John the Baptist", in the sacristy. From the tower (17th c.) there are extensive views.

Santa María del Prado

Another church of high artistic quality is San Pedro (14th–15th c.), with Gothic and Mudéjar doorways. In the Capilla del Sagrario in the south aisle can be seen the fine alabaster tomb of the Coca family.

San Pedro

Surroundings of Ciudad Real

The old Ermita de Alarcos, 8km/5 miles west of Ciudad Real, was built to commemorate the battle of Alarcos, probably fought in this area, in which Alfonso VIII's army was defeated by the Moorish cavalry in 1195.

Ermita de Alarcos

In the Footsteps of Don Quixote and Sancho Panza

The area around Ciudad Real is the setting of many of the adventures and misadventures of Don Quixote described in Cervantes' great novel. Here we suggest a route taking in some of the places associated with the Knight of the Rueful Countenance.

From Ciudad Real N 420 runs north-east to Daimiel, near which Don Quix-ote encountered the Yanguesian goatherds. The town has a beautiful Plaza Mayor and the remains of an Arab stronghold. To the north lies the Tablas de Damiel National Park (See Practical Information, National Parks).

Daimiel

Ciudad Real

Alcázar de San Juan

N 420 continues to Puerto Lápice, where the innkeeper dubbed Don Quixote a knight, and Alcázar de San Juan (alt. 643m/2110ft), a little town on the railway from Madrid with an important collection of Roman mosaics in the Museo Arqueológico Fray Juan Cobo, the 13th century church of Santa María, a Railway Museum and a number of the windmills so characteristic of La Mancha.

Campo de Criptana/Sierra de Molinos

8km/5 miles beyond this is Campo de Criptana, an attractive village which could have been the scene of Don Quixote's fight with the windmills. In the surrounding hills, the Sierra de Molinos, there are more than 30 windmills, several of them still working. Some of them (e.g. El Quimera and El Pilón) contain small museums.

El Toboso

From N 420, just beyond Campo de Criptana, a minor road runs 15km/9 miles north-east to the charming village of El Toboso, where Don Quixote found his mistress Dulcinea, a peasant's daughter. Visitors are shown her supposed home at the entrance to the village. The Town Hall has a collection of handsome editions of Cervantes' novel in many languages.

Mota del Cuervo

A minor road runs north-east from El Toboso to join N 301. A few kilometres along this road to the right is Mota del Cuervo, a typical La Mancha village in which Sancho Panza's crony Ricote el Monisco lived.

Tomelloso

From Mota del Cuervo N 420 leads south-west to Pedro Muñoz, from which a secondary road continues south to Tomelloso, an important La Mancha wine-producing centre. The 16th century parish church has a retablo of the Virgen de la Paz.

Argamasilla de Alba

Beyond Tomelloso is Argamasilla de Alba, where Cervantes was held prisoner in the Cueva de Medrano and began his famous novel. It is also supposed to be the village in which Don Quixote was born and to which he

Corral de Comedias, Almagro

returned to die. It has a windmill known as the Molino Dulcinea. 12km/
7½ miles south-east of the village is the Castillo de Peñarroya, a Moorish
stronghold which was taken by Alonso Pérez de Sanabria in 1198.

The return to Ciudad Real is by way of Manzanares (alt. 645m/2115ft), an   Manzanares
attractive little town on the Río Azuer which grew up around the castle of
Peñas Borras, built after the battle of Las Navas de Tolosa in 1212.

To the Lagunas de Ruidera

Almagro is situated 24km/15 miles from Ciudad Real in the middle of the   **Almagro**
Campo de Calatrava. Almagro was the headquarters of the Calatrava order.

The fine long Plaza Mayor is flanked by houses with arcaded passages and   Plaza Mayor
rows of balconies.

The most interesting building in the main square is the 16th century Corral   ★Corral de
de Comedias, the picturesque theatre-courtyard with red wooden galleries   Comedias
where the first Spanish comedies were presented.
· Many other interesting sights of Almagro are the former University of
Santo Domingo and the Dominican Monastery of La Asunción.

Ciudad Rodrigo   E 4

Province: Salamanca (SA). Telephone dialling code: 923
Altitude: 623m/2044ft. Population: 15,000

South-west of Salamanca, finely situated high above the Río Agueda, here
spanned by a bridge built on Roman foundations, is Ciudad Rodrigo, one of
the most interesting towns in the province of Salamanca, with charming
late medieval buildings. The whole town is protected as a national monument. Originally the Roman settlement of Mirobriga Vettorum, it was re-
founded in the 12th century by Count Rodrigo González Girón. As a border
fortress on the frontier with Portugal it saw much fighting down the centuries. In 1812 the Duke of Wellington captured it from the French and
thereafter was granted the title of Duke of Ciudad Rodrigo. Pigs and fighting bulls are now bred in the surrounding area.

Sights

The circuit of walls round the town is more than 2km/1¼ miles long and up   Town walls
to 13m/43ft high. The walls were originally built in the 12th century, but
were renovated and rebuilt down to the 18th century.

In the elongated Plaza Mayor are the Ayuntamiento (Town Hall), an impos-   Plaza Mayor
ing 16th century building flanked by round towers bearing coats of arms,
with a two-storey arcaded patio, and a number of handsome houses,
including the Palacio de los Cueto on the north side, which has a frieze of
relief decoration.

From the north-west corner of the Plaza Mayor it is a short distance to the   Capilla de
quiet and secluded Plazuela del Buen Alcalde, in the centre of which is a   Cerralbo
fountain. On the west side of the square is the Capilla de Cerralbo
(16th–17th c.), in Herreran style.

The Cathedral of Santa María was begun in the mid 12th century and much   Cathedral
altered in the 16th. It is entered through two richly decorated doorways.
Notable features of the interior are the beautiful choir-stalls by Rodrigo
Alemán (1498); the high altar by Gil de Hontañón, with a painting by

Cloister of the Cathedral, Ciudad Rodrigo

Fernando Gallego; and the altar in the north transept, with an alabaster Descent from the Cross. The cloister (13th–14th c.) contains a number of interesting tombs and has capitals depicting the Fall.

Palacio de los Castro

To the east of the Cathedral stands the Palacio de los Castro, with a Plateresque façade, and diagonally opposite it is the Palacio de Moctezuma. From here a narrow lane leads back to the Plazuela del Buen Alcalde.

Alcázar

Built against the walls on the south side of the town, above the river, is the Alcázar of Ciudad Rodrigo, the Castillo de Enrique II de Trastamara (14th–15th c.), which is now a parador. From the castle there is a view of the old bridge over the Río Agueda.

Coca

G 4

Province: Segovia (SG). Telephone dialling code: 911
Altitude: 790m/2592ft. Population: 2000

The little town of Coca lies amid extensive pine forests at the junction of the Río Eresma and Río Voltoya. It was originally a settlement of an Iberian tribe, the Vaccaei, and was known to the Romans as Cauca. It was the birthplace in A.D. 347 of Theodosius I, who became East Roman Emperor in 379 and in 394 reunited the Empire and made Christianity the state religion. In its magnificent Castillo de Fonseca the town has a unique example of a castle in Mudéjar style.

★ ★ Castillo de Fonseca

The castle, on a square plan, was erected by Moorish builders in the 15th century for Bishop Alfonso Fonseca. It is built entirely of brick, the material characteristic of the Mudéjar style, laid in decorative patterns. A bridge

Castillo de Fonseca, Coca

over the moat leads through the imposing main gateway, the Arco de la Villa, just inside the first defensive wall. At the corners of the walls, round which visitors can walk on the top, are massive polygonal towers, which in turn have defensive turrets. Between the battlements and through the countless cruciform loopholes there are views down into the moat far below. The central structure of the castle, which also has tall polygonal corner towers and round towers along the sides, is dominated by the keep to the right of the main gate, a massive square tower with battlemented turrets at the corners and two smaller turrets on the sides. To the right of the keep is the entrance to the castle courtyard. The castle is now occupied by an agricultural college.

The only feature of interest in the little town of Coca itself is the principal church, dedicated to Santa María, which has four handsome Gothic tombs belonging to members of the Fonseca family.

Santa María

Córdoba

G 7

Province: Córdoba (CO). Telephone dialling code: 95
Altitude: 119m/390ft. Population: 283,000

Córdoba, chief town of its province and the most important city in Andalusia after Seville, lies at the foot of the Sierra de Córdoba, an outlier of the Sierra Morena, in a plain which slopes gently down to the Río Guadalquivir.

Narrow winding streets, small squares and low whitewashed houses, most of them with beautiful patios which can be admired from the street, give the town a Moorish atmosphere inherited from its past. It is still a kind of western European Mecca, with the famous Great Mosque, now the Cathedral, which in spite of later alterations ranks with the Alhambra in Granada

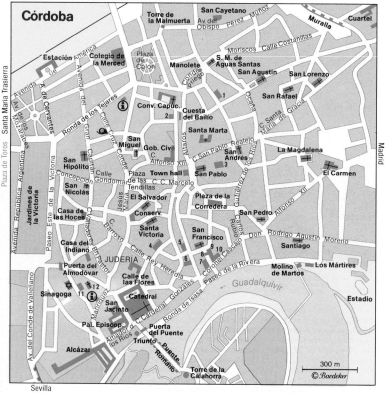

Sierra de Córdoba

Córdoba

[Map labels:] Torre de la Malmuerta, San Cayetano, Av. del Obispo, Pérez, Muñoz, Muralla, Cuartel, Estación, Colegio de la Merced, Plaza de Colón, Moriscos, Calle Costanillas, América, Manolete, Córdoba Otero, S. M. de Aguas Santas, San Agustín, San Lorenzo, Avenida del Gran, A. de Cervantes, Avenida de los Mozárabes, Ronda de los Tejares, Conv. Capuc., Calle Cruz Conde, Cuesta del Bailío, Santa Marta, Orcha, San Rafael, C. Santa María de Gracia, San Miguel, Gob. Civil, Alfaros, C. San Pablo, Realejo, San Andrés, La Magdalena, San Hipólito, C. Alfonso XIII, San Pablo, Gutiérrez de los Ríos, El Carmen, Calle Concepción, Calle Gondoma, Plaza de las Tendillas, C. C. Marcelo, San Nicolás, Jesús María, El Salvador, Plaza de la Corredera, San Pedro, Alfonso XII, Casa de las Hoces, Conserv., Carlos Rubio, Don Rodrigo Agustín Moreno, Casa del Indiano, Valladares En Pastor, Barroso, Santa Victoria, San Francisco, Santiago, Puerta del Almodóvar, Calle Rey Heredia, Coronel Cascajo, Paseo de la Rivera, Molino de Martos, Los Mártires, JUDERIA, Calle de las Flores, Sinagoga, Maimónides, Catedral, Don Gonzáles, Guadalquivir, Estadio, San Jacinto, Ronda de Isasa, Pal. Episcop., Amador de los Ríos, C. Cardenal Gonzáles, Alcázar, Av. del Conde de Vallellano, Triunfo, Puerta del Puente, Puente Romano, Torre de la Calahorra, Sevilla, Santa María Trasierra, Plaza de Toros, Madrid

300 m

© Baedeker

1 Palacio de los Marqueses de Viana
2 Casa de Fernández de Córdoba
3 Casa de los Villalones
4 Museo Provincial Arqueológico
5 Arco del Portillo
6 Casa de los Marqueses del Carpio
7 Posada del Potro
8 Fuente del Potro
9 Museo Provincial de Bellas Artes
10 Museo Julio Romero de Torres
11 Museo de Toros
12 San Bartolomé

as one of the two most splendid examples of Islamic art and architecture in western Europe.

Córdoba is also famed for its silverware and its leather goods. Around the old town has grown up a modern Córdoba, with metalworking plants, factories producing electrical goods and foodstuff industries. The surrounding country is still given up to agriculture.

History

Already a place of some consequence in Iberian times, Córdoba became chief town of the Roman province of Hispania Ulterior in 152 B.C. Under the Empire it alternated with Hispalis (Seville) and Italica (north of Savile) as capital of the province of Baetica. In Visigothic times it became the see of a bishop, but remained a place of no great importance. After the decisive defeat of the Visigoths by the Moors in 711, however, the town enjoyed a new period of prosperity under Arab rule, particularly from 756 under the Umayyad ruler Abderrahman I after his expulsion from Damascus. As capital of an independent Spanish caliphate under the rule of Abderrahman II and III, Al-Hakam II and Almansor, Vizier to Hisham II, Córdoba developed into one of the most brilliant cities in Europe and a centre of learning which attracted students from all over the western world and promoted active exchanges between Christian, Muslim and Jewish scholars.

With the fall of the Caliphate in 1031 the city's decline began. It fell successively under the control of Seville (1078), the Almoravids (1091) and the Almohads (1148); but after its capture by the Christians in 1236 the formerly flourishing city fell into oblivion. The magnificent buildings erected during the Moorish period fell into disrepair, the irrigation system was neglected, and the once fertile Campiña became an almost barren steppe. Commerce and industry collapsed, and it was three hundred years after the Christian reconquest before trade began to revive with the resumption of the production of leather wall-hangings.

Córdoba was the birthplace of many famous men, among them the Roman orator M. Annaeus Seneca (54 B.C.–A.D. 39), his son L. Annaeus Seneca (4 B.C.–A.D. 65) and his grandson the poet Lucan (A.D. 39–65); the Arab scholar Averroes (Ibn Rushd, 1126–98), translator and interpreter of Aristotle, Rabbi Moses Maimonides (1135–1204), the painter Bartolomé Bermejo (c. 1430–after 1496) and the poet Luis de Góngora (1561–1627).

★★La Mezquita-Catedral (Mosque-Cathedral)

The city's outstanding monument is the Cathedral, formerly the principal mosque of western Islam and still known as the Mezquita, one of the largest mosques in the world and the finest achievement of Moorish architecture in Spain, comparable in beauty and size with the great mosques of Mecca and Damascus, the El-Azhar Mosque in Cairo and the Blue Mosque in Istanbul.

Opening times
daily
10.30am–1.30pm
and 4–7pm,
in winter
3.30–5.30pm

The site on which the mosque stands was originally occupied by a Visigothic church, which the Moors used after the conquest as a mosque, though at first leaving part of it to the Christians. This part was acquired by Abderrahman I, and the building of the present mosque began in 785, with eleven aisles open to what is now the Court of Orange-Trees and the mihrab (prayer niche indicating the direction of Mecca) at the end of the central aisle, which was larger than the others. Building material from Roman and Visigothic buildings was used in the construction. During the reign of Abderrahman II, between about 830 and 850, the aisles were increased in length; in 951 Abderrahman III built the minaret (which has been altered since his time); and Al-Hakam II enlarged the mosque still further to its present length of 179m/587ft. In the course of this extension the unique "third mihrab" and the maqsura (enclosure for the Caliph) were added. Finally Almansor increased the width of the mosque, bringing it to its present dimensions, by building on eight additional aisles along the whole length of the structure, so that the prayer hall now has no fewer than nineteen aisles.

After the return of the Christians the mosques underwent little change for many years: Alfonso X replaced the mihrab of the second building phase by the Capilla Villaviciosa, and that was all. During the reign of Charles V, however, one of the most drastic changes in the mosque was carried out. In 1523 the decision was taken to build a large cathedral within the Muslim prayer hall. The city council of Córdoba recognised the danger and threatened death for anyone who sought to destroy the Moorish buildings; but on Charles V's orders the rebuilding went ahead under the direction of an architect named Hernán Ruiz. When, some years later, Charles came to Córdoba to inspect the work he is said to have remarked to the canons of the cathedral: "If I had known what you gentlemen had in mind I should not have permitted it; for what you have built can be seen everywhere, but what you have destroyed had not its like in the world."

Córdoba, seen from the left bank of the Guadalquivir

The building of the Cathedral was for all practical purposes completed by 1599, and about that time work began on the alteration of the minaret.

The Mosque
Exterior

The whole building is surrounded by a battlemented outer wall between 9 and 20m (30 and 65ft) in height, with countless tower-like buttresses. The principal entrance, on the north side, is the Puerta del Perdón (1377), in Mudéjar style. Adjoining it, forming the first stage of the minaret, is the 60m/200ft high Campanario (Bell-Tower) or Torre de Alminar, which was given its present form, showing the influence of the Herreran style, in 1593. It is now topped by a statue of the Archangel Michael, patron saint of the town.

★ Patio de
los Naranjos

The Puerta del Perdón leads into the picturesque Patio de los Naranjos (Court of Orange-Trees), planted with orange-trees and palms, where the ablutions prescribed by Islamic law were performed.

★★ Prayer hall

From here the Mudéjar-style Puerta de las Palmas (1531) gives access to the interior of the Mezquita–Catedral, the prayer hall of the mosque. This magnificently impressive hall, only 11.5m/38ft high, is seen in the semi-darkness as an apparently endless forest of columns, in vistas changing at every step. There is an astonishing impression of space. Altogether there are 856 marble, jasper and porphyry columns, linked longitudinally by red and white horseshoe arches. Some of the columns were taken from ancient buildings and Christian churches. At the Puerta de las Palmas and between the mihrabs (prayer niches), which mark the direction of Mecca, some of the colourful and richly carved roof structure of the mosque has been exposed.

★★ Mihrab Nuevo

The Mihrab Nuevo (the New or Third Mihrab), in which the Koran lay open, is an incomparable masterpiece of Islamic architecture and ornament.

Roofed with a high dome hewn from a single block of marble, it is covered with a great profusion of decoration in the form of floral and geometric patterns and verses from the Koran in Arabic script.

In front of the mihrab is a railing which separates the vestibule of the mihrab and the maqsura (the Caliph's prayer room) from the rest of the mosque. Here too there is a profusion of ornament and a great variety of arch forms demonstrating the skill of the Muslim craftsmen. The fine mosaics were a gift from the Byzantine Emperor.

Maqsura

To the left of the mihrab is the Sala Capitular (chapterhouse), which contains the cathedral treasury, including a silver monstrance by Enrique de Arfe (1517) and nine fine statues of saints by Alonso Cano.

Sala Capitular

The Capilla Villaviciosa, opposite the mihrab, was the first Christian chapel to be built in the Moorish mosque. It is notable for its fine columns and vaulting.

Capilla Villaviciosa

Adjoining the Capilla Villaviciosa is the Capilla Real, a masterpiece of Mudéjar architecture which was the burial chapel of Ferdinand IV and Alfonso XI of Castile.

Capilla Real

In the heart of the mosque, and built transversely across it, is the Cathedral, consisting of a Gothic choir with the Capilla Mayor. It was built between 1563 and 1599 and involved the destruction of 63 columns. The richly carved choir-stalls (18th c.) were the work of Pedro Cornejo. Over the red marble high altar (1618) is a painting by Palomino. There are two fine pulpits of mahogany and marble.

Cathedral

Around the Mezquita–Catedral

Diagonally opposite the Puerta de las Palmas, to the right, is a narrow street, off which there opens, again on the right, the picturesque Calleja de

Calleja de las Flores

Mezquita–Catedral de Córdoba

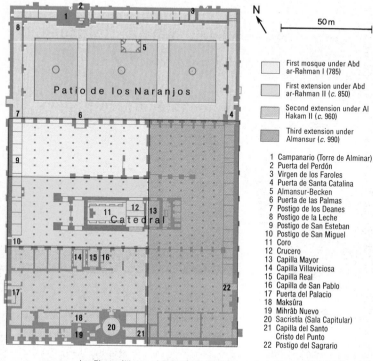

	First mosque under Abd ar-Rahman I (785)
	First extension under Abd ar-Rahman II (c. 850)
	Second extension under Al Hakam II (c. 960)
	Third extension under Almansur (c. 990)

1 Campanario (Torre de Alminar)
2 Puerta del Perdón
3 Virgen de los Faroles
4 Puerta de Santa Catalina
5 Almansur-Becken
6 Puerta de las Palmas
7 Postigo de los Deanes
8 Postigo de la Leche
9 Postigo de San Esteban
10 Postigo de San Miguel
11 Coro
12 Crucero
13 Capilla Mayor
14 Capilla Villaviciosa
15 Capilla Real
16 Capilla de San Pablo
17 Puerta del Palacio
18 Maksûra
19 Mihrâb Nuevo
20 Sacristía (Sala Capitular)
21 Capilla del Santo Cristo del Punto
22 Postigo del Sagrario

las Flores ("Lane of Flowers"), which owes its name to the profusion of flowers decking the white walls of the houses.

Museo Arqueológico

North-west of the Mezquita–Catedral, in Plaza Don Jerónimo Paez, is the Archaeological Museum, with Iberian objects, including sculptures of lions and a relief depicting a stag-hunt from Almodóvar del Río, Roman and Early Christian antiquities and a large collection of Moorish art, including a bronze stag of the 10th century and finds from Medina Azahara (see below).

Palacio Episcopal

Opposite the south-west corner of the Cathedral stands the Bishop's Palace, built in the 15th century on the ruins of the Caliph's palace and rebuilt in 1745.

Triunfo de San Rafael

South of the Bishop's Palace is the Triunfo de San Rafael, a tall column erected in 1765 bearing a statue of the Archangel Raphael.

★Puente Romano

Beside the Triunfo rises the Puerta del Puente, a Doric triumphal arch (16th c.) at the end of the 16-arched Puente Romano over the Río Guadalquivir. The bridge was originally built after Caesar's victory over Pompey, and a Moorish bridge, 223m/244yd long was later built on its foundations.

The forest of columns in the Mezquita ▶

Córdoba

Torre de la
Calahorra

At the south end of the bridge is the massive Torre de Calahorra, built in 1369, which now houses a modern museum on the history of the city. From this side of the bridge there is a magnificent view upstream of the city, rising above the right bank of the Guadalquivir, and downstream of a number of dilapidated old Moorish watermills.

★ Alcázar

Returning across the bridge, we turn left and come to the Alcázar de los Reyes Cristianos. Some parts of the massive walls and towers date from Moorish times, but most of them were built when Alfonso XI strengthened the fortress in the 14th century. It contains a number of very fine Roman mosaics. Around the Alcázar, within the walls, are beautiful gardens, with ornamental pools and fountains, which are illuminated on summer evenings. In front of the main building is a square called the Camposanto de los Mártires, said to have been the place of execution of Christian martyrs.

★ Judería

On the north side of the Camposanto lies the Judería, the old Jewish quarter. With its narrow lanes, its whitewashed houses and patios gay with flowers and its cosy little squares, it has a very distinctive atmosphere of its own.

Museo Taurino

In Plaza de las Bulas is the Casa Zoco, a 16th century house now occupied by the Museo Taurino (Bullfighting Museum), which has two sections devoted to the crafts of leatherwork and silversmithing in addition to the main section on bullfighting, which includes displays of bullfighting equipment and mementos of famous Córdoba-born toreros such as Lagartijo, Machaco, Guerrita, Manolete and El Córdobes.

Synagogue

To the north of the Bullfighting Museum is the Synagogue (1315), one of the oldest surviving synagogues in Spain.

Puerta de
Almodóvar

Farther north is the Puerta de Almodóvar, a well preserved Moorish gate at the entrance to the old Ghetto.

Around the Plaza de las Tendillas

In the centre of the town is the Plaza de las Tendillas, with an equestrian statue of the "Gran Capitán", Gonzalo Fernández de Córdoba (1453–1515), a native of the town who conquered the kingdom of Naples for the Crown of Aragon.

Avenida del
Gran Capitán

From the Plaza de las Tendillas Calle Conde de Gondómar runs west into the Avenida del Gran Capitán, lined with theatres, restaurants, hotels and cafés, which is a popular promenade, particularly on summer evenings.

San Nicolás

Opposite the end of the street stands the fortress-like 15th century church of San Nicolás, with an elegant octagonal tower, which has a valuable treasury.

San Hipólito

Farther north is the collegiate church of San Hipólito, built by Alfonso XI in 1340 and rebuilt in 1729. Flanking the high altar are the modern tombs of Ferdinand IV and Alfonso XI, who were originally buried in the Cathedral's Capilla Real.

Around the Plaza del Potro

Plaza del Potro

North-west of the Cathedral, near the river, is the Plaza del Potro, which gets its name from a fountain with a small figure of a colt *(potro)*. In the square can be seen an old inn, the Mesón del Potro, in which Cervantes once stayed.

Opposite the inn is the entrance to the Provincial Museum of Art, housed in the former Hospital de la Caridad. It has pictures by Spanish masters, including Ribera, Murillo and Goya, and numerous works by the Córdoba-born painter Antonio del Castillo y Saavedra (1616–68). | Museo Provincial de Bellas Artes

Adjoining the Museum of Art is the Museo Julio Romero de Torres, with a large collection of paintings by the artist of that name (1874–1930), who was the son of the director of the Museum of Art; they are mainly portraits of women. | Museo Julio Romero de Torres

To the east of the Plaza del Potro are the churches of San Pedro (13th c.), with Moorish apses and two doorways from the original church, and Santiago, which dates from the time of the Reconquista, with a tower which was originally the minaret of a mosque. | San Pedro, Santiago

North-Eastern Córdoba

On the way from the Plaza del Potro to the north-east of the city lies the Plaza de la Corredera, a square surrounded by arcaded houses in which bullfights used to be held. | Plaza de la Corredera

North of the Plaza de la Corredera, to the left of the Town Hall, are the remains of a large Roman temple of the 1st century A.D. | Templo Romano

In Calle San Pablo is the church of San Pablo (1241), with beautiful Mudéjar and Arab decoration in the interior and some fine sculpture. | San Pablo

Calle San Pablo, with a handsome Renaissance palace, the Casa de los Villalones, runs north-east to the Plaza San Andrés, from which Calle Enrique Redel leads north to the Palacio de los Marqueses de Viana, a princely residence with fourteen beautiful patios which now houses a collection of leatherwork, fine furniture and an exhibition on falconry. | Palacio de los Marqueses de Viana

North-east of Plaza San Andrés is the Romanesque and Gothic church of San Lorenzo, with a beautiful rose window and a tower of 1555. | San Lorenzo

Surroundings of Córdoba

★Medina Azahara

10km/6 miles west of Córdoba, reached by way of C 431 and a secondary road which in 8km/5 miles goes off on the right, stands Medina Azahara, a palace-town built by Abderrahman III from 936 onwards and named after his favourite wife Zahara which is said to have been large enough to house 30,000 people. In 1010 it was destroyed by the Almoravids and thereafter used as a quarry of building material; as a result it is now largely in ruins.

The palace, situated on a hill, was surrounded by terraced gardens. Some impression of its splendour can be gained from the partly rebuilt Palace of Abd ar-Rahman with its arched columns and its walls covered with reliefs, as well as the town-gate facing Córdoba. Finds from Medina Azahara can be seen in the site museum and in the Archaeological Museum in Córdoba. | Palace of Abd ar-Rahman

A short distance away above the Moorish town can be found the ruins of the monastery of San Jerónimo, situated at the foot of the Sierra de Córdoba. Built in 1408 the monastery was often visited by Isabella the Catholic. In 1492, after the Moors had been driven out of Granada (see entry) she left captured standards to the monastery for safe keeping. | San Jerónimo

In Medina Azahara

Almodóvar
del Río

15km/9 miles beyond this on C 431 we come to Almodóvar del Río, in the valley of the Guadalquivir, with an imposing castle on a hill above the town. The castle is reached by driving around the town and climbing a steep footpath.

Las Ermitas

From the Plaza de Colón, at the north-east end of the Ronda de los Tejares, the Carretera del Brillante runs north to the slopes of the Sierra de Córdoba (7km/4½ miles) and Las Ermitas. This is a group of hermitages belonging to the Congregation of the Brethren of Our Lady of Bethlehem. From the mirador below the 18th c. church there is a fine panorama.

Santa María
de Trassierra

On the north-western slopes of the Sierra is the church of Santa María de Trassierra, built in the period of the Reconquista on the site of an earlier mosque in the grounds of the ruined castle.

La Coruña/A Coruña   C 1

Province: La Coruña. Telephone dialling code: 981
Altitude: sea level. Population: 240,000

The port of La Coruña (Galician A Coruña), traditionally known in English as Corunna, lies in the north-western corner of Spain on a peninsula in the bay formed by the rías of El Ferrol, Ares, Betanzos and La Coruña. It is the largest city in Galicia, an important international port, capital of its province, a garrison town and a fishing port, with large fish-canning plants. The numerous glazed galleries *(miradores)* on the house-fronts have earned it the name of the *ciudad de cristal* ("city of crystal"). Although the first impression of La Coruña is of a not particularly attractive port and industrial town, there are many romantic nooks and corners in the hilly old part of the town.

La Coruña, originally an Iberian settlement, was used by the Romans as a port, under the name of Ardobirum Coronium; an imposing relic of the Roman period is the lighthouse known as the Torre de Hércules. It was occupied by the Moors, captured from them by the Portuguese and then taken from the Portuguese by Spain. In 1588 the "Invincible Armada", with 130 vessels and 29,000 men, sailed from here for the invasion of England

History

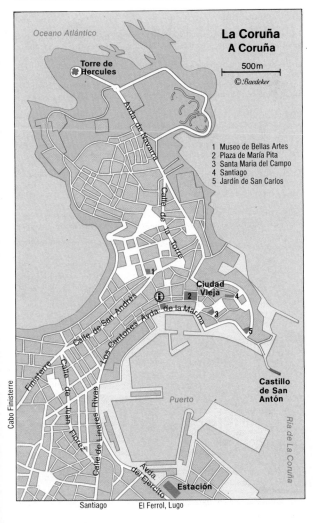

1 Museo de Bellas Artes
2 Plaza de María Pita
3 Santa Maria del Campo
4 Santiago
5 Jardín de San Carlos

but lost half its ships and half its men as a result of severe storms and English counter-attacks and returned defeated to La Coruña. In 1589 an English fleet commanded by Sir Francis Drake appeared in the bay and attacked the town; the attack was beaten off thanks to the courage of a local heroine named María Pita, but the town suffered much destruction.

During the Napoleonic wars, in 1809, a British and Spanish army under the command of Sir John Moore was defeated in a battle at Elviña, just outside the town, in which Moore was killed. During the fight for a liberal constitution at the beginning of the 19th century La Coruña was always on the side of the liberal forces.

The New Town (La Pescadería)

Avenida de la Marina

The multi-lane motorway which leads to the city centre runs through unattractive industrial districts and suburbs and into the Paseo de los Cantones and its continuation the Avenida de la Marina, the busiest streets on the new town, which grew out of a fishing village (La Pescadería) on the peninsula. The miradores of the houses in the Avenida de la Marina are among the finest in the city. Between these two streets and the harbour are the Jardines de Méndez Núñez, in which are a number of monuments.

Palacio Municipal

Off the Avenida de la Marina to the left lies the spacious Plaza de María Pita or Plaza Mayor, on the north side of which is the large Palacio Municipal (Town Hall). In addition to the municipal administration this also houses a gallery of contemporary pictures, a watch and clock museum and the archives of the Real Academia Gallega (Royal Galician Academy).

Museo de Bellas Artes

To the west of the Town Hall is the church of San Nicolás, which has an image of the Virgen de las Coruñenses, the Virgin of the Women of La Coruña. From here it is a short distance north to the Museum of Art in the

Glazed house fronts in the Avenida de la Marina, La Coruña

Plaza del Pintor Sotomayor, which has a fine collection of pictures, including works by Goya, Velázquez, Ribera, Murillo, Morales, Brueghel and Rubens, as well as ceramics, coins and exhibits illustrating the history of the city.

In a pavilion in the Parque de Santa Margarita, south-east of the city centre, is the Casa de las Ciencias (House of Science), which was opened in 1985. This is a museum designed to introduce visitors in popular fashion to physical laws and scientific knowledge. Thus much space is given up on the ground floor to personal computers, on which visitors can play or can be initiated into the mysteries of programming. On the first floor the dominant theme is physics, and here visitors can experience on their own bodies the force of gravity, centrifugal force and other natural laws. The second floor is used for special exhibitions, while on the third floor, in addition to a collection of stuffed animals, there are stereo-microscopes which visitors can use.

Casa de las Ciencias

Old Town (Ciudad Vieja)

The old town with its narrow and irregular streets lies on a spur of the promontory above the harbour, to the east of Plaza de María Pita. Its central feature is the Plaza de Azcárraga (Plaza de la Harina). To the south of this square, in the Plaza del General Franco, is the Capitanía General (1748).

From the Plaza de Azcárraga can be seen the apses of the church of Santiago (St James), the oldest church in the town (12th–13th c.), with fine doorways. Notable features of the interior are the stone pulpit and a figure of Santiago Matamoros (St James the Moor-Slayer).

Santiago

North of the Plaza de Azcárraga, on the highest point in the old town, is the church of Santa María del Campo (13th–15th c.), with a 14th century tower. It has beautiful doorways decorated with sculpture, the finest of them being the main doorway, with the Adoration of the Kings, and a large rose window. In the square in front of the church is a Gothic prayer column.

Santa María del Campo

South-east of Santa María by way of the quiet and picturesque Plazuela de Santa Bárbara, with the convent of Santa Bárbara, we come to the Baroque church of Santo Domingo, which has a number of fine chapels and a Churrigueresque altar. Nearby, in Calle de Herrerías, is the house of La Coruña's 16th century heroine María de la Pita, marked by a commemorative tablet.

Santo Domingo

A little way downhill, beyond the Casa de la Cultura, is the Jardín de San Carlos, laid out in 1834 on the site of an old defensive work. From here there is a good view over the harbour. In the gardens is the tomb of Sir John Moore.

Jardín de San Carlos

At the tip of the breakwater sheltering the harbour stands the Castillo San Antón, a massive 16th century fort which now contains the Museo Arqueológico (Archaeological Museum), with antiquities mostly from the surrounding area.

Castillo San Antón

*Torre de Hércules

On a crag 2km/1¼ miles north of the town is the Torre de Hércules, the oldest lighthouse in the world which is still operating; it is reached on a well signposted road skirting the old town (or by the bus labelled Torre de Hércules). It was built by the Romans in the 2nd century A.D., as a tablet at the foot of the tower records. There was originally an external spiral staircase to the top. The tower was rebuilt in its present form in the 18th century.

Both from the tower and from the tip of the promontory there are magnificent panoramic views of the sea, the city, the Ría de la Coruña and the bathing beaches of Playa Riazor and Playa del Orzán to the west.

Surroundings of La Coruña

⋆ Rías Altas

The Rías Altas (Upper Rías) are the fjord-like inlets cutting deep into the land to the north and north-east of La Coruña. The principal ones are the rías of La Coruña, Betanzos (see entry), Ares, El Ferrol, Cedeira and Ortigueira. Strictly speaking, the stretch of coast between Viveiro and Ribadeo in Lugo province is also part of the Rías Altas; it is described in the entry for Lugo (Surroundings).

Puentedeume/Pontedeume

From La Coruña N VI leads south-east to Betanzos and then turns north for El Ferrol. 21km/13 miles from Betanzos is Puentedeume (Galician Pontedeume), a fishing town and port on the Ría de Ares, once the seat of the powerful princely family of Andrade, of whose 14th century castle there survives only a single tower. The name of the town comes from the bridge which was built over the Río Eume in the 14th century. The 16th century church of Santiago contains the tomb of Count Fernando de Andrade.

Convento de Caaveiro

A detour can be made from Puentedeume on a secondary road along the Río Eume to the overgrown ruins of the monastery of Caaveiro, which was founded in the 10th century.

Monasterio de Monfero

Another possible excursion from Puentedeume is to the large derelict monastery of Monfero, south-east of the town (22km/14 miles) on LC 152. Originally founded in the 12th century, the monastery was rebuilt in the 17th. The façade of the impressively large church is decorated in a chequerboard pattern. It contains tombs of the Andrade and Moscoso families. There is a 16th century cloister.

El Ferrol

From Pontedeume the road continues north, passing the seaside resort of Cabañas, to El Ferrol, an industrial town noted particularly for its shipyards and Spain's principal naval base on the Atlantic. Around the commercial harbour is the old town with its narrow winding streets; the new town, laid out on a regular plan, is a typical example of the town planning of the 18th century, when Ferdinand VI and Charles III developed the town as a naval base and built massive fortifications and the Arsenal on the seaward side. El Ferrol was the birthplace of General Franco, and until a few years ago bore the honorific style of El Ferrol del Caudillo. The entrance to the harbour is defended by forts on either side of the river mouth a few kilometres from the town.

Cedeira

From El Ferrol a beautiful road (C 646) runs north-east to Cedeira, on the Ría de Cedeira, which has beautiful sandy beaches.

Sierra de la Capelada

A rather difficult road, with magnificent cliff scenery, leads round the Sierra de la Capelada, on a peninsula north-east of Cedeira, to Ortigueira, passing the pilgrimage chapel of San Andrés de Teixido.

Ortigueira

The easier route to Ortigueira is on a road which cuts across the peninsula to join C 642. Ortigueira is a little fishing town, magnificently situated on the Ría de Ortigueira, with beautiful beaches. Here a Celtic musical festival is held annually at the end of July, with musicians and visitors from Scotland, Ireland and Wales as well as Galicia and with the Galician bagpipes, the *gaita*, among the instruments used.

Punta de la Estaca de Bares

From Ortigueira it is 25km/16 miles to the Punta de la Estaca de Bares, the most northerly point in Spain, on which is a lighthouse.

★Costa de la Muerte/Costa da Morte

The stretch of coast extending south from La Coruña to Cabo Finisterre is known as the Costa de la Muerte (Galician Costa da Morte; the "Coast of Death") because so many ships have been wrecked on this rugged coast. The attractions of this area, for visitors who are not discouraged by the prospect of rain, are its grandiose, austere scenery, its long lonely beaches and its sleepy little fishing villages.

From La Coruña C 522 goes south-west to Carballo, from which a detour can be made to the beautifully situated little port of Malpica de Bergantiños, with a long sandy beach.

Malpica de Bergantiños

Camariñas, a little town in a sheltered bay which has long been renowned for its pillow lace *(enjaces)*, can be reached from Malpica de Bergantiños on a very beautiful coast road or from Carballo by way of Baio.

Camariñas

Farther south is the port of Corcubión, from which it is 12km/7½ miles south-west to Cabo Finisterre (Galician Fisterra), the most westerly point on the Spanish mainland. From this rugged granite promontory (light-house) there are magnificent views of the open Atlantic.

★Cabo Finisterre/ Cabo Fisterra

Costa Blanca

L–N 6–8

Provinces: Valencia (V), Alicante (A), Murcia (MU), Almería (AL)

The Costa Blanca ("White Coast") extends south from Setla on the promontory of La Almadraba, at the end of the Costa del Azahar, to the Cabo de Gata, taking in the coastal regions of the provinces of Alicante and Murcia and part of the coast of Almería. It is mainly flat and sandy, with numerous beaches. Thanks to its excellent climate it attracts visitors in winter as well as in summer.

Sights and Routes

See Alicante, Benidorm, Cartagena, Denia and Gandía

Costa Brava

P/Q 3

Province: Gerona (GE)

The description of the Costa Brava in this guide is abridged, since there is a full description in the AA/Baedeker guide "Costa Brava/Costa Dorada/Barcelona".

The most northerly stretch of the Spanish Mediterranean coast, the Costa Brava ("Wild Coast"), is one of the most popular holiday areas in Spain, favoured particularly by visitors from northern Europe because of its accessibility. Its reputation has suffered in recent years from the enormous development of hotels and tourist facilities which has ruined much of the coast and made the Costa Brava the very epitome of mass tourism.

★★The "Wild Coast"

Away from the main tourist centres, however, the Costa Brava still offers visitors magnificent scenery, great works of art and good bathing. The much indented coast is rocky for most of the way, and on the cliff-fringed promontories cannot usually be reached by car and is sometimes accessible only by boat. Between the promontories there are picturesque fishing villages and little towns with sandy beaches. Visitors who prefer to avoid the long drive along the coast road with its many bends can see the most beautiful places on the Costa Brava by following N II and the A 7 motorway (E 15), from which there are roads (usually of good quality) leading down to the coast.

Along the Costa Brava

Col de Balitres

Visitors entering Spain from France should take N 114 from Perpignan. This runs via Argelès-sur-Mer to the French frontier town of Cerbère, 49km/ 30 miles from Perpignan, from which the road winds its way up to the Col de Balitres (173m/568ft), on the frontier, with beautiful views of the coast.

Port-Bou/Portbou

Beyond the frontier another winding road (C 252) runs down to Port-Bou (Catalan Portbou; alt. 15m/50ft), a fishing port and the Spanish frontier town. It has an important railway station, since in view of the broader gauge of the Spanish railway system passengers must usually change trains here or wait while their carriages are adjusted to the Spanish gauge.

Colera

The road continues high above the cliff-fringed coast with its offshore islands to Colera, which lies below the road and has a stony beach.

Llansá/Llançà

Beyond this is Llansá (Catalan Llançà), a little walled town, off the road to the right, with the Baroque church of San Vicente (Catalan Sant Vinceç) and a 15th century defensive tower. There is a small beach by the harbour.

★San Pedro de Roda/Sant Pere de Rodes

From Llansá the coast road continues, with extensive views, to Puerto de la Selva (Catalan El Port de la Selva), charmingly situated at the foot of the Sierra de Roda. In the hills is the old Benedictine abbey of San Pedro de Roda (Catalan Sant Pere de Rodes), with a church going back to the 8th century; the Romanesque barrel vaulting is believed to be the oldest of the kind. The capitals have finely carved animals' heads and interlace ornament. Above the abbey is the Castillo de San Salvador, from which there are fine views. Puerto de la Selva has a seawater swimming pool and a boating marina.

★Cadaqués

At the next road junction the road on the left leads to Cadaqués (alt. 20m/65ft), a picturesque little town which in the early years of the 20th century drew many artists, including Max Ernst, Paul Eluard, André Breton and Salvador Dalí, who lived in nearby Port Lligat. The parish church (rebuilt in the 17th century) has a fine Baroque altar of 1727. The Museo Perrot-Moore has pictures of the 15th–17th centuries and works of the Modernist school.

The curving bay, flanked by rugged cliffs, offers only limited scope for bathing.

Cabo de Creus/ Cap de Creus

To the north of the Port Lligat promontory (accessible only by boat or on foot) the 80m/260ft high Cabo Creus (Catalan Cap de Creus), known to the Greeks as Cape Aphrodision, projects into the sea. It is the most easterly point on the Iberian peninsula.

Rosas/Roses

Returning from Cadaqués to the road junction, we turn left and in another 12km/7½ miles turn left again into the road to Rosas (Catalan Roses), originally founded by the Greeks under the name of Rhode. At the west end of the town, within the walls of a former citadel, are the remains of a church belonging to an early Christian cemetery. North-west of the town is the Aqua Brava water park, with several swimming pools, restaurants and seven water chutes.

Castelló de Ampurias/ Castelló d'Empúries

From Rosas C 260 runs round the Bahía de Rosas to Castelló de Ampurias (Catalan Castelló d'Empúries), an old market town with the church of Santa María (13th–15th c.), which has a fine doorway and a Gothic alabaster retablo.

Cadaqués

On the coast to the south-east of Castelló de Ampurias is the planned holiday settlement of Ampuriabrava (Catalan Empúria Brava), a well designed complex of holiday houses and apartments laid out round an artificial network of canals.

Ampuriabrava/
Empúria Brava

From Castelló de Ampurias a secondary road runs south by way of San Pedro Pescador (Catalan Sant Pere Pescador) and the archaeological site of Ampurias (Catalan Empúries: see entry) to the old fishing port of La Escala (Catalan L'Escala), attractively situated above the sea on a small promontory in the Golfo de Rosas. It is now a popular family holiday resort, with a beach of sand and pebbles.

La Escala/
L'Escala

From La Escala the road turns inland and runs south to join a secondary road coming from Gerona (see entry). This road runs via Ullá to Torroella de Montgrí (alt. 30m/100ft), situated on the Río Ter, a river with an abundant flow of water, amid wild coastal scenery. It has a fine Gothic church (15th c.) and a Renaissance mansion, the Palacio Solterra (Catalan Palau Solterra), which is now occupied by an art gallery. Above the town to the north-east, on Montgrí, is the 14th century Castillo de Torroella.

Torroella
de Montgrí

On the coast to the east is the not particularly beautiful resort of Estartit (Catalan L'Estartit), which is part of the commune of Torroella. From here there are boat trips to the Islas Medas (Catalan Islas Medes), a nature reserve with good diving grounds.

Estartit/
L'Estartit

From Torroella the road runs through level country (rice-fields) by way of Pals, an old-world little town picturesquely situated on the slopes of a hill, and Regencós to Bagur (Catalan Begur; alt. 220m/720ft), built round a castle situated on a cone-shaped crag, from which there are panoramic views. 2km/1¼ miles south-east of Bagur are the resorts of Playa de Fornells and Aiguablava, the latter of which has a small sandy beach and attractive coves with clear water.

Bagur/Begur

Barcelona, Gerona/Palamós

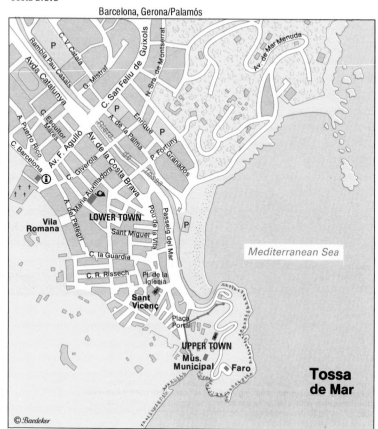

Palafrugell

South-west of Bagur, reached either on the direct road or via Regencós, is the little town of Palafrugell (alt. 65m/215ft), which along with the adjoining resorts of Llafranch, Tamariu and Calella de Palafrugell constitutes one of the major tourist centres on the Costa Brava, with a series of fine beaches. Palafrugell itself has the Gothic church of San Martín, with a 17th century retablo, and remains of its old town walls. From here roads run down to Calella (5km/3 miles), with a beautiful botanic garden on Cabo Roig; Llafranch (4km/2½ miles; also a short stretch of motorway); and to the picturesque Cabo de San Sebastián (4km/2½ miles), with the beautifully situated chapel of San Sebastián, and the little resort of Tamariu (5km/3 miles), from which there are boat trips to the sea caves of Cova del Bisbe and Cova d'en Gisbert.

Palamós

Beyond Palafrugell the coast road joins C 255, coming from Gerona, which continues south to Palamós, finely situated on an outlying promontory of the Sierra de las Gabarras. This old fishing village, in which fish auctions are still held, is now also a popular holiday resort. The handsome 14th century church of Santa María has a Flemish altarpiece. An unusual attraction is a dusty little museum in the Plaça del Forn with a collection of 5000 species of shellfish and snails from all over the world.

C 253 continues south-west, a short distance from the coast, to San Antonio de Calonge (with the beautifully situated inland holiday resort of Calonge 2.5km/1½ miles off on the right) and Playa de Aro (Catalan Platja d'Aro), a busy seaside resort comprehensively developed for tourism, with high-rise hotels lining the seafront promenade.

Playa de Aro/
La Platja d'Aro

South of Playa de Aro is S'Agaró, a high-class resort established only in 1923, with numbers of fine villas set in beautiful gardens. The resort is closed to non-local cars.

★S'Agaró

San Feliú de Guixols (Catalan Sant Feliu de Guíxols) is a port town, attractively situated at the head of a bay. As the main centre for the shipment of the cork produced in the surrounding area it is a port of call for ships of many nations, and it is also a very popular seaside resort with a good beach. In the town are the remains of a monastery built in the 13th century, with an iron entrance gate, the 11th century Porta Ferrada, and a defensive tower beside it. In the square, standing by itself, is a Baroque doorway. The Casa Berruguer contains a small museum with Iberian, Greek and Roman antiquities.

San Feliú de
Guixols/Sant
Feliu de Guíxols

From the beach, which is fairly short, a road runs up to the Mirador de Sant Elm. On the hill there is also an old hermitage.

Sant Elm

From San Feliú de Guixols the coast road runs south-west, high up on the slopes of the Puig de Cadiretas (519m/1703ft), and continues, with an endless succession of bends and magnificent views, to Tossa de Mar, a popular seaside resort delightfully situated in a bay, with a good beach and a seafront promenade with beautiful views.

★ **Tossa de Mar**

The upper town of Tossa de Mar, surrounded by medieval walls and towers, is protected as a national monument. The Municipal Museum, in a restored medieval house, has a collection of modern art (including Marc Chagall), Roman mosaics and Stone Age implements.

Upper town

On the west side of the crowded lower town are the scanty remains of a Roman settlement.

Lower town

Lloret de Mar is one of the most popular resorts on the Spanish Mediterranean coast. Once a modest fishing village, it is now a high-class holiday and tourist centre with a wide range of entertainment and leisure facilities, including the Waterworld leisure centre to the west of the town.

Lloret de Mar

The drive along the Costa Brava ends at Blanes, the last resort on this stretch of coast. Places of interest in the hinterland of the coast include Gerona, Figueras and Vich (see entries).

Costa Cálida

See Cartagena

Costa de la Luz

D–E 8/9

Provinces: Huelva (H), Cádiz (CA)

The Costa de la Luz ("Coast of Light") is the stretch of the southern Atlantic coast of Spain between the mouth of the Río Guadiana on the Portuguese frontier and the promontory of Tarifa on the Straits of Gibraltar. Along this coastal region, almost perpetually bathed in the warm light of the sun, are a succession of spacious sandy beaches, well away from main roads and

The★ "Coast of Light"

traffic routes. The coast of Huelva province in particular, with the extensive Playa de Castilla, is a bathers' paradise, bounded on the landward side by eucalyptus trees. Inland from the coast around Cádiz are vineyards and olive-groves. Almost all the villages along the coast live by fishing, though tourism is increasingly becoming an important source of revenue. To date there is only one resort at Matalascañas; further development has been prevented by protests from environmentalists who see the unique reserve of Coto de Doñana as being under threat.

Sights and Routes

See Cádiz and Huelva

Costa del Azahar

See Castellón de la Plana and Huelva

Costa del Sol

F–K 8/9

Provinces: Almería (AL), Granada (GR), Málaga (MA), Cádiz (CA)

The
★"Sunshine
Coast"

The Costa del Sol ("Sunshine Coast") extends along almost the whole of the Mediterranean coast of Andalusia, from Cabo de Gata, where the Costa Blanca ends, to the most southerly point in Spain at Tarifa, where the Costa de la Luz begins. The mild climate of this region (with an average annual temperature of over 18°C/64°F) has led to the development of a densely populated holiday and tourist region almost 300km/190 miles long which

Benalmadena, on the Costa del Sol

attracts hosts of foreign visitors. The stretch between Málaga and Manilva is particularly developed but in 1993 sewage plants were installed to improve the water quality and other measures were introduced to clean up the beaches. This is not the place to come for peace and quiet as the night life comes right up to the beach and there is no shortage of discos and bars. Inland the vivid colouring of the landscape and the luxuriant flora give the Costa del Sol its particular stamp. With its whitewashed houses, its agaves and cactuses, its farms and its cheerful villages, it is the very image of Andalusia.

Sights and Routes

See Almería, Algeciras, Estepona, Fuengirola, Gibraltar, Granada, Málaga, Nerja and Torremolinos

Costa Dorada/Costa Daurada   N–P 3–4

Provinces: Barcelona (B), Tarragona (T)

The description of the Costa Dorada in this guide is abridged, since there is a full description in the AA/Baedeker guide "Costa Brava/Costa Dorada/Barcelona".

The Costa Dorada ("Golden Coast"), extending south from the Costa Brava along the Mediterranean, takes in almost the whole coastline of the provinces of Barcelona and Tarragona. With a total length of some 260km/ 160 miles, it attracts many visitors with its gently sloping beaches of fine golden sand and its notably mild climate.

The ★"Golden Coast"

The Port Aventura Theme Park opened in 1995 is situated in Salou on the Costa Dorauda. The Park is divided into 5 different worlds, Mediterrania, China, Polynesia, Mexico and The Far West, it is open from mid-Mar. to Jun. 22nd and from Sept. 17th to Oct. 29th from 10am until 8pm. From Jun. 23rd to Sept. 16th from 10am until midnight. Visitor service information is available from the park on tel. 902 20 22 20 or from the Spanish Tourist office on tel. (0891) 669920.

Port Aventura Theme Park

Sights and Routes

See Barcelona, Sitges, Tarragona and Villanueva y Geltrú

Costa Verde

See Gijón

Cuenca   K 5

Province: Cuenca (CU). Telephone dialling code: 966
Altitude: 998m/3274ft. Population: 42,000

Cuenca, chief town of its province and the see of a bishop, is magnificently situated on the steep rocky slopes of the Serranía de Cuenca above the deep valleys of the Río Júcar and the Río Huécar. It is one of the most picturesque of Spain's old medieval towns, famous for its Casas Colgadas ("Hanging Houses").

★Situation

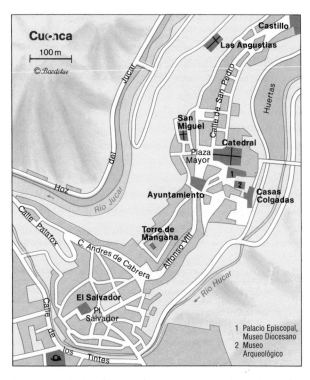

Cuenca

100 m

© Baedeker

1 Palacio Episcopal,
  Museo Diocesano
2 Museo
  Arqueológico

History

This was the Roman Conca, which later fell into the hands of the Visigoths and then of the Moors, from whom it was liberated by Alfonso VIII in 1177. Thereafter it enjoyed special privileges as a frontier town and became the headquarters of the knightly Order of Santiago.

Sights

★ Old town

The old town of Cuenca has preserved much of its medieval aspect, with handsome old mansions sporting the arms of the noble families to whom they once belonged. The principal sights cluster in the south-west of the town, around the Plaza Mayor, with the Ayuntamiento (Town Hall) on its west side.

★ Cathedral

In the Plaza Mayor stands the Norman/Gothic Cathedral (12th–13th c.); the façade was rebuilt after it collapsed in 1902. The richly decorated interior was left unscathed. The 18th century high altar by Ventura Rodríguez is separated from the rest of the church by magnificent grilles dating from 1557. The triforium in the ambulatory is the only one of its kind in Spain. In the north aisle is a very beautiful Renaissance arch, the Arco de Jamete. Two particular treasures are a "Mater Dolorosa" by Pedro de Mena (13th c.) in the sacristy and a "Crucifixion" by Yáñez de la Almedina in the Capilla de los Caballeros.

Treasury

Two carved walnut doors by Alonso de Berruguete give access to the chapterhouse, which contains the valuable cathedral treasury (though some of the finest items are in the Diocesan Museum).

Casas Colgadas, Cuenca

In the Museum of Abstract Art

Built on to the Cathedral is the Palacio Episcopal (Bishop's Palace), on the three lowest floors of which is the Diocesan Museum. Among its principal treasures are two paintings by El Greco ("Christ on the Cross", "Prayer in the Garden of Olives"), a 13th century Byzantine diptych from Mount Athos, fine pieces of goldsmith's work and valuable tapestries.

Museo Diocesano

To the south of the Diocesan Museum, reached by way of Calle Obispo Valero, are the famous Casas Colgadas which overhang the Río Huécar (here spanned by eight bridges), with their balconies projecting over the abyss.

★★Casas Colgadas

Some of the houses are occupied by the Museum of Spanish Abstract Art, which displays in a series of attractive rooms more than 700 works by the best known Spanish artists from the 1950s onwards. It is the largest collection of modern Spanish art in the country after the Museo de Arte Contemporáneo and the newly established Museo Nacional Centro de Arte Reina Sofia in Madrid.

★Museo de Arte Abstracto Español

Near the Hanging Houses is the Museo de Cuenca or Museo Arqueológico, which displays antiquities from the surrounding area. Among the most notable exhibits are a marble head of Lucius Caesar (1st c. A.D.), a reconstruction of a Roman kitchen, Iberian dolls and other Roman and Visigothic items.

Museo de Cuenca

North-west of the Plaza Mayor is the church of San Miguel, standing high above the gorge of the Río Júcar, which has a Mudéjar ceiling. Not far away is the octagonal church of San Pedro and further north the remains of the castle.

San Miguel

Surroundings of Cuenca

From Cuenca a road runs north up the wild and romantic valley of the Júcar, with beautiful views to the rear of the town and the valley, and

★★Ciudad Encantada

235

In the "Enchanted City"

comes in 36km/22 miles to the Ciudad Encantada ("Enchanted City") – not a city but a fascinating geological feature. Here, in the course of many thousands of years, erosion has hewn out of the sedimentary rocks a stony labyrinth of crags and caves and lakes and waterfalls which, with a little imagination, can be seen to resemble a ruined city with its houses and streets and squares.

Mirador de Uña

From the "Enchanted City" a road goes north and then east to Uña, with a viewpoint (mirador) from which there are fine views of the Río Júcar and the artificial lake of La Toba.

★Nacimiento del Cuervo

From Uña there is a more arduous excursion on a road which runs east and then north to Tragacete (35km/22 miles), from which it is another 12km/7½ miles to the Nacimiento del Cuervo, the source of the Río Cuervo. The effort is rewarded, however, by the beauty of the spring, with the water emerging from moss-covered caves and tumbling over rocks into a pool.

★Monasterio de Uclés

From Cuenca N 400 runs west to Carrascosa del Campo (57km/35 miles), from which a minor road (CU 701) leads south-west to the monastery of Uclés, built between the 16th and 18th centuries, which was the headquarters of the knightly Order of Santiago. It has a very beautiful patio. In the crypt of the church (1529) is the tomb of the poet Jorge Manrique (1440–79). The refectory has a magnificent panelled ceiling with carved medallions containing portraits of Grand Masters of the Order and of the Emperor Charles V.

Denia   L 4

Province: Alicante (A). Telephone dialling code: 965
Altitude: 12m/40ft. Population: 22,000

The seaside resort of Denia, set amid orange-groves on the Mediterranean coast, has a history going back to Greek and Roman times. It was known to the Greeks in the 8th century B.C. as Hemeroskopeion and to the Romans as Dianium. In the Moorish period, between 715 and 1253, it was a flourishing port which at one time was in control of Majorca. Its main sources of revenue are now tourism and fishing. There is a regular ferry service to San Antonio Abad on Ibiza.

Sights

The town lies at the foot of a hill crowned by a castle, which now houses an archaeological museum. From the top of the hill there are extensive views of the Gulf of Valencia. At the foot of the hill is an open-air theatre.

Castillo

The Baroque church of Santa María (1734) is faced with tiles.

Santa María

Denia's two beaches, the flat Playa de las Marinas and the rocky Playa de las Rotas (diving grounds), have been awarded the blue Europa flag for particularly well kept beaches.

Beaches

Surroundings of Denia

There is a rewarding climb to the summit of Montgó, with the remains of the Casa de Biot, an Iberian settlement of the 8th century B.C. From the top of the hill there are magnificent views of the coast and the sea. The ascent takes about 4 hours.

★Montgó

Farther south, below Montgó at the mouth of the Río Jalón, is the little port and seaside resort of Jávea, with old walls and towers, the Castillo de San Juan and a fortified Gothic church (14th c.).
   Near Jávea are two stalactitic caves, the Cueva del Organo and the Cueva del Oro.

Jávea

2km/1¼ miles east of Denia is Cabo de San Antonio (174m/571ft), with a lighthouse; from here there are far-ranging views.

Cabo de
San Antonio

4km/2½ miles south of Jávea is the Cabo de la Nao, the most easterly point in the Cordillera Bética (Andalusian Mountains). Around the cape are beautiful beaches. From the tip of the promontory there is a view to the south of the rocky mass of the Peñón de Ifach (383m/1257ft) rearing out of the sea off the Punta de Ifach (see Benidorm).

★Cabo de
la Nao

El Burgo de Osma

See page 165

Elche/Elx

M 7

Province: Alicante (A).
Telephone dialling code: 965
Altitude: 88m/289ft. Population: 180,000

Elche (Catalan Elx), situated on both banks of the Río Vinalopó in one of the hottest parts of Spain, is noted for its palm grove, a feature unique in Europe. There were Iberian, Phoenician and Greek settlements on the site, and the Romans founded the colony of Julia Ilici here. With its flat-roofed white houses and domed churches the old part of the town, set on the edge

In the palm grove, Elche

of an oasis of palms, has an Oriental air. Elche is now a centre of shoe manufacture.

Sights

Santa María

The 17th century church of Santa María, dedicated to the Virgen de la Asunción, is a prominent landmark with its large blue-tiled dome and its fortress-like tower, 37m/121ft high, from which there are fine views of the town and the palm grove. The richly decorated main doorway and the Baroque façade were the work of Nicolás de Busi. Every year on August 14th and 15th the Misterio de Elche (Catalan Misteri d'Elx) is performed in the church. This 13th century play is a dramatic presentation (by male actors only), with a musical accompaniment, of the Death, Assumption and Coronation of the Virgin.

★Misterio de Elche

La Calahorra

To the east of the church are the remains of the 14th century Moorish stronghold of La Calahorra.

Museo Arqueológico

North of the church, in the 15th century Palacio de Altamira, is the Archaeological Museum, with a fine collection of prehistoric, Iberian, Greco-Roman and Islamic antiquities.

The museum has only a copy of the famous "Lady of Elche", an Iberian figure of the 4th or 3rd century B.C. which was found at Elche in 1897 (illustration, page 57); the original is in the Archaeological Museum in Madrid.

Puente de Santa Teresa

There is a very fine view of the town from the Puente de Santa Teresa, a bridge in Gothic style (1705) which spans the Río Vinalopó a little way south-west of the Plaza Baix.

Museo de Arte Contemporáneo

Farther south is the Museum of Contemporary Art, with a collection of pictures, graphic art, sculpture and ceramics, mainly by Catalan and Valencian artists.

★ Palmeral de Europa

Immediately east of the town is the Palmeral de Europa, the largest palm grove in Europe. A visit takes about 2 hours; the best time in summer is in the early morning (guide advisable). The plantations, probably established by the Phoenicians but dating in their present extent from Moorish times, are surrounded by walls or hedges. Water for irrigation comes from a reservoir in the Vinalopó valley, 5km/3 miles away.

The date palm *(Phoenix dactylifera;* Spanish *palmera)* requires very careful culture. The dates (which are inferior in quality to those of the Sahara) are harvested between November and the spring; each tree bears dates (an average of 35kg/77lb) only every other year. From April onwards some of the male palms are bound up so that they become bleached, and the bleached fronds *(ramilletes)* are then sold all over Spain for Palm Sunday and hung from the balconies of houses.

★ Huerta
del Cura

The palms, usually between 20 and 25m (65 and 80ft) in height but sometimes reaching more than 35m/115ft, stand with "their feet in water and their heads in the fires of heaven", as an Arabic saying has it. Under them are planted pomegranate trees, in the shade of which fodder crops and vegetables are grown. Particular features of interest are the Huerta del Cura ("Priest's Garden"); the Palmera Imperial, a male palm said to be 200 years old, with seven lateral stems growing out of the main trunk; the Palmeras Romeo y Julieta; and the Villa Carmen, with a belvedere from which there are fine views.

El Escorial (San Lorenzo del Escorial)   G 4

Province: Madrid (M). Telephone dialling code: 91
Altitude: 1028m/3373ft. Population: 9000

The little town of San Lorenzo del Escorial (El Escorial for short), 50km/30 miles north-west of Madrid on the southern slopes of the Sierra Guadarrama, was once, during the summer months, a royal residence and the effective capital of the Spanish empire. The huge monastery-cumpalace with its inestimable treasures of art is now one of the most visited sights in Spain.

★★ Monasterio de San Lorenzo del Escorial

After the battle of Saint-Quentin on August 10th 1557 (St Lawrence's Day), in which Spanish troops defeated the French, Philip II vowed to build a monastery dedicated to St Lawrence. After careful preparations, including the consultation of astrologers, the little town of San Lorenzo was chosen as the site of a huge complex which was to include a monastery, a church, a royal palace, a mausoleum, a library and a museum and was conceived as a monument to Philip and his reign. Work began on April 23rd 1563 and was completed on September 13th 1584 in the presence of Philip himself, who had closely supervised the whole operation. The architects were Juan Bautista de Toledo, who died in 1567, and Juan de Herrera. The decoration was the work of numerous Spanish painters, and a major part was also played by Italian masters, including Pellegrino Tibaldi, Luca Giordano and the sculptors Pompeo and Leone Leoni.

Opening times
Tues.–Sun.
10am–7pm

From the outside the Escorial – a massive pile, built of greyish-white granite in the form of a rectangle 204m/669ft long by 161m/528ft wide – looks more like a fortress or a barracks than a monastery. Although conceived in the spirit of 16th century Italian classicism, it shows the begin-

Philip II's view of the Escorial

nings of the Spanish Baroque school. At the core of the whole complex is the church with its twin towers and its 90m/295ft high dome. To the west of this is the Patio de los Reyes, to the south the cloister, with the sacristy and the chapter rooms, to the east and north the royal palace. Altogether the Escorial has 16 courtyards, 2673 windows, 1250 doors, 86 staircases and 88 fountains, and the corridors have a total length of 16km/10 miles.

Puerta Principal

The main entrance to the Escorial, the Puerta Principal, is on the west side, opening off the main square, the Lonja. Over the doorway are St Lawrence's gridiron, the arms of the Habsburgs and a statue of St Lawrence by Juan Bautista Monegro.

Patio de los Reyes

The Puerta Principal leads into the Patio de los Reyes (Court of the Kings). This is dominated by the façade of the church, with the statues of Old Testament kings from which it takes its name, and by the two massive towers.

Church

The interior of the church, which has frescoes by Luca Giordano, is notable for its austerity and monumentality. The dome over the crossing admits a flood of cold light which illuminates the precious materials used in Herrera's 30m/100ft high retablo. Approached by a flight of 17 steps, this is a four-storey structure of jasper and red marble, with pictures by the Italian painters Zucaro and Tibaldi and statues of Fathers of the Church and Evangelists by Pompeo and Leone Leoni.

The Leonis were also responsible for the bronze monuments of the two greatest rulers of Spain in niches in the presbytery. On the left, facing the high altar, is a gilded bronze statue of Charles V, kneeling, with his wife Isabella, his daughter Maria and his sisters Eleanor and Maria; on the right Philip II is kneeling with his three wives (Anne of Austria, Isabelle of Valois and Maria of Portugal) and his son Don Carlos.

Panteón de los Reyes

Immediately underneath the church is the Panteón de los Reyes, the burial vault of the Spanish kings. A domed octagonal structure originally

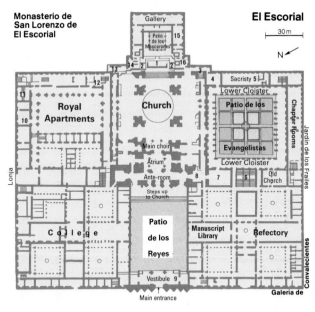

Monasterio de San Lorenzo de El Escorial

El Escorial

1 Presbytery and high altar
2 Royal oratories
3 Steps up to Coro Alto and down to Panteon
4 Ante-Sacristy
5 Altar of Sagrada Forma
6 Grand Staircase
7 Sala de la Trinidad

8 Sala de los Secretos
9 Entrance to Library
10 Entrance to Bourbon palace
11 Palace staircase
12 Entrance to 16th c. rooms and museum
13 Sala de Batallas

14 Apartments of the Infanta Isabel Clara Eugenia
15 Throne Room
16 Chamber, alcoves and Philip II's oratory

designed by Herrera was enlarged by Juan Gómez de Mora and completed in 1654. The black marble and gilded bronze decoration, by Giovanni Baptista Crescenti, reflects the Baroque taste of the period. On the left-hand side are identical granite sarcophagi containing the remains of almost all the Spanish kings from Charles V onwards, together with Isabella II; on the right are the queen mothers and Isabella II's husband Francisco de Asís.

Below the sacristy and the chapter rooms is the burial vault of Spanish princes and princesses and queens whose children did not succeed to the throne.

Panteón de los Infantes

In the south aisle of the church is a doorway leading through the ante-sacristy (with a ceiling painting by Nicola Granelo) into the sacristy, which contains more than 40 valuable pictures. Among them is Claudio Coello's "Festival of the Host" (1684), which covers a niche containing the Sagrada Forma, a Host which is said to have been desecrated by Dutch Calvinists in 1572.

Sacristy

On the south side of the church is the Lower Cloister (with frescoes by Tibaldi), within which is the Patio de los Evangelistas (Court of the Evangelists), named after the fountain-house (by Herrera) with figures of the four Evangelists which stands in the centre of the courtyard.

Patio de los Evangelistas

On the south side of the Lower Cloister are the Salas Capitulares (Chapter Rooms), with beautiful ceiling paintings. They contain numerous pictures,

Salas Capitulares

including works by Navarrete, Ribera and Luca Giordano, together with vestments and liturgical utensils.

Iglesia Antigua

The Iglesia Antigua (Old Church) adjoining the chapter rooms was used for worship while the Escorial was under construction. It contains a fine painting of "The Martyrdom of St Lawrence" (seen only with special permission).

Escalera Principal

The Escalera Principal (Grand Staircase), with two symmetrical flights, leads to the upper floor; it was designed by Herrera. The ceiling has a painting of the battle of Saint-Quentin by Luca Giordano; on the walls are portraits, including those of Juan Bautista de Toledo and Juan de Herrera.

Library

On the south side of the Patio de los Reyes, on the second floor, is the Library. Decorated with fine frescoes by Tibaldi depicting "The Foundations of Learning", it contains more than 40,000 volumes. Some of its most valuable incunabula, notably the Codez Aureus (1093) attributed to the German Emperor Conrad II, are displayed in cases, together with a manuscript of Alfonso the Wise's "Hymns to the Virgin", manuscripts in the hand of Santa Teresa de Ávila and Hebrew and Arabic writings.

Palacio Real

The Palacio Real (Royal Palace) extends over two floors of the Escorial. On the north side of the church is the administrative palace. Particularly impressive, in this part of the palace, is the Bourbon Suite. A staircase reconstructed by Villanueva in the 18th century leads up to the state apartments of Charles IV and Maria Luisa of Parma on the 3rd floor. They contain valuable furniture and porcelain of the 18th century, but their principal treasures are 338 tapestries, some from the Santa Bárbara manufactory in Madrid, some from Flemish workshops. They depict scenes from popular life (some after cartoons by Goya), allegories and hunting scenes (after cartoons by Teniers, Wouwerman, Bayeu and Maella).

Hall of Battles

In the north-east corner of the administrative palace is the Sala de Batallas (Hall of Battles), 55m/180ft long and 7m/23ft high, with paintings commissioned by Philip II of the principal battles of the Reconquista and the victories won during his reign.

Private
Apartments
of Philip II

The Hall of Battles leads into the private apartments of Philip II, laid out round the Patio de los Mascarones (Court of Masks) at the east end of the church. The most interesting rooms are the Alcoves of Philip II, from which he had direct access to the church and in which he died on September 13th 1598; the "Cell of Philip II", with Hieronymus Bosch's "Hay Wain" (possibly a copy) and eleven watercolours attributed to Albrecht Dürer; the Throne Room; and the apartments of the Infanta Isabel Clara Eugenia.

Nuevos Museos

In a series of rooms in the palace are housed the Nuevos Museos (New Museums), in which pictures and objets d'art from all over the palace and monastery have been brought together. They consist of a Museum of Architecture and a Picture Gallery.

The Museum of Architecture, in the east basement of the administrative palace, displays prints, models, apparatus and original plans illustrating the building of the Escorial.

The Picture Gallery, in the basement storey of Philip II's private apartments, the so-called Summer Palace, has a large collection of fine paintings, only a few of which can be mentioned here. In the first two rooms are works by Hieronymus Bosch ("The Crowning with Thorns"), Gerard David, Quentin Metsys, Marinus van Reymerswaele ("The Money-Changers") and Albrecht Dürer. In the next two rooms are Titian ("Last Supper", "St Jerome in Prayer"), Guido Reni, Tintoretto and Veronese. In the adjoining rooms are works by José de Ribera and Diego Velázquez ("Joseph's Robe"). Two rooms in the administrative palace contain important works by El Greco, including "The Martyrdom of St Maurice" (a representation of the saint's martyrdom which displeased Philip II).

Wall painting in the Hall of Battles

Surroundings of the Escorial

South-east of the monastery lie the Jardines del Príncipe (Prince's Gardens), with attractive walks shaded by tall ancient trees. In the lower part of the gardens stands the Casita del Príncipe, a miniature palace built in 1773 for the Prince of Asturias, later Charles IV; the interior, decorated and furnished in the style of the period, is open to the public.

Jardines del Príncipe

A smaller counterpart to the Casita del Príncipe is the Casita del Infante south-west of the Escorial, a retreat built for the Infante Gabriel, Charles IV's brother.

Casita del Infante

On a hill 3km/2 miles south of the Escorial are several blocks of stone in the form of seats, from which Philip II is said to have watched the building of the monastery/palace: hence the name Silla de Felipe II (Philip II's Chair). From here there is a magnificent view of the huge building set against the backdrop of the Sierra de Guadarrama. The best way to reach the hill is to drive past the golf course on the west side of the town to a road junction with a signpost to the Silla de Felipe II.

Silla de Felipe II

Valle de los Caídos

Some 13km/8 miles north of the Escorial is the Monumento Nacional de Santa Cruz del Valle de los Caídos, or Valle de los Caídos (Valley of the Fallen) for short, built by General Franco between 1940 and 1958 as a monument to the Nationalist dead of the Spanish Civil War. The entrance to the site lies several kilometres below the monument itself, which is reached by car on a hill road. From a bridge half way up there is a view of an 150m/490ft high cross above the memorial basilica – a textbook example of the architectural gigantomania of Fascism.

From the vast square in front of the basilica there are extensive views of the beautiful hilly countryside. Over the entrance to the basilica, which was blasted out of the rock, is a huge Pietà by Juan de Ávalos. The entrance leads into a vestibule which is smaller than the main hall but still of impressive size, with a barrel vault which re-echoes the slightest whisper. Beyond this extends the immense nave of the basilica, 262m/860ft long, its walls hung with copies of Brussels tapestries. The heart of this rock church is the altar, below the 42m/138ft high mosaic-decorated dome over the crossing. A grave slab in front of the altar marks the tomb of Primo de Rivera, founder of the Falange, and behind the altar is a similar slab under which Franco is buried. In vaults under the Capilla de los Caídos, to the right of the altar, are 40,000 sarcophagi with the remains of those who fell in the Civil War (not open to the public).

To the right of the basilica is a funicular going up to the foot of the gigantic cross.

Estella   K 2

Province: Navarra (NA). Telephone dialling code: 948
Altitude: 426m/1398ft. Population: 13,000

★Townscape

The ancient little town of Estella, lying on the Río Ega well away from the main traffic routes, was founded by King Sancho Ramírez in 1090 on the site of an earlier Roman settlement. During the Middle Ages it was an occasional residence of the kings of Navarre and a staging-point on the pilgrims' road to Santiago de Compostela, the Way of St James (see entry). A 12th century guide for pilgrims describes it as a hospitable city. The Jews and Franks (Frenchmen, foreigners) who were encouraged by the kings of Navarre to settle in Estella lived in their own separate quarters of the town and contributed to its prosperity – still evidenced by its many towers and palaces.

Sights

San Pedro de la Rúa

A prominent landmark of the town is the tower of the 12th century church of San Pedro de la Rúa, which is approached by a steep flight of steps. In its combination of pointed and cusped arches the doorway shows Moorish influence. An unusual feature of the interior (aisled, with three apses) is a column in the central apse formed of three intertwined snakes. In the Baroque Capilla de San Andrés in the north aisle is a silver shrine containing a relic of St Andrew, brought here in the 13th century by a bishop of Patras.

★Cloister

The cloister was damaged in 1573 by falling debris when the castle on the hill above was blown up, and only the north and west sides remain. It is of particular interest for its capitals, depicting the Massacre of the Innocents, scenes from Christ's life and Passion, the stories of St Lawrence and St Andrew, the arrest of St Peter, etc., together with animal and plant ornament.

★Palacio de los Reyes de Navarra

Below the church is the Plaza de San Martín, from the east side of which Calle San Nicolás leads to the Puerta de Castilla, through which pilgrims left the town. On this street is the Palacio de los Reyes de Navarra, the palace of the kings of Navarre, the basic structure of which goes back to the 12th century; the towers and gallery were added in the 16th century. On the main front of the palace are two columns with capitals depicting the fight between Roland and the Moorish giant Ferragut (on left) and devils tormenting misers and animal musicians (on right). The palace houses a museum with paintings by Gustavo de Maeztu (1887–1947).

Estella: a bird's eye view

In the Plaza de San Martín is the 16th century Ayuntamiento (Town Hall), with two very fine municipal coats of arms on the façade.

Ayuntamiento

From the Town Hall Calle de la Rúa leads east, lined by handsome burghers' houses and noble mansions, notable among them the 16th century Casa de Fray Diego de Estella and the 17th century Palacio del Gobernador (both on the left-hand side).

Calle de la Rúa

Farther along Calle de la Rúa, on the right, is the church of Santo Sepulcro, which was begun in the late 12th century. In the tympanum of the Gothic doorway are represented the Crucifixion, the Entombment and the Resurrection of Christ; flanking the doorway are fine statues of Apostles.

Santo Sepulcro

On the left bank of the Río Ega a flight of steps goes up to the Mercado Viejo, in which is the church of San Miguel Arcángel, in a style transitional between Romanesque and Gothic. Although at first sight the exterior of the church is plain, its north doorway is one of the finest examples of Romanesque sculpture in Navarre. The door is flanked by five columns on each side, with capitals depicting Christ's birth and childhood and the Massacre of the Innocents; the last two have hunting scenes and plant ornament. The figural ornament continues on the archivolts, and in the tympanum is a figure of Christ surrounded by the symbols of the Evangelists. Flanking the doorway are two masterpieces of sculpture: on left the Archangel Michael fighting a dragon and Michael and Abraham fighting devils for men's souls, on right the Resurrection.

San Miguel Arcángel

In the north aisle is a fine retablo of Santa Elena (1406).

Estepona

Province: Málaga (MA). Telephone dialling code: 952
Altitude: 21m/69ft. Population: 34,000

Estepona, the most westerly resort on the Costa del Sol, lying at the foot of the Sierra Bermeja on the coast road (N 340), has a history going back to Roman times. Nearby are the ruins of the thousand-year-old aqueduct of Salduba, and in the town itself are remains of an Arab fortress and medieval watch-towers. The old part of the town has retained something of its Andalusian character; otherwise Estepona is a typical modern tourist and holiday centre catering for an international public, with a boating marina, high-rise hotels, restaurants and bars surrounding the old town centre.

Sport and recreation

With 21km/13 miles of beaches, Estepona offers a varied range of facilities for bathing and water sports. Some of the beaches have earned the European Union's blue flag. The modern boating marina has moorings for 900 boats, and there are also a sailing club, good sea-angling, regattas and water-skiing facilities, as well as three golf courses and numbers of tennis courts.

Sierra Bermeja

For those who want to get away from it all there are many quiet little places amid beautiful mountain scenery in the Sierra Bermeja.

Figueras/Figueres   Q 2

Province: Gerona (GE). Telephone dialling code: 972
Altitude: 30m/100ft. Population: 28,000

Figueras (Catalan Figueres) lies 35km/22 miles north of the provincial capital, Gerona (Catalan Girona), and 15km/9 miles north-west of the Golfo de Rosas.

★★Museo/Museu Salvador Dalí

Opening times
Jul.–Sept. daily
9am–7.15pm; other
times Tues.–Sun.
10.30am–5.15pm

The Salvador Dalí Museum can be distinguished from a long way off by the perspex dome composed of honeycomb-like elements which now crowns the old Neo-Classical theatre (1850) housing the museum.

Photography prohibited

The Dalí Museum is not only the principal tourist attraction of Figueras but one of the most important sights in the whole of Catalonia and, after the Prado in Madrid, the most visited museum in Spain. Nowhere else can the work of the great Surrealist artist, a native of Figueras, be seen in so concentrated form. The museum is laid out on several floors corresponding to the different levels of the old theatre, the roof of which has been replaced by the perspex dome. In the windows and on the cornices are a host of plastic figurines in every conceivable pose.

The works displayed here in such numbers have an extraordinary fascination of their own. Here every trend in art is parodied and given a new turn, every technique is handled with the utmost virtuosity, every material is used in an unexpected way. Only a few particularly striking examples of Dalí's work can be mentioned. Thus on the first floor there is a large ceiling painting in the Baroque manner which carries the perspective effects of its models to a grotesque extreme: of two figures seen from below little is visible but the huge soles of their feet, while their bodies are lost in the depths of the scene. The former stage has been shut off by a high glass wall, behind which, in a space resembling the sanctuary of a church, is a monumental painting and, opposite it, like an altar, a smaller picture under a red baldachin. The outside walls and the monument in front of the entrance have also been distorted by Dalí in an unexpected way.
Dalí died on January 25th 1989, and his tomb is under the Museum's dome. Characteristically, it includes a representation of a Cadillac with Dalí himself at the wheel as well as a statue of "Esther" by the Viennese sculptor Ernst Fuchs.

At No. 2 on the Ramblas, the tree-shaded main street of the town, is the Museo del Ampurdán (Catalan Museu del Empordà), devoted to the history of the Empordà (Spanish Ampurdán) area to the south of the town. On the ground floor is a collection of works by contemporary local painters. On the first floor are displayed ancient glassware, bronze ornaments and implements, black-figure amphoras, terracottas, etc. The earlier material comes largely from the excavations of the Iberian settlement at Ullastret (see Gerona, Surroundings) and Ampurias (see entry). There are also examples of Romanesque and Gothic art, Baroque costumes and ship models.

Museo del Ampurdán/ Museu del Empordà

Near the wider part of the Ramblas, at No. 10, is the Museo de Juguetes (Toy Museum), housed in the Hotel Paris.

Museo de Juguetes

Fuengirola

G 9

Province: Málaga (MA). Telephone dialling code: 952
Altitude: sea level. Population: 30,000

The seaside resort of Fuengirola on the Costa del Sol, 29km/18 miles from Málaga on N 340 and 25km/16 miles from the Torremolinos airport, occupies the site of the Roman settlement of Suel.
Fuengirola is sheltered on the north by the Sierra de Mijas. Above the town are the ruins of the Moorish stronghold of Sohall, built in the 10th century by Abderrahman III.

Fuengirola is now an international holiday resort, conveniently situated and offering a great range of attractions – 7km/4½ miles of beaches, hotels and restaurants in all categories and recreational facilities which include a golf course, a zoo and training courses in many forms of sport and leisure activity.

The resort

9km/6 miles north of Fuengirola is Mijas, a little village which has been dressed up to cater for the needs of tourists, with many of its whitewashed houses now occupied by bars, restaurants and craft shops. On the way to Mijas there are fine views of the Mediterranean from the southern slopes of the Sierra de Mijas. There is a Museum of Miniatures and water lovers will enjoy the Aqualand Mijas Costas with numerous long water slides.

★Mijas

Gandía

M 6

Province: Valencia (V). Telephone dialling code: 96
Altitude: 22m/72ft. Population: 53,000

Gandía, once capital of a dukedom, lies in the richest and most populous huerta in the former kingdom of Valencia. It was the seat of the Borja (Borgia) family, which produced the notorious Pope Alexander VI, previously Bishop Rodrigo de Borja of Valencia. Alexander's great-grandson Francisco, who was born in Gandía in 1510, became the third General of the Jesuits and was later canonised.

Gandía consists of the town proper and the little port of El Grao (Catalan El Grau), 4km/2½ miles away; its long sandy beaches have made it one of the great centres of mass tourism on the Valencian coast.

Sights

At the highest point on the old town, at the east end of the Paseo de las Germanías (Catalan Passeig de les Germanies), which cuts through the town centre, stands the Palacio del Santo Duque (Catalan Palau Sant Duc),

Palacio del Santo Duque/ Palau Sant Duc

in which Francisco de Borja was born. The palace was given its present form in the 16th and 18th centuries. Its finest features are the Patio de las Armas with its magnificent staircase (16th c.) and the Baroque state apartments, particularly the 38m/125ft long Golden Gallery, which has a very beautiful mosaic floor.

There is a small museum commemorating the life and work of San Francisco de Borja.

La Colegiata

In Plaza de la Constitución (Catalan Plaça Constitució) is the Colegiata, a collegiate church with a tall tower which is a fine example of Catalan Gothic architecture. It was built in the 13th and 14th centuries on the site of a Moorish mosque and was renovated and enlarged in the 15th and 16th centuries. The south doorway and the Apostles' Doorway are richly decorated with sculpture.

Antigua
Universidad/
Antica Universitat

The Calle Mayor (Catalan Carrer Maior) runs north to the Old University (Spanish Antigua Universidad, Catalan Antica Universitat), which was founded by Francisco Borja. After the banning of the Jesuits the 16th century University building, now with a Baroque façade, was given to the Mercedarian Order.

El Grao/El Grau

El Grao (Catalan El Grau) was once a busy port which had an active fishing fleet and exported the citrus fruits grown in the huerta, but those days are gone. The town's economy now depends on its long white beaches, lined with hotels, apartment blocks, restaurants and bars.

Gerona/Girona

Q 3

Province: Gerona (GE). Telephone dialling code: 972
Altitude: 68m/223ft. Population: 88,000

Gerona (Catalan Girona), chief town of its province, lies 35km/22 miles inland from the Costa Brava on the Río Ter, which is joined here by the Onyar, the Güell and the Galligans.

History

Gerona was founded by the Iberians, probably in the period of the first Greek settlements, and has preserved remains of its Iberian walls. In Roman times it was known as Gerunda, and the Arabs (from whom it was briefly recaptured by Charlemagne in 785) called it Jerunda. Strategically situated on the most important road through the Pyrenees, it was frequently fought over and became known as the "town of a thousand sieges". In the late 10th century it became an independent County, and later became subject for a time to the Counts of Barcelona. During the rising against Napoleon, in 1809, Gerona withstood a French siege for seven months before surrendering. Thereafter the French occupation lasted until 1814.

Sights

New town

The new town of Gerona lies on the left bank of the Onyar. In the arcaded Plaza de la Independencia (Catalan Plaça de Independència), near the river, is a monument commemorating the town's heroic resistance to Napoleon's troops. On the north side of the town is the Parque de la Dehesa (Catalan Parc de la Devesa).

Old Town

The old town rises up the right bank of the Onyar. Between the railway bridge in the north and the Plaza de Cataluña (Catalan Plaça Catalunya) spanning the river in the south a colourful line of old houses flanks the river,

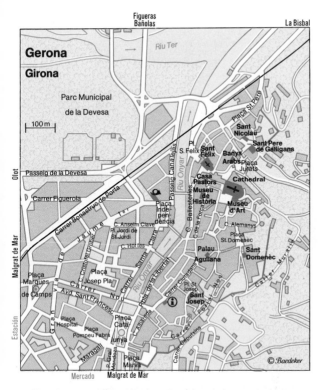

dominated by the church of San Feliú and the cathedral. Parallel to the riverbank is the Rambla de la Libertat (pedestrian zone), the main street of the old town, lined with arcades, shops and pavement cafés.

Near the north end of the old town stands the former collegiate church of San Feliú (11th–18th c.), a Gothic structure with very low aisles in which are Late Romanesque galleries with sculptured capitals. The choir was completed in 1318; the west front dates from the 17th century. The tall tower, originally Gothic, was struck by lightning in 1581 and was considerably altered in the subsequent rebuilding.

San Feliú/ Sant Fèlix

The church is entered through the doorway on the south side. There are no transepts, but on the north side is the vaulted Baroque chapel of San Narciso (dedicated to St Narcissus, bishop of Gerona in the time of Diocletian). In the choir, which has a carved Gothic altar, are a number of sarcophagi of the 2nd–6th centuries A.D.

Interior

Going along the south side of the church, we come to the Portal de Sobreportes, a massive town gate flanked by two towers, beside which is the Neo-Classical church of San Lucas (Catalan Sant Lluc). Beyond the gate is the little Plaza de la Catedral, most of which is taken up by the Baroque staircase of 90 steps (1690) leading up to the cathedral.

Opposite the foot of the steps is the palace of the Pastors family, which was given its present aspect in the 18th century. It is now occupied by the Law Courts.

Casa Pastors

The old town of Gerona on the Río Ter

Museo de
História/
Museu de
História

In Carrer de la Força, which runs south from the square in front of the cathedral, is an old Capuchin friary which now houses the Museo de História, a museum on the history of the town, concentrating particularly on the prehistory of the region and the age of industrialisation (19th–20th c.).

The part of the old town which extends south from here was until the 15th century the Jewish quarter of Gerona.

⋆Cathedral

The Gothic Cathedral which dominates the town was begun in 1312 and completed towards the end of the 16th century. At the top of a flight of steps is the Baroque main doorway (18th c.), with modern sculptural decoration. Outside the south side of the church with its Gothic doorway (lacking its original sculpture) is a small square.

Interior

The nave (aisleless) is one of the largest vaulted spaces in Gothic architecture, 50m/165ft long, 23m/75ft across and 34m/112ft high. The apse is considerably lower and, with its ambulatory and ring of chapels, is in accordance with the classical canon of forms. The high altar, under a baldachin, has a gilded retablo, a masterpiece of 14th century silversmith's work. Beyond this is the bishop's throne, a stone seat embellished with friezes of arabesques which is popularly known as the Throne of Charlemagne.

⋆⋆ Museum

On the north side of the church a doorway gives access to the Cathedral Museum. Among its principal treasures are (in the first room) a Romanesque Virgin (11th–12th c.), strongly resembling the Madonna of Montserrat (see entry), and an illuminated manuscript of the "Apocalypse"

(975). In the second room are a Late Gothic cross (1503–07) set with pearls and enamel inlays and a 14th century cross with champlevé enamel decoration. In a wall case in Room 3 are silver book covers (14th c.), and in the case in the centre of the room a fine collection of 15th century sculpture. Here too is a Bible which belonged to Charles V (14th c. Italian work) and two fine altar frontals (Nos. 41 and 42), one (14th c.) with gold and silver embroidery, the other (13th c.) with 21 scenes from the life of Christ.

Room 4 contains the finest thing in the museum, a magnificent tapestry (strictly speaking, not tapestry but silk embroidery) depicting the Creation. This 11th century work is based on Early Christian models (as is shown, for example, by the beardless figure of Christ as Creator of the world in the middle of the cycle, surrounded by the Latin text "And God said, Let there be light, and there was light").

★★"Creation" tapestry

From the Museum a short flight of steps leads down to the Romanesque cloister, trapezoid in plan, which dates from the 12th century. Some of the figural capitals of the columns are damaged, but they are still remarkable for their variety of subject-matter, including both Biblical themes and scenes from popular life. Under the vaulting are numerous grave slabs. Above the cloister rears the stump of a Romanesque tower, articulated by single and double-arched windows.

★Cloister

On the upper floor of the cloister are a fine collection of richly embroidered vestments. From one of the galleries there is an attractive view of the gardens to the north, the little Romanesque church of San Pedro de Galligans and a fragmentary stretch of the old town walls.

The Museum of Art, on the south side of the cathedral, has exhibits ranging in time from the pre-Romanesque period to the early 20th century.

Museo de Arte/ Museu d'Art

Paseo Arqueológico/Passeig Arqueològic

Starting from the cathedral, a signposted archaeological trail guides visitors to all the important sights in the old town. This leads through the Portal de Sobreportes and comes (on the left) to the Arab Baths (Baños Arabes, Banys Arabs), which probably developed out of a Jewish mikwe (ritual bath). The Late Romanesque vaulting has recently been restored.

Baños Arabes/ Banys Arabs

The Romanesque church of San Pedro de Galligans lies lower down, beyond the little Río Galligans. This sturdy 12th century building, which once belonged to a Benedictine abbey, is now deconsecrated, and the cloister houses an Archaeological Museum. The round-arched doorway of the church, now used for art exhibitions, has fine rosette and interlace ornament.

San Pedro de Galligans/ Sant Pere de Galligans

A short distance from San Pedro is the much smaller Romanesque church of San Nicolás (12th c.), now also deconsecrated and used for exhibitions.

San Nicolás/ Sant Nicolau

Surroundings of Gerona

Ullastret

Near the village of Ullastret, 30km/19 miles east of Gerona in the plain round the mouth of the Riu Ter, is the Iberian Village (Catalan Poblat Ibèric, Spanish Poblado Ibérico), an excavated Iberian settlement, now laid out as an archaeological park.

★ Poblado Ibérico/ Poblat Ibèric

The settlement is one of the largest of its kind in north-eastern Spain. The Puig de Sant Andreu and the Illa d'en Reixac, linked by a narrow isthmus of land, were already occupied by man in the Palaeolithic era, and here,

History

Iberian town walls, Ullastret

Medieval bridge, Besalú

probably from the 7th century B.C. onwards, a fortified settlement grew up. By the 6th century B.C. the Iberians, the original inhabitants of this region, had already developed active trading relations with the Phoenicians, the Etruscans and the Greeks. It was as a result of Greek influence that the Iberians began to build in stone and to use the potter's wheel. By the turn of the 5th century B.C. the Iberian town, now surrounded by a stout stone wall, was at the peak of its development and its prosperity. In the 3rd century, however, strong competition from the nearby Greek foundation of Emporion (see Ampurias) brought about its decline, and in the 2nd century B.C. the town was abandoned. It remained forgotten until the thirties of this century; then after its rediscovery systematic excavations began in 1947 and are still going on.

The site

A short distance from the entrance to the site are the walls on the west side of the town, with six large round towers set at fairly regular intervals of 30m/100ft. In this area too there are six gates through the walls.

The best place to start the tour of the site is Gate 1. From here a broad street (Street 1) leads to the upper town or acropolis, on the highest point of which is the Museum. Excavation has made most progress in this area, just inside the town walls. Here and there are large shafts driven vertically into the ground which no doubt served as store-rooms and cisterns. To the left of Street 1 is a residential district (Predis subirana), also with the foundations of buildings and a cistern. In the upper town the remains of two temples have also been excavated.

The area farther north is not yet open to the public. In the Camp Triangular ("Triangular Field") objects of the 5th and 4th centuries B.C. – the town's heyday – were recovered.

Museum

The Museum, on the highest point of the acropolis, displays agricultural implements, weapons, etc., of the Iberian period, a number of human skulls (some from victims of execution, some showing evidence of trepanation), fossil fauna, spinning whorls and loom weights, moulds for bronze fibulas and painted pottery (mostly imported Greek ware from Attica). In the main hall is a model of the site, and on the walls are large sketch maps showing the places of origin of the coins and pottery displayed and an archaeological map of Gerona province.

8km/5 miles south-west of Ullastret, on C 255, is the little town of La Bisbal (alt. 39m/128ft), a centre of pottery manufacture, with a wide range of products from simple and attractive ware to the merest kitsch. In the town can be seen a Romanesque castle, once the residence of the bishops of La Bisbal. | La Bisbal

Bañolas/Banyoles

The little town of Bañolas (Catalan Banyoles) has an archaeological museum (to the east of the Plaça Major) displaying finds from the surrounding area. On the east side of the town is the church of San Esteban (Catalan Sant Esteve), originally founded in the 9th century, destroyed by French troops in 1665 and thereafter rebuilt in Neo-Classical style. It contains a very beautiful Gothic retablo, the Retaule de la Mare de Deu de l'Escala (by Joan Antigo, 1437–39).

To the west of the town lies the Lago de Bañolas (Catalan Llac de Banyoles), the largest natural inland lake in Catalonia, which was the venue of the rowing events in the 1992 Olympic Games. At the south-west end of the lake is the village of Porqueras (Catalan Porqueres), with a beautiful little Romanesque church. | Lago de Bañolas/ Llac de Banyoles

★Besalú

16km/10 miles north-west of Bañolas on C 150, on the Río Fluvia (Catalan Riu Fluvià), is Besalú (alt. 151m/495ft), a little town which has preserved its medieval character. In the centre of the old town is the arcaded Plaza Mayor (Catalan Plaça Major).

North-west of the Plaça Major is the Late Romanesque parish church of San Vicente (Catalan Sant Vincenç), with a 16th century tower. On the south-east side is the fine Porta de Sant Rafael, with a round-headed arch and figural capitals. | San Vicente/ Sant Vincenç

South of the Plaça Major is the massive church of San Pedro (Catalan Sant Pere), one of the finest Romanesque churches in Catalonia. The columns on either side of the middle window in the otherwise undecorated west front have richly carved figural capitals and are flanked by two figures of lions. | San Pedro/ Sant Pere
Opposite the church is a handsome mansion, the Casa Cornelià.

On the road to the medieval bridge spanning the Fluvià, on the right, is a Jewish ritual bath (mikwe). The bridge, which was rebuilt in 1315, has a defensive tower in the middle and a gate with a portcullis at the end nearest the town. | Medieval bridge

Castellfullit (Catalan Castellfollit), 16km/10 miles west of Besalú on C 150, is fantastically situated on a spur of basalt which falls almost vertically down to the Riu Fluvià. Near the outermost tip of the crag, high above the abyss, is the old church. | ★Castellfullit/ Castellfollit

Other Sights in the Area

See Ampurias, Barcelona, Costa Brava, Figueras, Ripoll, Seo de Urgel and Vich.

Gibraltar

Status: British dependent territory
Area: 6.5 sq.km/2½ sq.miles
Telephone dialling code: 00 350
Altitude: 0–425m/0–1395ft
Population: 30,000

Entry

Gibraltar is entered from Spain at the La Linea frontier crossing (see Algeciras).

★★ Situation

International
Driving Plate

Gibraltar, long famous as the "key to the Mediterranean", which has been held by Britain since 1704, lies near the southern tip of the Iberian peninsula. The Rock of Gibraltar (Arabic Jebel al-Tarik) rears out of the sea on the east side of Algeciras Bay, linked with the mainland of Spain by a narrow isthmus. The town of Gibraltar lies on the west side of the Rock, which rises from the sea in a series of terraces. Since Gibraltar has for all practical purposes no sources of water of its own, large cisterns ("water catchments") have been hewn out of the rock at its higher east end. The only monkeys living wild in Europe are the Barbary apes of Gibraltar.

The population of Gibraltar is a mixture of people from all parts of the British Isles, from Spain, Portugal, Morocco and other Mediterranean countries, as well as some Indians. The language pattern is equally mixed: in addition to English in all its variations and of course to Spanish, Gibraltar has a dialect of its own, basically Spanish but with an admixture of English.

Since the withdrawal of most of the British troops and the loss in jobs which followed, Gibraltar has tried to attract investment from the EU and become a financial centre. Tourism (4.1 million in 1991), the sale of stamps, and the commercial harbour are significant sources of income together with a modest degree of industry (oil, foodstuffs). The currency is the Gibraltar pound and since 1991 a coin worth 70 ECU (=50 pounds) has been in circulation.

Transport

The runway of the civil airport is built out into Algeciras bay and is crossed by the road to the Spanish frontier (with traffic light control), there are flights to London and Tangier (Morocco). There are also ferry services to and from Tangier. Vehicles on Gibraltar drive on the right.

History and Constitution

★ Straits of
Gibraltar

Arms of Gibraltar

The Straits of Gibraltar, known in antiquity as the Fretum Gaditanum or Fretum Herculeum, are a strategically important link between the Atlantic and the Mediterranean. In ancient times the rock of Gibraltar, then known as Calpe, and its counterpart on the African side, Mt Abyla (Jebel Musa), near Ceuta (see entry), were known as the Pillars of Hercules – set up by Hercules, as legend had it, at the gateway to the great Ocean. In A.D. 711 the Moors landed here under their general Tarik, who named the rock Jebel al-Tarik ("Mount of Tarik"), which in course of time became Gibraltar.

In 1462 Spain at last recovered Gibraltar from the Arabs. During the War of the Spanish Succession, in 1704, it was taken by British troops, and under the treaty of Utrecht in 1713 it was formally assigned to Britain. All later attempts by Spain to recapture Gibraltar were unsuccessful. The Franco regime also sought to recover the territory, but in a referendum held in 1967 more than 95% of the inhabitants voted in favour of staying with Britain. In 1969 a new constitution came into effect under which the colony became the City of Gibraltar, under British sovereignty. Thereupon Spain closed the frontier with Gibraltar. Under a treaty signed at Lisbon in 1980 Britain and Spain agreed on the reopening of the frontier, though it was not in fact opened until 1985. In 1987 agreement was reached on the "joint use" of the territory so as to promote the development of tourist facilities and the use of the airport.

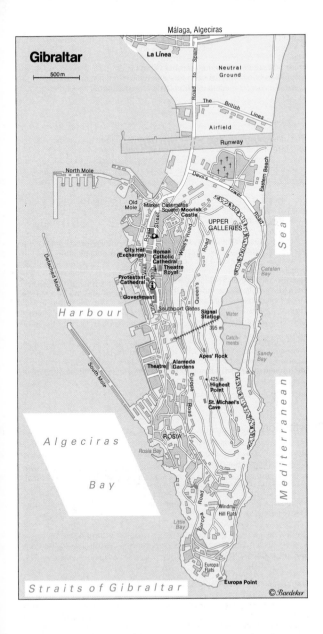

Gibraltar

Málaga, Algeciras

500 m

La Línea

Neutral
Ground

The British Lines

Airfield

Runway

North Mole

Devil's Tower

Eastern Beach

Old Mole

Market Casemates
Square Moorish
Castle

UPPER
GALLERIES

City Hall
(Exchange)

Roman
Catholic
Cathedral

Theatre
Royal

Protestant
Cathedral

Government

Southport Gates

Signal
Station

Water

395 m

Catchments

Catalan
Bay

S e a

Sandy
Bay

Apes' Rock

Theatre

Alameda
Gardens

• 425 m
Highest
Point

St. Michael's
Cave

M e d i t e r r a n e a n

H a r b o u r

Detached Mole

South Mole

A l g e c i r a s

B a y

ROSIA

Rosia Bay

Little
Bay

Windmill
Hill Flats

Europa
Flats

Europa Point

S t r a i t s   o f   G i b r a l t a r

© Baedeker

255

Gibraltar

Constitution

Gibraltar enjoys self-government in internal affairs, but Britain remains responsible for foreign affairs, defence and internal security. The head of state is the Governor as representative of the Queen and commander-in-chief, assisted by the nine-member Gibraltar Council. The executive, the Council of Ministers (between four and twelve in number), headed by the Chief Minister, is elected by Gibraltar's fifteen-member Parliament.

North Town (Old Town)

Moorish Castle

The old town of Gibraltar, North Town, begins beyond the airport, which is laid out on the isthmus of level ground, with Casemates Square. Above this, to the east, is the Moorish Castle, originally built in the 8th century and rebuilt by the Almohads in the 14th century, of which only the keep and a few fragments of masonry remain.

Harbour

North-west of the square is the harbour, and just beyond this the Old Mole, built in 1309, which along with the North Mole marks the northern end of Gibraltar's large harbour.

Main Street

From the square Main Street, in which are most of Gibraltar's hotels, shops and public buildings, runs past the Post Office and the Exchange (with the Town Hall to the rear) to the Roman Catholic Cathedral, a former mosque which was rebuilt in Gothic style in 1502. South-west of this are the Synagogue and, in Bomb House Lane, the Gibraltar Museum, the most striking item in which is a large model of the peninsula. In Cathedral Square stands the Moorish-style Anglican Cathedral (1821). Near the south end of Main Street is the Governor's Residence (the Convent), originally a Franciscan convent built in 1531.

Alameda

At the end of Main Street are the Southport Gates, beyond which is the Alameda, a public garden with luxuriant subtropical vegetation and an open-air theatre. At the north end of the gardens is a cableway running up to the Signal Station (395m/1295ft), near which are the Water Catchments (reservoirs).

South Town

Europa Road

On the east side of the Alameda is the beginning of Europa Road, a 5km/ 3 mile long scenic road which climbs steeply up the west side of the Rock between the houses and gardens of South Town and then runs down between the jagged rock faces of Europa Pass.

★★ Europa Point

At the southern tip of the peninsula is Europa Point, with a restaurant, a lighthouse and the old chapel of Nuestra Señora de Europa. From here there are magnificent views of Algeciras Bay, the African coast and Apes' Rock (see below).

On the east side of the Rock a road runs from north to south by way of Eastern Beach and Catalan Bay Village (tourist centre), below the Water Catchments, to Sandy Bay.

Around the Apes' Rock

Upper Galleries

From Main Street Willis' Road leads past the Moorish Castle into Queen's Road, a narrow road which runs along the Rock, half way up, affording fine views. At the near end of this road, on the left, are the Upper Galleries, which were hewn from the rock during the Franco-Spanish siege of Gibraltar in 1779–83 and still house cannon.

The Rock of Gibraltar

1.5km/1 mile farther south on Queen's Road is the Apes' Rock, home of the Barbary apes which are the only monkeys living wild in Europe. A British army corporal is assigned the duty of feeding these living symbols of Gibraltar. Visitors should be wary in their dealings with the apes, which tend to bite.

Apes' Rock

Beyond the Apes' Rock, on the left, a flight of steps leads up to the Highest Point (425m/1395ft).

★Highest Point

Farther south a track leads off Queen's Road to St Michael's Cave, the largest cave on the Rock, with fine stalactites and stalagmites. In summer the cave is used as a concert hall. At the end of Queen's Road there is a sharp bend turning back into Europa Road.

St Michael's Cave

Gijón

F 1

Province: Asturias (O). Telephone dialling code: 985
Altitude: sea level. Population: 262,000

The busy port and industrial town of Gijón is the largest city in Asturias, with one of the best harbours on the north coast of Spain. It lies between two sheltered bays on the south side of the former rocky island of Santa Catalina and on the deposits of alluvial soil which now link it with the mainland. Gijón is the economic centre of Asturias, and much of the coal mined in the province is shipped from its harbour at El Musel. There is a predominance of heavy industry (smelting works, shipyards, engineering plants); other products include glass and ceramics.

There was a Roman settlement called Gegio here, which developed in the 8th century into the residence of the Asturian kings. In 1588 the remnants of the "Invincible Armada" sought refuge in Gijón harbour. Here in 1744 was

History

born Gaspar Melchor de Jovellanos (d. 1811), the poet and liberal reformer who became one of the leaders of the resistance to Napoleon. The town was largely destroyed during the Spanish Civil War and thereafter was rebuilt on a modern plan, so that practically no old buildings have survived.

Old Town (Cimadevilla)

The original core of Gijón is the old fishing quarter of Cimadevilla with its steep and irregular streets, between the old fishing harbour on the west and the Playa de San Lorenzo on the east. Above the houses rises Monte Santa Catalina, from which there are extensive views, westward to Cabo de Peñas, eastward to Cabo de San Lorenzo and south-eastward to the Picos de Europa.

Plaza Mayor

The Plaza Mayor, lined with cafés and bars, lies between the old town and the newer districts of Gijón. On its east side is the Ayuntamiento (Town Hall).

Roman baths

North of the Town Hall, in Plaza Jovellanos, stands the Palacio de los Valdés (1590), in the cellars of which were found remains of Roman baths dating from the 1st century A.D.

Museo Casa
Natal Jovellanos

On the opposite side of the square is the house in which Gaspar Melchor de Jovellanos was born, an imposing building with a long wrought-iron balcony, in which Jovellanos founded the Instituto Jovellanos in 1794. It is now a museum, with pictures by contemporary Asturian painters and material illustrating Gijón's industrial history.

Palacio de
Revillagigedo

To the west of the Plaza Mayor, in Plaza del Marqués, is the Palacio de Revillagigedo, with two tall towers (15th–16th c.).

New Town

Plaza del
6 de Agosto

From Plaza del Marqués Gijón's busy main street, the Corrida, runs south to the Plaza del 6 de Agosto, the central feature of the new town. In the centre of the square is a monument to Gaspar Melchor de Jovellanos. To the north-east is the present-day Instituto Jovellanos, originally founded as a school for the practical study of the natural sciences, now the Provincial College of Industry and Nautical Science.

Playa de
San Lorenzo

On the east side of the Santa Catalina promontory is the Playa de San Lorenzo, a beach lined with high-rise hotels and apartment blocks which extends south-east for more than a kilometre (¾ mile) to the Río Piles.

Pueblo de
Asturias

On the far side of the Río Piles, opposite the Parque Isabel la Católica, lies the Pueblo de Asturias (Asturian Village), an open-air ethnographic museum in which visitors can see typical Asturian buildings, including *hórreos* (maize stores), farmhouses and a factory producing *gaitas* (Asturian bagpipes).

Universidad
Laboral

On a hill on the south-eastern outskirts of the city (5km/3 miles from the town centre on the Santander road) is the extensive campus of the Universidad Laboral (Workers' University), founded in 1955. It is centred on a building with a 120m/395ft high tower which has more of the appearance of a Baroque church than of a university. There are some 4000 students studying science, technology and agriculture.

★★ Costa Verde

The stretch of coast between Ribadeo in the west and San Vicente de la Barquera in the east, known as the Costa Verde ("Green Coast"), offers some of the finest coastal scenery in northern Spain. Here a strip of land only a few kilometres wide extends between the sea on the one hand and the green slopes of the high Cantabrian Mountains (Cordillera Cantábrica) on the other. The inhabitants of the coastal strip live by fishing, stock-farming and the growing of cereals. For tourists the Costa Verde is one of the most varied regions in Spain: the picturesque little coves and sandy beaches which occur at intervals along the generally rocky coast offer attractive bathing, while there is endless scope for walkers in the hills, with the chance of encountering some of the shy mountain fauna.

★ Cabo de Peñas

Cabo de Peñas, north-west of Gijón, divides the Costa Verde into an eastern and a western half. 6km/4 miles west of Gijón on N 632 a side road branches off on the right and runs north to the fishing village of Candás. In the church is a famous image of Christ from Ireland which is much venerated by seamen.

Candás

Beyond this is Luanco, which has a small Museum of the Sea (Museo del Mar).

Luanco

The road continues to Bañagues, and soon after this, at a junction, the road to the right leads to Cabo de Peñas, from which there are extensive views.

★ Mirador

Along the Coast to the West

From Gijón it is possible either to follow the route described above to Cabo de Peñas and continue from there to Avilés (see entry) or to take the direct road to Avilés, either the A 8 motorway or N 632.

From Avilés the coast road (N 632) runs west, passing Salinas, a seaside resort with one of the broadest beaches in Asturias.

Salinas

The road continues by way of Soto del Barco to the fishing town of Cudillero, its houses straggling picturesquely along the slopes of the coastal hills. It has a very attractive little plaza and harbour.

Cudillero

9km/6 miles farther on is Soto de Luiña, just beyond which a side road goes off on the right to Cabo Vidio, from which there are splendid views of the sea and Cabo de Peñas.

★ Cabo Vidio

At Canero N 632 runs into N 634 (E 50). Luarca, which lies on both banks of the Río Negro, here spanned by several bridges, is a charming little town – though the effect is spoiled by the heavy goods traffic on this narrow European highway. The town centre with its 18th and 19th century houses is separated from the sea by a spur of hill. A road descends along the Río Negro to the district bordering the large fishing harbour. A long breakwater extends round the harbour to its entrance, from which there is the best view of the houses and of the boats in the harbour. Above the town, on a rocky spur once occupied by an old fortress, are a church and cemetery.

★ Luarca

Navia, 20km/12½ miles west of Luarca at the mouth of the Río Navia, is another charming little fishing town.

Navia

From Navia a detour (4km/2½ miles south-west) can be made to Coaña, where there is an excellently preserved Celtic village, with the remains of circular huts, fortifications and cisterns.

Coaña

Beyond Navia the road crosses the river and climbs by way of Valdepares to the little fishing village of Tapia, near the cliff-fringed bay next to Cabo

Castropol

Cebes. Beyond this, on the high east bank of the Ría de Ribadeo (the estuary of the Río Eo), is the little port of Castropol, a fishing town which also ships the local timber.

Ribadeo

Across the estuary from Castropol can be seen the Galician town of Ribadeo, which is most easily reached by way of a high bridge on N 634, the Puente de los Santos.

Along the Coast to the East

Villaviciosa

From Gijón N 632 runs east, following a hilly and winding route which takes it over the Alto del Infanzón and then down to Villaviciosa, an old-world little port and fishing town on the Ría de Villaviciosa which is also a centre of cider manufacture. In September 1517 the town was honoured by an unexpected visit from the Emperor Charles V (Charles I of Spain), who was paying his first visit to Spain, when his ship put in here by mistake instead of Santander. In the attractive Plaza Mayor is the Gothic church of Santa María de la Oliva (13th c.), with a richly decorated doorway. Nearby is a secluded little square. From Villaviciosa a detour (10km/6 miles south-west) can be made to the old Cistercian abbey of Santa María de Valdediós (see Oviedo, Surroundings).

★Mirador del Fito

The coast road then crosses the Alto de Buenos Aires and descends to the village of Colunga, situated on rising ground. The sea now comes into sight; and soon after the resort of La Isla, situated in a beautiful bay, a side road branches off on the right to the Mirador del Fito (12km/7½ miles), from which there is a magnificent view of the Picos de Europa (see entry).

★Ribadesella

N 632 continues to Ribadesella, an attractive fishing town and seaside resort at the mouth of the Río Sella (good fishing). The river, which is spanned by a wide bridge, divides the town into two parts: to the left the newer part of the town, with hotels, holiday villas and a very beautiful beach (unspoiled by tower blocks), to the right the harbour and the old town (17th and 18th c.) with the little Plaza Vieja and friendly sidrerías (cider bars), in which the drinks are poured in traditional fashion from high above the glass. Every year at the beginning of August there is a very popular canoe race on the river.

★Cuevas de Tito Bustillo

A few hundred metres from Ribadesella (cross the bridge to the new town and at once turn left) are the Cuevas de Tito Bustillo, a much ramified cave system with animal paintings between 15,000 and 20,000 years old. The caves were discovered in 1968 by a team of speleologists and are named after a member of the group who died young. The conducted tour (in Spanish) takes visitors through a series of huge chambers with bizarre stalactitic formations to the cave containing the paintings and engravings, with figures of horses and stags painted in colour and outlined in black.

Cuevas del Mar

9km/6 miles beyond Ribadesella N 632 joins N 634 (E 50), and shortly after the junction a road goes off on the left to the Cuevas del Mar, sea-caves which are under water at high tide.

San Antolín de Bedón

A few kilometres farther on, to the left of the road, are the remains of the 11th century Benedictine abbey of San Antolín de Bedón.

★Llanes

Llanes, which lies a little way off the main road, is a charming little town, in the centre of which is a harbour linked with the sea by a canal. North of the harbour in an attractive square, the Plaza del Cristo Rey, stands the 13th century church of Santa María. The church has a fine doorway under a porch with interlaced arcading and contains a 16th century Flemish altarpiece. Behind it are remains of the old town walls, beyond which is a beautiful little beach.

The newer part of the town, to the north-west, is also attractive.

Llanes

The road continues, with no view of the sea, through wooded hilly country, in which several megalithic tombs (dolmens) have been found, to La Franca. Soon after this little town a road goes off on the left to the Cueva del Pindal, a sea-cave containing scratched drawings and paintings, including an unusual figure of a mammoth, showing the heart, and several drawings which appear to represent wounded animals.

★ Cueva del Pindal

Beyond this is Colombres, where the most recent attraction for visitors is the Archivo de Indianos, the principal contribution made by Asturias to the 500th anniversary of the discovery of America which is to be celebrated in 1992. Housed in a handsome blue-painted villa, it documents the emigration of Spaniards to America and their relations with the native Indians. It thus supplements the Museo de América in Madrid (see entry), which is concerned with research on the native peoples of America, and the Archivo de Indias in Seville (see entry), which is devoted to colonial history.

Colombres
★ Archivo de
Indianos

A number of rooms on the first floor are used for special exhibitions on a variety of subjects.

The Costa Verde ends at San Vicente de la Barquera, a popular holiday resort with a sandy beach. Around the Plaza Mayor are a number of handsome old houses. The fortress-like church of Nuestra Señora de los Angeles (13th–16th c.) contains a number of fine carved tombs.

San Vicente
de la Barquera

Granada

H 8

Province: Granada (GR). Telephone dialling code: 958
Altitude: 662–780m/2170–2560ft. Population: 262,000

The famous old Moorish capital of Granada, now chief town of its province, the see of an archbishop and a university town, is magnificently situated at

★★ Situation

Granada and the Alhambra

the foot of the Sierra Nevada between two outlying hills which fall steeply down to the fertile vega of the Río Genil (often waterless in summer).

History

Granada is thought to have originally been an Iberian foundation. In A.D. 711, after the defeat of the Visigoths, it fell into the hands of the Arabs, who called it Gharnatha and built a castle on the Alhambra hill. After the fall of the Caliphate of Córdoba, in 1031, the governor of Granada declared the independence of the town and surrounding area. Thereafter Granada was ruled by the Almoravids and Almohads; then in 1241 Ibn al-Ahmed, of the Beni Nasr tribe, founded the Nasrid dynasty, taking the title of Mohammed I, and made Granada the wealthiest city in the Iberian peninsula. After 250 years of splendour the town passed to the Catholic Monarchs under the treaty of Santa Fe in 1491, and on January 2nd 1492 Ferdinand and Isabella made their entry into Granada, while Boabdil, the last Moorish ruler, was leaving his kingdom. Thereafter the town remained in Christian hands and enjoyed a fresh period of prosperity during the Renaissance. The bloody repression of a Moorish rising in 1569 was followed by a decline. The town's recovery began with the renovation of the irrigation system in the vega and the introduction of new crops in the early 20th century.

The ★★Town

The more northerly of the two hills between which Granada lies is Albaicín, on which the older part of the city is built; the Alhambra hill to the south is separated from Albaicín by the gorge of the Río Darro, a normally meagre stream which flows underground below the town to join the Río Genil. Crowned by the Alhambra palace on its hill, Granada has been declared a national monument in virtue of its many well preserved remains of a rich alien culture and art and as the scene of great events in the history of Spain.

Old Town and Albaicín

★Cathedral

A short distance north-west of the Plaza de Isabel la Católica is the Cathedral of Santa María de la Encarnación, a memorial to the victory of Christian Spain and the country's finest Renaissance church. It was begun in Gothic style by Enrique Egas in 1523, continued in Plateresque style by Diego de Siloé from 1525 onwards and consecrated in 1561 while still unfinished. The massive west front (1667) was built by Alonso Cano and his successor José de Granados. Over the main doorway (Puerta Principal) is a large relief by José Risueño (1717). On the north-west side of the cathedral are the Puerta de San Jerónimo, with sculpture by Siloé, Juan de Maeda and others, and the richly decorated Puerta del Perdón, completed in 1537.

The cathedral is entered by the doorway on the Gran Via de Colón, which also leads to the Capilla Real. The interior was not completed until after 1703. With double aisles and a transept, it is richly furnished with sculpture and pictures, mostly by Alonso Cano and Juan de Sevilla. Particularly magnificent is the domed Capilla Mayor, 47m/154ft high, with beautiful 16th century stained glass and seven large paintings by Alonso Cano. On the entrance arch pillars are statues of the Catholic Monarchs by Pedro de Mena and, above them, heads of Adam and Eve by Alonso Cano. The bronze statues of Apostles date from 1614. In the choir are two large Baroque organs. The cathedral treasury, the finest items in which are a large silver monstrance and a number of Flemish tapestries, is now housed in the former chapterhouse in the north-west corner. From the south aisle a Gothic doorway (usually closed) gives access to the Capilla Real.

Interior

★Capilla Mayor

On the south-east side of the cathedral is the Sagrario, a Baroque structure built between 1705 and 1759 on the site of the town's principal mosque.

Sagrario

★★Capilla Real

In the south aisle of the cathedral is the entrance to the Capilla Real, the Late Gothic burial chapel of the Catholic Monarchs, built on to the cathedral in 1506–21. An elaborately wrought grille by Bartolomé de Jaén encloses the richly decorated royal tombs: to the right Ferdinand (d. 1516) and Isabella (d. 1504), in a tomb of Carrara marble (1522) by the Florentine sculptor Domenico Fancelli; to the left Philip the Handsome (d. 1506) and Joan the Mad (d. 1555), by Bartolomé Ordóñez.

Beyond the royal tombs is a large and beautifully carved retablo by Felipe Vigarny, with statues of the Catholic Monarchs by Diego de Siloé. In the transepts are finely carved and richly decorated *relicarios* (side altars) by Alonso de Mena (1623); also in the north transept is the famous Triptych of the Passion by Dierik Bouts. Steps lead down to the Crypt, with simple lead sarcophagi containing the remains of other kings and princes.

Sacristy

The sacristy of the Capilla Real contains a number of outstanding works of art, including pictures by Botticelli ("Christ on the Mount of Olives"), Rogier van der Weyden ("Pietà") and Hans Memling ("Descent from the Cross"), polychrome wood figures of the Catholic Monarchs in prayer by Felipe Vigarny, Ferdinand's sword, Isabella's crown and sceptre, and a missal which belonged to the Catholic Monarchs.

Between the Capilla Real and the Sagrario is the Lonja (the old Stock Exchange), with a beautiful loggia (1518–22).

Lonja

Directly next to the entrance of the cathedral is the Madraza, a Baroque building but originally constructed by Jusuf I, in 1349 as a Moorish university.

Madraza

Around the Cathedral

Facing the west front of the cathedral, in Plaza de Alonso Cano, is the Archbishop's Palace, mostly dating from the 18th century.

Palacio Arzobispal

Behind the Archbishop's Palace is the Plaza de Bib-Rambla, which takes its name from one of the old Moorish town gates, the Bab al-Ramia. In the centre of the square is the Fuente de los Gigantones.

Plaza de Bib-Rambla

The Corral del Carbon (14th c.) east of the cathedral is the only remaining caravanserai in Spain. Following the expulsion of the Moors in 1531 it served as a coal depot and later as a theatre and residential house.

★ Corral del Carbon

Plaza Nueva

North-east of the cathedral, in the busy Plaza Nueva, is the Audiencia (Law Courts), built between 1531 and 1587 as the Real Cancillería (Royal Chancellery). It has a beautiful two-storey arcaded courtyard and a magnificent staircase with a fine timber ceiling. From the Plaza Nueva the Cuesta de Gomérez ascends to the Alhambra, above the town to the east.

Plaza Santa Ana

Along the Río Darro

Santa Ana

At the north-east end of the Plaza Nueva the Río Darro emerges from underground. Here too is the Renaissance church of Santa Ana (1541–48), with a Plateresque doorway and a minaret-like tower (1563).

Bañuelo

Along the north side of the Río Darro runs the Carrera del Darro, one of the oldest streets in Granada, from which there are fine views of the Alhambra. At No. 31 is the Bañuelo, an 11th century Moorish bath-house, of which survive the changing room and three bathing rooms with Moorish arches.

Casa de Castril/
Museo
Arqueológico

Farther along, on the right, is the church of San Pedro y San Pablo and opposite this, on the left, the Casa de Castril, a Renaissance mansion with a Plateresque doorway probably designed by Diego de Siloé. This now houses the Archaeological Museum, with prehistoric, Iberian and Moorish antiquities and a number of fine Egyptian vases.

Sacromonte

From the Carrera del Darro the Cuesta del Chapiz branches off on the left. At the Casa del Chapiz, a fine example of a house belonging to a well-to-do Morisco family of the 16th century, the Camino del Sacromonte turns off on the right and ascends the hill (fine views), passing large numbers of cave dwellings occupied by gipsies *(gitanos)*, whose presence in Granada is attested since 1532, to the former Benedictine abbey of Sacromonte (12th c.), which is much favoured by the gipsies. Other footpaths, steep in places, climb through deeply indented gullies (loose stones) to the Ermita San Miguel de Alto, from which there are magnificent views.

Albaicín

San Salvador

From the Cuesta del Chapiz Calle del Salvador leads into the picturesque little lanes of the Albaicín quarter, parts of which still have something of a Moorish character. In this area is the Mudéjar church of San Salvador, built on the site of an earlier mosque.

★ View from
San Nicolás

Beyond San Salvador is the church of San Nicolás (1525), the heart of the Albaicín quarter. From here there is a splendid view, frequently painted, of the Alhambra and the Sierra Nevada.

Arab walls

From the nearby Puerta Nueva (Puerta de los Estandartes) a well preserved stretch of the town's Arab walls (Muralla árabe) runs west to the Puerta Monaitia. The best view of the walls is from the Cuesta de la Alhacaba, which leads to the Plaza del Triunfo. In this square is the Puerta de Elvira, once the town's principal gate, which dates from the 9th century.

Around the University

Hospital Real

North-west of the Plaza del Triunfo, in Calle Ancha de Capuchinos, is the Hospital Real, a Renaissance building (by Enrique Egas, 1504–22) now occupied by the University.

★ La Cartuja

1km/¾ mile north of the Plaza del Triunfo is the Cartuja (Charterhouse), a Carthusian monastery founded in 1516, the finest part of which is the church, with an interior remodelled in Baroque style in the 17th century. The ceiling paintings in the nave were the work of Pedro Anastasio Bocanegra. The most striking feature of the church, however, is the sacristy, designed by Luis de Arévalo, with a riot of elaborate stucco ornament.

Hospital
San Juan de Dios

South-west of the Paseo del Triunfo is the Hospital San Juan de Dios (Hospital of St John of God). The tomb of St John of God, who founded the Hospital in 1552, is behind the outsize retablo of the adjoining church, which has rich Baroque decoration.

A little farther south-west is the Convento de San Jerónimo, which was founded in 1492. The walls of the church are completely covered with 18th century wall paintings. In the splendid Capilla Mayor is the tomb of the "Gran Capitán", Gonzalo Fernández de Córdoba (d. 1515). Flanking the high altar (after 1570) are kneeling figures of Gonzalo and his wife.

Convento de
San Jerónimo

From San Jerónimo Calle de la Duquesa runs south-east to the 18th century building, with a fine Baroque façade, which since 1759 has been occupied by the University. It was originally a Jesuit college.

University

Alhambra Hill

The Alhambra can be reached on foot by way of the Cuesta de Gomérez and the short but steep Cuesta Empedrada. There is also a bus service. Cars can drive up the Cuesta de Gomérez and continue past the Puerta de las Granadas on the Paseo de la Alhambra to the signposted car parks.

Access

★ Alameda de la Alhambra

From the Plaza Nueva the Cuesta de Gomérez runs up some 250m/275yd to the Puerta de las Granadas, the main entrance to the Alameda de la Alhambra (Alhambra Park). The gate was built in 1536, replacing an earlier Moorish gate.

Puerta de
las Granadas

On Monte Mauror, above the road to the right, can be seen the Torres Bermejas, Granada's oldest defensive work. The towers were given their present form in the 13th century, but were originally part of an earlier stronghold.

Torres Bermejas

From the Puerta de las Granadas the Cuesta Empedrada climbs steeply up through the Alhambra Park, which covers a large area on the slopes above a gorge between the Alhambra Hill and Monte Mauror, to the Puerta de la Justicia at the entrance to the Alhambra proper, a massive gateway built in 1348, during the reign of Yusuf I.

Puerta de
la Justicia

Beyond the Puerta de la Justicia is the Puerta del Vino, which leads into the Plaza de los Aljibes (Square of the Cisterns). From here there are fine views of the Darro valley, Albaicín and Sacromonte.

Plaza de los
Aljibes

Alcazaba

On the west side of the square is the Alcazaba, the earlier royal castle begun in the reign of Mohammed I (13th c.), of which there remain only the outer walls with their massive towers. The Puerta de la Alcazaba leads into the Jardín de los Adarves on the south side of the castle, from which there is a fine view of the town. There are even more extensive views from the 26m/85ft high Torre de la Vela at the west end of the terrace.

★ View from
Torre de la Vela

★ Palacio de Carlos V

On the east side of the Plaza de los Aljibes is the palace built for the Emperor Charles V by Pedro Machuca. Begun in 1526 but never completed, the palace was paid for by a special tax imposed on Moors who had remained in Granada after its reconquest. The palace is a massive structure 65m/207ft square and 17m/57ft high. Even in its unfinished state the palace, with its sober façade, is the finest example of High Renaissance architecture in Spain. Apart from the façade the only part completed is the pillared inner courtyard, a two-storey rotunda with Doric columns in the lower gallery and Ionic columns in the upper gallery.

Granada

Museo Provincial
de Bellas Artes

On the upper floor of the palace is the Provincial Museum of Art, which is mainly devoted to artists of the Granada school. The sculpture on display includes an "Entombment" by Jacobo Florentino, Alonso Cano's "St John of God" and figures by Pedro de Mena and Diego de Siloé. The pictures include many by Alonso Cano and works by Fray Juan Sánchez Cotán (who lived in the Cartuja), Pedro de Raxis, Pedro Anastasio Bocanegra, Juan Ramírez and Juan de Sevilla.

Museo Nacional
de Arte
Hispano-
Musulmán

On the ground floor of the palace the National Museum of Hispano-Muslim Art has a large collection of decorative objects from the period of Moorish rule in Spain, including many items from the Alhambra. These include glassware, ceramics, ornamental friezes and – the Museum's principal treasure – the 1.3m/4ft 3in. high Alhambra Vase (Jarro de la Alhambra), which dates from 1320.

Santa María

On the east side of the palace stands the church of Santa María, built between 1581 and 1618 on the site of the Alhambra mosque, in which the first mass after the recapture of Granada was said. To the right of the main doorway is a column commemorating the death of two Christian martyrs in 1397.

★★ Alhambra Palace

Opening times
Mon.–Sat.
9am–8pm, Sun.
9am–6pm;
night opening:
Tues., Thur. and
Sat. 10pm–
midnight

On the north side of Charles V's palace is the entrance to the Alhambra Palace (Casa Real, Alcázar), residence of the Moorish rulers of the Nasrid dynasty. Work on the building of the palace began in the reign of Yusuf I (1333–54) and was substantially completed in the reign of Mohammed V (1354–91). Like all Moorish secular buildings, it is externally plain and unpretentious: it depends for artistic effect on its carefully contrived ground plan and its sumptuous decoration, one of the finest achievements of Moorish art. The palace, surrounded by its walls and numerous towers, was known to the Arabs as Medinat al-Hambra, the "Red City", after the colour of the stone. The entrance ticket has a time limit of half an hour to allow for entering. The visiting time itself is not restricted.

Tour of the
Alhambra

The interior is an outstanding example of Islamic palace architecture, with its careful articulation into three sections – the Mexuar, used for the public administration of justice and for large assemblies; the royal palace proper (the Divan or Serrallo); and the women's apartments or Harem, designed for the private and family life of the monarch. In each section all the rooms open off a central courtyard, as in the old Greco-Roman house; in the Divan this has a large ornamental pond (Court of Myrtles), in the Harem a fountain (the Lion Fountain).

Mexuar

An antechamber leads into the azulejo-clad Mexuar, originally an audience chamber and court-room, which after the Christian conquest was used as a chapel. Adjoining the Mexuar is the Patio del Mexuar, on the left of which is the Cuarto Dorado (Golden Chamber), on the right one of the Alhambra's finest façades.

★ Patio de
los Arrayanes
(Court of Myrtles)

The Patio del Mexuar leads into the Patio de los Arrayanes or Patio de los Mirtos (Court of Myrtles), which takes its name from the hedges of myrtle round the central pond. The court is 37m/121ft long by 23m/75ft across, with a graceful arcade at each end. At its north end, beyond the Sala de la Barca (Hall of Blessing), is the 45m/148ft high Torre de Comares.

★★ Sala de
los Embajadores

In the Torre de Comares is the Sala de los Embajadores (Hall of the Ambassadors). In this room (11m/36ft square, 18m/59ft high), also used as a

In the Alhambra ▶

Granada

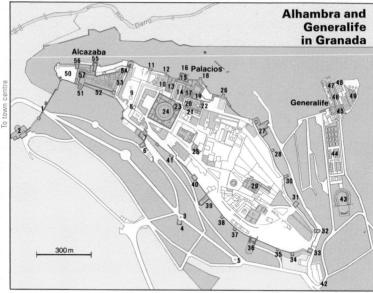

Alhambra and Generalife in Granada

To town centre

Sierra Nevada

300 m

throne room, the rulers of Granada received foreign envoys. With its magnificent larchwood dome, its many tall windows and its profusion of ornament (over 150 different patterns, including verses from the Koran and floral and geometric themes), this is one of the richest and most beautiful apartments in the Alhambra.

From the south-east corner of the Court of Myrtles the tour continues through the Sala de los Mozárabes into the Patio de los Leones (Court of Lions), the central feature of the royal winter residence built by Mohammed V, with the adjoining Harem. In the centre of this spacious court (28m/92ft by 16m/52ft) is the Lion Fountain, its basin supported by twelve marble lions. The arcading round the court, with its 124 columns, is of extraordinary lightness and delicacy.

★★Patio de los Leones (Court of Lions)

On the north side of the Court of Lions is the Sala de las Dos Hermanas (Hall of the Two Sisters) which together with the succeeding apartments was probably the women's winter lodging. Its tile and stucco decoration is perhaps the finest in the whole of the Alhambra. The honeycomb dome, the largest of all Arab stalactitic vaults, has some 5000 celles. The hall owes its name to the two large identical slabs of marble let into the floor.

★★Sala de las Dos Hermanas

Opening off the Hall of the Two Sisters is the Sala de los Ajimeces. Between its two arched windows (*ajimeces*) is the Mirador de Lindaraja (or de Daraxa), a charming little enclosed balcony with three windows reaching down almost to the floor and overlooking the Patio de Lindaraja. This room is, however, usually closed.

Sala de los Ajimeces

At the east end of the Court of Lions is the Sala de los Reyes (Hall of the Kings) or Sala de la Justicia. It is divided into seven sections with high stalactitic domes. In its alcove-like recesses are well preserved 15th c. ceiling paintings. Highly unusual are three paintings on leather of scenes

★Sala de los Reyes

Court of Lions

from court life and possibly portraits of rulers. The paintings show a consultation between ten magnificently attired councillors, a hunting scene and a representation of the rescue of a maiden from the clutches of a wild man.

★★Sala de los Abencerrajes

On the south side of the Court of Lions is the Sala de los Abencerrajes, named after a powerful aristocratic family who probably celebrated their winter festival here. In the centre of the room, which is crowned by a mighty stalactitic dome, is a twelve-sided marble fountain.

Patio de Lindaraja

Leaving the palace buildings and going down a staircase, twice turning left, the visitor comes to the Patio de Lindaraja, formerly the inner palace garden, which is planted with cypresses and orange-trees. The garden was not laid out until the victory of the Christian kings; the fountain formerly stood in the courtyard of the Mexuar.

Tocador de la Reina

From the Hall of the Two Sisters we pass along the gallery on the west side of the Jardín de Daraxa and through two other rooms in the outer gallery on the north side of the palace into the Tocador de la Reina (Queen's Dressing-Room) on the upper floor of the Torre del Peinador, from which there are fine views, particularly to the east of the Torre de las Damas and the Generalife.

Baños

On the south side of the Patio de la Reja are the Baños (Baths), an extensive complex of underground rooms dating from the time of Yusuf I: first the Sala de las Camas, with a gallery for girl singers, then a small bath, a steam bath and two women's baths.

★Towers

It is also well worth visiting the towers of the Alhambra. Immediately east of the Alhambra Palace is the Torre de las Damas, a defensive tower with an adjoining vaulted hall, a pool and a small mosque. Farther east, at the Puerta de Hierro or del Arrabal (where there is a path down to the Paseo de los Tristes), stands the Torre de los Picos ("Battlemented Tower"). Beyond this is the Torre del Candil, with a view (to right) of the former Convento de San Francisco, Granada's oldest religious house, converted in 1495 from an Arab palace and now a Parador Nacional. Then comes the Torre de la Cautiva (Tower of the Girl Captive), with a small patio and a splendidly decorated principal apartment. The Torre de las Infantas, beyond this, has a richly decorated hall and affords extensive views from the upper platform. At the east end of the hill is the Torre del Agua, with the cistern which supplied the Alhambra with water, and round the corner, on the south side, are two smaller towers, the Torre de Juan de Arce and Torre de Baltasar de la Cruz, followed by the tower of the Puerta de los Siete Suelos ("Gate of Seven Storeys"), two other small towers, then the Torre de las Cabezas ("Tower of the Heads") and finally the Torre de los Carros ("Tower of the Wagons"), at the exit.

★Palacio del Generalife

To the east of the Alhambra, on the slopes of the Cerro del Sol, is the Palacio del Generalife (Arabic Jennat al-Arif, the "Architect's Garden"), the summer palace of the Moorish kings, which was completed in 1319, during the reign of Ismail I. From the outer gate at the east end of the Alhambra complex a beautiful avenue of cypresses (Paseo de los Cipreses) leads to the 16th century gatehouse. Beyond this is a large court planted with myrtle and laurel hedges and orange-trees through which flows the Acequia del Generalife. At the north end of this court is the Sala de los Reyes (Hall of

Kings), adjoining which is a room with an enclosed balcony affording a magnificent view of the Alhambra and the Darro valley; from the belvedere above the hall there is a far-ranging prospect.

To the east a beautiful park extends up the hill, reminiscent of the garden of an Italian Renaissance villa with its terraces, grottoes, flowerbeds, fountains and carefully trimmed hedges.

★Park

From the continuation of the Paseo de los Cipreses, leading away from the Generalife, the Callejón de Falla goes off on the left. In this street is a house once occupied by the composer Manuel de Falla (1876–1946), who lived for many years in Granada; it is now a museum devoted to the composer.

Casa Museo Falla

Surroundings of Granada

To the Costa del Sol

Leave Granada on N 323, which runs south through the suburban district of Armilla and the fertile countryside beyond, with fine views of Granada to the rear, and then climbs to the Puerto del Suspiro del Moro (865m/2838ft), the "Pass of the Moor's Sigh", where the last Moorish king of Granada, Boabdil, is said to have wept as he took his last look at the city he was leaving.

Puerta del Sospiro del Moro

N 323 continues south by way of Beznar, where a very beautiful road goes off on the left into the wild hill scenery of the Alpujarras (see Almería, Surroundings), to Motril, beautifully situated at the foot of the coastal hills, with a fishing and boating harbour. It has two fine churches, one of which, on a hill, occupies the site of a Moorish castle in which Boabdil's mother lived.

Motril

The coast road (N 340) leads east through the fishing village of Calahonda to Castell de Ferro, a village dominated by the tower of a Moorish castle which lives by fishing, vegetable-growing and now increasingly – thanks to its long beach – by tourism.

Castell de Ferro

To the west N 340 crosses the Río Guadalfeo, passes through Salobreña, a charmingly situated little town of whitewashed houses, and comes to Almuñécar, a picturesque town, originally a Phoenician foundation, which is now a popular seaside resort. Its main features of interest are a ruined Moorish castle, the remains of a Roman aqueduct and its principal church, which was built by Juan de Herrera.

Almuñécar

Through the Sierra Harana

Leave Granada on N 342 (the road to Murcia), which runs north-east over the Puerto de la Mora (1360m/4462ft), the highest point on the road, to Purullena, a very interesting village of cave dwellings in a region of tufa hills.

Purullena

A few kilometres farther on (55km/34 miles from Granada) is Guadix (alt. 949m/3114ft), an episcopal town on the river of the same name, with an old Moorish castle dominating the town. Its most notable building is the cathedral (16th–18th c.), built on the foundations of an earlier mosque, with a massive tower and a Baroque façade; it has fine choir-stalls and contains a museum of religious art. In the Barrio de Santiago many of the inhabitants still live in cave dwellings hewn from the local tufa.

Guadix

Guadalajara
J 4

Province: Guadalajara (GU). Telephone dialling code: 911
Altitude: 641m/2103ft. Population: 57,000

Guadalajara, chief town of its province, situated above the left bank of the Río Henares some 56km/35 miles from Madrid, is now very much under the influence of the capital. Its name is derived from the Arabic Wad al-Hajarah ("river of stones"). The powerful Mendoza family, who gained possession of Guadalajara in the 14th century, left their mark on the town. During the Spanish Civil War, in March 1937, the "battle of Guadalajara" between Republican and Italian forces was fought at Brihuega, north-east of the town.

Sights

★ Palacio del Duque del Infantado

The Palacio del Duque del Infantado, in a style which mingles Late Gothic and Mudéjar features, was built for the Mendoza family between 1461 and 1480 by the French-born architect Juan Guas, and ranks as one of his finest achievements. King Francis I of France was sumptuously received in the palace after being taken prisoner in the battle of Pavia (1525), and Philip II married Elisabeth de Valois here. During the Civil War the palace was largely destroyed but was subsequently rebuilt. The façade has faceted stonework and is topped by a projecting gallery with finely carved columns. It has a beautiful two-storey Isabelline patio. The interior is magnificently decorated, and now houses the Museo de Bellas Artes (Museum of Art), with a collection consisting mainly of 15th–17th century works.

San Ginés

The church of San Ginés (begun in 1557) contains tombs of the Infantado and Tendilla families and has 16th century bas-reliefs on the high altar.

Santa María de la Fuente

The 13th century church of Santa María de la Fuente, built on the site of an earlier mosque, has a minaret-like tower in Mudéjar style and contains a number of 15th century tombs.

Convento de la Piedad

The Convento de la Piedad, a nunnery founded by Doña Brianda de Mendoza about 1530, is now an institute. The finest part of the building is the cloister, which has Plateresque doorways and double arcades. The foundress is buried in an alabaster tomb.

Surroundings of Guadalajara

Through the Montes de Encinas

Torija

Leave Guadalajara on N II, which runs north-east over the Castilian plateau in the direction of Zaragoza, coming in 18km/11 miles to Torija (alt. 964m/3163ft), with a 13th century Templar castle which was destroyed by Juan Martín el Empecinado in 1811 but has been restored in recent years. The parish church contains some fine pieces of goldsmith's work.

Sigüenza

N II cuts through the Montes de Encinas in a long straight stretch and continues to a junction where C 204 goes off on the left to Sigüenza (see entry).

Medinaceli

From the turn-off for Sigüenza N II climbs through Algora (alt. 1116m/3662ft) into the Sierra Ministra, from which there is a fine view of Sigüenza. It then continues by way of Saúca (alt. 1200m/3940ft) to Alcolea del Pinar (alt. 1205m/3955ft), where it turns north to Medinaceli.

At Alcolea del Pinar we turn right into N 211, which climbs to the Puerto de Maranchón (1250m/4100ft) and then descends to Molina de Aragón, a picturesque little town with a history going back to pre-Arab times. On a hill above the town is an imposing stronghold surrounded by walls and towers, the finest of which is the Torre de Aragón (11th c.).

Molina de Aragón

Features of interest in the town are the old Jewish quarter and the 12th century church of San Gil, which contains the tomb of Doña Blanca, Duchess of Molina (d. 1283).

To the Mar de Castilla

From Torija (see above) C 201 runs east to the old fortified town of Brihuega (alt. 886m/2907ft), situated above the valley of the Río Tajuña. The village of Villaviciosa, a short distance away, was the scene of a battle in 1710 which decided the result of the War of the Spanish Succession and brought Philip V to the throne. Above Brihuega can be seen the ruins of the 12th century Castillo de Piedra Bermeja, and in the town itself are the parish church of Santa María de la Peña, with a fine retablo, the arcaded Plaza Mayor and the gardens round the Real Fábrica de Paños (the old Royal Cloth Manufactory).

Brihuega

From Brihuega the road (C 201, then N 204) continues to Cifuentes, at the foot of the Sierra de Megorrón. The town, which takes its name from the numerous springs in the area, has a handsome Plaza Mayor and a church (12th–13th c.) with a Late Romanesque doorway. On a hill above the town is a castle built by Juan Manuel in 1324.

Cifuentes

South of Cifuentes on N 204 is the Mar de Castilla ("Sea of Castile"), a very beautiful lake district, with two large artificial lakes, the Embalse de Entrepeñas and Embalse de Buendía, and a smaller one, the Embalse de Bolar-

Mar de Castilla

Molina de Aragón

Guadalupe

que. The water stored in these reservoirs is used for irrigation and for the production of hydro-electricity. At the Embalse de Zorita, to the south of the lake district, there is also an atomic power station. These great expanses of water and the country round them are a popular recreation area for the people of Madrid.

Pastrana

N 204 crosses the Embalse de Entrepeñas half way down its length and joins N 320 at Sacedón. From N 320 a secondary road runs south to Pastrana, which has a fine 14th century Gothic church, with a retablo by Juan de Vigarny (16th c.) and the tomb of a Princess of Éboli who was exiled to Pastrana. The church's greatest treasures, however, are four 15th century Tournai tapestries depicting the Moroccan campaigns of the Portuguese king Afonso V.

★ Tapestries

Guadalupe   F 5

Province: Cáceres (CC). Telephone dialling code: 927
Altitude: 640m/2100ft. Population: 3000

The village of Guadalupe is famed for its fortress-like monastery, founded in 1340, occupied by Hieronymites from 1359 until its dissolution in 1832 and reoccupied by Franciscans in 1928. It stands on the spot where in the early 14th century a shepherd is said to have found the effigy of a black Virgin believed to have been made by St Luke. The monastery was founded by Alfonso XI in 1340, after the battle of the Río Salado, and in addition to its religious function became the seat of a celebrated faculty of medicine. The veneration of the Virgin of Guadalupe reached a climax in the 15th and 16th centuries, when the Spanish navigators, before setting out on their voyages of discovery, made her patroness of the whole "Hispanidad", the territories conquered by Spain in America. Columbus named one of the islands he discovered after the Virgin of Guadalupe (Guadeloupe); and the patroness of Mexico is also the Virgin of Guadalupe, who is said to have appeared in 1531 to an Aztec convert to Christianity. Guadalupe is still one of the great religious centres of Spain, with great fiestas and processions on September 8th and 30th and October 12th.

★ **Monasterio de Guadalupe**

The monastery buildings were erected at various times between the 14th and the 18th century, and as a result show great diversity of architectural style. The west front of the church with its two square flanking towers, the Torre de Santa Ana and Torre de la Portería, dates from the 15th century.

★ **Church**

The church, which is entered through two bronze doors with scenes from the lives of Christ and the Virgin, was originally built in the 14th century and was rebuilt in the 17th and 18th centuries. The sculptural decoration of the Baroque retablo was the work of Giraldo de Merló and the paintings are by Vicente Carducho and Eugenio Caxès. The aisles are separated from the nave by finely wrought grilles; the richly carved choir-stalls and the two organs by Churriguera are Baroque. Among the numerous tombs are those of Henry IV of Castile and his mother María of Aragon.

★★ Sacristy

To the right of the Capilla Mayor is the Sacristy, sumptuously decorated in Baroque style, with ceiling paintings and eight portraits (1638–47) by Francisco de Zurbarán of leading members of the Hieronymite order. On the altar of the adjoining Capilla de San Jerónimo is one of Zurbarán's finest works, "The Apotheosis of St Jerome", and the chapel also contains a trophy from the battle of Lepanto (1571) in the form of a lamp from the Turkish flagship.

Capilla de
San Jerónimo

Camarín

Behind the Capilla Mayor, approached by a flight of red jasper steps, is the Rococo Camarín, which houses the image of the Virgin of Guadalupe. It

276

The monastic church, Guadalupe

contains nine pictures by Luca Giordano and statues of female figures from the Bible. On the wall facing the Capilla Mayor is the modern throne (1953), decorated with enamels, of the Black Virgin; it can be rotated so that the image faces into the church. The statue itself is of oak and is clad in a magnificent brocade robe. On feast days it is decked in a crown covered with precious stone, which can be seen, together with other precious garments, liturgical utensils and relics, in the octagonal reliquary chamber adjoining the Camarín. Other valuable objects are displayed in the Treasury (Joyel).

Beyond the church is the two-storey Mudéjar Cloister (14th c.), with fine horseshoe arches. In the centre is a fountain-house in the form of a temple (by Juan de Sevilla, 1405). | Mudéjar Cloister

On the west side of the cloister is the former Refectory, now housing the Museo de Bordados (Embroidery Museum), with beautiful embroidered vestments and altar-cloths of the 14th–18th centuries, mostly made in convents. | Museo de Bordados

Adjoining the Mudéjar Cloister is the Gothic Cloister, with three galleries (14th–16th c.). | Gothic Cloister

Museo de Libros Miniados	In the former Chapterhouse (in the wing to the left of the monastery façade) is the Museo de Libros Miniados (Museum of Illuminated Books), which displays 86 illuminated books of hours and missals produced in the monastery, a Flemish triptych of the Three Kings, a picture by Juan de Flandes and a number of small pictures by Zurbarán.
The village	The village of Guadalupe itself is worth seeing, with its picturesque narrow streets and its Plaza Mayor, centred on a Gothic fountain.

Guernica y Luno/Gernika-Luno   J 1

Province: Vizcaya (BI).Telephone dialling code: 94
Altitude: 4m/13ft. Population: 18,000

The town of Guernica (Basque Gernika), the "holy city of the Basques", lies in the valley of the Río Mundaca (also known as the Río de Guernica). In a square in the town, the Gernikazarra, under an ancient oak-tree, the Council of Elders (Batzarra) of Vizcaya (Basque Bizkaia) met every two years from the early Middle Ages to discuss matters of common concern and transact business. The feudal lords of the region were required to appear before this assembly to guarantee the rights and privileges (*fueros*) of the Basques. The town of Guernica grew up around the Gernikazarra.

The name of Guernica is now forever associated with the first mass air attack on an inhabited town. On April 16th 1937 several waves of bombers of the German "Condor Legion", which supported Franco in the Civil War, appeared over the town and within two hours had reduced it to rubble and ashes and killed 1645 of the inhabitants. Guernica was deliberately used by the Luftwaffe as a test-bed for the technique of area bombing. The massacre inspired Picasso's famous and controversial painting, "Guernica", which during the Franco period was hung in the Museum of Modern Art in New York and is now in the new Museo Nacional Centro de Arte Reina Sofía (see Madrid).

Sights

Casa de Juntas	The Casa de Juntas, built in 1824–33 around the old oak, is now the meeting-place of the provincial assembly of Vizcaya. Adjoining the council chamber is a chapel faced with coloured tiles depicting the lords and the Estates of Vizcaya. On one side of the main entrance, below a classical-style temple, is the stump of the oak-tree. Behind the building is a tall oak, grown from a seedling of the original tree in 1860. The 1937 air raid is commemorated by a piece of sculpture by Eduardo Chillida. The Casa de Juntas also houses a library and the largest archives in Vizcaya.
Santa María	The church of Santa María, begun in 1418 and completed in 1715, is notable particularly for a series of works by modern sculptors including Inurria, José Capuz and Moisés Huerta.
Frontón	Guernica is a great centre of the game of frontón (jai alai, pelota), which is played on Saturdays, Sundays and Mondays in the Guernica Jai Alai Hall in Artekale Carlos and also in the Frontón Santanape.

Surroundings of Guernica

Cuevas de Santimamiñe	6km/4 miles north-east of Guernica are the Santimamiñe Caves, in which paintings of bison, stags, horses and bears dating from the Magdalenian period (15,000–10,000 B.C.) were discovered in 1917.

Huelva

Province: Huelva (H). Telephone dialling code: 955
Altitude: 56m/184ft. Population: 140,000

Huelva, chief town of its province, lies near the Atlantic coast of Andalusia (the Costa de la Luz) on the left bank of the Río Odiel, here 4km/2½ miles wide and navigable by ocean-going vessels. A town on this site was known to the Romans as Onuba, and some scholars believe that it was the legendary ancient city of Tartessus (Tarshish).

The commercial harbour of Huelva is one of the leading ports in Spain in terms of traffic handled, mainly due to the shipment of ore from the Río Tinto and Tharsis. The tunny and sardine fisheries and the associated fish-canning industry also make important contributions to the town's economy. The establishment of oil refineries and other petro-chemical industries, with a consequent uncontrolled building boom, has led to a dramatic deterioration in the local environment.

Sights

The effects of the Lisbon earthquake of November 1st 1755 were felt as far away as Huelva, and much of the town was destroyed, leaving it with little in the way of historic buildings.

Churches

Of the older buildings that survived the earthquake only a few churches are of any note – Cathedral de la Merced (17th c.) which contains an image of "La Cintra" the town's patroness; San Pedro (15th–16th c.), built on the ruins of an earlier mosque, which was restored after the earthquake; La Concepción (14th c.), which has two small pictures by Zurbarán; and Nuestra Señora de la Cinta, which contains azulejo tiles commemorating Columbus's visit to the church.

At the south end of the town at Punta del Sebo an imposing 34m/112ft high statue of Columbus (Monumento a Colón) guards the bridge over the Rio Tinto (1929).

Columbus statue

Surroundings of Huelva

Although Huelva itself has relatively little in the way of tourist sights, there is much of historical interest in the surrounding area.

Round Trip to La Rábida

Leave Huelva on the Seville road (N 431), and just beyond San Juan del Puerto (14km/9 miles) take a road on the right which crosses the Río Tinto and comes to Moguer (alt. 51m/167ft), a little town situated on a hill 21km/13 miles from Huelva. In the 16th century this was the starting-point of many voyages to America. The church of Santa Clara, which belonged to a once important convent founded in 1348, contains the very beautiful alabaster tombs of members of the Portocarrero family, founders of the convent, as well as a statue of the Virgin by Montañés and fine choir-stalls. The birthplace of the poet and Nobel Prize winner Juan Ramón Jiménez (born in Moguer in 1881) is now a museum.

Moguer

The road continues south-west, running close to the Río Tinto, to the old port of Palos de la Frontera, now silted up and decayed, which provided experienced seamen for many voyages to the New World in the age of discovery. Columbus sailed from here on August 3rd 1492 and returned here from the New World on March 15th 1493, and Hernán Cortés landed in Palos de la Frontera after his conquest of Mexico. The church of San Jorge dates from 1473.

Palos de la Frontera

La Rábida

Farther downstream is the Franciscan friary of La Rábida, finely situated on a hill at the mouth of the Río Tinto. A cross at the entrance, erected in 1892, commemorates Columbus's stay here. After failing in 1485 to win the support of John II of Portugal for his plans Columbus and his son were given a friendly reception in the monastery and found an advocate in Prior Pérez de Marchena, Queen Isabella's confessor. After long negotiations Isabella was persuaded to conclude an agreement, signed and sealed in Santa Fe, making Columbus viceroy of any lands discovered. The 14th century church has a Mudéjar cloister and a small museum with mementoes of the Conquistadors.

Punta del Cebo

The return to Huelva is by way of the bridge over the Río Tinto, from which there is a view of the 34m/112ft high Columbus Monument on the Punta del Cebo. Beneath the monastery a modern open-air theatre, the "Foro Ibero-americano" has been built.

To the Río Tinto Copper-Mines

Trigueros

Leave Huelva on N 431 and at San Juan del Puerto (14km/9 miles) turn left into N 435, which runs north into the Sierra Aracena. Off this road on the left is Trigueros, near which, at La Lobita, is the interesting Dolmen de Soto, believed to date from the 2nd millennium B.C.

Río Tinto mining area

The road continues via Valverde del Camino (alt. 270m/886ft), at the beginning of the Río Tinto mining area, within which almost all vegetation has been killed, to Zalamea la Real (alt. 387m/1270ft), where we turn east into C 421. The chief places on this road are Minas de Río Tinto and Nerva, in the heart of the copper-mining area. The mines in this area are among the richest in the world, and were already being worked in Iberian and Roman times. The pyrites found here, lying close to the surface, have a sulphur content of 85% and between 0.5 and 2% of copper. The mines, which can be visited, were originally British-owned, and the towns have something of the character of British mining towns. In Minas de Río Tinto the Mining Museum covers the history of mining in the area and features a coach designed for Queen Victoria for a journey to India which never took place. The railway, once vital to the mining industry, is now a tourist train travelling 20km/12 miles through the Río Tinto area (afternoons Sat., Sun. and pub. hols.).

★Aracena

From Minas de Río Tinto a local road runs north through the beautiful Sierra Aracena to the little hill town of Aracena (alt. 682m/2238ft), surrounded by plantations of olives, figs and almonds, with an excellent climate which has made it a popular health resort. The Convento de Santa Catalina has a fine doorway. On the Cerro del Castillo are remains of a Moorish stronghold which was taken over by the Templars. The 13th century church, originally a mosque, has a 12th century Mudéjar minaret as its tower. In the hill are the Cuevas de las Maravillas, a 1200m/1300yd long cave system with magnificent stalactites and stalagmites and an underground lake. From Aracena an excursion to the wonderful scenery of the Sierra de Aracena with its cork and holm oaks and to Jabugo, famous for its ham, is recommended.

Huesca   M 3

Province: Huesca (HU). Telephone dialling code: 974
Altitude: 488m/1601ft. Population: 44,000

Huesca, chief town of its province and the see of a bishop, lies on the slopes of a hill above the Río Isuela. A typical Pyrenean town, it is an important market centre for the agricultural produce of the surrounding area.

The Iberian settlement of Osca became the Roman Urbs Victrix Osca, headquarters in the 1st century B.C. of the rebel Quintus Sertorius, a supporter of Marius, who was able to maintain his independence of Rome for almost ten years. After the expulsion of the Moors by Pedro I Huesca was capital of Aragon from 1096 to 1118. In the Napoleonic period the town was occupied by French troops, and during the Spanish Civil War there were two years of bitter fighting for control of the town.

Sights

Cathedral

On the highest point in the town, occupying the site of an earlier mosque, stands the Gothic cathedral (13th–16th c.), which has a beautiful main doorway (14th c.) with rich figural decoration and a rose window in the apex of the arch. The most notable feature in the interior is the magnificent alabaster high altar, the masterpiece of Damián Forment, on which he worked for thirteen years (1520–33). The beautiful reliefs in the middle register depict three scenes from Christ's Passion, and the sculptor has immortalised himself and his daughter in medallions at the end of the lowest row. Also notable are the Renaissance choir-stalls (c. 1590), the cathedral treasury in the sacristy and the chapel of Santa Ana, with a retablo attributed to Alonso de Berruguete. The Museo Episcopal (Episcopal Museum), in the chapterhouse, displays Romanesque and Gothic wall paintings, reliquaries, book illuminations and an alabaster group by Damián Forment, "Adoration of the Kings".

In the adjoining parish church is the famous alabaster Retablo de Monte Aragón, a masterpiece by Gil Morlanes (1495) which was originally in the fortified monastery of Monte Aragón.

Parish church

Opposite the cathedral is the 16th century Casa Consistorial (Town Hall), with a Renaissance façade. On the first floor is a gruesome representation of the "Bell of Huesca" (see below).

Casa Consistorial

To the north of the cathedral and the Town Hall, housed in the Baroque premises of the former Literary University, is the Provincial Museum, with eight rooms of prehistoric and Roman antiquities, Gothic frescoes (including 13th century Passion scenes from San Fructuoso de Bierge) and pictures of the 15th–19th centuries. Among the pictures are four Virgins by an unknown Italian master (15th–16th c.), works by Francisco Camilo, Guido Reni and Claudio Coello, and four drawings by Goya.

Museo Provincial

The University was built over the old 12th century Aragonese royal palace. One of the surviving rooms was the scene of a grisly event in 1136 which became known as the "Bell of Huesca", when King Ramiro II summoned his rebellious nobles to meet here and had sixteen of them beheaded: fifteen of the heads were then laid on the ground in the shape of a bell, with the sixteenth suspended above them as the clapper.

In the Mercado Nuevo, to the south of the cathedral, is the church of San Pedro el Viejo, one of the oldest Romanesque churches in the region, built in the 12th century on the remains of a Benedictine abbey, with a hexagonal tower. In the tympanum of the main doorway is a representation of the Three Kings. In the Capilla de San Bartolomé are the tombs of Ramiro II and Alfonso I of Aragon. The Romanesque cloister has finely carved capitals.

San Pedro el Viejo

The church of San Lorenzo (17th c.), to the south of San Pedro, has a fine carved and gilded altar.

San Lorenzo

Surroundings of Huesca

Santuario de San Jorge	2km/1¼ miles south-west of Huesca on N 123, above the road on the right, is the Santuario de San Jorge, built in 1554 on the remains of earlier walls on the site of the battle of Alcoraz (in which Pedro I of Aragon defeated the Moors in 1096). From here there is a fine view of Huesca.

★Into the Pyrenees on N 330

Arguis	C 136 (good for most of the way, but hilly and winding) runs north up the valley of the Río Isuela towards the Pyrenees, with the Sierra de Guarra (2076m/6811ft) on the right. Beyond Nueno are a number of short tunnels. The road then skirts the green waters of the Embalse de Arguis and comes to Arguis (alt. 1200m/3940ft), a popular holiday resort from which there is a
★View	magnificent view of the plain to the rear.
Puerto de Monrepós	The road continues uphill, with many bends and fine views, and through a tunnel to the Puerto de Monrepós (1262m/4141ft). It then descends into the valley of the Río Gállego and comes to the industrial town of Sabiñánigo. 2km/1¼ miles beyond the town is a road junction at which C 134 goes off on the left to Jaca (see entry).
Biescas	C 136 continues north up the Gállego valley to Biescas (alt. 865m/2838ft), a little market town situated astride the Gállego, with some handsome old houses.
★Parque Nacional de Ordesa, Monte Perdido	From Biescas a detour can be made on C 140, which runs east over the Puerto de Cotefablo (1423m/4669ft) to Torla and, beyond this, the magnificent Parque Nacional de Ordesa (1320m/4331ft), an area of rich and varied vegetation with numerous gorges, waterfalls, etc., in the valley of the Río de Ordesa below Monte Perdido (3352m/10,998ft). This is splendid walking and climbing country (see Practical Information, National Parks).

Torla: a Pyrenean village

From Biescas C 136 continues north up the Gállego valley, through beautiful mountain scenery. Above the road on the right is the convent of Santa Elena, a pilgrimage centre.

Monasterio de Santa Elena

15km/9 miles from Biescas a road branches off on the right and runs north-east through the narrow Gargantas de Escalar to the spa of Balneario de Panticosa (alt. 1659m/5443ft; radioactive sulphurous water), magnificently situated on a lake in a rocky cirque. Many people come to take the cure here, but the resort also attracts large numbers of skiers; there are eleven downhill pistes and two langlauf trails at Panticosa, 8km/5 miles away.

★ Gargantas de Escalar
★ Balneario de Panticosa

Beyond the turning for Balneario de Panticosa C 136 follows the Gállego valley to Sallent del Gállego (alt. 1310m/4298ft), in good climbing and winter sports country. The Spanish frontier post is here.

Sallent del Gállego

From Sallent the road continues uphill at a moderate gradient to the winter sports resort of El Formigal (alt. 1500m/4920ft), with 22 pistes in all grades of difficulty and several ski-lifts.

El Formigal

The Puerto de Portalet (1792m/5880ft) lies on the Spanish–French frontier. The crossing is closed from November to May.

Puerto de Portalet

Into the Pyrenees via Barbastro

From Huesca N 240 leads east to Barbastro (51km/32 miles), beyond which we turn left into C 138, a narrow and winding road which heads north up the valley of the Río Cinca. The river is pounded by dams to form a series of artificial lakes. After passing through El Grado and Naval (ruined castle) the road climbs to the Alto del Pino (857m/2812ft), from which there is a view (below, to the right) of the Embalse de Mediano.

To the National Park

C 138 now runs down to the charming village of Ainsa, once capital of a petty kingdom, with a 12th century collegiate church, an imposing ruined castle and the remains of a 9th century monastery.

Ainsa

At Ainsa C 138 turns west and comes to Boltaña, a pretty little town in the valley of the Río Ara. It then continues up the valley, with the Sierra de Bolave on the right. Beyond Brotó it runs into the road coming from Biescas, which it follows north to the Parque Nacional de Ordesa (see above, page 282).

Boltaña

A variant of the route just described is to turn off C 138 shortly before El Grado into C 139, which runs north-east to Graus, at the junction of the Río Esera and the Río Isábena. From here the road runs up the Esera valley, through magnificent scenery, and comes in 70km/45 miles into the Benasque valley, which offers endless scope for walks and climbs, and in winter for skiing, with 24 pistes at Cerler, a few kilometres from Benasque.

Into the Benasque valley

Towards Pamplona

From Huesca N 240 runs north-west over the fertile plain of La Hoya and then climbs, with many bends and fine views of the Pyrenees to the right, on to the Meseta, and comes to the little town of Ayerbe (alt. 560m/1837ft), with the 15th century Palacio de los Marqueses de Ayerbe.

Ayerbe

8km/5 miles north-east, at the foot of the Sierra de Loarre, is Loarre. On a crag above the village stands the Castillo de Loarre, one of the finest Romanesque castles in Spain. It was built by King Sancho I Ramírez from 1076 onwards on the site of the Roman fort of Calagurris Fibularia, and was a royal residence until the 12th century. The castle is surrounded by a double circuit of walls with round towers, above which rise the rectangular keep and the church of Santa María. The church, built over a crypt, origi-

★ Castillo de Loarre

nally belonged to an Augustinian monastery within the castle. The columns in the nave have beautiful floral capitals.

Mallos de Riglos — Beyond Ayerbe N 240 crosses the Río Gállego and traverses a gorge-like valley, with the mighty crags of the Mallos de Riglos on the right, followed by the Embalse de la Peña.

★ Puerto de Santa Bárbara — N 240 continues to a road junction at Santa María de la Peña (alt. 542m/1778ft), where N 330 branches off on the right, crosses the Puerto de Oroel (1080m/3543ft) and comes to Jaca (see entry). N 240 continues up the valley of the Río Asabón, with the Sierra de la Peña on the right. Going over the Puerto de Santa Bárbara (864m/2835ft), from which there are extensive views, it runs down to Puente la Reina de Jaca, in the valley of the Río Aragón, where N 240 turns west for Pamplona.

South-East of Huesca

★ Fraga — From Huesca a beautiful road (C 1310) leads south-east via Sariñena and Villanueva de Sigena, with the monastery of Sigena (Romanesque church), to enter the valley of the Río Cinca, follow the river downstream and join N II, the main road linking Zaragoza and Lérida. A short distance along this to the left (135km/84 miles from Huesca) is the little town of Fraga (alt. 120m/395ft), picturesquely situated above the left bank of the Río Cinca. Its main features of interest are a number of noble mansions and the church of San Pedro, which occupies the site of an earlier mosque; originally Romanesque (12th c.), it was later rebuilt.

Jaca   M 2

Province: Huesca (HU). Telephone dialling code: 974
Altitude: 820m/2690ft. Population: 15,000

Jaca, situated on a hill above the Río Aragón, was the first capital of the kingdom of Aragon which was established in 1035. It is now the see of a bishop, and in summer becomes a branch of Zaragoza University, which runs language courses here. On the first Sunday in May every year the "Moros y Cristianos" festival commemorates a victory over the Moors in 760. In the Middle Ages Jaca was an important staging-point on the Way of St James (see entry), and evidence of its importance is still provided by the Puente San Miguel on the outskirts of the town.

Sights

Fortifications — There are remains of the old town walls, dating from the 10th century, and the Castillo (begun in 1571).

Ayuntamiento — The 16th century Ayuntamiento (Town Hall) has a fine Plateresque façade with wrought-iron window grilles.

★ Cathedral — Jaca's most important building is the Romanesque Cathedral (1040–76), which in later centuries was altered and given Plateresque decoration. The square tower, the outer walls, the main doorway and the south doorway are all Romanesque. There is very fine figural decoration on the south doorway and its porch; particularly notable are the capitals, with representations of Abraham's sacrifice, David playing the lute, etc.

In the choir and the dome of the central apse are frescoes by Bayeu (1792). Beneath the high altar are the remains of Santa Orosia and the tomb of a 16th century bishop.

In the cathedral cloister is the Diocesan Museum, which in addition to a variety of religious objects displays a magnificent collection of Romanesque wall paintings from churches in the Aragonese Pyrenees, second in importance only to the collection in the Museo de Arte de Cataluña in Barcelona (see entry).

Museo
Diocesano

Surroundings of Jaca

Sierra de la Peña

N 330 runs south from Jaca, goes over the Puerto de Oroel (1080m/3543ft; fine views), on the western slopes of the Peña de Oroel (1769m/5804ft; rewarding climb, 3 hours from Jaca) and comes to Bernués. From there a mountain road runs 11km/7 miles west to the monastery of San Juan de la Peña (alt. 1115m/3658ft), magnificently situated in wooded country under an overhanging wall of rock. The monastery was founded in the 9th century but in its present form dates mainly from the 10th–12th centuries. From that period date the chapterhouse (10th c.), the Mozarabic crypt (originally the lower church; dating in part from the 9th century) and the upper church, which was consecrated in 1094. In the sacristy of this church is the burial-place of the kings of Aragon, which was given its present form in the 18th century. Among those buried here are King Ramiro I and King Sancho Ramírez, and also, it is said, Doña Jimena, the Cid's wife. In front of the church is a small court with tomb recesses for the nobility of Aragon on the left-hand side. Of the cloister, which is built into the rock, there remain only two wings, with finely carved capitals of the highest quality.

Puerto de Oroel

★San Juan
de la Peña

From the monastery the road descends to Santa Cruz de la Serós, where in the 11th century there was a rich convent, of which only the Romanesque church, with an octagonal tower, is left. The most notable feature in the interior is a holy water stoup supported on small columns from the cloister.

Santa Cruz
de la Serós

★Pyrenean Valleys

From Jaca C 134 runs west, following the Río Aragón. The river is joined by a series of tributaries coming down from the mountains through extraordinarily beautiful and thinly populated valleys, which can be explored on narrow roads following the course of the streams – the Valle del Hecho, the Valle del Ansó, with a narrow gorge, the Hoz de Biniés, and the Valle del Roncal, formed by the Río Esca. The road up the Roncal valley crosses the Collado de la Piedra San Martín to enter France.

Jaén

Province: Jaén (J). Telephone dialling code: 953
Altitude: 573m/1880ft. Population: 100,000

Jaén, chief town of its province and an old-established episcopal see, lies at the foot of the Sierra de Jabalcuz and Sierra de la Pandera, the slopes of which, to the south of the town, are covered with large plantations of olives. The province of Jaén is one of the largest olive-growing areas in the world.

There was a Carthaginian walled town here which was captured by the Romans and given the name of Auringis. The local silver-mines were already being worked in Roman times, and the town is still known as "silver Jaén". During the Moorish period it was capital of the kingdom of Jayyan, and after its recapture by Ferdinand III in 1246 it became an outpost of the Reconquista. In 1492 the Christian armies assembled here for the assault on Granada, the last Arab stronghold on the Iberian peninsula.

History

View of Jaén

Sights

★ Castillo de Santa Catalina

On a ridge to the west of the town stands the Castillo de Santa Catalina which occupies the site of a Moorish stronghold and which was captured in 1246 by Ferdinand III; it is now a Parador Nacional. It is best reached by car on a road signposted to the parador (5km/3 miles). When approaching from the old town remains of the old defensive walls can still be seen, and from the top of the hill, towering up like the prow of a ship, there is a viewpoint (not for the fainthearted) marked with a cross, which offers a magnificent panorama of the town and the surrounding olive groves.

★ Cathedral

On an elevation in the Old Town, rising out of a tangle of narrow streets on the site of an earlier mosque, stands the massive cathedral (16th–19th c.). which was begun by Andrés de Vandelvira in 1500. The west front is flanked by two towers and has a carving of the Madonna by Pedro Roldán as well as figures of rulers and saints. The most notable features of the interior are the fine 15th century choir-stalls and – in a shrine by the high altar – the "napkin of St Veronica", with which the saint is said to have wiped Christ's face on the way to Calvary. In a chapel nearby on the left is an almost kitschy representation of Christ carrying the Cross, and on the right the entrance to the chapter-house with retablo-painting by Pedro Machuca. The Cathedral Museum, in the sacristy, displays pictures and church utensils and ornaments, including a large silver monstrance.

La Magdalena

North-west of the cathedral is the former Moorish old town of La Magdalena, at the foot of the hill.

Baños Árabes

We come next to the Palacio Villardompado, underneath which extensive 11th c. Arab bathing establishment (Spanish: Baños Árabes) was discovered. The palace itself contains a museum of art and folk traditions.

Capilla de San Andrés

Farther east is the Capilla de San Andrés, founded in 1515 by Gutiérrez González Doncel, treasurer to Popes Leo X and Clement VII, which is believed to occupy the site of a former synagogue. In the Capilla de la Purísima can be seen a statue of the Virgin (Andalusian school) and a painting of the Virgen del Pópulo. There is also a very fine choir screen by a local master named Bartolomé.

Past the Convento de Santo Domingo lies the church of La Magdalena; built on the site of an Arab mosque this is probably the oldest church in Jaén. It has a Late Gothic doorway and a fine retablo, but especially a beautiiful patio. Opposite the church can be seen the "Raudal de la Magdalena", a fine fountain which was used by the Romans.

Iglesia de la Magdalena

Near the Plaza de los Caños to the north of the cathedral, stands the 13th c. Monasterio de Santa Clara, the oldest sacral building in the town. It has a beautiful cloister and a fine figure of Christ, the "Cristo de Bambú".

Monasterio de Santa Clara

The busy New Town of Jaén begins to the north of the cathedral near the Plaza de la Constitución, with its main axis the Paseo de la Estación.

New Town

In this street in buildings dating from 1920 is housed the Museo Provincial with the art gallery on the first floor and an archaeological section on the ground floor. The most interesting exhibits are a Roman mosaic and Iberian sculpture.

Museo Provincial

There are palaces and mansions of important families on the many squares.

Mansions

Surroundings of Jaén

11km/7 miles south-east of Jaén on a minor road is the little town of La Guardia de Jaén, with the remains of ancient buildings which bear witness to its Roman origin. It also has a ruined castle, an interesting parish church and a courtyard (designed by Vandelvira) which is all that remains of a Dominican monastery founded in the 16th century.

La Guardia de Jaén

Ruta de las Batallas

The Ruta de las Batallas ("Battle Trail") leaves Jaén on N 323, following a winding course northwards above the valley of the Río Guadalbuilón, and comes in 24km/15 miles to Mengíbar (alt. 323m/1060ft), the ancient Ossigi, once a Moorish stronghold, of which only the tower remains.

Mengíbar

The road crosses the Río Guadalquivir and continues north to Bailén (alt. 349m/1145ft), where the Roman consul Scipio the Elder defeated the Carthaginian general Hasdrubal in 208 B.C. Here too, in 1808, Spanish troops commanded by General Castaños defeated a French army for the first time. The general is buried in the church of La Encarnación (16th c.), which also contains a sculpture by Alonso Cano.

Bailén

15km/9 miles east of Bailén is the mining town of Linares (alt. 418m/1371ft). The Archaeological Museum displays Iberian, Carthaginian and Roman finds from the site of Cástulo (5km/3 miles north), the largest Iberian settlement in the lead- and silver-mining area on the upper Guadalquivir. Other features of interest in Linares are the church of Santa María la Mayor (12th–13th c.) and a fine 16th century retablo in the church of San Francisco.

Linares

30km/19 miles west of Bailén on N IV is Andújar (alt. 212m/696ft), on the right bank of the Guadalquivir, here spanned by a bridge which goes back to Roman times. The town, lying near the ancient Iberian settlement of Illiturgo (Los Villares), is a centre of olive oil production and is also noted for its fine pottery (*alcarrazas, jarras*). The streets are lined with handsome old

Andújar

houses and churches. The Gothic church of Santa María has a painting by El Greco, "Christ in the Garden of Olives", housed in a chapel which is closed off by a finely wrought grille. The church of San Miguel has fine carved woodwork.

★Virgen de la Cabeza

Just before Andújar a winding mountain road branches off on the right and runs north to the Santuario de la Virgen de la Cabeza, a chapel founded in the 13th century, totally destroyed during the Civil War and subsequently rebuilt, from which there are tremendous panoramic views.

La Carolina

The Ruta de las Batallas continues north from Bailén on N IV, which passes a side road to Baños de la Encina (fine 10th c. castle) and after going through Guarromán (alt. 349m/1145ft) reaches the little town of La Carolina (alt. 605m/1985ft). Like other places in this area, La Carolina was founded by French and German settlers whom Charles III had brought into the Sierra Morena between 1767 and 1769. The once rich lead-mines in the surrounding area are now in ruins. The town itself has a number of handsome old mansions.

Las Navas de Tolosa

Just north of La Carolina, 2.5km/1½ miles off N IV to the right, is Las Navas de Tolosa (alt. 694m/2277ft), another attractive old settlers' village. Here on July 16th 1212 the united army of Castile, Aragon and Navarre inflicted an annihilating defeat on the Almohads – an event commemorated by a monument outside the town.

★Santa Elena

From Las Navas de Tolosa N IV climbs gradually to Santa Elena (alt. 742m/2435ft), a pretty little place situated on a hill from which there are extensive views, near the boundary between Andalusia and New Castile.

Jerez de la Frontera   E 8

Province: Cádiz (CA). Telephone dialling code: 956
Altitude: 55m/180ft. Population: 200,000

Jerez de la Frontera lies in a fertile upland region on the southern edge of the Andalusian plain, some 35km/22 miles north-east of Cádiz. The town is world-famed for the sherry to which it has given its name (and which is also distilled to produce Spanish brandy). Equally important to the economy of

Jerez
de la Frontera

1 San Dionisio
2 Museo Arqueológico
3 San Juan de
   los Caballeros
4 Fundación Andaluza
   de Flamenco
   (Flamenco-Museum)

Bodegas (Wine stores)

300 m

© Baedeker

the area is the breeding of pedigree horses, particularly the fiery Andalusian breed. Jerez is famous, too, as a centre of flamenco dancing and the *cante jondo*. All these activities come together in two great annual festivals – the Fería del Caballo (Horse Show) in the first half of May and the Fiesta de la Vendimia (Vintage Festival) in the first half of September, which includes a flamenco festival.

The area between Jerez and Cape Trafalgar was the scene of the decisive battle in 711 between Visigoths and Moors which condemned Christian Spain to many centuries of subjection under alien peoples from the East. Another great battle fought here in 1340 ended in a Christian victory which prevented the last invasion from North Africa. Jerez has borne the style "de la Frontera" ("on the Frontier") – along with other towns on the frontier with the Moorish East – since 1379. | History

Most people think of Jerez mainly as the centre of sherry production. There are some 36 bodegas (cellars) in the town devoted to the making and selling of sherry. The process of manufacture is a lengthy one. When the young wine has completed its fermentation it is classified, according to its character, as Fino, Amontillado or Oloroso. It is then poured into casks, which take their place in the rows (*soleras*) containing wine of similar character but different ages. At the beginning of the row is the young wine, at the far end the oldest. From time to time some of the younger wine is taken out and blended with the older wines, until the vintner is satisfied that the sherry is sufficiently mature. The best sherries are those which come from the same row; but as a rule wine from different soleras is blended, and sometimes sweetened. A fino, the most typical sherry, is pale yellow in colour, dry or very dry, with little blending or sweetening (alcohol content 15.5–17%). Amontillado is amber-coloured, fuller in body than fino but still dry (alcohol content 16–18%); it is traditionally made from selected finos, left to age in cask. An oloroso is dark golden in colour and sweeter (alcohol content 18–20%). Other types are dulce, which is sweetened, dark in colour and heavy, and cream sherry, which is still heavier and fuller. The neighbouring town of Sanlúcar de Barrameda produces manzanilla, a light-coloured, very dry wine with a salty tang. | ★ Sherry

Almost every visitor to Jerez tours one or more of the bodegas. Among the best known are Garvey, Guadalete 14; González Byass, Manuel María González 12; Pedro Domecq, San Ildefonso 3; John Harvey & Sons, Alvar Núñez 53, Sandeman, Pizarro 10; Williams & Humbert, Nuño de Cañas 2. Guided tours of one of the bodegas (with tasting) can usually be made between 10am and 1pm; prior notice is advisable. | Bodegas

Sights

The main square, the Alameda Fortún de Torres, is in the southern part of the town. On its south side is the Alcázar, a massive Almohad stronghold dating from the 11th century. Within its walls are a Gothic chapel, Arab baths and the palace, rebuilt in Renaissance style. From the keep there are fine views. | Alcázar

A visit can be made to the Flamenco Museum at Calle Quintos 1, south of the Alcázar; on display are costumes and musical instruments. | Flamenco Museum

To the east of the Flamenco Centre is the church of San Miguel (1430–1512), with a richly decorated west front of 1672 and a blue tiled tower. Harmoniously proportioned interior. The high altar has a retablo with reliefs by Martínez Montañés and Juan de Arce (1625). | San Miguel

North-west of the Alcázar stands the Baroque collegiate church of San Salvador (begun 1695), built on the foundations of an earlier mosque. From the free-standing bell-tower there are very fine views. The church, which is approached by a Baroque staircase, contains a painting by Zurbarán. | La Colegiata

Casa del Cabildo	To the north-east of the church and the Alcázar we reach in the Plaza de la Asunción the Plateresque Casa del Cabildo, the former town hall, which was erected in 1575.
San Dionisio	In the same square stands the Mudéjar-style church of San Dionisio which has a fine Baroque retablo.
Museo Arqueológico	The archaeological museum can be found in the north-west of Jerez, near the church of San Mateo.
★Fundación Andaluza de Flamenco	A little further north in the Palacio de Pemartin in the Plaza San Juan is the Fundación Andaluza de Flamenco (Andalusian Flamenco Foundation). Here visitors can learn all about flamenco dancing from a variety of displays, video films and demonstrations and from the library.
★Real Escuela Andaluza del Arte Ecuestre	In Avenida Duque de Abrantes, in the north of the town, is the Real Escuela Andaluza del Arte Ecuestre (Royal Andalusian Riding School). Every Thursday at noon a show entitled "Cómo bailan los Caballos Andaluces" ("How Andalusian horses dance") takes place here. On other weekdays between 11am and 1pm visitors can watch a training session and visit the stables.
Museo de Relojes La Atalaya	One of the finest bodegas in Jerez, in the north-west of the town, is now occupied by the Atalaya Clock Museum, with more than 300 antique clocks, some of them very valuable, from all over Europe.
Parque Zoológico	In the west of the town lies the Parque Zoológico (Zoo), the largest in Andalusia. With it is associated a very attractive Botanical Garden.

Surroundings of Jerez de la Frontera

Circuito de Jerez	10km/6 miles north-east of Jerez on N 342 is the Circuito de Jerez, a motor-racing track on which the Spanish Grand Prix and other world championship races are run. Near here is Sherryworld, a leisure and entertainment park with an area of 63 hectares/156 acres.
Cartuja	A few kilometres south-east of Jerez is the Cartuja (Charterhouse), a former Carthusian monastery founded in 1477. Here in the 16th century German, Italian and Andalusian horses were crossed to produce the "Carthusian" breed. In the mid 18th century Charles III presented several Cartuja stallions to the Austrian Empress Maria Theresa, and these became the ancestors of the famous Lipizzaner horses of the Vienna Riding School. The monastery has a magnificent Renaissance gateway (1571) and a Gothic church with a richly decorated façade of 1667.

La Coruña

See page 222

León   F 2

Province: León (LE). Telephone dialling code: 987
Altitude: 837m/2746ft. Population: 131,000

León, chief town of its province and the see of a bishop, lies at the confluence of the Río Torío and the Río Bernesga in the north-western part of the central Spanish plateau, the Meseta, under the south side of the Cantabrian Mountains. It is the chief place in an iron- and coal-mining region and an important trading centre for the cattle reared in the surrounding area.

León owes its name to the Roman Seventh Legion, having developed out of the Legion's camp in the 1st century A.D. The town was destroyed at the end of the 10th century by Almansor's Moorish army but was rebuilt in the reign of Alfonso V (999–1027). Its heyday was in the 10th–12th centuries, when it was for a time capital of the kingdom of León, which extended from the Atlantic Ocean to the Rhône. It lost this status, however, when the kingdoms of León and Castile were reunited in 1230, and thereafter it declined. During the Middle Ages León was an important staging-point on the Way of St James (see entry) for pilgrims travelling to Santiago de Compostela (see entry).

History

★★ Cathedral

León's principal street, Calle del Generalísimo Franco, leads to the Plaza de Regla, in which stands the Cathedral of Santa María de Regla (13th–14th c.), the work of a number of different architects. It is an impressive structure, 91m/299ft long, one of the great masterpieces of Early Gothic architecture in Spain, showing close affinities with the French cathedrals of Reims and Amiens.

Particularly impressive is the west front with its two imposing towers, the 65m/213ft high Torre de las Campanas (on left) and the 68m/223ft high Torre del Reloj, which flank the nave with its large rose window and three doorways, richly decorated with sculpture. The finest of the doorways is the middle one, the Puerta de Nuestra Señora la Blanca, with a figure of Santa María la Blanca on the central column and a representation of the Last Judgment on the tympanum, the frieze and the archivolts. On the right-hand doorway, the Puerta de San Francisco, are figures of prophets and the Coronation of the Virgin; on the Puerta de la Regla, to the left, are the Natiivity and Childhood of Christ.

West front

The south front, similar in form to the west front, with a triple doorway and large rose window, is also very fine.

South front

The incomparable beauty of the harmonious interior is due particularly to the astonishing light effects produced by the traceried windows, which are up to 12m/39ft in height. The 1800 sq.m/19,400 sq.ft of stained glass range in date from the 13th to the 20th century, the oldest glass being in the middle choir chapels and the rose windows on the west and north fronts.

Interior

★★ Stained glass

The magnificent choir-stalls, carved by Flemish craftsmen, date from the 15th and 16th centuries.

★ Choir-stalls

The richly gilded alabaster Trascoro was the work of Esteban Jordán (1575). It is designed in such a way that it is possible to look up through an opening into the nave.

Trascoro

In the centre of the Capilla Mayor is a modern retablo incorporating 15th century paintings by Nicolás Francés from the original winged altar; particularly notable is the "Entombment" on the left-hand panel. In a silver shrine (by Enrique de Arfe) in front of the high altar are the relics of the town's patron saint, San Froilán (bishop of León from 900 to 905). Other notable features are a "Pietà" by Rogier van der Weyden (on the left) and the richly carved bishop's throne.

Capilla Mayor

The chapels opening off the ambulatory contain numerous handsome monuments, notable among them the richly decorated tomb (early 14th c.) of Ordoño II (d. 924). The Capilla de Santiago has very beautiful Renaissance stained glass.

Choir chapels

On the north side of the cathedral is a large Plateresque cloister, originally built in the 14th century and altered in the 16th. The frescoes are by Nicolás Francés.

★ Cloister

Adjoining the cloister is the Cathedral Museum (Museo Catedralicio): to reach it, leave the cathedral by the main doorway and turn right round the

Cathedral Museum

León Cathedral, south front

north front, as indicated by a sign. The Museum has a large collection of sacred articles and religious art, including some very valuable items. Among them are the 11th century "Lex Romana Wisigothorum", a 6th century palimpsest, a 10th century Visigothic Bible, a crucifix by Juan de Juní (1576), works of sculpture and pictures.

Diocesan Museum

The Diocesan Museum (Museo Diocesano), housed in the Seminario Mayor facing the south front of the cathedral, also has an interesting collection.

★ Old Town

Plaza Mayor

To the south of the Diocesan Museum lies the arcaded Plaza Mayor, on the west side of which is the handsome twin-towered Old Town Hall (Consistorio Viejo) of 1677. The square has an appealing charm, particularly on market days, when it is a bustle of activity. Equally lively are the little streets of the old town leading to the Plaza de San Martín (with the 13th century church of San Martín) and the Plazuela de San Marcelo. An evening stroll around the old town can be pleasantly combined with a visit to some of the *tapa* bars with their variety of enticing appetisers.

Around the Plazuela de San Marcelo

San Marcelo

In the Plazuela de San Marcelo, the hub of the town's traffic, are a number of important buildings. The square takes its name from the church of San Marcelo (1588–1627), with a reliquary containing the saint's remains. Opposite the church is the Renaissance Ayuntamiento (Town Hall).

Casa de Botines

The most striking building in the Plazuela de San Marcelo, however, is the Casa de Botines on the north side of the square, a Neo-Gothic building by the Catalan architect Antoni Gaudí (1894). It is now occupied by a bank.

On the north-east side of the square stands the Palacio de los Guzmanes (1560), a building in the style of an Italian palazzo which is now occupied by the Diputación Provincial. It has an imposing façade, with round-headed arches, large corner towers and wrought-iron balconies.

Palacio de los Guzmanes

★Colegiata de San Isidoro

From the Palacio de los Guzmanes it is a few minutes' walk along Calle del Cid (behind the Palacio), passing the Jardín Romántico, to the collegiate church of San Isidoro.

The church can be reached from the cathedral by following the well preserved old town walls (north-east of the choir), going north and then turning west. The walls, which date in part from the 3rd century A.D. and are reinforced by numerous round towers *(cubos)*, lead to one of the old town gates, the massive Puerta del Castillo (1759), south-west of which, by way of Plaza del Castillo, is the Plaza de San Isidoro.

The square is dominated by the Colegiata de San Isidoro, which originated as a 10th century church but which was completed in its present form in 1149. It is of great importance to Spanish Catholics as the last resting place of San Isidoro, bishop of Seville and the greatest Visigothic doctor of the church, whose remains were brought here from Seville by Ferdinand I in 1063. At the west end of the church rises a massive Romanesque tower. The finest features of the exterior are the two Romanesque doorways on the south front, which faces on to the square: on the left the Puerta del Cordero (Doorway of the Lamb), the main doorway, with sculptured figures of San Isidoro and San Pelayo and the Lamb of God, and on the right the Puerta del Perdón, with a relief of the Crucifixion.

The most notable feature of the rather dark interior is the 16th century Capilla Mayor. In the north transept are the Capilla de San Martín and the Capilla de los Quiñones, which has Romanesque frescoes.

The Treasury and the Library contain many valuable items, including (in the Library) a Bible of 960, a 15th century breviary with miniatures by Nicolás Francés and the embroidered "Banner of Baeza" and (in the Treasury) the 11th century reliquary of San Isidoro, the agate Chalice of Doña Urraca (11th c.), a casket decorated with Limoges enamels and a processional cross by Juan de Arfe.

The highlight of a visit to San Isidoro, however, is the Panteón Real (Royal Pantheon), the burial vault of the kings, princes and nobles of León, which

★Panteón Real

was built on to the west end of the church in 1054–66. The groined vaulting of the Pantheon is borne on two marble columns which, like the columns round the walls, have capitals carved with plant and animal motifs. The ceilings and vaulting along the east and south walls are covered with superb frescoes painted in the reign of Ferdinand II (1157–88). The glowing colour of these paintings, which depict Biblical scenes, hunting scenes and the labours of the months, interwoven with animal and plant ornament, have earned the Pantheon the name of the "Sistine Chapel of Romanesque art".

★Monasterio de San Marcos

On the north-west side of the town, on the banks of the Río Bernesga, is the former monastery of San Marcos, now a luxurious parador. The main (south) front, over 100m/330ft long, is unsurpassed in the richness and delicacy of its Plateresque decoration. The eastern half was built between 1533 and 1541, the western half, with the doorway and the tower, between 1708 and 1716. Over the main entrance is a Baroque figure of Santiago (St James) in his legendary role as the Moor-Slayer (Matamoros).

The site was occupied from the 12th century onwards by the mother house of the knightly Order of Santiago, which protected pilgrims travelling to Santiago de Compostela. In gratitude for their exploits the Catholic Monarchs ordered the building of a new monastery for the order.

Iglesia de San Marcos	At the east end of the monastery is the church of San Marcos (consecrated in 1541), which has beautiful choir-stalls of 1543 and sculpture by Juan de Juni and Juan de Horozco.
Museo Arqueológico Provincial	The sacristy (by Juan de Badajoz, 1549), the cloister and the adjoining chapter rooms are now occupied by the Provincial Archaeological Museum, which has a rich collection of material. Its greatest treasure is an 11th century ivory figure of Christ; other exhibits include an altar dedicated to Diana, Roman and Celtic antiquities, sculpture, carved ivories and pictures.

Lérida/Lleida   N 3

Province: Lérida (L). Telephone dialling code: 973
Altitude: 154m/505ft. Population: 110,000

Lérida (Catalan Lleida) is chief town of its province and the largest city in western Catalonia, the Terres de Ponent. It lies on the Río Segre, half way between Barcelona and Zaragoza, in one of Spain's leading agricultural regions, made fertile by irrigation. Lérida has been the see of a bishop since 1149, and from 1300 to 1717 it had a university, the first in Catalonia, founded by King Jaime II. It is now a marketing centre for agricultural produce.

History — Lérida was originally an Iberian foundation, which became Roman in the 2nd century B.C. under the name of Ilerda. During the Roman civil war the armies of Caesar and Pompey met here. Between 713 and 1117 the town was under Moorish rule for most of the time; then in 1149 it was taken by Ramón Berenguer IV. In later centuries it suffered repeated destruction in successive wars – in 1707 during the War of the Spanish Succession, in 1810 during a siege by the French, in 1936 during the Spanish Civil War.

Lower Town

Puente Viejo/ Pont Vell — There are good views of the lower town and the castle hill from the Old Bridge (Puente Viejo, Catalan Pont Vell) over the Río Segre.

To the east of the bridge, reached by way of the Plaza de San Juan (Catalan Plaça de Sant Joan), the town's main square, and Calle de San Juan, are the offices of the provincial government, the Diputación (Catalan Diputació), where visitors can see collections of coins and of weapons.

Diputación/
Diputació

To the west of the bridge is an arcaded square, the Plaza de la Pahería (Catalan Plaça de la Paeria), where the Calle Mayor (Catalan Carrer Major) begins. At the near end, on the left, is the Pahería (Paeria), which in the Middle Ages was the seat of the Paer, an officer responsible for maintaining law and order in the town; it is now the Town Hall. Several times rebuilt or renovated, it has an attractive façade with round-headed Romanesque windows. It houses a museum on the history of the town.

La Pahería/
La Paeria

At the end of the Calle Mayor, on the right, is the Neo-Classical Catedral Nueva (Catalan Catedral Nova), the New Cathedral (1781), with a Corinthian portico.
    In the chapterhouse is a museum (valuable liturgical utensils, Flemish tapestries, etc.).

Catedral Nueva/
Catedral Nova

Opposite the portico of the cathedral is the Hospital de Santa María (15th–16th c.), originally a hospice for the poor and sick. The façade, in Catalan Gothic style, is plain, but there is a very handsome inner courtyard with an 18th century staircase. The building is now occupied by the Archaeological Museum, with material from the town and surrounding area.

Hospital de
Santa María

A short distance north-west of the New Cathedral, adjoining the modern Bishop's Palace, is the little church of San Lorenzo. Built between 1270 and 1300 and much altered in later centuries, it is said to occupy the site of a Roman temple which had been converted into a mosque. Its most notable features, apart from its octagonal tower, are its fine retablos (14th–15th c.), particularly one depicting scenes from the life and martyrdom of San Lorenzo (St Lawrence).

San Lorenzo/
Sant Llorenç

Cloister, Lérida Cathedral

295

Lérida/Lleida

Museo Diocesano/ Museu Diocesà	West of the Bishop's Palace, in a former Seminary on the Rambla de Aragón (Catalan Rambla d'Aragó), is the Diocesan Museum (Museo Diocesano, Catalan Museu Diocesà), with a collection of medieval painting and church utensils and ornaments.
El Roser	To the east of the New Cathedral El Roser, a Baroque convent now occupied by the Museu d'Art Jaume Morera, houses a museum of modern art displaying works by contemporary Catalan artists.

On the Castle Hill

Castell La Suda	From the Bishop's Palace the Calle de la Tallada (Catalan Carrer de la Tallada) and a stepped path lead up to the 12th century Castell La Suda; an easier way up is to take the lift from the Plaza de San Juan. This massive structure with its four towers was originally a Moorish stronghold and later became a palace of the kings of Aragon. From the gardens of the castle there are good views of the town.
★Seo Antigua/ La Seu Vella	Within the walls of the castle stands the Old Cathedral (Seo Antigua, Catalan La Seu Vella), which dates from the 13th century but was not completed until the 16th. It was built on the site of an earlier mosque: hence the position of the cloister on the west end of the cathedral, like the forecourt of a mosque. The cloister is the most striking feature of the cathedral, with its high traceried windows (offering fine views of the town), its finely carved capitals depicting fabulous beasts, intertwining plants and scenes from everyday life and the tall octagonal bell-tower (1416) at its north-west corner. The sculptural decoration of the church and the beautiful doorways shows the same consummate skill as the carving of the capitals. Particularly fine is the Porta dels Fillols in the south aisle – an outstanding example of the sculpture of the Lérida school which also shows Mozarabic influence.

★ Into the Pyrenees

	Lérida is an ideal base for excursions into the valleys of the Pyrenees and to Andorra (see entry).

To Tremp

Balaguer	Leave Lérida on C 1313 and in 27km/17 miles turn left into C 148, which crosses the Río Segre to enter Balaguer, chief town of the Noguera district. The monastery of Santo Domingo (Catalan Sant Domenec) is a fine example of Catalan Gothic architecture. Also of interest are the large Plaça del Mercadal and remains of the town walls.
Castellón de Farfaña/Castelló de Farfanya	8km/5 miles west of Balaguer is Castellón de Farfaña (Catalan Castelló de Farfanya), with a ruined Moorish castle and the fine Gothic church of San Miguel (Catalan Sant Miquel).
Avellanes	From Balaguer there are alternative routes to Tremp: either an attractive secondary road by way of Avellanes and the Puerto de Ager (fine views) which joins C 147 above the Embalse de Camarasa – the route which is described below – or on C 147 all the way, along the left bank of the Río Segre past the artificial lakes. The secondary road runs north-west from Balaguer through the Sierra de Montroig to Avellanes. On a hill to the right of the road is the Premonstratensian monastery of Bellpuig de les Avellanes, founded in 1166, once the place of burial of the Counts of Urgel, with a Romanesque cloister.
Ager/Àger	After passing through Font de Pou (Catalan Fontdepou) the road climbs to the Puerto de Ager (912m/2992ft) and then goes down to Ager (Catalan

Ager), an old town with some remains of Roman walls and the ruins of the 12th century collegiate church of San Pedro (Catalan Sant Pere).

The road now follows the slopes of the Sierra de Montsech (1677m/5502ft) and descends into the valley of the Río Noguera Pallaresa. Below this point the river is enlarged into an artificial lake, the Embalse de Camarasa, by a dam 151m/165yd long and 92m/302ft high some kilometres downstream. The water of the lake supplies a hydro-electric station with an output of 700,000 kW.

Embalse de Camarasa

The road crosses the river and joins C 147, the direct road from Balaguer. This passes through the tunnels of the Portell dels Terradets, between the hills of the Sierra de Montsech, and along the Embalse de Terradets to Tremp (alt. 507m/1663ft), situated on a hill above the right bank of the Río Noguera Pallaresa, which still preserves remains of its old walls. To the north of the town is the Embalse des Talarn, formed by a dam 206m/225yd long and 82m/269ft high which supplies a hydro-electric station with an output of 300,000 kW.

Tremp

From Tremp C 144 continues north, passes through the medieval village of Talarn and comes to a road junction at Pobla de Segur (alt. 540m/1772ft), where the Río Flamisell flows into the Río Noguera. Pobla de Segur, a timber-working and dairy-farming town, is a good base for walkers and climbers as well as for excursions into the Pyrenees by car. The local rivers and streams, well stocked with fish, are a paradise for anglers.

Pobla de Segur

To the Valle de Arán via Pont de Suert

From Pobla de Segur there are two different ways into the uniquely beautiful mountain world of the Pyrenees – the present route via Pont de Suert and the alternative route, described on page 298, over the Puerto de la Bonaigua.

From the road junction at Pobla de Segur the left-hand road (C 144) runs north to Senterada and then climbs north-west, with many bends, to the Puerto de Perves (1350m/4429ft). Above the pass on the left is the summit of the Sierra de San Gervás (1839m/6034ft).

Puerto de Perves

The road then crosses the Puerto de Viu (1325m/4347ft), runs down into the valley of the Río Noguera Ribagorzana, here dammed to form the 8km/5 mile long Embalse de Escalas, and reaches the modern little town of Pont de Suert, where C 144 joins N 230, coming from Lérida.

Pont de Suert

N 230 continues up the valley to Vilaller, below the east side of Maladeta (Pico de Aneto, 3404m/11,169ft), the highest peak in the Pyrenees.

★Maladeta

After passing through the Tunel de Viella the road comes to Viella (Catalan Vielha; alt. 975m/3200ft), chief town of the Valle de Arán. The 13th century church of San Miguel (Catalan Sant Miquel), with a 16th century tower, has a Romanesque figure of Christ, the "Crist del Mig Arán".

Viella/Vielha

The Valle de Arán, in which the source streams of the Garonne (Spanish Garona) rise, is a valley of great natural beauty, with endless scope for walks and climbs in magnificent scenery, good fishing in the mountain streams and two skiing resorts, Vaqueira-Beret and Tuca-Betrén. The people of the valley still speak Aranese, a Romance dialect related to Gascon – demonstrating the valley's racial and geographical affinity with France and also its many centuries of isolation, which came to an end only with the construction of a road over the pass in 1925 and the Viella tunnel in 1948. The valley has been part of Spain since 1308.

★Valle de Arán/ Vall d'Arán

From Viella a detour can be made (N 230 to Les Bordes, then a minor road on the left) to the wooded Güells de Joeu area, where the Garona de Joeu rises.

Güells de Joeu

Bosost/Bossost | N 230 continues up the Garona valley to Bosost (Catalan Bossost; alt. 765m/2510ft), which has a well preserved Romanesque church (12th c.), notable particularly for the black marble figures on the north doorway.

Into France | From Bosost the road continues by way of the little spa of Lés (alt. 635m/2083ft; Spanish frontier control) to the Pont de Rey (alt. 580m/1903ft) spanning the Garona on the Spanish–French frontier.

Through the Bohí Valley

★Tahull/Taüll | Just beyond Pont de Suert a side road branches off N 230 on the right into the valley of the Río Noguera de Tor (the Bohí valley), in which can be found some of the finest Romanesque churches in the Pyrenees. After passing through Bohí (Catalan Boí) the road comes to the village of Tahull (Catalan Taüll), with the churches of Sant Climent and Santa María (12th c.). These are very typical of the Romanesque churches of the Pyrenees, with a large nave, three apses and a free-standing bell-tower. Both churches had very fine wall paintings, the originals of which are now in the Museum of Catalan Art in Barcelona (see entry); the paintings to be seen in Taüll are copies.

Caldes de Bohí | At the end of the valley, in a beautiful setting, is the little spa of Caldes de Bohí, the western entrance to the Aigües Tortes National Park.

To the Valle de Arán over the Puerto de la Bonaigua

★Desfiladero de Collegats | At the road junction at Pobla de Segur take the road to the right (C 147). This runs up the valley of the Río Noguera Pallaresa, which here receives many tributaries tumbling down over waterfalls, and through a wild limestone

Pyrenean Romanesque: Sant Climent, Tahull

gorge, the Desfiladero de Collegats, with the Bou Mort (2082m/6831ft) on the right.

Just beyond the gorge is Gerrí de la Sal, which takes its name from the salt-pans on the banks of the river. In the village is a former Benedictine monastery (12th c.).

Gerrí de la Sal

Beyond Gerrí de la Sal the road traverses another long gorge, at the far end of which is the village of Sort (alt. 692m/2270ft), with a ruined castle. 12km/7½ miles north-west is the winter sports resort of Llesuí (alt. 1400m/4600ft).

Sort, Llesuí

After another defile the Río Cardós comes in on the right. A narrow road runs up its beautiful green valley.

Cardós valley

C 147 continues to Escaló, with the ruined 10th century monastery of Sant Pere del Burgal, which preserves some Romanesque wall paintings.

Escaló

6km/4 miles off the road to the left is the winter sports resort of Espot (alt. 1340m/4400ft), with a chair-lift and ski-lifts to the skiing centre of Super Espot.

Espot

Espot is the eastern entrance to the Parque Nacional de Aigües Tortes (Catalan Parc Nacional d'Aigüestortes). Its particular charm lies in its numerous glacier lakes, among them the Llac de Sant Maurici. Ibexes can still be encountered in the National Park. Information about walks and climbs can be obtained in Espot and Caldes de Boí.

★National Park

Beyond Esterrí de Aneu (alt. 1000m/3300ft) C 147 enters the valley of the Río Bonaigua and then climbs, passing the parador of Farga de los Abetos and the Santuario de los Ares (alt. 1728m/5670ft), to the Puerto de la Bonaigua (2072m/6798ft), on the watershed between the Mediterranean and the Atlantic.

Puerto de la Bonaigua

The road now winds its way down, with many sharp bends, into the Valle de Arán and comes to Tredós (alt. 1295m/4249ft), lying off the road to the left, which has an old Templar church (12th c.) with a Gothic altarpiece.

Tredós

C 147 continues to Salardú (alt. 1265m/4150ft), where it enters the valley of the Río Garona, and then runs down, passing the spa of Artiés (sulphurous springs) on the left of the road, to the winter sports resort of Betrén, from which there is a chair-lift to the skiing centre of La Tuca (alt. 1560m/5118ft). Soon after this, at Viella, C 147 joins N 230, coming from Lérida.

Logroño   J 2

Province: La Rioja (LO). Telephone dialling code: 941
Altitude: 384m/1260ft. Population: 120,000

Logroño, chief town of the province of La Rioja, situated on the banks of the Ebro in a famous wine-growing region, was originally the Roman settlement of Varea Lucrosus. It is an industrial town, with few historic old buildings. The main industries of Logroño are textiles and metalworking; the town is also important as the centre of the Rioja wine trade.

Rioja is famed for its full-bodied red wines, though it also produces white wines. It is divided into the hilly Rioja Alta (Upper Rioja), west of the Río Leza, with the towns of Haro and Santo Domingo de la Calzada (see entry), and the flatter Rioja Baja (Lower Rioja) to the east of the river. The Ebro valley offers optimum conditions for vine-growing; and in addition Rioja Baja is an important vegetable-growing region, which produces almost the whole of the Spanish asparagus crop.

Rioja wines

Sights

Santa María del Palacio	The church of Santa María del Palacio, on the banks of the Ebro, is a relic of the palace of Alfonso VII, which he presented to the Knights of the Holy Sepulchre in 1130. The most striking feature of the church, which was much altered in the 16th century, is the 45m/150ft high spire over the crossing, the Aguja del Palacio. It has a fine high altar by pupils of Berruguete.

San Bartolomé — A short distance away the church of San Bartolomé (12th c.), has a Romanesque/Gothic doorway, one of the finest of its kind in Rioja.

Santa María la Redonda — The Cathedral of Santa María la Redonda (15th–18th c.) – the name is a reminder of its original circular ground-plan – has a handsome twin-towered Baroque façade. Notable features of the interior are the finely carved altars and choir-stalls.

Santiago el Real — The façade of the church of Santiago el Real is dominated by a monumental statue of Santiago Matamoros (St James the Moor-Slayer).

On the Way of St James

Nájera — The pilgrims' road to Santiago de Compostela runs west from Logroño on N 120 to Navarrete and Nájera (alt. 481m/1578ft), a little town on the Río Najerilla which was once a royal residence. Legend has it that in the 11th century King García Sánchez, while hunting in this area, discovered a hidden cave containing an altar dedicated to the Virgin and thereupon founded the monastery of Santa María la Real. The church, which dates from the 15th century, has fine choir-stalls. Much more important, however, is the Panteón de los Reyes (Royal Pantheon), the mausoleum of the kings and princes of Navarre and León. The finest of the tombs is the stone sarcophagus of Queen Blanca of Navarre (12th c.); the other sarcophagi mostly date from the 15th and 16th centuries. A small 13th century figure of the Virgin marks the spot where García Sánchez is supposed to have found the altar of the Virgin. The cloister of 1522 (in which historical plays are performed in June) has flamboyant Gothic tracery.

San Millán de la Cogolla — 16km/10 miles south of Nájera, on the northern slopes of the Sierra de la Demanda, is San Millán de la Cogolla (alt. 738m/2421ft), which was visited by many pilgrims on their way to Santiago de Compostela. It takes its name from San Millán de la Cogolla (St Emilian of the Cowl), a hermit who died here in 574. The little town is famed for its two monasteries, both of which have been declared national monuments.

Monasterio de Yuso — The Monasterio de Yuso (Lower Monastery), in the valley, was founded in 1053; attached to it was a hospice for pilgrims. The present buildings, which have been called the "Escorial of Rioja", date from the 16th–18th centuries. Until 1835 it was occupied by Benedictines, and thereafter lay empty until it was reoccupied by Augustinians in 1878. The 16th century church has a retablo with paintings by Juan Rizzi. In the sacristy are two finely wrought reliquaries with ivory decoration (11th c.) containing the remains of San Millán and San Felice. There are several cloisters, the finest of which is the Claustro de San Agustín (1572). The monastery library possesses valuable incunabula and manuscripts.

Monasterio de Suso — The Monasterio de Suso (Upper Monastery) is built into the rock higher up the hill, and is older than the Monasterio de Yuso. The small Mozarabic church, which is divided into two halves by horseshoe arches, was consecrated in 984, and contained San Millán's sarcophagus until its transfer to the newer monastery in 1053. It still preserves the tombs of the Seven Infantes of Lara (who were treacherously murdered in the 10th century while trying to free their imprisoned father), and also an effigy of San Millán. From the monastery there is a fine view of the valley of the Río Cárdenas.

Monasterio de Yuso

From Nájera there is an attractive excursion (30km/19 miles south on C 113) up the beautiful valley of the Río Najerilla to the 11th century monastery of Valvanera, on the edge of the Sierra de la Demanda nature reserve.

Monasterio de Valvanera

The pilgrims' route continues west from Nájera on N 120 and in 19km/ 12 miles reaches Santo Domingo de la Calzada (see entry).

Lorca

K 7

Province: Murcia (MU). Telephone dialling code: 968
Altitude: 327m/1073ft. Population: 67,000

Lorca, lying astride the Río Guadalantín below a 13th century castle, was known to the Romans as Illurco and to the Moors as Lurka, and was the see of a bishop as early as the Visigothic period. It is now best known for its magnificent Holy Week processions.

The celebrations of Holy Week (Semana Santa) in Lorca, which are among the most splendid in Spain, have a long tradition behind them. Two brotherhoods, the "Blues" (Azules) and the "Whites" (Blancos), seek year by year to outdo each other in the magnificence with which they deck their *pasos* (life-size figures associated with Christ's Passion), crosses, etc., in valuable fabrics, embroideries and other precious materials and the lavishness of their contribution to the procession which enacts the mystery play of the Passion, complete with Roman soldiers, the populace looking on and the suffering figure of Christ.

★Semana Santa

Sights

Around the Plaza Mayor (Plaza de España), in the centre of the town, are a number of handsome Baroque buildings, including the Court-House and

Plaza Mayor

San Patricio, Lorca

Town Hall (Casa Consistorial; 17th–18th c.), which contains large paintings of battle scenes by Miguel Muñoz (1723) and a display of captured Arab flags. From the square it is a pleasant walk up to the Castillo.

San Patricio

Also in the square is the handsome church of San Patricio (16th–17th c.; tower 1772). Over the fine Baroque doorway is a statue of the saint. The church has a magnificent high altar with a painting by Camacho.

★Casa de
los Guevara

South of the Plaza Mayor, in Calle Lope Gisbert, is the 17th century Casa de los Guevara, now occupied by the Tourist Office. The house has a sumptuous Baroque doorway with four finely turned columns and rich heraldic ornament, flanked by wrought-iron balconies.

La Corredera

To the north of the Casa de los Guevara, in the street called La Corredera, are a series of other handsome Baroque houses.

Lugo   C 2

Province: Lugo (LU). Telephone dialling code: 982
Altitude: 465m/1526ft. Population: 75,000

Lugo, situated on the upper Miño (Galician Minho), in the uplands of Galicia in north-western Spain, is chief town of its province and the see of a bishop. It is a town with a long history: there was a Celtic settlement on the site, and the Romans developed it into an important city and military base under the name of Lucus Augusti. The town has preserved most of its circuit of Roman walls, with numerous towers. When the Moors, under their general Muza, attacked the town in 714 they were unable to destroy the walls and had to content themselves with burning the place down.

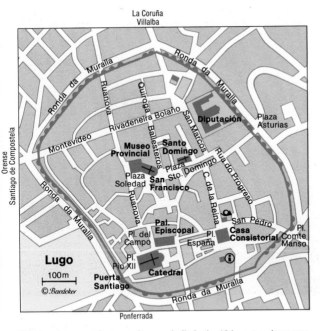

La Coruña
Villalba

Ponferrada

Within a few years, however, it was rebuilt. In the 10th century Lugo was captured by Norman raiders, but after they were driven out the town enjoyed a relatively peaceful existence until the Napoleonic wars of the early 19th century.

Lugo is now the centre of a beautiful, largely agricultural region. Around the outskirts of the town are rather dreary and unappealing districts of high-rise apartment blocks, but within the old walls Lugo is a lively town which also has many peaceful nooks and corners and handsome old buildings.

★★Town Walls

The town centre is completely enclosed by the old town walls, built by the Romans in the 2nd and 3rd centuries A.D. and renovated or rebuilt in the 14th century. They have a total length of 2131m/2330yd, an average height of 11m/36ft and an average thickness of 4.5m/15ft. Of the original total of 85 towers 50 have survived the various sieges of the town. There are ten gates, the oldest of which are the Puerta de Miñá, Puerta de Falsa and Puerta de Nova. The Puerta de Santiago, opposite the cathedral, was built in the 18th century and is surmounted by a figure of Santiago Matamoros, St James as the Moor-Slayer. At the gates there are steps up to the wall-walk, and a walk round it, which takes about half an hour, affords interesting glimpses of the town, including its back yards, and views of the surrounding hills.

★Town Centre

The lively hub of the town's life is the Plaza de España (Plaza Mayor), a spacious square with car parking in the Alameda, a tree-shaded avenue, a

Plaza de
España

Lugo

Town walls, Lugo

bandstand and a wide boulevard along the north side with rows of café tables tempting the sightseer to relax and watch the world go by. The east side of the square is dominated by the Casa Consistorial (Town Hall, *c.* 1735) with its handsome Baroque façade.

Palacio Episcopal

From the west end of the Alameda steps lead down to the Plaza de Santa María, on the right-hand side of which is the plain ashlar façade, decorated with coats of arms, of the Bishop's Palace (18th c.).

Cathedral

Opposite the Bishop's Palace is the tower on the north front of the granite cathedral (Santa María), begun in 1129 by Raimundo de Monforte but not completed until the 18th century; it is thus a conglomerate of many styles. The north doorway and porch, with a very beautiful figure of Christ in the act of blessing, are among the oldest parts of the building. A narrow street along the north side leads into the large but peaceful Plaza Pio XII, in which is the Baroque west front of the Cathedral with its twin towers, the last part of the structure to be built (1768). On the right is the cloister, which also dates from the 18th century. On the far side of the square is the Puerta de Santiago, with a broad flight of steps leading up to the top of the walls.

Interior

The cathedral can be entered either by the north doorway or by the main doorway. The interior, like the exterior, shows a variety of styles. The richly decorated choir-stalls (by Francisco Mouro) date from 1625. In both transepts are altars with carved retablos; the one in the north transept was the work of a Dutchman, Cornelis de Holanda (16th c.). In the Capilla Mayor the Host is permanently exposed. Behind the Capilla Mayor is the Capilla de Nuestra Señora de los Ojos Grandes (Our Lady of the Large Eyes), one of the finest examples of Baroque architecture, built by Fernando Casas y Novóa, the architect responsible for the west front of the Cathedral of Santiago de Compostela (see entry). The chapel contains a painted alabaster statue of the Virgin (12th c.).

To the north of the cathedral, beyond the Bishop's Palace, lies the picturesque old town of Lugo with its irregular streets. Its most attractive square
is the little Plaza del Campo, surrounded by arcaded houses, with a fountain in the centre.

★ Plaza del Campo

From the Plaza de España the Calle de la Reina runs north into the elongated Plaza de Santo Domingo, in the centre of which is a tall column
topped by an eagle. On the north side of the square the monastic church of
Santo Domingo (begun in 1280) has a beautiful Romanesque doorway and
Churrigueresque retablos.

Santo Domingo

Immediately west of the Plaza de Santo Domingo is the Provincial
Museum, with a collection which includes Roman antiquities, Galician craft
products, pictures, prints, coins and ceramics. A particular attraction is a
fully-equipped kitchen such as would be found in an old peasant's house.

Museo Provincial

In Calle San Marcos, in the newer part of the town centre, is the Neo-
Classical building (1886) occupied by the Diputación Provincial, the provincial government authority.

Diputación
Provincial

Surroundings of Lugo

Leave Lugo on N 640, going south, and in 4km/2½ miles turn right into the
road to Friol, from which a narrow road on the left is signposted to Bóveda.
This passes through a verdant region of woodland and meadows, with
areas of pastureland and small fields enclosed by granite walls. The tiny
village of Bóveda is worth seeing for its own sake, with its low slated
granite houses enclosed by walls and its *hórreos* (maize stores) – the very
picture of a typical old Galician village. Its particular attraction, however, is
the little church of Santa Eulalia de Bóveda, in the basement of a house on

★ Santa Eulalia
de Bóveda

The village of Bóveda

Lugo

the left at the entrance to the village, which has been declared a national monument (closed Monday). The church is believed to have originally been a Roman nymphaeum (shrine housing a sacred spring) which was converted to Christian use. In the centre of this underground chamber, which was of pre-Christian origin, is the basin of the spring, and on the walls are paintings of birds, animals and Christian symbols.

On the Way of St James to Santiago de Compostela

Leave Lugo on N 640 and just beyond Guntín de Pallares (18km/11 miles) turn right into C 547, which runs through pleasant country to Santiago de Compostela, passing through a number of staging-points for pilgrims on the Way of St James (see entry).

Puertomarín/ Portomarín	Before heading west for Santiago, however, it is worth making a detour to Puertomarín (Galician Portomarín), an earlier point on the pilgrim route, by continuing on N 540 and turning left into C 535; the total distance from the junction with C 547 is 21km/13 miles. The original village of Puertomarín was drowned in the waters of a new reservoir, the Embalse de Belesar, but the village and its historic old buildings were re-erected on higher ground above its old site. Particularly notable are the massive fortress-like church of San Juan (12th c.), with a rose window over its west doorway, and the church of San Pedro, which also dates from the 12th century.
★ Vilar de Doñas/ Vilar de Donas	The first place of interest on the road to Santiago is the village of Vilar de Doñas (Galician Vilar de Donas), which lies just off the road on the right some 12km/7½ miles from the road junction at Guntín. At the entrance to the village, on the right, stands a very simple granite-built church (13th c.). A plain Romanesque doorway leads into the dark and rather damp interior, which has faded 15th century wall paintings of Christ surrounded by SS Paul, Luke, Peter and Mark and the female figures (Galician *donas)* from which the church takes its name. Against the right-hand wall of the nave are a number of grave slabs of knights of the Order of Santiago, with their coats of arms, including a particularly fine one with the figure of a knight in full relief.
Palas de Rey/ Palas de Rei	A few kilometres farther on is Palas de Rey (Galician Palas de Rei), with a Romanesque church which provided accommodation for pilgrims.
Arzúa	One of the last staging points on the pilgrim route before Santiago de Compostela was Arzúa, which also has a church visited by pilgrims.

★ Mondoñedo

	Leave Lugo on N VI (the road to La Coruña) and at Rábade (13km/8 miles) turn right into C 641, which runs north to Villalba (22km/14 miles). From there the route continues on N 634, which crosses the Puerto de la Xesta (590m/1936ft) and then descends to Mondoñedo (alt. 200m/660ft), which can be seen picturesquely situated in the valley below. In the centre of this old episcopal town stands the Cathedral of La Asunción, which dates from the 13th century; the towers flanking the Gothic doorway were added in the 18th century. The most notable feature of the interior, in addition to the Plateresque choir and the two organs, below which are 14th century frescoes, is the figure of Nuestra Señora la Inglesa, originally in St Paul's Cathedral in London, which was brought here by English Catholics during their persecution by Henry VIII.
Cathedral	
Museo Diocesano	Attached to the cathedral is the Diocesan Museum (liturgical objects, pictures, sculpture, vestments, furniture).
Plaza de España	The cathedral stands on one side of the very beautiful, slightly sloping Plaza de España, which is surrounded by typical Galician houses, their

projecting upper storeys supported on timber columns. A stroll through the streets of the town will reveal many old noble mansions bearing coats of arms.

Madrid   H 4

Autonomous Community
Province: Madrid (M). Telephone dialling code: 91
Altitude: 655m/2150ft. Population: 3,500,000

The description of Madrid in this guide is abridged, since there is a separate Baedeker/AA guide to the city.

★★Madrid, the National Capital

Madrid, capital of Spain and its largest city, with a population of nearly 3.2 million living within its area of 605.8 sq.km/233.9 sq.miles, lies in the heart of Spain on a plateau below the south side of the Sierra de Guadarrama, above the little Río Manzanares, a river with a meagre flow of water and now partly canalised.

Madrid was a political creation by the Spanish kings on a site lacking all the natural conditions for development. It was only in the 19th and 20th centuries that the building of railways and construction of modern roads made Madrid the centre of the country's communications and stimulated the rapid growth of the city, which is now Spain's largest industrial centre after Barcelona. The airport of Madrid–Barajas, 14km/9 miles east of the city, links Madrid with all the world's capitals and is an important link in communications between Europe and South America.

As a result of its high altitude Madrid has wide temperature variations, which may be as much as 17°C/31°F in the course of a day. In spring and autumn, therefore, visitors should take precautions against catching a chill. The summers are hot (up to 43°C/109°F), the winters cold (down to –12°C/+10°F). The air of Madrid, once lauded as clear, if piercing, is now increasingly being polluted by the uncontrollable growth in traffic and by industrial emissions.

Climate

Madrid is the intellectual and cultural capital of Spain, though Barcelona makes great efforts to rival it. It has two universities and is the headquarters of a Papal University and the Open University for Science, and with the National Dramatic Centre, the National Ballet, the National Orchestra, the new Concert Hall opened in 1988 and over 30 theatres it is the centre of Spanish theatrical and musical life. Some of the most important Spanish newspapers are published in Madrid – "El Pais", "Diario 16" and "ABC" – and the state television station TVE is based here. No other Spanish city has such an abundance of museums, some of them of international standing, headed by the Prado Museum, the National Archaeological Museum and the Museo Nacional Centro de Arte de Reina Sofia, opened in 1986. With the acquisition on loan (for 9½ years) of much of the Thyssen-Bornemisza collection, on display in the handsome Palacio de Villahermosa since 1993, Madrid has enhanced its reputation as one of the cultural centres of Europe and indeed ws nominated "European City of Culture" in 1992.

Cultural capital

Madrid was late in becoming the economic and financial centre of Spain. Today more than 15% of Spanish industrial goods are produced in the Madrid region including trucks (Pegaso), tractors, electrical goods (Zanussi, Marconi, AEG, Siemens), cosmetics and textiles. 70% of the multi-national firms operating in Spain are located in Madrid, over half the

Spain's economic metropolis

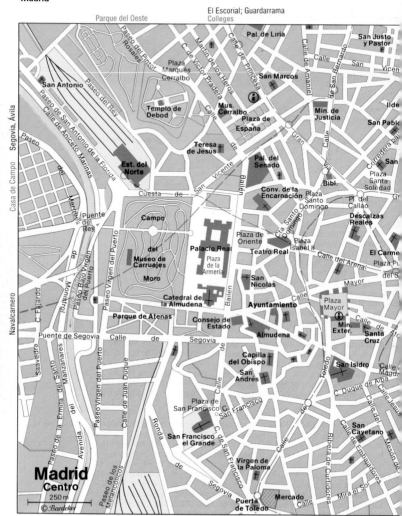

Parque del Oeste

El Escorial; Guardarrama
Colleges

Pal. de Liría
San Justo y Pastor
C. de Victor Pradera
Martín de los Heros
Calle de Princesa
Calle de Amaniel
Calle de San Bernardo
San Vicen
San Marcos
Plaza Marqués Cerralbo
San Antonio
Paseo del Pintor Rosales
Paseo del Rey
Paseo de San Antonio de la Florida
Calle de Aniceto Marinas
Ilde
Min. de Justicia
San Pablo
Mus. Cerralbo
Plaza de España
Templo de Debod
Correrra ba
San
Teresa de Jesús
Pal. del Senado
Gran
Plaza Santa Soledad
Vicente
Bailén
Est. del Norte
Bibl.
Conv. de la Encarnación
Plaza Santo Domingo
Pl. del Callao
Cuesta de
San
Gr
Descalzas Reales
Campo
Puente del Rey
Paseo Virgen del Puerto
Cta Santo Domingo
Plaza de Oriente
El Carme
del
Plaza Isabel II
Museo de Carruajes
Palacio Real
Teatro Real
Plaza PU del S
Plaza de la Armería
Calle del Arenal
Moro
Mayor
San Nicolás
Bailén
Calle
Catedral de la Almudena
Ayuntamiento
Plaza Mayor
Parque de Atenas
Consejo de Estado
Min. Exter.
Calle de
Santa Cruz
Puente de Segovia
Calle
de
Segovia
Almudena
Toledo
San Isidro
Calle de Malga
Capilla del Obispo
C. Duque de Alba
Calle de Jesús
San Andrés
Paseo de la Ermita del Santo
Avenida del Manzanares
Calle de Juan Duque
Ronda
Plaza de San Francisco
San Francisco
San Cayetano
Paseo de los Melancólicos
San Francisco el Grande
Calle de San Francisco
Calle
Ribera de Curtidores
Calle de Embajadores
Meson de
Virgen de la Paloma
Madrid Centro
de
Segovia
Mercado
250 m
Puerta de Toledo
Calle
Mira el Sol
© Baedeker

Segovia, Ávila

Casa de Campo

Navalcarnero

Saavedra

C. Fajardo

Monstrol

Marques

Paseo

Calle de Anita marinas

country's research institutes with 5000 scientists, and the leading high-tech concerns are represented here. In addition 80% of Spanish publishing companies are located in Madrid together with the State Bank (Banco de España) and three of the five major private banks – Banco Central, Banco Hispanoamericano and Banco de Crédito. Barcelona, Bilbao and Madrid dominate the Spanish stock exchange. This continually expanding metropolis is one of the most important centres of commerce, residential building and tourism.

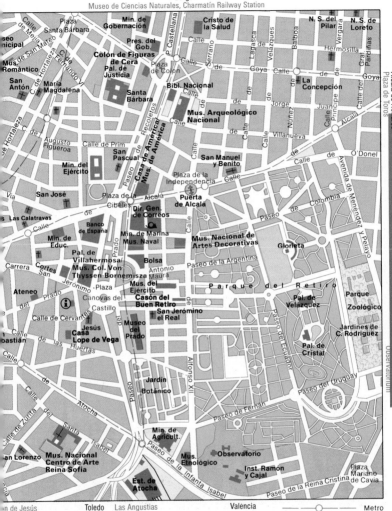

Burgos
Museo de Ciencias Naturales, Charmatín Railway Station

Madrid's rise from a provincial administrative centre to an international metropolis has had catastrophic effects on the housing market. A tremendous property boom has driven house prices sky-high, and in the suburban districts round the city, where the building boom is still continuing, prices have doubled within the last few years. In the worldwide ranking list for rents Madrid now occupies the 13th place, ahead of cities like Amsterdam and Frankfurt. In a similar comparison of incomes per head Madrid comes off much worse, ranking only 27th.

The housing market in disarray

As a result of speculative activity many houses in Madrid are at present empty: a figure of some 200,000 dwellings is mentioned, belonging to a 14% minority of the city's property-owners. Some 170,000 people have left Madrid because of the housing shortage and high prices and settled in the rural areas around the capital. As a result they are faced with long commuter journeys every day, which – given the high level of car ownership – means increasing pollution of the air by exhaust gases. The more prosperous members of the population are moving to the north-west of the city, where, on the slopes of the hills, the air is better. The poorer residents are crammed into the tower blocks of the built-up areas to the south of the city with the poorest of the poor, the "marginados", those marginalised by society, living in the 2500 so-called "chabolistas" – hovels. There are corresponding divergences in income patterns: the average household income in the north-western districts is five times the figure for the districts to the south.

Traffic chaos

Madrid's position in the middle of the country means that all the major roads meet at the Puerta del Sol. Even though the long-distance roads bypass the city and are of motorway standard and much of the heavy traffic is diverted onto the ring road motorways (M30 and M40) the city is choked up with traffic as almost every third person in Madrid owns a car. The townplanners need to develop a traffic strategy which puts an end to the right to drive a car in the city but so far there are no integrated tickets for public transport and the construction of the much heralded express rail link to Barajas airport is no closer.

History

In the 10th century the site of the present Royal Palace was occupied by the little Moorish town and fortress of Majrit, which was captured by King Alfonso VI in 1103. In 1239 Ferdinand IV summoned the first Cortes to meet in "Madrit", which thereafter became a frequent residence of the king. It was only in the time of the Emperor Charles V, however, that the old Alcázar

The heart of Madrid: Puerta del Sol

was converted into a palace. In 1561 Philip II finally moved the court from Toledo to Madrid, which then had a population of some 30,000. This was the period that saw a great flowering of Spanish literature and art: Cervantes wrote the second part of "Don Quixote" in Madrid, while Lope de Vega, Velázquez and Calderón lived for varying periods in the new capital. In the 18th century, under the Bourbons, the present Palacio Real was built to replace the older palace which had been destroyed by fire. In the early 19th century the French occupying forces demolished many convents and whole districts of the city in order to open up the crowded old town. The rising by the people of Madrid against the French on May 2nd 1808 was the signal for further risings throughout the country. Madrid's development into a modern city began towards the end of the 19th century. On April 14th 1931 the Republic was proclaimed in Madrid. During the Civil War the city underwent a grim siege by Franco's forces, beginning with a two-week battle in November 1936, mainly around the University City; but in spite of heavy bombardment by German and Italian aircraft Madrid held out until March 28th 1939.

Description of the City

The following description of Madrid is divided into convenient sections, which are grouped in three broad areas: first the central area, with the old town and the Royal Palace (the Centro ward of the city), bounded by the Gran Vía on the north, the Paseo del Prado on the east, the Ronda de Toledo and Ronda de Valencia on the south and the Río Manzanares on the west; secondly the north-eastern districts (Retiro and Salamanca wards), along the north–south axis formed by the Paseo del Prado, Paseo de Recoletos and Paseo de la Castellana; and the north-western districts (Chamberi and Moncloa wards) from the Gran Vía to the Ciudad Universitaria.

Visitors who have only one day for seeing Madrid should confine themselves to a tour of the central area, with perhaps a brief visit to the Prado Museum. The best starting-point of a tour is the Metro station in Plaza de la Cibeles, in which also is the imposing Head Post Office. From here it is a short distance down the Paseo del Prado to the Prado Museum, from which the Carrera San Jerónimo runs west to the Puerta del Sol, the hub of the city's traffic; then along the Calle Mayor to the Plaza Mayor, the historic centre of Madrid. Farther west is the Calle de Bailén, which runs north past the Plaza de Oriente, with the Royal Palace and the Theatre Royal. From here it is a short distance east, passing the Monasterio de las Descalzas Reales, back to the Puerta del Sol. To the north is the Gran Vía, Madrid's principal shopping street. The day can be rounded off with dinner in one of the numerous restaurants or by a visit to some of the *tapa* bars around the Plaza Mayor.

A second day could be devoted – depending on individual preference – to visiting the Prado, the Archaeological Museum or some of Madrid's many other museums, the Royal Palace, the Museo Nacional Centro de Arte Reina Sofia or the Monasterio de las Descalzas Reales. For rest and relaxation after intensive sightseeing a walk in the Parque del Retiro can be recommended.

A third day will provide an opportunity for seeing something of the outer districts of the city and the surrounding area, with a visit to the Escorial, Segovia, Aranjuez or Toledo as a possibility. Those who have done enough sightseeing may prefer a shopping trip among the shops in the old town and on the Gran Vía or the more exclusive establishments in Calle Serrano and Calle Velázquez in the Salamanca district.

Football fans will find plenty to interest them at the weekend. Madrid has three teams in Spain's First League – the famed Real Madrid, whose home games are played in the large Estadio Santiago Bernabéu in the north-east of the city, Atlético de Madrid, whose base is the Estadio Vicente Calderón,

Sightseeing programme

Football

south-west of the city centre, and Rayo Vallecano, who play in Estadio del Rayo Vallecano, south-east of the city centre.

Transport

Driving your car in central Madrid is to be avoided. Apart from the difficulty of parking, driving in the city's congested streets is no pleasure.

Metro

Madrid's Metro is the quickest means of getting about the city. Its ten lines will enable visitors to get to, or near, the principal sights without difficulty. The Metro runs from 6 in the morning to 1.30 on the following morning; the busiest times are between 7.30 and 9.30am, 1.30 and 2.30pm, and 7.30 and 9pm. There is a flat fare.

◀ **Metro** ▶

Buses

There are 170 bus routes operating from 6am to midnight and eleven night services running between midnight and 6am. The night services all intersect in the Plaza de Cibeles (every 35 minutes between midnight and 3am, every hour between 3 and 6am). There is a flat fare.

Taxis

Madrid's ubiquitous taxis are white, with a transverse red band on the sides and the Madrid heraldic bear on the passenger doors. A green *Libre* sign on the windscreen or a green light on the roof indicates that a taxi is free. The fare is made up of a flat-rate hiring charge plus so much per kilometre. There is an additional charge for journeys between 11pm and 6am, on Sun. and pub. hols. and to/from the airport, bus and train stations, the bullring and football stadiums.

Central Area
Around the Puerta del Sol

Metro station
Puerta del Sol
(Lines 1, 2, 3)

The Puerta del Sol ("Gate of the Sun"), the point ("kilometre zero") from which distance on the main roads radiating from the capital is measured, is the hub of the city's life. It lies at the junction of the city's main traffic arteries and the principal bus and Metro lines, and is thus a good base from which to start a sightseeing tour. The town gate from which the square takes its name, long since demolished, was a plain brick-built structure with six towers. The Puerta del Sol is now surrounded by shops, bars, cafés and restaurants and is busy all day long. The handsomest building in the square is the old Post Office building (1786) on the north side, designed by the French architect Jacques Marquet, which is now the seat of the regional government. An upright bear nibbling at a madroño tree, the symbol of Madrid, also stands in the square.

Museo de la
Real Academía
de Bellas Artes
de San Fernando

From the Puerta del Sol the Calle de Alcalá, the broadest street in the city centre, runs north-east to the Plaza de Cibeles. At No. 13, on the left, is a Baroque palace now occupied by the Royal Academy of Art. The Academy has a collection of drawings, including works by Titian and Raphael, and pictures (Veronese, Correggio, Rubens, van Dyck, Mengs, Fragonard, Zurbarán, Murillo, etc.); Goya is particularly well represented. (Open: Tues.–Fri. 10am–7pm, Sun.–Mon. 10am–2pm.)

Farther along the street, on the left, is the Iglesia de las Calatravas (17th c.), the church of the knightly Order of Calatrava, and beyond this, on the right, the Círculo de Bellas Artes (1926), a monumental building crowned by a tower which is used for art exhibitions.

★Real Monasterio de las Descalzas Reales

Metro station
Puerta del Sol
(Lines 1, 2, 3)
Opera
(Lines 2, 5)

A little way north-west of the Puerta del Sol is the Plaza de las Descalzas Reales, in which is the Real Monasterio de las Descalzas Reales, a convent founded in the 16th century by Joan of Austria, daughter of the Emperor Charles V, in a Renaissance palace which was converted for the purpose. It was intended for ladies of the royal house and the higher nobility: hence the very valuable works of art which it possesses.

There is a magnificent Baroque staircase decorated with frescoes by Claudio Coello (ceiling), Colonna, Mitelli and Antonio de Pereda ("Calvary"). Open: Tues.–Thur. and Sat. 10.30am–12.30pm and 4–5.15pm, Fri. 10.30am–12.30pm; closed Sun. and Mon.

In the rooms and passages of the convent there are numerous portraits of Habsburg rulers. The Gran Sala de Tapices contains a unique series of Brussels tapestries, "The Triumph of the Eucharist", after cartoons by Rubens.

Rooms

The fine collection of pictures in the former dormitory includes works by Hans Memling, Adriaen Isenbrant, Dierik Bouts, Rogier van der Weyden, Zurbarán, Murillo, Ribera, Brueghel the Elder ("Adoration of the Kings") and Titian ("The Tribute Money").

Pictures

Of the various richly decorated chapels the most notable is the Capilla de la Dormición, with a ceiling painting by Luca Giordano.

Chapels

⋆ Gran Vía

The Gran Vía, Madrid's principal shopping street and the very epitome of its big-city character, runs to the north of the Puerta del Sol from its junction with the Calle de Alcalá in the east to the Plaza de España in the west. The construction of the street began, after much demolition of buildings in the cramped old town, in 1910, and the first section, from the Calle de Alcalá to the Red de San Luis, still has a very 19th century character, with such buildings as the Gran Peña (No. 2) and the Ybarra House (No. 8). Between the Red de San Luis and the Plaza de España the street has a distinctly American air, with buildings such as the Telefónica (1929) in the Red de San Luis, the Palacio de la Prensa (Palace of the Press, 1924), the Capitol cinema which projects into the Plaza de Callao like the bow of a ship, and other Broadway-style cinemas between the Plaza de Callao and Plaza de España.

Metro stations
Gran Vía
(Lines 1, 5)
Callao (Lines 3, 5)
Plaza de España
(Lines 3, 10)

An imposing bank in the Gran Vía

Madrid

Museo Municipal

From the Red de San Luis Calle de Fuencarral runs north. At No. 78, near the Tribunal Metro station (Lines 1, 10), stands the former Hospicio de San Fernando, with a magnificent Baroque doorway by Pedro de Ribera. It is now occupied by the Municipal Museum, with a collection of material on the history of the city, including in particular the earliest plan of Madrid (1656) and a model of the city as it was in 1830. (Open: Tues.–Sat. 10am–2pm and 5pm–9pm; Sun. 10am–2pm; closed Mon.) However, check locally as the new Museo de la Ciudad (City Museum) has opened near the Auditorio Nacional de Música on Calle Príncipe de Vergara.

Museo Romántico

Near the Tribunal Metro station in Calle de Fuencarral Calle de San Mateo goes off on the right. On the left-hand side of this street is the Museo Romántico, which with its architecture, furniture and works of art – including pictures by Zurbarán, Mengs, Murillo and Goya – conjures up the atmosphere of aristocratic and upper middle class life in Madrid in the time of Isabella II. (Open: Tues.–Sun. 9am–3pm; closed Mon. and in August.)

Around the Plaza Mayor

★Plaza Mayor

From the Calle Mayor, which runs west from the Puerta del Sol, a passage on the left leads into the Plaza Mayor, now a traffic-free pedestrian zone. This large square, completed in 1619 by Juan Gómez de Mora on the basis of plans by Juan de Herrera, is remarkable for its architectural unity. In the past it was used for festive events, tournaments, horse races and bullfights, and also for executions. Now surrounded by arcaded cafés and bars, it is a popular meeting-place for the people of Madrid. In the centre of the square can be seen an equestrian statue of Philip III, modelled by Giovanni Bologna and cast by his pupil Pietro Tacca in Florence in 1613. On the north side is the Casa Panadería (1672), decorated with frescoes; originally the municipal bakery, it is now occupied by municipal offices. Opposite it, on the south side of the square, is the Casa Consistorial.

From the south-west corner of the Plaza Mayor a steep flight of steps runs down under the Arco de los Cuchilleros into a crowded quarter of the old town, with numerous shops, bars and restaurants.

San Isidro

From the Arco de los Cuchilleros Calle de Toledo runs south to the Cathedral of San Isidro, a handsome granite building erected between 1622 and 1651 which was Madrid's principal church until the completion of the Cathedral of Nuestra Señora de la Almudena. It was dedicated in 1769 to the city's patron saint, San Isidro Labrador (St Isidore the Ploughman), whose remains are preserved in the choir.

El Rastro

300m/330yd south, in Plaza de Cascorro, is the beginning of Madrid's flea-market, El Rastro (Metro stations: Tirso de Molina, line 1, and Puerto de Toledo, line 5), which extends over a number of neighbouring streets and lanes, with innumerable shops and stalls selling furniture, craft products, jewellery and ornaments, and a great variety of other wares of varying antiquity. Sunday morning is the time for the large open-air market.

Puerta de Toledo

At the south end of Calle de Toledo stands the Puerta de Toledo, one of Madrid's two surviving town gates. It was begun in the reign of Joseph Bonaparte and inaugurated in 1813, after the expulsion of the French, as a symbol of victory.

Around the Plaza de la Villa

Casa del Ayuntamiento

To the west of the Plaza Mayor along the Calle Mayor is the Plaza de la Villa, one of the finest squares in the old town. On its west side is the many-towered Casa del Ayuntamiento (Town Hall), the building of which took

Plaza de la Villa

more than a century (1586–1696). It contains beautiful tapestries and pictures by Goya.

The Casa de Cisneros, which is connected with the Town Hall by a covered bridge, is the residence of the Mayor of Madrid. Its main front is one of the city's few Plateresque façades. It contains a number of valuable tapestries.

Casa de Cisneros

Opposite the Town Hall can be seen the Torre de los Lujanes, which together with the adjoining Municipal Newspaper Archives is the oldest part of the Plaza de la Villa. After being taken prisoner in the battle of Pavia (1525) Francis I was confined here, but enjoyed considerable liberty.

Torre de los Lujanes

A little way north of the Plaza de la Villa, in Plaza San Nicolás, is the church of San Nicolás, Madrid's oldest church and one of the few examples of Mudéjar architecture in the city (though only the brick-built Mudéjar tower survives). It has a retablo by Juan de Herrera, the architect of the Escorial.

San Nicolás

To the south of the Plaza de la Villa is the Capilla del Obispo, built in the 16th century to house the shrine of San Isidro. The Plateresque retablo (1547) is by Francisco Giralte, who is buried in the chapel.

Capilla del Obispo

Adjoining the Capilla del Obispo stands the church of San Andrés, built in the 17th c. to receive the shrine of San Isidro on its transfer from the chapel.

San Andrés

Farther to the south-west is the domed church of San Francisco el Grande, built in 1761–70 on the site of an earlier Franciscan friary. In the first side chapel on the left is "San Bernardín" by Goya; the church also has pictures by Bayeu, Maella and González Velázquez.

San Francisco el Grande

★★ Palacio Real

To the west of the Puerta del Sol, above the Río Manzanares, is the imposing granite-built Palacio Real (Royal Palace). After a fire in 1734 which

Metro station
Opera (Line 2)

Madrid

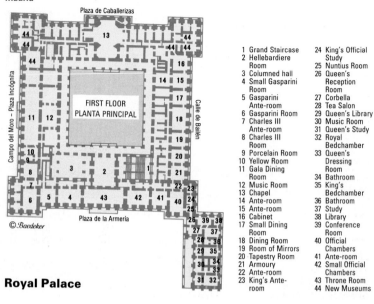

Plaza de Caballerizas

Plaza de Caballerizas

FIRST FLOOR
PLANTA PRINCIPAL

Campo del Moro – Plaza Incógnita

Calle de Bailén

Plaza de la Armería

© *Baedeker*

Royal Palace

1 Grand Staircase
2 Hellebardiere Room
3 Columned hall
4 Small Gasparini Room
5 Gasparini Ante-room
6 Gasparini Room
7 Charles III Ante-room
8 Charles III Room
9 Porcelain Room
10 Yellow Room
11 Gala Dining Room
12 Music Room
13 Chapel
14 Ante-room
15 Ante-room
16 Cabinet
17 Small Dining Room
18 Dining Room
19 Room of Mirrors
20 Tapestry Room
21 Armoury
22 Ante-room
23 King's Ante-room
24 King's Official Study
25 Nuntius Room
26 Queen's Reception Room
27 Corbella
28 Tea Salon
29 Queen's Library
30 Music Room
31 Queen's Study
32 Royal Bedchamber
33 Queen's Dressing Room
34 Bathroom
35 King's Bedchamber
36 Bathroom
37 Study
38 Library
39 Conference Room
40 Official Chambers
41 Ante-room
42 Small Official Chambers
43 Throne Room
44 New Museums

Opening times
Mon.–Sat. 9am–6pm (9am–5pm Oct.–Mar.), Sun. 9am–3.15pm (9am–2pm Oct.–Mar.), closed during official functions

destroyed the old Habsburg castle (originally a Moorish alcázar) Philip V commissioned the Italian architects Juvara and Sacchetti to build a new palace in its place. After Juvara's death Sacchetti completed the building in the form of a closed square with an inner courtyard and projecting elements at the corners. The main front of the palace facing the Plaza de la Armería, with the royal coat of arms, was modelled on the Louvre in Paris. In the inner courtyard are statues of the four Spanish-born Roman Emperors, Trajan, Hadrian, Theodosius and Honorius. Conducted tours.

Main floor

From the main entrance an imposing staircase, with a fresco by Giaquinto, "The Triumph of Religion and the Church", leads up to the main floor of the palace. The first room entered is the Salón de los Alabarderos (Hall of the Halberdiers), which has a ceiling painting by Tiepolo, "The Apotheosis of Aeneas".

★★Apartments of Charles III

The next rooms, the Apartments of Charles III, are the finest in the palace. Two small rooms with ceiling paintings by Mengs are followed by the Salón de Gasparini, with its chinoiserie and furniture a consummate masterpiece of Rococo style. Beyond this is the Salón de Carlos III, in which the king died. The Sala de Porcelana, its walls faced with porcelain plaques from the Buen Retiro manufactory, is followed by the Sala Amarilla (Yellow Room), with its decoration of yellow silk, and the State Dining Room, which has frescoes by Mengs, Bayeu and González Velázquez, Brussels tapestries, Sèvres vases and Chinese porcelain. Off the Dining Room to the right is the Music Room, with a valuable collection of clocks.

Chapel

The Chapel, in the north wing, was the work of Sacchetti and Ventura Rodríguez (1749–57).

Bourbon Apartments

The Bourbon Apartments, in the east wing and part of the south wing, were occupied by Spanish monarchs from Isabella II to Alfonso XIII. They are furnished in a variety of styles and contain many personal mementoes. The most magnificent room is the Salón del Trono (Throne Room) over the main entrance, its walls clad in red velvet, with a ceiling painting by Tiepolo. The Throne Room is still used on great state occasions.

The palace's splendid collection of tapestries is housed in a number of special rooms. Among the oldest items in the collection are a series of tapestries, "The Triumph of the Mother of God", after cartoons by Quentin Metsys (c. 1490), and 16th century Brussels tapestries. In addition to Flemish and French tapestries there are also fine examples from the Madrid and Buen Retiro manufactories.

Tapestry Collection

The New Museums bring together many pictures which formerly hung in various rooms in the palace; many are now also in the Prado. The pictures on display include works by Hieronymus Bosch, Rogier van der Weyden, Caravaggio, Velázquez, El Greco and Goya. The Museums also contain embroideries and a variety of decorative objects in glass, porcelain, precious metals, rare woods, etc.

New Museums

The Royal Library, established by Philip V, contains 300,000 books, together with numerous manuscripts, drawings, sheets of music and maps.

Ground floor
Library

Also on the ground floor is the Real Farmacía (Royal Pharmacy), with old instruments and drug jars.

Real Farmacía

At the south end of the west wing of the palace is the Armería (Armoury). Here, on two floors, is housed a museum of arms and armour with over 3000 exhibits, the most valuable of which are the parade armour of Charles V and Philip II and the swords of the Cid, Boabdil, Cortés and Pizarro.

★ Armería

The former Winter Garden in the Campo del Moro, as the palace gardens are called, now houses the Museo de Carruajes (Carriage Museum), with a collection of royal coaches and carriages, including the litter in which the Emperor Charles V was carried to the monastery of Yuste.

Museo de Carruajes

Around the Royal Palace

Beyond the palace gardens, on the far side of the Río Manzanares, is the large Casa de Campo park, originally a royal forest, which now contains an amusement park, the Madrid Zoo, a swimming pool and other attractions. The park, which is crowded with visitors at weekends, is steadily being encroached on by the growth of the city. From the Paseo del Pintor Rosales, to the north of the Royal Palace, there is a cableway across the river into the park.

Casa de Campo

Metro stations
Lago, Batán (Line 10)

To the south of the Plaza de la Armería is the unfinished cathedral of Nuestra Señora de la Almudena. Work on the construction of the Cathedral began in 1883 but was suspended in 1940; it has recently been resumed. The cathedral was consecrated by Pope John Paul II in 1993 and contains fine examples of religious art. (Open: 10am–2pm and 6–8.30pm.)

Nuestra Señora de la Almudena

Opposite the east wing of the Royal Palace, on the far side of Calle de Bailén, is the Plaza de Oriente, laid out during the reign of Joseph Bonaparte. In the centre of the square is an equestrian statue of Philip IV by the Florentine sculptor Pietro Tacca on the basis of models by Martínez Montañés. Around the square are 44 statues of Visigothic and Spanish kings.

Plaza de Oriente

On the east side of the Plaza de Oriente is the Teatro Real (Theatre Royal). Work began on the construction of the theatre, on the site of the old Caños de Peral theatre, in 1818, and it opened in April 1850 with a performance of Donizetti's "La Favorita".

Teatro Real

This convent of Augustinian nuns, to the north of the Plaza de Oriente, was built by Juan Gómez de Mora, a pupil of Juan de Herrera. Furnished in period style, it is now a museum of 17th century art. The collection includes pictures by Ribera, Juan Carreño, Bartolomé Román, Carducho

★ Convento de la Encarnación

and Antonio de Pereda, Peter van der Meulen's "Entrega en el Bidasoa" (the marriage of Louis XIII of France and Anne of Austria on an island in the Bidasoa) and some fine sculpture, including works by Gregorio Fernández and Pedro de Mena. (Open: Wed. and Sat. 10.30am–12.30pm and 4–5.30pm; Sun. 11am–1.30pm.)

Eastern and Northern Districts

★Plaza de la Cibeles

Metro station
Banco (Line 2)

The Plaza de la Cibeles lies at the intersection of Madrid's main north–south and east–west traffic arteries. In the centre of the square can be seen the 18th century Fountain of Cybele (by José Hermosilla and Ventura Rodríguez), with a figure of the Greek goddess Cybele in a chariot drawn by two lions.

Banco de
España

At the end of Calle de Alcalá is the Banco de España, Spain's national bank. Unusually for a bank, it is furnished with pictures by such famous masters as Murillo, Mengs and Goya.

Dirección
General de
Correos

On the opposite side of the street is the Dirección General de Correos (Head Post Office, 1905–18), a fantastic building in "wedding-cake" style with Art Nouveau features designed by Joaquín Otamendí, who was the target of much criticism for his work. It is worth looking into the building to see the palatial main hall.

Palacio de
Buenavista

At the north-west corner of the square is the large Palacio de Buenavista, built in 1777 for the Duchess of Alba. The palace was acquired by the city in 1802 and presented to Manuel Godoy, Charles IV's minister. It is now occupied by the Ministry of Defence (Ministerio del Ejército).

Plaza de la Cibeles

On the north-east corner of the square is the Palacio de Linares (1875), restored and re-opened in 1922 as the Casa de América, a Spanish/Latin American cultural centre. It houses the Museo de América containing a wealth of material on the history of America both before and after its discovery by Columbus.

Casa de América/
Museo de América

★Paseo del Prado

From the Plaza de la Cibeles the Paseo del Prado runs south to the Plaza del Emperador Carlos V. *Prado* means "meadow", and the Paseo del Prado still preserves a green, tree-shaded avenue between the carriageways. The Paseo was laid out in the 18th century at the behest of Charles III.

In Calle de Montalbán, which branches off on the left at the Museo Naval, is the National Museum of Decorative Art, with ceramics, furniture and other forms of applied and decorative art.

Museo Nacional
de Artes
Decorativas

Farther down the Paseo is the beautiful Plaza de la Lealtad, with the imposing Ritz Hotel. In the centre of the square is an obelisk commemorating those killed on the "Dos de Maio" (May 2nd 1808).

Plaza de
la Lealtad

Beyond this is the Plaza de Cánovas del Castillo, in the centre of which stands the Neptune Fountain. On the right is the Palacio de Villahermosa, which since 1993 has housed the famous Thyssen-Bornemisza Collection (a private collection second only to that of Queen Elizabeth II). It comprises some 800 pictures, including Holbein's "Portrait of Henry VIII", works by Dürer, Caravaggio and Rubens, and a number of paintings by Impressionists and Expressionists, otherwise poorly represented in Madrid. (Open: Tues.–Sun. 9am–7pm, closed Mon.)

**Palacio de
Villahermosa/**
★Museo de la
Colección Von
Thyssen-
Bornemisza

From Plaza Cánovas del Castillo Calle de San Jerónimo leads off on the right to the Cortes, the Spanish Parliament. The entrance to the Neo-Classical building (1843–50) is guarded by two bronze lions, cast from cannon captured in the Moroccan war of 1860.

Cortes

At No. 11 in Calle de Cervantes, in the old part of the town to the south of the Cortes, can be seen a reproduction of a house once occupied by the dramatist Lope de Vega, now a museum. (Open: Mon.–Fri. 9.30am–2.30pm, Sat. 10am–1.30pm; closed Sun. and in Aug.)

Casa de Lope
de Vega

East of the Plaza Cánovas del Castillo, in the direction of the Parque del Retiro, is the Casón del Buen Retiro (El Casón for short), an annexe of the Prado Museum housed in the 17th century Real Sitio del Buen Retiro, once a royal residence. Here are displayed the Prado's collections of Spanish artists of the 19th century, divided into four sections: 19th century historical painting (Gisbert's "Shooting of Torrijos", Degrain's "Lovers of Teruel"), Spanish Realism (Madrazo, Vicente López), Spanish Impressionists (Fortuny, Rosales) and Catalan artists. (Open: Tues.–Sat. 9am–7pm, Sun. 9am–2pm; closed Mon.)

★Casón del
Buen Retiro

Just to the north of El Casón, in the only surviving part of the Palacio del Buen Retiro, is the Museo del Ejército (Army Museum), with a display of weapons and other military equipment (open: Tues.–Sun. 10am–2pm; closed Mon.). The Museum is due to become an annexe of the Prado and to house works of art from the Prado collection.

Museo del
Ejército

South-west of El Casón is the church of San Jerónimo el Real, from 1528 to 1833 the meeting-place of the Cortes, in which the heir to the throne, the Príncipe de Asturias, still takes the oath.

San Jerónimo el
Real

From the Plaza Cánovas del Castillo the Paseo del Prado continues south past the Prado (see below). Just beyond it, on the left, lies the Real Jardín Botánico, which was laid out by Juan de Villanueva and opened in 1781. It is enclosed by iron railings, with two Neo-Classical entrance gates. The gar-

★Real Jardín
Botánico

Madrid

dens are famous for their plants from America and the Philippines. (Open: 10am–7pm or sunset.)

★ **Museo Nacional Centro de Arte Reina Sofía**

Opening times
Mon.–Wed., Sat.
10am–9pm, Sun.
10am–2.30pm;
closed Tues.

The Paseo del Prado ends in the Plaza del Emperador Carlos V, on the left of which is the Atocha Station. Opposite it is the Museo Centro de Arte Reina Sofía, Madrid's new gallery of contemporary art, opened in 1986. It occupies the massive 18th century Hospital San Carlos, which stood empty from 1965 to 1977 before being converted in 1980 and which is slightly reminiscent of the Pompidou Centre in Paris. The main collection of the museum is from the Museo Español de Arte Contemporáneo, situated in the north of the city, with works by Spanish artists such as Andrés Alfaro, Alvaro Delgado, Salvador Dalí, Juan Gris, Juan Miró, Antonio Saura and Pablo Picasso together with foreign artists such as Francis Bacon, Pierre Bonnard, Georges Braque, Markus Lüpertz, Pierre Kandinsky and Henry Moore. Since the summer of 1992 the museum's *pièce de résistance* has been Picasso's anti-war painting "Guernica" which is now permanently housed here.

Paseo de la Infanta Isabel

From the Atocha Station the Paseo de la Infanta Isabel runs south-east to the Museo Nacional de Etnológia (National Museum of Ethnology) in a building, like the core of its eclectic collection, dating from 1975. (Open: Tues.–Sat. 10am–6pm, Sun 10am–2pm.) Just off the Paseo are the Observatorio Astronómico (on the south side of the Parque del Retiro), the Panteón de los Hombres Ilustres (Pantheon of Famous Men) and the Real Fábrica de Tapices, the old Royal Tapestry Factory.

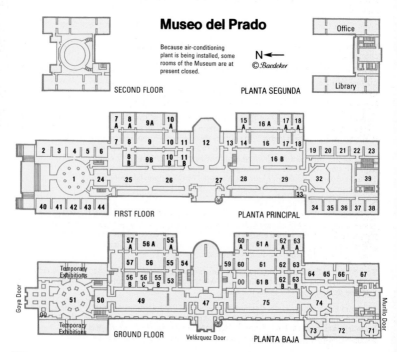

Museo del Prado

★★Museo del Prado

The Prado Museum is one of the oldest and most famous art galleries in the world, and a visit to it is undoubtedly one of the high spots of a stay in Madrid. It was in origin a royal collection, begun by the Habsburgs and carried on by the Bourbons. The decision to erect a new building to house the collection, with Juan de Villanueva as the architect, was taken in the reign of Charles III, and the gallery was opened in 1819 as the "Museum of the Royal Picture Collection".

The Prado possesses some 5000 pictures, only about half of which are on show to the public in its 120 rooms, on three floors. With such an over-whelming abundance, it is not possible in this guide to give any detailed account of the Prado's treasures; and in any event the buiding work which has been in progress for many years means that some rooms may be temporarily closed and the position of pictures changed. No plan showing the location of particular works of art is available: all that visitors can get in the Prado is a complete catalogue of the collections and a "Key to the Prado" which lists the most important works in the various schools. The best plan is to enter the Prado by the Murillo Entrance, since there is a large sales counter by the ticket office where a guide can be bought. Here we can mention only some of the principal works of the most important artists represented in the Prado, bearing in mind that changes are always possible.

Pending completion of the building work, the early Dutch and Flemish artists are to be found in Rooms 53–55 on the ground floor. They include Hieronymus Bosch, known in Spain as El Bosco ("Garden of Earthly Delights", "Hay Wain"), Pieter Brueghel the Elder ("Triumph of Death"), Rogier van der Weyden ("Descent from the Cross"), Hans Memling and Gerard David. Dürer is represented by a self-portrait and "Adam and Eve".

Opening times
Tues.–Sat.
9am–7pm,
Sun. 9am–2pm;
closed Mon.

Early Dutch and Flemish artists; Dürer

Velázquez Entrance of the Prado

Madrid

17th century Dutch and Flemish artists

17th century Dutch and Flemish painters are in Rooms 59–65 on the ground floor. They include Rubens ("Three Graces", "Judgment of Paris", "Peasants' Dance"), van Dyck ("Charles I of England"), Jordaens ("The Jordaens Family in the Garden") and Rembrandt ("Self-Portrait").

Italian painting

Most of the works by Italian painters are on the upper floor (Rooms 2–10 and 41–44). The artists represented include Fra Angelico, Botticelli, Raphael, Correggio, Giorgione, Titian and Tintoretto.

Spanish painting

Part of the Spanish collection is on the ground floor in rooms 49, 50, 51C and 55–57 (Berruguete, Juan de Flandres) but the majority of the other rooms on the upper floor are devoted to Spanish paintings. In Room 12 and adjoining rooms 14–15, in the central block, are some of Velázquez's finest works – "Triumph of Bacchus", "Vulcan's Smithy", "Surrender of Breda" ("Las Lanzas"), the famous portraits of the dwarfs of the Spanish court, "The Spinning Women" and one of his best known pictures, "Las Meninas" ("Ladies of the Court"). There are also works by Murillo, including "The Good Shepherd" and "Holy Family with Bird", works by El Greco ("Nobleman with his Hand on his Breast", "Resurrection", "Pentecost"). Among other Spanish masters represented are Ribera ("Jacob's Dream"), Alonso Cano, Ribalta, Valdes Leal and Olivares (16A, 17A, 18A).

Goya

Goya is particularly well represented, occupying several rooms on the ground and first floor of the right-hand wing. In addition to many of his early cartoons for the Madrid tapestry manufactory there are his paintings of "The Family of Charles IV", "Maja Desnuda", "Maja Vestida", "The Colossus", "Los Fusilamientos del Dos de Mayo", "The San Isidro Meadow", "Saturn eating his Children", the so-called "black pictures" and, in a side room on the ground floor, the drawings for his series of etchings, which are exhibited in rotation.

Monument to Alfonso XII in the Retiro Park

★ Parque del Retiro

Beyond the Prado, flanking Calle de Alfonso XII, is the Parque del Retiro, once a royal park and the scene of brilliant festivities, which was presented to Philip IV by the Duke of Olivares in 1632. In the 18th century part of the park was thrown open to the public, and in 1869 the whole park became the property of the city. It is now a popular place of recreation, with open-air cafés, fountains, monuments, open-air museum, a "Crystal Palace" and a large boating pond, on the shores of which is an imposing monument to Alfonso XII, topped by an equestrian statue of the king.

Metro station
Retiro (Line 2)

The main entrance to the park is at its north-west corner, in the Plaza de Independencia. In the centre of the square is the Puerta de Alcalá, one of the landmarks of Madrid, built in 1769–78 by Sabatini.

Puerta de Alcalá

From the Puerta de Alcalá Calle de Serrano, an elegant shopping and commercial street, runs north into the Salamanca district.

Calle de Serrano

Calle de Alcalá leads north-east from the Puerta de Alcalá and comes in 2km/1¼ miles to the Plaza de Toros (bullring) of Las Ventas, for aficionados the centre of the bullfighting world. Attached to the bullring is the Museo Taurino (Bullfighting Museum).

Las Ventas

★★ Museo Arqueológico Nacional

From the Plaza de la Cibeles the Paseo de Recoletos runs north to the Plaza de Colón, at the south-east corner of which is the National Archaeological Museum, Madrid's most important museum after the Prado. The Museum was founded in 1867, and moved in 1895 to its present premises in the Biblioteca Nacional (National Library).

The tour of the museum should begin in the garden, in which there is an underground gallery containing reproductions of the cave paintings of Altamira (see entry).

Metro stations
Serrano, Colón (Line 4)

Opening times
Tues.–Sat. 9.30am–8.30pm, Sun. 9.30am–2.30pm; closed Mon. and pub. hols.

Museo Arqueológico

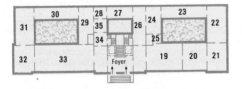

FOURTH FLOOR
PLANTA CUARTA

THIRD FLOOR
PLANTA TERCERA

SECOND FLOOR
PLANTA SEGUNDA

323

Madrid

Prehistory	Rooms 1–16 on the second floor display material from Spain, North Africa, Egypt, the Near East and Italy, together with a fine collection of Greek vases.
Iberian art	Room 20, on the third floor, is devoted to Iberian art. Among the most notable exhibits are the famous figures of the Dama de Elche (illustration, page 57), the Dama de Baza and the Dama de los Cerros Santos.
Roman art	Rooms 21–26 are devoted to Roman art. Particularly notable is the fine collection of mosaics.
Visigothic and Islamic art	Rooms 27–29 display Visigothic art. The central feature of Room 29 is the Treasure of Guarrazar (Toledo), a collection of votive crowns set with gold and precious stones. The next two rooms display Islamic ceramics, metalwork and fragments of stucco.
Medieval Christian art	In rooms 32 and 33 is an impressive collection of Romanesque religious art.
Gothic, Renaissance, modern times	Rooms 34–36, on the fourth floor, display funerary monuments, sculpture, reredoses, etc., illustrating the consummate skill of the artists of the Gothic period. Room 37 contains the royal collection of Italian Renaissance bronzes and 16th century Talavera ware. The last three rooms are devoted to glass, pottery, porcelain and silver of the 17th–19th centuries.
Plaza de Colón	The Plaza de Colón in its present form is a product of the 1970s. On the east side of the square are the Jardines del Descubrimiento (Gardens of Discovery), with a monument to Columbus. On the west side is the Colón de Figuras de Cera (Wax Museum), with more than 400 wax figures in scenes from Spanish history. (Open: daily 10am–2pm and 4–8.30pm.)
Salesas Reales	One block south of the Plaza de Colón is Calle de Braganza, which runs west to the Palacio de Justicia (Law Courts) and the church of the Salesas Reales, with the tomb of Ferdinand VI.

Paseo de la Castellana

	From the Plaza de Colón the wide Paseo de la Castellana goes north. In recent years its bars and restaurants and the green avenue between the carriageways have been popular meeting-places for the gilded youth of Madrid. The pedestrian underpass between Calle de Juan Bravo and Calle de Eduardo Dato, just south of the Glorieta de Emilio Castelar, is a kind of open-air museum of sculpture.
Museo Sorolla	From the Glorieta de Emilio Castelar Calle General Martínez Campos runs west to the Museo Sorolla, a villa which belonged to the Spanish Impressionist Joaquín Sorolla, with more than a hundred of his works dating from 1890 to 1920. (Open: Tues.–Sat. 10am–3pm, Sun. 10am–2pm; closed Mon.)
Museo Lázaro Galdiano	North-east of the Glorieta, in Calle Serrano, is the Museo Lázaro Galdiano, which displays the rich art collection assembled by the financier Lázaro Galdiano, including works by Velázquez, Zurbarán, Murillo, Ribalta, Hieronymus Bosch, van Dyck, Metsys, Jordaens, Reynolds and Constable. There is also a large collection of weapons, coins, ivories, tapestries, jewellery and much else besides. (Open: Tues.–Sun. 10am–2pm; closed Mon. and Aug.)
Museo Nacional de Ciencias Naturales	Farther up the Paseo de la Castellana, on the right, is the Museo Nacional de Ciencias Naturales (National Museum of the Natural Sciences), with zoological, geological, palaeontological and entomological collections. (Open: Tues.–Fri. 10am–6pm, Sat. 10am–8pm, Sun. 10am–2.30pm; closed Mon.)
Nuevos Ministerios	Just beyond this is the huge complex of the Nuevos Ministerios (New Ministries), the headquarters of three government departments.

The Paseo de la Castellana continues north to the Chamartín Station, passing on the right the Estadio Santiago Bernabéu, the home ground of Real Madrid.

South-east from Plaza Cardinal Cisneros, in Avenida Reyes Católicos, is the Museo de América. After years of restoration this museum of American history re-opened in the autumn of 1995. Its extensive collection of American ethnologial and archaeological items has new works added. (Open: Tues.–Sat. 10am–3pm, Sun. 10am–2.30pm.)

North-Western Districts

Around the Plaza de España

At the north-west end of the Gran Vía is the Plaza de España, where Habsburg and Bourbon Madrid meets the modern city. The modernisation of the square, which in the 18th and 19th centuries was surrounded by barracks, began in the 1920s. It is now dominated by the 107m/350ft high Edificio de España (1948), which has a swimming pool at 96m/315ft, and the 124m/407ft high Torre de Madrid, a block of offices and flats erected in 1957. In the centre of the square can be seen a large monument in honour of Cervantes, with figures of his two heroes Don Quixote and Sancho Panza.

A little to the west of the Plaza de España, in Calle de Ferraz, the Museo Cerralbo, houses a privately-owned collection of archaeological material, Meissen and Sèvres porcelain, weapons, furniture and pictures, including works by El Greco, Ribera, Alonso Cano and Goya. (Open: Tues.–Sat. 9.30am–2.30pm, Sun. 10am–2pm; closed Mon. and Aug.)

Opposite the Museo Cerralbo is the Montaña del Príncipe Pío, from which there is an excellent view of the Royal Palace and the surrounding district. In a small lake here is a monument one would hardly expect to find in Madrid: the Templo de Debod, an Egyptian temple of the 4th century B.C. dedicated to the god Amun, which in 1960 was presented to Spain by the Egyptian government in gratitude for Spanish help in saving monuments threatened by the Aswan High Dam. (Open: daily 10am–1pm and 4–7pm.) From here the Parque del Oeste extends to the north-west.

Below the hill to the west can be seen the railway lines leading to the Northern Station (Estación del Norte). Beyond the railway is the Ermita de San Antonio de la Florida, a plain Neo-Classical chapel in which Goya is buried. Declared a national monument in 1905, the dome has frescoes by Goya, painted in August–December 1798. (Open: Tues.–Fri. 10am–2pm and 4–8pm (mid Jul.–end Aug. 9.30am–2.30pm), Sat. and Sun. 10am–2pm; closed Mon.)

In Calle de la Princesa, which runs north-west from the Plaza de España, stands the 18th century Palacio de Liria, residence of the Dukes of Alba. It contains a rich art collection, including works by Titian, Veronese, Rembrandt, Ruisdael, Rubens, El Greco, Velázquez and Goya (seen Saturday mornings only by appointment: tel. 2 47 53 02).

★ Ciudad Universitaria

In north-western Madrid, flanking the main road to La Coruña, lies the Ciudad Universitaria (University City), founded in 1927 by King Alfonso XIII. During the Civil War the University City was the scene of fierce fighting between the defenders of the Republic and Franco's troops.

In recent years there has been much new building on the campus. In this area too is the large Palacio de Moncloa, official residence of the prime minister.

To the west of the Plaza Cardinal Cisneros, a busy traffic intersection, rises the tower block formerly housing the Museo Español de Arte Contemporáneo (Museum of Contemporary Art), whose collection is incorporated in the Museo Nacional Centro de Arte Reina Sofía now houses the Museo Nacional de Antropología (National Museum of Anthropology). Currently holding temporary exhibitions, in time the museum will have a permanent collection. (Open: Tues.–Sat. 10am–6pm, Sun. 10am–2pm.)

Museo Nacional de Antropología

Other Museums and Collections

Calle San Roque 9
Open: Mon.–Fri. 10am–12.30pm and 4–6pm,
Sat. and Sun.
Convent museum with picture collection

Convento de San Plácido

Paseo Delicias 61
Open: Tues.–Fri. 10am–3pm, Sat. and Sun. 10am–3pm
Railway museum, in an old station

Museo del Ferrocarril

Calle Príncipe de Vergara 140
Open: Tues.–Fri. 10am–2pm and 4–6pm, Sat. and Sun. 10am–2pm
New municipal museum

Museo de la Ciudad

Ciudad Universitaria, Facultad de Farmacia
Open: Sun.–Fri 11am–2pm by appointment
History of pharmacy

Museo de la Farmacia Hispana

Instituto Tecnológico Geominero, Calle Rios Rosas 23
Open: Mon.–Sat. 9am–2pm
Minerals and mining

Museo Geominero

Calle Doctor Esquerdo 36
Open: Wed.–Fri. 10am–2.30pm and 5–7.30pm, Sat. and Sun. 10am–2pm
The Mint: coins, dies, punches, etc.; also stamps

Casa de la Moneda

Palacio Comunicaciones, Calle Montalbán
Open: Mon.–Fri. 10am–1.30pm and 5–7pm, Sat. 10am–1.30pm
Museum of postal services and telecommunications

Museo Postal y Telecomunicaciónes

Universidad Autónoma, de Canto Blanco, Facultad de Filosófia y Letras
Open: Mon.–Fri. 11am–2pm, Tues. and Thu. also 5–8pm
Folk traditions and folk art

Museo de Artes y Tradiciones Populares

Carretera de Extremadura, km. 10.5
Open: Tues.–Sun. 10am–2pm
Aviation and aerospace museum, in an old hangar

Museo del Aire

Calle Sebastián Herrera 2
Open: Sun.–Fri. 11am–2pm by appointment; closed Aug. and pub. hols.
History of military pharmacy

Museo de la Farmacia Militar

Calle Conde Duque 9–11
Open: Mon.–Fri. 9am–9pm
Collection of musical instruments, scores, photographs illustrating history of music

Biblioteca Musical Municipal

Calle Velázquez 144
Open: Mon.–Fri. 10am–1pm by appointment
Mementoes of the physician Ramón y Cajal

Museo Ramón y Cajal

◀ *Cervantes Monument and Edificio de España, Plaza de España*

Madrid

★ Museo Naval   Paseo del Prado 5
Open: Tues.–Sun. 10.30am–1.30pm
History of Spanish navy and sea travel including famous nautical map of
Juan de la Cosa from 1500

Real Fábrica de   Calle Fuenterrabia 2
Tapices   Open: Mon.–Fri. 9am–12.30pm
History, manufacture and examples of famous tapestries.

Surroundings of Madrid

★ El Pardo

Leave Madrid on N VI, going north-west, and at the Puerta de Hierro turn
right into C 601, which runs through a former royal deer park, noted for its
holm-oaks, to the little town of El Pardo, in the middle of the park.

Palacio   The palace of El Pardo, built in 1543 and enlarged in 1772, was for long the
summer residence of the Spanish kings, and in more recent times was
occupied by General Franco until his death. The palace, which has a plain
exterior but contains fine furniture and a collection of tapestries after
cartoons by Goya, Bayeu and González Ruiz, is now open to the public.

Casita del   The Casita del Príncipe is a little 18th century summer palace built for
Príncipe   Charles III's wife María Luísa, sumptuously decorated and furnished in the
style of the period, with fine silk embroidery and pictures by Luca
Giordano.

Convento del   To the west of the palace can be found the Convento del Santo Cristo, with a
Santo Cristo   polychrome wood figure of Christ by Gregorio Fernández in the church.

Into the Sierra de Guadarrama

Colmenar Viejo   Leave Madrid on N I, going north, and soon after Fuencarral (9km/6 miles)
turn left into C 607, which runs north-west to Colmenar Viejo (alt.
885m/2904ft), a town with no particular features of interest apart from a fine
Plateresque retablo of 1579 in the 14th century parish church.

★ Manzanares   C 607 continues to Cerceda, where a road branches off on the right to
el Real   Manzanares el Real (alt. 908m/2979ft), which has a magnificent 15th century castle in Gothic/Mudéjar style, recently restored.

Miraflores de   From Manzanares el Real a minor road follows the Embalse de Santillana to
la Sierra   Soto el Real, from which a side road runs north to Miraflores de la Sierra, a
little town beautifully situated under the south side of the Sierra de Guadarrama, much favoured by the people of Madrid as a summer resort.

★ Monasterio   From Miraflores de la Sierra a road leads north-west over the Puerto de la
del Paular   Morcuera (1796m/5893ft) and down the beautiful valley of the Río Lozoya
to the Monasterio del Paular (alt. 1153m/3783ft), a Carthusian house
founded in 1390. The conventual buildings, laid out around a beautiful
cloister, are now a hotel. Notable features of the church, which was rebuilt
in Baroque style after the 1755 earthquake, are the richly decorated Capilla
del Tabernáculo (1724) and a magnificent 15th century marble high altar of
Dutch workmanship.

★ Puerto de   From the monastery C 604 climbs up through beautiful scenery to the
Navacerrada   Puerto de Navacerrada (1860m/6103ft), from which there are fine views of
the surrounding hills. On the pass is a skiing station, with a lift. From here
M 601 descends to the pretty little town of Navacerrada, from which
C 600 continues south-west to Guadarrama.

A detour can be made from Guadarrama to the Escorial (see entry), 12km/7½ miles south-west.

Málaga

Province: Málaga (MA). Telephone dialling code: 952
Altitude: 8m/26ft. Population: 503,000

Málaga, picturesquely situated on the south coast of Spain at the foot of the Montes de Málaga amid luxuriant subtropical vegetation, is one of the oldest Mediterranean ports. The wide sweep of Málaga Bay is bounded on the east by the Punta de los Cántales and on the west by the Torre de Pimentel. Half way round the bay is the hill of Gibralfaro, crowned by its castle. To the west of the town extends the fertile Vega or Hoya de Málaga, in which oranges, figs, bananas, sugar-cane, cotton and other crops flourish. Málaga is particularly famed for its raisins (*pasas*) and its excellent wines, already well known in Moorish times, notably the sweet Pedro Ximenes and the Dulce and Lágrimas muscatel wines. Málaga's proverbially mild climate has made it the chief centre of the Costa del Sol, and almost five million holidaymakers fly in every year to its international airport (which is to be expanded to handle up to ten million passengers a year). Málaga was the birthplace of Pablo Picasso, and the 17th century sculptor Pedro de Mena lived and died in the town.

The processions and passion plays which take place during Holy Week are particularly extravagant and spectacular in Málaga.

★ Semana Santa

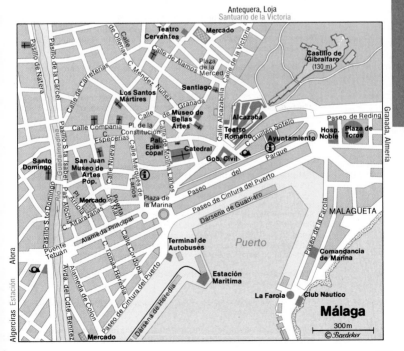

Málaga

300m
© Baedeker

Málaga

History   Málaga was founded by the Phoenicians, who established a settlement here for the trade in salt fish; and this seems to be the origin of its name (Phoenician *malac,* to salt). It later became a Carthaginian stronghold, which the Romans conquered and made into a colony. They were succeeded by the Visigoths, who were driven out by the Moors in 711. It then became a petty Moorish kingdom which refused to submit to the Emirs of Córdoba. In 1487 Málaga was recaptured by the Catholic Monarchs, and thereafter many churches were built in the town. In May 1931, after the proclamation of the Republic, more than forty churches were set on fire and destroyed, and the town also suffered severely during the Civil War.

Sights

Alameda Principal   Málaga's main traffic artery is the Alameda Principal, which extends westward for 420m/460yd, with a breadth of 42m/138ft, from the Plaza de la Marina to the Río Guadalmedina and is continued beyond the Puente de Tetuán by a wide modern street leading to the western suburbs. From the Alameda side streets lead north to the Mercado (Market Hall), which is seen at its liveliest during the morning fish market.

Musseo de la Semana Santa   From the west end of the Alameda across the Puente de Tetuán is the church of San Pedro which houses the Museo de la Semana Santa (Museum of Holy Week). Figures, costumes and carts which are used on the processions during Holy Week are exhibited.

Paseo del Parque   To the east of the Plaza de la Marina the Paseo del Parque extends along the harbour, flanked by promenades shaded by palms and plane-trees. On its north side are the former Custom House (Aduana 18th c.), now the seat of the provincial government (Gobierno Civil), and the Ayuntamiento (Town Hall, 1912–19), with a richly decorated interior. Of the fountains on the Paseo the one opposite the Town Hall, the Fuente de Neptuno (1560), is particularly notable.

Plaza de Toros   On the Paseo de Reding, the continuation of the Paseo del Parque, is the Plaza de Toros (Bullring, 1874).

Cathedral   From the Plaza de la Marina Calle Molina Larios leads into the old town, which is dominated by the cathedral with its twin-towered façade. This massive limestone building, on the site of an earlier mosque, was begun in 1538 to the design of Diego de Siloé, partly destroyed by an earthquake in 1680 and rebuilt from 1719 onwards. From the 86m/282ft high north tower there are extensive views.

Interior   The finely proportioned interior, with lateral aisles, is 115m/377ft long. ★ Choir-stalls   Particularly notable is the choir (1592–1631) with its beautiful stalls (1658). The 40 carved wooden statues of saints on the stalls, together with other figures, were the work of Pedro de Mena and José Micael. In the Capilla del Rosario (the third chapel in the south aisle) is a painting of the "Virgin with Saints" by Alonso Cano, and on the left-hand wall of the Capilla de los Reyes (the first choir chapel on the right) are kneeling figures of the Catholic Monarchs by Pedro de Mena and a statuette of the Virgin which Ferdinand and Isabella are said to have carried with them on all their campaigns. The modern altar in the Capilla Mayor has Passion scenes of 1580.

Palacio Episcopal   Opposite the cathedral stands the 18th century Bishop's Palace, now occupied by the Diocesan Museum.

Sagrario   The Sagrario, a small chapel on the north side of the cathedral, has a very fine Isabelline doorway.

Museo de Bellas Artes   North of the cathedral, in Calle San Agustín, is the Renaissance Palacio de Bellavista, now occupied by the Museo Provincial de Bellas Artes (Pro-

Moorish stronghold and Roman theatre

vincial Museum of Art). On the ground floor are works by Spanish painters of the 16th–20th centuries, including Alonso Cano, Ribera, Murillo, Luis de Morales and Zurbarán, and sculpture by Pedro de Mena; on the upper floor are works by Málaga artists, including Picasso (represented only by two early paintings, etchings and painted pottery) and his first teacher, Muñoz Degrain.

From the Museum Calle San Agustín passes the church of Santiago el Mayor (1490), on the right and reaches the large Plaza de la Merced, in which (No. 15) is the house in which Picasso was born.

Picasso Birthplace

Farther north, reached by way of Calle de la Victoria, is the church of Nuestra Señora de la Victoria, built on the spot where the Catholic Monarchs set up their camp. It contains a 15th century figure of the Virgen de la Victoria, patroness of the town, and two works of sculpture by Pedro de Mena.

Nuestra Señora de la Victoria

From the Plaza de la Merced Calle del Mundo Nuevo ascends to the Alcazaba, which occupies the site of the earliest settlement. This old stronghold of the Moorish kings was begun in the 9th century, but has been much rebuilt and restored since then. Three circuits of wall surround the hill. The principal remains of the original structure are the Torre de la Vela and the Arco de Cristo, The castle now contains an archaeological museum, with finds of Roman material, a collection of Hispano-Arab pottery and models of the castle. The great charm of the Alcazaba lies in the beautiful gardens in the castle courtyards.

Alcazaba

★ Gardens

From the Alcazaba there is a good view of Gibralfaro (170m/558ft), on which are fortifications dating from the 13th century. The name of the hill is derived from the Arabic Jabal-Faruk ("Hill of the Lighthouse"). From the walls there are fine views of the town, the harbour and the surrounding area.

Gibralfaro

Roman theatre On the west side of the castle hill are the remains of a Roman theatre dating from the time of Augustus, in which theatrical performances are given from time to time.

Marbella F 9

Province: Málaga (MA). Telephone dialling code: 952
Altitude: 14m/46ft. Population: 85,000

Marbella, lying between Málaga and Algeciras, was originally a Phoenician foundation. It is now the most fashionable resort on the Costa del Sol and one of the principal tourist centres on the Spanish Mediterranean coast, with beautiful long beaches and every facility for shopping and entertainment.

Marbella's entry into the world of tourism began in the mid fifties, when Prince Alfonso von Hohenlohe founded the Marbella Club, still a favourite haunt of the jet set. He was followed by members of the European nobility, industrialists, playboys and their friends and associates, and the little town of Marbella became the scene of constant parties and luxurious living. Then in the early seventies the seriously rich began to come to Marbella. Arab potentates, including the king of Saudi Arabia and the emirs of Abu Dhabi and Qatar, chose Marbella for their summer retreat and built veritable palaces; and although they live a relatively secluded life their immense financial power has greatly increased the prosperity of the town – not always to the satisfaction of the local people. The society of Marbella is further enlarged by a group of residents who might not care to be asked about the source of their wealth: famous or notorious arms-dealers and a colony of British citizens who, having arrived before an extradition agree-

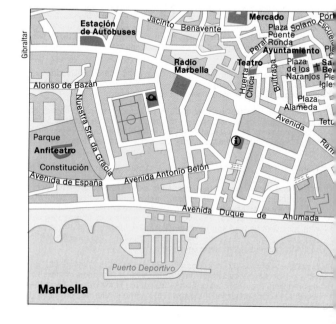

Marbella

ment between Britain and Spain came into effect in 1986, are able to lead a carefree life on the Costa del Sol.

Sights

The old part of the town with its whitewashed houses has preserved some remains of its medieval walls, with two battlemented towers.

Old town

Above the town are the well preserved remains of a Moorish stronghold (walls, courtyard, keep).

Castillo

The new mosque of Marbella, with its whitewashed walls, was built by Prince Salman, governor of the Saudi Arabian capital Riyadh. For the convenience of its wealthy worshippers it is provided with stables and a helicopter landing pad!

Mosque

Marbella has numbers of exclusive restaurants, night clubs, bars, a casino and other places of entertainment, where the prices are in direct proportion to the number of Rolls-Royces, Jaguars and Ferraris parked outside them. The long beaches offer facilities for all kinds of water sports. In addition there are seven golf courses, numerous tennis courts, riding stables, three boating harbours and sailing clubs.

Sport and recreation

Surroundings of Marbella

A few kilometres inland, north-east of Marbella, lies Tivoli, a large amusement park.

Tivoli

West of Marbella, at the Nueva Andalucía holiday village, is an ultra-modern marina with more than 900 moorings.

Puerto Banús

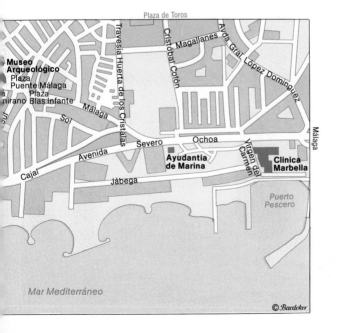

Medina del Campo   F 3/4

Province: Valladolid (VA). Telephone dialling code: 983
Altitude: 721m/2366ft. Population: 20,000

The little town of Medina del Campo, on the Río Zapardiel, is an important
rail and road junction on the N VI, the main road from Madrid to La Coruña.
Until the 16th century Medina del Campo was one of Europe's most important commercial towns, and the Catholic Monarchs made it a royal residence. Isabella the Catholic died in the town in 1504.

Sights

★Castillo de
la Mota

Above the town is the 15th century Castillo de la Mota, one of the finest
castles in Spain. Brick-built, it was erected by Fernando Carreño in 1440. It
was a favourite residence of Isabella the Catholic, who died in the castle.
Her daughter Joan the Mad also frequently stayed here. Cesare Borgia
(César Borja) was imprisoned in the keep from 1504 to 1506.

San Antolín

The collegiate church of San Antolín (1503) has a large and impressive
retablo which was the work of many artists, including Juan Rodríguez and
Cornelis de Holanda. Capilla de los Quiñones has a relief by Juan de Juni.

Hospital

The town's Hospital was built by Simón Ruiz, a 16th century merchant and
banker, and visitors can still see the wards. The church has a very fine
retablo by Juan de Ávila, with sculpture by Pedro de la Cuadra.*

Palacio de
las Dueñas

The Palacio de las Dueñas in Calle Santa Teresa is a magnificent mansion
decked with coats of arms, with a Renaissance gallery and a beautiful inner
courtyard.

Castillo de la Mota

Province: Málaga (MA). Status: *plaza de soberanía*
Telephone dialling code: 952
Altitude: 0–30m/0–100ft. Population: 60,000

There are regular connections with Almería, Barcelona, Madrid and Málaga in mainland Spain. The Iberia office is at Avenida Juan Carlos 1.

Air services

Trasmediterránea runs weekly services to Almería and daily services to Málaga; the crossing takes about 8 hours in each case. The ferries sail from the harbour (Marina 1), which is reached by way of the Paseo del General Macias.

Ferry services

The port, garrison town and free-trade zone of Melilla (Arabic Mlilya or Ras el-Querk, Berber Tamlilt) is a Spanish enclave *(plaza de soberanía)* of 12.3 sq.km/4¾ sq.miles on the Mediterranean coast of Morocco. It is strategically situated on the east side of a small bay on the peninsula of Beni Sicar or Gelaia, 25km/15 miles south of Cabo Tres Forcas and 14km/9 miles north of the Moroccan town of Nador. For administrative purposes Melilla is part of the province of Málaga. Most of the inhabitants have Spanish nationality; some 10% are Muslims.

Situation and characteristics

Melilla is a town of purely Andalusian character. The old part of the town, surrounded by stout defensive walls, lies at an altitude of 30m/100ft on a small peninsula and has remained almost unchanged since the 16th century. The newer part, with its wide, straight streets and beautiful parks and gardens, grew up around 70 years ago. Melilla is almost totally dependent on Spain for its supplies. Most goods come in by sea; air transport – in spite of the town's new airport – plays a relatively minor role. The port, which during the Spanish protectorate over Morocco shipped iron and lead ore from the eastern foothills of the Atlas Mountains, is now again a port of transhipment for iron ore and steel, which comes from and via Nador by rail. More important for the port of Melilla, however, are the sardine fisheries, much of the catch being processed in canning factories in Melilla. The ferry services to and from Málaga, Ceuta and Almería also make some contribution to the economy. The local craft industries, which cover a remarkably wide range, are also of considerable importance.

Melilla was originally a Phoenician foundation under the name of Rusadir – the oldest Phoenician settlement in Morocco after Lixius. It suffered the same fate as other Phoenician settlements, becoming successively Carthaginian, Roman, Vandal, Byzantine and finally Arab. In 705, during their second campaign of conquest, the Arabs completely destroyed the town. They rebuilt it in the 10th century, and from the 13th century onwards, during the period of Merinid rule, developed it into one of the leading ports on the North African coast.

History

Spain conquered Melilla in 1497. Thereafter it was frequently attacked – most recently by Abd el-Krim in 1921 – but always remained in Spanish hands, and became an important port, protected by strong fortifications.

After becoming a customs-free zone in 1887, and during the Spanish protectorate over Morocco (1914–56), Melilla enjoyed a second economic heyday; but when Morocco became independent it lost its hinterland, and when Algeria also became independent in 1962 it lost the customers for duty-free goods who had previously come from there, and decline set in, as evidenced by a fall in population from 100,000 to around 60,000.

Sights

The town extends in a semicircle round the harbour and the bay. It is a place of typically Spanish aspect, with wide streets intersecting at right angles, large squares and parks. In the past the population was almost exclusively Spanish, but more recently numbers of Moroccans have come in, legally or illegally, and settled on the outskirts of the town.

Old town
(Medina Sidonia, Ciudad Vieja)

The best starting-point for a tour of the town is the Plaza de España. To the west of this square is the new town of Melilla (Ciudad Nueva); to the east, on a small, rather higher, peninsula edged by cliffs falling steeply down to the sea, is the old town, known as Medina Sidonia or Pueblo (the "Village"). The whole of the old town, which is ringed by 16th century walls and bastions, has been declared a national historical monument. It is reached by way of the Paseo del General Macias, which runs east from the Plaza de España. At the end of the Paseo are steps leading up to the top of the massive town walls. Round the walls to the left stands the handsomest of the town gates, the Puerta de Santiago, with the coat of arms of the Emperor Charles V on the outer wall. The gate gives access to the Plaza de Armas, near which is a small chapel dedicated to Santiago (St James).
From the walls there are fine views of the town and the coast.

La Purísima
Concepción

Melilla's oldest church is the Purísima Concepción (16th c.), which has a number of beautiful Baroque altars. On the retablo is a 17th century statue of the Virgen de Victoria, the town's patroness. Opposite this is a fine and much venerated 16th century figure of Christ, the Cristo de Socorro.

Museo
Municipal

North of the church is the Municipal Museum, with a collection of prehistoric antiquities, including Palaeolithic stone implements, Carthaginian and Roman pottery, coins and pieces of ironwork, and weapons, flags and plans from more recent periods in the town's history.

New town
(Ciudad Nueva)

The Avenida de Juan Carlos I, which leads north-west from the Plaza de España, is the main shopping street of the new town. Other shopping streets are Calle del Ejército Español/Calle López Moreno, parallel to the Avenida on the north, and various side streets running at right angles to them.

Parque Hernández

To the west of the Plaza de España lies the Parque Hernández, planted with many different species of palms.

Beach

At the south end of the town is a beautiful sandy beach 2km/1¼ miles long.

Cabo Tres Forcas

An excursion can be made, on a poor road, to the tip of the peninsula, Cabo Tres Forcas (25km/15 miles north). This outpost of the Moroccan coast, reaching far out into the Mediterranean, falls vertically down to the sea in 400m/1300ft high cliffs. From the lighthouse there are magnificent views. On the way back it is worth making a detour to Playa Charranes, a beautiful sandy beach on the north-west coast of the Beni Sicar (Gelaia) peninsula. This whole area belongs to Morocco, so that this excursion means crossing the frontier.

Mérida   E 6

Province: Badajoz (BA). Telephone dialling code: 924
Altitude: 196m/643ft. Population: 41,000

★ Roman remains

Mérida, the Spanish town which is richest in remains of the Roman period, lies on a flat-topped hill on the right bank of the Río Guadiana, on the sparsely populated plateau of Extremadura which adjoins the Portuguese frontier.

History

Mérida was founded by the Romans in 25 B.C., under the name of Augusta Emerita, as a colony for veterans of the Vth and Xth Legions. The town prospered and became capital of the province of Lusitania; with a population of 50,000, it was the largest Roman town in Iberia and the political and cultural centre of the whole peninsula. After Christianity was adopted as the state religion of the Roman Empire Mérida was one of the first Roman cities to become the see of an archbishop. It retained its position after its conquest by the Visigoths in the 5th century, but its decline began after it fell to the Moors in 713. The decline continued after its reconquest by Alfonso IX of León, who granted it in 1229 to the knightly Order of Santiago.

Sights

The hub of the town's traffic is the arcaded Plaza de España (Plaza Mayor), at the north-west corner of which stands the church of Santa María la Mayor (13th–15th c.). It was founded by Alonso de Cárdenas, Grand Master of the Order of Santiago, who is buried in the church along with his wife.

Santa María la Mayor

A little way north of the square, at the junction of two streets, the Arco de Trajano or Arco de Santiago, is a Roman triumphal arch almost 13m/43ft high, with four rows of columns, which was the north gate of the Roman town.

Arco de Trajano

To the west of the Plaza de España, at the corner of Calle Romero Leal Sagasta, is the Temple of Diana (not in fact dedicated to Diana but to some unknown cult), which was converted into a noble mansion in the 16th century.

Templo de Diana

South of the Plaza de España, on the banks of the Guadiana, is the Alcazaba, a Moorish castle created in 855 by the enlargement of an earlier Roman and Visigothic building, which was later converted by the Order of Santiago into a monastery. The Moors restored the Roman cistern in the basement of the fortress and built a flight of steps down to it, re-using Roman and Visigothic stones.

Alcazaba

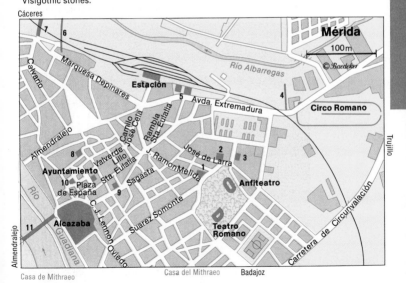

1 Museo Nacional de Arte Romano	4 Acueducto Moderno	8 Arco de Trajano
2 Termas (Baths)	5 Santa Eulalia	9 Templo de Diana
3 Casa Romana	6 Acueducto Los Milagros	10 Santa María
	7 Puente de Albarregas	11 Puente Romano

Mérida

★ Puente Romano On the west side of the Alcazaba is one of Mérida's principal sights, the Roman bridge over the Guadiana, probably built in the reign of Augustus but frequently renovated or rebuilt in later centuries. With 64 granite arches, it has a total length of 792m/866yd.

New Bridge Just below the Roman bridge Méridas' new symbol spans the river, the arches of the Santiago Calatrava bridge.

Casa del Mithraeo From the Alcazaba Calle de Oviedo runs south to the Plaza de Toros (Bullring), beyond which is the Casa del Mithraeo, a large Roman villa named after a mithraeum which was found here, with very fine mosaics depicting the origin of the world.

★ Museo Nacional de Arte Romano Mérida's most important Roman monuments are at the east end of the town. On the way there from the Temple of Diana is the new National Museum of Roman Art, opened in 1986. Built on the scale of the Arco de Trajano, the Museum contains a fine collection of Roman coins, including many from the local mint, sculpture, including a head of Augustus in Carrara marble, a collection of Roman glass and wall paintings from the Roman theatre. The Museum is built over part of the Roman town, and on prior appointment visitors can see the foundations of Roman buildings and other remains in the basement.

★ Teatro Romano Opposite the Museum is an area containing the largest Roman architectural remains. To the right is the Theatre, built by the Roman general Agrippa in 16 B.C. and rebuilt after a fire in the reign of Hadrian (2nd c. A.D.). The well preserved semicircular auditorium could seat 6000 spectators. The rear wall of the stage buildings, which suffered most damage in the fire, has sculptural decoration dating from the 2nd century rebuilding. Here there

Roman theatre, Mérida

was a garden which served as a foyer. The theatre has recently been restored and is used in an annual summer festival of drama.

Adjoining the theatre are the excavated remains of the Roman Amphitheatre, built in 8 B.C., in which 15,000 spectators could watch gladiatorial contests. The amphitheatre could be flooded, so that ships could sail in and naval battles could be fought. After gladiatorial contests were banned material from the amphitheatre was used for repairing the bridge over the Guadiana.

Anfiteatro Romano

On the opposite side of the street from the amphitheatre are the remains of Roman baths.

Termas

To the right of the baths is the Casa Romana, a Roman villa of the 1st century A.D. with remains of wall painting and very beautiful pavement mosaics.

Casa Romana

North-west of the amphitheatre, beyond the railway, are the remains of a hippodrome, the only one of its kind in Spain. The site is now much overgrown.

Circo Romano

Adjoining the site of the hippodrome, on the far side of Calle Teniente Coronel Yagüe, can be seen the 140 arches of the Acueducto Moderno, the "modern" aqueduct built by the Moors.

Acueducto Moderno

From here the Avenida Extremadura runs along the railway to the station, just before which stands the church of Santa Eulalia, built in the 4th century on the site of a Roman temple and completely rebuilt in the 13th century.

Santa Eulalia

Farther along the railway line is the massive Acueducto de los Milagros ("Aqueduct of the Miracles"), a Roman aqueduct, built of granite and brick, of which there survive 37 piers and ten arches up to three storeys high. It brought water to Mérida from the Prosérpina reservoir 10km/6 miles away.

★Acueducto de los Milagros

A little way west of the Roman aqueduct the Puente de Albarregas, another Roman bridge, 125m/137yd long, spans the little Río Albarregas.

Puente de Albarregas

Montserrat

O 3

Province: Barcelona (B). Altitude: up to 1241m/4072ft

The hill of Montserrat, famed for its monastery, is some 50km/30 miles north-west of Barcelona.

Montserrat can be reached from Barcelona by taking the A 2 motorway to Martorell and continuing from there on C 1411, which runs via Olesa to Monistrol. Soon after Olesa a bridge crosses the valley and leads to the lower station of the cableway (large signpost to "Aeri" – officially the Funicular Aeri del Montserrat), the upper station of which is just beside the monastery. There is also a road to the monastery, with many bends but scenically magnificent, from Monistrol.
   There is also a direct rail link from Barcelona to the cableway, starting from the junction under the Plaza de España (Catalan Plaça d'Espanya).
   Visitors approaching Montserrat from the north will do well to avoid the built-up area of Barcelona. The best plan is to take the A 7 motorway, which runs parallel to the coast some distance inland, as far as Cerdanyola and then follow the motorway spur which runs north-west to Tarrasa, continuing on the ordinary road to Monistrol.

Access

Montserrat was formerly identified, wrongly, with the castle of Monsalvat in the story of the Grail (now thought more probably to have been at the little pilgrimage centre of Salvatierra on the southern slopes of the Pyrenees). According to legend the monastery was founded in 880 in honour of

History

a wonderworking image of the Virgin. In 976 it was granted to the Benedictine order, and in 1025 it was occupied by monks from the Catalan monasteries of Ripoll and Vich. In 1409 Pope Benedict XIII raised it to the status of an independent abbey, and towards the end of the century a printing press was established in the abbey. In 1522 Ignatius Loyola, later to become the founder of the Jesuits, stayed for some time in the abbey. During the Napoleonic wars most of its enormous wealth was lost, and in 1811 the abbey was destroyed by the French. It suffered further losses while it was closed during the Carlist wars (1835–60). The monastery still runs the Escolanía, a school of church music founded in the 15th century, whose pupils sing the "Salve" of the Ave Maria (1pm) and at Vespers.

The ★ ★ Site

Montserrat, the "jagged mountain", and to the Catalans Montsagrat, the sacred mountain, is one of Spain's major tourist attractions by virtue both of its scenic magnificence and its famous monastery. This great massif of conglomerate, 10km/6 miles long and 5km/3 miles across, rears out of the Catalonian upland plain on the right bank of the Río Llobregat in splendid isolation, with steep rock faces on every side, looking from a distance, with its fantastically eroded crags and terraces, like some gigantic fortress. The highest peak is San Jerónimo (Catalan Sant Jeroni; 1241m/4072ft). On the south-east side the range is cleft by a huge fissure, known as the Valle Malo (Catalan Vall Malalt, the "Bad Valley"), at the mouth of which, on a projecting spur of rock, stands the monastery (alt. 725m/2380ft). The north-eastern slopes are covered with forests of pines, the flanks and summit of the hill with evergreen scrub. Much of the celebrated flora of Montserrat (with some 1500 species) was destroyed by fires in 1986.

The ★ Monastery

The monastery, with its church and the various subsidiary buildings, is a little city on its own. The road ends at the extensive car parks, near which is a large outlook terrace, with a modern monument to the Catalan poet and mystic Ramón Llull. The eight stages of the monument, in the form of a spiral, represent the eight stages of awareness (stone, flame, plant, animal, man, heaven, angel, God).

The monastery complex proper is reached by way of the Plaza de la Cruz (Catalan Plaça de la Creu), which is flanked by a restaurant, souvenir shops, a post office, payphones and a bureau de change.

Museo/Museu de Montserrat

Beyond this is a spacious square, the Plaza de Santa María (Catalan Plaça de Santa Maria). To the right of the broad central section leading to the

Montserrat

1 Main entrance to Monastery
2 Audio-visual information
3 Museum (two buildings)
4 Hotel
5 Gothic Cloister
6 Gatehouse
7 Basilica
8 Singing Academy (Escolania)
9 Memorial to Ramon Llull
10 Restaurant
11 Cableway (Aeri)
12 Memorial to Pablo Casals
13 Funicular to the Holy Grotto (Santa Cueva)
14 Funicular to Saint Joan (San Juan)
15 Police Station (Guardia Civil)
16 Via Crucis (Way of the Cross)

church is the entrance to the modern part of the Museum, under the square, which contains works by 19th and 20th century Catalan painters, generally of no more than local importance. The older part of the Museum, to the left of the church, contains a small Egyptological collection, Neolithic material, Roman and Byzantine pottery and jewellery, coins, antique glassware and Jewish cult objects.

At the far end of the square is a gatehouse (1942–68), with five round-headed arches on the lower level and three on the upper level. Reliefs in the three upper arches depict (from left to right) St Benedict, the Assumption of the Virgin (following its definition by Pope Pius XII in 1950) and St George, patron saint of Catalonia. To the left of the gatehouse are remains of the old Gothic cloister (15th c.).

Church

Between the gatehouse and the church is a small inner courtyard, with a statue of St Benedict (1927), beside which is the entrance to the monastery (public not admitted). In the gatehouse, entered from the courtyard, is the baptismal chapel, its entrance decorated with 20th century reliefs.

The church, which contains the much revered image of the Virgin of Montserrat, dates from the 16th century, but underwent much renovation and alteration in the 19th and 20th centuries. The façade shows Renaissance forms, but the figures of Christ and the Apostles date only from around 1900.

There are two entrances to the church: the main doorway leads into the nave, while the one on the right gives direct access to the image of the Virgin (one-way traffic). The nave is 68m/223ft long, 21m/69ft wide and 33m/108ft high, and is rather dimly illuminated by the numerous candles lit by worshippers. The furnishings are modern.

Interior

Above the high altar is the image (Spanish Santa Imagen, Catalan Santa Imatge) of the Virgin of Montserrat, one of the most revered images in the whole of Spain. It is approached from the transepts by flights of steps with silver mountings. The image, of polychrome wood, dates from the 12th or 13th century. The face and hands are black with age: hence the Catalan name of the image, la Moreneta (*moreno* = "dark"). The legend is that the image was made by St Luke and brought to Spain by St Peter.

★★ Virgin of Montserrat

The exit from the church is in the north transept. Outside, on the rock face, are large numbers of ex-votos (among them wax models of parts of the body, offered in gratitude for a cure) and votive candles. Here too is the Sacred Spring (Catalan Mistica Font del Aigua de la Vida), with a coloured majolica painting of the Virgin.

In the Plaça de l'Abat Oliva is the beginning of the Via Crucis (Way of the Cross), with fourteen large statuary groups set up between 1904 and 1919 and restored after the Civil War.

At the end of the Way is the chapel of the Virgen de la Soledad. At the 14th station a path goes off to the Ermita de San Miguel (Catalan Sant Miquel), a 19th century chapel replacing a 10th century predecessor.

Way of the Cross

From the Plaça de la Creu a road goes past the upper station of the cableway from the valley road to the Cueva Santa (Catalan Cova Santa), with a 17th century chapel. In this "Sacred Cave" the image of the Virgin of Montserrat, hidden during the Moorish period, is said to have been rediscovered by shepherds.

Cueva Santa/ Cova Santa

In Plaça de la Creu is the lower station of the cableway to the Ermita de San Juan (Catalan Sant Joan). Nearby, by the roadside, is a monument to the Catalan cellist Pau (Pablo) Casals.

San Juan is one of the many hermitages round Montserrat, originally thirteen in number. From the upper station of the cableway there is a fine view of the monastery. There is a rewarding walk from here to San Jerónimo (Catalan Sant Jeroni).

San Juan/ Sant Joan

Murcia

<table>
<tr><td>★★ San Jerónimo/
Sant Jeroni</td><td>A 680m/745yd long cableway (difference in height 535m/1755ft), the oldest of its kind in Spain, runs up from the Manresa road to the Capilla de Sant Jeroni, from which it is a 5 minute walk to the summit of Sant Jeroni, the highest peak in the Montserrat range.</td></tr>
</table>

Murcia   L 7

Province: Murcia (MU). Telephone dialling code: 968.
Altitude: 43m/141ft. Population: 305,000.

Murcia, situated in the hot coastal plain of south-eastern Spain, is the chief town of its province and the seat of a university. The fertile Huerta de Murcia, in which fruit and vegetables flourish, supplies a large canning industry.

Murcia was the birthplace of the sculptor Francisco Salzillo or Zarcillo (1707–83), whose works are to be seen in many churches.

<table>
<tr><td>★ Semana Santa</td><td>The Semana Santa (Holy Week) celebrations in Murcia are among the most famous religious festivals in Spain, with impressive nocturnal processions in which *pasos* by Francisco Salzillo are carried round the town. Particularly striking is the procession on the morning of Good Friday.</td></tr>
<tr><td>History</td><td>The Moorish town of Mursiya was founded by Abderrahman II about 830. From 1224 Murcia and the surrounding area became an independent Moorish kingdom (*taifa*), which was conquered by Castile only nineteen years later. During the War of the Spanish Succession the huerta round the town was flooded to defend it against attack by Austrian troops. In 1936, during the Civil War, many churches in the town were set on fire or otherwise destroyed.</td></tr>
</table>

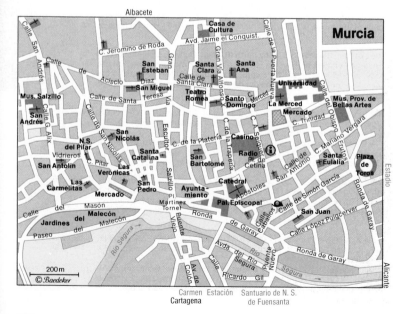

★ Cathedral

Murcia's most important monument is the Cathedral of Santa María, to the north of the Palacio Episcopal (Bishop's Palace). Begun in 1358 in Gothic style on the site of an earlier mosque, it was partly rebuilt in the 16th century and much altered from 1748 onwards, when the ornate Baroque west front was built. The side doorways are also richly decorated: in the south transept the Gothic Portada de los Apóstoles (by Antonio Gil), in the north transept 16th century Portada de las Cadenas. From the top of the 92m/302ft high tower (begun in 1521 but completed only in 1792) there are fine panoramic views of Murcia and the Huerta.

Exterior

The finest of the side chapels is the fourth chapel in the south aisle, the Capilla de Junterón, in consummate Renaissance style (by Jerónimo Quijano, 1525 onwards). The central altar (probably Italian work) has a representation of the Adoration of the Shepherds.

Interior

The Capilla Mayor, enclosed by a *reja* of 1497, has a gilded retablo (19th c.). In a recess on the left is an urn containing the entrails of Alfonso the Wise; on the right are the relics of St Fulgentius and St Florentina. The choir, separated from the nave by an ornate screen, has fine Plateresque stalls (1571). The most notable of the chapels round the ambulatory is the Capilla de los Vélez (4th on right), the burial chapel of the Vélez family (1491–1507), with an extraordinary Isabelline doorway, delicate figural and plant ornament reminiscent of Arab work and a high dome.

The Portada de la Antesacristía in the north aisle leads into the sacristy, which has very fine panelling by Jerónimo Quijano.

The Diocesan Museum is housed in the cloister and chapterhouse. Among its principal treasures are a Roman sarcophagus, three works of sculpture by Salzillo, a monstrance coated with gold leaf from Toledo (1678), an 18th century silver monstrance and the large silver "Maundy Thursday chest".

Museo Diocesano

Murcia Cathedral

Around the Cathedral

Calle de la Trapería	From the cathedral Calle de la Trapería, once Murcia's main street, runs north through the old town. Together with Calle de la Platería, which branches off it on the left, it is the heart of a busy pedestrian zone well provided with shops. One of the most striking buildings in Calle de la Trapería is the Casino (on right), a gentleman's club built in the 19th and 20th centuries, with an Arab-style patio, a restaurant, a glazed gallery, a billiard room, a ballroom and a library.
Plaza de Santo Domingo	Calle de la Trapería ends in the Plaza de Santo Domingo, with the handsome twin-towered church of Santo Domingo (17th–18th c.). Behind it, to the west, is the Teatro Romea.
Museo Arqueológico	To the north of the Plaza de Santo Domingo, in the Casa de Cultura, the Archaeological Museum houses prehistoric, Iberian, Greek and Roman antiquities and a collection of pottery, including in particular Moorish ware.
Museo de Bellas Artes	From the Plaza de Santo Domingo Calle de la Merced runs east to the University, just beyond which, in Calle del Obispo Frutos, is the Museum of Art, with frescoes and pictures by the Murcia-born painter Nicolá Villacis (1616–94), a pupil of Velázquez, works by many local artists and pictures by Ribera, Degrain and Picasso.
Museo de la Muralla Árabe	In Plaza Santa Eulalia, south of the Museum of Art, Moorish and medieval town walls have been brought to light. Objects found in the excavations are to be displayed in the Museo de la Muralla Árabe (Museum of the Arab Town Walls) which is due to open shortly.
Along the Río Segura	A short distance south of the cathedral, on the street along the left bank of the Río Segura, is the Glorieta de España, a beautiful public garden with the Ayuntamiento (Town Hall) on its northern side. At its west end is the Plaza de Martínez Tornel, from which Murcia's main traffic artery, the Gran Vía del Escultor Salzillo, runs north. To the west of the Plaza de Martínez Tornel are the Plano de San Francisco and beyond this the Paseo del Malecón, a promenade along the embankment offering no shade from summer sun.

Western Districts

Churches	The most interesting of the numerous churches in the western districts of the town are San Nicolás, in the Plaza Mayor, with a Baroque interior and sculpture by Alonso Cano, Pedro de Mena and Salzillo, and San Miguel, adjoining the Jardín de San Esteban, which has several figures on the altar by Salzillo and his family workshop.
★Museo Salzillo	At the west end of the town, in the Plaza de San Agustín, is the Ermita de Jesús, a round Baroque chapel (1777) which now houses the Salzillo Museum, devoted to the work of the Murcia-born sculptor Francisco Salzillo. Among the works on exhibition are the famous processional figures (*pasos*) carried in the Holy Week processions (particularly notable being a representation of the Last Supper), clay models and a magnificent Nativity scene with more than 500 figures dressed in 18th century Murcian costume.
Museo del Traje Folklórico	The Museo Internacional del Traje Folklórico (International Museum of Folk Costume), which has a collection of traditional costumes from all over Spain, is due to move to new premises, not yet determined.

Nerja

Province: Málaga (MA). Telephone dialling code: 952
Altitude: 21m/69ft. Population: 12,000

The Balcón de Europa on the Costa del Sol

Nerja is a popular seaside resort situated at the mouth of the Río Chillar on a steeply sloping site below the Sierra de Mihara. The coast road along the Costa del Sol (N 340) runs through the town. The town was known to the Arabs as Narixa ("abundant spring"). The tourist boom has not left Nerja unscathed, as the mass of new buildings and some rather dreary beaches will bear witness.

★Balcón de Europa

The Balcón de Europa ("Balcony of Europe") is an outlook terrace, high above the sea on a promontory in the middle of the town, from which there are magnificent views of the varied coastal scenery.

Surroundings of Nerja

A few kilometres north-east of the town are the Cuevas de Nerja, a cave system discovered in 1959, with four chambers containing bizarrely shaped stalactites and stalagmites and prehistoric rock paintings.

Cuevas de Nerja

In summer the Sala de la Cascada serves as a concert hall for the Festival of Music and Dance. At the entrance to the caves are a restaurant and a small archaeological museum.

Olite

K 2

Province: Navarra (NA). Telephone dialling code: 948
Altitude: 380m/1247ft. Population: 3000

The old-world little town of Olite lies on the Río Cidacos, south of Pamplona. There was a settlement here in Roman times, but the town's heyday was in the 15th century, when the kings of Navarre made it their residence and built the huge castle, a labyrinth of passages and rooms.

Sights

★ Palacio de los
Reyes de Navarra

In 1406 Charles III of Navarre commissioned French architects to alter and enlarge the original castle, making it a combination of fortress and palace. Although partly destroyed in the 19th century, the castle is still over-whelmingly impressive with its fifteen slender towers and battlemented walls. Within the castle, dominated by the keep (Torre de Homenaje), there were once beautiful gardens. The rooms had azulejo-clad walls and fine timber ceilings.

Santa María
la Real

The 14th century church of Santa María la Real, below the castle, has a very beautiful Gothic doorway, in the centre of which is the Virgin, surrounded by the Apostles. It has a 16th century retablo and a Gothic figure of Christ.

San Pedro

The church of San Pedro (12th–13th c.) is distinguishable by its two dissimi-lar towers. The doorway, with scenes from the life of St Peter, is flanked by two eagles symbolising power and goodness.

Orense/Ourense

C 2

Province: Orense (OR). Telephone dialling code: 988
Altitude: 125m/410ft. Population: 96,000

Orense (Galician Ourense), chief town of its province and the see of a bishop, lies in southern Galicia. It has been famed since ancient times for its healing sulphurous springs (Las Burgas). It was known to the Romans as Aurium, a name probably derived from the legendary gold (Spanish *oro*) of the Río Miño. In the 6th and 7th centuries it was the residence of the Suevian kings, and after the expulsion of the Moors it suffered for many years from Norman and Arab raids.

★ Cathedral

Near the Plaza Mayor stands the Cathedral of San Martín, the finest cathe-dral in Galicia after that of Santiago de Compostela (see entry). It was built in the 12th and 13th centuries and rebuilt in the 16th and 17th centuries after severe damage by earthquakes and war. Both the side doorways have rich sculptural decoration, and even finer is the rich Romanesque sculpture of the Pórtico del Paraíso ("Porch of Paradise") on the west front (accessi-ble only from inside the cathedral), which is modelled on the Pórtico de la Gloria in Santiago. On the central arch can be seen figures of the 24 Elders of the Apocalypse, and on the central pier of the doorway are the Virgin and the Apostle St James (Santiago), with the four Evangelists to the right and four prophets to the left.

Interior

The presbytery, with an equestrian statue of St Martin, is closed off by a fine Plateresque screen. In the north transept is the tomb of Bishop Vasco Mariño. Behind the altar is a large Gothic retablo (14th c.). The Capilla del Cristo (1567–74), a masterpiece of Galician Baroque, has an altar with a baldachin and a very ancient figure of Christ with natural hair, traditionally believed to have been washed ashore on the Galician coast in the 14th century.

Museo Diocesano

The Diocesan Museum in the chapterhouse contains fine 13th century enamels and eight 10th century chessmen in rock crystal.

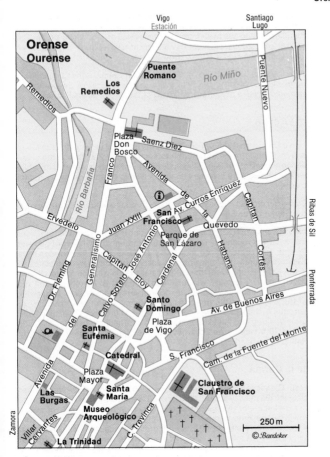

Map: Orense / Ourense, 250 m scale. © Baedeker

Around the Plaza Mayor

A few paces from the cathedral is the arcaded Plaza Mayor, the central feature of the old town. At its south end stands the Romanesque Palacio Episcopal (Bishop's Palace; scheduled as a national monument), with a beautiful arcaded courtyard, which now houses the Archaeological Museum and Provincial Archives. The museum has two sections, one devoted to archaeology (including prehistoric material) and the other to religious painting and sculpture.

Museo Arqueológico

In the south of the town is the Romanesque church of La Trinidad (13th c.), with two round towers and a Gothic doorway.

La Trinidad

In public gardens to the south-west of the Plaza Mayor are the three hot springs (66–68°C/151–154°F) of Las Burgas, which have been known since ancient times.

Las Burgas

Puente Romano	North of the Plaza Mayor, on the way to the railway station, the Puente Romano (Roman Bridge) crosses the Miño; it was built in 1230 on Roman foundations and has been frequently renovated or rebuilt since then. The central arch, 38m/125ft high, has a span of 43m/141ft. A short distance upstream is the Puente Nuevo (New Bridge).
Campo de los Remedios	At the near end of the bridge, on the banks of the Miño, is the Campo de los Remedios, in which is the pilgrimage chapel of Nuestra Señora de los Remedios, with a much revered image of the Virgen de los Remedios.

Surroundings of Orense

★San Esteban de Ribas de Sil	Leave Orense on C 546, which ascends the beautiful valley of the Río Miño, and in 17km/11 miles turn right into a narrow road leading to the abandoned monastery of San Esteban de Ribas de Sil, finely situated on a hill, with a 10th century cemetery chapel, a Gothic church and two beautiful cloisters.
★Gargantas de Sil	Below the monastery the Río Miño flows through a wild and narrow gorge, the Gargantas de Sil.
★Monasterio de Osera	Leave Orense on N 525, going north-west, and in 20km/12½ miles turn right into a narrow secondary road which runs through the villages of Cea and Coletas and comes to the monastery of Santa María la Real de Osera (Galician Oseira). This imposing monastery was founded by the Cistercians in the 12th century. From that period dates the plain interior of the church, which has 17th century wall paintings; the rest of the church and the conventual buildings were rebuilt in Baroque style after a fire. The façades of the church and the monastery are particularly ornate examples of Baroque architecture. The finest part of the church is the sacristy, with groin vaulting and fan-like columns (16th c.). There are two cloisters, one of the 18th century and the other of the 16th, with some remains of Romanesque work.

To the Portillo de la Canda

Allariz	From Orense N 525 runs south-east, heading for Zamora (see entry). After crossing the railway just outside Orense it winds its way up the valley of the Río Barbaña and through an upland region, with large tracts of forest, towards the mountains. 24km/15 miles from Orense is Allariz (alt. 470m/1542ft), capital of Galicia during the Reconquista, which still preserves a 1km/¾ mile long circuit of walls. There are many handsome old mansions in the town, particularly notable being the Casa de Armoeiro, the two parts of which are linked by an arch over the street. The most interesting of the town's ecclesiastical buildings are the Romanesque church of Santiago (begun 1205), which has a figure of the Virgin by Juan de Juni, and the Monasterio de Santa Clara, with a huge Baroque cloister and a church containing the tombs of Alfonso X's children.
Verín	The road continues via Ginzo (Galician Xinzo) de Limia (alt. 620m/2034ft) and through the valley of the Río Támega to Verín (alt. 612m/2008ft), a little town with thermal springs, beautifully situated at the meeting of several valleys.
★Castillo de Monterrey	4km/2½ miles west of Verín rises the mighty Castillo de Monterrey, a fortress guarding the frontier with Portugal which was later used as a prison and is now a parador. Over the centuries the castle developed into a little fortified town surrounded by three circuits of walls. Within the walls are a 13th century church with a very fine doorway and a beautiful retablo, a Jesuit college, a 13th century pilgrim hospice and the 14th century Torre de las Damas.

From Verín N 525 follows an up-and-down easterly course through the hills, and finally climbs to the Portillo de la Canda (1262m/4141ft), on the boundary between Galicia (Orense province) and Castile (Zamora province).

Portillo de la Canda

Towards Portugal

Leave Orense on N 540, going south, which comes in 26km/16 miles to Celanova (alt. 645m/2116ft). In the Plaza Mayor is the famous Benedictine monastery of San Rosendo, founded in 936 but now mainly Baroque. The church has a magnificent façade by Melchor de Velasco, and on entering it the visitor will be overwhelmed by the Baroque splendour of the retablos, particularly the one in the Capilla Mayor. The beautiful cloister (1550) and the panelled stair-wells are also magnificent examples of Baroque art. Of the original monastery there survives the church of San Miguel (10th c.) in the monastery garden.

★ Celanova

Oviedo

E 1

Province: Asturias (O). Telephone dialling code: 985
Altitude: 228m/748ft. Population: 200,000

Oviedo lies on the slopes of a hill some 30km/20 miles from the north coast of Spain, on a fertile plateau enclosed by the foothills of the Cantabrian Mountains. Chief town of the province, it is also the spiritual and intellectual centre of Asturias, the see of a bishop and a university town. Its economy is centred on mining and industry (arms production). The town itself is not particularly attractive, though there are some pleasant squares around the cathedral.

The town grew up in the 8th century around a monastery on the site of ancient Ovetum. Alfonso II moved the Asturian court to Oviedo, which from 810 to 924 was capital of the kingdom then warring against the Moors, until Asturias was united with León and Castile. Oviedo's development into an industrial town started in the 18th century, when mining began in the surrounding coalfield and the Royal Arms Manufactory was established. Most of the town dates from this period. During the 1934 rising of the Asturian miners and the almost two-year-long siege of the town by Republican forces during the Civil War (1936–37) many buildings, including the Cámara Santa, the cathedral and the university, were severely damaged. Since then a whole new district has been developed to the south-west of the town.

History

From the Parque de San Francisco to the Plaza Mayor

The central feature of the town is the Parque de San Francisco (area 6 hectares/15 acres), at the north-east corner of which are the Plaza de la Escandalera and the premises of the Consejo Regional de Asturias. To the north, in Plaza del Progreso, is the Theatre. From the Plaza de la Escandalera Calle de Uría, Oviedo's main street, which is particularly busy in the afternoon and evening, runs north-west to the Northern Station (Estación del Norte).

Plaza de la Escandalera

From the Plaza de la Escandalera the busy Calle de Fruela runs south-east to the arcaded Plaza Mayor. At the south-west corner of the square is the former Jesuit church of San Isidoro (1578), and on its north side the Ayuntamiento (Town Hall; by Juan de Naveda, 1662).

Plaza Mayor

South-west of the Plaza Mayor the quiet Plaza Daoiz y Velarde is surrounded by Baroque houses.

Plaza Daoiz y Velarde

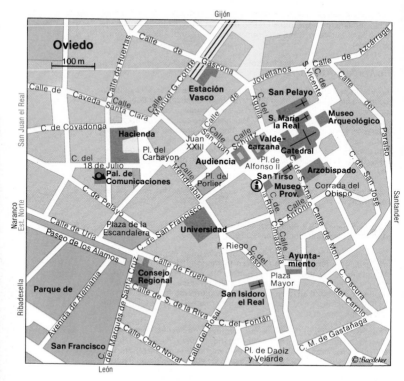

＊Cathedral

From the Plaza Mayor Calle la Rúa goes north to the Gothic Cathedral (the Basílica del Salvador, 1388–1498), on the site of an earlier church built by King Fruela I in the 8th century. The west front has three dissimilar doorways, with a Baroque relief of the Transfiguration on the central doorway. The 82m/269ft high tower, completed in 1539, is one of the finest in Spain. From the top there are extensive views.

Interior
＊Retablo

The most striking feature of the harmonious interior is the huge and magnificent retablo in the Capilla Mayor (by Giralte de Bruxelles and Juan de Balmaseda, 1520), with numerous panels depicting scenes from the life of Christ. Also in the Capilla Mayor can be seen the Gothic tomb of Archbishop Arias de Villar (c. 1500).

In the north aisle is the Baroque Capilla de Santa Eulalia, with an 11th century silver gilt casket containing the relics of Santa Eulalia. Opening off the north transept is the Capilla del Rey Casto, which Alfonso II, the Chaste, made the Panteón de los Reyes, the burial-place of the Asturian kings (though in fact it contains only a single royal sarcophagus, dating from the 8th century).

＊＊Camara Santa

From the south transept a flight of steps leads to the Cámara Santa, in which is preserved the Arca Santa (Holy Chest), a precious reliquary brought to Asturias for safety after the Visigothic kingdom of Toledo fell to the Moors. Many pilgrims travelling to Santiago de Compostela also visited Oviedo to do honour to it.

The reliquary chapel is preceded by an ante-chapel, enlarged in the 12th century, with very beautiful figures of Apostles, in pairs, against the right-hand wall and a head of Christ over the door, all dating from the 12th century. In the reliquary chapel itself is the Arca Santa, covered with silver plates adorned with reliefs, which contains relics from the Holy Land, together with a variety of other treasures – the 9th century Angels' Cross (Cruz de los Ángeles), a cedarwood cross adorned with gold filigree and precious stones; the Victory Cross (Cruz de la Victoria), which Pelayo is said to have carried in the battle of Covadonga (see Picos de Europa) and which Alfonso III refurbished in 1908; an agate chest of the same period; a 6th century Byzantine diptych; and two 13th century diptychs, one of silver and the other of ivory.

Under the Cámara Santa is the Capilla de Leocadia, which contains 12th century tombs.

Adjoining the south transept is a beautiful cloister (9th–15th c.), with a number of monuments and pilgrims' gravestones.

Cloister

Around the Cathedral

In front of the cathedral is the spacious Plaza de Alfonso II, in which are a number of notable buildings. At the west corner of the square stands the 17th century Palacio de Valdecarzana, and beyond this, in the little Plaza Porlier, the 18th century Palacio de Camposagrado, now the Audiencia (Law Courts). Also in Plaza Porlier is the 17th century Palacio de Toreno. Just south of this, at a street intersection, is the plain building occupied by the University, founded in 1608 by Archbishop Fernando Valdés Sala (with a bronze statue of the archbishop in the courtyard). In the middle of the south-east side of the Plaza de Alfonso II is Oviedo's oldest secular building, the Casa de la Rúa (15th c.), adjoining which is the church of San Tirso, originally dating from the 9th century but rebuilt in its present form in the 18th century.

Plaza de Alfonso II

To the south of San Tirso, in Calle de Santa Ana, is the Baroque Palacio de Velarde, now occupied by the Provincial Museum of Art, with a collection which includes works of the Renaissance and Baroque periods as well as pictures by contemporary Asturian painters.

Museo Provincial de Bellas Artes

On the south side of the cathedral can be seen the Bishop's Palace (16th–18th c.)

Palacio Episcopal

Behind the cathedral, in the cloister of the old Convento de San Vicente (founded in the 8th century and rebuilt in the 15th), is the Archaeological Museum. The ground floor is devoted to pre-Romanesque and Romanesque art, mainly from Asturias, including the altar-stone of Santa María de Naranco (see below); on the first floor are Roman coins, sculpture, mosaics and other relics of the period of Roman rule in Iberia; and the second floor displays Stone Age material from the surrounding area.

Museo Arqueológico

From the Archaeological Museum a passage leads into the Plaza Feijido, on the left of which stands the late Renaissance church of Santa María la Real (1592), with the tombs of prominent local people.

Santa María la Real

Immediately north of the cathedral, Santa María la Real and the Archaeological Museum is the large Convento de San Pelayo (11th–18th c.).

Convento de San Pelayo

In the outlying district of Santullano (reached by way of Calle G. Conde, on the Gijón and Avilés road) is the largest pre-Romanesque church in Spain, San Julián de los Prados, measuring 25 by 30m (82 by 98ft). An unusual

Santullano

feature is the two-level apse, with the altar on the lower level and a concealed chamber above it.

Surroundings of Oviedo

★ Naranco

2km/1¼ miles north-west of Oviedo, on the slopes of the Sierra de Naranco (1233m/4045ft), is the little town of Naranco, which has two churches of great historical and architectural interest. To reach Naranco, leave on Calle de Uría, in the direction of the Northern Station (Estación del Norte), and shortly before reaching the station turn left into Calle Independencía and immediately right to cross the railway on the Viaducto Ingeniero Marquina; then turn right into a road signposted to Naranco.

★ Santa María de Naranco

The little church of Santa María de Naranco lies below the road on the left, in a grassy area surrounded by trees from which there is a fine view of Oviedo. Originally a hall in the palace of Ramiro I of Asturias (*c.* 850), it was converted into a church in the 10th and 11th centuries. At each end of the building, which is in the form of an elongated rectangle, is an open porch or loggia with a three-arched opening. On the side facing the road a staircase leads up to the doorway of the church. Both here and in the interior of the church note the twisted columns of Asturian type, with Corinthian capitals outside and trapezoid capitals inside. Between the arches are medallions with relief ornament.

★ San Miguel de Lillo

A little higher up is the church of San Miguel de Lillo, originally the chapel of a 9th century royal palace but altered in the 15th century. Externally the church has a strikingly sturdy appearance. Here too, and in the aisled

Santa María de Naranco

interior, are the typical Asturian twisted columns. Flanking the entrance are two similar Byzantine-style bas-reliefs depicting a consul accompanied by dignitaries. The delicate carving of the windows has recently been protected from destruction by sheets of glass.

Palencia

G 3

Province: Palencia (P). Telephone dialling code: 988
Altitude: 700m/2300ft. Population: 75,000

The ancient town of Palencia, once the stronghold of an Iberian tribe, the Vaccaei, under the name of Pallantia, lies between Burgos and Valladolid on the Meseta of Old Castile, on the left bank of the Río Carrión. Around it is the Tierra de Campos, a corn-growing plain made fertile by irrigation with water from the Canal de Castilla. The town owes its industrial development to the textile and automobile industries. Palencia is now a lively modern town with few relics of its long history.

Palencia was destroyed three times in the course of its history – first by the Romans, then by the Visigoths and finally by the Moors. After this last

History

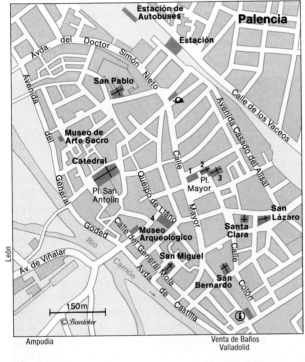

1 Ayuntamiento
2 La Soledad

3 San Francisco
4 Nuestra Señora de la Calle

visitation the town was not rebuilt until the 11th century. Its heyday was in the 12th century, when it was the residence of the kings of Castile and the meeting-place of the Castilian Cortes. In the 13th century Alfonso VIII of Castile founded Spain's first university in the town.

★ Cathedral

In the Plaza de San Antolín, to the west of the Plaza Mayor, stands the imposing Cathedral of San Antolín, built between 1321 and 1516. It incorporates the remains of a 7th century Visigothic chapel which was rebuilt by King Sancho of Navarre and became a crypt. The exterior of the cathedral is notable for its unfinished tower and its fine doorways: on the main front the 15th century Puerta del Obispo (to left), with a statue (by Diego Hurtado de Mendoza) of San Antolín on the apex of the arch, the 16th century Puerta de los Novios (to right) and in the north transept the Plateresque Puerta de los Reyes, with rich sculptural decoration.

Interior

The interior is 130m/427ft long and 28m/92ft high. The Trascoro has fine sculptural decoration by Simón de Colonia and Gil de Siloé and an altarpiece by Juan de Holanda (1505). Behind it is a Plateresque staircase leading down to the crypt, the original church of the 7th and 11th centuries, which contains the relics of San Antolín, the town's patron saint.

The Capilla Mayor (1520), with a beautiful *reja* (lattice-work screen) by Cristóbal Andino, has a magnificent Plateresque retablo, with sculpture mainly by Felipe Vigarny, a Crucifixion by Juan de Valmaseda and twelve painted panels by Juan de Flandes. In the Capilla Mayor Vieja, behind the present one, are the tombs of Inés de Osorio (15th c.) and Queen Urraca of Navarre (12th c.).

The choir has a fine *reja* of 1555 and choir-stalls of 1519.

San Antolín, Palencia

Of the side chapels, which all have very beautiful grilles, the ones of most interest are the Capilla del Sagrario and the Capilla de San Ildefonso; both have fine retablos, that in the Capilla de San Ildefonso being by Juan de Balmaseda. In the south transept is an interesting old clock.

Among the exhibits in the Cathedral Museum, housed in the cloister and chapterhouse, are four 15th century Flemish tapestries, pictures by El Greco, Zurbarán and Cerezo, sculpture and monuments. Attached to the museum is the Treasury, among the most notable items in which are a silver monstrance by Juan de Benavente (16th c.) and a portrait of the Emperor Charles V by Cranach.

Museum

Other Sights

The Museum of Sacred Art is housed in the Palacio Episcopal (Bishop's Palace), to the north of the cathedral.

Museo de Arte Sacro

South-east of Plaza San Antolín, in the Plaza del Cordón, is the Archaeological Museum, with a valuable collection of Iberian and Roman antiquities.

Museo Arqueológico

Near the Archaeological Museum, in the little Plaza Isabel la Católica, stands the modest 16th century church of Nuestra Señora de la Calle, with an image of the Virgen de la Calle, patroness of the town, and Baroque altars.

Nuestra Señora de la Calle

Farther south is the Gothic parish church of San Miguel (13th–14th c.), with a massive battlemented tower. In this church the Cid, Spain's national hero, was married to Doña Jimena.

San Miguel

The attractive Plaza Mayor, to the west of the cathedral, is the hub of the town's life, with bars and cafés. On the north side of the square is the Town Hall, on its east side the church of San Francisco, and in the centre a modern monument to the 16th century sculptor Alonso Berruguete, who was born in the nearby village of Paredes de Nava. The town's principal shopping street, the Calle Mayor, flanks the west side of the square.

Plaza Mayor

At the south end of the Calle Mayor, in Calle San Bernardo, is the Capilla de San Bernardo, with an imposing façade (national monument).

San Bernardo

North-east of San Bernardo, in Calle de Burgos, is the Convento de Santa Clara (late 14th c.), with a beautiful doorway and an impressive recumbent figure of Christ.

Convento de Santa Clara

In the north of the town, near the railway station, the 15th century church of San Pablo has a 17th century façade. In the Capilla Mayor, which has a large Plateresque retablo, are tombs of the Rojas family (16th c.). There is a fine Late Gothic carved altar in the choir.

San Pablo

Surroundings of Palencia

32km/20 miles north of Palencia on N 611, just beyond the Canal de Castilla, is Frómista, which was an important staging-point for pilgrims on the Way of St James (see entry). Its most notable monument is the brick-built church of San Martín (1066), which belonged to an 11th century Benedictine monastery. It is a magnificent example of Spanish Romanesque architecture, with two round towers on the plain west front and an octagonal tower over the crossing. The church of Santa María has a large 15th century retablo.

★ Frómista

From Palencia N 611 runs south towards Valladolid and in 10km/6 miles is joined by N 620, coming from Burgos. Near the junction is Venta de Baños (alt. 731m/2398ft), a small industrial town and railway junction, and 2.5km/1½ miles east of this is the little spa of Baños de Cerrato, where the

★ Baños de Cerrato

The ancient church of Baños de Cerrato

Visigothic king Recceswinth was cured of a stone. In gratitude for his cure he built the little church of San Juan Bautista in 661 (rebuilt in the 9th century), one of the oldest churches in the Iberian peninsula. The three aisles are separated by plain columns with leaf capitals supporting horseshoe arches. The date of foundation is inscribed on the large arch in front of the apse, which contains an alabaster figure of St John the Baptist.

Pamplona/Iruñea   K 2

Province: Navarra (NA). Telephone dialling code: 948
Altitude: 449m/1473ft. Population: 200,000

★ Fiesta de
San Fermín

The ancient city of Pamplona (Basque Iruñea), chief town of the province of Navarra and the most important town in the Spanish Pyrenees, lies on a hill above the left bank of the Río Arga, at the western end of the Pyrenees. Pamplona is famed for the Fiesta de San Fermín, celebrated every year from July 6th to 14th, with impressive parades of Gigantes (Giants) and Cabezudos (Bigheads) and a procession in honour of San Fermín (St Firmianus) on July 7th. Throughout the week there are bullfights, and every morning the fighting bulls are driven through the streets, which have been closed off for the purpose, to the Plaza de Toros, while large numbers of daring young men (and in recent years also women) confront them and race ahead of them through the streets, cheered on by the bystanders. This "running of the bulls" (*encierro*) is vividly described by Ernest Hemingway in his novel "Fiesta" ("The Sun also Rises").

History

The settlement of Pompaelo, which became Pamplona, is said to have been founded by the Roman general Cn. Pompeius Magnus in the winter of 75 B.C. during his campaign against Sertorius. The Goths conquered the

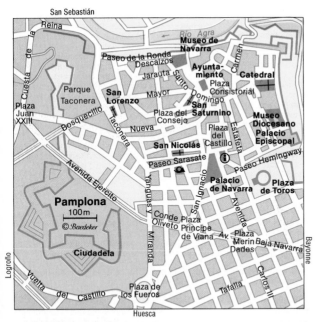

The "running of the bulls", Pamplona

town in the 5th century but were driven out in the 8th century by the Moors, with whom the inhabitants had concluded a pact. This was the assembly point of the Arab army which was defeated at Tours and Poitiers in 732. In 778 Charlemagne slighted the town's defences, and thereafter it sank into insignificance for several centuries. The pilgrimage to Santiago de Compostela on the Way of St James (see entry) gave Pamplona a fresh lease of life, and three separate settlements developed – the Navarrería in which the old-established inhabitants lived, the new district of San Cernín, mainly inhabited by French merchants and craftsmen, and another new district, San Nicolás. Antagonisms between these three communities flared up in the 13th–15th centuries, when the kings of Aragon and Castile were at odds with the French kings of Navarre over the possession of Pamplona and sought allies in the different parts of the town, which fought against each other in changing coalitions. These conflicts were finally settled in 1423, but the inhabitants of Pamplona maintained their stout resistance to any aggressor, as the Castilians found out in 1512 and the French in 1808.

Old Town

Diputación Foral

The central feature of the town, which is still partly surrounded by its old walls, is the spacious Plaza del Castillo. At the south-west corner of the square stands the Diputación Foral or Palacio de Navarra (built 1847, enlarged 1932), the seat of the provincial assembly. In the magnificent Throne Room is a portrait of Ferdinand VII by Goya.

Archivo General

On the south side of the Diputación Foral is the interesting Archivo General, with a valuable collection of medieval manuscripts.

San Ignacio

Adjoining the Archivo General is the church of San Ignacio (1694), which is said to be built on the spot where Ignacio de Loyola, the future founder of the Jesuits, was wounded while serving as a captain in the Castilian army during a siege of Pamplona by the Navarrese.

Paseo de Sarasate

From the Plaza del Castillo the Paseo de Sarasate, the town's principal promenade, runs south-west. At its near end is the Monumento de los Fueros, an allegorical representation of the rights and privileges (*fueros*) granted to the town.

San Nicolás

Half way along the Paseo de Sarasate, on the right, is the church of San Nicolás, originally Romanesque. This fortress-like building served as a stronghold for the San Nicolás quarter, but was largely destroyed when the Castilians entered the town.

Parque Taconera

The Paseo leads to the romantic Parque Taconera, with an old town gate, the Puerta de San Nicolás, moved here from its original position. To the south is the Ciudadela (Citadel), now also an attractive park.

Ayuntamiento

North-west of the Plaza del Castillo, in the little Plaza Consistorial, stands the 17th century Ayuntamiento (Town Hall; restored 1953), with a beautiful Baroque façade in dark-coloured stone which is crowned by lions bearing coats of arms and a trumpet-blowing angel. The Town Hall was built at the point where the three separate parts of the town met.

San Saturnino

Just to the west of the Plaza Consistorial is the town's oldest church, San Saturnino (13th–14th c.), with two Romanesque towers. Notable features of the church are the north doorway and a retablo in the baptistery.

Museo de Navarra

North-west of the Town Hall is the interesting Museo de Navarra, housed in the old pilgrim hospice of Nuestra Señora de la Misericordia, of which the Plateresque façade (1556) survives. The museum's collection, displayed in 34 rooms, includes Roman sculpture and pavement mosaics, Romanesque capitals from the cathedral cloister, Gothic wall paintings, pictures by

Morales and Becerra, and Goya's fine portrait of the Marquese de San   ★ Goya portrait
Adrián. A particular treasure is a Moorish ivory casket from Córdoba (1004–
05) found in the monastery of Leyre.

★ Cathedral

North-east of the Plaza del Castillo, just inside the town walls, rises the
massive cathedral, mostly dating from the 15th century, with a Neo-
Classical façade and towers of 1780. In the nave, in front of the choir, is the
alabaster tomb of Charles III, the Noble, and his wife Leonora de Trastamara (c. 1420), by the Flemish master Jean de Lomme. The choir has
magnificent stalls by Miguel de Ancheta (1530), and in the Capilla Mayor is
a retablo of 1507.

A richly gilded doorway in the south aisle, with a beautiful 14th century   ★ Cloister
tympanum ("Death of the Virgin"), gives access to the 14th century cloister,
with its tall arches one of the finest in Spain. On the east side is the Capilla
Barbazana, with the tomb of its founder, Cardinal Arnaldo de Barbazán
(1318–55). On the south side is the 14th century Puerta Preciosa, which
leads into the Sala Preciosa, once the meeting-place of the Cortes of
Navarre.

The Diocesan Museum is housed in rooms opening off the cloister. Particu-   Museo Diocesano
larly impressive are the richly decorated refectory, with a carving of the
"Maiden and the Unicorn" on the lector's pulpit, and the huge kitchen with
a chimney 27m/89ft high. The other rooms contain the rich Cathedral
Treasury, which includes a 13th century Gospel book, a French reliquary of
the Holy Sepulchre, the Lignum Crucis (believed to be a fragment of the
True Cross), pictures and sculpture.

Eastern and Southern Districts

East of the Plaza del Castillo, in Calle de Amaya, is the Plaza de Toros   Plaza de Toros
(Bullring). In front of it can be seen a monument to Ernest Hemingway
(1899–1961), a great lover of Spain and aficionado of bullfighting.

From the south side of the Plaza del Castillo the Avenida de Carlos III, lined   Plaza del Conde
by modern buildings, runs south-east, crosses the wide Avenida de la Baja   de Rodezno
Navarra and comes to the spacious Plaza del Conde de Rodezno, with the
temple-like Monumento de los Caídos (Monument to the Fallen), commemorating the Nationalist dead of the Civil War.

★ Valle de Baztán

N 121 leads north from Pamplona, passing through Villava and then up the   Puerto de Velate
valley of the Río Ulzama to the Puerto de Matacola (662m/2172ft). There-
after it continues climbing to the Puerto de Velate (847m/2779ft), from
which there are extensive views, before descending, with many bends and
fine views, into the valley of the little Río Bidasoa and continuing to
Mugaire.

From Mugaire N 121 runs north-east up the picturesque Valle de Baztán.   Valle de Baztán
This isolated valley in the Basque Pyrenees comprises fourteen communes
which from the medieval period on enjoyed self-government and their own
system of justice. Something of the old traditions of the valley still survives
in the local dialect, costume, music and dances. On the green slopes of the
valley livestock are reared and maize is grown on terraced fields.

The chief place in the valley is the old-world little town of Elizondo (alt.   Elizondo
196m/643ft), with many old houses and palaces decked with coats of arms,

notably the Baroque Palacio de Arizcunenea and the 18th century Ayuntamiento (Town Hall).

From Elizondo N 121 winds its way up the valley, crosses the Puerto de Otsondo (602m/1975ft) and continues to the Spanish–French frontier at the Puente de Dancharinea.

*Roncesvalles

From Pamplona C 135 goes north-east up the valley of the Río Arga, passes through Zubiri and climbs to the Puerto de Erro (801m/2628ft). It then continues up the valley to Burguete (alt. 910m/2986ft) and Roncesvalles (981m/3219ft), just below the pass which was the most important way through the Pyrenees in the early Middle Ages and which was made famous by the "Chanson de Roland". The monastery and hospice which was established here to care for pilgrims following the Way of St James (see entry) to Santiago de Compostela developed into one of the largest and most famous establishments of the kind on the pilgrim route.

Real Colegiata de Roncesvalles

The Augustinian abbey was founded in 1130. The 13th century church has sumptuous gilded retablos, and on the high altar is a carved wooden figure of the Virgin of Roncesvalles, richly clad in silver and gold. In the chapterhouse, which opens off the cloister, is the tomb of Sancho VII, the Strong, during whose reign, in 1219, the church was consecrated. The recumbent figure of the king is 2.25m/7ft 4½in. long, which is said to have been his actual height.

Museum

Among the exhibits in the Museum housed in the conventual buildings are a Gospel book which belonged to the kings of Navarre, several reliquaries in precious materials, a collection of outsize weapons said to have been the property of Sancho VII, a precious stone from the turban of the Arab leader at the battle of Las Navas de Tolosa, in which the Arabs were decisively defeated, and valuable paintings, including a triptych ascribed to Hieronymus Bosch.

Capilla Sancti Spiritus

Near the monastery is the much visited Gothic pilgrimage church of the Holy Spirit, traditionally believed to have been built by Charlemagne to house Roland's tomb.

★ Puerto de Roncesvalles

The road continues up to the Pass of Roncesvalles (1057m/3468ft), by which the various invaders from Northern Europe entered Spain in the early Middle Ages. This, according to legend, was the scene of the battle in 778 in which the rearguard of Charlemagne's army returning from Zaragoza was destroyed. The rearguard was commanded by Roland, one of Charlemagne's paladins, who was killed in the battle together with eleven other paladins. There was in fact a battle in the year 778 between the Franks and an army of Basques, Asturians and Navarrese seeking revenge for Charlemagne's destruction of Pamplona; the Moors were probably not involved. This relatively minor engagement, however, provided the subject matter of the 12th century "Chanson de Roland", which lauded the heroism of Roland and presented Charlemagne as the saviour of Christendom from Antichrist.

From the top of the pass there are fine views. A modern chapel has replaced an earlier one which provided shelter for pilgrims on the way to Santiago de Compostela, and there is a stone commemorating Roland (Roldán in Spanish).

To the Monasterio de Leyre

★ Sangüesa

From Pamplona N 243 runs south-east and in 43km/27 miles reaches the little town of Sangüesa (alt. 404m/1326ft), which was fortified in the 12th century by Alfonso el Batallador (Alfonso I of Aragon, the "Battler"). In the 15th and 16th centuries many noble families built handsome mansions in the town, the finest of which are the Palacio del Príncipe de Viana (now the Town Hall) and the Palacio Vallesantoro (now the Casa de Cultura) with its imposing doorway and elaborately carved canopy.

The south doorway of the Romanesque church of Santa María la Real (11th–13th c.) is covered with a profusion of fine sculpture. In the tympanum is the Last Judgment; on the arches are animals, fabulous beasts and human figures; and above the arches are Christ, Apostles and prophets. The spandrels, too, are filled with fabulous beasts and other figures.

Santa María la Real

Other interesting churches are the Virgen del Carmen and San Francisco, which has a Gothic cloister.

The road continues over the plateau to Yesa (alt. 492m/1614ft), at the west end of the Embalse de Yesa, an artificial lake which offers facilities for water sports, including sailing and wind-surfing.

Embalse de Yesa

4km/2½ miles south of Yesa is Javier (alt. 476m/1562ft), with a 14th century castle which was the birthplace of St Francis Xavier (San Francisco Javier, 1506–62), patron saint of Navarre and a missionary in Japan, India and China, where he died. The castle has been restored, and visitors are shown a number of rooms, including the armoury and the saint's room.

Castillo de Javier

Just before N 240 reaches Yesa a road branches off on the left and climbs up to the monastery of Leyre, commandingly situated on a hill below the south side of the Sierra de Leyre. Most of the present buildings date from the 17th and 18th centuries, but the original abbey was founded in the 11th century and became the burial-place of the kings of Navarre. The apse dates from that period; the nave is Gothic (14th c.). A chapel in the north aisle contains the tombs of the early kings of Navarre. The undecorated crypt, of almost primitive aspect, is the oldest part of the church. The west doorway, the Puerta Speciosa, has a rich assemblage of Romanesque sculpture.

★Monasterio de Leyre

Other Excursions from Pamplona

See Bilbao, Olite, San Sebastián, Tudela, Vitoria-Gasteiz

Picos de Europa

F/G 1/2

Provinces: Asturias (O), Cantabria (S), León (LE).

The ★★Mountains

The Picos de Europa are a wild and majestic range of mountains, with steeply scarped peaks and deeply slashed valleys, lying between the rivers Deva and Sella near the north coast of Spain. The whole range is now a nature reserve. The massif (Spanish *macizo*) is divided into three parts by torrential mountain streams well stocked with fish. To the west, between the Río Sella and the Río Cares, is the Macizo de las Peñas Santas (Macizo de Occidente), with the Peñas Santas de Castilla (2596m/8517ft) as its highest peak; in this area is the Parque Nacional de Covadonga (see Practical Information, National Parks). Between the Río Cares and the Río Duje lies the Macizo de Urrieles (Macizo Central), the wildest section of the Picos de Europa, rising to 2645m/8678ft in the Torre de Cerredo. To the east, between the Río Duje and the Río Deva, is the Macizo de Andarra (Macizo de Oriente), the highest peak of which is the Pico Cortés (2470m/8104ft). This mountain barrier, extending parallel to the coast for a distance of almost 40km/25 miles, is separated from the sea by the lower Sierra de Cuera, reaching to within 20km/12½ miles of the Bay of Biscay at its nearest point.

The inhabitants of this mountain region are mainly engaged in agriculture and stock-farming. They produce a well-known blue cheese, Cabrales, made from cow's, ewe's and goat's milk, which is somewhat similar to Roquefort. In the sheltered Liébana area around the little town of Potes cherries and walnuts are grown.

Walking and climbing

The Picos de Europa are splendid walking and climbing country, offering endless scope for everything from hill-walks to Alpine climbs. As in any mountain area, walkers and climbers should take sensible precautions: in particular they should be properly equipped and should not over-estimate their own capabilities. For difficult climbs a guide is essential. The mountain huts run by the Spanish Climbing Federation (Federación Española de Montañismo) and the communes (local authorities) are open to all, and provide good bases for further exploration. Information about the availability of accommodation in huts and about walks and climbs can be obtained from the local tourist office or town hall, which will also be able to provide guides.

This section covers a tour of the Picos de Europa, starting from Cangas de Onis and taking in many places which are good bases for walks and climbs, or for drives in cross-country vehicles, which can be hired locally. The roads are sometimes testing, but are asphalted and in good condition. The tour suggested here can be done in a single day, but this would leave no time for detours; if two days are allowed for the trip this will give the opportunity not only of enjoying the mountain scenery but also of exploring it on foot.

Tour of the Picos de Europa

★ Covadonga

Before setting out on the tour it is worth while making an excursion to Covadonga and the Covadonga National Park. Leave Cangas de Onis on C 6312, going east, and in 4km/2½ miles, at Soto de Cangas, turn right into a beautiful little road (O 220) which runs up a mountain valley to the little town of Covadonga (8km/5 miles from Cangas de Onis), situated on a hill spur. This is one of the great Spanish shrines and a much frequented place of pilgrimage.

Birthplace of Spain

Covadonga is regarded as the birthplace of Spain. After the Moorish incursion and the destruction of the Visigothic kingdom a handful of Christian warriors under the leadership of Pelayo withdrew into these inaccessible mountains and defied the invaders. In 722 they won the first Christian victory over the Moors when they routed an army sent against them by the Emir of Córdoba. Pelayo and his men attributed their victory to the Virgin and set up an altar to her in a cave, the Santa Cueva. The name given to the spot, Covadominica (the "Virgin's Cave"), developed into the present name of Covadonga. The Reconquista then started from the newly founded kingdom of Asturias, with its capital at Cangas de Onis: hence the title of Prince of Asturias borne by the heir to the Spanish throne.

Church

A steep road, with many hairpin bends, winds its way up to the church of Covadonga (1891). To the left of the church can be seen a statue of Pelayo, with the Asturian cross above his head. The church itself is of little interest, but the museum opposite it contains the church treasury, with precious relics and votive offerings, including the Virgin's diamond-encrusted crown.

Treasury

Santa Cueva

Across the square from the church and to the left is a tunnel leading to the Santa Cueva (Holy Cave), high up on the rock face above a pool into which a waterfall tumbles. In front of a tiny chapel is the altar with the figure of the

A mountain lake in the Picos de Europa

Virgin of Covadonga (18th c.), which is always surrounded by worshippers. In a recess on the right is a sarcophagus which is believed to contain the mortal remains of Pelayo, his wife Gaudiosa and his sister Hemisinda.

From the Hotel Pelayo, near the shrine, a steep but rewarding road (with gradients of up to 18%) winds its way up to the Mirador de la Reina (8km/ 5 miles south-east), from which in clear weather there are superb views of the mountains and the sea.

★Mirador de la Reina

From the Mirador de la Reina the road descends to the Lago Enol (3.5km/2 miles). 1.5km/1 mile beyond this, on a gravel road, is the Lago de la Ercina. Both lakes lie amid the beautiful mountain scenery of the Covadonga National Park, and both are the starting-points of waymarked footpaths and tracks. A colourful Shepherds' Festival is held annually on July 25th at the Lago de la Ercina.

Lago Enol/ Lago de la Ercina

Through the Cares Valley

The starting-point of our tour of the Picos de Europa is Cangas de Onis (alt. 195m/640ft), in the 8th century the first capital of the Asturian kings and now a base for walkers, climbers and anglers. At the entrance to the town the Río Sella is spanned by a fine three-arched 13th century bridge, from the central arch of which hangs a reproduction of the cross which Pelayo is said to have carried at the battle of Covadonga; the original is in the Cámara Santa of Oviedo Cathedral (see entry). Beside the modern Ermita de la Santa Cruz, which occupies the site of a 5th century chapel rebuilt in the 8th century, is a prehistoric dolmen with incised drawings. The Palacio de Cortés is a handsome 16th century mansion.

Cangas de Onis

2km/1¼ miles east of Cangas de Onis on C 6312 a side road on the left leads to the Cueva del Buxu, with Palaeolithic cave paintings (25,000–30,000 B.C.)

Cueva del Buxu

Las Arenas de Cabrales	C 6312 continues east, passing the turning for Covadonga, and comes in 27km/17 miles to the valley of the Río Cares. It then runs down the valley to Arenas de Cabrales (alt. 120m/394ft), where the famous Cabrales cheese is made.
★Upper Cares valley	At Las Arenas a steep and narrow mountain road (tunnel) goes off on the right and climbs the upper Cares valley to Poncebos (6km/4 miles), at the foot of the Torre de Cerredo. From here there is a long but not particularly difficult walk (about 3½ hours each way) along the magnificent gorge of the Río Cares to Caín. Experienced climbers can undertake the ascent of the Torre de Cerredo (10 hours, with guide), on difficult mountain tracks by way of the village of Buinés and the Refugio (mountain hut) de Camburero.
Panes de Peñamellera	C 6312 follows the Río Cares down to Panes de Peñamellera, where the Cares flows into the Río Deva.

Through the Deva Valley

★Desfiladero de la Hermida	From Panes C 621 runs south through the narrow gorge of the Río Deva, the Desfiladero de la Hermida (magnificent views), which takes its name from the little spa of La Hermida.
Nuestra Señora de Lebeña	A few kilometres beyond La Hermida is Lebeña, with the little 10th century church of Nuestra Señora de Lebeña, a notable example of Mozarabic church architecture.
Potes	Potes, 27km/17 miles from Panes, is a picturesque little town in a beautiful setting, the centre of the fruit- and wine-growing district of Liébana and a good base from which to explore the south-eastern Picos de Europa. The 15th century Torre del Infantado is now the Town Hall.
★Santo Toribio de Liébana	From Potes a minor road (signposted) runs 3km/2 miles west to the monastery of Santo Toribio de Liébana, which was founded in the 7th century but in its present form is Late Romanesque, Gothic and Baroque. In the Capilla de la Santísima Cruz can be seen what is claimed to be the largest surviving piece of the True Cross, brought here from Jerusalem in the 5th century by Bishop Toribio. A monk from this monastery, Beatus of Liébana, wrote a famous commentary on the Apocalypse directed against the Arians which was frequently copied in magnificent manuscripts. One such copy is preserved at Seo de Urgel (see entry).
★Fuente Dé	From Potes C 621 runs 25km/15 miles west by way of Espinama (fonda), the last village in the valley, to Fuente Dé (alt. 1000m/3280ft), where there is a parador. Beside it is the lower station of a cableway which runs steeply up to the Balcón del Cable (alt. 1840m/6037ft), from which there are breathtaking views of the mountains. From the upper station of the cableway a path leads east to Áliva (1780m/5840ft); the walk takes 1½ hours. The Balcón del Cable is also a good starting-point for climbs of some of the surrounding peaks (guide essential).

Over the Puerto de San Glorio

Mirador de Llesba	From Potes a road goes south up a lateral valley of the Río Deva to La Vega de Liébana and then follows a winding course, with many sharp bends, to the Puerto de San Glorio (1609m/5279ft), from which it is a half-hour walk (to the right) to the Mirador de Llesba (views).
★Puerto de Pandetrave	From the pass the road descends the valley of the Río Lechada to Portilla de la Reina, on the Río Yuso, from which a side road runs north to the Puerto de

Pandetrave (1562m/5125ft), in the heart of the Picos de Europa. Here too there are magnificent views of the surrounding peaks.

The road continues down the valley of the Río Yuso to Riaño (alt. 1040m/3412ft), 56km/35 miles from Potes, a little town in the upper Esla valley, in the province of León.

Riaño

Through the Sella Valley

From Riaño C 637 runs north to Vegacerneja, on the Río Sella, and continues to a junction just before the Puerto del Pontón where a side road branches off on the right and winds its way up to the Puerto de Panderruedas, amid beautiful mountain scenery. From the pass it is a 20 minutes' walk to the Mirador de Piedrafitas (views).

★Puerto de Panderruedas

C 637 continues over the Puerto del Pontón to Oseja de Sajambre, from which a minor road leads up to the Mirador de Oseja de Sajambre, with a view down into the deep and narrow gorge of the Río Sella.

Oseja de Sajambre

From Oseja de Sajambre C 637 winds its way down the picturesque gorge of the Río Sella, the Desfiladero de los Beyos, and continues to Cangas de Onís, the starting-point of the tour.

Desfiladero de los Beyos

Plasencia

E 5

Province: Cáceres (CC). Telephone dialling code: 927
Altitude: 316m/1037ft. Population: 36,000

The old-world episcopal town of Plasencia, founded by Alfonso VIII in 1159 under the name of "Ut Deo placeat" ("May it please God"), lies on a hill encircled by the deep gorge of the Río Jerte, in the foothills of the Sierra de Gredos.

Cathedral

The town's most notable building is the cathedral, which consists of two parts. The original Romanesque church was built in the 13th and 14th centuries, and a new part was begin in Gothic style in 1498 and continued in the 16th century in Plateresque style but never completed. Francisco de Colonia, Gil de Hontañón and other leading masters of the day worked on the new cathedral, the most notable features of which are the Plateresque north front with its graceful columns and the beautiful Puerta del Enlosado in the north transept, and, in the interior, the Capilla Mayor (by Juan de Álava, Diego de Siloé and Alonso de Covarrubias), the magnificent *reja* (1604), the choir-stalls (1520), carved with Biblical scenes and scenes from country life, and the retablo, with a relief of the Assumption of the Virgin (1629) by Gregorio Fernández.

Catedral Nueva

A doorway leads into the older part of the cathedral, the parish church of Santa María, which has a Romanesque doorway, the Puerta del Perdón, and contains a 13th century polychrome statue of the Virgin. There is a small museum in the chapterhouse, the most valuable items in which are pictures by Ribera and Morales.

Santa María

From the cloister (14th–15th c.) a flight of steps by Gil de Hontañón leads to a terrace from which there is a good view of the dome of the sacristy.

Cloister

On the corner opposite the cathedral stands the Palacio de los Marqueses de Mirabel, who from the 15th century bore the title of Condes de Plasencia. The palace is built round a courtyard and garden, in which are some archaeological remains. The finest room in the palace itself is the Salón de Carlos V, which contains a bust of the Emperor Charles V by Pompeo Leoni.

Palacio de los Marqueses de Mirabel

Pontevedra

Ciudad Vieja

Between the cathedral square, the Plaza de San Nicolás and the Plaza Mayor extends the most interesting part of the old town, with beautiful churches, noble mansions and whitewashed houses with gallery-like projections on the façades.

Town walls

The town is surrounded by a double circuit of walls, with 68 towers, dating from the time of its foundation. There are fine views from the wall-walk, particularly on the north-east side.

Surroundings of Plasencia

★ Monasterio de Yuste

46km/29 miles north-east of Plasencia on C 501 is the Hieronymite monastery of San Jerónimo de Yuste, founded in 1404, devastated by the French in 1809 and later partly restored. It is famed particularly as the last retreat of the Emperor Charles V, who abdicated in favour of his son Philip II in 1556, withdrew to Yuste and died there in 1558. The apartments occupied by the Emperor are shown to visitors, including his dining room, his study and his bedroom (the room in which he died), directly adjoining the church. On the high altar of the church (1508) is a copy of a painting by Titian depicting Charles and his wife Isabella of Portugal with Philip II and Maria of Hungary. Adjoining the church is a Plateresque cloister. From the covered terrace there is a fine view of the fertile surrounding countryside, extending to the Sierra de Guadalupe.

Jarandilla
de la Vera

The little town of Jarandilla de la Vera, a few kilometres east of the monastery, has a 15th century castle of the Counts of Oropesa, now a parador.

Pontevedra   B 2

Province: Pontevedra (PO)
Telephone dialling code: 986
Altitude: 19m/62ft
Population: 66,000

The lively town of Pontevedra, finely situated on the Ría de Pontevedra in the delta of the Río Lérez, the Río Alba and the Río Tomeza, is the chief town of its province, and in the Middle Ages was a considerable port under the name of Pontis Veteris ("Old Bridge"). From that period date some remains of town walls. Legend has it that Teukros, brother of the Greek hero Ajax, landed here on his return from the Trojan War.

Sights

Museo Provincial

The Provincial Museum, housed in two 18th century mansions, the Casa de los Monteaguedos and the Casa de los García Flórez, has a very large and interesting collection. The first house contains the department of prehistoric and early historical antiquities, with a Celtiberian gold hoard as one of its greatest treasures, and a picture gallery with works by Zurbarán, Murillo, Ribera, Giordano and Veronese. In the second house is the Museum's collection of sculpture, including a series of processional crosses of the 13th–19th centuries. There is also a section devoted to the Spanish navy, with a reproduction of the admiral's cabin on the "Numancia", flagship in 1866 of the Spanish fleet commanded by Admiral Méndez Núñez in the war with the former colonies of Chile and Peru.

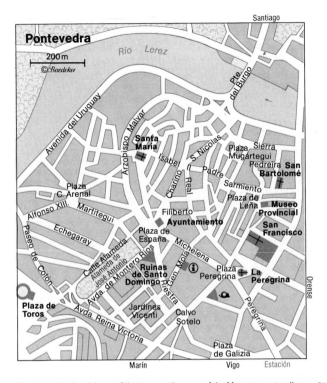

The streets in the old part of the town to the west of the Museum, extending northward to the river, have an aspect very typical of Galicia, their tall houses fronted by glazed balconies.

Old town

South of the Museum is the 14th century church of San Francisco, with a 13th century doorway. Originally belonging to the Mendicant Friars, it contains a number of Gothic tombs, including that of Don Payo Gómez Chariño, who took part in the capture of Seville in 1248.

★ San Francisco

A little farther south is the chapel of La Peregrina (by Fernando Souto, 1776), one of the finest examples of Galician Baroque, on an unusual circular ground-plan, with a convex façade and slender towers. It contains a much revered image of the Virgen de la Peregrina, patroness of the town.

La Peregrina

From the Peregrina chapel Calle Michelena runs north-west into the Plaza de España, on the south side of which are the ruins of the church of Santo Domingo, with five tall 14th century apses containing a number of Gothic tombs. These and other Roman and medieval carved stones now form part of a Lapidarium, an annexe of the Provincial Museum.

Santo Domingo

To the north of the Plaza de España, on the west side of the old town centre, stands the Gothic church of Santa María la Mayor (16th c.), which has a magnificent west front by Cornelis de Holanda in the form of a retablo. On the side doorway on the right is a fine figure of Christ, the Cristo del Buen Viaje. Like Santo Domingo, the church contains a number of Gothic tombs.

Santa María la Mayor

367

Province: Gerona (GE). Telephone dialling code: 972
Altitude: 682m/2238ft. Population: 12,000

The little industrial town of Ripoll lies well inland on the southern slopes of
the Collado de Ares, over which runs the Spanish–French frontier, at the
junction of the Río Freser with the Río Ter. There are a number of coal-
mines in the surrounding area.

Monasterio de Santa María

On the main square in the town centre is the large Benedictine monastery
of Santa María de Ripoll, originally founded in the 6th century by the
Visigothic king Reccared. The first church was consecrated in the 9th
century and was enlarged in the 11th, giving it the form of a five-aisled
basilica. The monastery became a great centre of learning and culture;
among those who studied here was the Benedictine monk Gerbert of
Aurillac (c. 940–1003), the future Pope Silvester II.

The great Romanesque church was almost completely destroyed by fire
in 1835, and the present church was built to replace it in 1883. Although
very obviously a new church, it is modelled on the old one and excellently
reproduces the Romanesque spatial effect.

★ Doorway

The most considerable remnant of the Romanesque church, reasonably
well preserved, is the 12th century main doorway, which is now given
some protection from the elements by a glazed porch.

The doorway is covered with a profusion of sculpture on Old and New
Testament themes. In the uppermost register are scenes from the Apocalypse (Christ enthroned, flanked by angels and the symbols of the Evangelists). Lower down, on the left of the doorway, are scenes from the Book of
Kings; on the right are scenes from the Book of Exodus. Below this again
are King David, with musicians, and fabulous beasts. On the archivolts are
scenes from the life and martyrdom of SS Peter and Paul, the story of Jonah
and the whale and the story of Cain and Abel.

Interior

The five-aisled interior of the church has an effect of sombre majesty. Just
inside the doorway, let into the floor, is a gravestone of 1909 surrounded by
a mosaic. The massive chancel has three subsidiary apses on either side of
the main apse. In the south transept is the tomb of Berengar III (d. 1131).

Cloister

To the right of the doorway steps lead down to the cloister (12th–15th c.). Its
sculptural decoration is later than that on the west front and artistically of
less significance.

Museum

To the left of the church of Santa María, housed in the deconsecrated
church of San Pedro (Catalan Sant Pere), is a museum with exhibits illustrating the history and folk art of the region, including weapons, pottery,
objets d'art and textiles.

Surroundings of Ripoll

**San Juan de
las Abadesas**

10km/6 miles north-east of Ripoll on C 151 is the little town of San Juan de
las Abadesas (Catalan Sant Joan de les Abadesses). In the centre of the
town is the large church of San Juan (Sant Joan) – the third church on
the site, consecrated in 1150, when the convent had been made over to the
Augustinians.

Interior
★ Descent from
the Cross

In the otherwise undecorated interior of the church can be seen a major
work of Romanesque art, the carved "Descent from the Cross" group
(c. 1250) known as the "santissim misteri de Sant Joan de les Abadesses".

A Late Romanesque work, it already shows Gothic features. The group consists of Christ, Mary, the two thieves (the original of the Good Thief was destroyed in 1936 and has been replaced by a copy), St John, Nicodemus and Joseph of Arimathea.

In the south transept is the alabaster Lady Altar (Gothic, 1423). The church also contains the 14th century sarcophagus of Miró, a canon of Sant Juan, whose recumbent figure is on the lid.

Lady Altar

To the left of the west front of the church is a gatehouse with a doorway giving access to St Michael's Cloister, with delicate Gothic arcades and a coffered ceiling.

Cloister

The exhibits in the Museum come almost entirely from the former monastery and other churches in the town.

Museum

25km/15 miles north-east of Ripoll on C 151 lies Camprodón, an attractive little town of narrow streets and tightly packed houses with a shady Plaza Mayor. In the square is the parish church, and behind it, on higher ground, a former monastic church, built in the 11th century on the site of an earlier 10th century church.

Camprodón

The industrial town of Olot, 36km/22 miles east of Ripoll on C 150, has little to offer the visitor apart from a number of museums – the Regional Museum, the Museum of Modern Art, a museum of religious art and a house furnished in the style of the 17th–19th centuries.

Olot

Around Olot is the dramatic volcanic landscape of the Garrotxa area. The largest crater is the Crater de Santa Margarida, north-west of the town, which has a diameter of 350m/380yd.

★ Zona Volcano

In the villages in the surrounding area there are many Romanesque churches.

Ronda

F 8

Province: Málaga (MA). Telephone dialling code: 952
Altitude: 850m/2790ft. Population: 31,000

Ronda, in the Andalusian Mountains, owes its great attraction as one of the leading tourist sights in southern Spain to its extraordinary situation. The town is built on a triangular plateau, with its apex towards the south, which rears out of a fertile plain at the foot of the Serranía de Ronda (highest point Torrecilla, 1919m/6296ft), with almost vertical rock faces on the west side, and is divided into two by the gorge of the Río Guadalevín, between 40m/130ft and 90m/295ft wide and up to 150m/490ft deep. At the southern tip of the plateau is the old town (La Ciudad), occupying the site of the Roman settlement of Arunda, with the barrio (outer district) of San Francisco below it to the south. The northern part of the plateau is occupied by the new town (Mercadillo), founded by the Catholic Monarchs after their reconquest of Ronda from the Moors in 1485. The old and the new town are linked by three bridges spanning the gorge.

★★ Situation

Mercadillo (New Town)

The main shopping street of the new town, where most of Ronda's shops and services are concentrated, is the Carrera de Espinel (pedestrian zone), which leads into Calle Virgen de la Paz.

Carrera de Espinel

Near the junction of the two streets is the Plaza de Toros (Bullring) of 1785, Spain's second oldest bullring, notable for its two tiers of arcaded galleries

★ Plaza de Toros

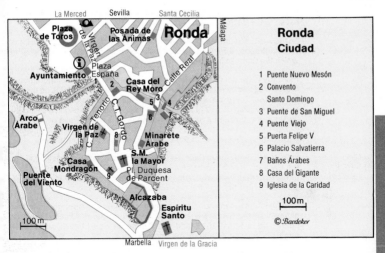

La Merced   Sevilla   Santa Cecilia

Ronda

Plaza de Toros · Posada de las Ánimas · Ayuntamiento · Plaza España · Casa del Rey Moro · Arco Árabe · Virgen de la Paz · Minarete Árabe · S.M. la Mayor · Casa Mondragón · Puente del Viento · Pl. Duquesa de Parcent · Alcazaba · Espíritu Santo

Marbella   Virgen de la Gracia

Ronda Ciudad

1 Puente Nuevo Mesón
2 Convento Santo Domingo
3 Puente de San Miguel
4 Puente Viejo
5 Puerta Felipe V
6 Palacio Salvatierra
7 Baños Árabes
8 Casa del Gigante
9 Iglesia de la Caridad

100 m

© *Baedeker*

for the spectators. Ronda was the home of the Romero dynasty of bull-fighters (Francisco, Juan and Pedro), who developed the rules of the present-day bullfight in the 18th and 19th centuries.

Calle Virgen de la Paz leads to the Alameda de José Antonio, a beautiful park with fine views from projecting spurs of rock (protected by railings) of the river gorge, here almost 200m/650ft deep, and over the plain to the mountains.

Alameda de José Antonio ★ view

Farther north, beyond the church of La Merced, is the Hotel Reina Victoria, where the German poet Rainer Maria Rilke stayed in 1912–13. The room he occupied contains mementoes of the poet, and there is a statue of him (by N. Díaz Piquero, 1966) in the hotel gardens.

Hotel Reina Victoria

At the south end of Calle Virgen de la Paz is the Plaza España, with the Ayuntamiento (Town Hall) and tourist information office.

Plaza de España

Beyond the Plaza España the Puente Nuevo (New Bridge) of 1788 spans the gorge of the Río Guadalevín at its narrowest point (70m/77yd); here the gorge is over 100m/330ft deep. From the bridge there is a breathtaking view into the gorge.

★ Puente Nuevo

★ La Ciudad (Old Town)

On the far side of the bridge, high above the gorge, lies the old town of Ronda, La Ciudad. From the bridge Calle del Teniente Gordo runs south to the picturesque Plaza de la Duquesa de Parcent, in which is the church of Santa María la Mayor. Originally a mosque, the church has preserved four Moorish domes; the Gothic aisles flanking the nave and the tall Plateresque Capilla Mayor were added in Christian times. The church has fine Renaissance stalls and a Moorish mihrab (prayer niche indicating the direction of Mecca).

Santa María la Mayor

Beyond the church, at the southern tip of the plateau, is the old Moorish Alcazaba, which was destroyed by the French in 1808. From here the Paseo

Alcazaba

◀ Ronda: view of the Guadalevín gorge from the Puente Nuevo

de San Francisco leads down through a Moorish gate, the Puerta de Almocávar, to the district of San Francisco.

Casa de
Mondragón

To the west of Santa María la Mayor, on the edge of the plateau, is the Casa de Mondragón, a Renaissance mansion with an interesting doorway, in which the Catholic Monarchs once stayed.

El Tajo

★★ View

From the Plaza del Campanillo, to the right of the Casa de Mondragón, a footpath descends the side of the crag to the ruined water-mills on the Río Guadalevín. There is a choice between continuing on the main path which pursues a zigzag course to the lower mills (½ hour), and taking a side path on the right, through a small Moorish gate, the Arco Árabe or Arco del Cristo, to the power station (20 minutes) and the upper mills. From either path there are fine views of the waterfalls and the Puente Nuevo.

Casa del
Rey Moro

From the Puente Nuevo Calle del Comandante Linares (to the left) leads to the Casa del Rey Moro (House of the Moorish King), a mansion with a terraced garden from which there are fine views. From here a flight of 365 steps tunnelled through the rock goes down to the river.

Lower bridges

Calle del Comandante Linares continues downhill and through an arched gateway to the two lower bridges over the gorge, the Puente Viejo or Puente de la Mina (1616) and the Puente de San Miguel, which may originally have been built by the Romans.

Baños Árabes

To the right of the Puente Viejo is a Moorish bath-house (13th–14th c.) with horseshoe arches.

Surroundings of Ronda

★ Serranía
de Ronda

South-east of Ronda are the barren rocky hills of the Serranía de Ronda. Part of the range, the Coto de la Serranía de Ronda, is a nature reserve in which ibexes and other wild animals can be seen.

★ Cuevas de
la Pileta

C 339 (the Jerez road) crosses the river and runs north-west through beautiful scenery. In 12km/7½ miles a side road turns off on the left and goes via Montejaque to Benaoján (11km/7 miles), near which are the very interesting Cuevas de la Pileta, stalactitic caves with realistic Stone Age paintings of animals, like those of Altamira (see entry) but older (c. 10,000–25,000 B.C.).

Setenil

Setenil, 25km/15 miles north of Ronda on a secondary road, has a large Gothic church; but more interesting than this are the many dwellings hewn from the rock.

Sagunto
M 5

Province: Valencia (V). Telephone dialling code: 96
Altitude: 46m/151ft. Population: 55,000

★ Saguntum

Sagunto lies near the Spanish Mediterranean coast on the right bank of the Río Palancia, 25km/15 miles north of Valencia, in the centre of a large agricultural region. Above the town, on a steep-sided crag 170m/558ft high, are the imposing remains of the famous ancient stronghold of Saguntum, founded by the Iberians.

History

The destruction of Saguntum by the 28-year-old Carthaginian general Hannibal in 219 B.C. sparked off the Second Punic War. The people of Saguntum had allied themselves with Rome in 221 B.C., although the town lay south of the Ebro in an area which had been recognised, under a treaty of 226 B.C. between Rome and Carthage, as falling within the Carthaginian

Sagunto: the castle and the Roman theatre

sphere of influence. Thereupon Hannibal laid siege to the town, until, after holding out for many months, the Saguntines, in despair at receiving no effective assistance from Rome, set fire to the town and burned themselves to death. When Hannibal crossed the Ebro and headed for Italy, however, the Romans took action and in 214 B.C. recaptured the town. The importance of the Saguntum in Roman times is demonstrated by the remains of the theatre and other buildings. To the Moors, who were briefly driven out of the town by the Cid in 1099, it was known as Murbiter (from *muri veteres,* "old walls"), which became Muviedro. In 1874 Alfonso XII was proclaimed king here, and in 1877 the town reverted to its ancient name of Sagunto.

Sights

In the arcaded Plaza Mayor, the central feature of the town, stands the Gothic parish church of Santa María (begun 1334), which has alabaster windows and a gilded 18th century high altar.

Santa María

The old Jewish quarter, the Judería, is better preserved in Sagunto than in most other Spanish towns. It extends around the medieval gate at the entrance to the Jewish quarter in Calle Sang Vella and on the way up to the castle.

Judería

From the Plaza Mayor Calle del Teatro Romano runs south-east to the well preserved Roman theatre half way up the hill which is crowned by the castle. The auditorium, 50m/165ft in diameter, could accommodate 6000 spectators, who would have a view over the stage towards the sea.

★Teatro Romano

From the Roman theatre a road winds its way up the hill, with fine views, to the Castillo de Sagunto, which extends for some 800m/880yd along the

★Castillo

373

summit of the hill. Here there are remains of buildings erected or altered by the Iberians, the Carthaginians, the Romans, the Moors and the French, who besieged the town in 1811. The extensive circuit of walls, from which there are fine views of the town and the coast, dates mostly from the Arab period and from the French occupation.

Museo Arqueológico

Near the entrance is a small archaeological museum, with finds from the Carthaginian and Roman town.

Salamanca   F 4

Province: Salamanca (SA). Telephone dialling code: 923
Altitude: 802m/2631ft. Population: 168,000

The ancient and famous university town of Salamanca, chief town of its province and the see of a bishop, lies in south-western León on the right bank of the Río Tormes. The climate of the almost treeless plateau shows sharp contrasts: the winter is severe and often bitterly cold, the summer sometimes almost unbearably hot.

★★The town

Salamanca is one of Spain's great tourist attractions. With its many old and historic buildings, including some particularly fine examples of Plateresque architecture, which here reached its highest point, the whole town has been declared a national monument and listed by UNESCO as part of the world's cultural heritage. In the clear light of the Meseta the old town, all built of golden-yellow stone from Villamayor, is of overwhelming effect. The best view of the town is from the Ávila road on the left bank of the Río Tormes. The narrow streets around the University and the Plaza Mayor, crowded with students, still preserve something of the atmosphere of the old university of Salamanca.

History

Salamanca, the Roman Salmantica, was captured by Hannibal in 217 B.C. and by the Moors in the 8th century A.D. During the long wars between Christians and Moors the town was almost completely destroyed, and only recovered some measure of importance around 1100, in the reign of Alfonso VI of Castile. Salamanca's international reputation was established, however, by its University, founded by Alfonso IX of León, which vied with the universities of Bologna, Paris and Oxford and transmitted Arab science and learning to the rest of Europe. In the 16th century the University had more than 7000 students. The establishment of a bishopric in Valladolid (1593), which had previously been within the diocese of Salamanca, and the expulsion of the Moriscos in 1610, led to the decline of Salamanca, from which it has recovered only in recent times. During the occupation of Spain by French troops during the Napoleonic wars Salamanca was frequently a French base. In 1811 British troops defeated a French army in the Arapiles valley, to the south of the town, and thus initiated Napoleon's withdrawal from the Iberian peninsula.

★★Plaza Mayor

The central feature of Salamanca is the Plaza Mayor, a regular square (actually trapezoid in shape) of arcaded three-storey buildings in uniform architectural style which was begun in 1729 to the design of Alberto de Churriguera and completed in 1755. In its unity of conception and execution it is one of the most magnificent squares in Spain, a splendid setting for ceremonial occasions, in which bullfights were still being held in the 19th century. With its many cafés and bars under the arcades, it is a lively scene in the evening.

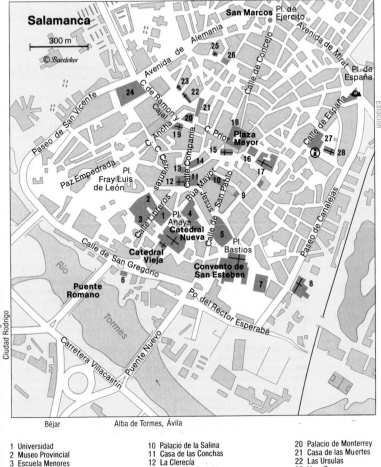

Salamanca

300 m

© Baedeker

Valladolid, Zamora

San Marcos

Pl. de Ejercito

Avenida de Mira

Pl. de España

Estación

Avenida de Alemania

25
26

Calle de Concejo

C. de Ramón y Cajal

23
22

24

21

20

C. Prior

Plaza Mayor

Calle de España

27
28

C. Ancha

19

18

C. C. Cervantes

Calle Compañia

15

16

17

Paseo de San Vicente

Paz Empedrada

Pl. Fray Luis de León

13

14

11

Rúa Mayor

10

Calle de San Pablo

9

12

2

Calle Libreros

Pl. Anaya

4

Paseo de Canalejas

3

Catedral Nueva

5

Calle de Jesús

Pl. Bastios

Catedral Vieja

Calle de San Gregorio

Convento de San Esteban

6

7

8

Río

Puente Romano

Po. del Rector Esperabé

Ciudad Rodrigo

Tormes

Carretera Villacastin

Puente Nuevo

Béjar

Alba de Tormes, Ávila

1 Universidad
2 Museo Provincial
3 Escuela Menores
4 Palacio de Anaya
5 Convento de Dueñas
6 Santiago
7 Calatrava
8 Las Bernardas
9 Torre del Clavero

10 Palacio de la Salina
11 Casa de las Conchas
12 La Clerecía
13 Universidad Pontífica
14 San Benito
15 San Martín
16 Mercado
17 San Julián
18 Ayuntamiento
19 La Purísima

20 Palacio de Monterrey
21 Casa de las Muertes
22 Las Ursulas
23 Vera Cruz
24 Colegio Arzobispo Fonseca
25 San Juan de Barbalos
26 Casa de Santa Teresa
27 Torre del Aire
28 Sancti Spiritus

On the north side of the square stands the Ayuntamiento (Town Hall), in the style of José de Churriguera, built by Andrés García de Quiñones. The bell-cote was added in 1852.

Ayuntamiento

Opposite the Town Hall is the Pabellón Real, by Alberto de Churriguera, with a bust of Philip V, at whose behest the square was built.

Pabellón Real

Between the Plaza Mayor and the University

San Martín

Adjoining the south-west corner of the Plaza Mayor is the little Plaza Corillo, with the church of San Martín (12th c.), in Late Romanesque style, which has a 13th century relief of St Martin on the north doorway and Plateresque decoration on the south-west doorway. It contains several Gothic tombs and a retablo by Alberto de Churriguera (1731).

★Casa de las Conchas

From Plaza Corillo the Rúa Mayor runs south-west to a small square, at the corner of which, on the right, is the Casa de las Conchas (House of the Scallop-Shells), built in 1514. This was the town mansion of Talavera Maldonado, a knight of the Order of Santiago, who decorated the façade of his house lavishly with the scallop-shells associated with St James, who create changing patterns of light and shade according to the position of the sun. Note also the finely wrought window grilles. Visitors are shown round the house, which has a very handsome two-storey courtyard and a staircase well with a beautiful coffered ceiling.

La Clerecía

Opposite the Casa de las Conchas is the Clerecía, a large domed Baroque church with an imposing twin-towered façade by Quiñones. It has a magnificent Churrigueresque high altar.

Universidad Pontificia

Abutting on the church is the Pontifical University, in which theology, philosophy and canon law are taught. A staircase leads up to the first-floor gallery surrounding the very handsome Baroque courtyard.

★★University

Opening times
Mon.–Fri.
9.30am–1.30pm
and
4.30–6.30pm;
Sat. and pub. hols.
10am–1pm

From the Clerecía it is a short distance south-east along Calle Libreros to the once world-famed University of Salamanca (on the left). Among those who taught here were the humanist Fray Luis de León (1527–91), the mystic John of the Cross (Juan de la Cruz, 1542–91) and the philosopher Miguel de Unamuno (1864–1936), who also became Rector of the University. Cervantes was a student here. The Copernican system was recognised at Salamanca University at a time when this was still a grave heresy.

★★Main front

The original building (1415–33) was relatively plain; then in 1534 it was given its present façade with its lavish profusion of Plateresque ornament – the unsurpassed masterpiece of that style in Spain. Above the two doorways are three registers of finely carved panels separated by pilasters. At first floor level, in the centre of the façade, is a medallion with likenesses of the Catholic Monarchs; above this is the coat of arms of Charles V, flanked by the double-headed imperial eagle and the eagle of St John; and above this again is the Pope, surrounded by cardinals, with figures of Venus, Priam and Bacchus to the right and Hercules, Juno and Jupiter to the left. On the right-hand pilaster in the first register, above a skull, can be seen a frog, regarded by students as a bringer of good luck.

Ground floor

The University is built around a large two-storey courtyard, which is surrounded by lecture halls on the ground floor. Visitors are taken on a conducted tour, turning left from the entrance, passing through two smaller halls to the lecture hall in which Fray Luis de León taught, with a desk for the lecturer and rough wooden benches for the students. Beyond this is the Paraninfo or Great Hall, used for the granting of degrees and other ceremonial occasions, which was originally the lecture hall for canon law; in it hangs a Brussels tapestry with a portrait of Charles IV after a cartoon by Goya. After seeing other rooms visitors come to the Capilla de San Jerónimo, in the right-hand wing, which was formerly the Library. It was remodelled in marble in 1767; some of the ceiling paintings from this room are now to be seen in the Escuelas Menores. Here too can be seen the diploma conferring an honorary doctorate on St Theresa of Ávila. From here the tour continues by way of the Sacristy and the Rector's Room to the

Plaza Mayor, Salamanca

Music Room, which contains fine tapestries and two pictures by Juan de Flandes.

The staircase leading to the upper floor (16th c.) is decorated with finely carved scenes of tournaments, Moriscos and hunting, and on the keystone are the arms of the University. A corridor with a fine artesonado ceiling leads to the Isabelline doorway of the Library, which was founded in 1254. The library hall, originally Gothic, was remodelled in 1749. From that period date the bookcases, which contain some 50,000 books and 3500 manuscripts. The most valuable items (incunabula, manuscripts and miniatures) are kept in a separate room.

Upper floor

★Patio de las Escuelas

Opposite the front of the University is the Patio de las Escuelas, in the centre of which can be seen a monument to Fray Luis de León (1869). Around it are buildings in pure Plateresque style, giving it a very characteristic atmosphere of its own.

The south-west side of the square is occupied by a long range of buildings with ornamental openwork battlements crowning the façade. The left-hand doorway leads into the Hospital del Estudio, built in 1533 as a hospice for students; it is now the Rector's Office.

Hospital del Estudio

The right-hand half of the building is occupied by the Escuelas Menores (Lesser Schools), the courtyard of which is entered through a double-arched doorway, splendidly decked with coats of arms, followed by a vestibule. The Sala Calderón de la Barca has decorative elements from the old University Library, including particularly the fine ceiling painting by

Escuelas Menores

Salamanca

★ "Cielo de Salamanca"

Fernando Gallego (c. 1480) known as the "Cielo de Salamanca", which illustrates the state of knowledge of astronomy in the late 15th century. Some of the painting has been lost, but it is still possible to see the signs of the Zodiac, a number of constellations and the four winds. Other items of interest are works of sculpture by Felipe de Vigarny and pictures by Juan de Vigarny.

Museo Provincial de Bellas Artes

On the far side of the square is the entrance to the Provincial Museum of Art, housed in the Palacio de los Abarca Alcaraz, which was built in the late 15th century by Isabella the Catholic's personal physician. The main front faces on to the Plaza Fray Luis de León. The collection, displayed in nine rooms, consists mainly of pictures of the 16th–20th centuries.

★ Catedral Nueva

A narrow street runs round the University buildings to the New Cathedral, the tower of which can be seen from the Patio de las Escuelas. Begun by Juan Gil de Hontañón in 1513, this imposing building was not completed until 1733, and thus shows a mingling of Late Gothic, Plateresque and Baroque features. Particularly rich are the Plateresque doorways. notably the triple west doorway and the north doorway (the Puerta de Ramos), which has a relief of Christ's entry into Jerusalem.

Tower

The 110m/360ft high tower, with a beautiful dome (probably by Joaquín de Churriguera), has reinforcement walls round its lower storeys, built in 1755 as a precaution against earthquakes.

Interior

The richly furnished interior, 104m/341ft long by 48m/157ft across, achieves an effect of spaciousness and height (38m/125ft) in spite of the insertion of the choir, which has beautifully carved Baroque stalls and Baroque sculpture by Alberto de Churriguera. The chapels contain numerous works of art, including the tomb of Sánchez de Palenzuela in the Capilla Dorada which he founded and the figure of the Virgen de la Cueva, patroness of Salamanca, in the Capilla del Mariscal. At the head of the ambulatory, in the Capilla del Cristo de las Batallas, is an 11th century crucifix said to have been presented by the Cid to his comrade in arms Jerónimo, later bishop of Salamanca. Other notable features are the Sacristy, decorated in Rococo style, and the Reliquary Chapel.

★ Catedral Vieja

Immediately adjoining the south side of the New Cathedral is the Romanesque Old Cathedral of Santa María de la Sede, which is entered from the south aisle of the New Cathedral. It is difficult to get a general view of both cathedrals; the best view of the exterior of the Old Cathedral, however, is from the Patio Chico, which is reached from a doorway in the south aisle of the New Cathedral.

The Old Cathedral, one of the most splendid buildings of its period in Spain, was begun about 1100 and was probably completed before 1200. From the Patio Chico there is a view of the chancel, with a magnificent tower-like dome over the crossing, known as the Torre del Gallo from the figure of a cock which surmounts it.

Interior

In the principal apse is a monumental retablo with 53 scenes from the life of Christ and the life of the Virgin. Like the large fresco of the Last Judgment in the vaulting of the apse, it was the work of Nicolás Florentino (1445 onwards). In the centre of the retablo is a 12th century statue of the Virgen de la Vega, plated with bronze and decked with precious stones.

In the Capilla de San Martín, in the tower, are wall paintings, which, like those in the aisles, show French influence.

Salamanca's two cathedrals, dominating the skyline

The 12th century Cloister was badly damaged in the 1755 earthquake and rebuilt from 1785 onwards, so that little Romanesque work is left. Among Romanesque features that survive are the Mudéjar-style Capilla de Talavera, with sculpture by Alonso Berruguete and the tomb of the founder (owner of the Casa de las Conchas), and the 14th century Capilla de Santa Bárbara, in which candidates for the doctorate spent the night before their final examination and appeared before their examiners.

★Claustro/
Museo Diocesano

The Diocesan Museum, in the former chapterhouse, which contains fine works by Fernando Gallego ("Virgin with the Rose" triptych, "Coronation of the Virgin"), a triptych by Juan de Flandes, a 13th century ivory figure of the Virgin and a Renaissance organ from the University.

Around the Cathedrals

In front of the New Cathedral is the Plaza de Anaya, laid out in 1811.

Plaza de Anaya

Opposite the west front of the New Cathedral stands the former Palacio Episcopal (Bishop's Palace), now housing the Municipal Museum, with a collection of material on the history of the town.

Museo Municipal

South-west of the Old Cathedral, on the banks of the Río Tormes, lies the Plaza del Puente, from which the old Roman bridge spans the river. Of the bridge's 27 arches fifteen, at the near end, are still Roman. Near the bridge is the plain Romanesque church of Santiago, a modern reproduction (1980) of the original church.

Puente Romano

A little way upstream is the Puente Nuevo (New Bridge), from which the south-western end of which radiate the roads to Ávila, Plasencia and Ciudad Rodrigo. From the near end of the bridge the Avenida de los Reyes leads to the Dominican monastery of San Esteban (on right, on higher ground), with

★Convento de
San Esteban

a church built between 1524 and 1610, its façade covered with a riot of Plateresque decoration. It has a gilded high altar of 1693 by José de Churriguera, one of the sculptor's greatest works, and three side altars by pupils of his. To the left of the high altar is the tomb of the Duke of Alba, governor of the Spanish Netherlands. On the west wall, above the raised choir, can be seen a large fresco by Antonio Palomino, "The Triumph of the Church" (1705).

Cloister

Adjoining the church is the two-storey Cloister, with very fine medallions, figural ornament and a staircase by Gil de Hontañón.

Convento de las Dueñas
★Cloister

Just north of San Esteban, on the far side of the Avenida de los Reyes, is the Convento de las Dueñas, with a Plateresque façade of 1533. Visitors can see the beautiful two-storey Renaissance cloister, with capitals depicting fabulous beasts and human figures, possibly based on Dante's "Divine Comedy".

Palacio de la Salina

From the Convento de las Dueñas Calle Juan de la Fuente goes up past the Plaza de Colón to join Calle San Pablo, along which, to the right, is the Plaza Mayor. In this street, on the left, is the Palacio de la Salina, built in 1516 for Archbishop Fonseca. The façade has four tall round-headed arches with sculptured medallions, behind which is a beautiful patio.

Torre del Clavero

At the far end of the side street opposite the Palacio de la Salina can be seen the massive 15th century Torre del Clavero, with eight corner turrets, all that is left of a fortress-like mansion built by Francisco de Sotomayor.

North and East of the Playa Mayor

Sancti Spiritus

Farther to the east is the 16th century church of Sancti Spiritus (Espíritu Santo), with a Plateresque doorway. Notable features of the interior are the fine high altar (1659) and the Sagrario. The cloister dates from the 13th century.

San Marcos

At the north end of the old town is the 12th century church of San Marcos. Circular in form, it has two apses containing Gothic wall paintings.

West of the Plaza Mayor

Palacio de Monterrey

From the south-west corner of the Plaza Mayor Calle del Prior leads west to the handsome Palacio de Monterrey (built c. 1540), flanked by two finely articulated low towers.

Convento de las Agustinas

Opposite the palace is the Convento de las Agustinas (1598–1636), with the church of La Purísima, which contains a number of fine pictures by Ribera, including the "Immaculate Conception" (1635), one of his finest works.

Colegio Mayor del Arzobispo Fonseca

Farther west is the former Colegio Mayor del Arzobispo Fonseca (1527–78), also known as the Colegio de los Irlandeses, having originally been built for Irish students in Salamanca. The doorway is Plateresque, and the church itself has a beautiful retablo by Alonso Berruguete and pictures by pupils of his. The two-storey courtyard with its fine capitals and medallions containing busts was designed by Diego de Siloé.

Convento de las Úrsulas

North-east of the Colegio Fonseca, in the beautiful tree-shaded Calle de las Úrsulas, is the Convento de las Úrsulas, a convent of Ursuline nuns which contains the magnificent alabaster tomb (by Diego de Siloé) of Archbishop Alonso Fonseca.

In the convent is a small museum with works by Michelángelo, Morales, Juan de Borgoña and other artists.

At the end of Calle de las Úrsulas lies a little square with a monument to the writer and philosopher Miguel de Unamuno, who was also Rector of the University. Opposite it is the Casa de las Muertes, a 15th century mansion in Plateresque style which takes its name from the skulls on the upper part of the façade. In a medallion over the doorway is a bust of Archbishop Fonseca.

Casa de las Muertes

Surroundings of Salamanca

28km/17 miles north of Salamanca on N 630, off the road to the right, is the little town of Villanueva de Cañedo, dominated by the massive round towers of the Castillo de Buen Amor ("Castle of True Love").

Castillo de Buen Amor

The castle, built by Alfonso VII of León in the 13th century, was used by the Catholic Monarchs as a base in their conflict with Isabella's half-sister Juana la Beltraneja for the crown of Castile. The most notable features of the castle are the inner courtyard and the sumptuous decoration of the interior, in particular the Mudéjar-style panelled ceiling in the Great Hall.

San Sebastián/Donostia

K 1

Province: Guipúzcoa. Telephone dialling code: 94
Altitude: sea level. Population: 175,000

San Sebastián (Basque Donostia), chief town of the Basque province of Guipúzcoa and Spain's most fashionable bathing resort, lies on the Bay of Biscay near the French frontier. It is beautifully situated on alluvial land between the canalised Río Urumea and the crescent-shaped Bahía de la Concha, which is bounded on the east by Monte Urgull and on the west by Monte Igueldo and sheltered on the seaward side by the island of Santa Clara.

★★ Situation

San Sebastián's rise to become a resort of worldwide reputation began in the 19th century, when Queen María Cristina chose it as her summer

The ★★ resort

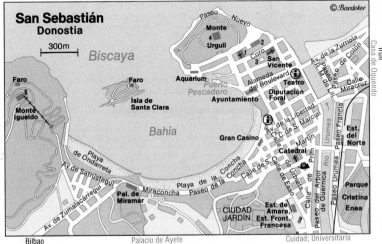

© Baedeker

San Sebastián Donostia

300m

1 Basílica de Santa María del Coro
2 Museo de San Telmo
3 Plaza de la Constitución
4 Castillo de Santa Cruz de la Mota mit
5 Parque de Atracciones

Museo Histórico Millitar

residence. Since then it has developed into an international resort where the boulevards, restaurants, cafés and Casino still preserve something of the fashionable atmosphere of the 19th century, attracting visitors from all over the world with a summer programme of major events such as the International Film Festival, the Jazz Festival and the Semana Grande in August. San Sebastián has practically no old buildings, since a great fire in 1813 destroyed much of the town.

Sights

Alameda del Boulevard

The hub of the town's life is the tamarisk-shaded Alameda del Boulevard with its shops, restaurants and cafés. At its west end are the fishing harbour, the Club Náutico and the Town Hall, housed in the former Gran Casino, the west front of which overlooks the Bahía de la Concha with its beach.

Paseo de la Concha

To the south of the Town Hall is the Parque Alderdi-Eder ("beautiful place"), from which the Paseo de la Concha encircles the bay to the large bathing beach of La Perla and the royal bathing pavilion, the Caseta Real.

New Town

Palacio de la Diputación

To the east of the Paseo de la Concha and the south of the Alameda lies the new town of San Sebastián, with the Avenida de la Libertad, its main street, and the Plaza de Guipúzcoa. On the west side of this square is the Palacio de la Diputación (1885), which has busts of notable figures on the façade. It contains pictures by Ignacio Zuloaga (1870–1945), and the library has a large collection of books on Basque literature and history.

Cathedral

In the southern part of the new town, beyond the busy Calle de San Martín, stands the Neo-Gothic Cathedral of the Buen Pastor (Good Shepherd), which was begun by Manuel de Echave in 1880 and completed in 1897. Its 75m/246ft high tower is a city landmark.

Gran Casino del Kursaal

To the west of the cathedral, in the Paseo de la Concha, is the Gran Casino del Kursaal, opened in 1922. Gambling in the Casino – as in the rest of Spain – stopped only two years later, in 1924, and was not resumed until 1978.

Old Town

Plaza de la Constitución

North of the Alameda, extending to Monte Urgull, is the old town of San Sebastián, which is at its liveliest in the evening. Its central feature is the arcaded Plaza de la Constitución, in which bullfights used to be held. To the east of the square is the Fish Market (Pescadería).

San Vicente

North-east of the Plaza de la Constitución stands the Gothic church of San Vicente (1507), the town's oldest church, with a richly carved retablo of 1584.

Museo Municipal San Telmo

To the north-west of San Vicente is the former monastery of San Telmo, a Renaissance building of the 16th century which is now occupied by the Municipal Museum. On the ground floor, around the cloister, are gravestones, stelae, mill-wheels, etc., from the Basque country. There is also an ethnographic collection (craftsmen's tools and implements, pottery, porcelain, etc.) as well as a prehistoric section.

Picture gallery

On the first floor is a collection of pictures by Spanish masters, including works by El Greco, Morán, Ribera and Coello. Among Basque artists represented are Ugarte, Zubiaurre, Echagüe, Salaberría, Arteta, Amarica and Zuloaga.

The church has wall paintings by José María Sert on themes from Basque history.

South-west of San Telmo is the church of Santa María del Coro (1764), a Baroque building with a rich Churrigueresque façade. It has an altarpiece with side wings painted by Robert Michel.

Santa María

From the church of Santa María a stepped path leads up Monte Urgull (135m/443ft), a sandstone hill which was once an island. On top of the hill is the Castillo de la Mota, which now houses a museum of military history. The chapel of the Sacred Heart is crowned by a 12m/40ft high statue of Christ.

Monte Urgull

Below the south side of Monte Urgull, to the west of the old town, is the harbour, from which a boat can be taken to the island of Santa Cristina. The Aquarium, to the west of the harbour at the near end of the Bahía de la Concha, has an interesting Oceanographic Museum; the exhibits include the skeleton of a large whale, ship models, navigational instruments and documents.

Aquarium/
Museo
Oceanográfico

From the Aquarium the Paseo Nuevo encircles Monte Urgull, above the rocky shore, to the mouth of the Río Urumea, affording fine views. The river is spanned by the Puente Zurriola, beyond which a seafront promenade runs east to just before Monte Ulía.

★ Paseo Nuevo

To Monte Igueldo

From the west end of the Paseo de la Concha the Miraconcha continues through a tunnel under the Palacio de Miramar, formerly a royal summer residence, to the district of Antiguo with its beautiful Playa de Ondarreta.

Palacio
de Miramar

At the far end of the Playa de Ondarreta is the Royal Tennis Club, from which a funicular and a winding road go to the top of Monte Igueldo (184m/604ft), where there are a terrace restaurant, an amusement park, an observatory and an outlook tower, from which there are magnificent views of the town, the sea and the Basque mountains.

★ Monte Igueldo

★ Monte Ulía

7km/4½ miles east of the town centre Monte Ulía (230m/755ft) rises above the outlying district of Gros. A road winds up to the top of the hill, where there are a garden restaurant and three outlook terraces.

Surroundings of San Sebastián

To the French Frontier

The motorway and N I cross the Río Urumea to the industrial town of Rentería, on the Río Oyarzun. North of Rentería is the port of Pasajes (Basque Pasaia), at the mouth of the inlet of the same name.

Pasajes/Pasaia

Pasajes is made up of three parts – San Pedro, the commercial port of Ancho (Basque Antxo) and the little port of Pasajes de San Juan (Basque Pasaia Donibane) which is situated in a beautiful land-locked bay and which consists of a single street. Lafayette sailed from here in 1777 to aid the American revolutionaries. Victor Hugo lived in the village for some time in 1843.

From here the road crosses the Basque hills to the frontier town of Irún, the most notable features of which are the 16th century church of Nuestra

Irún

San Sebastián Bay from Monte Igueldo

Señora del Juncal, with a Romanesque figure of the Virgin, and the 17th century Ayuntamiento (Town Hall) in the Plaza de San Juan.

★ Fuenterrabía/
Hondarribia

3km/2 miles north, on the bay at the mouth of the Río Bidasoa, is the little fishing town and holiday resort of Fuenterrabía (Basque Hondarria), formerly a frontier stronghold which was frequently the scene of fighting. In the picturesque little streets of the old town, which is entered through the 15th century Puerta de Santa María, are many old houses with coats of arms on the façade. In the church of Nuestra Señora de la Asunción (Gothic; enlarged in the 18th century) was celebrated the marriage of Louis XIV of France and the Infanta María Teresa of Spain – though the Infanta herself was not present, being represented by a Spanish minister. From the terrace of the 12th century Palacio del Rey Carlos V (now a parador), in the Plaza de Armas, there is a fine view of the mouth of the river and the lighthouse on Cabo Higuer to the north, probably on the site of an ancient temple of Venus.

★ Jaizquibel

From Fuenterrabía there is a very attractive road up the bare sandstone ridge of Jaizquibel (Basque Jaizkibel; 584m/1916ft), with the pilgrimage church of Nuestra Señora de Guadalupe and the commandingly situated Hostal Provincial de Jaizquibel (alt. 448m/1470ft).

★★ Along the Cantabrian Coast

Usúrbil

Leave San Sebastián on N I, heading south, and after passing through the Antiguo district turn right into N 634, which runs west through the Basque uplands to Usúrbil (alt. 45m/148ft), with a handsome church and the old mansion of the Soroa family.

Orio

The road continues through the broad valley of the Río Oria to Orio (alt. 34m/112ft), a little fishermen's and seamen's town on the fjord-like estuary of the river, with a beach at its mouth.

After crossing the Col d'Orio the road descends to Zarauz (Basque Zarautz), a little town on the flat and sandy coast, at the west end of a plain surrounded by hills; it was a summer residence of Queen Isabella II in the 19th century. With its long and beautiful beach it is still a popular holiday resort. In the 16th century Zarauz was famed for its shipyards; among the ships built here was the "Victoria", in which Juan Sebastián Elcano, the companion of Magellan, carried out the first circumnavigation of the globe in 1519–22. In the picturesque streets of the town are a number of handsome old buildings, including the 18th century Casa Consistorial (Town Hall), the 15th century Palacio del Marqués de Narros, with a beautiful park, and the massive Torre Lucea (15th c.).

Zarauz/ Zarautz

At Zarauz begins the Cornisa Cantábrica (Cantabrian Corniche), a magnificent road running close to the rocky coast. The fishing port of Guetaria (Basque Getaria) is picturesquely situated on a promontory, its harbour sheltered by the fortified island of San Antonio, which is connected with the mainland by a causeway. From the lighthouse at the tip of the promontory there are fine views. In the town's main street stands a tall monument (1922) to the navigator Juan Sebastián Elcano (1487–1526), a native of Guetaria, who ended his circumnavigation of the globe in his home town. In the Town Hall are frescoes by Zuloaga (1922) depicting Elcano's voyage round the world. Below the 13th century Gothic church of San Salvador lies the harbour, with attractive fish restaurants.

★ Guetaria/ Getaria

The coast road continues to the resort of Zumaya (Basque Zumaia), at the foot of Monte Santa Clara. At the entrance to the town is the Villa Zuloaga, built by the painter Ignacio Zuloaga (1870–1945) on the ruins of the 12th century monastery of Santiago Echea. His house is now a museum, which displays the artist's collection, including works by El Greco, Zurbarán and Goya. The Gothic church of San Pedro has a retablo by the Basque artist Juan de Anchieta.

Zumaya/Zumaia

Zarauz

Deva/Deba

N 634 continues, with many bends, to the little resort of Deva (Basque Deba), at the mouth of the Río Deva. The beautiful 14th century church of Nuestra Señora de la Asunción, which was restored in the 17th century, has a fine 13th century doorway and contains Romanesque bas-reliefs, also of the 13th century.

Eibar

From Deva N 634 turns inland and comes in 21km/13 miles to Eibar (alt. 120m/394ft), where the Spanish Republic was proclaimed in 1931. During the Civil War the town suffered much destruction. Along with Elgóibar, Eibar is a centre for the manufacture of arms and munitions.

To Arantzazu

Azpeitia

From just beyond Zumaya, on the Cantabrian Corniche, C 6317 runs south through the Urola valley, between wooded hills, to Azpeitia (alt. 85m/279ft), a small industrial town with handsome old patrician houses. The Gothic church of San Sebastián, in which St Ignatius of Loyola was baptised, has a fine portico by Ventura Rodríguez (1767).

★**Monasterio de San Ignacio de Loyola**

C 6317 continues up the Urola valley to the monastery (off the road to the left) of San Ignacio de Loyola (alt. 115m/377ft), an extensive range of buildings erected between 1689 and 1888 to the design of Carlo Fontana, a pupil of Bernini. The monastery now houses a Jesuit college.

Church

The church, with a 65m/213ft high dome by Joaquín de Churriguera, is one of the finest of its kind in Spain; it was completed only in the mid-18th century. The interior is richly decorated with marble and semi-precious stones, and on the sumptuous Baroque high altar, between twisted columns, is a silver statue of St Ignatius.

Santa Casa

In the left wing of the monastery is the Santa Casa, the house in which St Ignatius of Loyola was born, which has a Mudéjar-style exterior. Visitors are shown the room in which the saint was born and the sickroom in which he resolved to abandon a military career.

Zumárraga

After passing through Azcoitia (alt. 130m/427ft), an old market town in a beautiful situation, the road continues on a winding course to Zumárraga (alt. 357m/1171ft), on the right bank of the Río Urola, a road and railway junction and the birthplace of Miguel López de Legazpi, conqueror of the Philippines, who is commemorated by a monument erected in 1897.

Vergara/ Bergara

From Zumárraga C 6322 winds its way up to the Puerto de Descarga (487m/1598ft), from which there are fine views, and then runs down to Vergara (Basque Bergara; alt. 145m/476ft), at the junction of the Río Anzuola with the Río Deva. The church of San Pedro has a figure of Christ by Montañés (1657). Also of interest is the 16th century Palacio Jaúregui with its very individual façade.

Oñate/Oñati

C 6322 then continues south in the direction of Mondragón (Basque Arrasate). Just before that town, at San Prudencio, a road branches off on the left and traverses beautiful scenery to Oñate (Basque Oñati). This little town, once famous for its university, has preserved a fine university building (16th c.) with a richly sculptured Plateresque façade. The monastery of Bidauerreta has a Renaissance façade. The most notable feature of the 15th century church of San Miguel is the cloister, with a stream flowing through it.

★ Arantzazu

From Oñate a narrow road leads up to the shrine of Arantzazu (alt. 800m/2625ft), where a shepherd is said to have discovered a figure of the Virgin in 1469. The original 16th century chapel was replaced in 1950 by a modern church decorated by contemporary artists. From the church there are magnificent views of grand mountain scenery.

Other Excursions from San Sebastián

See Bilbao, Pamplona and Vitoria-Gasteiz

Santander

H 1

Province: Cantabria (S). Telephone dialling code: 942
Altitude: 15m/50ft. Population: 184,000

The port of Santander in Old Castile, chief town of its province and the see of a bishop, lies in a beautiful bay on the north coast of Spain, ringed by hills and within easy reach of the highest peaks in the Cantabrian Mountains, the Picos de Europa.

Santander was a considerable port in Roman times, and is still one of the leading ports of northern Spain, handling a large export and import trade. In the Middle Ages it shipped the agricultural produce of Castile, and from the 16th to the 19th century it was involved in the American trade, particularly in the export of flour. Nowadays its economic importance depends on the export of ore and coal and on the industry which has been attracted by the port. Its beautiful beach and mild climate also make Santander a popular holiday place – a tradition which began in the 19th century when it became a fashionable bathing resort and a summer residence of the Spanish royal family; and with the summer courses run by its University and its International Festival of music and drama Santander is also one of Spain's cultural metropolises.

Sights

After a great fire which destroyed forty streets in the city centre on the night of February 15th–16th 1941 the area was rebuilt with wide streets and buildings restricted to a height of five storeys. The central feature of Santander is now the broad Avenida de Alfonso XIII, which runs inland from the harbour, crosses the town's main traffic artery, the Avenida de Calvo Sotelo/Paseo de Pereda, and ends in Plaza Porticada.

The town

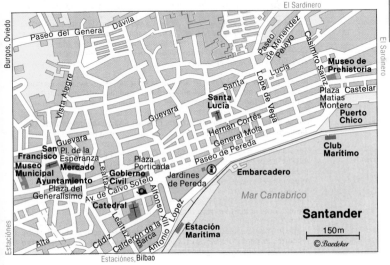

387

Market, Santander

Cathedral

Just to the west of the Avenida de Alfonso XIII, on the eastern edge of the old town, stands the Cathedral, originally Gothic (13th c.), which was restored after the fire. In its large crypt, the Iglesia del Cristo (*c.* 1200), are the remains of two martyred saints, Celedonius and Emeterius. In the cloister (rebuilt) is the tomb of the Santander-born writer and scholar Marcelino Menéndez y Pelayo (1856–1912).

Harbour

To the east and south-west of the Avenida de Alfonso XIII, extending along the Muelle de Maliaño and beyond this to the south-west, is the harbour, with the Custom House and the Marine Station (Estación Marítima). A specially cut channel allows large vessels to enter the industrial harbour of El Astillero, in the south of the bay.

Museo Municipal de Bellas Artes

From the Avenida de Alfonso XIII, going west along the Avenida de Calvo Sotelo and turning right into Calle Cervantes and then left into Calle Rubio, we come to the Municipal Museum of Art, which contains a portrait of Ferdinand VII and several etchings by Goya, as well as a rich collection of works by regional artists and Italian, Flemish and Spanish painters of the 17th and 18th centuries.

Biblioteca Menéndez y Pelayo

The same building houses the Menéndez y Pelayo Library, the library of 40,000 volumes assembled by the scholar of that name, with his study preserved in its original condition. On the far side of the garden is the house in which Menéndez y Pelayo worked and died, now a museum.

From the west end of the Avenida de Calvo a tunnel under the hill on which the old town is built leads to the railway stations.

Museo Marítimo del Cantábrico

From the Avenida de Alfonso XIII the Paseo de Pereda runs east, flanked by beautiful gardens, to the Puerto Chico (Little Harbour). At its east end is the Museo Marítimo del Cantábrico, an interesting museum and aquarium, with preserved specimens of marine fauna, objects and documents illustrating the life of fishermen and ship models.

A little way north of the Puerto Chico the Regional Museum of Prehistory and Archaeology has a large collection of finds from prehistoric caves (notably Altamira: see entry), including the so-called "bâtons de commandement" made from stags' antlers, the function of which is not known. The collection includes Roman antiquities and some very interesting funerary stelae erected by the pre-Roman Celtic population of the area.

★ Museo Regional de Prehistoria y Arqueología

Calle Castelar and the Avenida de la Reina Victoria (fine views) continue east from the Paseo de Pereda to the peninsula of La Magdalena, on which is the summer palace of Alfonso XIII (1912), now occupied by Santander's International University.

La Magdalena

On the north side of the peninsula is the beautiful beach of El Sardinero, which still preserves something of the atmosphere of the Belle Epoque with its seafront terraces, its Gran Casino and its numerous hotels and restaurants.

★ El Sardinero

Surroundings of Santander

3km/2 miles north of El Sardinero is the Cabo Mayor, with a lighthouse and the Puente Forado, a large natural bridge in the local limestone rocks.

Cabo Mayor

Along the Cantabrian Coast

From Santander N 611 runs inland to Barreda, from which C 6316 turns west for Santillana del Mar (see entry); from there a detour can be made to the caves and museum of Altamira (see entry).

Santillana del Mar/ Altamira

C 6316 continues west to Oreña and follows a winding course to the picturesque little town of Comillas, which in the reign of Alfonso XII was a fashionable bathing resort. The central feature of the town is the paved Plaza Mayor, with the parish church. West of this is the park of the Palacio de los Marqueses de Comillas, in which is a pavilion designed by Gaudí. On the far side of the main road, on a hill between the town and the sea, is the massive brick-built complex of the former Pontifical University (Universidad Ponteficia), from the forecourt of which there are fine views of the park and the town; from the rear of the building there is a prospect of the sea and a number of beautiful beaches.

★ Comillas

C 6316 finally joins N 634, which continues along the coast to La Revilla and San Vicente de la Barquera, an old-world little port town with a large beach which makes it also a popular holiday resort. It lies at the mouth of the Río Escudo, which is crossed on a long bridge. It preserves part of an old battlemented wall, a ruined castle and the fortress-like church of Santa María de los Angeles (13th–16th c.), with a Romanesque doorway and Gothic monuments.

San Vicente de la Barquera

Santander to Bilbao

N 634 runs south from Santander and then round the Bahía de Santander in a wide curve to Solares, a little spa, beautifully situated on the Río Miera, which is also noted for its table water.

Solares

The route continues on a good road through hilly country. 20km/12½ miles beyond Solares C 629 goes off on the left to Santoña (10km/6 miles), a small port situated on a peninsula which Napoleon planned to make a northern

Santoña

Gibraltar, as the remains of fortifications still bear witness. The Romanesque collegiate church (12th–13th c.) has a 16th century retablo. In the convent of San Sebastián de Anó is the tomb of Barbara Blomberg (d. 1597 at Colindres), the daughter of a German commoner who became the mistress of Charles V and mother of Don John of Austria, the victor of Lepanto. North of the town is the beach of Playa Berria.

Limpias

N 634 continues through the fertile delta of the Río Asón to Colindres, where a road branches off on the right up the Asón valley to the pilgrimage centre of Limpias (7km/4½ miles). In the parish church is the much venerated 17th century image of Santo Cristo de la Agonía, which is said to have shed tears of blood in 1919.

Laredo

Beyond this is Laredo, beautifully situated in Santoña Bay, which has become one of the leading resorts on the Cantabrian coast, with a continually expanding modern district adjoining the crowded old town. The 13th century church of Nuestra Señora de la Asunción, with a 16th century doorway, contains some fine sculpture and pictures.

On June 24th every year Laredo celebrates the Noche de San Juan (Midsummer Night), when the young men of the town dress in women's clothes and wash their feet in the sea.

Castro Urdiales

Beyond Laredo the road begins to climb, with beautiful rearward views of the town and the wide sweep of Santoña Bay. Thereafter it follows a winding course to the Punta de Sonabia, after which there is a magnificent stretch along the rocky coast to Castro Urdiales (see Bilbao, Surroundings). From there N 634 continues to Bilbao.

Santiago de Compostela   B 2

Province: La Coruña (C). Telephone dialling code: 981
Altitude: 260m/853ft. Population: 94,000

The old capital of the kingdom of Galicia, Santiago de Compostela, the see of a metropolitan archbishop and the seat of an ancient university, lies in north-western Spain some 35km/22 miles from the Atlantic coast. Northwest of the town, which is one of the rainiest places in Spain, is Monte Pedros (735m/2412ft).

★ ★ Pilgrimage
centre

Santiago is Spain's most celebrated place of pilgrimage, with a magnificent cathedral which is one of the country's outstanding tourist sights. According to legend the Apostle St James the Great (known in Spain as Santiago) preached the Gospel in Spain, and after his martyrdom in A.D. 44 his body was miraculously brought back to Spain, lost for many centuries and then rediscovered in 813 on the site of the present Cathedral. Thereafter St James became the patron saint of Spain and pilgrims flocked from all over Europe along the Way of St James (see entry) to visit his shrine, which ranked with Jerusalem and Rome as one of the three great places of pilgrimage in Christendom.

Under a special privilege granted by Pope Callistus (Calixtus) II, every year in which the feast of St James (July 25th) falls on a Sunday is a Holy Year. In the Holy Year of 1993 seven million visitors came to Santiago, 100,000 of whom were issued with "compostelas", pilgri. certificates. The next Holy Year will be 1999.

The Puerta Santa,
opened only in a
Holy Year

The Apostle's feast day, the Fiesta de Santiago, is celebrated with a great procession and the swinging of a huge censer, the Botafumeiro, across the transept of the cathedral.

Note

Much of the old town of Santiago and the area around the cathedral is closed to traffic. Visitors travelling by car will do well to leave their car in the

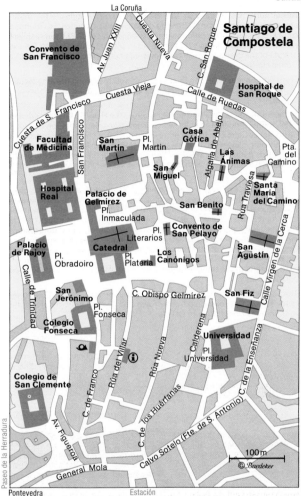

Santiago de Compostela

La Coruña

Convento de San Francisco

Av. Juan XXIII

Cuesta Nueva

C. San Roque

Hospital de San Roque

Cuesta Vieja

Calle de Ruedas

Cuesta de S. Francisco

San Francisco

Facultad de Medicina

San Martín

Pl. Martín

Casa Gótica

Algalia de Abajo

Las Ánimas

Pta. del Camino

San Miguel

Santa María del Camino

Rúa Travíesa

Hospital Real

Palacio de Gelmírez

Pl. Inmaculada

San Benito

Palacio de Rajoy

Pl. Literarios

Convento de San Pelayo

Calle Virgen de la Cerca

Catedral

Pl. Obradoiro

Pl. Platería

Los Canónigos

San Agustín

San Jerónimo

C. Obispo Gelmírez

San Fiz

Colegio Fonseca

Pl. Fonseca

Calle de Trinidad

Rúa del Villar

Rúa Nueva

Calderena

Universidad

Pl. Universidad

Colegio de San Clemente

C. de Franco

C. de los Huérfanas

C. de la Enseñanza

Av. Figueroa

Calvo Sotelo (Fte. de S. Antonio)

Paseo de la Herradura

General Mola

100 m

© Baedeker

Pontevedra

Estación

multi-storey car park at the northern end of Calle San Francisco, to the north of the Plaza del Obradoiro.

★Plaza del Obradoiro

The objective of all visitors to Santiago is the Plaza del Obradoiro (Plaza de España), a spacious square surrounded by handsome buildings below the west front of the Cathedral. The square, which lies on the west side of the old town, with its old-world arcaded streets and its many churches and convents, is one of the finest and best preserved squares in Spain.

391

Santiago de Compostela

Convento de San Francisco

At the north end of Calle de San Francisco, directly opposite the multi-storey car park, stands the Convento de San Francisco, which was founded by St Francis on his first pilgrimage to Santiago between 1213 and 1215 and rebuilt between 1618 and 1783. There is a modern monument to St Francis in front of the doorway of the twin-towered church. There are remains of a Gothic cloister.

From the convent Calle San Francisco runs south, passing the long façade of the Faculty of Medicine, to enter the Plaza del Obradoiro at its north-east corner.

★ Hospital Real

At the north end of the Plaza del Obradoiro is the Hospital Real, founded in 1489 by the Catholic Monarchs, which is now a luxurious parador, the Hotel de los Reyes Católicos. In the centre of the main front facing the square is a magnificent Plateresque doorway. The Hospital is laid out round four courtyards dating from the 16th–18th centuries. In the centre of the building is the Gothic chapel, with beautifully carved piers at the crossing and a grille of 1556.

Palacio de Gelmírez

On the east side of the square, adjoining the cathedral, stands the Palacio del Arzobispo (Archbishop's Palace), a plain building which incorporates the restored palace of Archbishop Gelmírez (12th–13th c.), one of the most important Romanesque secular buildings in Spain. On the upper floor is the 30m/100ft long Salón de Fiestas, with splendid groined vaulting springing from finely carved consoles depicting Alfonso IX's wedding banquet. On the lower floor is another large vaulted hall, beyond which is a medieval kitchen.

To the right of the cathedral is the west wing of the cloister, with an open pillared gallery.

Palacio de Rajoy

The west side of the Plaza del Obradoiro is dominated by the Palacio de Rajoy (1777), now occupied by the Town Hall and the government of the Autonomous Community of Galicia.

Palacio de Rajoy and Hospital Real, Plaza del Obradoiro

At the south end of the square is the former Colegio de San Jerónimo, now the Institute of Galician Studies. It is the smallest and plainest building on the square, with a fine sculptured doorway of 1490 (originally belonging to an old pilgrim hospice).

Colegio de San Jerónimo

Beyond the Colegio de San Jerónimo, to the south, is the Colegio de Fonseca (1544) now houses the Faculty of Pharmacy and the main part of the University Library. This is also the meeting-place of the Galician parliament. The building is laid out round a two-storey patio.

Colegio de Fonseca

★★ Cathedral

The Cathedral, one of the outstanding monuments of Early Romanesque architecture, was built between 1060 and 1211 on the site of an earlier 9th century church destroyed by Almansor's Moorish army in 997 – though Almansor, respecting the religion of his enemies, left the relics of the Apostle undisturbed. The new building was begun in the reign of Alfonso VI, and after the completion of the main structure new elements were added in later centuries, culminating in the Baroque transformation of the exterior in the 16th–18th centuries. The interior of the Cathedral, however, is still in the purest Early Romanesque style.

Building history

The west or Obradoiro front, facing the Plaza del Obradoiro, is one of the most impressive church façades in Spain, built in lavishly decorated Baroque style between 1738 and 1747 by Fernando Casas y Novoa. The central gable, which is flanked by two richly articulated towers 76m/249ft high, is topped by a statue of St James. A handsome double staircase of 1606 leads up to the doorway.

★★ West front

On the north side of the Cathedral, in the Plaza de la Inmaculada, is the Puerta de la Azabachería (1769). In the Plaza de los Literarios, at the east

Doorways

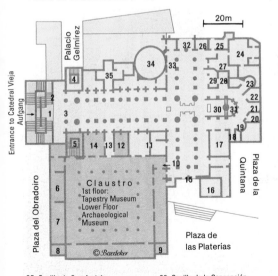

Catedral de Santiago de Compostela

1 Staircase
2 Obradoiro façade
3 Pórtico de la Gloria
4 Torre de la Carraca
5 Torre de las Campanas
6 Biblioteca
7 Sala Capitular
8 Torre de la Corona
9 Torre del Tesoro
10 Entrance to Museum
11 Sacristía
12 Tesoro
13 Vestíbulo
14 Capilla de las Reliquias
15 Puerta de las Platerías
16 Torre del Reloj
17 Capilla del Pilar
18 Capilla de Mondragon
19 Capilla de San Pedro
20 Puerta Santa
21 Capilla del Salvador
22 Capilla de N. Sra. Blanca
23 Capilla de San Juan
24 Capilla de la Corticella

25 Capilla de San Andrés
26 Capila de San Fructuoso
27 Capilla del Espíritu Santo
28 Capilla de San Bartolomé

29 Capilla de la Concepción
30 Capilla Mayor
31 Apostle statue, entrance, crypt below

32 Puerta de la Parroquia
33 Capilla de Santa Catalina
34 Capilla del Corazón
35 Capilla del Cristo de Burgos

end of the Cathedral, is the Puerta Santa, which is opened only during Holy Years; built in the 17th century, it is decorated with 12th century sculpture representing prophets, apostles and fathers of the church. Over the doorway are statues of St James and his disciples Athanasius and Theodore (1694). The oldest surviving doorway of the Cathedral is the Puerta de las Platerías on the south side, a double doorway richly decorated with 12th and 13th century Romanesque sculpture. In the tympana are the Nativity, the Adoration of the Kings and the Temptation. Above the arches of the doorways, in the centre, is the figure of Christ in the act of blessing, flanked by St James and Moses, and below this are the Creation of Adam, the Expulsion from Paradise and Abraham emerging from the tomb.

Catedral Vieja

Below the staircase leading up to the west doorway can be found the oldest surviving part of the Cathedral, the vaulted Romanesque chamber known as the Old Cathedral, though in fact it is merely a crypt built in the early 12th century to compensate for the fall in ground level.

★★ Pórtico de la Gloria

Immediately inside the west doorway of the Cathedral is the Pórtico de la Gloria, part of the old west front now concealed by the 18th century Baroque façade. This triple doorway with its profusion of sculpture (which was originally painted) is one of the largest and most magnificent collections of Romanesque sculpture that have come down to us, carved by one Master Mateo between 1166 and 1188.

The sculpture in the arch of the central doorway (the only one with a tympanum) is of overwhelming power and abundance. In the centre is Christ as the Saviour of the world, surrounded by the four Evangelists, two angels with censers and eight angels holding the instruments of the Passion. In the archivolt are the twenty-four Elders of the Apocalypse.

The central pier of the doorway is still the first objective of all pilgrims. The wearing away of the stone and the holes in the base of the column, which represents the Tree of Jesse, are evidence of the age-old practice of

The end of the pilgrimage: the Pórtico de la Gloria

touching or kissing the column to mark the end of the pilgrimage. On the top of the Tree of Jesse is an impressive figure of St James; the capital of the column represents the Holy Trinity.

The clustered columns to the left of the main doorway have figures of Moses, Isaiah, Daniel and Jeremiah; to the right are Peter, Paul, James and John.

In the archivolt of the left-hand doorway is Christ with the Jews, in that of the right-hand doorway Christ with the Gentiles.

The Romanesque interior of the Cathedral (94m/308ft long, nave 24m/79ft high, dome 33m/108ft) is dominated by the elaborately decorated Capilla Mayor, built over the Apostle's tomb. The high altar consists of a super-structure of jasper, alabaster and silver with numerous figures (1665–69) and the altar proper (by Figuera, 1715). In the centre is a 13th century wooden figure of the Apostle, richly decked with silver, gold and precious stones added about 1700. On either side of the altar are narrow staircases leading up behind the figure of St James, so that pilgrims go up and kiss the Apostle's cloak – the culminating act of the pilgrimage.

Interior
★★Capilla Mayor

Under the altar is a crypt (entered by steps on the right) with the remains of the Apostle and his two disciples Theodore and Athanasius. The silver casket containing the Apostle's remains is 19th century work.

Crypt

In the dome over the crossing (1445) can be seen the device (installed in 1604) for swinging the huge Botafumeiro (censer), 2m/6½ft high, which is set in motion on great feast days by a team of eight men. When not in use it is kept in the Library (see below).

Botafumeiro

Only a few of the chapels in the aisles and transepts of the Cathedral, all sumptuously decorated and furnished, can be mentioned here: the Capilla del Sagrado Corazón, a tall circular marble chapel in the north aisle, with bishops' tombs; the Capilla del Espíritu Santo in the north transept, which also has fine tombs; the adjoining Capilla de la Concepción, with the tomb of Canon Rodríguez Agustín by Cornelis de Holanda; and the Capilla de Mondragón in the south ambulatory, with a finely wrought ceiling.

In the Capilla de las Reliquias or Relicario, the first chapel in the south aisle, are the tombs of kings and queens of the 12th–15th centuries.

Chapels

The Capilla de San Fernando in the south aisle contains the Cathedral Treasury (Tesoro), with splendid vestments and silverware. A particular treasure is a silver monstrance by Antonio de Arfe (1545).

Treasury

In the south transept, to the right of the Puerta de las Platerías, is the entrance to the Plateresque Cloister (1521–86), one of the largest and finest in Spain, measuring 35m/115ft each way, with walks 5.8m/19ft wide.

★Cloister

At the north-west corner of the cloister is the entrance to the rooms sur-rounding it. The first of these, on the ground floor, is the Library (Biblio-teca), in which are displayed a number of large and very beautiful hymnals, manuscripts and two examples of the Botafumeiro.

Library

In the adjoining Chapterhouse (Sala Capitular) the walls are hung with fine 17th century tapestries by Juan Raés and others from the Madrid manufactories.

Chapterhouse

The Tapestry Museum, in four rooms on the upper floor of the cloister, displays Flemish tapestries and tapestries from the Real Fábrica de Madrid after cartoons by Teniers, Rubens, Goya, Bayeu and other artists, most of them on country themes and depicting scenes of aristocratic life. From the last room a passage leads to the outer gallery, from which there is a good general view of the Plaza del Obradoiro.

Tapestry Museum

In three rooms on the lower floor is a small archaeological museum illus-trating the different stages in the building of the Cathedral. The first room is

Archaeological
Museum

devoted to carving in stone (sculpture, architectural elements), the second to carving in wood (sculpture, fragments of retablos), the third to 17th and 18th century plans and drawings of the Cathedral and some very fine examples of book illumination.

Plaza de las Platerías

The south doorway of the Cathedral, the Puerta de las Platerías, leads down a flight of steps into the picturesque Plaza de las Platerías, in the centre of which is a handsome fountain. On the far side of the square is the Baroque Casa del Cabildo, with a regularly articulated façade. On the south front of the Cathedral, flanking the doorway, are the Torre del Tesoro (on the left), the counterpart to the Torre de la Corona on the Plaza del Obradoiro, and the 14th century Gothic Torre del Reloj (Clock-Tower), with a bell 2.5m/8ft in diameter. To the left of the doorway is the outer wall of the Cloister (by Gil de Hontañón).

★ Plaza de los Literários/Plaza de la Quintana

Casa de
los Canónigos

On the east side of the Cathedral (in which is the Puerta Santa) extends the majestic Plaza de los Literários (Plaza de la Quintana), one of Santiago's most popular meeting-places. On the south side of the square is the long colonnade of the Casa de los Canónigos (17th–18th c.), once the residence of the Cathedral canons.

Convento de
San Pelayo

The whole of the east side of the square is occupied by the sober, almost forbidding, façade of the Convento de San Pelayo, which was given its present aspect in the 18th century.

On the north side of the square a grand flight of steps leads to the Plaza de la Inmaculada on the north front of the Cathedral.

North of the Cathedral

Monasterio de
San Martín Pinario

The Plaza de la Inmaculada is dominated by the former Benedictine house of San Martín, founded in 899, which is now a seminary. It has a massive pillared doorway (begun 1590) and a handsome courtyard.

San Martín

Within the seminary complex is the church of San Martín, with its main front on Plaza San Martín (reached by a street on the east side of the seminary). The church (by Mateo López, 1590) has a sumptuous retablo by Fernando Casas y Novoa and Miguel de Romay and beautiful choir-stalls of 1644.

Old Town

To the south of the Cathedral and the Plaza de las Platerías is the old town of Santiago, centred on two parallel streets, Rúa del Villar (with the 18th century Casa del Deán at its near end, on left) and Rúa Nueva (Galician Nova). These two arcaded streets with their bars and restaurants and souvenir shops are the hub of the town's life. Half way along Rúa Nueva stands the Romanesque church of Santa María Salomé (12th c.).

Santa María
Salomé

University

Farther east, in the Plaza del Instituto, we come to the University (late 18th c.), which was originally founded in 1532. It has a very valuable library, including important 16th century works.

Paseo de
la Herradura

On the south-west side of the old town, off the broad Alameda, is the Paseo de la Herradura, a large park-like area from which there is a fine view of the

Cathedral and the town. In the park is the church of Santa Susana (begun 1105). To the south lies the University City.

Outside the Central Area

On the east side of the town, beyond the Puerta del Camino (a square on the site of the old gate through which pilgrims entered the town), is the 18th century monastery of Santo Domingo. One wing of the monastery houses the Museo do Pobo Gallego (Museum of the Galician People) and the Municipal Museum.

Monasterio de
Santo Domingo

In the Barrio de Sar, on the south-east side of the town, is the 12th century church of Santa María de Sar, the columns and walls of which are considerably off the vertical, probably because of an unstable site. It has a fine 13th century cloister, partly preserved, with rich sculptural ornament by Master Mateo.

Santa María
de Sar

In San Lorenzo, 2km/1¼ miles west of the town, is the early 13th century church of San Lorenzo de Transouto, with a marble altar (1525) and sculptured figures by Montañés.

San Lorenzo
de Transouto

Santillana del Mar   G 1

Province: Cantabria (S). Telephone dialling code: 942
Altitude: 100m/330ft. Population: 4000

Santillana del Mar, lying a little inland of the Cantabrian coast, is a charming little town which preserves the atmosphere of the past and is now protected as a national monument. With its old mansions flaunting their coats of arms, Santillana – now bearing the marks of a thriving tourist trade – gives a unique picture of the way of life of the old country nobility of Spain, even though some of the houses are now occupied by souvenir and craft shops. The town grew up in the 5th century around the Monasterio de Santa Juliana and was granted its municipal charter in the 13th century. Two centuries later, with the creation of the marquisate of Santillana, many noble families moved to the town and built the palaces and mansions which give the town its special character.

Santillana is also known as the fictional birthplace of Gil Blas, hero of the picaresque novel "Gil Blas de Santillane" by the 18th century French writer Alain-René Lesage.

The ★Town

A little out of the town centre, near the large car park, the Convento de Regina Coeli now houses a museum of religious art.

Convento de
Regina Coeli

Santillana must be explored on foot. A walk round the town will reveal the charm of its old houses with their plain façades relieved by magnificent coats of arms and by balconies decked with flowers in summer.
   The town is entered by Calle de Santo Domingo, on the right-hand side of which is the 18th century Casa de la Villa (now a hotel), notable for its semicircular balconies. Keeping left where the street divides, we come into the Plaza de Ramón Pelayo, in which, on the right, is the 17th century Palacio Barreda-Bracho, now the Parador Nacional Gil Blas. On the left rises the massive Torre Borja-Barreda (15th c.), with a Gothic-arched doorway. From here Calle de las Lindas leads into Calle del Cantón, at the corner of which is the Casa de los Valdivieso. In Calle del Cantón are the Palacio del Marqués de Santillana and the Casa de los Hombrones, with a coat of arms

Tour of
the town

Coat of arms in
Santillana

Casa de los Velarde

supported by two warriors. From here we turn left, following a small stream which feeds a cattle-trough in the Plaza de la Colegiata, the square in front of the church. The most notable houses in the square are the Renaissance-style Casa de Quevedo and the Baroque Casa de Cossío. Beyond the church, to the right, is the Plaza de las Arenas, with the three-storey battlemented Casa de los Velarde, an unusually massive house for Santillana.

La Colegiata

The collegiate church of Santillana, the most important church of the kind in Cantabria, occupies the whole of the north side of the Plaza de la Colegiata. It was built in the 12th century on the site of an earlier church in which the relics of St Juliana were preserved, and has an image of the saint over the main doorway. The interior of the church, remodelled in Gothic style, has groined vaulting. Its most notable features are the sarcophagus of St Juliana (15th c.), a retablo with paintings by Jorge Inglés (1453), a Mexican silver altar frontal and Romanesque sculpture on the high altar.

★Cloister

On the north side of the church is a beautiful Romanesque cloister dating from the late 12th century. The three surviving sides have paired columns with finely carved capitals.

Santo Domingo de la Calzada   J 2

Province: La Rioja (LO). Telephone dialling code: 941
Altitude: 638m/2093ft. Population: 5500

The little town of Santo Domingo de la Calzada, on the Río Oja, was one of the principal staging-points for pilgrims travelling to Santiago de Compostela on the Way of St James (see entry). Its old 24-arched stone bridge is a memorial to the hermit, born in the nearby village of Viloria, who built this bridge, a church, a hospice and a stretch of paved road for pilgrims and is now revered as Santo Domingo de la Calzada, St Dominic of the Causeway.

Sights

The Romanesque/Gothic Cathedral (1180) occupies the site of an earlier church built by Santo Domingo. The free-standing Baroque tower was built in 1767, the doorway in 1769. The high altar has a magnificent retablo by Damián Forment. To the right of the altar is a Gothic baldachin over the 12th century tomb of Santo Domingo.

★Cathedral

High up on the wall opposite the saint's tomb is an unusual feature for a church – a Gothic-style cage containing a cock and a hen. This commemorates a remarkable miracle attributed to the saint. A young man travelling to Santiago with his parents was wrongly accused of theft and was hanged; but when his sorrowing parents returned from their pilgrimage they found him still alive on the gallows. They hastened to the local judge, who was at dinner, with a roast cock and hen on the table before him. He refused to believe that the boy was still alive, declaring that he would as soon believe that the cock and hen were alive: whereupon the birds jumped up from the dish and crowed. The boy was returned to his parents, and since then a cock and hen have been kept in the Cathedral to commemorate the miracle.

The most notable of the side chapels are the Capilla de Santa Teresa, with the sarcophagus of a knight; the Capilla de Santa Verónica, with a 15th century statue of the saint; and the Capilla de San Juan Bautista, which has a magnificent Late Gothic retablo.

Opposite the Cathedral is the old pilgrim hospice, the Hospital del Santo, now a parador.

Hospital del Santo

The 16th century church of the Convento de San Francisco has a carved stone retablo (also 16th c.) by Bernardo de Fresneda.

Convento de San Francisco

The old town of Santo Domingo de la Calzada is enclosed by a 14th century wall built by Pedro the Cruel and contains a number of handsome old houses.

Old town

Segovia

G 4

Province: Segovia (SG). Telephone dialling code: 911
Altitude: 1000m/3300ft. Population: 53,000

Segovia, chief town of its province and the see of a bishop, is built on a rocky hill almost 100m/330ft high, encircled by the little rivers Eresma and Clamores, on the northern slopes of the Sierra de Guadarrama. Its picturesque situation, its unique Roman aqueduct and its numerous old medieval buildings make Segovia one of the most popular tourist destinations in Spain.

★★Situation

★★Townscape

Originally an Iberian foundation and a centre of resistance to the Romans, Segovia was for several centuries a place of considerable importance. Under the Romans, who captured it in 80 B.C., it lay at the junction of two military roads. After the Visigothic and Moorish periods the town was resettled by the Counts of Castile, and it was for long a favourite residence of the kings of Castile, including Alfonso X, the Wise. Isabella the Catholic was proclaimed Queen of Castile here in 1474. Juan Bravo, one of the leaders of the rising of the Comuneros against Charles V, was born in Segovia, and was also beheaded there. Segovia enjoyed further periods of

History

prosperity under the Trastamara dynasty, and after falling into oblivion for a time rose to fresh brilliance in the 18th century under the Bourbons. Something of this splendour can still be felt in the modern town.

★★ Roman Aqueduct

Plaza del Azoguejo

The hub of the town's traffic is the Plaza del Azoguejo, in a depression below the old town, where all the roads to Segovia meet.

The square is traversed by the magnificent Roman aqueduct (Acueducto romano), probably built in the late 1st century A.D. in the reign of Trajan, which ranks with the walls of Tarragona (see entry) as one of the two largest surviving Roman structures in Spain. The water channel, still bringing water from the Sierra de Fuenfría, 17km/11 miles away, is carried over the deep valley now occupied by the outlying districts of the town on 118 arches, built of granite blocks laid without mortar or metal cramps, with a total length of 818m/895yd. The arches range in height between 7 and 28.5m (23 and 96ft), and 43 of them, covering 276m/302yd of the total length, starting from a sharp bend in the southern part of the town, are double-tiered. The aqueduct conveys the water to the upper town, ending at the Alcázar in an underground channel.

San Justo

Just to the east of the aqueduct, higher up, is the church of San Justo, which has vivid Romanesque frescoes in the apse.

San Antonio el Real

On the southern outskirts of the town, at the end of the aqueduct, is the monastery of San Antonio el Real, founded by Henry IV in the 15th century. The church has a beautiful artesonado ceiling and several Flemish retablos.

Eastern Old Town

San Juan de los Caballeros

From the Plaza del Azoguejo steps beside the aqueduct ascend to the upper town. From the top a street to the right leads to the Plaza Colmenares, on

Roman aqueduct

Plazuela San Martín

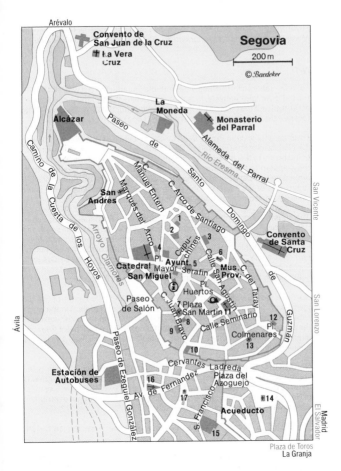

Segovia

200 m

© Baedeker

Arévalo

Convento de
San Juan de la Cruz
La Vera
Cruz

La
Moneda

Alcázar

Monasterio
del Parral

Camino de la Cuesta de los Hoyos

Paseo de Santo Domingo

Río Eresma

Alameda del Parral

San Vicente

San
Andres

C. Manuel Enter

C. Marqués del Arco

C. Arco de Santiago

1
2

Convento
de Santa
Cruz

3

4

Capuchines

6

Catedral

Pl. Ayunt. 5
Mayor

Calle San Agustín

Mus.
Prov.

San Salvador

C. del Taray

San Lorenzo

San Miguel

Serafín

Pl.
Huertos

Paseo
de Salón

C. Juan Bravo

7 Plaza
San Martín 11

8

12
Pl.
Colmenares

Madrid El Salvador

Guzmán

9

Calle Seminario

13

10

Cervantes

Ladreda
Plaza del
Azoguejo

Estación de
Autobuses

16

14

17

Acueducto

Paseo de Ezequiel González

Av. de Fernandez

S. Francisco

15

Ávila

Plaza de Toros
La Granja

1 San Esteban	10 Casa de los Picos
2 Palacio Episcopal	11 San Agustín
3 Torre de Hercules	12 San Juan de los Caballeros
4 Palacio del Marqués del Arco	(Museo Zuloaga)
5 La Trinidad	13 San Sebastián
6 San Nicolás	14 San Justo
7 San Martín	15 Academia de Artillería
8 Torreon de los Lozoya	16 San Millán
9 Palacio de los Condes de Alpuente	17 San Clemente

the east side of the old town. In this square is the church of San Juan de los
Caballeros, once the place of burial of the leading families of Segovia, now
deconsecrated and occupied by the Museo Zuloaga, with works by the
painter Ignacio Zuloaga and the potter Daniel Zuloaga.

In the Plaza de San Pablo, a short distance west of Plaza Colmenares, are
two fine noble mansions, the 14th century Casa de Lozoya and the Palacio
del Conde de Villares, once the seat of the Inquisition.

Plaza de
San Pablo

Museo Provincial
de Bellas Artes

From the Plaza de San Pablo Calle San Agustín leads to the Provincial Museum of Art (pictures, engravings), housed in the Casa del Hidalgo.

Western Old Town

Casa de
los Picos

Calle Cervantes climbs steeply up from the aqueduct to the western part of the old town (alternatively, take the steps beside the aqueduct and turn left at the top) and the Casa de los Picos (so called after the faceted stones of the façade), the 15th century palace of Pedro López de Ayala.

★ Plazuela
San Martín

From here Calle Juan Bravo, lined by shops, bars and restaurants, leads to the picturesque little Plazuela de San Martín (on the right, above the street). In the centre of the square is a fountain, with two figures of mermaids. From the steps up to the square, to the west, can be seen a house with a four-arched gallery between two larger houses. This was the birthplace of Juan Bravo, one of the leaders of the rising of the Comuneros. To the left is the massive Torreón de los Lozoya (16th c.).

★ San Martín

The square takes its name from the 12th century Romanesque church of San Martín. This has pillared Romanesque galleries on the north, south and west sides which have richly carved capitals with floral motifs and Biblical scenes. The Gothic Capilla de Herrera contains tombs of the Herrera family, and the Capilla Mayor has a fine recumbent figure of Christ by Gregorio Fernández. There is a valuable church treasury.
Adjoining the church is the old Prison.

Plaza Mayor

North-west of San Martín is the Plaza Mayor, the lively centre of the old town, with pavement cafés and a bandstand in the middle. On the north side is the plain Ayuntamiento (Town Hall; 17th c.), on the south-east side the church of San Miguel (by Gil de Hontañón, 1558), which has a fine high altar of 1572 and a number of tombs. Isabella the Catholic was proclaimed queen in this church.

★ San Esteban

North of the Plaza Mayor, in the slightly sloping Plaza de San Esteban, is the church of San Esteban with its tall tower, which consists of six segments relieved by arches and is topped by a steeple with a weathercock. Like most of Segovia's Romanesque churches, San Esteban has a loggia or atrium in which meetings of the guilds were held.

Palacio Episcopal

The Bishop's Palace, in the same square, dates from the 16th–18th centuries.

Plaza de
la Trinidad

Close by is the Plaza de la Trinidad, with the Torre de Hércules and the church of La Trinidad.

★ Cathedral

On the highest point in the old town stands the cathedral, an imposing Late Gothic structure in yellow stone built by Juan and Rodrigo Gil de Hontañón between 1525 and 1593. It is of impressive effect with its vigorously articulated exterior and its 100m/330ft high tower topped by a dome and lantern (1558).

Interior

The light interior, 105m/345ft long and of great height, has rich stellar vaulting, vivid stained glass and fine sculpture and altars in the chapels, which are closed by grilles. On the marble high altar is a 14th century ivory figure of the Virgen de la Paz. On the south side of the ambulatory is the Capilla del Santísimo Sacramento, with a richly decorated altar. In the north aisle, to the right of the doorway, the Capilla de la Piedad has a polychrome wood "Lamentation" by Juan de Juni (1571) and a triptych by

Segovia Cathedral against the backdrop of the Sierra de Guadarrama

the Flemish artist Ambrosius Benson. Opposite the Capilla de la Piedad, beyond the choir, is the Capilla del Cristo del Consuelo, which has a richly decorated doorway and contains the tombs of Bishops Raimundo de Losana and Diego de Covarrubias.

From the Capilla del Cristo del Consuelo we continue into the Cloister (Claustro), built between 1524 and 1530, mostly with material from the cloister of the old cathedral near the Alcázar which was destroyed in the 16th century. In the rooms opening off the cloister and in the Archive Room on the upper floor is the Cathedral Museum (Museo Catedralicio), with valuable church furnishings, including pictures by Ribera and others. Its principal treasures, however, are its very fine 16th and 17th century Brussels tapestries, in particular a series on the story of Queen Zenobia of Palmyra. The Chapterhouse (Sala Capitular) has a beautiful artesonado ceiling.

Cloister

★ Alcázar

From the Plaza de la Catedral Calle del Marqués del Arco runs north-west, passing the Romanesque church of San Andrés (12th c.), which has a Baroque interior.

San Andrés

Calle de Daoiz leads to the Plaza del Alcázar, from which there are fine views, particularly of the churches in the valley to the east.

Plaza del Alcázar

The Alcázar, built on a steep-sided crag between the valleys of the Eresma and the Clamores, which join here, is a magnificent example of the military architecture of Old Castile, originally dating from the 11th century. It was rebuilt by Alfonso the Wise in the 13th century and enlarged and embellished in the 15th and 16th centuries. The marriage of Philip II and Anne of

History

Alcázar: courtyard . . .   *. . . and view from the Río Eresma*

Austria was celebrated here. The Alcázar was badly damaged by fire in 1862 but was subsequently restored.

The castle is entered through the Torre de Juan II, which is ringed by ten semicircular turrets (*cubos*). This tower and the round helm-roofed Torre del Homenaje at the opposite end of the Alcázar both date from the 14th century. The laborious climb up the Torre de Juan II – laborious because of the cramped conditions – is rewarded by superb views of the town, the Sierra de Guadarrama and the Meseta.

A tour of the castle gives some idea of the life-style of the high nobility in the 15th and 16th centuries. Visitors are shown eleven rooms built round two inner courtyards. The first notable room on the tour is the Sala del Trono (Throne Room), with a magnificent gilded ceiling. Beyond this is the Sala de la Galera, with arched windows from which there are fine views of the river valley. Then follow a number of rooms furnished in period style, with tapestries, arms and armour, and the chapel. From the small courtyard below the Torre de Homenaje the tour turns back, passing through three rooms containing a museum of military history.

Outside the Walls

A road encircles the hill outside the walls of the old town, affording fine views of the walled town and passing a number of interesting churches.

San Clemente

From the Plaza del Azoguejo the Avenida de Fernández Ladreda runs south-west to the Romanesque church of San Clemente (13th c.), with an interesting apse. To the right of the Capilla Mayor are 13th century wall paintings.

San Millán

Farther on is another Romanesque church, San Millán, which was built between 1111 and 1124 and is thus one of Segovia's oldest churches. The interior, predominantly Baroque, is decorated with frescoes. There are also remains of Romanesque frescoes in the chancel.

Beyond San Millán we reach the little road which runs round the hill beneath the circuit of walls, still almost complete. The walls, which are built on Iberian foundations, were improved and strengthened by the Romans and restored in the 11th and 12th centuries. At intervals in the walls are 86 semicircular towers (*cubos*), and there are three imposing gates.

Town walls

The road curves round the north-eastern tip of the town, crosses the Río Eresma and turns right. From this point there is a good view of the Alcázar in all its towering majesty.

★View of Alcázar

Just beyond the bridge a narrow road goes off on the left to three ecclesiastical buildings. First, in a low-lying area to the left of the road, stands the massive 17th century pilgrimage church of the Virgen de la Fuencisla, beyond which is the Convento de San Juan de la Cruz, a house of Discalced Carmelites founded in 1576 by St John of the Cross, of which he was prior for some time; it is now an old people's home.

Convento de San Juan de la Cruz

On the opposite side of the road, standing alone, is the round church of the Vera Cruz (Holy Cross), built in 1208–17. Originally a Templar church, it was modelled on the church of the Holy Sepulchre in Jerusalem and has 13th century wall paintings.

Vera Cruz

A few hundred metres farther on another side road branches off the "ring road" on the left, crosses the Eresma and comes to the Monasterio del Parral, a Hieronymite house founded by Henry IV in 1447 and financed by the Marqués de Villena. The church, in Isabelline style, has a massive 16th century retablo and contains two alabaster tombs of 1528, one being that of the founder.

Monasterio del Parral

Almost opposite the monastery on the left bank of the river, at the bridge, is the old Mint (Moneda), in which Spanish coins were minted until 1730.

Moneda

The road below the town walls, now returns to the Plaza del Azoguejo, passing on the left the Convento de Santa Cruz (founded 1217), which has an Isabelline doorway.

Convento de Santa Cruz

From the Convento de Santa Cruz a road leads to the church of San Lorenzo, in the outer district of that name. Its tower and tripartite apse are magnificent examples of Mudéjar architecture.

San Lorenzo

Surroundings of Segovia

C 605 runs north-west from Segovia to Santa María la Real de Nieva (28km/17 miles), with a church which has a particularly beautiful cloister.

Santa María la Real de Nieva

N 110 leads south-west from Segovia to the major junction with N VI, just beyond which is Villacastín (alt. 1040m/3412ft). This little town on the western slopes of the Sierra de Guadarrama has old mansions and a notable parish church (15th–17th c.) with two fine retablos and a number of tombs.

Villacastín

A minor road which branches off N 603 within the built-up area of Segovia runs south-west to the country mansion of Riofrío, built by Philip V's widow, who did not wish to return to La Granja. The house now contains a Hunting Museum.

★Riofrío

★★La Granja de San Ildefonso

N 601, going south-east from Segovia into the Sierra de Guadarrama, comes in 11km/7 miles to the little town of San Ildefonso (alt. 1040m/

The Rococo gardens of La Granja

3412ft), a favourite resort of the people of Madrid, particularly at weekends. The town, beautifully situated at the foot of the massive peak of Peñalara, grew up around a monastic grange (*granja*) and hospice.

In the early 18th century Philip V chose San Ildefonso, with its good air, as the site of a palace modelled on Louis XIV's Versailles which was built between 1721 and 1739.

Palace

Visitors approach the palace from its rear front, which is dominated by the imposing palace church. A conducted tour of the palace takes in the Throne Room and other apartments which have superb Flemish, French and Spanish tapestries. In the church is the red marble tomb of Philip V and his wife Isabella Farnese.

Gardens

The beautiful gardens below the main front of the palace, reached by way of the magnificent Grand Cascade, were designed by the French landscape architects Etienne Boutelou and René Carlier. Framed in old trees, the gardens are filled with an extraordinary profusion and variety of fountains and sculpture, mostly the work of René Fremin and Jean Fermy. Round almost every corner visitors will encounter another lively allegorical group.

Fountains

The whole complex of fountains makes an impressive display. They are turned on only at Easter and on May 30th, July 25th and August 25th at 5.30pm.

Puerto de Navacerrada

Beyond San Ildefonso N 601 climbs into the wooded hills of the Sierra de Guadarrama. On the pass, the Puerto de Navacerrada (1860m/6103ft), is a ski resort much frequented by winter sports enthusiasts from the Madrid area.

Castles Tour

Turégano

Leave Segovia on N 601, going north-west, and in 9.5km/6 miles turn right into N 603, which runs north-east to (34km/21 miles) Turégano (alt.

936m/3071ft), a little episcopal town with an arcaded Plaza Mayor over which looms a partly ruined castle of the 13th–15th centuries with a massive keep. Within its battlemented walls is the Romanesque church of San Miguel, with a striking bell-cote.

15km/9 miles beyond Turégano on C 603 lies Cantalejo, 24km/15 miles north of which is Fuentidueña, with the ruins of two Romanesque churches and a formidable castle.   Fuentidueña

From Cantalejo a minor road runs 15km/9 miles north-east to the picturesque little town of Sepúlveda (alt. 1032m/3386ft), situated high above a loop on the Río Duratón. This was the Roman settlement of Septempublica, and it still has well preserved Roman walls as well as several Romanesque churches. Lower down is the commandingly situated 11th century church of El Salvador, with a galleried portico and a free-standing bell-tower, from which there is a breathtaking panoramic view. The Castillo was founded by Fernán González.   Sepúlveda

From Sepúlveda follow SG 233 south-west towards Pedraza. At the road junction known as the Cuatro Carreteras a road goes off on the left to Castilnovo (12th–15th c.), originally a Moorish stronghold.   Castilnovo

Pedraza claims to be the birthplace of the Emperor Trajan. The little town is dominated by a massive castle on a high rocky crag. Around the attractive Plaza Mayor, a very typical Castilian square, are the Romanesque Torre San Juan and the Casa de la Inquisición, now an inn.   Pedraza

10km/6 miles beyond Pedraza SG 233 joins N 110, which continues south-west by way of Collado Hermoso to Segovia.

Other Excursions from Segovia

See Ávila, Arévalo, Coca, El Escorial and Madrid.

Seo de Urgel/La Seu d'Urgell   O 2

Province: Lérida (L). Telephone dialling code: 973
Altitude: 700m/2300ft. Population: 10,000

In the wide valley of the Río Segre, framed by the Pyrenees, is the little episcopal town of Seo de Urgel (Catalan La Seu d'Urgel, or La Seu for short), which now lives by dairy farming, textile processing and, increasingly, tourism. The Bishop of Seo de Urgel is one of the co-rulers of the little state of Andorra, the other being the President of France.

Sights

The Cathedral of Seo de Urgel, La Seu, which is dedicated to the Virgin, stands on the site of an earlier church consecrated in 839. It was founded in 1116 by Bishop Hermengol (St Hermengaudius) and built mainly by a master builder from Italy, Ramón Llombard, between 1175 and 1183; Italian influence can be detected in the four subsidiary apses at the end of the aisles and the design of the façades. After being rebuilt in the 18th century the Cathedral was restored to its original Romanesque form at the beginning of the 20th century. It has a Gothic high altar and contains a number of fine reliquaries. Its great glory, however, is the cloister, built in the 13th century by a master from Roussillon, as is indicated by the carved capitals of the columns. The east side was restored in the early 17th century.   Cathedral

Cathedral cloister, Seo de Urgel

Museo Diocesano/ Museu Diocesà	The principal treasure of the Diocesan Museum is an 11th century copy of Beatus of Liébana's Commentary on the Apocalypse, magnificently illuminated. Outstanding among other exhibits are a papyrus Bull of Pope Sylvester II (1001) and the silver shrine of St Hermengaudius by Pedro Llopart (18th c.).
San Miguel/ Sant Miquel	Adjoining the Cathedral cloister, and accessible from it, is the 11th century church of San Miguel (Catalan Sant Miquel; also called Sant Père), which has fine Romanesque wall paintings.
Barrio Medieval	Around the Cathedral extends the Barrio Medieval, the old medieval quarter, with the Bishop's Palace (Catalan Palau Episcopal) and other old houses, particularly in the Carrer Major and Carrer dels Canonges.

Surroundings of Seo de Urgel

Winter sports	Seo de Urgel is the chief place in the Alt Urgell district, which offers ideal conditions for langlauf skiing. Within easy reach of the town, around the skiing stations of Sant Joan de l'Erm and Tuixént-La Vansa, are prepared cross-country trails running through the beautiful Pyrenean forests, of various lengths and all degrees of difficulty. There are also facilities for langlauf in the Cerdanya region to the east, near Núria, La Molina, Lles and Aránser.
Summer sports	In summer the two principal rivers of Alt Urgell, the Río Segre and the Río Valira, are popular with fast-water canoeists. The fast-water canoeing events of the 1992 Summer Olympics were held in Seo de Urgel.
	The slopes of the Pyrenees offer endless scope for hill walkers and climbers, and the rivers and streams provide good sport for anglers.

Seo de Urgel is the southern gateway to the Pyrenean republic of Andorra   Andorra
(see entry), which is within easy reach for a day trip.

Seville   E 8

Province: Sevilla (SE). Telephone dialling code: 954
Altitude: 10m/33ft. Population: 678,000

★★ Capital of Andalusia

Sevilla (in Spanish Sevilla), Spain's fourth-largest city, chief town of its
province and capital of Andalusia, the see of an archbishop and a university
town, lies in a fertile plain on the left bank of the Río Guadalquivir. Here the
Guadalquivir emerges into the Andalusian lowlands, and at high tide – the
effect of which is felt for more than 100km/60 miles up the river – it is
possible for seagoing vessels of some size to reach the river port of Seville,
87km/54 miles from the sea, using a channel which bypasses the last bend
on the river before the town. In 1948–49 the main channel of the Guadalquivir was diverted to the west side of the town; the port installations,
however, are still on the old river-bed. Seville is also an important industrial
town (foodstuffs, textiles, metal-processing).

With the abundance of art and architecture which it has inherited from
many centuries of history and the lively and bustling activity of a southern
Mediterranean town which is also a port, Seville fully justifies the old
saying, "Quien no ha visto Sevilla, no ha visto maravilla" ("If you have not
seen Seville you have missed a marvel").

Seville was the birthplace of two famous painters, Diego Velázquez
(1599–1660) and Bartolomé Esteban Murillo (1617–82). Many commemorative tablets in the streets of the town recall scenes from the works of
Cervantes. Seville is also famous as the setting of Mozart's "Don Giovanni"
and "Marriage of Figaro" and of Bizet's "Carmen"; and a number of streets
claim the honour of having Figaro's barber shop in Rossini's "Barber of
Seville".

Seville has one of the hottest climates in mainland Europe (up to   Climate
48°C/118°F). Accordingly the houses usually have patios, decked with
flowers and a plashing fountain, often tantalisingly glimpsed from the
street, which provide a cool retreat in the heat of summer.

When the Romans arrived here about 205 B.C. they found a town which they   History
named Hispalis, perhaps an Iberian or Phoenician foundation. In the time of
Caesar it became an important port under the name of Colonia Julia
Romula. In the 5th century A.D. it was successively the capital of the Vandals
(411) and the Visigoths (441). In 712 the Moors captured the town, which
they called Ihbiliya. Subsequently it was ruled by the Umayyads (from 913),
the Almoravids (from 1091) and the Almohads (from 1147). Under Yusuf
Abu Yakub (1163–84) and Yakub ibn Yusuf (1184–98) many splendid buildings were erected in Seville, and for a time the city exceeded even Córdoba
in population. In 1248 Ferdinand III of Castile recaptured the town and
made it his residence. The king most popular in Seville – in spite of his
name – was Pedro the Cruel (1350–69). On his return from his first voyage
to the New World, on March 31st 1493, Columbus was given a ceremonial
reception in Seville.

Amerigo Vespucci planned his voyage to America in the town, and
Magellan sailed from here on his circumnavigation of the globe. Thereafter
Seville gained a monopoly of overseas trade and became Spain's principal
port. Later the town's importance declined, but its prosperity revived following the regulation of the Guadalquivir, which brought seagoing trade
back to Seville.

The world exhibition EXPO '92 brought considerable improvements to the   EXPO '92
infrastructure of Seville. These included the expansion of the airport,

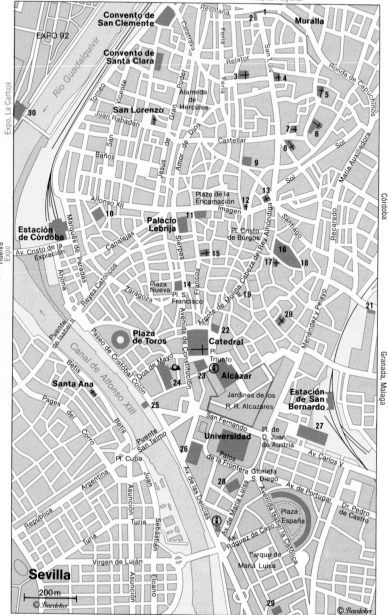

Hospital Regional

Convento de San Clemente

EXPO 92

Convento de Santa Clara

Muralla

Río Guadalquivir

San Lorenzo

Alameda de Hércules

Castellar

Estación de Córdoba

Palacio Lebrija

Plaza de la Encarnación

Pl. Cristo de Burgos

Plaza Nueva

Pl. S. Francisco

Plaza de Toros

Catedral

Pl. Triunfo

Alcázar

Santa Ana

Universidad

Jardines de los R. R. Alcázares

Estación de San Bernardo

Pl. de D. Juan de Austria

Palos de la Frontera

Glorieta S. Diego

Plaza España

Parque de María Luisa

Sevilla

200 m

© Baedeker

Expo. La Cartuja

Huelva Expo

Córdoba

Granada, Málaga

Dr. de Pedro de Castro

Museo Arqueológico Jerez

rebuilding of Santa Justa railway station for the high speed AVE train to Madrid and completion of the motorway link with Madrid. The townscape was also dramatically altered by the construction of spectacular bridges over the Guadalquivir "La Barqueta" and "Alamillo". However, the high expectations concerning job creation and economic revival were only partly met. By the end of the spectacle the initial euphoria had gradually given way to disillusion.

★★ Fiestas

The Semana Santa (Holy Week) celebrations in Seville are one of the most impressive festivals in Spain. Particularly striking are the processions of the brotherhoods (*cofradías, hermandades*) from the different quarters of the town, clad in penitents' garb and carrying richly decked figures of saints (*pasos*), and the main procession in the night before Good Friday and on Good Friday morning. The ceremonies in the Cathedral during Holy Week are of particular splendour.

Semana Santa

The April Fair is a six-day secular festival, during which *sevillanas* are sung and danced in the streets.

Feria de Abril

The Romería del Rocio, in Whit week, is one of the most celebrated pilgrimages in Spain, in which groups of pilgrims from Seville, Huelva, Cádiz, Jerez and other towns travel on horseback, on mules or in ox-carts to Almonte in Huelva province to pay honour to Nuestra Señora del Rocio in her azulejo-clad church in the presence of the Archbishop of Seville.

Romería del Rocio

★★ Cathedral

Seville Cathedral, one of the largest and richest Gothic cathedrals in Christendom, unmatched in its impressive spatial effect and its abundance of art treasures, was built between 1402 and 1506 on the site of the town's principal mosque.

Entrance Puerta de San Cristobel (south transept)

On the east side of the cathedral, between the Puerta de los Palos and the Puerta de Oriente, which gives access to the Patio de los Naranjos, rises the Giralda ("Weathercock"), the 93m/305ft high tower which is the landmark and emblem of Seville. The tower was originally built in 1184–96 as the minaret of the Great Mosque; the bell-chamber added in 1568 is topped by a weathervane 4m/13ft high, the Giraldillo, in the form of a female figure representing Faith and carrying the banner of Constantine. From the first gallery, with 24 bells, at a height of 70m/230ft, there are extensive views of the city and surrounding area. Above this gallery is the Matraca, a timber structure housing the rattles which are used during Holy Week instead of bells.

★★ Giralda

The imposing Puerta del Perdón on the north side of the cathedral, which dates from the Moorish period, leads into the Patio de los Naranjos (Court of Orange-Trees), originally the forecourt of the mosque. The octagonal

★ Patio de los Naranjos

1 Puerto Macarena	12 San Pedro	22 Palacio Arzobispal
2 San Gil	13 Santa Catalina	23 Casa Lonja
3 Omnium Sanctorum	14 Ayuntamiento	(Archivo de Indias)
4 Santa Marina	15 San Salvador	24 Hospital de la Caridad
5 San Julián	16 Convento de	25 Torre del Oro
6 Convento de Santa Paula	San Leandro	26 Palacio San Telmo
7 Santa Isabel	17 San Ildefonso	27 Estación de Autobuses
8 San Marcos	18 Casa de Pilatos	28 Teatro Lope de Vega
9 Casa de la Dueñas	19 Monolitos Romanos	29 Museo de Artes y
10 Museo de Bellas Artes	20 Santa María la Blanca	Costumbres Populares
11 Pabellón Sevillanos Illustres	21 Acueducto	30 Entrance to Expo '92

Visigothic fountain in the centre is a remnant of the Islamic *midha,* the fountain for religious ablutions.

In the south-east corner of the courtyard is the Capilla de la Granada, another relic of the old mosque, with a fine horseshoe arch. On the east side is the Biblioteca Colombina, founded in the 13th century and enriched by a bequest from Fernando Colón, Columbus's son, which contains rare works on the discovery of America and valuable manuscripts, including some by Columbus himself.

Doorways

The finest of the cathedral's doorways, all of which are richly decorated with statues and reliefs, are the Puerta del Bautismo (Doorway of the Baptism) and the Puerta del Nacimiento (Doorway of the Nativity), to left and right of the Puerta Mayor on the west front, with figural decoration by Lorenzo Mercadante and Pedro Millán. In the south transept is the modern Puerta de San Cristóbal or Puerta de la Lonja; on the east side are the Puerta de las Campanillas (Doorway of the Little Bells) and the Puerta de los Palos.

Interior

The five-aisled interior (117m/384ft long, 76m/249ft wide, 40m/130ft high) is one of the most impressive among the Gothic churches of Spain, notable for the clarity of its proportions and the beauty of its lines as well as for the abundance of art treasures it contains (only a selection of which can be mentioned here). Of the 75 stained glass windows (16th–19th c.) the oldest are those by Cristóbal Alemán (1504) and Arnao de Flandes (1525–57).

At the west end of the nave is the tomb of Columbus's son Fernando (d. 1539).

Side chapels

The side chapels contain numerous tombs and altarpieces. Particularly notable among the altarpieces are two by Murillo, the "Guardian Angel" to the right of the Puerta Mayor and another in the Capilla de San Antonio (the second in the north aisle), with the "Baptism of Christ" and "The Infant Christ appearing to St Antony of Padua"; this chapel also has a picture by Jordaens. Among the finest of the tombs are the Gothic monument of Juan de Cervantes in the Capilla de San Hermenegildo and the Plateresque tomb of Archbishop Mendoza in the Capilla de la Antigua.

Choir

The Choir has a beautiful *reja* (grille) of 1519 and Gothic choir-stalls of 1475–79.

★ Capilla Mayor

In the Capilla Mayor, which also has a large and richly wrought *reja,* the dominant feature is the resplendent retablo, a masterpiece of Gothic wood-carving. In the centre is a silver image of the Virgen de la Sede surrounded by 45 scenes from the life of Christ and the life of the Virgin.

Monument of Columbus

In the south transept, just inside the Puerta de San Cristóbal, can be seen the monument of Columbus (by Arturo Mélida), originally erected in Havana Cathedral in 1892 and brought here after the loss of Cuba in the Spanish-American War of 1898.

★ Capilla Real

Behind the Capilla Mayor, at the east end of the Cathedral, is the Capilla Real, a Renaissance structure 38m/125ft long with a high dome, built between 1551 and 1575 on the site of an earlier royal funerary chapel. Behind the grille (1773) are the tombs of King Alfonso the Wise and his mother Beatrice of Sweden. In the apse are two altars: one in front, with a silver shrine (1729) containing the remains of St Ferdinand, and the other to the rear with a 13th century figure of the Virgen de los Reyes, patroness of the town. Steps beside the front altar lead down to the Panteón, with the tombs of Pedro the Cruel, his wife María de Padilla and several infantes.

To the left of the Capilla Real is the Puerta de los Palos.

The Giralda, landmark of Seville ▶

Seville

Sacristía de los Cálices

The Sacristía de los Cálices, to the right of the Capilla Mayor, contains a famous crucifix by Montañés as well as numerous pictures, including works by Goya, Zurbarán, Morales and Murillo.

★Sacristía Mayor

The Sacristía Mayor, which is entered through an antechamber (admission charge), is a magnificent 16th century structure with a beautiful domed ceiling. It contains a number of fine pictures, a large candelabrum and a crucifix by Pieter de Kempeneer, and also houses the rich Cathedral Treasury, which includes the key of Seville (1248) and the crown of the Virgen de los Reyes, decked with precious stones.

Chapterhouse

In the south-east corner of the Cathedral the Plateresque Chapterhouse (Sala Capitular; 1530–92) contains Murillo's "Immaculate Conception".

Sagrario

On the north side of the Cathedral, reached through the Puerta del Sagrario (on left), is the Sagrario (1618–62), a handsome Baroque building, now serving as the parish church. It has a retablo with a "Descent from the Cross" by Pedro Roldán.

Between the Cathedral and the Alcázar

Casa Lonja
(Archivo General de Indias)

South of the Cathedral is the Plaza del Triunfo, on the south-west side of which is the Casa Lonja, the former Exchange, a High Renaissance building by Juan de Herrera (1583–98). On the first floor, housed here since 1781, is the General Archive of the Indies, with many thousands of documents relating to the discovery and conquest of America and the Philippines,

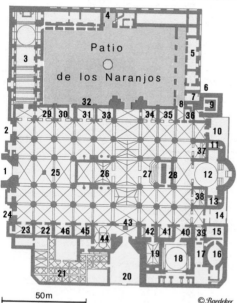

Patio de los Naranjos

50m
© Baedeker

1 Puerta Mayor
2 Puerta del Bautismo
3 Sagrario
4 Puerta del Perdón
5 Biblioteca Colombina
6 Puerta de Oriente
7 Capilla de la Granada (Granatapfelkapelle)
8 Puerta del Lagarto (Eidechsenporte)
9 Giralda
10 Puerta de los Palos
11 Sala Capitular
12 Capilla Real
13 Sakristei
14 Puerta de las Campanillas (Portal der Glöckchen)
15 Contaduría Mayor
16 Sala Capitular
17 Antecabildo
18 Sacristía Mayor
19 Sacristía de los Cálices (Sakristei der Kelche)
20 Puerta de San Cristóbal (Puerta de la Lonja)
21 Dependencias de la Hermandad Sacramental
22 Capilla de Santa Ana
23 Capilla de San Laureano
24 Puerta del Nacimiento
25 Grabstein des Fernando Colón

26 Coro
27 Capilla Mayor
28 Sacristía Alta
29 Capilla de San Antonio
30 Capilla de Escalas
31 Capilla de Santiago
32 Capilla Sacramental

33 Capilla de San Francisco
34 Capilla de las Doncellas
35 Capilla de los Evangelistas
36 Capilla del Pilar
37 Capilla de San Pedro
38 Capilla de la Concepción Grande
39 Capilla del Mariscal

40 Antesala (Vorraum)
41 Capilla de San Andrés
42 Capilla de Dolores
43 Grabdenkmal des Kolumbus
44 Capilla de la Antigua
45 Capilla de San Hermenegildo
46 Capilla de San José

including autograph documents of Magellan, Pizarro and Cortés, Columbus's diary and plans of Spanish foundations in the New World.

In Calle Santo Tomás, which flanks the south side of the Casa Lonja, is the Museum of Contemporary Art, housed in the Old Chapterhouse.

Museo de Arte Contemporáneo

To the east of the Alcázar lies the picturesque Barrio de Santa Cruz, which in Arab times was the Jewish quarter (Judería). It is now a district of flower-decked squares and streets, with many attractive patios.

★Barrio de Santa Cruz

In this area is the Asilo de Venerables Sacerdotes, a hospice for aged priests, which contains a number of fine works of art, including frescoes by Valdés Leal in the chapel, an ivory figure of Christ by Alonso Cano and works by Rubens and Roelas.

Asilo de Venerables Sacerdotes

Farther east, at Calle Santa Teresa 8, is a house which is believed to have been occupied by the painter Bartolomé Esteban Murillo.

Casa Murillo

Still further east is the church of Santa María la Blanca, which until 1391 was a synagogue. The dome has a painting of 1659.

Santa María la Blanca

★Alcázar

On the south-east side of the Plaza del Triunfo stands the Alcázar, the stronghold of the Moorish and later of the Christian kings. The present structure, still with the aspect of a medieval fortress, was built by Moorish architects in the second half of the 14th century, in the reign of Pedro the Cruel. The entrance leads into the Patio de las Banderas, planted with orange-trees, and through the Jardín del Crucero into the Patio de la Montería, the Court of the Royal Bodyguard, on the south side of which is the richly articulated main front of the Alcázar proper.

The Alcázar is entered through the Puerta Principal, from which a narrow passage to the left leads into the Patio de las Doncellas (Court of the Maids of Honour), built between 1369 and 1379, with magnificent cusped arches and open arabesque work above, borne on 52 marble columns; the glazed gallery was added in the 16th century.

Tour of the Alcázar
★Patio de las Doncellas

On the north side of the Patio de las Doncellas the Salón de Carlos V has a beautiful coffered ceiling, and adjoining this are the apartments of María de Padilla, Pedro the Cruel's favourite, and the long Dining Room (Comedor). This leads into the Salón de Embajadores (Hall of the Ambassadors), the oldest room in the Alcázar, with a superb cedarwood stalactitic dome (1420), inscriptions in Arabic script and decorative friezes. From here, passing through Philip II's Bedchamber, we come into the little Moorish Patio de las Muñecas (Court of the Dolls), the inner courtyard of the private apartments. To the left of this is the Dormitorio de Isabel la Católica, the Queen's Bedchamber, preceded by the Salón del Príncipe. To the right is the beautifully tiled Dormitorio de los Reyes Moros, the Bedchamber of the Moorish Kings.

Ground floor

★Salón de Embajadores

From the Patio de la Montería a magnificent staircase leads to the upper floor, on which are the apartments of the Catholic Monarchs. Particularly fine is the Chapel Royal, with an azulejo-clad altar by Nicoloso Pisano.

Upper floor

To the left of the Patio de la Montería, through the Jardín del Crucero, are the Apartments of Charles V. The private chapel is richly decorated with azulejos; the other rooms are hung with Flemish tapestries of the 16th–18th centuries, the most interesting of which are those depicting the conquest of Tunis.

Apartments of Charles V

The gardens of the Alcázar, laid out by Charles V, are divided into two by a rocaille wall. Their most notable features are an underground bath-house and the Pabellón de Carlos V (1540).

★ Alcázar Gardens

North of the Cathedral

Plaza
San Francisco

The central feature of the town, a little way north of the Cathedral, is the Plaza San Francisco, once the scene of executions, tournaments and bullfights.

★ Ayuntamiento

On the west side of the square stands the Ayuntamiento (Town Hall), an imposing Renaissance building (1527–64) with a richly decorated east front, one of the most charming examples of Plateresque style. It contains a number of valuable pictures by Zurbarán and other artists.

Plaza Nueva

On the west side of the Town Hall lies the spacious palm-shaded Plaza Nueva, surrounded by banks and offices.

★ Calle de
las Sierpes

On the north side of the square is the narrow Calle de las Sierpes ("Street of the Snakes"), Seville's main shopping street, now a pedestrian zone lined with shops, cafés and restaurants.

San Salvador

In Calle Jovellanos Gallegos, a turning on the right off Calle de las Sierpes, is the church of San Salvador, built in the 16th century and radically remodelled in Churrigueresque style at the end of the 18th century. It contains works by Montañés, including an "Ecce Homo", and a painting by Murillo.

Palacio Lebrija

In Calle de la Cuna, which runs north from the Plaza San Salvador, is the Palacio Lebrija, a good example of a Sevillian noble mansion, with a large staircase leading up to the entrance and an artesonado ceiling.

Universidad Vieja

The church of the Universidad Vieja (Old University), founded in 1502, which lies a short distance to the right of the Palacio Lebrija, has a large and elaborately decorated retablo and pictures by Roelas, Alonso Cano, Pacheco and other artists.

★ Casa de Pilatos

Some 500m/550yd east of San Salvador by way of Calle de Aguilas, in the Plaza de Pilatos, is the 16th century Casa de Pilatos, built by Moorish and Christian architects, which is popularly believed to be a copy of Pilate's house in Jerusalem. It shows a charming variant of the Mudéjar style, modified by Gothic and Renaissance features. The house is laid out round a beautiful patio decorated with azulejos and pieces of antique sculpture. The interior is also in Mudéjar style. Particularly fine are the Salón Dorado (Golden Room), with faience decoration and a coffered ceiling, the Grand Staircase and the private chapel. A number of rooms are occupied by a museum of Roman sculpture.

San Pedro

From the Plaza de Pilatos Calle de Caballerizas runs north-west past the twin-towered Baroque church of San Ildefonso. Beyond this Calle de los Descalzos continues into the long Plaza del Cristo de Burgos, on the north-west side of which is the Gothic church of San Pedro (14th c.), with a beautiful Mudéjar tower. Velázquez was baptised in this church.

Santa Catalina

A little way east of San Pedro is the church of Santa Catalina, with a tower which was originally the minaret of a mosque.

★ Palacio de
las Dueñas

From Santa Catalina Calle Gerona runs north-west to the 15th century Palacio de las Dueñas, which has a beautiful Mudéjar-style patio.

Around the Alameda de Hércules

Alameda de
Hércules

The continuation of Calle de las Sierpes to the north, Calle Amor de Dios, goes past the Plaza del Duque to the Alameda de Hércules, a fine promenade laid out in gardens, at the south end of which are two tall granite columns from a Roman temple, set up here in 1574, bearing statues of Hercules and Julius Caesar.

To the west of the Alameda de Hércules stands the church of San Lorenzo, with a beautiful high altar by Montañés and a much venerated figure of Christ, Nuestro Señor del Gran Poder (by Juan de Mesa), in a side chapel.

San Lorenzo

On the north side of the old town, between the Puerta de Córdoba and the Puerta de la Macarena, extends a considerable stretch of the old town walls, built on Roman foundations.

Town walls

To the left of the Puerta de la Macarena can be found the Basílica Macarena, with an image of the Virgen de la Macarena by Pedro Roldán. In a museum attached to the church are displayed the jewels and ornaments with which the image is decked on special occasions, together with the costumes worn by celebrated bullfighters.

Basílica
Macarena

★★ Museo de Bellas Artes

In the western part of the old town, reached from the Plaza del Duque by way of Calle de Alfonso XII, is the 17th century Convento de la Merced, now occupied by the Museum of Art, which has the finest collection of pictures in Spain after the Prado in Madrid, particularly of the works by 17th century Spanish painters. The museum is currently undergoing a thorough reorganisation, with the result that only two rooms are at present open where the most important paintings of the collection are on show. In the smaller room Spanish masters of the 18th to 20th centuries are represented; in the fine main room are works of the 15th to 17th c., including:

Opening times
Tues.–Sun.
9am–3pm

"St Hieronimus", "St Bruno visits Pope Urban II", "Apotheosis of Thomas Aquinas" and "Jesus on the Cross".

Zubarán

"St Thomas of Villanueva distributes alms", "Immaculate Conception", "St Justa and St Rufina" and "Vision of St Francis".

Murillo

"Portrait of his son Jorge Manuel".

El Greco

"Portrait of the Orantes couple".

Pacheco

"The Holy Family".

Uceda

"Transfiguration of St Hermengildus".

Uceda/Vazquez

"Calvary".

Cranach

"The Last Judgment".

de Vos

On the Banks of the Guadalquivir

On the south-west side of the old town, along the left bank of the Guadalquivir, here canalised (Canal de Alfonso XIII), is the Paseo de Cristóbal Colón, beginning at the Puente de Isabel II. On this stretch of the river, extending south along the Avenida de las Delicias, are the port installations.

Paseo de
Cristóbal Colón

Not far from the bridge is the Plaza de Toros, with seating for 14,000 spectators, the largest and one of the most important bullrings in Spain. There is also a bullfighting museum.

Plaza de Toros

A little farther along the left bank stands the La Maestranza cultural centre which was built for the World Exhibition.

La Maestranza

Seville

Hospital de la Caridad

On the east side of a square half way along the Paseo de Cristóbal Colón, between the Puente de Isabel II and the Puente San Telmo, stands the Hospital de la Caridad (1661–64), founded by Miguel de Mañara, who is supposed to have been the prototype of Don Juan. The church, entered from a pillared courtyard, has five azulejo pictures on the façade and contains pictures by Valdés Leal (just inside the entrance) and six paintings by Murillo in the aisles.

Torre del Oro/ Museo Marítimo

Just beyond this, on the banks of the river, rises the hexagonal Torre del Oro (1220, with additions in 1760), originally a Moorish defensive tower clad with gold azulejos and later, in the reign of Pedro the Cruel, used as a treasury and a prison. It now houses the Maritime Museum.

Palacio de San Telmo

In the Avenida de las Delicias, beyond the Puente San Telmo, is the Palacio de San Telmo, built in 1743 as a naval college and now a seminary for the training of priests (Universidad Pontificia), with a handsome Baroque doorway.

Fábrica de Tabacos

To the east, in Calle de San Fernando, is the former Fábrica de Tabacos (Tobacco Factory), a Baroque building (1757) which is now occupied by University lecture rooms.

★Parque de María Luisa

Plaza de España

To the south of the Tobacco Factory, in the Avenida de Isabel la Católica, is the main entrance to the large Parque de María Luisa, laid out by the Infanta María Luisa Fernanda de Borbón. The Ibero-American Exhibition of 1929–30 was held in the park, and a number of the buildings still remain – the Palacio Centrale, with two 82m/269ft high towers at the corners, in the semicircular Plaza de España and the Pabellón Mudéjar, Pabellón Real and Palacio del Rinacimiento in the Plaza de América.

In the Plaza de España

In the Pabellón Mudéjar the Museum of Folk Art and Costume, has a large collection, displayed on two floors, of 19th century costumes, folk arts and crafts, furniture, domestic equipment, etc.

Museo de Artes y Costumbres Populares

The Archaeological Museum displays in its 27 rooms prehistoric, Phoenician, Greek and Roman antiquities, including a magnificent statue of Diana, gold jewellery and finds from Itálica (see below, Surroundings).

★ Museo Arqueológico

Barrio de Triana

On the right bank of the Guadalquivir lies the Barrio de Triana, a working-class district which has been from time immemorial the potters' quarter of Seville, producing the best azulejos in the city. From here, near the Puente San Telmo, Magellan set out on his voyage round the world.

On the left bank of the river, near the Puente de Isabel II, stands the Mudéjar-style church of Santa Ana, built by Alfonso the Wise, which contains a "Virgen de la Rosa" by Alejo Fernández, a fine retablo and an interesting treasury.

Santa Ana

★ Former site of EXPO '92

From April 20th to October 12th 1992 Seville was home to the World Exhibition EXPO '92 in which 109 countries, 22 international organisations, the 17 autonomous regions of Spain and important manufacturers took part. The main theme "Age of Discovery" was to commemorate the 500 year anniversary of Colombus's voyage of discovery in 1492. The island of La Cartuja in the Guadalquivir river, north of the district of Triana, was chosen as the site for the exhibition and was linked to the old town of Seville by a monorail, a cablecar (telecabina) and two bridges. The exhibition was to be a showpiece of modern architecture and some spectacular buildings were constructed: the different countries' pavilions such as the Japanese pagoda (the largest wooden building in the world), the British water pavilion, the Norwegian pavilion in the shape of a North Sea pipeline, the four pavilions on the themes of "15th century", "Sea journey", "Age of Discoveries" (which actually burned down during the exhibition) and "Present and Future" – the viewing tower and spectacular bridges Alamillo and La Barqueta by Santiago Calatrava. However, the centrepiece of the exhibition was the Royal Pavilion, the only old building on the island, the former Carthusian monastery Santa Maria de las Cuevas founded in 1401 in which Colombus planned his Atlantic voyage and was used as a ceramics factory by the Englishman Pickman from 1839 onwards. The old kilns can be seen in the Pickman museum.

On balance the outcome of the exhibition was positive for the organisers: the desired number of visitors was reached, the infrastructure was improved and jobs were created. Yet it is this which the critics of the exhibition dispute. They maintain that not enough long term jobs were created, the future use of the site had not been thought out and the cost of living in Seville has since risen noticably. Of the 76 national pavilions 26 have since been demolished: the four theme pavilions, the Spain pavilion, the buildings of the autonomous regions and two panoramic cinemas have been turned into an amusement park. The remaining national and commercial pavilions are slowly being transformed into the technology park "Cartuja 93".

Outcome of EXPO '92

Surroundings of Seville

★ Itálica

Leave Seville on the Huelva road and after crossing the Guadalquivir turn right into N 630, which runs north to the village of Santiponce (8km/

Santiponce

View from the Giralda over Seville

Hall of the Ambassadors in the Alcázar, Seville

5 miles), with the much dilapidated monastery of San Isidoro del Campo, founded by Guzmán el Bueno in 1298. The church has a very beautiful carved Gothic altar and contains the tombs of the founder and his wife.

A short distance beyond the village a road goes off on the left to the Roman site of Itálica, a town founded about 205 B.C. by Scipio Africanus the Elder, later the birthplace of the Emperors Trajan and Hadrian.

Itálica

The remains include an amphitheatre with seating for 25,000 spectators and traces of houses and fountains. The fine mosaics which were found here are now mostly in the Archaeological Museum in Seville; only a few remain in situ.

＊Carmona

From Seville N IV runs east, passing the airport and continuing through a fertile upland region to Carmona (alt. 215m/705ft), the Roman Carmo and Moorish Karmuna, 30km/19 miles from Seville. This little country town, dominated by its Alcázar and still ringed by its Roman walls, lies on a bare ridge rising above the rich Vega de Corbones. On the right of the main road through the town is the church of San Pedro, with a tower resembling Seville's Giralda. Other features of interest are the church of Santa María (15th–16th c.), with a high white interior; the Plaza Mayor, surrounded by handsome old houses; and a number of old noble mansions in the town's picturesque little streets.

A signpost on the left (Necrópolis Romana) points the way to the nearby Roman cemetery, where more than 900 tombs have been brought to light, some of them with forecourts and benches for the funeral meal. The most interesting are the three-room Triclinio del Elefante, which takes its name from a stone figure of an elephant, and the large Tumba de Servilia, a beehive-shaped family tomb.

＊Roman cemetery

＊Osuna

92km/57 miles south-east of Seville on N 334 lies the historic old town of Osuna (alt. 450m/1475ft), known to the Romans as Urso and to the Moors as Oxuna. Its main features of interest are the ruined palace of the Dukes of Osuna; the collegiate church (1534), with a "Christ on the Cross" by Ribera and the family vault of the Osuna family; and the four-towered former University (1549–1824; now occupied by a school), which is mentioned in "Don Quixote".

Sierra de Gredos

F/G 4/5

Provinces: Ávila (AV), Salamanca (SA), Cáceres (CC)

The Sierra de Gredos thrusts across the Castilian plateau like a mighty rock wall, dividing it into two. Along with the lower ranges of the neighbouring Sierra de Guadarrama and Sierra de Béjar it forms the central Spanish mountain chain.

The ＊ Mountains

The central massif of the Sierra de Gredos, with its perpetually snow-capped peaks, is a region of magnificent mountain scenery and one of Spain's most popular climbing areas. The highest peak is Almanzor

Walking and climbing

(2592m/8504ft). Below the north face of Almanzor is the Laguna de Gredos, which can be reached from the Club Alpino mountain hut on a good and well waymarked path. From the Laguna de Gredos there are waymarked paths (caution required) to five picturesque mountain lakes, the Cinco Lagunas, and to Almanzor, rearing above them to the south.

Note

Information about walking and climbing in the Sierra de Gredos can be obtained from tourist information offices in Ávila, Arenas de San Pedro and El Barco de Ávila and in the Parador Nacional.

★Parador Nacional de Gredos

From Ávila C 502 runs south-west into the Sierra de Gredos. At Venta Rasquilla C 500, coming from the high valley of the Río Albeche, goes off on the right and runs below the north side of the sierra to the Parador Nacional de Gredos (alt. 1650m/5414ft), 62km/39 miles from Ávila, magnificently situated in the wooded foreland of the sierra. The parador is popular both as a health resort and as a winter sports centre. Much of this region, in which ibexes and chamois still live, is now a National Park.

Sierra Nevada   H/J 8

Province: Granada (GR)

★★Mountain scenery

The Sierra Nevada is a massive mountain chain extending for a distance of almost 110km/70 miles between the Río Almería and the Valle de Lecrín, with the highest peaks in the Iberian peninsula, the Cerro de Mulhacén (3481m/11,421ft) and the Pico de Veleta (3428m/11,247ft).

★Winter Sports

From November to June the Sierra Nevada offers magnificent facilities for winter sports, and as the most southerly winter sports region in Europe usually has a blue sky and brilliant sunshine as well as snow. Throughout the area much effort has been devoted to improving the available facilities, with ski-lifts and ski schools: the existing pistes are constantly supervised and are being extended. In addition to hotels there are numerous mountain huts provided by various skiing and climbing organisations.

★★To the Pico de Veleta

This is an enchanting trip (which can be made by bus as well as by car) into the glorious mountain world of the Sierra Nevada on a good asphalt road

Sierra Nevada

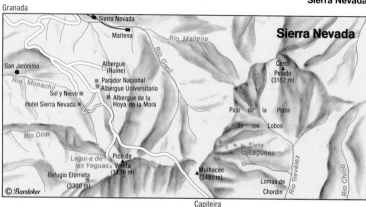

Granada

Capileira

which climbs from 640m/2100ft to 3392m/11,129ft, making it one of the highest mountain roads in Europe. This continuous ascent of almost 35km/22 miles, without any shelter from the sun, calls for an early start, and warm clothing should be taken for protection from the cold and the wind on the top. A striking feature of the run is the contrast between the lush southern landscape of the Vega de Granada and the snow-capped peaks of the mountains.

From Granada (see entry) the road runs east along the slopes above the right bank of the Río Genil and reaches in 6km/4 miles Cenes de la Vega (alt. 737m/2418ft). Farther up the valley the road crosses the river, passes a side road on the left to Pinos Genil and winds its way uphill, with gradients of 8–12%, between slopes which are still covered with olive-groves; there are magnificent views to the rear down the valley, extending in clear weather as far as Granada. After 20km/12½ miles or so the road passes the 1500m/4920ft mark, and soon afterwards the trees disappear.

In another 8km/5 miles the 2000m/6560ft contour is reached. This is the beginning of the winter sports region of Solynieve (Sol y Nieve = "Sun and Snow"), at altitudes of between 2000m/6560ft and 2600m/8530ft, well provided with hotels, chalet colonies and blocks of flats, mountain huts, ski-lifts and cableways. | Solynieve

From Solynieve there is a road (4km/2½ miles) to the regularly if unimaginatively planned resort of Pradollano (alt. 2100m/6890ft), from which a chair-lift goes east to the Parador Nacional (alt. 2500m/8200ft) and a cabin cableway south to the hotel village of Borreguiles (alt. 2600m/8530ft). From Borreguiles there are chair-lifts and ski-tows to pistes at higher levels, including one to the Pico de Veleta. | Pradollano

It is also possible to drive round the Solynieve region, remaining on the main road and bearing left to reach the Parador Nacional Sierra Nevada, beyond which, off the road to the left, is the Residencia Universitaria (alt. 2550m/8365ft). The road to the Pico de Veleta continues through the bare mountain landscape and comes to a side road on the right which leads in 2km/1¼ miles to a beautiful mountain lake, the Laguna de las Yeguas (alt. 2970m/9745ft; mountain hut). After another 5km/3 miles the road ends at an altitude of 3392m/11,129ft on a rocky platform just below the Pico de Veleta (3428m/11,247ft), the second highest peak in the Sierra Nevada. On its slopes, at a height of 2850m/9350ft, is a 30-metre radio-telescope for space research established by the Franco-German Institute of Radio-astronomy. | ★Pico de Veleta

From the Pico de Veleta a narrow unasphalted road winds up first round the summit and then descends in hairpin bends on the south side of Mulhacén to the picturesque village of Capileira (alt. 1436m/4712ft), 37km/23 miles from the Pico de Veleta, in the wild mountain region of the Alpujarras. From here there is a good road (20km/12½ miles) to the beautifully situated little town of Orgiva (alt. 417m/1368ft), with the Palacio de los Condes de Sástago. The road then continues west by way of Lanzarón (alt. 687m/2254ft) to join N 323, which runs north to Granada. | Las Alpujarras

Sigüenza   J 4

Province: Guadalajara (GU). Telephone dialling code: 911
Altitude: 982m/3222ft. Population: 6500

The little episcopal town of Sigüenza, on the left bank of the Río Henares, can look back on a long history. As Segontia it was a Celtiberian base in 195 B.C. during the conflict with Rome, and under the Visigoths it became the see of a bishop.

Sigüenza

★Cathedral

The cathedral (12th–14th c.) is one of the finest Late Romanesque buildings in Spain, with some Gothic and Plateresque features. With its two battlemented towers it has the aspect of a fortress.

Capilla de Santa Librada

The Capilla de Santa Librada (by Alonso de Covarrubias) in the north aisle contains the tomb of the town's patron saint and the Gothic monument of Don Fadrique of Portugal.

Capilla Mayor

The Capilla Mayor has a retablo by Giraldo de Merlo (1619) and a fine *reja*. It contains the tombs of Cardinal Carillo de Albornoz and two bishops.

★Capilla del Doncel

The Capilla del Doncel contains one of the finest examples of Late Gothic sculpture in Spain, the figure of Martín Vázquez de Arce, squire to Isabella the Catholic, who was killed fighting the Moors at Granada in 1486.

Sacristy

The Sacristy has a beautiful coffered ceiling by Alonso de Covarrubias.

Cloister

The Gothic Cloister is entered from the north aisle through a fine doorway of 1503.

Museo de Arte Antiguo

The Museum of Ancient Art, opposite the cathedral, is mainly devoted to religious art from the Romanesque to the Baroque period. Among the most notable exhibits are tomb figures by Pompeo Leoni and an "Annunciation" by El Greco.

Old town

The picturesque old town of Sigüenza, with its fine noble mansions and burghers' houses, is best explored on foot. To the south of the cathedral is the Plaza Mayor, with the Ayuntamiento (Town Hall) of 1511.

From the Plaza Mayor we go past the church of San Vicente and the Arco de San Juan to the 12th century Castillo, now a parador, from which there are fine views.

The "Doncel"

Sitges

Province: Barcelona (B). Telephone dialling code: 93
Altitude: sea level. Population: 12,000

Sitges, lying on the Costa Dorada between Barcelona and Tarragona, is one
of the oldest seaside resorts on the Spanish Mediterranean coast. It has
suffered less from mass tourism than other Spanish resorts, and still
attracts a clientele of summer visitors with cultural interests as well as
money. Many well-to-do Barcelona families have a second home in Sitges.
G. K. Chesterton was a frequent visitor and created his famous character
Father Brown here.

Sights

In 1891 the painter and art collector Santiago Rusiñol bought two houses in
Sitges and attracted numbers of other artists and admirers to the town,
which then became known as a centre of culture and as a bathing resort. His
house near the Baroque church of Santa María, Cau Ferrat, is now a
museum, with his large collection of Catalan Art Nouveau paintings (including works by El Greco and Picasso) and drawings.

Museu Cau Ferrat

Adjoining the Museu Cau Ferrat is the Museu Maricel de Mar (opened
1970), with the collection of Jesús Pérez Rosales, a conglomeration of
furniture, glass, porcelain and other objects ranging in date from the
Middle Ages to modern times. Of particular interest are wall paintings by
the Catalan artist José María Sert.

Museu Maricel
de Mar

The Museu Romàntic, housed in the Casa Llopis, a late 18th century mansion, displays period furniture and other objects. On the upper floor is the
Lola Anglada Collection of dolls of the 17th–19th centuries in a great variety
of materials.

Museu Romàntic

Within the territory of Sitges are the three boating harbours of Aiguadolç,
Garraf and Port Ginesta and a sailing club; for bathers there are 4km/
2½ miles of well maintained beaches; and other sporting facilities include a
golf club and tennis courts.

Sport and
recreation

An International Film Festival specialising in science fiction films is held
annually in Sitges at the beginning of October.

Film Festival

Soria

Province: Soria (SO). Telephone dialling code: 975
Altitude: 1063m/3488ft. Population: 32,000

The old-world town of Soria, situated in the bleak upper valley of the Río
Duero, on the right bank of the river, was an important frontier town in the
Middle Ages, lying as it did on the Duero line which separated Christian
from Moorish Spain. Now chief town of its province, it is still a relatively
undeveloped small town. Its wealth of Romanesque buildings, however,
makes it well worth a visit.

★Townscape

Nothing is known of the origins of the town. It was captured from the Arabs
by Alfonso el Batallador, king of Aragon, and soon afterwards became part
of the kingdom of Castile. Thereafter it played no significant part in history.
A number of noted Spanish writers lived in the town, among them Gustavo
Becquer, the essayist Miguel de Unamuno and the great lyric poet Antonio
Machado (1875–1939).

History

Soria

Sights

San Juan de Duero	The most notable of Soria's many churches and religious houses is the 13th century monastery of San Juan de Duero, a former Templar house, outside the town on the left bank of the Duero. Round the ruins is a small open-air archaeological museum. The Romanesque/Gothic cloister displays an astonishing variety of arch forms, the most unusual of which are the intersecting pointed arches.
San Saturio	Also on the left bank of the river, beyond the railway, is the octagonal chapel of San Saturio (18th c.).
Castillo	From the hill on the right bank of the Duero which is crowned by the ruined castle there are fine views of the town and surrounding country. There is now a modern parador on the hill.
San Pedro	On the right of the road into the town from the bridge over the Duero is the Co-Cathedral of San Pedro (12th–16th c.), which has a fine Plateresque doorway and a Romanesque cloister (12th c.) with paired columns and richly carved capitals. The finest thing in the church itself is a Flemish triptych of 1559 in the Capilla de San Saturio.
Palacio Gómara	Farther into the town, in Calle de Aguirre, is the Palacio de los Condes de Gómara, a magnificent Renaissance mansion (16th c.) with an elegant square tower. It is the most sumptuous building dating from the heyday of the Mesta, the corporation of wealthy sheep-farmers which from the 13th to the 19th century controlled the summer migration of sheep from Extremadura into the more temperate regions of eastern Spain and exercised considerable political and economic power.
San Juan de Rabanera	Diagonally opposite the Palacio Gómara, on the left, Calle San Juan leads to the 12th century Romanesque/Byzantine church of San Juan de

Rabanera. The tympanum with its rich figural decoration came from the church of San Nicolás. The church has a retablo by Juan de Baltanás and Francisco de Ágreda.

To the north of San Juan, in Calle Aduana Vieja, stands the church of Santo Domingo (second half of 12th c.), with the finest Romanesque façade in Soria. The sculpture on the doorway depicts Old and New Testament scenes; on either side of the doorway are two rows of blind arches with capitals telling the story of the Creation. The church has a beautiful retablo and good sculpture.

Santo Domingo

In Plaza General Yagüe is the Museo Numantino, with Iberian and Roman material from the nearby Iberian site of Numantia.

Museo Numantino

Tarazona

K 3

Province: Zaragoza (Z). Telephone dialling code: 976
Altitude: 475m/1558ft. Population: 12,000

The little episcopal town of Tarazona, originally the Iberian settlement of Turiasso, is picturesquely situated on the Río Queiles to the north of the Sierra de Moncayo, which rises to over 2300m/7550ft, where seams of iron ore were already being worked in Roman times. For a time Tarazona was a residence of the kings of Aragon.

Sights

Tarazona Cathedral dates from the 12th and 13th centuries, but was much altered in the 16th and 18th centuries. The brick-built tower (1588) is a

★Cathedral

Sculptured figures, Tarazona Cathedral

typical example of Mudéjar architecture. The sculpture and reliefs on the beautiful north doorway were the work of Juan de Talavera. The Capilla de los Calvillo on the north side of the ambulatory contains the sumptuous alabaster tombs of Cardinal Calvillo and his brother, Bishop Pedro. The beautiful altarpiece was painted by the Sephardic artist Yojanan Levi, a convert to Christianity. The other chapels also have fine retablos and monuments. The large Mudéjar cloister dates from the 16th century.

Palacio
Episcopal

The Bishop's Palace (14th–15th c.) was once the palace of the kings of Aragon. It has a fine artesonado ceiling.

The old Jewish quarter lay behind the palace, and the streets in this area preserve the old layout.

★ Casa
Consistorial

The façade of the 16th century Casa Consistorial (Town Hall) is richly decorated with reliefs on the story of Hercules and elaborate coats of arms and topped by an elegant arcaded gallery.

Churches

Tarazona has a number of other interesting old churches, including San Francisco (16th c.), La Magdalena (the town's oldest church, with a Mudéjar tower) and La Merced (17th c.).

Surroundings of Tarazona

★ Monasterio
de Veruela

Leave Tarazona on N 122, going south-east, and at Vera de Moncayo take a road on the right to the Monasterio de Veruela. This imposing monastery, surrounded by a battlemented wall, was begun by the Cistercians in the 12th century and completed in the 15th. The poet Gustavo Adolfo Bécquer (1836–70) lived for some years in the monastery while writing his "Letters from my Cell", a poetic journey through the landscape of Aragon. The transition from Romanesque to Gothic is reflected in the architecture of the monastery, and the Gothic cloister is a good example of the Cistercian style. It contains abbots' tombs and, in the chapterhouse, a small museum of modern art.

Borja

Farther east on N 122, 26km/16 miles from Tarazona, is the little town of Borja, in the centre of a wine-producing area. The town, originally the Iberian settlement of Bursao, was the ancestral seat of the Borja family, an offshoot of which was the Italian Borgia family. The Borja castle is a ruin.

Tarragona   O 4

Province: Tarragona (T). Telephone dialling code: 977
Altitude: 60m/200ft. Population: 109,000

The old port town of Tarragona, chief town of its province and the see of an archbishop, is picturesquely situated, some 100km/60 miles south-west of Barcelona, on a hill rising 160m/525ft above the Mediterranean. On the highest point of the hill, which was the site of an ancient fortified settlement, is the Cathedral. No other Spanish town except Mérida (see entry)

★ Roman remains

has so many remains of the period of Roman rule in the Iberian peninsula. As an important centre of the wine trade Tarragona has numbers of large bodegas (wine-cellars) in which wine from the Campo de Tarragona, the Campiña de Reus and the Priorato is stored. When the monks of the Grande Chartreuse near Grenoble were expelled from their monastery they came to Tarragona and made their famous liqueur here between 1903 and 1929.

History

The origins of the ancient stronghold known to the Romans as Tarraco go back to the 3rd millennium B.C. The first town walls were built by an Iberian tribe, the Cessetani. After its capture by the Romans in the Second Punic

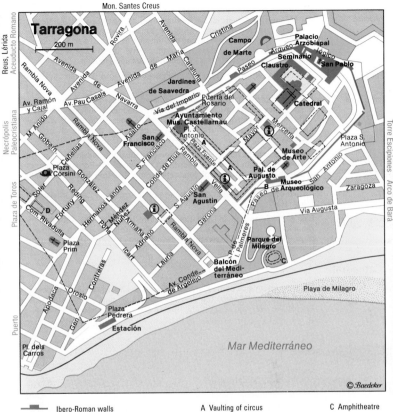

Tarragona

Ibero-Roman walls
Ancient remains (some underground)

A Vaulting of circus
B Remains of ancient buildings

C Amphitheatre
D Forum

War (218 B.C.) the town became the main Roman base in Spain and from the time of Augustus capital of the whole province of Hispania. The remains of many splendid buildings still testify to the wealth of ancient Tarraco. In later centuries the town was several times destroyed – in 475 by the Visigoths, in 713 by the Moors, who held it until the beginning of the 9th century, and in 1811 by the French.

Around the Rambla Nova

The town's principal traffic artery is the broad tree-lined Rambla Nova. At its south end is the Balcón del Mediterráneo (Catalan Balcó del Mediterraní), from which there are extensive views of the sea and the coast.

★ Balcón del Mediterráneo/ Balcó del Mediterraní

From the Balcón steps (to right) lead down to the railway station and the harbour (Puerto), which is sheltered by the Dique de Levante, a breakwater 1700m (over a mile) long, with a lighthouse.

Harbour

Tarragona

**Anfiteatro/
Amfiteatre**

Below the Balcón (on the left) extends the Parque del Milagro (Catalan Parc del Milagre), in which is the Roman amphitheatre (Spanish Anfiteatro romano, Catalan Amfiteatre romà), which was excavated in 1952. The amphitheatre, which dates from the time of Augustus, had seating for 12,000 spectators. It was the scene of the martyrdom in A.D. 259 of Bishop Fructuosus and two deacons named Augurius and Eulogius.

Playa del Milagro

Beyond the railway is the beach of Playa del Milagro (Catalan Platja del Miracle).

Rambla Vella

To the east of the Balcón del Mediterráneo is the Paseo de les Palmeres, a beautiful avenue laid out in terraces. From its near end the Rambla Nova, a wide boulevard with gardens along the middle, goes off on the left, with the handsome Baroque church of San Agustín and the church of San Francisco.

**Plaza de
la Fuente/
Plaça de la Font**

Half way along the Rambla Vella a turning on the right leads to the Plaza de la Fuente (Catalan Plaça de la Font), on the site of the Roman Circus, of which there are remains of foundations and vaulting in the adjoining buildings.

On the north side of the square is the early 19th century Casa Consistorial (Town Hall).

**Museu
Castellarnau**

East of the Town Hall, in Calle (Catalan Carrer) Ferrers, is the 15th century mansion of the Castellarnau family, fully furnished, which is now a museum (ceramics, glassware, metalwork, coins and items illustrating the history of the town).

★ Cathedral

From the south side of the Plaza de la Fuente the Bajada de la Misericordia (Catalan Baixada Misericòrda) and its continuation, the Calle Mayor (Carrer Major), the old main street of the Roman town, ascend to the Cathedral.

Roman amphitheatre, Tarragona

The Cathedral, mainly built in the 12th and 13th centuries on a site which had previously been occupied by a Roman temple of Jupiter and later a Moorish mosque, is one of the most splendid examples in Spain of the transition from Romanesque to Gothic. On the west front (begun 1278; upper part unfinished) is a deep Gothic doorway with rich sculptural decoration, flanked by massive buttresses, above which is a magnificent rose window. The Romanesque side doorways are also very fine. The oldest part of the Cathedral is the fortress-like apse.

Exterior

The interior of the Cathedral creates an impression of great austerity. Over the crossing is an octagonal dome, and in the transepts are fine rose windows of 1574. The choir (14th c.) has carved stalls of 1478–93 and an organ of 1563. The dominant feature of the Capilla Mayor is the retablo (by Pere Joan, c. 1430), with statues of the Virgin and Child and SS Paul and Thecla. To the right of the high altar is the tomb of Archbishop Juan de Aragón, who died at the age of 33. At the end of the south aisle is the pentagonal Capilla de los Sastres (14th c.), with wall paintings and an Early Gothic altar dedicated to the Virgin. The Capilla de Montserrat in the north aisle has a very fine retablo by Lluis Borrasà. There are other richly decorated chapels of various dates and styles.

Interior

★Retablo

To the left of the Capilla de los Sastres a finely carved Romanesque doorway leads into the Cloister (begun in 13th c.), one of the finest in Spain. The beautifully laid out cloister garth, shaded by trees, is surrounded by large Gothic arches, each enclosing three smaller round-headed arches. In the west wing is a mihrab (prayer niche) from the mosque which once stood on this site.

★Cloister

At the north-east corner of the cloister is the Diocesan Museum, with ecclesiastical vestments, 52 tapestries of the 15–17th centuries and ancient and medieval sculpture.

Museo Diocesano/ Museu Diocesà

Adjoining the cloister the little 12th century church of Santa Tecla houses the Diocesan Museum's collection of gravestones and sculpture.

Santa Tecla

To the north of the Cathedral, in the Plaza del Palacio (Catalan Plaça del Palau), stands the early 19th century Archbishop's Palace. Adjoining the palace is an old defensive tower, the Torre del Arzobispo, standing on the highest point in the town, on the site of the Roman castrum (fine views). In the courtyard of the palace are a number of gravestones.

Palacio Arzobispal/ Palau Arquebispal

Paseo Arqueológico/Passeig Arqueològic

From the north end of the Rambla Vella the Vía del Imperio runs east to the Puerta del Rosario (Catalan Portal de Roser), which dates from the 6th or 5th century B.C. This is the starting-point of the Paseo Arqueológico round the massive ancient cyclopean walls (*murallas ciclópeas*) enclosing the highest part of the town, which are preserved almost without interruption for a length of 1000m/1100yd, standing to heights of between 3 and 10m (10 and 35ft). The lower part of the walls – the remains of the Iberian town walls of the 6th century B.C. – is built of huge irregularly shaped blocks up to 4m/13ft long. Above this lie the Roman walls, built by the Scipios from 218 B.C. onwards; native workmen were employed in the construction, and many of the stones bear Iberian masons' marks. Higher still are the remains of the Augustan walls. The six surviving gates all date from the earliest period.

★★Cyclopean walls

West of the Puerta del Rosario is a section of Moorish wall, built with blocks of rammed earth.

The Paseo Arqueológico, which is pleasantly shaded by cypresses and affords extensive views from each end, passes a bronze statue of Augustus gifted by Italy in 1934, the Torre del Arzobispo and a seminary for the training of priests at the east end of the hill.

Tarragona

★Museo Arqueológico/ Museu Arqueològic	From here the Paseo de Torroja (Catalan Passeig de Torroja) and Paseo de San Antonio (Passeig de Sant Antoni) go past the Puerta de San Antonio (Portal i Creu de Sant Antoni) to the Archaeological Museum, which has one of Spain's finest collections of Roman art. Particularly notable are a number of mosaics, including a fine Medusa's head and a Bacchic scene. Other items include architectural elements from Tarragona, Roman sculpture and pottery, and an ivory doll 23cm/9in. long (4th c. A.D.) found in a child's tomb. In the basement of the museum are the excavated foundations of Roman walls.
Pretorio Romano	Adjoining the modern Museum building rises the massive Roman Praetorium (Praetor's Palace), also known as the Torreón de Pilatos because Pilate is supposed to have been born in it. It is not in fact a palace but one of the towers bounding the Forum, which lay to its rear. The tower now houses a museum on the history of the town.
Museo de Arte Moderno/Museu d'Art Modern	North-east of the Archaeological Museum, in Calle (Catalan Carrer) Santa Ana, is the Museum of Modern Art. To the south of this extends the former Jewish quarter of Tarragona.
	From the Archaeological Museum it is a short distance west to the south end of the Rambla Vella.

Western Districts

Forum	To the west of the Rambla Nova is the Plaza (Catalan Plaça) Corsini, near which are remains of the Roman Forum (reached from Calle Lérida/Carrer Lleida) and many Roman houses, dating from the time when Tarraco was capital of the province.
Early Christian necropolis	Some distance farther west, beyond the Plaza de Toros (Bullring) on the banks of the Río Francolí, are the remains of an early Christian necropolis (3rd–6th c.), discovered during the building of a tobacco factory. The most important finds from the site (lead and marble sarcophagi, urns, mosaics, jewellery and ornaments, etc.) are displayed in the Museo Paleocristiano (Catalan Museu Paleocristià).

Surroundings of Tarragona

Beaches	From the Balcón del Mediterráneo promenades affording fine views run along high above the sea to the beaches to the east, from Rabasada and Sabinosa to the Punta de la Mora. To the south-east are Playa de la Pineda and Salou where there is good bathing.
Alto del Olivo	1.5km/1 mile north-east of the Puerta del Rosario stands the ruined fort of Alto del Olivo, from which there are fine views of the town and the coast.
Mausoleum of Centcelles	6km/4 miles north-west of the town centre on the Constantí road is the late Roman mausoleum of Centcelles, probably built in the 4th century A.D. for Constans, son of the Emperor Constantine. It has a well preserved Christian mosaic in the dome depicting Biblical scenes like "Daniel in the Lions' Den".

On the Barcelona Road

Torre de los Escipiones	From Tarragona the coast road (N 340) runs east. 6km/4 miles from Tarragona, to the left of the road, is the Torre de los Escipiones (Tower of the Scipios), a square structure 8m/25ft high dating from the 1st century A.D. There is no basis for the association with the Roman generals of that name,

Gnaeus and Publius Cornelius Scipio, who were killed in the 3rd century B.C. There are two statues of the Phrygian divinity Attis.

2km/1¼ miles farther on a road branches off on the left to the Roman quarry (*cantera*) of El Medol, in the centre of which is a monolithic block indicating the original height of the rock.

Cantera del Medol

Continuing along a pleasant road flanked by lemon-groves, we come to Tamarit, which preserves part of its 14th century circuit of walls. The Castillo, directly on the sea, is now a museum.

Tamarit

Beyond Torrembara the road passes the Arco de Barà, a 12m/40ft high triumphal arch of the 2nd century A.D. dedicated to Lucius Licinius Sura, a wealthy friend of the Emperor Trajan.

★ Arco de Barà

N 340 now leaves the coast and runs inland to El Vendrell (alt. 50m/165ft). This little town, attractively situated on a hill in a famous wine-producing region, was the birthplace of the cellist Pau (Pablo) Casals (1876–1973). There is a Prehistoric Museum in the town.

El Vendrell

On the Lérida Road

From Tarragona N 240 runs north, passing under the motorway, and comes in 4km/2½ miles to a path leading to the Roman aqueduct of Las Ferreras (Catalan Els Ferreres), popularly known as the Puente del Diablo (Devil's Bridge), which carried water from the Río Gayà over a side valley of the Río Francolí. Probably dating from the early Empire, this is one of the most impressive Roman remains in Spain. The 25 arches cover a total length of 217m/712ft, with a lower tier 73m/80yd long at the deepest part of the valley. The water channel had a total length of 35km/22 miles.

★ Acueducto de las Ferreras

The road continues up the valley of the Río Francolí to Valls (alt. 215m/705ft), with a much revered image of Nuestra Señora de la Candela in the parish church, which is partly decorated with azulejos.

Valls

From Valls a secondary road leads 18km/11 miles north to the Cistercian monastery of Santes Creus, founded in 1157. The Romanesque church (1254) with its fortress-like façade and octagonal tower over the crossing, contains the handsome tombs of a number of kings of Aragon, including Pedro III and Jaime II and his wife Blanche of Anjou.

★ **Monasterio de Santes Creus**

The monastery has two cloisters – the Gothic New Cloister, with finely carved capitals and a simple fountain-house, and the Romanesque Old Cloister, entered from the north-west corner of the New Cloister, in which is an old wine-cellar. Other features of interest are the Chapterhouse, with the gravestones of canons set into the floor, the Dormitory and the Palacio Real, in which the kings of Aragon spent Easter week.

★ Cloisters

From Valls the road winds its way through the Sierra de Cogulla and over the Puerto de Lilla (581m/1906ft) to Montblanch (Catalan Montblanc; alt. 310m/1017ft). This picturesque little town, still ringed by its old walls and towers, is dominated by the large 14th century church of Santa María, which has a fine Baroque doorway. In the Casa Josa-Andreu, adjoining the church, is a small museum of pottery, prehistoric finds and craft products from the surrounding area.

★ Montblanch/ Montblanc

N 240 now turns west, passing the little spa of Espluga de Francolí, off the road on the left. From here a detour can be made to the monastery of Santa María de Poblet, 3km/2 miles south-west. This Cistercian house was founded in 1151 by Ramón Berenguer IV and was completed in all essentials by the end of the 14th century. It was partly destroyed in the early 19th

★ **Monasterio de Poblet**

Altar and tombs, Poblet monastery

century, but was reoccupied by Cistercian monks in 1940. Famed as the burial-place of the Aragonese kings, it is still highly impressive. The whole complex, including various associated buildings as well as the conventual buildings proper, is surrounded by a protective wall.

Within the outer gate and the inner "Golden Gate" (Catalan Porta Daurada) are the hospital (to left) and the hospice (to right). Beyond this is an open court, dominated by the Baroque façade of the church.

Church

The most notable feature of the Romanesque church is the magnificent alabaster high altar (1527) by Damián Forment. Flanking the altar, on depressed arches, are the tall Gothic tombs of the kings and queens of Aragon, with recumbent figures of the occupants.

From the church a staircase leads up to the Dormitory of the Novices and the Royal Palace.

Conventual buildings

The conventual buildings, which are surrounded by a high wall, are reached from the central court by way of the Royal Doorway (Catalan Porta Real), flanked by two massive towers. Passing the large parlour on the right and the wine-cellar on the left, and then the kitchen and the refectory, we enter the Early Gothic cloister, which is of impressive size. The side nearest the church was begun in Romanesque style and completed in Gothic. On the opposite side is a fountain-house with 30 spouts. Opening off the cloister are the magnificent chapterhouse, with numerous abbots' tombs, and beyond this, on the left, the library, formerly the scriptorium. The dormitory, above the wine-cellar, is now a museum in which the church treasury is displayed.

The Southern Costa Dorada

For this trip along the southern part of the Costa Dorada (Catalan Costa Daurada; the "Golden Coast") there are alternative routes out of Tarragona

– either N 340, going west, or the short stretch of motorway which runs south-west from the town.

After crossing the Río Francolí the road comes to Salou, a port and popular seaside resort in a bay sheltered by Cabo Salou, with holiday chalets and high-rise hotels and apartment blocks, good beaches and a boating harbour. King Jaime I sailed from Salou in 1229 on his expedition to conquer Majorca.

Salou

From Salou the coast road continues to Cambrils, which, like many other places on the Mediterranean coast, has developed from a fishing village into a resort with more pleasure boats than fishing boats in the harbour. The church in the old part of the town has a fortress-like tower. For bathers and sunbathers there is the beach of Cambrils Playa.

Cambrils

The road continues south-west, keeping close to the coast. After passing several camping sites it passes through Miami Playa and past a number of other beaches to Hospitalet del Mar, which owes its name to an old pilgrim hospice situated close to the sea. A short distance away is the Vandellós atomic power station, an accident in which – fortunately without serious consequences – made the headlines in October 1989.

Hospitalet del Infante

After passing the fishing villages of L'Ametlla de Mar and Ampolla, both now developing holiday resorts, the road follows the west side of the Ebro delta. At Amposta-Aldea C 235 goes off on the right to Tortosa (see entry), 14km/9 miles west.

★ Ebro delta

Soon afterwards N 340 crosses the Ebro and comes to Amposta, a little town noted for its rice. The Ebro delta in which it lies, a marshy area with countless little waterways and pools, is well suited for the growing of rice. The river has two mouths, the Gola del Norte and Gola del Sur, with the island of Buda between them. The whole delta is a paradise for birds, the haunt of many different species (see Practical Information, Nature Parks).

Other Excursions from Tarragona

See Barcelona, Lérida, Sitges

Tarrasa /Terrassa

P 3

Province: Barcelona (B). Telephone dialling code: 93
Altitude: 277m/909ft. Population: 160,000

The industrial town of Tarrasa (Catalan Terrassa) lies in the fertile Vallés district on the right bank of the Río Palau. Its principal industry is textiles, in particular the production and processing of silk. Until its conquest by the Moors the town, then known as Egara, was the seat of a Visigothic bishopric founded in 450, and it has preserved three early Christian churches, all lying to the south-east of the present-day railway station.

Sights

The church of Santa María was a Visigothic basilica which was enlarged in the 12th century in Catalan Romanesque style. In front of the church are remains of a 4th century mosaic. The church itself has very interesting wall paintings depicting the story of St Thomas Becket, the murdered archbishop of Canterbury. The magnificent Gothic retablos were the work of Jaume Huguet, Lluis Borrassà, Jaume Cirera and Guillerm Talarn.

★ Santa María

The church of San Miguel (Catalan Sant Miquel), originally built in the 6th century as a baptismal chapel, shows Byzantine and Visigothic influences.

★ San Miguel/ Sant Miquel

Its most notable features are the octagonal baptistery, surrounded by columns, and the 7th century painting in the crypt.

★ San Pedro/
Sant Pere

San Pedro (Catalan Sant Pere) was originally a burial chapel. In the Byzantine apse are remains of a mosaic; the nave is Romanesque. This church too has wall paintings.

Museo
Municipal

The Municipal Museum, in the Cartuja de Vallparadis, displays Catalan ceramics, pictures and sculpture.

Museo de
Textil

The Textile Museum has a collection of old weaving looms and old fabrics and textiles from all over the world.

Teruel

L 4

Province: Teruel (TE). Telephone dialling code: 974
Altitude: 915m/3000ft. Population: 28,000

★ Mudéjar towers

Teruel, chief town of its province, lies on a hill on the Río Turia, surrounded by gorges. A town of Iberian origin (Turba), it was devastated by the Romans in 215 B.C. Long after the Reconquista it retained its Moorish inhabitants, who enjoyed special rights and were able to develop freely, losing their last mosque as late as 1502. To this continuing Moorish presence the town owes its fine examples of Mudéjar architecture, including particularly the magnificent towers which still span certain streets. Teruel also had a large Jewish community, who lived in peaceful coexistence with Christians and Moors until a pogrom in 1486 which ended the concord between the different religions and initiated the town's decline. During the Spanish Civil War Teruel was the scene of a decisive battle (Dec. 1937 to Feb. 1938) which caused great destruction in the town.

Sights

San Salvador

Above Calle del Salvador, in the south of the town, soars the tower (1277–1315) of the church of San Salvador, one of Teruel's finest Mudéjar towers with its intricately patterned brickwork, its chequered tile insets and its battlemented top.

San Pedro

At the north end of Calle del Salvador is the Plaza de Carlos Castell, the central feature of the town, in the centre of which is the Fuente del Torico. To the right of the square stands the church of San Pedro, with a 14th century tower similar in structure and decoration to that of the Cathedral. The chancel is also Mudéjar; other parts of the church were altered in the 18th century. The 16th century retablo on the high altar is ascribed to Gabriel Joly, a Picard.

"The Lovers
of Teruel"

Leaving the church and passing under the tower, we come to a chapel containing a rather gruesome sight, two mummified bodies housed in glass coffins. These are said to be the remains of the "Lovers of Teruel" (Los Amantes de Teruel), the story of whose love has been celebrated by several Spanish poets. The story goes that in the 13th century Diego García de Marcilla wanted to marry Isabella de Segura but was turned down by her father, who wanted a rich bridegroom for his daughter. Diego thereupon went abroad, made his fortune and returned to Teruel after five years, on the very day of Isabella's marriage to another man. Thereupon, his heart broken, he died, and on the next day Isabella followed him into the grave.

The Mudéjar tower of San Salvador, Teruel ▶

The Lovers of Teruel

Cathedral	On the north side of Plaza General Mola rises the tower of the Cathedral, which was begun in the 13th century and given its present form in the 16th century. Typical of the Mudéjar style are the use of glazed bricks and the decoration with green and black azulejos. The tower over the crossing is also Mudéjar. The church itself, which was given cathedral status only in the 16th century, dates from the 12th and 13th centuries. The Capilla Mayor has a magnificent retablo (1535) by Gabriel Joly. The fine choir screen was made in Teruel. The Capilla de la Coronación in the north aisle has a fine Flemish-style retablo.
★Artesonado ceiling	The finest feature of the Cathedral, however, is its artesonado ceiling, beautifully painted in the 13th and 14th centuries with scenes of contemporary life, including hunting scenes, craftsmen at work and scenes of court life, framed in Moorish flower patterns, geometric designs and Arabic inscriptions. In the sacristy are two fine silver monstrances 3m/10ft high, a Romanesque processional cross and other valuable items.
Palacio Episcopal	Passing through the arch of the Cathedral tower we come into a square in which is the Bishop's Palace, housing the small collection of the Diocesan Museum.
San Martín	To the west of the Cathedral is the church of San Martín, with the last of Teruel's Mudéjar towers (1315–16), which vies in beauty with that of San Salvador.
Los Arcos	In the north of the town, spanning a gorge, is the aqueduct of Los Arcos, built in 1558 on the Roman model. Its lower tier is also a pedestrian bridge.

Surroundings of Teruel

★Albarracín	Some 40km/25 miles west of Teruel, in the Sierra de Albarracín, lies the little town of Albarracín (alt. 1182m/3878ft), situated on the slopes above the Río

Guadalaviar. In the 11th century Albarracín was a petty Moorish kingdom; later it became an independent territory held by the Azagra family; and at the beginning of the 14th century it was incorporated in Aragon. The whole town, with its picturesque narrow streets and circuit of walls, is now protected as a national monument. Something of the atmosphere of the Middle Ages still lingers in the town, particularly around the Plaza Mayor. The fine Cathedral (13th–16th c.) contains a museum, housed in the sacristy and chapterhouse, the most valuable items in which are 16th century Brussels tapestries.

Near Albarracín (respectively 4km/2½ miles and 6km/4 miles south) are two caves, El Callejón de Plou and the Cueva del Navazo, with interesting prehistoric paintings, including hunting scenes.

Caves

From Teruel N 234 runs north-west via Torrelacárcel to Monreal del Campo (alt. 940m/3084ft), below the east side of the Sierra de Menera, in which are the rich iron-mines of Ojos Negros. The church of Santa Eulalia del Campo has a Plateresque doorway.

Monreal del Campo

Toledo

H 5

Province: Toledo (TO). Telephone dialling code: 925
Altitude: 529m/1736ft. Population: 58,000

With its unique situation, its picturesque townscape and its magnificent old buildings, Toledo, chief town of its province and the see of an archbishop, the Primate of Spain, is one of the great tourist cities of Spain, an essential goal for every visitor interested in art and history.
    Toledo has long been famed for its sword blades and its gold and silver inlay work, a craft tradition brought in by the Moors.

★★Situation

Toledo is one of the oldest towns in Spain. The capital of an Iberian tribe, the Carpetani, it was captured by the Romans in 192 B.C. and given the name of Toletum. Under the Visigoths, between 534 and 712, it again enjoyed the status of a capital and was the meeting-place of many church councils. At the Council of Toledo in 589 the Visigothic king Recarred, an Arian, was converted to the Catholic faith. During the Moorish period (712–1085) the town was known as Tolaitola, and until 1035 was the seat of an emir subject to the Caliph of Córdoba. Thereafter it became an independent kingdom and rose to prosperity through the manufacture of weapons and its silk and woollen industries. Science and learning were also eagerly cultivated in the town. The Christian inhabitants, known as Mozarabs ("servants of the Arabs" or "pseudo-Arabs"), adopted the Arabic language, which remained in use alongside Spanish for centuries and was not finally prohibited until 1580.
    In 1087 Toledo became the residence of the kings of Castile and the ecclesiastical centre of the whole of Spain, and the Cardinal Archbishops of Toledo – Mendoza, Jiménez, Albornoz and others – were involved in all the great events of their period. In the reigns of Ferdinand III and Alfonso X, the Wise, Toledo became a centre of learning, notable for the mutual tolerance of the three great religions, Christianity, Judaism and Islam. The Jewish community of Toledo was the largest in the Iberian peninsula. The mid-14th century saw the first pogroms, followed in subsequent decades by others; and with the establishment of the Inquisition in Spain in 1485 and the expulsion of the Jews in 1492 the heyday of Jewry in Spain came to an end.
    The revolt of the Comuneros in the 16th century began in Toledo. With the transfer of the capital to Madrid by Philip II (who resided in Toledo between 1559 and 1561) the town lost all political importance. During the

History

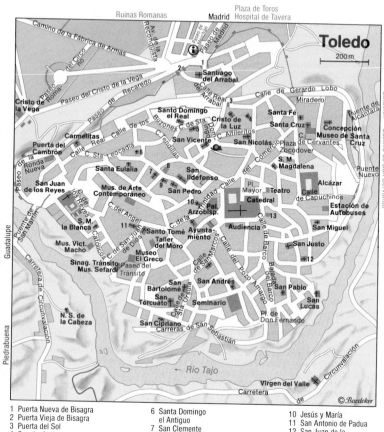

Civil War Republic forces laid siege to the Alcázar, which was totally destroyed.

The ★★Town

Toledo lies on a granite hill surrounded on three sides by the deep gorge of the river Tagus (Tajo). With its ring of Gothic and Moorish walls, its towering Alcázar and its Cathedral it presents a picture of incomparable effect. The layout of the town, with its irregular pattern of narrow streets and numerous blind alleys, reflects its Moorish past. The blank walls, the windows with their iron gratings and the open courtyards of the houses also betray Oriental influence. The architecture of the Christian period is represented by numerous churches, convents and hospices. Thus the city as a whole is a kind of open-air museum illustrating the history of Spain, which has been listed by UNESCO as part of mankind's cultural heritage.

Toledo

★★ Cathedral

On the east side of the Plaza del Ayuntamiento stands the Cathedral, the city's principal landmark and the Catedral Primada of Spain. Spain's finest Gothic cathedral after that of Burgos, it was built between 1227 and 1493 on the site of the Moorish Great Mosque, which itself had replaced an earlier Visigothic church. In the 90m/295ft high north tower (1380–1440), from which there are fine views, is the famous bell known as the Campana Gorda, cast in 1753 and weighing 17 tons. The south tower, which was left unfinished, has a Baroque dome.

On the west front are three handsome Gothic doorways (1418–50), richly decorated with sculpture and reliefs. On the central doorway, the Puerta del Perdón, is a carving by Juan Alemán depicting the Virgin handing a vestment to San Ildefonso. Of the beautiful side doorways the most notable is the richly decorated Gothic Puerta de los Leones (1458–66) at the end of the south transept. On the north side of the church, between the cloister and the sacristy, is the oldest of the doorways, the 13th century Puerta de la Chapinería. From the cloister the Puerta de Santa Catalina leads into the church.

The Cathedral is entered by the Puerta de Mollete (*mollete* = "muffin"), at which food was distributed to the poor. The interior (110m/360ft long without the Capilla de San Ildefonso), with its 88 richly articulated clustered columns, is of impressive effect. The beautiful stained glass windows are 16th century.

The Choir, screened by a Plateresque *reja* of 1548, has choir-stalls of walnutwood which are masterpieces of Renaissance carving. The stalls in the lower tier (*sillería baja;* by Rodrigo Alemán, 1495) are carved with 54 historical reliefs of scenes from the conquest of Granada. The upper tier

Exterior

Doorways

Interior

Choir
★ Choir-stalls

441

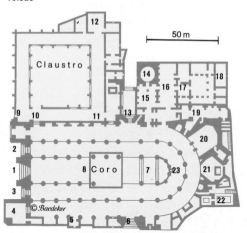

Catedral de Toledo

1 Puerta del Perdón
2 Puerta de la Torre
3 Puerto de los Escribanos
4 Capilla Mozárabe
5 Puerta Llana
6 Puerta de los Leones
7 Capilla Mayor
8 Trascoro
9 Puerta del Mollete
10 Puerta de la Presentación
11 Puerta de Santa Catalina
12 Capilla de San Blas
13 Puerta de la Chapinería
   (Puerta del Reloj)
14 Ochavo
15 Capilla del Virgen del Sagrario
16 Sacristía
17 Vestuario (Robing room)
18 Ropería (Vestment store)
19 Capilla de Reyes Nuevos
20 Capilla de Santiago
21 Capilla de San Ildefonso
22 Sala Capitular
23 Transparente

(*sillería alta*), completed in 1543, has Biblical scenes by Alonso Berruguete and an alabaster "Transfiguration" in the left-hand section and carving by Felipe Vigarny on the right. On the free-standing altar in the choir can be seen a Romanesque stone figure of the Virgen Blanca (*c.* 1500).

★Capilla Mayor

The richly gilded Capilla Mayor has a finely decorated Plateresque *reja* of 1548. The huge retablo of gilded and painted larchwood (1504) has four tiers of New Testament scenes with life-size figures; in the centre is a magnificent pyramidal monstrance. On either side of the high altar are royal tombs (*sepulcros reales*) – on the left Alfonso VII, on the right Sancho II and his son. Farther left is the tomb of Cardinal González de Mendoza.

Behind the high altar, the sides of which are decorated with numerous reliefs and figures of saints, are the tomb of Cardinal Diego de Astorga and the Transparente, a huge marble altar in Churrigueresque style dedicated to the Virgin, surmounted by a painted openwork dome (1722).

Ambulatory

★Capilla de Santiago

The chapels round the ambulatory all contain finely carved tombs. In the central chapel, the Capilla de San Ildefonso, is the tomb of Cardinal Albornoz; to the left of this is the richly decorated Gothic Capilla de Santiago, which contains the magnificent Gothic marble monuments of Condestable Álvaro de Luna and his wife (1488).

Capilla de Reyes Nuevos

Immediately to the left of the Capilla de Santiago is a doorway giving access to the Capilla de Reyes Nuevos, splendidly decorated in Plateresque style, which contains the tomb of Henry II of Trastamara.

★Chapterhouse

From the ambulatory a magnificent doorway gives access to the Chapterhouse (Sala Capitular) of 1512, which has a beautiful artesonado ceiling. The thirteen wall paintings with portraits of archbishops of Toledo are mostly the work of Juan de Borgoña; two are by Goya.

Sacristy

To the left of the ambulatory is the entrance to the Sacristy (1592–1616), which is now a small picture gallery. On the altar is El Greco's "Disrobing of Christ" ("El Spolio", 1579); to the right of the altar is Goya's "Arrest of Christ" (1788); and on the walls are a cycle of 16 Apostles by El Greco. There are also pictures by Morales, van Dyck, Raphael, Titian and Mengs and a sculpture of St Francis by Pedro de Mena. The collection extends into the adjoining Vestry (Vestuario) and the Salas Nuevas, recently incorporated in the Cathedral Museum.

Retablo in Capilla Mayor, Toledo Cathedral

On the west side of the Sacristy lies the Ochavo, an octagonal chamber with a high dome (ceiling paintings by F. Ricci and J. Carreño) which contains some 400 relics. The adjoining Capilla de la Virgen del Sagrario has a much venerated image of the Virgin enthroned (*c.* 1200), clad in costly garments.

Ochavo

The Cathedral Treasury (Tesoro Mayor) is in the Capilla de San Juan, under the north tower. Its principal treasure is the famous monstrance by Juan de Arfe (1524), which is almost 3m/10ft high and weighs 172 kg/380lb, with 260 silver gilt statuettes.

★Tesoro

Immediately on the right of the main entrance, in the south tower, is the Mozarabic Chapel (1504), in which mass is celebrated every morning about 9.45 according to the Visigothic (Mozarabic) rite.

Capilla Mozárabe

In the south aisle can be seen the inside of the Puerta de los Leones, decorated with fine 16th century wood reliefs. Above it is the "Imperial Organ" of 1594, with a stone sounding-board.

On the north side of the Cathedral is the Cloister (begun 1389). On the south and east sides of the lower cloister (*claustro bajo*) are frescoes by Francisco Bayeu and Mariano Maella (1776). At the north-east corner is the Capilla de San Blas (not open to the public), with Florentine ceiling paintings of the early 15th century. In a room off the upper cloister (*claustro alto*), entered

Cloister

from Calle Hombre de Palo, are the *gigantones,* the huge figures some 6m/20ft high, clad in 18th century costume, which are carried in procession in the town's fiestas.

Around the Cathedral

Plaza del Ayuntamiento

Outside the main front of the Cathedral is the Plaza del Ayuntamiento, on the north-west side of which is the Palacio Arzobispal (Archbishop's Palace). On the south-west side stands the Ayuntamiento (Town Hall; 1618), with two handsome corner towers and a beautiful tiled frieze (1595) by El Greco's son Jorge Manuel Theotocopouli in the chapterhouse.

San Ildefonso

North-west of the Cathedral are a number of fine churches. Calle del Nuncio Viejo leads into Calle Alfonso X. In a square on the left-hand side of this street is the imposing Baroque façade of the twin-towered church of San Ildefonso, which contains two works by El Greco.

San Román

A little to the west can be seen the Moorish tower of the 13th century church of San Román, now occupied by the Museo de los Concilios y de Cultura Visigoda (Museum of Councils and Visigothic Culture), with a collection of Visigothic antiquities, including crowns, sculpture and jewellery in addition to the frescoes which form part of the decoration of the church.

Santo Domingo el Antiguo

Farther north-west is the monastery of Santo Domingo el Antiguo where El Greco is buried in the church.

Alcázar

On the eastern slopes of the hill on which the town is built is the Alcázar, reached from the Plaza de Zocodover. On the site of an earlier Roman fort and laid out in a square, with corner towers, this imposing structure was built by Covarrubias and Herrera in the 16th century. It was burned down by the French in 1810 but was subsequently restored. In 1882 it became a military college, and in the early days of the Civil War the Nationalist garrison held out for more than two months against Republican forces until it was blown up and the defenders were forced to surrender. After restoration it became a museum on the Civil War, and is still regarded by Franco supporters as a monument to the heroism of its defenders.

★★Museo de Santa Cruz

★Hospital de Santa Cruz

To the east of the Plaza de Zocodover, through the Moorish Arco de la Sangre, is the old Hospital de Santa Cruz (15th–16th c.), a Renaissance building designed by Enrique de Egas for Cardinal Mendoza, Isabella the Catholic's confessor, with an early Plateresque doorway showing the Cardinal kneeling at the Cross, surrounded by SS Peter, Paul and Helen.

The rebuilt Alcázar

The old Hospital houses the Museo de Santa Cruz.

The archaeological section, in the rooms around the patio, contains prehistoric, Roman and Visigothic antiquities.

The museum's collection of pictures begins in the three rooms on the ground floor. Particularly notable items are Flemish tapestries of the 15th and 16th centuries and a tapestry with the signs of the Zodiac which was woven for the Cathedral. Among the old masters displayed here are a Flemish portrait of Philibert II of Savoy and a picture by Morales, "Christ in Chains". Here too is the standard flown by Don John of Austria in the battle of Lepanto (1571). On the first floor are the museum's most valuable works, including a retablo dedicated to the Virgin with figures by Alonso Berruguete, works by Luis Tristán, a pupil of El Greco's, Ribera and the Master of Sigena, a "Crucifixion" by Goya and above all a superb collection of pictures by El Greco, among them his "Assumption of the Virgin", a late work.

On the first floor there is also the section of applied and decorative art.

Below the Hospital, to the east, the deep gorge of the Tagus is spanned by the Puente de Alcántara (no cars). Originally a Roman structure, the bridge was completely rebuilt by the Moors in 866, and in its present form dates mainly from the 13th and 14th centuries. At the west end is a gate tower, the Puerta de Alcántara (1484), at the east end a Baroque gateway of 1721. From the bridge there is a magnificent view of the town, rising steeply up from the river, and of the Alcázar.

Downstream can be seen the Puente Nuevo (New Bridge; 1933) and the remains of a Roman aqueduct. High above the left bank of the river is the 11th century Castillo de San Servando.

Around the Plaza de Zocodover

The real centre of Toledo is the triangular Plaza de Zocodover, which is surrounded by arcaded houses.

From the square Calle de Armas descends into the Paseo del Miradero, a promenade with a raised outlook terrace from which there are views extending in clear weather as far as the Sierra de Gredos (see entry).

Along the Paseo to the left rises the massive twin-towered Puerta del Sol (14th c.), in Mudéjar style.

Going through the Puerta del Sol and turning left, we come to the Puerta del Santo Cristo de la Luz, beyond which is the Ermita del Santo Cristo de la Luz. This little chapel, originally a mosque (10th c.), has nine Moorish domes and columns which came from a Visigothic church. The choir, added in Christian times, has remains of Romanesque wall paintings.

To the Hospital de Tavera

From the Puerta del Sol Calle Real del Arrabal leads down in a north-westerly direction to the outer district (arrabal) of Santiago, in which is the 13th century Mudéjar church of Santiago del Arrabal.

Near the church, in the town walls, is the Puerta Vieja de Bisagra, a 9th c. Moorish town gate, with a horseshoe arch flanked by towers. Alfonso VI is said to have made his entrance to Toledo in 1085 through this gate.

Along the town walls to the right is the Puerta Nueva de Bisagra, a double gateway dating in its present form from 1550 which is a magnificent example of military architecture. On the town side an inner gate flanked by towers leads into a court containing a statue of Charles V; on the outside of the main gate, which is flanked by massive round towers, is a large Imperial coat of arms.

Hospital de Tavera

From the Puerta Nueva de Bisagra the Paseo de Merchán, laid out in gardens, leads to the outlying district of Las Covachuelas, in which is the Hospital de Tavera, a large complex of buildings erected between 1541 and 1599. The church (1561) has a marble façade by Alonso Berruguete, and under the dome is the fine tomb, also by Berruguete (his last work) of Cardinal Tavera, founder of the Hospital. The retablo was designed by El Greco.

★ Museo Tavera

Some of the residential apartments in the Hospital, decorated and furnished in 17th century style, are open to the public. Their main interest lies in the valuable pictures they contain, including works by Titian, Claudio Coello ("Portrait of the Infanta Clara Eugenia"), El Greco (including his last work, the "Baptism of Christ"), Tintoretto ("Birth of the Messiah") and Zurbarán. The 16th century Pharmacy, faithfully restored to its original form, is unfortunately not open to the public. Visitors can, however, see the Library and Archives (with El Greco's "Holy Family").

Judería

Santo Tomé

To the west of the Cathedral, on the edge of the old Jewish quarter, the Judería, is the Plaza de Santo Tomé, with the church of Santo Tomé. Originally a mosque, the church was rebuilt by the Count of Orgaz in Gothic style in the 14th century, with a beautiful Mudéjar tower. In an annexe to the church is displayed El Greco's "Burial of the Count of Orgaz" (1586), one of his finest works. It reflects the legend that the dead man was conveyed to paradise by St Stephen and St Augustine.

★★ "Burial of the Count of Orgaz"

Museo de Arte Contemporáneo

North of Santo Tomé, in Calle de las Bulas, is the Museum of Contemporary Art, with a collection of 20th century figurative art.

Taller del Moro

A little way south of Santo Tomé can be found the Taller del Moro ("Moor's Workshop"), actually a 15th century palace, which now houses a small Museum of Mudéjar Art, with examples of Moorish carving and sculpture.

Palacio de Fuensalida

In the same square is the Palacio de Fuensalida, in which Isabella of Portugal, wife of Charles V, died in 1539.

★★ Casa y Museo El Greco

Calle de los Alamillos leads to Calle Samuel Leví, in which is the Casa El Greco. It is not certain that El Greco actually lived in this house or died there in 1614; but at any rate it is the only survivor of the houses adjoining the synagogue of El Tránsito, the property of the Marquese de Villena, in one of which El Greco is known to have lived. The building was renovated in 1906 and equipped with furniture and sculpture belonging to El Greco.

In the adjoining building is the Museo El Greco (opened in 1910). On the first floor are three rooms containing more than twenty works by El Greco, including the famous "View of Toledo", "Christ with the Apostles", the "Crowning with Thorns" and "San Bernardino". The other rooms have paintings by other Spanish painters, including Zurbarán and Miranda.

★★ Sinagoga del Tránsito/ Museo Sefardí

A short distance away is the Mudéjar-style Sinagoga del Tránsito, built in 1366 by Samuel ha-Levi, treasurer to Pedro I of Castile. After the expulsion of the Jews in 1492 the synagogue was given to the knightly Order of Calatrava. In the aisleless interior are decorative friezes and Hebrew inscriptions in praise of Jahweh, Samuel ha-Levi and Pedro I, both above and below the magnificent windows with their cusped arches. The ceiling is also very fine. In the adjoining rooms is the Sephardic Museum, devoted to the history and culture of the Jews in Spain, the Sephardim. A particularly notable item is the Sarcófago de Tarragona, with a trilingual inscription in Hebrew, Latin and Greek.

The Mudéjar church of Santa María la Blanca, built in 12th and 13th c., was also a synagogue. After the reconquest of Toledo it was given to the Order of Calatrava and in 1405 became a Christian church. It has an artesonado ceiling and 28 horseshoe arches with pine-cone capitals.

★ Santa María la Blanca

★ San Juan de los Reyes

North-west of the Judería is the Franciscan convent of San Juan de los Reyes, founded in 1476 after the victory over the Portuguese in the battle of Toro as the burial-place of the Catholic Monarchs and their descendants but not completed until the 17th century. The church, begun in 1553, has an Isabelline doorway by Covarrubias, and on the outer walls are the chains of Christians freed from Moorish captivity. Notable features of the sumptuous interior (by Juan Guas) are the friezes of the arms of the Catholic Monarchs supported by eagles in the transepts, the vaulting of the choir gallery and the retablo by Felipe Vigarny and Francisco de Comontes.

The cloister (1504), to the south-east, is one of the finest achievements of Late Gothic architecture in Spain. The upper gallery has a very decorative artesonado ceiling.

North-west of the church, lower down, stands the imposing Puerta del Cambrón ("Gate of the Thorn-Bush"), a double gateway dating from Visigothic times, which was rebuilt in the 11th century by the Moors and again in the 16th century.

Puerta del Cambrón

From the Puerta del Cambrón a road goes down, passing under the road encircling the north side of the town, to the Ermita del Cristo de la Vega outside the town walls. It occupies the site of a small 4th century church which was rebuilt after 660, when St Leocadius is said to have appeared to St Ildefonso, archbishop of Toledo. Of that church only the apse survives.

Ermita del Cristo de la Vega

From the Puerta del Cambrón a road follows the town walls, from which there are extensive views, to the 30m/100ft high Puente de San Martín, built in 1212 and renovated in 1390, from which there is a magnificent view of the Tagus gorge.

Puente de San Martín

★★ Circuit of the Town

There is a very attractive circuit round the town from the Puerta Nueva de Bisagra on the Paseo de Recaredo, past the Puerta Vieja de Bisagra and the Puerta del Cambrón, to the Puente de San Martín; over the bridge and up the hill to the west of the Ermita de Nuestra Señora de la Cabeza, from which there is a magnificent view of the town; then along the Carretera de Circunvalación, on the high ground to the south of the Tagus valley, to the Ermita de la Virgen del Valle; from there northward down to the Puente Nuevo (New Bridge) and along the east bank of the Tagus to the Puente de Alcántara and the Castillo de San Servando; and finally over the modern Puente de Azarquiel and back to the starting-point of the circuit.

Surroundings of Toledo

La Mancha

Leave Toledo on N 401 (the Madrid road), which traverses the outer district of Las Covachuelas and comes in 34km/21 miles to Illescas (alt. 588m/1829ft), a fine old town in which the Emperor Charles V met the captured Francis I of France after the battle of Pavia (1525). In the church of the Hospital de la Caridad are five pictures by El Greco ("Annunciation", "Nativity of Christ", "Coronation of the Virgin", "Compassion", "San Ildefonso"). The parish church has a very handsome Mudéjar tower.

Illescas

Puente de San Martín

Esquivias	A kilometre or two beyond Illescas a minor road branches off N 401 on the right to Esquivias, with the church of Santa María, which preserves the record of Cervantes's marriage.
Ocaña	From Esquivias the road continues east to join N VI, which runs south via Aranjuez (see entry) to Ocaña (alt. 730m/2395ft), an ancient little town still partly surrounded by the dilapidated remains of its walls. It has a neat 18th century Plaza Mayor, a number of interesting churches, including the Renaissance church of Santa María, San Juan and San Martín, and the Isabelline palace of the Dukes of Frías.
Quintanar de la Orden	From Ocaña N 301 runs south-east by way of Villatobas and after crossing the Río Cigüela comes to Quintanar de la Orden (alt. 691m/2267ft), a little town, formerly held by the knightly Order of Santiago, in the corn- and vine-growing district of La Mancha in which Cervantes set the adventures of Don Quixote.
El Toboso	9km/6 miles south-east of Quintanar de la Orden we come to the village of El Toboso, home of Don Quixote's mistress Dulcinea. The Town Hall has a collection of editions of "Don Quixote" in many languages.
★ Tembleque	From Quintanar de la Orden C 402 runs west to Tembleque (which can also be reached from Ocaña on N IV), a typical little La Mancha town. It has an attractive 17th century Plaza Mayor with three tiers of arcaded galleries. Other features of interest are the Baroque Palacio de los Torres and the parish church.
★ Consuegra	From Tembleque N IV runs south, passing numbers of the typical local windmills, to Madridejos (alt. 674m/2211ft), from which C 400 runs 8km/5 miles west to Consuegra (alt. 704m/2310ft), once the chief place in a territory held by the Order of St John. Above the town are a ruined castle

Consuegra: castle and windmills

and hills topped by thirteen windmills, from which there are fine views of La Mancha.

C 400 now turns north-west and skirts the Montes de Consuegra to Mora (alt. 717m/2352ft), a little town with a fine Gothic church and interesting Roman remains.

Mora

10km/6 miles south-west of Mora on C 402 is Orgaz (alt. 744m/2441ft), with a massive 14th century castle which is visible long before the town is reached, an old Roman bridge and a typical Plaza Mayor.

Orgaz

From Mora C 401 goes north-west to Toledo. Off the road to the left stands the imposing Castillo de Guadamur, a well preserved 15th century castle, furnished in period style, which can be visited.

★Castillo de Guadamur

Castles Tour

From Toledo N 403 runs north-west, crosses the Río Guadarrama and comes to Torrijos (alt. 526m/1726ft), a picturesque little town with a Late Gothic church (fine Plateresque doorway) and the Palacio de Altamira.

Torrijos

Shortly before Torrijos a minor road branches off on the right to Barcience which has an imposing 15th century Gothic castle.

Barcience

12km/7½ miles from Torrijos N 403 crosses N V. Just beyond the junction is the old-world little town of Maqueda (alt. 483m/1585ft), the main features of interest in which are the church of Santa María (15th–16th c.), with a carved wood retablo of 1554, and a castle with five round towers, originally a Moorish stronghold.

Maqueda

A few kilometres north of Maqueda is Escalona, with the ruins of a 15th century alcázar.

Escalona

Oropesa

From Maqueda N V runs south-west by way of Talavera de la Reina to Oropesa (alt. 420m/1378ft), a little town famed for its embroidery which has preserved something of a medieval atmosphere. The magnificent Castillo de los Duques de Frías (14th c.) is now the Parador Nacional Virrey de Toledo.

Tordesillas F 3

Province: Valladolid (VA). Telephone dialling code: 983.
Altitude: 702m/2303ft. Population: 7500

The old Castilian market town of Tordesillas, situated on a hill above the Río Duero, lies at an important road junction and was once a frequent residence of the kings of Spain. Here in 1494, following a decision of Pope Alexander VI, Spain and Portugal signed the Treaty of Tordesillas, which divided the New World and other territories yet to be discovered between the two countries: all the lands to the east of a line running from pole to pole 370 miles west of the Cape Verde Islands were assigned to Portugal, all the lands to the west of the line, with the exception of Brazil, to Spain (see map, page 46).

Patio Árabe in the Real Monasterio

After her husband's death Joan the Mad spent the last years of her life in the convent of Santa Clara here. During the rebellion of the Comuneros the town was the headquarters of their Junta Santa ("Sacred League").

Sights

The 16th century church of San Antolín, with a graceful tower, is now a museum. The Capilla de Alderete has a beautiful retablo and contains the tomb of the founder, Pedro González de Alderete; both are by Gaspar de Tordesillas (1550).

San Antolín

The Real Monasterio de Santa Clara, a convent of Clarissine nuns, was originally a palace built by Alfonso XI in the 14th century. Pedro the Cruel chose it as a residence for his illegally married second wife María de Padilla and rebuilt it in Moorish style, modelled on the Alcázar in Seville. After Pedro's death it was occupied by the Clarissines.

★ Real Monasterio de Santa Clara

Moorish influence is evident particularly in the horseshoe and cusped arches in the Patio Árabe and the dome of the adjoining Capilla Dorada, which has 16th century frescoes. A variety of objects are displayed in this chapel, including Joan the Mad's harmonium and a clavichord which Charles V and Philip II are said to have played. The most sumptuous of the chapels in the Gothic church is the Capilla Mayor, with a superb artesonado ceiling which came from Alfonso XI's throne room. In the Capilla del Contador Saldaña is a Flemish retablo with paintings by Nicolás Francés.

★ Artesonado ceiling

Torremolinos

G 8

Province: Málaga (MA). Telephone dialling code: 952
Altitude: 40m/130ft. Population: 40,000

Torremolinos is a popular resort, much favoured by package tour operators, on the coast road (N 340) between Málaga and Algeciras (see entries). Lying in a wide bay with a beach almost 9km/6 miles long, it owes its excellent climate to the shelter provided by the Síerra Tejada to the north and the Sierra Nevada to the south.

In the 19th century a mere village which had grown up around the towers and windmills (torres, molinos) from which it takes its name, Torremolinos is now a long range of concrete buildings – hotels, high-rise apartment blocks and places of entertainment – lining the beach. The life of the town centres on the old Calle San Miguel, while the former fishermen's quarters of La Carihuela and El Bajondilla have developed into heavily built-up holiday settlements.

Around Torremolinos are numerous modern developments with holiday homes and apartments, which make this area, together with Fuengirola (see entry) to the south-west and Málaga to the north-west, one of the largest tourist complexes in Europe – though one that still lacks a sewage plant.

The leisure activities offered by Torremolinos include every kind of water sport, fishing, scuba diving (with facilities for the hire of boats and equipment), sailing, a Wine Museum and a Wax Museum, bullfights, golf, tennis and riding.

Sport and recreation

Tortosa

N 4

Province: Tarragona (T). Telephone dialling code: 977
Altitude: 10m/33ft. Population: 31,000

Tortosa is an old episcopal town on the Ebro, situated between high hills just above its delta. Above the town are the ruins of an Arab stronghold.

Tortosa is identified with the Roman town of Derosa, founded by Scipio Africanus on the ruins of the Iberian settlement of Hibera. It was recovered from the Moors by Ramón Berenguer V in 1148. In 1938 the surrounding area was the scene of the battle of the Ebro, one of the bloodiest engagements of the Civil War, which raged for four months and cost 150,000 lives. The economy of the town is centred on agriculture (olives, rice, citrus fruits) and also on tourism.

Sights

Cathedral

The Cathedral, built between 1347 and 1557, has a Moorish tower and a Neo-Classical façade, but the interior shows a surprising unity of Gothic style. The choir-stalls date from 1588; the retablo on the high altar is by Jaime (Catalan Jaume) Huguet. Other notable features are two stone pulpits, one with reliefs of the Evangelists and the other with Fathers of the Church, and a font bearing the arms of Antipope Benedict XIII and a relief symbolising the schism of the Church (see Castellón de la Plana, Peñíscola). To the left of the font is the 18th century Capilla de Nuestra Señora de la Cinta (Catalan Mare Déu de la Cinta), which preserves as a sacred relic what is believed to be the Virgin's girdle.

A Baroque side doorway leads into the 13th century cloister.

Palacio Episcopal

The Bishop's Palace (1316) has a two-storey patio in typical Catalan Gothic style, with a beautiful chapel on the upper floor.

Colegio de San Luis

The Colegio de San Luis was established by Charles V in 1544 for the education of young Moriscos (Muslims converted to Christianity). It has a handsome three-storey patio decorated with busts of the kings of Aragon.

Santo Domingo

The 16th century church of Santo Domingo now houses the Municipal Archives and Museum.

Tortosa, on the Ebro

Trujillo

Province: Cáceres (CC). Telephone dialling code: 927
Altitude: 485m/1591ft. Population: 11,000

Originally the Roman town of Turgalium, Trujillo was held by the Moors for many centuries before being recovered by Christian forces in the 13th century. The town now calls itself the "Cradle of the Conquistadors", having been the birthplace of many men who went out to seek their fortune in the New World and conquered vast territories for Spain. Chief among them was Francisco Pizarro, conqueror of Peru, who was born in Trujillo in 1475. Other notable figures were Francisco de Orellana, the first man to sail up the Amazon; Diego García Paredes, the "Samson of Extremadura", a man strong as an ox, who founded Trujillo in Venezuela; and Ñuflo de Chaves, who founded the Bolivian town of Santa Cruz. They and their descendants brought some of their wealth back to Trujillo and built great palaces which still give the town its distinctive stamp.

★ Townscape

Around the Plaza Mayor

The central feature of the old town is the Plaza Mayor, in which stands an equestrian statue of Pizarro, erected in 1927. Flanking the square are a number of palaces built by Conquistadors.

Plaza Mayor

At the south-east corner of the square is the Palacio de Piedras Albas, a Gothic mansion with a Renaissance gallery.

Palacio de Piedras Albas

At the north-east corner stands the Palacio de San Carlos, a Renaissance building with a two-storey patio which is now occupied by a convent of nuns. Above a corner balcony can be seen a two-headed eagle, the heraldic emblem of the Vargas-Carvajal family.

Palacio de San Carlos

Adjoining the Palacio de San Carlos, on higher ground, is the church of San Martín (15th–16th c.), with two dissimilar towers; it contains the tombs of two Conquistadors, Orellana and Vargas-Carvajal.

San Martín

In the higher part of the square is the Casa de la Cadena ("House of the Chain"), seat of the Chaves-Orellana family, and in the street behind it the Torre del Alfiler ("Needle Tower").

Casa de la Cadena

At the south-west corner of the Plaza Mayor stands the Plateresque Palacio de la Conquista, the most imposing of the palaces in the square. Along the edge of the roof are twelve statues symbolising the Months, and the windows have elaborate grilles. The palace was built by Hernán Pizarro, half-brother and also son-in-law of Francisco Pizarro. On either side of the corner window are busts of Francisco Pizarro and his wife, the Inca princess Yupanqui, their daughter Juana and Hernán Pizarro himself, who married his own niece. Over the window can be seen the magnificent coat of arms of the Pizarro family.

Palacio de la Conquista

To the west of the Palacio de la Conquista is the Palacio Orellana-Pizarro, with a Renaissance façade flanked by two towers.

Palacio Orellana-Pizarro

Within the Town Walls

From the Palacio Orellana-Pizarro it is a short distance to the Gothic Puerta de San Andrés, which leads into the part of the old town within the walls. Here too there are numerous noble mansions. Immediately inside the gate, to the right, is a small square with the 15th century Palacio de Escobar.

Palacio de los Escobar

Palacio de la Conquista, Trujillo

Pizarro Monument

Alberca	Diagonally opposite the palace are the remains of Roman baths of the Augustan period, including an 11m/36ft deep cistern.
Santa María la Mayor	Farther north, to the left, is the Gothic church of Santa María la Mayor (13th c.), with the tombs of Diego García de Paredes (b. Trujillo 1466) and Juana Yupanqui, daughter (and also daughter-in-law) of Francisco Pizarro. The retablo has paintings by Fernando Gallego. In the square in which the church stands is the birthplace of Francisco de Orellana.
Santiago	The 12th century church of Santiago contains a statue of St James (Santiago), the town's patron saint, and a Gothic retablo. Adjoining the church is an old town gate, the Puerta de Santiago.
Castillo	From the church of Santiago a street leads up to the Castillo, built in Moorish times on the remains of a Roman fort and given its present form in the 15th and 16th centuries.

Tudela

K 3

Province: Navarra (NA). Telephone dialling code: 948
Altitude: 275m/902ft. Population: 26,000

Tudela, situated on the right bank of the Ebro, is the second largest town in the province of Navarra and the chief place in the Ribera district. The town was originally a Moorish settlement, founded in 802 by Amrus, a Muslim ruler subordinate to the Caliph of Córdoba. After its reconquest by Alfonso I in 1119 Tudela offered an admirable example of peaceful coexistence between Christians, Muslims and Jews, each living in their own quarters of the town (which can still to some extent be identified on the ground). The Jewish quarter of the town produced such eminent figures as the rabbi and geographer Benjamin of Tudela, the poet Abraham ben Ezra and the philosopher Yehuda Halevi. It was not until 1512 that Tudela submitted to its incorporation in the kingdom of Castile.

Sights

The town's most important building is the Cathedral, built on the site of an earlier mosque in the 12th and 13th centuries, in a style transitional between Romanesque and Gothic. It has an octagonal bell-tower and a smaller tower with a helm roof. Over the west doorway, in its eight archivolts, is a superb Last Judgment, with innumerable figures. The most notable features of the interior are the retablo, painted by Diego Díaz de Oviedo in 1489–94, remains of Romanesque wall paintings, the Romanesque image of Santa María la Blanca, the magnificent choir-stalls and the Capilla de Santa Ana, lavishly decorated in Baroque style. In the Capilla de Nuestra Señora de la Esperanza are the splendid sarcophagi (15th c.) of Francisco Villaespesa, chancellor of Navarre, and his wife Isabel de Ujué. The Romanesque cloister has finely carved capitals.

Cathedral

The church of La Magdalena (13th–16th c.) has a very beautiful 12th century doorway and a fine 16th century retablo.

La Magdalena

San Nicolás is a brick-built church with a Romanesque doorway which owes its present form to an 18th century rebuilding. It contained the tomb of Sancho the Strong (d. 1234) until its transfer to Roncesvalles (see Pamplona, Surroundings).

San Nicolás

In one of the narrow streets near the Cathedral is the 16th century Casa del Almirante, with a painted façade and two balconies supported by Atlas figures.

Casa del Almirante

The central feature of the town is the Plaza de los Fueros, the finest building in which is the Casa del Reloj, with a small clock-tower. In the centre of the square is a bandstand.

Plaza de los Fueros

Túy/Tui

B 3

Province: Pontevedra (PO). Telephone dialling code: 986
Altitude: 45m/148ft. Population: 16,000

The old Spanish frontier town of Túy (Galician Tui), picturesquely situated on a hill above the right bank of the Río Miño (Galician Minho), was originally the Iberian settlement of Tude, which put up a long resistance to the Romans before being finally conquered. In the 8th century it became capital of the Visigothic kingdom of Galicia, and in the 11th century it was briefly held by a Viking chieftain called Olof before being recaptured by Alfonso V.
    Túy is the Spanish frontier control post on the frontier with Portugal, which is formed by the Río Miño. The river is spanned by a lattice girder bridge 333m/364yd long.

Sights

On the highest point in the town stands the fortress-like Cathedral with its twin towers (11th–13th c.), which was begun in Romanesque style and much altered in later centuries. Within a porch on the west front is a 14th century Gothic doorway, with a representation of the Adoration of the Shepherds and the Three Kings in the tympanum and finely carved figures on either side. Notable features of the interior are a number of Gothic and Renaissance tombs and the choir-stalls, carved with scenes from the life of

Cathedral

San Telmo, the town's patron saint. The cloister is also Gothic. From the wall-walk on the roof there is a fine view of the town.

San Telmo   San Telmo was a Dominican friar from Portugal who died in Túy in 1240. Near the north doorway of the Cathedral is the late 16th century church dedicated to him which contains his relics.

San Bartolomé   Just outside the town centre can be seen the 10th century church of San Bartolomé, one of the oldest churches in Galicia.

Úbeda   H 7

Province: Jaén (J). Telephone dialling code: 953.
Altitude: 757m/2484ft. Population: 29,000

★ Townscape   The town of Úbeda, the Moorish Obdah, lies near the upper Guadalquivir amid extensive olive plantations. Its numerous Renaissance buildings, forming a remarkably unified and harmonious whole, have earned it the name of the "Andalusian Salamanca". After its reconquest by Christian forces in 1234 Úbeda became one of the main bases in the fight to recover Andalusia from the Moors.

Sights

★ Plaza de
Vázquez Molina   The magnificent central feature of the town is the long Plaza de Vázquez Molina, surrounded by remarkable Renaissance buildings.

★ El Salvador   The finest building in the square is the Renaissance church of El Salvador on the north-east side, built in the first half of the 16th century to the design

El Salvador, Úbeda

Parador in the Sierra de Cazorla

of Diego de Siloé and Andrés de Vandelvira. The west front with its rich sculptural decoration is flanked by two low round towers. The large semicircular Capilla Mayor with a high dome, of impressive size even from outside, is closed by a superb choir screen and has a retablo with a carved "Transfiguration" by Alonso Berruguete. The sacristy, by Vandelvira, is equally magnificent.

On the right-hand side of the square are the Parador Nacional Condestable Dávalos, in an old noble mansion, and the Casa de los Cadenas, now the Town Hall, which was designed by Vandelvira; over the entrance is a coat of arms supported by two lions.

Casa de los Cadenas

Diagonally opposite the Town Hall, on the left-hand side of the southeastern part of the square, is a 16th century palace built by the Marqués de Mancera, Viceroy of Peru.

Palacio de Mancera

On the far side of this part of the square is the church of Santa María de los Reales Alcázares, with two slender towers. Much altered and rebuilt over the centuries, the church has richly decorated Gothic chapels and a Renaissance choir screen by Maestro Bartolomé of Jaén.

Santa María de los Reales Alcázares

On the left of the church can be seen the old Cárcel del Obispo, the Bishop's Prison.

Cárcel del Obispo

To the north of Plaza Vázquez de Molina, in Plaza 1 de Mayo, is the church of San Pablo, built at the time of the Reconquista, with an apse of 1380. The main doorway still shows Romanesque features; the south doorway is Isabelline. Set into the outside wall is a fountain of 1559. The most notable feature of the interior is the Plateresque Capilla del Camarero Vago.

San Pablo

In Calle del Obispo Cobos, in the western part of the town, is the Hospital de Santiago, a long range of buildings designed by Vandelvira (1587).

Hospital de Santiago

A walk round the town will reveal many other old mansions, usually bearing the coat of arms of the family.

Surroundings of Úbeda

From Peal de Becerro (40km/25 miles south-east of Úbeda) C 328 runs 15km/9 miles east to the picturesque little town of Cazorla, dominated by its castle. This is the chief place in the Sierra de Cazorla, in which the Guadalquivir rises, and a good base for walks and climbs in the sierra and in the Coto Nacional de Cazorla nature park. From here a narrow road crosses the Puerto de las Palomas (1290m/4232ft), with magnificent scenery (possibility of an overnight stop in the Parador Nacional El Adelantado), and through the Guadalquivir gorge to Villacarrillo, from which it is 35km/22 miles back to Úbeda.

★ Sierra de Cazorla

See entry

Baeza

Valencia

M 5

Province: Valencia (V). Telephone dialling code: 96
Altitude: sea level. Population: 752,000

Valencia, the old capital of the kingdom of Valencia and now chief town of its province, Spain's third largest city, the see of an archbishop and a university town, lies close to the Mediterranean on the right bank of the Río Turia (known to the Arabs as the Guadalaviar, the "White River"), in the fertile Huerta de Valencia.
    Described in an ancient saying as "a piece of heaven fallen to earth", Valencia is a typically southern town with its bustling streets and the

brightly coloured azulejo domes of its many churches. The climate is unusually mild and predominantly dry.

El Grao

Valencia's port of El Grao, 4km/2½ miles east of the city centre, is mainly engaged in shipping the huerta's considerable exports of agricultural produce (oranges, wine, raisins, oil and rice). There has also been a considerable development of industry (metal-processing, shipbuilding, chemicals, textiles) in this area.

★Fallas

Every year in March Valencia celebrates the fiesta of San José, a spring festival during which large tableaux known as *fallas,* with figures made of papier mâché and rags (*ninots*), are set up in the streets and burned at midnight on the last day of the fiesta. The custom originated in the Middle Ages, when carpenters and other craftsmen used to burn up left-over scraps of wood and other materials on the feast of St Joseph.

History

Originally a Greek settlement, Valencia later fell into the hands of the Carthaginians, and in the 2nd century B.C. became the Roman colony of Valentia, which rose to prosperity in the reign of Augustus. In 413 it passed to the Visigoths and in 714 to the Moors, who called it Medina bu-Tarab ("City of Joy"). After the fall of the Caliphate of Córdoba Valencia and the adjoining coastal region became an independent kingdom, which was conquered by the Almoravids in 1092. Two years later it was recovered by the Cid, but in 1102 it again fell into Moorish hands. Under Mohammed ibn Said it became the capital of a Moorish kingdom until its reconquest by Jaime I of Aragon (Jaime el Conquistador) in 1238. During the War of the Spanish Succession at the beginning of the 18th century Valencia supported the Habsburgs. In 1808 the town rose against the French. During the Civil War, in 1936–37, it was the seat of the Republican government, and it was the last Republican stronghold to fall to Franco on March 30th 1939, two days after Madrid.

Fallas, celebrating the fiesta of San José

Porta Coeli, Teruel, Castellón

1 N. Sra. de los Desamparados
2 San Esteban

3 Palacio del Marqués
  Dos Aguas

4 Corpus Christi
5 Colegio del Patriarca

Around the Plaza del Ayuntamiento

The hub of the city's life and traffic is the long Plaza del Ayuntamiento, surrounded by hotels, cafés and offices, with a remarkable musical fountain. A colourful flower market is held in the square.

On the west side of the square is the Ayuntamiento or Casa Consistorial (Town Hall), in which are the Municipal Library and the Municipal Historical Museum, with pictures, weapons and jewellery and a valuable collection of books.

Ayuntamiento

To the south of the Plaza del Ayuntamiento, beside the Estación del Norte, is the Plaza de Toros, one of Spain's largest bullrings, with seating for 18,000. Attached to it is the interesting Museo Taurino (Bullfighting Museum).

Plaza de Toros

At the northern tip of the Plaza del Ayuntamiento, running north-east/south-west, is Valencia's main street, Calle de San Vicente, the northern part of which is particularly busy.

Calle de
San Vicente

★Cathedral

Calle de San Vicente leads north into the Plaza de la Reina, the central square of the old town.

On the north side of the square stands the Cathedral (La Seo), built between 1252 and 1482 on the site of an earlier mosque. It is an imposing building with a predominantly Gothic exterior but a Baroque façade. At its south-west corner is the 68m/223ft high bell-tower (unfinished) known as the Torre del Miguelete (Micalet), with the bell of the same name (originally consecrated on Michaelmas Day 1418), which with its chimes formerly regulated the irrigation of the huerta. From the outlook platform at a height of 50m/165ft (entrance from north aisle) there is a magnificent view of the city. In the south transept is the Romanesque Puerta del Palau, in the north transept the Gothic Puerta de los Apóstoles, richly decorated with sculpture and surmounted by a 14th century rose window. Every Thursday morning the ancient Water Court (Tribunal de las Aguas) meets in this doorway to deal with disputes over water rights in the huerta.

★Torre del Miguelete

Interior

The interior of the Cathedral (98m/322ft long) was completely remodelled in the 18th century. It contains many valuable pictures, including works by Goya (in the 2nd chapel in the south aisle) and Palomino. The choir has fine 16th century stalls. Over the crossing is a majestic octagonal dome (*cimborio*). The Capilla Mayor has a magnificent 15th century high altar, with side panels painted by Fernando de Llanos, a pupil of Leonardo da Vinci, and Fernando Yáñez de la Almedina (1509). In the Capilla de la Buen Muerte, behind the Capilla Mayor, are a crucifix by Alonso Cano and an alabaster altar with a reliquary containing San Vicente Mártir's forearm.

★Capilla del Santo Cáliz

The Capilla del Santo Cáliz, originally the chapterhouse (1369), with fine Gothic stellar vaulting, is entered from the south aisle. In this chapel is preserved the Santo Cáliz (Holy Chalice), set with rubies and pearls, which is believed to be the cup used at the Last Supper and by some is thought to be the legendary Holy Grail in which Christ's blood was caught at the Crucifixion. Until the 15th century the chalice was kept in the monastery of San Juan de la Peña in the Pyrenees (see Jaca, Surroundings).

The Cathedral Museum has pictures by Zurbarán and by Juan de Juanes and other artists of the Valencian school.

West of the Cathedral

Santa Catalina

On the west side of the Plaza de la Reina is the Gothic church of Santa Catalina, with a richly decorated hexagonal tower.

★Lonja de la Seda

Farther west, in the long Plaza del Mercado (once the scene of tournaments and festivals), stands the Lonja de la Seda (or Lonja de los Mercaderes), the old Silk Exchange in which the trade in the famous Valencian silk, sold all over Europe, was carried on. This magnificent Late Gothic building, erected in 1498 on the site of a Moorish alcázar, has richly decorated doorways and windows and fine gargoyle water-spouts (*gárgolas*). The main hall has rich stellar vaulting borne on twisted columns. From the tower (144 steps) there are fine views of the town.

Mercado Central

Opposite the Lonja is the Mercado Central (Central Market), built in 1928 and lavishly decorated with azulejos, with some 1300 market stalls selling all the produce of Spain.

Los Santos Juanes

The church of the Santos Juanes (1368) immediately adjoining the Market has a beautiful façade and a ceiling painting by Palomino, both dating from about 1700.

Valencia Cathedral   *Lonja*

To the north of the Plaza del Mercado is the church of San Nicolás, built on the site of an earlier mosque, which has a "Crucifixion" by Rodrigo de Osona in the baptismal chapel and a retablo by Juan de Juanes in a side chapel on the left.

San Nicolás

South-East of the Cathedral

To the south of the Plaza de la Reina, in Calle San Vicente, stands the Gothic church of San Martín (1372), with a Baroque doorway crowned by a bronze equestrian statue of St Martin (15th c. Dutch work).

San Martín

A little way east of San Martín is the handsome 18th century Palacio del Marqués de Dos Aguas, with a richly decorated alabaster doorway by Ignacio Vergara, which now houses the National Ceramic Museum, Spain's leading collection of ceramics. Founded in 1947, with the González Martí collection as its nucleus, the Museum has over 5000 examples of traditional pottery from Valencia and the surrounding area (Alcora, Paterna, Manises), azulejos from Teruel, faience from Toledo and Seville, Greek, Roman and Arab ware, Chinese and Japanese porcelain, and modern pieces by Mariano Benlliure and Picasso. The pride of the collection is a fully equipped early 19th century Valencian kitchen completely faced with tiles.

★ Museo Nacional de Cerámica

South of the Museum is the church of San Andrés, built in 1686 on the site of a mosque, which has many pictures by Valencian artists and hand-painted azulejos from Manises.

San Andrés

To the east of San Andrés we find the Renaissance-style Colegio del Patriarca, with an arcaded courtyard, which was built between 1586 and 1610 to house a seminary for the training of priests founded by Juan de Ribera, Archbishop and Viceroy of Valencia. The Capilla de la Concepción

★ **Colegio del Patriarca**

461

contains valuable 16th century Flemish tapestries. On the first floor, in the Rector's Lodging, are a collection of old masters (Dierick Bouts, Rogier van der Weyden, Juan de Juanes, Ribalta, Morales, El Greco, etc.) and fine Brussels tapestries.

Corpus Christi   At the south corner of the building is the church of Corpus Christi (1586), with a superb "Last Supper" by Ribalta (1606) on the high altar. The Miserere service in this church (every Friday about 10) is an impressive occasion, during which Ribalta's picture disappears and a curtain is suddenly pulled aside to reveal a wooden crucifix (believed to be of 16th century German workmanship).

University   Facing the Colegio, to the south, is the University (1830), with a valuable library of some 87,000 volumes, including many incunabula and manuscripts.

Convento de Santo Domingo   East of the University, in the direction of the Río Turia, lies the Plaza Porta de la Mar, with a triumphal arch in the centre. To the north of this square is the Convento de Santo Domingo. The church of Santo Domingo (also called the Capilla de San Vicente Ferrer), rebuilt at the end of the 18th century, is entered by a handsome doorway adjoining the uncompleted tower. To the right of the entrance is the 15th century Capilla de los Reyes, with the tomb of Marshal Rodrigo Mendoza. Part of the convent, including the cloister, is now a barracks.

North of the Cathedral

Capilla de Nuestra Señora de los Desamparados   On the north side of the Cathedral and linked with it by an arch, is the Capilla de Nuestra Señora de los Desamparados, built in 1667 and decorated with frescoes by Palomino. On the high altar can be seen a much venerated image (1416) of Our Lady of the Helpless, patroness of Valencia.

Almudín   North-east of the chapel is the old public granary, the Almudín, now occupied by the Palaeontological Museum, with a collection of prehistoric animal remains from South America.

★ Palacio de la Generalidad   North-west of the Cathedral, in Calle de Caballeros, stands the Palacio de la Generalidad (Audiencia), built between 1510 and 1579 to house the parliament of the kingdom of Valencia and now occupied by the Diputación Provincial. Particularly notable among the sumptuous rooms of the palace are, on the first floor, the Salón de Cortes, with a coffered ceiling and an azulejo frieze, and the Sala Dorada, with a superb artesonado ceiling.

★ Torres de Serranos   On the north side of the old town are the Torres de Serranos, the old north gate of the town, built in 1398 on Roman foundations and restored in 1930. From the massive towers there are good views of the town. Temporarily housed in the towers is the Maritime Museum, which displays antiquities recovered from the sea.

★ Museo Provincial de Bellas Artes

Just north of the Torres de Serranos the Puente de Serranos crosses the Río Turia (usually dry), beyond which is the Plaza de Santa Mónica, with the church of Santa Mónica. Down the far bank of the river to the right is the Museo Provincial de Bellas Artes (Provincial Museum of Art), also known as the Museo de Valencia.

As the name indicates, the museum is mainly devoted to artists of the Valencian school. On the ground floor are displays of archaeological material and sculpture, with the museum's collection of pictures on the first floor. Among them are the anonymous altarpiece of Fray Bonifacio Ferrer (14th c.), a triptych of the Passion by Hieronymus Bosch, pictures of the early Valencian school by Rodrigo de Osona ("Pietà"), Nicolás Falcó, Jacomart and others, works by painters of the main Valencian school including Ribalta ("Last Supper", "St Bruno"), Ribera ("St Jerome"), Macip and Espinosa, pictures by other Spanish painters (Velázquez, Murillo, El Greco, Goya, Morales) and works by the Italian masters Pinturicchio and Andrea del Sarto.

On the second floor can be seen pictures by 19th and 20th century Valencian artists; the third floor is devoted to historical painting.

Adjoining the Museum of Art are the Jardines del Real or Viveros Municipales, with numerous modern monuments, and the exhibition building of the International Trade Fair (Feria de Muestras). Opposite the Trade Fair grounds the Puente del Real (1598), with statues of San Vicente Mártir and San Vicente Ferrer (17th c.) crosses the Turia. From the bridge the Paseo de la Alameda runs down the left bank of the river to the Puente de Aragón. | Jardines del Real

Other Sights

From the Palacio de la Generalidad Calle de Caballeros and its continuation Calle de Cuarte run west to the Torres de Cuarte (or Puerta de Cuarte), an old town gate (1440–90) similar to the Torres de Serranos. | Torres de Cuarte

A little way east, beyond the Avenida de Guillén de Castro, lies the Botanic Garden, with thousands of species of plants. | Jardín Botánico

North-west of the Botanic Garden, in Calle de la Corona, is the Museum of Ethnology and Prehistory. The ethnological collection includes agricultural implements, furniture, kitchen equipment, etc.; the prehistoric section is being built up. | Museo de Etnología y Prehistoria

The Museo Etnográfico de las Fallas, in the Avenida de la Plata (south-east of the town centre, some distance out), is devoted to the history and traditions of Valencia's famous fiesta of the Fallas. | Museo Etnográfico de las Fallas

Valladolid   G 3

Province: Valladolid (VA). Telephone dialling code: 983
Altitude: 694m/2277ft. Population: 330,000

Valladolid, chief town of its province, the see of an archbishop and a university town, lies on the Río Pisuerga just above its confluence with the Duero, on the fertile plateau of Old Castile. In recent decades the town has enjoyed a considerable economic upswing through the rapid development of industry, particularly car production; but as a result it is now surrounded by rather dreary industrial suburbs and the central area as a whole is not particularly attractive either. It does, however, preserve some splendid buildings and works of art, the legacy of a great past when it was the residence of the Spanish kings and attracted great artists working in the Isabelline, Renaissance and Herreran styles. | ★ Art and architecture

There was a settlement here in the time of the Arabs, who called it Velad-Olid or Balad-Walid ("Town of the Governor"). In 1469 the Catholic Monarchs, Ferdinand and Isabella, were married in Valladolid, and in 1504–06 Columbus, an ailing and disappointed man, spent the last two years of his life in the town. For brief periods during the 16th and 17th centuries, during the reigns of Philip II and III, Valladolid was the seat of the Spanish court. It was Napoleon's headquarters in 1809. | History

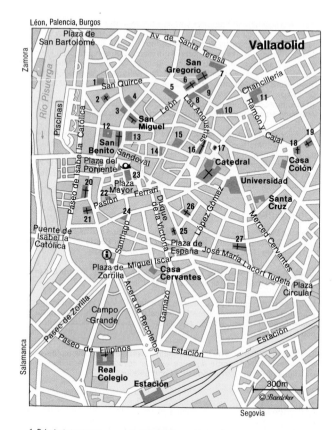

Léon, Palencia, Burgos

Av. de Santa Teresa

Valladolid

Zamora

Rio Pisuerga

Plaza de San Bartolomé

San Gregorio

Chancillería

San Quirce

1

2

3

4

5

6

7

8

9

10

11

12

San Miguel

13

14

15

16

17

18

19

León

Las Angustias

Ramón y Cajal

Piscinas

Paseo de Isabel la Católica

San Benito

Sandoval

Plaza del Poniente

Catedral

Casa Colón

20

21

22

23

24

25

26

27

Plaza Mayor

Ferrari

Pasión

Duque de la Victoria

López Gómez

Universidad

Santa Cruz

Merced

Cervantes

Puente de Isabel la Católica

Santiago

Plaza de España

José María Lacort

Tudela

Plaza Circular

Plaza de Zorrilla

Miguel Iscar

Casa Cervantes

Acera de Recoletos

Gamazo

Paseo de Zorrilla

Campo Grande

Paseo de Filipinos

Estación

Estación

Salamanca

Real Colegio

Estación

300m

© Baedeker

Segovia

1 Palacio de los Condes de Benavente	9 Casa del Marques de Villena	19 Las Huelgas
2 Santa Catalina	10 San Martín	20 San Lorenzo
3 Palacio de los Marqueses de Valverde	11 Palacio de los Vivero	21 Santa Ana
4 Museo Arqueológico	12 Patio Herreriano	22 La Pasión (Museo de Pintura)
5 Palacio Real	13 Casa de Berruguete	23 Ayuntamiento
6 San Pablo	14 La Cruz	24 Santiago
7 Casa del Sol	15 Palacio Arzobispal	25 Porta Coeli
8 Palacio de los Pimentel	16 Las Angustias	26 El Salvador
	17 Santa María la Antigua	27 La Promesa
	18 La Magdalena	

Around the Plaza Mayor

Ayuntamiento

The hub of the city's life is the spacious arcaded Plaza Mayor, on the north side of which stands the Ayuntamiento (Town Hall; 1908).

San Benito

A short distance north-west of the Town Hall is the church of San Benito (1499–1504), with a massive open porch below the tower. The choir is enclosed by a beautiful wrought-iron screen of 1571.

Museo Arqueológico

Farther north, diagonally opposite the church of San Miguel (retablo by Adrián Álvarez), we come to the Palacio de Fabio Nelli, which now houses the Provincial Archaeological Museum (prehistoric and Roman antiquities, including mosaics and busts; Gothic frescoes, sculpture, arts and crafts).

Opposite the Museum is the palace of the Valverde family, a typical example of a Renaissance noble mansion.

Palacio de los Valverde

West of the Plaza Mayor, in Calle de la Pasión, stands the church of the Pasión, now a picture gallery, with works by 16th and 17th century Spanish masters, notably Vicente Carducho (1578–1638) and Gregorio Martínez (1547–97), a native of Valladolid.

Museo de Pinturas

The church of the convent of Santa Ana, south-west of the Museo de Pinturas, contains paintings by Goya and Bayeu.

Santa Ana

From the Plaza Mayor Calle de Santiago runs south, passing the church of Santiago (St James), which has a fine retablo by Alonso Berruguete and a figure of Christ by Francisco de la Mata in one of the side chapels.

Santiago

Around the Plaza de Zorrilla

From the church of Santiago Calle de Santiago continues south to the Plaza de Zorrilla, the town's busiest traffic intersection. Beyond it is the Campo Grande, a large park, along the west side of which is a broad promenade, the Paseo del Campo Grande. This leads to the Plaza de Colón, in which is a large monument to Columbus (1905).

Campo Grande

From the Plaza de Colón the Paseo de Filipinos runs east past the Augustinian Convento de los Filipinos, now occupied by the Oriental Museum, which displays objets d'art from China and the Philippines collected by Augustinian missionaries in the Far East. The Chinese collection includes bronze objects of 1600–200 B.C., Sung and Ming porcelain, jade and lacquer ware and watercolours; the Philippines are represented by weapons, musical instruments and Christian sculpture.

★ Museo Oriental

To the east of the Plaza de Zorrilla, in the short Calle del Rosario, can be found the Casa de Cervantes, a little gem lost in a rather unattractive part of the city. Calle Miguel Iscar, going east from the square, runs past a high wrought-iron railing through which there is a glimpse of a small garden with a fountain in the centre. On the far side of the garden is the house, overgrown with ivy and wild vines, in which Cervantes lived from 1603 to 1606 and probably wrote the first part of "Don Quixote". The Río Esgueva, spanned by a small bridge, once flowed past the house; but of this no trace is left in the modern town. On a conducted tour of the house (in Spanish only) visitors are shown the dining room, Cervantes's desk, the alcove, the kitchen and other rooms, giving them an idea of the way of life in a better-off 16th century Spanish household.

★★ Casa de Cervantes

Around the Cathedral

Some 500m/550yd east of the Plaza Mayor stands the Cathedral, begun by Juan de Herrera in 1580 on an ambitious scale, continued by Alberto Churriguera from 1730 onwards but never completed. Herrera's design for Valladolid Cathedral provided a model followed by many churches in Spain and its South American colonies, its plain and massive architecture marking a break with the elaborate ornament of the Plateresque style. Of the four corner towers which were planned only the south tower was built (restored in 1885 after its collapse in 1841). The most notable features of the spacious interior (122m/400ft long, 62m/203ft wide) are the high altar by Juan de Juni (1561; originally in the church of Santa María la Antigua), the fine Renaissance choir-stalls and an "Assumption of the Virgin" by Velázquez.

Cathedral

MUSEO
NACIONAL
ESCULTURA

In the adjoining collegiate church is the Diocesan Museum. Among its principal treasures are a 2m/6½ft high silver monstrance in the form of a temple, Juan de Arfe's masterpiece (1590), sculpture (including an "Ecce Homo" by Gregorio Fernández) and paintings (retablo of St Anne, 15th c.).

Museo Diocesano

To the east of the Cathedral, in the Plaza de la Universidad, is the University (founded 1346), with a fine Baroque façade of 1715 by the brothers Diego and Narciso Tomé.

University

South-east of the University the former Colegio de Santa Cruz (by Lorenzo Vázquez, 1492), one of the earliest Renaissance buildings in Spain, has a handsome three-storey patio. On its richly sculptured façade can be seen a figure of Cardinal Pedro González de Mendoza, founder of the college, which is now occupied by a number of University institutes and a valuable library of 52,000 volumes.

Colegio de Santa Cruz

From the Colegio de Santa Cruz Calle del Cardenal Mendoza runs north-east into Calle de Colón. In this street is the Casa de Colón, the house in which Columbus (Cristóbal Colón) died on May 31st 1506. He is commemorated by a small museum in the adjoining house.

Casa de Colón

Adjoining, to the north-east, is the 16th century church of La Magdalena, with medallions containing coats of arms on the façade.

La Magdalena

Farther along the street we come to the Convento de las Huelgas, with a 16th century church which contains sculpture by Gregorio Fernández ("Adoration of the Shepherds") and Juan de Juni.

Convento de las Huelgas

North-west of the Plaza de la Universidad is the church of Santa María la Antigua (12th–14th c.), the oldest church in the town, with a Romanesque tower. The interior has an air of quiet elegance.

Santa María la Antigua

Close by is the church of Las Angustias (1597–1604). In a side chapel in this church is a masterpiece by Juan de Juni (1560), the much venerated Virgen de los Siete Cuchillos (Virgin of the Seven Knives).

Las Angustias

From here Calle de las Angustias leads north to the Plaza de San Pablo, on the right-hand side of which is the church of San Pablo, founded in 1276. The soaring façade (by Simón de Colonia, 1492), flanked by plain towers, vies in richness of decoration with the Colegio de San Gregorio (below). Above the doorway is a representation of the Coronation of the Virgin. Notable features of the interior are the fine Plateresque doorways into the transepts and a statue of Santo Domingo (St Dominic) by Gregorio Fernández.

San Pablo

★ Façade

Facing San Pablo is the Renaissance-style Royal Palace (Palacio de Felipe II), now occupied by the Capitanía General (military headquarters).

Palacio Real

On the south-east side of the Plaza de San Pablo, on the corner of Calle de las Angustias, is the Palacio de los Pimentel, in which Philip II was born in 1527.

Palacio de los Pimentel

★ Colegio de San Gregorio/★★ Museo Nacional de Escultura

Adjoining the church of San Pablo rises Valladolid's principal architectural showpiece, the former Colegio de San Gregorio, built between 1488 and 1496 for Isabella the Catholic's confessor Alonso de Burgos, bishop of Palencia. The sumptuously decorated façade (ascribed to Gil de Siloé), with its numerous statues, coats of arms and naturalistic ornament, is a masterpiece of Isabelline architecture.

★ Façade

◀ *Façade of San Gregorio*

Patio of the Colegio de San Gregorio

★ Patio	No less magnificent is the second patio, which is entered from another, more modest, courtyard. Over an arcaded gallery with plain twisted columns on ground level is an upper gallery with richly carved double arches, and along the edge of the roof are water-spouts in the form of fabulous animals.
★★ Museum of Sculpture	The College is now occupied by the Museo Nacional de Escultura (National Museum of Sculpture), with the finest collection of religious sculpture in wood (as well as religious paintings) in Spain and one of the most important collections of its kind in Europe, in which the leading artists of the 16th and 17th centuries are represented. The thirty rooms of the Museum (with beautiful timber ceilings) contain so many fine works of polychrome and gilded sculpture that only the most important can be mentioned here.
Rooms I–III	Rooms I to III on the ground floor are given up to the works of Alonso Berruguete (1489–1561). Outstanding among them are a retablo carved for the church of San Benito in Valladolid (Room II) and the "Martyrdom of St Sebastian" in Room III.
Room X	From Room III a staircase leads up to the first floor, on which Room X is of particular interest. It contains a five-part retablo of the Passion by an unknown Flemish artist of the 15th century, with the Descent from the Cross in the central panel, a "Holy Family" by Diego de Siloé and a Pietà which is thought to be of German origin.
Room XI	This large room is almost completely taken up by the magnificent choir-stalls from the church of San Benito (1525–29).
Room XV	In Room XV is one of the great masterpieces of Spanish religious sculpture, Juan de Juni's "Entombment" (1544; illustration, page 64).
Room XXI	Room XXI is mainly devoted to works by Pedro de Mena (1628–88), including a "Mary Magdalene" of 1664.

Rooms IV and V, reached at the end of the tour, contain works by Gregorio Fernández (1566–1636), including a fine "Pietà". Room V also has a picture by Zurbarán ("Santa Faz", 1658).

Opposite the Colegio de San Gregorio is the Plateresque façade of the Casa del Sol (16th c.).

Surroundings of Valladolid

The part played by the Valladolid region in the history of Spain has left it with many castles, and on excursions in the surrounding area visitors will frequently come upon imposing medieval strongholds.

11km/7 miles south-west of Valladolid, above the little town of Simancas (alt. 725m/2379ft) on the Río Pisuerga, is the formidable Castillo de Simancas, in which Charles V installed the Spanish national archives (more than 30 million documents, housed in 52 rooms).

19km/12 miles beyond Simancas on N 620 is Tordesillas (see entry).

Along the Río Duero

From Valladolid N 122 runs east along the south side of the Duero to Quintanilla de Onésimo, from which a detour can be made to Valbuena de Duero, on the north bank, to see the very interesting convent of Santa María, with a ruined 12th century Cistercian church and a fine Late Gothic cloister.

Returning to N 122, or following the road along the north bank and passing through the typical little Castilian town of Pesquera de Duero, we continue to Peñafiel, with an imposing castle (211m/231yd long, with twelve round towers and a 24m/80ft high keep) founded by the Count of Castile in the 10th century. Other features of interest in the town are the 14th century Mudéjar-style Convento de San Pablo and the large Plaza del Corso, in which bullfights used to be held.

On the Segovia Road

N 601 leads south-east from Valladolid, crosses the Canal de Castilla and comes to Arrabal del Portillo. Off the road to the left is Portillo, with a stoutly walled castle which was used as a state prison for political offenders.

N 601 continues into Segovia province and, 50km/31 miles from Valladolid, reaches Cuéllar (alt. 775m/2543ft). A settlement on this site was captured by the Romans in 96 B.C. and given the name of Colenda. The Catholic Monarchs frequently stayed in the town. There is a well-preserved 15th century castle with a Gothic chapel and a fine Renaissance courtyard. The little walled town itself has preserved many old palaces and a number of brick-built Romanesque churches which are among the oldest in Spain.

On the León Road

From Valladolid N 601 runs north-west up the slopes of the wide Duero valley to Villanubla (alt. 843m/2766ft), off the road to the left, with Valladolid's airport.

From Villanubla a minor road runs south-west to Wamba, with the church of Santa María, which incorporates part of a 12th century Mozarabic building. The Visigothic king Recceswinth died in Wamba in 672.

Torrelobatón	Beyond Wamba on the same minor road is Torrelobatón, which has a well-preserved 13th century castle with massive round towers and an imposing keep (Torre del Homenaje).
Fuensaldaña	From Villanubla a secondary road branches off on the right to the village of Fuensaldaña, with the 15th century Castillo de Vivero, which has a massive square tower with six defensive turrets.
★ Medina de Rioseco	N 601 continues through the Montes de Torozos to Medina de Rioseco (alt. 735m/2412ft), an old-world little town with six notable churches dating from the 15th–17th centuries. The church of Santa María de Mediavilla has two *rejas* of 1532 and 1554, an altar by Esteban Jordán (1590) and the Plateresque Capilla de los Benavente (1546); the church of Santiago has a sumptuous Churrigueresque altar. The main street of the town is lined with typical Castilian houses.

Other Excursions from Valladolid

See Arévalo, Coca, Medina del Campo, Palencia

Vich/Vic   P 3

Province: Barcelona (B). Telephone dialling code: 93
Altitude: 494m/1621ft. Population: 28,000

The old town of Vich (Catalan Vic), the see of a bishop since 616, lies in a wide valley some 60km/37 miles north of Barcelona, on the site of the Roman settlement of Ausa. It was the birthplace of the noted philosopher, mathematician and publicist Jaume Balmes (1810–48).

Cathedral	The Cathedral, on the edge of the old town, was originally founded in 1040, but was almost completely rebuilt between 1803 and 1821. It was badly damaged in 1936, during the Civil War, and subsequently restored. On the north side of the nave is a beautiful Romanesque tower.
Interior	The Cathedral is entered by a small doorway on the north side. The nave with its flanking aisles is in a massive, heavy Baroque style. The walls above the side chapels, the inner surface of the west front and the apse are covered with monumental wall paintings (1926–30) by José (Catalan Josep) María Sert, which reflect something of the spirit of their Baroque models. In a chapel closed by a grille in the north aisle, near the entrance, is a silver sarcophagus (18th century) containing the remains of a local saint, San Bernardo Calvo (Catalan Bernat Calbó).
★ Alabaster altar	In the ambulatory is a Gothic altar (by Pere Oller; 15th c.) of painted and richly gilded alabaster, originally the high altar, which miraculously survived the destruction of the church during the Civil War. The central figures are the Virgin and Child with St Peter (recognisable by his papal crown and keys); on either side are twelve scenes from the life of Christ and the life of St Peter; and on the predella are Apostles and Evangelists, with Christ as the Man of Sorrows in the middle.
Chapterhouse	The chapterhouse, crypt and cloister can be seen only in the company of the sacristan. The Gothic chapterhouse has a painted keystone with the figure of St Peter.
★ Cloister	From the chapterhouse visitors enter the Gothic part (14th c.) of the cloister, which is on three levels (Romanesque, Gothic and Renaissance). In the centre is the bombastic monument of Jaume Balmes, who was for a time an adviser to Pope Pius IX (of whom there is a portrait bust in the cloister).

This part of the cloister is notable for its lightness and transparency. The arcading has rich tracery.

The crypt, which dates from the early 11th century, incorporates stone from Visigothic and Arab buildings. Notable features are the fine capitals and the alabaster windows in the apse.

Crypt

Immediately opposite the north side of the Cathedral is the Episcopal Museum, much the most important part of which is the department of Romanesque art.

★**Museo Episcopal/Museu Episcopal**

Room I contains a world-famous carving of the Descent from the Cross (*c.* 1123); wall paintings from Romanesque churches in the surrounding area, including a complete apse from a 12th century church with paintings of the Creation of Man and the Fall; other apses; and many panel paintings of fine quality.

Room II moves on to Gothic art. Among the most notable items are a large alabaster altarpiece with a representation of the Passion, a large group of figures (*c.* 1467) from a Holy Sepulchre in the Cathedral and a number of Gothic altarpieces.

The next seven rooms are devoted to 14th and 15th century Gothic painting. Among the artists represented are Pedro Serra, Ramón de Mur, Jaume Ferrer I and II, the Master of Preixana, Lluis Borrassà, Bernard Martorell and Jaime Huguet.

On the first floor is the department of Baroque art. Here too are prehistoric antiquities, Roman amphoras, terra sigillata and glass, a large collection of embroidered vestments, and examples of folk art.

Immediately adjoining the Baroque façade of the church of Nuestra Señora de la Piedad, in the eastern part of the old town, are the remains (considerably restored) of a Roman temple of the 2nd century A.D. To the right are the remains of medieval walls and vaulting.

Roman temple

The focal point of the old town (now surrounded by a circuit of streets on the line of the old walls) is the Plaza Mayor (Catalan Plaça Major), in the northern part of the town. From its south-east corner a narrow street leads to the Casa Consistorial (Town Hall), originally built in Gothic style and enlarged in the 16th and 17th centuries. It contains a portrait gallery of the town's most distinguished sons and part of the municipal archives.

Plaza Mayor/ Plaça Major

Vigo

B 2

Province: Pontevedra (PO). Telephone dialling code: 986
Altitude: 28m/92ft. Population: 300,000

The important naval and commercial port of Vigo, one of the largest centres of sardine-fishing in Europe, lies in the west of Spain on the south side of the Ría de Vigo, a long inlet which penetrates 30km/19 miles inland. It is the largest town in Galicia, with an economy which depends on car manufacture and shipbuilding as well as on fishing and fish-processing. As a modern town Vigo has little to offer in the way of old buildings, but it has other attractions in the form of the beautiful coastal scenery of the Ría de Vigo, with a mild climate in which even oranges flourish.

★ Situation

After its destruction by Almanzor in 997 Vigo was not resettled until the 12th century. In the 16th century the American trade brought it prosperity but also made it the target of piratical raids, including one by Sir Francis Drake in 1588. In 1702, at the beginning of the War of the Spanish Succession, an Anglo-Dutch fleet attacked the Spanish silver fleet in Vigo harbour, captured part of the treasure it was carrying and sank many of the ships in the deep waters of the bay, from which they have never been recovered.

History

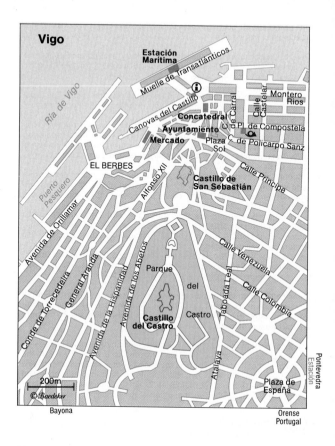

Sights

Forts
★ Views

Vigo lies on the slopes of a hill crowned by two old forts, the Castillo de San Sebastián (alt. 55m/180ft) and the Castillo del Castro (125m/410ft), from which there are extensive views in clear weather.

New town

On the east side of the hill is the newer part of the town, with modern tower blocks, broad avenues and beautiful parks. The town's main traffic arteries are the Avenida de García Barbón and its continuation Calle de Policarpo Sanz, on the northern slopes of the hill, Calle Urzaiz, which ascends the hill, and its continuation Calle del Príncipe, Vigo's main commercial and shopping street.

Below Calle de Policarpo Sanz is the Plaza de Compostela (Alameda), with numerous monuments. This is continued eastward by the Avenida de Felipe Sánchez, which runs alongside the Puerto Comercial (Commercial Harbour).

Old town

North-west of the new town, between the hill and the sea, is the old town of Vigo with its narrow and usually steep and winding streets. In its centre is Vigo's principal church, the Neo-Classical Colegiata de Santa María, built in the early 19th century.

Nearby, below the pier (Muelle), is the Fish Market (Pescadería), the scene of lively activity when a fish sale is in progress. The Muelle de Transatlánticos, built out onto the ría (estuary), is used by ocean-going vessels.

To the south-west is the old-world fishing quarter of El Berbés, with the Dársena del Berbés, the busy fishing harbour. Above the harbour, on the slopes of the hill, extends the Paseo de Alfonso XIII, from which there are fine views of the town, the harbour and the ría.

On the south-western outskirts of the town is the Parque Quiñones de León, with a large open-air theatre. Also in the park is the 17th century Pazo de Castelos, flanked by two large battlemented towers, which now houses the Provincial Museum. This has a collection of pictures, mainly by Galician artists, and a section containing prehistoric antiquities and exhibits illustrating the history of the town.

Within easy reach of the town are the beaches of Alcabre, Samil, Coruxo, O Bao, Canido and Saians.

Surroundings of Vigo

1km/¾ mile north-east of the town is the Mirador de la Guía, from which there are fine views of the ría and the offshore islands.

The Islas Cíes, in the Ría de Vigo, were already inhabited in Celtic times. They shelter the ría from the winds and waves of the Atlantic and thus help to give it its mild climate. The islands of San Martín and Monteagudo have been declared a nature reserve in order to protect their flora and fauna. The boat trip from Vigo takes 45 minutes.

Ría de Vigo

★ Rías Bajas/Rías Baixas

The long inlets which cut into the coast north and south of Vigo are known as the Rías Bajas (Galician Rías Baixas), the Lower Rías. The coastal landscape is less rugged than in the Rías Altas (see La Coruña, Surroundings). The inhabitants live mainly by fishing, but the summer tourist traffic to the seaside resorts is becoming increasingly important.

North of Vigo
Cangas

The coast road (C 550) goes round the Ría de Vigo to Cangas, facing Vigo across the ría. Cangas, originally a fishing village, is now a seaside resort. There is a ferry service between Cangas and Vigo.

Marín

C 550 continues north to the Ría de Pontevedra. 7km/4½ miles along its south side is the naval base and shipbuilding town of Marín, which has a picturesque old fishing quarter.

★ La Toja/
A Toxa

The road passes through Pontevedra (see entry) and round the ría to the seaside resort of Sangenjo (Galician Sanxenxo), from which a detour can be made to the former spa (thermal springs) of La Toja (Galician A Toxa), one of the most attractive little towns on the northern Atlantic coast of Spain, magnificently situated at the tip of a promontory.

Cambados

La Toja lies on the Ría de Arosa (Galician Arousa) opposite the interesting little town of Cambados. In the centre of the town is the beautiful Plaza de Fefiñanes, lined with arcaded houses, a fine 17th century mansion and the church of San Benito. The church of Santa Mariña is in ruins. Around Cambados are grown the grapes which produce the fruity Albariño wine.

Padrón

From Cambados C 550 continues along the Ría de Arosa to Padrón, at the mouth of the Río Ulla. It was here, according to legend, that the ship carrying the body of the Apostle St James (Santiago) was miraculously brought to land. Beneath the high altar of the church of Santiago, which occupies the site of earlier Romanesque and Gothic churches, is a large stone to which the ship is said to have been moored.

★ Mirador de
la Curota

From Padrón the road runs along the north side of the ría to the Mirador de la Curota, from which there are views of all the Rías Bajas.

Noya/Noia

A secondary road leads north-west from Padrón to Noya (Galician Noia), a little port which was known in antiquity as Noega. In the 12th century the town was surrounded by a massive circuit of walls, now largely destroyed; but Noya still preserves something of a medieval atmosphere, with a number of very handsome mansions such as the Casa de los Churruachos and the Palacio Peña de Oro and several old churches, the most interesting of which are San Martín (15th c.), with a richly sculptured façade and a fine rose window, and Santa María Nova, with a churchyard containing over 200 graves, some of them very old.

Muros

C 550 continues round the Ría de Muros y Noya to the little fishing port of Muros, where the catches are mostly of sardines. A stroll through the charming quarters of A Cerca and A Xesta will reveal many of the typical old Galician houses with glazed balconies.

From Noya it is only 37km/23 miles to Santiago de Compostela (see entry).

South of Vigo
Panjón/Panxón

From Vigo C 550 leads south past the fishing port of Bouzas and then bears south-west, running close to the Ría de Vigo. A narrow road turns off on the right to the seaside resort of Panjón (Galician Panxón), beyond which, on a promontory, is a memorial to the dead of the Spanish merchant fleet.

Bayona/Baiona

The road crosses a bridge spanning the inlet at the mouth of the Río Muiño (Galician Muinho) and comes to Bayona (Galician Baiona), a beautifully situated little port town which is now a popular seaside resort. Bayona was

Celtic hut, Monte Santa Tecla

the first town to hear of the discovery of America, when the "Pinta" put in here in 1493 after its transatlantic voyage. From the walls of the 16th century Castillo Monte Real, now a parador, there are breathtaking views of the sea. Near the Romanesque/Gothic collegiate church (12th–13th c.) is a beautiful park centred on a granite figure of the Virgin.

Farther down the rocky coast is Oya (Galician Oia), with the Benedictine monastery of Santa María la Real, in transitional Romanesque/Gothic style. It has an interesting 16th century cloister and a façade of 1740.

Oya/Oia

The road continues along the coast to La Guardia (Galician A Garda), a little port near the estuary of the Río Miño (Galician Minho), which forms the frontier between Spain and Portugal.

La Guardia/ A Garda

South of La Guardia, at the tip of a promontory, is Monte Santa Tecla. Here, on the wooded hillside, a large settlement was discovered in 1913 which had been inhabited by a Celtic tribe from 500 B.C. to the 1st century A.D. and was then occupied by the Romans. It is estimated that there were more than 1000 round stone huts with thatched roofs on the site, two of which have been reconstructed. There is a small museum displaying finds from the different periods of occupation.

★Monte Santa Tecla

From La Guardia it is 28km/17 miles up the north side of the Miño estuary to Túy (see entry).

Vitoria-Gasteiz

J 2

Province: Álava (VI). Telephone dialling code: 945
Altitude: 525m/1725ft. Population: 193,000

Vitoria-Gasteiz, chief town of the Basque province of Álava and administrative centre of the Autonomous Community of the País Vasco, lies to the south of the Cantabrian Mountains in a plain below the north side of the Montes de Vitoria. In recent decades a busy industrial area (mainly engineering and foodstuffs) has grown up around the town, but agriculture is still an important source of income.

History

This was probably the Visigothic settlement of Gasteiz: hence its double name. It began to develop into a town of some consequence in the 12th century, when, after a Navarrese victory, Sancho the Wise renamed it Vitoria. In 1813 Wellington's troops defeated a French army commanded by General Jourdan in a battle fought to the south of the town, compelling the French to withdraw from Spain.

Old Town

Plaza de la
Virgen Blanca

In the centre of Vitoria-Gasteiz, at the south end of the old part of the town, is the Plaza de la Virgen Blanca, surrounded by tall houses with glazed balconies. A monument in the square commemorates the battle of Vitoria in 1813. Every year in August the culminating ceremony of the Fiesta de la Virgen Blanca takes place in the square, when a figure holding an umbrella sails over the heads of the spectators on a rope stretched diagonally across the square from the tower of the church of San Miguel and everyone is then supposed to light a cigar.

Plaza de
España

From the Plaza de la Virgen Blanca a passage leads to the Plaza de España, which was laid out in 1791 on the model of the Plaza Mayor in Salamanca (see entry). On the north side of the square is the Ayuntamiento (Town Hall).

San Miguel

On the north side of the Plaza de la Virgen Blanca stands the 14th century Gothic church of San Miguel, with a statue of the Virgen Blanca (White Virgin), patroness of the town, on the façade. The church, entered through a richly sculptured doorway, has a retablo by Juan de Velázquez and Gregorio Fernández on the high altar. In a niche on the outside of the apse, in the Plaza del Machete, is an axe (*machete*), on which the royal governor of the town was required to swear that he would act in the interests of the town, on the understanding that he would be beheaded with the axe if he did not.

San Pedro

North-west of the Plaza de la Virgen Blanca is the 14th century Gothic church of San Pedro, with a fine doorway. In the Capilla Mayor are tombs of the Álava family.

Catedral Viejo

From here Calle Correría leads to the northern part of the old town, on a low hill. In this area is the Catedral Viejo (Old Cathedral) of Santa María (14th–15th c.), with a magnificent tripartite doorway, richly decorated with statuary, under a porch (scenes from the life of the Virgin in the centre, the Last Judgment on the right, scenes from the life of San Egidio/St Giles on the left). The Gothic Puerta de Santa Ana, on the south side, was opened up only in 1962. The most notable features of the interior are the various side chapels, some of which contain fine pictures, including a "Pietà" in the style of van Dyck (north aisle) and Carreño's "Immaculate Conception" (south aisle).

El Portalón

At the far end of Calle Correría, to the left of the Cathedral, are a number of very handsome old brick-built houses, including a 15th century merchant's house known as El Portalón, now occupied by a restaurant.

Museo de
Arqueológico

Opposite El Portalón is the Casa Armera de los Gobeo-Guevara-San Juan, which now houses the Archaeological Museum, with Celtiberian and Roman antiquities from the nearby site of Iruña.

Vitoria-Gasteiz

1 Palacio Escoriaza-Esquivel

2 Casa del Cordón

3 Palacio de los Álava-Esquivel

4 Ayuntamiento

5 Los Arquillos

6 Gorbierno Civil

7 Estación de Autobuses

8 El Portalón

150 m

© Baedeker

From the Cathedral Calle de Fray Zacharias returns to the south end of the old town, passing the 16th century Palacio de Escoriaza-Esquivel, which has a Plateresque doorway and a handsome inner courtyard.

Palacio de Escoriaza-Esquivel

At the end of the street are the Arquillos, a row of buildings erected in the 18th century to accommodate the difference in level between the old and the new town. Here too is the church of San Vicente.

Los Arquillos

New Town

To the south of the old town is the much larger area of the new town. On its west side, adjoining the park of La Florida, is the Catedral Nueva (New Cathedral), begun in 1907 but not consecrated until 1969.

Catedral Nueva

To the east of the New Cathedral is the Neo-Classical Parlamento Vasco (Basque Parliament).

Parlamento Vasco

South-west of the New Cathedral, in the Paseo de Fray Francisco de Vitoria, are four interesting museums: the Museo Provincial de Bellas Artes (Provincial Museum of Art), with a collection consisting mainly of religious art from the former Diocesan Museum (including pictures by Ribera and Alonso Cano); the Museo del Naipe, in the same building, which has the very interesting Fournier collection of playing cards, with examples going back to the 15th century; the Casa Museo de Arte Vasco (works by contemporary Basque artists); and the Museo de Armería (arms and armour).

Museums

Way of St James/Camino de Santiago/Camino Francés

B–L 1/2

The Way of St James (Camino de Santiago) was the ancient route followed by pilgrims from northern and central Europe on their journey to the tomb of the Apostle St James (Santiago) at Santiago de Compostela (see entry) in Galicia. The route was lined by Romanesque monasteries, churches and chapels, hospices and hostels, many of which still survive, marking out one of the most important pilgrim routes in Christendom.

★★ Medieval pilgrim route

History

Legend

The pilgrimage to Santiago was initiated by the discovery of the Apostle's tomb in western Galicia around the year 813. According to church tradition James was sent to preach the Gospel in Spain, but after several years there returned to Palestine, where he was beheaded in A.D. 44 on the orders of Herod Agrippa. His disciples recovered his body and put it on board a ship, which, guided by an angel, sailed back to Galicia. There the Apostle was buried, and his grave was forgotten until in the early 9th century it was rediscovered by a hermit, guided to the place by a star. Thereupon Alfonso II had a church built on the site, around which the town of Santiago de Compostela grew up. According to legend, at the battle of Clavijo in 844 the Apostle appeared riding a horse and led the Christian armies to victory over the Moors. Thereafter he was often represented on horseback as Santiago Matamoros, St James the Moor-Slayer. The first pilgrims from Europe began to make their way to Santiago in the middle of the 10th century, travelling through France and over the Pyrenees. Many of them were French, and so the way to Santiago also came to be known as the Camino Francés, the French Way. The heyday of the pilgrimage was in the 11th and 12th centuries, when the pilgrim route to the Holy Places in Palestine was blocked by the Turks. Thereafter the numbers of pilgrims declined, and the robbers, often disguised as pilgrims, who infested the pilgrim roads made the journey increasingly unsafe. When an English fleet commanded by Sir Francis Drake appeared off the Galician coast in 1589 the relics of the Apostle were hidden in a safe place – so safe that all knowledge of it was lost. At last, in 1879, the relics were rediscovered, and after their authenticity had been confirmed by Pope Leo XIII large numbers of pilgrims once again began to make their way to the Apostle's shrine.

The Pilgrims

The pilgrims flocked to Santiago de Compostela from all over Europe and from countries farther afield, most of them in profound piety, some in penitence for a sin or offence they had committed, and some false pilgrims also, such as the 15th century French poet François Villon, who set out with the idea of robbing the true pilgrims.

The pilgrims were easy to recognise. For safety's sake they usually travelled in groups, wearing a cloak and a broad-brimmed hat with the scallop-shell which was the emblem of the pilgrimage and carrying a stout staff, a leather bag and a water flask. All along the pilgrim route they found churches and pilgrim hospices and hostels run by monks, mostly Cluniacs and Benedictines, around which there grew up in course of time inns, shops and workshops, and finally towns such as Puente la Reina and Santo

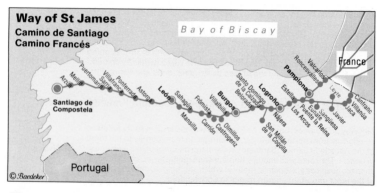

Domingo de la Calzada. The pilgrim route, the accommodation for pilgrims along the way, the dangers of the journey and the dishonesty of innkeepers were described in the "Liber Sancti Jacobi" (in a manuscript known as the Codex Calixtinus), written by a French monk named Aimery Picaud in the first half of the 12th century, which related the legends about St James and gave a variety of practical advice for pilgrims: in effect a guidebook to the whole pilgrim route.

Nowadays the pilgrimage is no longer an adventure: it is now possible to fly to Santiago, and much of the pilgrim route can be travelled by car. The numbers of pilgrims are greatest during a Holy Year: that is, when St James's Day (July 25th) falls on a Sunday.

The Pilgrim Route

The Way of St James was not so strictly defined as the route shown on the map (page 478) would suggest. There was an extensive network of routes running from east to west, though they tended to converge on the main route; and pilgrims might diverge from the route to visit some particular shrine on the way.

There were four main routes through France. Three of them ran from Paris, Vézelay and Le Puy, joined at Ostabat, on the French side of the Pyrenees, and then crossed the pass of Roncesvalles into Spain; the fourth, starting from Arles, went over the Somport pass and joined the others at Puente la Reina. From here the main Camino de Santiago continued west for another 740km/460 miles via Estella, Logroño, Santo Domingo de la Calzada, Burgos, León and Astorga to Santiago de Compostela (see entries).

An alternative, more hazardous, route followed the Basque, Asturian and Galician coasts by way of Irún, San Sebastián, Bilbao, Oviedo, Betanzos and La Coruña to Santiago.

Zamora

E/F 3

Province: Zamora (ZA). Telephone dialling code: 988
Altitude: 649m/2129ft. Population: 59,000

The old-world town of Zamora, chief town of its province, lies on a rocky hill above the Río Duero, which some 50km/30 miles downstream reaches the Portuguese frontier, in the southern part of the old kingdom of León. With its numerous Romanesque churches of the 12th and 13th centuries it has been called a "museum of Romanesque art".

★ "Museum of Romanesque art"

Zamora was originally a Moorish foundation, and during the fighting between Christians and Moors it was the scene of many fierce engagements, reflected in the Spanish national epic, the "Cantar de mio Cid".

Henry IV granted Zamora the style of "most noble and most loyal city". Ferdinand I called it the "well fortified city of Zamora" and bequeathed it to his daughter Doña Urraca. Her brother Sancho II was treacherously murdered while besieging the town, an event commemorated by the Portillo de la Traición (Treason Gate).

Zamora was also the scene of fierce fighting in the 15th century, during the conflict between the supporters of Isabella the Catholic and Juana la Beltraneja.

History

Sights

In the southern and rather higher part of the old town, still surrounded by its old walls and gates, is the Cathedral, standing above the right bank of the Duero. Built between 1151 and 1174, it is still mainly Romanesque. The plain square tower is topped by an unusual dome of scale-like stone slabs

★ Cathedral

with four corner turrets. On the south side of the church, facing the Bishop's Palace, is the richly sculptured Puerta del Obispo (Bishop's Doorway). Notable features of the interior are the fine dome and the choir-stalls of 1480 by Rodrigo Alemán, carved not only with figures of saints and famous men of antiquity but also with vigorous and earthy scenes of country life. The Capilla Major has a beautiful marble retablo, and the high altar is flanked by two Mudéjar pulpits. In the Capilla del Cristo de las Injurias, to the right of the south doorway, is a large figure of Christ by Gaspar Becerra. The Cathedral contains numerous tombs; particularly notable is the filigree carving on tomb of Dr Grado in the Capilla de San Juan at east end. Capilla del Cardenal, also at the east end, has an altar by Fernando Gallego.

Museum

The Cathedral Museum, in the 17th century cloister, is notable particularly for its fine Flemish tapestries of the 15th–17th centuries depicting scenes

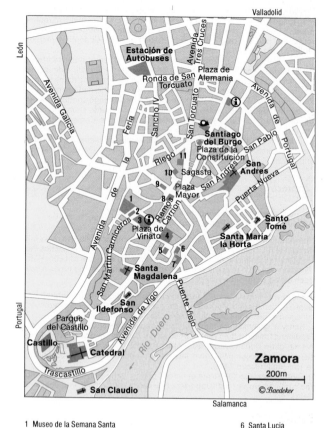

1 Museo de la Semana Santa
2 Santa María la Nueva
3 Diputación Provincial
4 Palacio de los Condes
  Alba y Aliste
5 San Cipriano

6 Santa Lucia
7 Museo Provincial
8 San Juan
9 Ayuntamiento
10 San Vicente
11 Palacio de los Momos

from the Trojan War, Hannibal's Italian campaign and the life of Tarquin, the Etruscan king of Rome. Another particular treasure is a Late Gothic monstrance of 1515.

North-west of the Cathedral stands the Castillo, with magnificent views of the town and the river from the keep.

Castillo

To the south of the Cathedral, outside the town walls on the banks of the Duero, is the 11th century church of San Claudio de Olivares.

San Claudio de Olivares

From the Cathedral Calle de los Notarios runs north-east, passing (on right) the church of San Ildefonso (11th c., with later alterations). The Capilla Mayor contains relics of the town's two patron saints, San Atilano and San Ildefonso.

San Ildefonso

From here Calle Ramos Carrión leads north to the little Romanesque Templar church of Santa Magdalena (12th c.), which has a splendid arched doorway with lions' and dragons' heads, surmounted by a rose window.
  The interior has finely carved capitals and reliefs and two richly decorated 13th century tombs.

Santa Magdalena

Calle Ramos Carrión continues to the little Plaza de Claudio Moyano, on the south side of which is the 12th century Romanesque church of San Cipriano, with fine relief decoration on the outer walls. The screen in the apse is believed to be the oldest in Spain.

San Cipriano

Passing the Palacio de los Condes Alba y Aliste (now a parador), in the Plaza de Cánovas, we reach the Plaza Mayor, with the Ayuntamiento (Town Hall; 1622) and the Late Gothic church of San Juan.

Plaza Mayor

South-west of the Plaza Mayor is the church of Santa María la Nueva, which dates from the 7th century. The apse has remains of Romanesque wall painting.

Santa María la Nueva

Opposite the church can be found the Museum of Holy Week, devoted to the Holy Week processions which are celebrated with particular ceremony in Zamora. The museum displays a large collection of *pasos,* the figures which are carried in procession through the streets by various confraternities.

Museo de la Semana Santa

A little way north of the museum rises the Puerta de Doña Urraca, an old town gate flanked by massive towers.

Puerta de Doña Urraca

South-east of the Plaza Mayor, near the river, the 12th century church of Santa María de la Horta has an imposing tower, a beautiful doorway and a Gothic retablo.

Santa María de la Horta

To the east of the Plaza Mayor, in the Plaza de Sagasta, is the 16th century Palacio de los Momos, now the Audiencia (Law Courts). It owes its name to the *momos* ("wild men") supporting the coat of arms on the palace's Renaissance façade.

Palacio de los Momos

From the Puente Viejo (Old Bridge) over the Duero, built on Roman foundations, there is an attractive view of the town.

Puente Viejo

Surroundings of Zamora

Leave Zamora on N 122, going west, and in 12km/7½ miles, after Venta del Puerto, turn right into a minor road which goes north-west to Campillo, on an artificial lake on the Río Esla. Here can be seen the Visigothic church of San Pedro de la Nave, re-erected in 1931 after being removed from its

★ San Pedro de la Nave

Bridge over the Duero

original site several kilometres away, now submerged by the lake. The church, which is thought to date from around 681, is notable for its magnificent carved capitals, which rank among the finest sculpture produced in Christian Spain before the arrival of the Moors.

Zaragoza   L 3

Province: Zaragoza (Z). Telephone dialling code: 976
Altitude: 200m/655ft. Population: 591,000

Zaragoza (traditionally in English Saragossa), once the residence of the kings of Aragon and now chief town of its province and the seat of a famous university, lies in the Ebro basin, on the right bank of the river, and from time immemorial has been the principal crossing point for traffic from the Pyrenees into Castile. The Huerta de Zaragoza, well watered by the Canal Imperial and the rivers Ebro, Huerva and Gallego, is a region of great fertility, and Zaragoza is accordingly an important agricultural centre, as well as possessing considerable industry (principally metal-processing and engineering).

History

The old Iberian settlement of Salduba was renamed by Augustus Colonia Caesaraugusta, from which its present name is derived. It fell into the hands of the Suevi in 452 and of the Visigoths in 476. In 712 it was conquered by the Moors, who held it for more than four centuries. After its recapture by Alfonso I of Aragon in 1118 it became the residence of the kings of Aragon and rose to considerable importance. In the 15th century, however, the court moved to Castile, and Zaragoza's importance declined.

It put up a heroic defence against the French in 1808–09, half of the population being killed before the honourable surrender of the town. After the expulsion of the Carlists, who captured the town in a surprise attack in March 1838, Zaragoza earned the style "siempre heróica e inmortal" ("always heroic and immortal").

★ Cathedral (La Seo)

At the east end of the long Plaza del Pilar, part of which is laid out in gardens, is the little Plaza de la Seo, in which stands the Cathedral (La Seo), dedicated to San Salvador. Built between 1119 and 1520 on the site of the town's principal mosque, it has double lateral aisles. The main doorway dates from 1795, the dome over the crossing from 1520 and the slender tower from 1686. The chancel has preserved its beautiful Mudéjar form.

Interior

The Choir has a superb grille and Late Gothic stalls. The Trascoro, with the Capilla del Santo Cristo, is a masterpiece of Renaissance architecture. In the Capilla Mayor, behind the high altar, can be seen a large alabaster retablo with three large painted panels (1473–77) by a German artist known as Juan de Suabia. On either side of the Capilla Mayor are the tombs of Aragonese nobles.

There are numerous side chapels. The Capilla de San Bernardo (to the left of the south-west doorway) contains the tombs of Archbishop Fernando de Aragón and his mother Ana Gurrea (1552), both by Diego Morlanes. The Capilla de San Martín (to the left of the main entrance), which serves as the parish church, has the Gothic tomb of Archbishop Lope Fernández de Luna (d. 1382). In the Capilla de San Pedro Arbués is the tomb of Pedro Arbués, an inquisitor who was murdered in the Cathedral in 1485 and canonised in 1867.

Museums

The Diocesan Museum, in the Sacristy, displays the rich Cathedral treasury, which consists mainly of gold and silver vessels and utensils, including a large silver monstrance (1541) made up of 24,000 parts. On the first floor is a Tapestry Museum, which possesses 60 valuable Gothic and Renaissance tapestries from Brussels and northern France (only a proportion of them being on show).

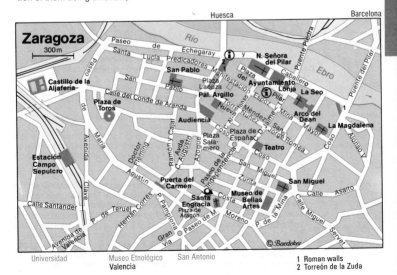

483

★ Basílica de Nuestra Señora del Pilar

Legend

Between the Plaza del Pilar and the Ebro is Zaragoza's second cathedral, the pilgrimage church of Nuestra Señora del Pilar, or Virgen del Pilar, the best view of which is from the opposite bank of the Ebro. The church was built on the spot where, according to the legend, the Virgin appeared on January 2nd in the year 40 to the Apostle James, then on his way to Compostela. A chapel was later built round the pillar on which she stood, and the latest successor to the original chapel still contains a much venerated marble pillar.

Exterior

The present church is a rectangular structure, 132m/433ft long by 67m/220ft across, with a large central dome, ten smaller azulejo-clad domes and four tall corner towers. Begun by Francisco Herrera the Younger in 1681 and continued by Ventura Rodríguez in 1753, it was completed in its present form only at the end of the 19th century.

Interior

The interior is in Neo-Classical style. The Choir has a fine *reja* of 1574 and magnificent Plateresque stalls of 1548. In the Capilla Mayor is a Gothic alabaster retablo (1484–1515) by Damián Forment and others.

Capilla de Nuestra Señora del Pilar

Near the east end of the church is its principal shrine, the Capilla de Nuestra Señora del Pilar, with fine ceiling paintings by Alejandro González Velázquez and paintings by Bayeu (1781) and Goya (1771) in subsidiary domes. On the west wall of the chapel, above three altars laden with candles, can be seen a small early 15th century alabaster figure of the Virgin on a marble pillar faced with silver; the Virgin's mantle is changed daily.

Between the chapel and the high altar, in the north aisle, is a stone bearing what is believed to be the Virgin's footprint which is kissed by many of the faithful. The Museo Pilarista displays offerings made to the Virgin and jewellery with which the statue is decked on feast days, together with sketches for the ceiling paintings by Velázquez, Goya and Bayeu.

Sacristía Mayor

In the Sacristía Mayor are displayed liturgical utensils, church silver and numerous brocaded mantles for the statue of the Virgin.

Old Town

★ Lonja

Between the two cathedrals, in the Plaza del Pilar, stands the former Lonja (Exchange), a handsome Renaissance building (1551) with a plain exterior. It contains a single large hall with heraldic decoration and a fine vaulted ceiling. The Lonja is open to the public only on special occasions.

Ayuntamiento

In the same square is the Ayuntamiento (Town Hall). The interior is worth seeing; among items of interest is a Roman statue of Augustus.

Palacio Arzobispal

Between the Cathedral and the Ebro is the 18th century Archbishop's Palace.

La Magdalena

South-east of the Cathedral rises the beautiful Mudéjar tower of the church of La Magdalena. Most of the rest of the church was rebuilt in the 18th century.

Plaza de César Augusto

Near the west end of the Plaza del Pilar is the little Plaza de César Augusto, in which are the Torreón de la Zuda, a 14th century Mudéjar-style tower, and the 18th century church of San Juan de los Panetes, with a leaning tower. Adjoining the south side of the Torreón are considerable remains of the Roman town walls.

Audiencia

South of the Plaza de César Augusto, at the end of Calle del Coso, is the Audiencia (Court of Appeal; 1537), popularly known as the Casa de los Gigantes after the two huge guardian figures flanking the entrance.

Nuestra Señora del Pilar, on the banks of the Ebro

Tower of the church of La Magdalena

San Pablo — In the western part of the old town stands the Romanesque/Gothic church of San Pablo (c. 1259), with an interesting octagonal tower in Mudéjar style (14th c.). It has a fine interior, with a sumptuous high altar by Damián Forment (1511).

★La Aljafería

On the west side of the town is the Castillo de la Aljafería, built by the Moors in the 11th century, which later became the residence of the kings of Aragon and was largely destroyed in 1809. The Catholic Monarchs stayed in the castle, and it was later occupied by the Inquisition.

The Aljafería, the only surviving Moorish building in Zaragoza, contains a number of very fine rooms, notably the beautiful little mosque on the ground floor. A magnificent Gothic staircase with a coffered ceiling leads to the apartments on the upper floor, the palace of the Catholic Monarchs. The focal point of the palace is the Throne Room, with an over-ornate carved and painted artesonado ceiling. In the Sala de Santa Isabel St Elizabeth of Portugal was born in 1271.

In the days of the Inquisition the Torre del Trovador was used as a prison. It provided a setting for part of Verdi's opera "Il Trovatore".

Around the Paseo de la Independencia

Santa Engracia — The Paseo de la Independencia, which runs south from the Plaza de España, half way along Calle del Coso, is a fine avenue with arcades along the west side. Near the end of the street, beyond the post office (on the left), is the former convent of Santa Engracia, an elaborately decorated Plateresque building (15th–16th c.) which was almost completely destroyed in 1809 (restored 1898); only the alabaster doorway is original. In the crypt are two Early Christian marble sarcophagi.

Museo Provincial de Bellas Artes — Farther east, in the Plaza de José Antonio, is the Provincial Museum of Art. On the ground floor are Roman antiquities, including a mosaic of Orpheus, Moorish art, and Romanesque and Gothic sculpture. The picture gallery is mainly devoted to works by both older and contemporary Spanish artists, Ribera, Goya and Bayeu being well represented, but there are also pictures by Italian and Flemish painters.

Ciudad Universitaria — At the south end of the Paseo de la Independencia is the oval Plaza de Aragón, and some 2km/1¼ miles farther south, to the right of the Paseo de Fernando el Católico, lies the Ciudad Universitaria (University City). Still farther south, on the Paseo de Isabel la Católica, is the Trade Fair Building, in which the National Trade Fair is held annually in October.

Parque Primo de Rivera — To the east in the beautiful Primo de Rivera Park is the Museum of Ethnology and Natural History.

Surroundings of Zaragoza

★Sos del Rey Católico — Leave Zaragoza on N 232, going north-west, and in 24km/15 miles turn right into a secondary road which leads to Tauste, on C 127. From there C 127 runs north via Ejea de los Caballeros to Sádaba, crosses the Puerto de Sos (856m/2809ft) and comes to Sos del Rey Católico, a little walled town which has largely preserved its medieval aspect. Ferdinand of Aragon, "el Rey Católico", was born here in 1452 in the 12th century Palacio de Sada. In the Plaza Mayor are the Renaissance Town Hall and the Lonja (Exchange), and nearby the Romanesque parish church of San Esteban (11th–12th c.), with a sculptured doorway and excellently preserved 14th century wall paintings.

Practical Information from A to Z

Accommodation

See Camping and Caravanning, Hotels and Paradors

Airlines (Líneas Aéreas)

Iberia (Iberia Líneas Aéreas de España) flies both international and domes- Iberia
tic services. (For international services, see Getting to Spain.) Addresses of
some Iberia offices are given below.

Aviaco (Aviación y Comercio) apart from two routes from the United King- Aviaco
dom (see Getting to Spain) only operates domestic services. For information about domestic services apply to Aviaco's Madrid office (address
below).

Viva Air, a subsidiary of Iberia, flies direct from the United Kingdom to Viva Air
Alicante and Palma de Mallorca (see Getting to Spain). Reservations can be
made through Iberia offices.

Binter Canarias, a subsidiary of Iberia, flies services within the Canaries. Binter
Reservations can also be made through Iberia offices. Canarias

Binter Mediterráneo, another recently established subsidiary of Iberia, Binter
serves the east coast of Spain and the Balearic Islands. Information about Mediterráneo
services can be obtained from Iberia offices.

Iberia Offices in the United Kingdom

First Floor McLaren Building, 35 Dale End
Birmingham B4 7LN; tel. (021) 643 1953

Third Floor, Venture House, 27–29 Glasshouse Street
London W1R 6JU; tel. (0171) 830 0011

Room 1, Level 7, Manchester Airport
Manchester M22 5PA; tel. (0161) 436 6444

Telephone numbers of Iberia offices at London airports:
Heathrow (0181) 897 3445
Gatwick (01293) 502469
Stansted (01279) 662394

Iberia Offices in the United States

6500 Wilshire Boulevard (suite 1900)
Los Angeles CA 90048; tel. (213) 852 4733

150 SE Second Avenue (suite 1308)
Miami FL 33131; tel. (305) 358 8800

509 Madison Avenue (ground floor)
New York NY 10022; tel. (212) 644 8843

Airline Offices in Spain

Iberia	Head office: Iberia Líneas Aéreas de España Calle de Velázquez 130, E-28006 Madrid tel. (91) 3 29 57 67 (Desks at all Spanish airports)
Aviaco	Maudes 51, Edificio Minister E-28003 Madrid 3; tel. (91) 2 54 93 76 and 2 34 42 00
Binter Canarias	Calle Alcalde Ramírez Bethancourt 8 E-35003 Las Palmas de Gran Canaria; tel. (928) 37 21 11

Airports (Aeropuertos)

The airport of Madrid, and to a lesser extent Barcelona, handle the greatest volume of air traffic in Spain. The main tourist airports are Palma de Mallorca, Santa Cruz de Tenerife and Málaga. Barcelona, Seville and Palma de Mallorca airports have recently been modernised.

Major Spanish Airports

Alicante	Aeropuerto de Alicante (12km/7½ miles south), tel. (96) 5 28 50 11
Almeria	Aeropuerto de Almeria (8km/5 miles east), tel. (951) 22 41 14
Barcelona	Aeropuerto de Barcelona (12km/7½ miles south), tel. (93) 3 01 39 93
Bilbao	Aeropuerto de Bilbao (9km/6 miles north), tel. (94) 4 53 06 40
Gran Canaria	Aeropuerto de Gran Canaria (23km/14 miles south from Las Palmas de Gran Canaria), tel. (928) 25 41 40
Madrid	**N.B.**: Passengers who have to change at Madrid Airport should bear in mind when making their bookings that it takes around an hour to transfer to another flight.
	International airport: Aeropuerto de Madrid/Barajas (16km/10 miles east; airport buses from Plaza de Colón), tel. (91) 3 05 83 44
Majorca	Aeropuerto de Palma de Mallorca (11km/9 miles east), C'an Pastilla, tel. (971) 26 42 12
Málaga	Aeropuerto de Málaga (10km/6 miles west), tel. (952) 2 24 00 00
Santiago de Compostela	Aeropuerto de Santiago de Compostela (10km/6 miles east), tel. (981) 59 75 50
Seville	Aeropuerto de Sevilla (12km/7½ miles west), tel. (95) 4 67 29 81
Tenerife	Aeropuerto del Tenerife Sur Reina Sofía (62km/39 miles south-west from Santa Cruz de Tenerife), tel. (922) 77 13 75
Valencia	Aeropuerto de Valencia (8km/5 miles west), tel. (96) 3 70 95 00

Air Travel

International flights	Spain is linked with the international network of air services both by the national airline, Iberia (including Aviaco and Viva Air; see Airlines), and by numerous foreign airlines.

In addition there are numerous charter flights (often as part of a package including accommodation) to mainland Spain, the Canaries and the Balearics.

Charter flights

Domestic services are flown by Iberia, Aviaco and Iberia's subsidiaries Binter Canarias and Binter Mediterráneo (see Airlines, Airports).

Domestic services

Approximate Flight Times between Madrid and Other Spanish Destinations

Barcelona:	55 minutes
Bilbao:	50 minutes
Canaries:	2½ hours
Palma de Mallorca:	1 hour
Seville:	50 minutes
Valencia:	30 minutes

Banks

See Currency

Bathing Beaches

There are over 2000km/1242 miles of beaches in Spain. In the past there have been complaints about the dirty water caused by industrial effluence and the lack of sewage plants and about the poor beach facilities. The Spanish government has invested considerably in improving conditions and sewage plants have been built in the main tourist areas along the Coasta del Sol. In Catalonia the beaches are regularly checked to maintain standards.

General

Many of the beaches are supervised with coloured flags flown to indicate conditions:

Beach warning service

green = bathing is safe
yellow = bathing is dangerous
red = bathing is forbidden

The following is a list of Spanish beaches which have been awarded the Blue Flag by the European Foundation for Environmental Education. This "distinction" has been criticised by many environmental organisations as it is not awarded on the basis of independent investigation but is applied for by the regional authority who fill in a questionnaire themselves after checking their own beaches. The Blue Flag is therefore highly subjective especially with regard to water quality but it may give an indication of good beach facilities. During the summer months the Spanish environment authority operates a telephone complaints line (Mon.–Fri. 9.30am–3pm, tel. 9 00 17 15 17).

Blue flags

The Costa Brava ("Wild Coast") is the most northerly stretch of coastline on the Mediterranean Sea, extending from Port Bou on the French border to Blanes. The coast is extremely rugged and frequently rocky with small coves and longer expanses of beach in places. The steep promontories are often only accessible on foot or by boat.
    The first real sandy beaches are in the Bay of Rosas.
    Blue flag: Castelló d'Empúries, Torroella de Montgri (Estartit), Begur (Sa Tuna), Palafrugell (Calella), Palamós (Playa de Bahía, La Fosca). Calonge

Costa Brava

489

Bathing Beaches

(San Antoni de Calonge), Castillo Playa de Aro (Playa de Aro). San Feliú de Guixols, Tossa de Mar (Platja Gran), Lloret de Mar.

Costa Dorada

The Costa Dorada ("Golden Coast") extends along almost the whole coastal strip of Barcelona and Tarragona provinces from the mouth of the Rio Tordera (Malgrat) to the mouth of the Ebro (San Carlos de la Rápita). It includes the smaller coastal region of Costa del Maresme in the north of the province of Barcelona and Costa de Garraf in the south. It has gently sloping beaches of fine golden-yellow sand, often separated from their hinterland by the road and railway.

Blue flag: Calella (Calella de la Costa), Castelldefels, Sitges (La Ribera, San Sebastian), Villanueva y la Geltrú (Ribes Roges), Cubelles (Playa Larga), Calafell-Salou (La Pineta, Platje Levant) El Vendrell (Comarruga, San Salvador, El Francés), Montroig del Camp (Playa Cristal), Cunit, Vilaseca.

Costa del Azahar
Costa de Valencia

The Costa del Azahar ("Orange Blossom Coast") including the Costa de Valencia extends from Vinaroz, south of the Ebro estuary, along the coast of Castellón province and the wide open gulf of Valencia to Denia. It has extensive flat beaches and a mild climate, but it is much polluted, particularly by industrial effluents.

Blue flag: Peñiscola (Playa Norte), Alcalá de Chivert (Cargador de Alcocéber), Torreblanca (Torrenostra), Oropesa (La Concha, Morro de Gos), Benicasim (La Almadraba, Torre de San Vicente), Castellón de la Plana (El Pinar), Burriana (El Arenal), Canet d'en Berenguer (Rincón del Mar), Sagunto (L'Armarda), Valencia (El Saler), Cullera (San Antonio, El Faro, El Dosel), Tabernes, Jaraco (Norte), Gandia (Norte), Sueca (Mareny Blau), Oliva (Agua Blanca, Terra Nova).

Costa Blanca
Costa Cálida

The Costa Blanc ("White Coast") extends from Setla (Punta de la Almadraba) to Cabo de Gata, taking in the coast of Alicante province and part of Murcia province. The beaches are mainly flat and of fine white sand. The winters in this region are very mild. The Costa Cálida adjoins the Costa Blanca.

Blue flag: Denia (Les Marines, Les Rotes), Jávea (Las Aduanas del Mar, El Arenal), Teulada de Moraira (El Portet, L'Ampolla), Calpe (La Fosa, El Arenal), Alfaz de Pi (L'Albir), Benidorm (Levante, Poniente, Mal Pas), Finestrat (La Cala), Villajoyosa (El Paraíso), Campello (El Carrer de la Mar), Alicante (San Juan, La Albufereta, Isla de Tabarca, El Postiget), Elche (Los Arenales, El Pinet), Santa Pola (Levante, Varadero, Gran Playa, Playa Lisa), Guardamar del Segura (Playa del Centro, Las Roquetas), Torrevieja (Torrelamata, Los Locos), Orihuela (Campoamor, La Zenai), Pilar de la Horada (Mil Palmeras), Benisa (Calafustera), Cartegena (Mar de Cristal).

Costa de Almeria

The Costa de Almeria refers to the stretch of coastline between Cabo de Gata and Motril. Here, away from the tourist hordes, deserted and clean, often pebbly, beaches can be found in rocky inlets.

Blue flag: Berja (Balanegra), Vera (Puertorey, El Payaro), Roquetas de Mar (Playa Serena), El Egido (Poniente Almerímar).

Costa del Sol

The Costa del Sol ("Sunshine Coast") comprises practically the whole Mediterranean coast of Andalusia, from Motril to Tarifa, Spain's most southerly point. It is now a densely populated tourist region and it is here that efforts have been made in the last few years to improve the water quality and cleanliness of the beaches. In the hinterland are many places of artistic and cultural interest, as well as picturesque Andalusian villages and a rich and varied flora.

Blue flag: Benalmadena (Santa Ana), Mijas (Cale de Mijas), Fuengirola (promenade), Motril (Carchuna, Calahonda), Marbella (La Fontanilla).

Costa de la Luz

The Costa de la Luz ("Coast of Light") takes in the southern Atlantic coast of Spain between the Tarifa promontory and the mouth of the Rio Guadiana on the Portuguese frontier. It has fine, long sandy beaches and relatively unspoiled dunes where large-scale tourist development has so far been avoided owing to the efforts of environmentalists.

Blue flag: Matalascañas, Punta Umbria, Ayamonte (Isla Canela), Lepe (La Antilla), Barbate (El Carmen), Chiclana (La Barrosa), Cádiz (La Victoria), El Puerto de Santa Maria (Valdelagrana), Rota (La Costilla), Chipiona (Playa de la Regla).

The Costa Gallega comprises the heavily indented Atlantic coast in the far north-west of Spain in the provinces of Vigo, La Coruña and Lugo. Sandy beaches are interspersed with rugged, rocky stretches of coastline and the tides are much higher than in the Mediterranean Sea. **Costa Galega**

Blue flag: Vigo (Cies), Sanxenxo (Silgar), O Grove (A Lanzada), Puebla de Caramiñal (Lombiña), Muros (San Francisco), Oleiros (Bastigueiros), Miño (Playa Grande), Foz (A Rapadoira), Carballo (Raro Baldaio), Cervo (Tomo).

The coast of Asturia deserves the name "Green Coast": behind the beaches the wooded, green mountains of the Cordillera Cantábrica rise up. In contrast with the indented coastline of Galicia there are long, white beaches which are not particularly busy. **Costa Verde**

Blue flag: Luarca (Salinas), Muros del Nalón (Aguilár), Gijón (San Lorenzo), Villaviciosa (Rodiles).

The Cantabrian coast is similar to Asturia. **Coast Cantábrica**

Blue flag: San Vicente de la Barquera (El Rosal), Pielagos (Valdearenas), Santander (El Sardinero), Ribanmontán al Mar (Somo), Noja (Ris), Santoña (Berria).

The Basque coast has beautiful stretches of beaches, which have the same features as in Asturia and Cantábria, but there are also areas of polluted water especially around the estuary of the Rio Nervión de Bilbao. **Costa Vasca**

Blue flag: Gorliz, Sopelana, Guetaria, San Sebastian/Donostia (La Concha, Ondarreta).

Blue flag: Alcudia, San Llorenç des Cardassar (Cala Millor, Sa Coma), Santany (Cala Mondragó), Ses Salines (Platja des Dolç), Palma de Mallorca (Playa de Palma), Calvia (Paguera), Andraitx (San Telmo). **Balaeric Islands**
Mallorca

Blue flag: Ferrerias: (Cala Galdana), Capdepera (Cala Agulla), Son Servera (Cala Millor) **Menorca**

Blue flag: San Antonio Abad (Cala Sabada, Santa Eulalia). **Ibiza**

Blue flag: San Bartolomé de Tirajana (Playa del Inglés/Maspalomas, Las Canteras). **Canary Islands**
Gran Canaria

Blue flag: Icod de los Vinos (San Marcos), Puerto de Santiago (La Arena), Adeje, Arona (Playa de las Américas). **Tenerife**

Blue flag: Teguise (Las Cucharras) **Lanzarote**

There are wonderful, long deserted beaches on Fuerteventura which do not have the Blue Flag award. **Fuenteventura**

Bus Services

All of the larger and small towns in Spain are linked by a dense network of bus services, mostly operated by private companies. Nearly every town has a bus station (*Estación de Autobuses*) where tickets are on sale and the timetables are displayed. Bus travel is cheaper than rail travel but at the weekend the buses are very crowded.

Business Hours (Horas de apertura)

Banks	See Currency
Chemists	See entry
Churches Museums Castles	The opening times of museums, churches and castles vary considerably and are subject to frequent change. They are likely to be closed during the long lunch break (broadly between 1 and 4pm) and are generally closed on Mondays.
Exchange offices	See Currency
Post offices	See Post, Telegrams, Telephone
Public holidays	See entry
Restaurants	See entry
Shops	Most shops usually open: Mon.–Fri. from 9–9.30am–1.30pm and from 5–8pm, Sat. 9am–1pm. As there are no statutory closing hours in Spain supermarkets and other shops in tourist areas may stay open during the traditional siesta hours, and stay open later and open on Sundays.
Tabernas	Tabernas are required to close at midnight.

Camping and Caravanning

Spain has more than 800 camping sites (*campings, campamentos*) with a total capacity of over 400,000 places. There are sites all over the country, more than two-thirds of them on the coast.

Categories

The sites are officially classified in four categories – L (luxury), 1, 2 and 3.

Reservation

During the main holiday season it is advisable to book a place in a camping site in advance. The addresses and telephone numbers of sites are given in the Spanish camping guide (see below).

Information

Information about camps and camping in Spain can be obtained from national camping organisations.

The Spanish Federation of Camping Sites publishes an annual "Guía de Campings", which lists sites, with illustrations, sketch plans and an introduction in English.

Address:
Federación Española de Empresarios de Campings y Ciudades de Vacaciones, General Oráa 52–2°D
E-28006 Madrid; tel. (91) 5 62 99 94

A free map ("Mapa de Campings") is also obtainable.
Lists of camping sites produced by national and local authorities can be obtained from tourist information offices.

Reservations:
RACETOUR (Royal Automobile Club), José Abuscal 10, E-28003 Madrid, tel. (91) 4 45 14 55, telefax (91) 4 47 79 48.

"Wild" camping

Before camping in open country campers should check that "wild" camping is not prohibited in the area – as it may be, for example, because of the danger of fire during the dry season or because there is an official site in the vicinity. Before camping on private land permission should, of course, be obtained from the owner.

Car Ferries

Map of ferry services: see page 558   Map

Owners of trailer and motor caravans should check with the shipping company or through a travel agency about possible size limits.   Caravans

SERVICE	FREQUENCY	COMPANY
Britain–Spain		
Plymouth–Santander	twice weekly (less January to mid-March)	Brittany Ferries
Portsmouth–Bilbao	twice weekly	P&O European Ferries
Spain–Balearics		
Barcelona–Palma de Mallorca	daily	Trasmediterránea
Barcelona–Mahón	2–6 times weekly	Trasmediterránea
Barcelona–Ibiza	3–6 times weekly	Trasmediterránea
Valencia–Palma de Mallorca	6 times weekly	Trasmediterránea
Valencia–Mahón	weekly	Trasmediterránea
Valencia–Ibiza	1–5 times weekly	Trasmediterránea
Denia–Ibiza	daily	Flebasa, San Antonio
Balearics (inter-island)		
Palma de Mallorca–Mahón	weekly	Trasmediterránea
Palma de Mallorca–Ciudadela	weekly	Trasmediterránea
Palma de Mallorca–Ibiza	twice weekly	Trasmediterránea
Palma de Mallorca–Cabrera	weekly	Trasmediterránea
Ciudadela–Puerto de Alcudia	4 times weekly	
Spain–Canaries		
Cádiz–Santa Cruz de Tenerife–Las Palmas de Gran Canaria–Puerto del Rosario (Fuerteventura)–Arrecife (Lanzarote)	weekly (Jan.–May)	Trasmediterránea
Cádiz–Las Palmas de Gran Canaria–Santa Cruz de Tenerife	weekly (June–Dec.)	Trasmediterránea

Canaries (inter-island)
Trasmediterránea runs regular services between:
Tenerife–Gran Canaria, Fuerteventura, Lanzarote, La Palma, Hierro;
Gomera: Gran Canaria–Tenerife, Fuerteventura, Lanzarote, La Palma, Hierro

Spain–Morocco		
Algeciras–Tangier	daily	Trasmediterránea
Algeciras–Tangier	daily in season	Limadet Ferry, Tangier
Tarifa–Tangier	daily	Tourafrica

Car Rental

SERVICE	FREQUENCY	COMPANY
Spain–Ceuta and Melilla		
Algeciras–Ceuta	daily	Trasmediterránea
Almería–Melilla	6 times weekly–daily	Trasmediterránea
Málaga–Melilla	6 times weekly–daily	Trasmediterránea
Gibraltar–Morocco		
Gibraltar–Tangier	twice weekly	Tourafrica

N.B.   A passport is required for the crossing to Tangier.

Information and Bookings on Car Ferries

Brittany Ferries
Brittany Ferries, Millbay Docks
Plymouth PL1 3EW; tel. (01752) 221321

P&O European Ferries
P&O European Ferries
Channel House, Channel View Road; Dover CT17 9TJ
tel. (0181) 575 8555

Trasmediterránea
c/o Southern Ferries
1st Floor, 179 Piccadilly
London W1V 9DB; tel. (0171) 491 4968

Tourafrica
Tourafrica International Ltd
Unit G10, International Commercial Centre
Main Street, Gibraltar; tel. (350) 7 76 66 and 7 91 40

Car Rental (Alquiler de Coches)

The main international car rental firms have branches throughout Spain, particularly at airports, railway stations, bus stations, etc. Bookings can be made in advance through one of the company's home branches. There are also numerous Spanish rental firms with whom arrangements can be made locally.

When hiring a car, ask for the cheapest rates, since there may be special offers which will not always be volunteered.

Anyone renting a car must be at least 21 years of age.

The easiest way to make payment, and avoid having to put down a deposit, is by credit card.

Telephone Numbers of International Car Rental Firms in Spain

The following is merely a selection.

Avis
Barcelona: (93) 2 15 78 72 / 38
Bilbao: (94) 4 44 31 90
Madrid: (91) 4 57 97 06 / 07 / 13 / 17

Hertz
Barcelona: (93) 3 23 10 62
Barcelona, Estación Ferrocaril Sants: (93) 3 22 97 52 and 2 17 80 76
Barcelona, El Prat Airport: (93) 2 41 13 81
Madrid: (91) 5 42 10 00

Madrid, Barajas Airport: (91) 3 05 84 52
Palma de Mallorca, Airport: (971) 26 08 09

Barcelona: (93) 3 17 57 03–58 76   Europcar
Barcelona, El Prat Airport: (93) 3 79 90 51 and 3 71 91 60
Bilbao: (94) 4 42 28 49 and 4 42 22 26
Bilbao, Sondica Airport: (94) 4 53 33 39
Madrid: (91) 5 97 15 00 and 5 56 15 00
Madrid, Barajas Airport: (91) 3 05 51 63
Palma de Mallorca: (971) 45 48 00 and 45 44 00
Palma de Mallorca, Airport: (971) 26 38 11 and 49 01 10

Some firms (e.g. Europcar) have motor caravans and mobile homes available for hire. Hertz has minibuses suitable for families.

Castles

Most of the castles in this list are referred to in the "Spain from A to Z"
section of this guide.

 1 Castillo de Moeche (14th c.)
 2 Villalba: Castillo de Andrade (14th–15th c.)
 3 Bayona: Castillo Monte Real (16th c.)
 4 Castillo Monterrey (12th–15th c.)
 5 Castillo de Monforte de Lemos
 6 Benavente: Castillo de los Pimentel (15th c.)
 7 Castillo de Valencia de Don Juan (12th–15th c.)
 8 Castillo de Grajal de Campos (16th c.)
 9 Castillo de Aguilar de Campóo (12th c.)
10 Fuenterrabía: Palacio del Rey Carlos (12th c.)
11 Castillo de Olite (13th–15th c.)

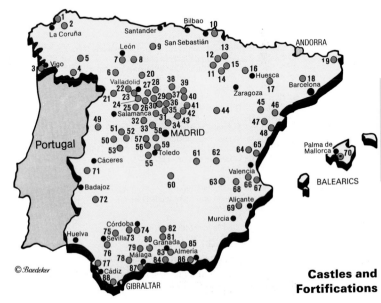

**Castles and
Fortifications**

12 Sangüesa: Castillo del Príncipe de Viana
13 Castillo de Javier (14th c.)
14 Castillo de Sádaba (13th c.)
15 Castillo de Uncastillo (12th c.)
16 Castillo de Loarre (11th c.)
17 Castillo de Monzón (10th–12th c.)
18 Castillo de Cardona (10th–12th c.)
19 Perelada: Castillo de Rocaberti (14th–17th c.)
20 Castillo de Fuensaldaña (13th–15th c.)
21 Zamora: Castillo and town walls (11th–12th c.)
22 Castillo de Torrelobatón (15th c.)
23 Castillo de Simancas (14th c.)
24 Medina del Campo: Castillo de Mota (14th c.)
25 Castillo de Arévalo (14th–15th c.)
26 Castillo de Coca (15th c.)
27 Castillo de Portillo (15th c.)
28 Castillo de Peñafiel (10th–13th c.)
29 Castillo de Cuéllar (15th c.)
30 Castillo de Turégano (13th–15th c.)
31 Segovia: Alcázar (12th c.)
32 Ávila: town walls (11–12th c.)
33 Castillo de las Navas del Marqués (16th c.)
34 Castillo de Manzanares el Real (15th c.)
35 Castillo de Pedraza (14th–15th c.)
36 Castillo Castilnovo (12th–15th c.)
37 Ayllón: town walls and Castillo
38 Castillo de Coruña del Conde
39 Castillo de Gormaz (10th–13th c.)
40 Castillo de Berlanga de Duero (15th c.)
41 Castillo de Sigüenza (12th c.)
42 Jadraque: Castillo del Cid (15th c.)
43 Hita: town walls (15th c.) and Castillo de Torija (13th c.)
44 Castillo de Molina de Aragón (11th–12th c.)
45 Alcañiz: Castillo de los Calatravos (12th c.)
46 Tortosa: Castillo de la Zuda
47 Morella: town walls and Castillo
48 Castillo de Peñíscola (11th–15th c.)
49 Ciudad Rodrigo: Castillo (14th c.) and town walls (12th c.)
50 Castillo de Jarandilla de la Vera (14th c.)
51 El Barco de Avila: Castillo de Valdecomeja (14th c.)
52 Arenas de San Pedro: Castillo de la Triste Condesa (15th c.)
53 Castillo de Oropesa (12th–15th c.)
54 Castillo de Trujillo (15th c.)
55 Castillo de Guadamur (15th c.)
56 Castillo de Maqueda (12th–15th c.)
57 Castillo de Escalona (11th–15th c.)
58 Castillo de Villaviciosa de Odón (14th–15th c.)
59 Toledo: Alcázar and Castillo de San Servando (14th c.)
60 Castillo de Calatrava la Nueva (12th c.)
61 Castillo de Belmonte (15th c.)
62 Castillo de Alarcón (13th c.)
63 Castillo de Chinchilla (15th c.)
64 Segorbe: Castillos and town walls (14th c.)
65 Castillo de Sagunto
66 Castillo de Alacuas
67 Játiva: Castillo Mayor (14th–15th c.)
68 Castillo de Almansa (13th c.)
69 Novelda: Castillo de la Mola (13th–14th c.)
70 Palma de Mallorca: Castillo de Bellver (13th c.)
71 Castillo de Alburquerque (13th c.)
72 Zafra: Alcázar (15th–16th c.)
73 Castillo de Almodóvar del Río

74 Córdoba: Alcázar
75 Carmona: town walls and Castillo
76 Castillo de Alcalá de Guadaira (12th c.)
77 Jerez de la Frontera: Alcázar (12th–15th c.)
78 Castillo de Zahara (11th c.)
79 Castillo de Antequera
80 Castillo de Loja
81 Alcalá la Real: Forteza de la Mota (14th c.)
82 Jaén: Castillo de Santa Catalina
83 Granada: Alhambra
84 Almuñécar: Castillo de San Miguel (11th–16th c.)
85 Guadix: Alcazaba (10th–15th c.)
86 Almería: Alcazaba (10th–15th c.) and Castillo de San Cristóbal
87 Málaga: Alcazaba (14th c.) and Castillo de Gibralfaro (14th c.)
88 Tarifa: Alcázar (10th–13th c.)

Caves

Something like 10,000 caves have been found in Spain, concentrated mainly in the karstic regions in the north, north-east, east and south of the country. In many areas there has not been any systematic prospecting or exploration.

The following list gives only a very small selection of caves which are of interest either for their prehistoric rock paintings or their stalactitic or other formations and can be seen without too much difficulty.

Since air temperatures in the caves are very different, even in the height of summer, from outside temperatures, warm or waterproof clothing should be worn when visiting a cave, and stout footwear is essential.
    For visiting caves without artificial lighting a good electric torch should be taken. In exploring a complicated cave system great care should be taken – and a ball of cord or other means of marking the way back.

Caves open to the public

Location: Province of Vizcaya; in Mont Ereñusarre, 4.5km/3 miles north-east of Guernica.
    Features: Beautiful coloured stalactites and stalagmites. Stone Age paintings and engravings in two small chambers (difficult of access) 150m/165yd from entrance. Conducted tour.

1 Cueva de Santimamiñe (Cueva de Basondo)

Location: Province of Cantabria; at Ramales, 36km/22 miles south-east of Santander.
    Features: Two long galleries; in the right-hand one (70m/77yd long), paintings in red (stags, bisons).

2 Cueva de Covalanas

Location: Province of Cantabria; in the Pico del Castillo, near Puerto Viesgo, 22km/14 miles south-west of Santander.
    Features: Several galleries (total length 300m/330yd); palaeontological finds (in Prehistoric Museum, Santander); 750 figures of animals.

3 Cueva del Castillo

Location: Province of Cantabria; in the Pico del Castillo, south-west of Santander (guide at Cueva del Castillo, No. 3).
    Features: A maze of passages, with well preserved monochrome Palaeolithic paintings.

4 Cueva de la Pasiega

Location: Province of Cantabria; 2km/1¼ miles south-west of Santillana del Mar.

5 Cueva de Altamira

497

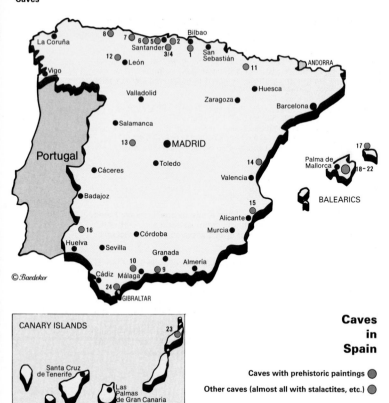

Caves
in
Spain

Caves with prehistoric paintings ⬤

Other caves (almost all with stalactites, etc.) ⬤

Features: A horizontal gallery (total length 270m/295yd); large painted ceiling in a chamber near the entrance, with the famous polychrome figures of animals (bisons, stags, horses, wild pigs). See Spain from A to Z, Altamira Caves.

6 Cueva del Pindal

Location: Province of Asturias; in the cliffs near Pimiango, 59km/37 miles south-west of Santander (guide at San Emérito lighthouse).
Features: A wide gallery 360m/395yd long, with numerous figures of animals.

7 Cueva de Tito Bustillo

Location: Province of Asturias; on outskirts of Ribadesella.
Features: A series of galleries with magnificent stalactites and stalagmites; polychrome wall paintings, including hand-prints.

8 Cueva de Cándamo (Cueva de San Román)

Location: Province of Asturias; at San Román, 20km/12½ miles north-west of Oviedo.
Features: A series of chambers leading to a large hall; some 60 figures of animals (paintings and engravings); fine sinter formations.

Location: Province of Málaga; at Nerja, 51km/32 miles east of Málaga.

9 Cueva de Nerja

Features: A series of chambers of considerable size. The lower gallery, well arranged for visitors, is about 800m/880yd long; upper gallery about 2000m/2200yd long. Many sinter formations, some very large (one pillar 60m/200ft high, 18m/60ft in diameter). Palaeolithic wall paintings (stags, horses, goats, dolphins), particularly in upper gallery. Important excavations (fragments of skulls). Music, coloured lighting; frequent concerts, ballet performances, etc.

Location: Province of Málaga; at Benaoján, 11km/7 miles south-west of Ronda.

10 Cueva de la Pileta

Features: Large main gallery with several chambers and side passages; smooth white stalactites, pools of water. Total length 1500m/1640yd. Palaeolithic engravings (horses, bisons, stags, ibexes, a rhinoceros, fishes), older than those of Altamira (No. 5).

Location: Province of Huesca; at Villanua, 12km/7½ miles north of Jaca (guide).

11 Cueva Vieja

Features: Large stalactites and stalagmites.

Location: Province of León; at Valporquero, 35km/22 miles north of León.

12 Cuevas de Valporquero

Features: Large gallery 1.8km/1 mile long, with many branches and chambers. Numerous sinter formations in different colours; waterfalls, pools and lakes.

Location: Province of Ávila; about 60km/37 miles south-west of Ávila, 6km/4 miles south-west of Arenas de San Pedro.

13 Cueva del Aguila

Features: Numerous sinter formations of all kinds; only one large chamber (18,900 sq.m/22,600 sq.yd) open to the public.

Location: Province of Castellón; at Val de Uxo, 26km/16 miles south-west of Castellón de la Plana.

14 Gruta de San José

Features: A long gallery (about 800m/880yd), traversed for part of the way by an underground river (boats). Many fine sinter formations (stalactites, etc.). Coloured lighting, music.

Location: Province of Alicante; at a height of 700m/2300ft on the northern slopes of the Sierra de Cabeza de Oro, 10km/6 miles ESE of Jijona and 3km/2 miles north of Busot.

15 Cueva de Canalobre

Features: A large sloping hall 150m/165yd long, with a profusion of stalactites and stalagmites. Coloured lights, music, stage for folk performances and concerts. Good view of the coast from the entrance.

Location: Province of Huelva; at Aracena, 75km/47 miles north-west of Seville; entrance in a house.

16 Gruta de las Maravillas

Features: A system of passages and chambers up to 70m/230ft high; lakes, many colourful sinter formations, crystals. Illuminations, music; conducted tour (1200m/1300yd; 1 hour).

Location: Province of Balearics; on Minorca, 4km/2½ miles south of Ciudadela at Cala Blanca.

17 Cueva de S'Aigu/Cova de S'Aygo

Features: Total length 215m/235yd; large lake of brackish water 80m/90yd long, in which the vividly coloured stalactites and stalagmites are reflected.

Location: Province of Balearics; on Majorca, 4.5km/3 miles west of Palma at Génova; entrance beside a house.

18 Cueva de Génova

Features: A series of chambers, with large numbers of delicate stalactites and stalagmites in a variety of colours. Conducted tour.

Location: Province of Balearics; on Majorca, 37km/23 miles north-east of Palma at Campanet.

19 Cueva de Campanet

Features: A large cave with a variety of sinter formations, many of them needle-like in shape. Conducted tour (1300m/1420yd); music.

20 Cueva de Artà	Location: Province of Balearics; on Majorca, about 70km/43 miles east of Palma, 9.5km/6 miles ESE of Artà at Cabo Vermell; entrance on coast. Features: Huge chambers with stalagmites up to 22m/72ft high. Total length 450m/490yd. Conducted tour (1km/¾ mile; 1 hour).
21 Cuevas del Drach	Location: Province of Balearics; on Majorca, about 60km/37 miles east of Palma at Porto Cristo; entrance on coast. Features: A series of four large chambers with several lakes (one of them 177m/195yd long and 12m/40ft deep). Large numbers of colourful sinter formations. Total length about 2km/1¼ miles. Coloured lighting; boat trips; classical concerts, with the musicians on illuminated boats. Conducted tour, with music (1km/¾ mile; 2 hours).
22 Cuevas dels Hams	Location: Province of Balearics; on Majorca, at Porto Cristo, about 2km/1¼ miles north-west of Cuevas del Drach (No. 21). Features: Beautiful chambers formed by an underground river; several lakes. Varied sinter formations, in particular delicate hook-shaped white stalactites (*hams* = "fish-hooks"). Part of the caves arranged for concerts, etc. Conducted tour.
23 Cueva de los Verdes	Location: Province of Las Palmas de Gran Canaria; on north coast of Lanzarote, 28km/17 miles north-east of Arrecife, at the foot of the Corona volcano. Features: Long galleries on several levels. Volcanic rock (no sinter formations); underground lakes. Total length 6km/4 miles. Large hall at entrance used for concerts, etc. Conducted tour.
24 St Michael's Cave	Location: Gibraltar; on the west side of the Rock at a height of 300m/980ft. Features: A series of chambers running down to a depth of 76m/250ft. Numerous sinter formations of varied shape and colour; small pools. Illuminations in changing colours, music; concerts, etc.

Chemists (Farmacias)

Chemists' shops are identified by a green cross on a white background.

Opening times follow normal shopping hours, generally from 9.30am to 2pm and from 4.30 to 8pm, Sat. 9am–12.30pm.

Arrangements are made for certain pharmacies to be open on a rota basis outside normal hours and on Sundays and public holidays. The address of the pharmacy on duty is given on a notice (*farmacia de guardia*) in chemists' windows and in the newspapers.

See also Emergencies, Medical Care

Consulates

See Embassies and Consulates

Currency

The unit of currency is the peseta (pta). There are coins for 1, 5, 10, 25, 50, 100, 200 and 500 ptas and notes in denominations of 1000, 2000, 5000 and 10,000 ptas. New coins were issued in mid 1993.

Current exchange rates can be found in national newpapers and may be obtained from banks and tourist offices.

Exchange rates (subject to fluctuation)

There are no restrictions on the import of Spanish or foreign currency (cash or cheques). It is advisable, however, to declare large sums of currency (over the equivalent of 1,000,000 ptas).

The export of local or foreign currency is permitted up to the equivalent of 500,000 ptas, or a larger sum if declared on entry.

Spanish regulations require a minimum of 5000 ptas per visitor per day on entry, or a total amount of 50,000 ptas. This, however, does not apply to visitors that travel on a package holiday.

Import and export of currency

Outside the opening hours of banks (generally Mon.–Fri. 9am–2pm, Sat. 9am–1pm, during the summer months banks close on Saturdays) money can be changed in exchange offices and travel agencies and at the reception desk of the larger hotels. Money is changed at the official rate, but a varying rate of commission may be charged.

Banks Exchange

It is advisable to take money in the form of Eurocheques, traveller's cheques or Postcheques of the British Girobank.

One bank in Madrid which makes no difficulty about cashing Eurocheques is the Banco Extranjero de España, Carretera de San Jerónimo 36 (Metro Sol).

All branches of the Caja de Madrid are also theoretically obliged to cash Eurocheques.

Eurocheques, etc.

Postcheques can be cashed at a post office up to the equivalent of 30,000 pesetas per cheque.

Most of the international credit cards are accepted by banks and by many hotels, restaurants and shops.

Credit cards

Holders of Eurocheque cards can draw cash from more than 4500 Eurocheque cash dispensers in Spain. Holders of credit cards (Visa, Access, American Express, etc.) can also draw cash from dispensers bearing the appropriate symbol. American Express has more than 150 of its own dispensers which will issue traveller's cheques as well as cash.

Cash dispensers

The loss of a Eurocheque card or credit card should be reported at once by telephone to the issuing organisation.

Loss of cards

Drugs

Drug dealers are active particularly in the Spanish ports (Barcelona, Cádiz, Málaga, Algeciras, etc.).

The penalty for the possession of drugs is a prison sentence of up to 20 years.

Electricity

The normal voltage in Spain is 220 volts AC, with a frequency of 50 cycles per second. Spain is committed to introducing the international norm (adopted in 1983) of 230 volts AC by the year 2003.

Power sockets are of the usual European two-pin type. An adapter is necessary for British and American-type plugs, in addition American appliances require a voltage transformer.

Embassies and Consulates in Spain

United Kingdom

Embassy:
Calle de Fernando el Santo 16, Madrid; tel. (91) 3 19 02 00

Consulates:
Avenida de las Fuerzas Armadas 11, E-11202 Algeciras
tel. (956) 66 16 00 and 66 16 04

Plaza Calvo Sotelo 1–2 (1st floor), E-03001 Alicante
tel. (96) 5 21 60 22

Edificio Torre de Barcelona (13th floor)
Diagonal 477, E-08036 Barcelona; tel. (93) 3 22 21 51

Alameda de Urquijo 2–8, E-48008 Bilbao
tel. (94) 4 15 76 00, 4 15 77 11 and 4 15 77 22

Avenida Isidoro Macabich 45 (1st floor), E-07800 Ibiza
tel. (971) 38 18 18 and 30 33 16

Calle Rubicón 7, Arrecife, Lanzarote; tel. (928) 81 59 28

Centro Colón, Calle Marqués de la Ensenada 16 (2nd floor)
E-28004 Madrid; tel. (91) 3 08 52 01

Edificio Duquesa, Calle Duquesa de Parcent 4
E-29001 Málaga; tel. (952) 21 75 71

Calle Torret 28, E-07710 San Luis, Minorca
tel. (971) 36 64 39

Plaza Mayor 3, E-07002 Palma de Mallorca
tel. (971) 71 24 45, 71 20 85 and 71 60 48

Edificio Cataluña (3rd floor), Calle Luis Morote 6
E-35007 Las Palmas de Gran Canaria; tel. (928) 26 25 08

Suarez Guerra 40 (5th floor), E-38002 Santa Cruz de Tenerife
tel. (922) 28 68 63

Paseo de Pereda 27, E-39004 Santander; tel. (942) 22 00 00

Plaza Nueva 87, E-41001 Seville; tel. (95) 4 22 88 75

Calle Real 33, E-43004 Tarragona; tel. (977) 22 08 12

Plaza de Compostela 23 (6th floor), E-36201 Vigo
tel. (986) 41 71 33 and 43 84 01

United States

Embassy:
Calle Serrano 75, Madrid; tel. (91) 5 77 40 00

Consulates:
Vía Layetana 33, Barcelona; tel. (93) 3 19 95 50

Avenida del Ejército 11–3, Bilbao; tel. (94) 4 35 83 00

Calle Franchy Roca 5, Las Palmas de Gran Canaria
tel. (928) 27 12 59

Embassy:
Edificio Goya, Calle Núñez de Balboa 35, Madrid
tel. (91) 4 31 43 00

Canada

Consulates:
Vía Augusta 125, Atico 3A, Barcelona; tel. (93) 1 09 06 34

Edificio Horizonte, Plaza de la Malagueta 3, Málaga
tel. (95) 2 22 33 46

Avenida de la Constitución 30 (2nd floor), Seville; tel. (95) 4 22 94 13

Emergencies

Dial 091 (throughout mainland Spain and in Balearics and Canaries).

Police

There are emergency telephones along almost the whole length of the Spanish motorways.

On motorways

In case of breakdown or accident, help can be obtained from the Guardia Civil de Tráfico, the traffic police, who have patrols on motorways and main roads, or, within towns, from the Policía Municipal (tel. 092). The Spanish Red Cross (Cruz Roja) also provides help in emergency.

Other services

The Real Automóvil Club de España (RACE) runs a 24-hour breakdown service throughout Spain:
   for English-speaking assistance tel. (91) 5 93 33 33.

Breakdown assistance

Events

There are so many events – fiestas, religious occasions, entertainments and sporting events – all over Spain throughout the year, particularly during the summer months, that it is not possible to list them all here. Events of more than local importance are mentioned in the "A to Z" section of this guide. Information about all events can be obtained from local tourist information offices (see Information) or from hotel reception desks.

See also Festivals, Public Holidays and Facts and Figures: Folk Traditions

Ferries

See Car Ferries

Festivals

The following is merely a selection of the most important international festivals. Information about these and other festivals can be obtained from local tourist information offices.

Semanas de Música Religiosa (Festival of Religious Music), Cuenca

End of March

Festival Internacional de Música y Danza (International Festival of Music and Dance), Granada: concerts, operas; zarzuelas (Spanish operettas); classical and modern ballet; flamenco. Theatre festival in Merida.

June/July

Food and Drink

July/August	Festival Internacional de Santander (Santander International Festival): music, dance, drama.
September	Festival de Teatro Clásico (National Festival of Classical Theatre), Almagro: performances of classical plays by Spanish and international dramatists. International Film Festival, San Sebastián
Sept./Oct.	Festival Internacional de Música (International Musical Festival), Barcelona: solo recitals, choral and orchestral concerts.
Mid Sept./ beginning Oct.	Autumn Festival, Madrid: concerts and operatic, dramatic and ballet performances (classical and modern).
October	International Film Week, Valladolid

Food and Drink

Mealtimes	The Spaniards eat lunch at about 2pm and the evening meal around 10pm. In restaurants (see entry) lunch is served from 1pm and dinner from 9pm.
Meals	Breakfast (*desayuno*) in Spain is rather simple and is usually taken in a bar. It consists of a cup of coffee and toast or a small cake, or, particularly in the south, *churros*, deep fried doughnuts. Hotels in the tourist resorts catering for foreign visitors offer a more substantial breakfast or buffet. Lunch (*almuerzo*) and dinner (*cena*) are more substantial and the Spaniards like to linger over these meals. Both meals consist of three or four courses.
	The tourist menu (*menu del día*) is usually better value than eating *à la carte*.
Spanish cuisine	Spanish cooking makes much use of garlic and olive oil. Egg dishes, rice dishes and fish, sea food and stews are typical throughout the country. The cooking of Andalusia makes use of spices from Moorish times: pepper, cinnamon, nutmeg, caraway seed and saffron. Good quality restaurants offering regional cuisine can be found in the paradors (see Hotels and Paradors).
Tapas	On offer all day in little bowls on the counters of bars everywhere are *tapas*. These are appetisers to be enjoyed with a glass of beer, wine or sherry and consist of salads, tortillas, various seafoods, offal, fish, ham, cheese or olives (for a full selection see Reading the Spanish Menu). Visiting a selection of bars and trying a different tapas in each one has the advantage not only of meeting lots of people but of providing a substantial snack making a main meal unnecessary. For those people with a larger appetite there are *raciones* which are a double portion of *tapas*. *Tapas* originate from Seville but are now popular throughout Spain, especially in tourist areas. It is customary to serve them free of charge when a drink is ordered.

Typical Spanish dishes

Hors d'oevres and soups	Hors d'oevres include spicy sausage (*chorizo*), ham (*jamón serrano, de Jabugo* and Trevélez), seafood such as prawns, shellfish (scallops = *vieira*, mussels= *percebes*), spiny lobsters (*langostinos, cigalas*) and olives (particularly Manzanilla and Gordal olives).
	Among Spanish soups are gazpacho, a cold Andalusian speciality made from tomatoes, cucumbers, onions, garlic and peppers with vinegar, oil, spices and breadcrumbs and often served with small dishes of chopped vegetables. Other soups are the Castilian garlic soup made with eggs and the *sopa al cuarto de hora* (quarter-of-an-hour soup), *pote* and *caldo* in Galicia and Asturia, the Basque soup *sopa zarauztarra*, soup from the Levante made from roasted rice and the *ajo blanco con uvas* (white garlic and grapes).

The first main course (*plato fuerte*) is often *tortillas*, omelettes made from eggs and potatoes, in numerous varieties both sweet and savoury. The various local dishes combining both meat and vegetables are both nourishing and substantial. Among them are the Castilian *cocido*, stew of meat, chickpeas, bacon, potatoes and other vegetables, the exact composition varying from one part of the country to another and the Asturian *fabada*, a rich stew of white beans. *Callos* (tripe) is a Madrid speciality and *paella* from Valencia is now widespread throughout Spain, a rice dish made from chicken, meat, fish, seafood, beans and peas.

Meat is mostly grilled or roasted with pork being the most popular with the Spaniards. Roast suckling pig, roast lamb and roast rabbit or rabbit stew are available almost everywhere. In southern Navarra and Aragon poultry, lamb, rabbits and veal are cooked *a la chilindron*, in a sauce of onions, tomatoes and stewed in oil with strong seasoning. An Andalusian speciality is *rabo de buey* (oxtail stew).

Fish is served in many forms. *Zarzuela de mariscos* is a highly seasoned stew of different kinds of fish, *merluza a la vasca* is hake with green sauce, *bacalao* (dried cod) is eaten in the Basque country with a tomato sauce or slowly simmered *al pil pil*, in Navarra trout are stuffed with slices of ham. Any kind of fresh fish is excellent simply fried in oil. Fish are also served as *tapas* such as small pieces of fried squid and sardines in a vinegar and garlic marinade.

Spain has excellent cheeses such as the *queso manchego* from La Mancha or *queso cabrales* from Asturia and delicious desserts: *turrón* (a kind of nougat made from honey and almonds) and marzipan date from Moorish times, in addition there are pastries, particularly on Mallorca (*ensaimadas*), spiced cakes, egg jelly, flan (*creme caramel*), candied yolk of egg and magnificent fruit, figs, dates and pine nuts.

Reading the Spanish Menu

aceitunas: olives
albóndigas: meat balls
boquerones en vinagre: small marinaded herrings
caracoles: snails
chipirones: small octopus
chorizo: spicy sausage
ensaladilla rusa: Russian salad
jámon serrano: dried ham
morcilla: black pudding
pulpo: octopus
tortilla: potato omelette

aceitunas: olives
ensalada: salad
ostras: oysters
anchoas: anchovies
sardinas: sardines
jamón: ham
rábanos: radishes
mantequilla: butter
pan: bread
panecillo: roll

sopa de legumbres (de yerbas, de verduras): vegetable soup
sopa con guisantes: pea soup
sopa de lentejas: lentil soup
sopa con tomates: tomato soup
sopa de fideos: noodle soup
sopa de arroz: rice soup
sopa de pescado: fish soup

Food and Drink

caldo: bouillon
gazpacho: cold vegetable soup

Egg dishes (platos de huevos)

huevo: egg
crudo: raw
fresco: fresh
duro: hard-boiled
pasado por agua: soft-boiled
tortilla: omelette
huevos revueltos: scrambled eggs
huevos frites (huevos al plato): fried eggs
huevos con tomate: eggs fried with tomato

Fish (pescado) and seafood (mariscos)

frito: fried
asado: roasted
cocido: boiled
ahumado: smoked
a la plancha: roasted on a griddle

anguila: eel
arenque: herring
atún: tunny
bacalao: cod
besugo: sea bream
carpa: carp
esturión: sturgeon
gado: haddock
lenguado: sole
merluza: hake
rodaballo: turbot
salmón: salmon
sollo: pike
trucha: trout

almeja: clam
bogavante: lobster
calamar: squid
camarón: shrimp, prawn
cangrejo de mar: crab
cangrejo de río: crayfish
gamba: prawn
langosta: spiny lobster
ostras: oysters

Meat (carnes)

asado: roast
carne ahumada: smoked meat
carne estofada: stew
carne salada: salt meat
chuleta: chop, cutlet
fiambre: cold meat
jamón: ham
serrano: smoked
salchichón: salami-type sausage

bistec: steak
buey: beef
carnero: mutton
cerdo: pork
cochinillo, lechón: sucking pig
cordero: lamb
rosbif: roast beef
ternera: veal

tocino: bacon
vaca: beef

faisán: pheasant
ganso: goose
pato: duck
perdiz: partridge
pichón: pigeon
pollo: chicken

Poultry
(aves)

ciervo: venison (red deer)
corzo: roe-deer
jabalí: wild boar
liebre: hare

Game (caza)

alcachofas: artichokes
apio: celery
cebollas: onions
col de Bruselas: Brussels sprouts
coliflor: cauliflower
col lombarda: red cabbage
ensalada: salad
escarola: endive
espárragos: asparagus
espinacas: spinach
garbanzos: chick peas
guisantes: peas
judias: beans
lechuga: lettuce
patatas: potatoes
patatas fritas: chips
pepinillo: gherkin
pepino: cucumber
pepollo: cabbage
tomates: tomatoes
zanahorias: carrots

Vegetables
(verduras)

aceite: oil
mostaza: mustard
pimienta: pepper
sal: salt
vinagre: vinegar

Condiments
(condimentos)

barquillos: wafers
bollo: bun
compota: compote
dulces: sweets
flan: caramel cream
helado: ice
  de chocolate: chocolate ice
  de frambuesa: raspberry ice
  de vainilla: vanilla ice
con nata: with whipped cream
membrillo: quince jelly
pastel: cake
queso: cheese
tarta: tart
torrijas: fritters

Desserts
(postres)

cerezas: cherries
chumbos: prickly pears
dátiles: dates

Fruit
(frutas)

fresas: strawberries
higos: figs
limón: lemon
mandarinas: mandarines
manzana: apple
melocotón: peach
melones: melons
naranjas: oranges
nueces: walnuts
pera: pear
piña: pineapple
plátano: banana
uvas: grapes

Miscellaneous	bocadillo: sandwich
	butifarra: Catalan sausage
	chorizo: red paprika sausage
	cubierto: table-setting, cutlery
	cuchara: spoon
	cucharita: teaspoon
	cuchillo: knife
	plato: plate
	servilleta: napkin
	sacacorchos: corkscrew
	taza: cup
	tenedor: fork
	torreznos: rashers of bacon
	vaso: glass

Drinks (bebidas)

Non-alcoholic drinks	As well as the usual internationally recognised brands of soft drinks there are numerous types of freshly-pressed fruit juices. Mineral water is also widely drunk, the best known coming from Lanjarón in the Sierra Nevada.
Sangría	This popular refreshing drink is a mixture of red wine, brandy, mineral water, orange and lemon juice with chunks of fruit, served with ice cubes.
Horchaterías	Good refreshing drinks can be had in summer in the *horchaterías*, which specialise in *horchata*, a drink made from earth almonds (*chufas*) or real almonds with lemonade, iced water, etc.
Beer	Beer has become almost as popular as wine. Lighter Pilsner-type beers served in small glasses (*cañas*) are preferred.
Wine and sherry	See Wine
Cider	In Asturia the visitor should really try cider (*sidra*) in one of the *sidrerías*. This apple wine is traditionally poured into the glass from the bottle which is held high so that it forms a large arc as it pours.
Spirits	After the meal a brandy is a popular drink, usually from the Andalusian town of Jerez de la Frontera or El Puerto de Santa Maria. *Chinchón* is an aniseed liqueur from Madrid, *orujo* is a clear spirit from northern Spain. The herb liqueurs of Galicia and Ibiza are famous as are *pacharán* (made from bilberries) from Navarra and absinthe from the Levante.
Coffee	After or during the meal the Spaniards like to drink *café solo*, a black expresso coffee served in small cups. *Café con leche* is more often drunk at breakfast; *café cortado* is coffee with just a drop of milk.

agua minerale: mineral water (con gas: carbonated, sin gas: still)
aguardiente: schnapps
amontillado: medium dry sherry
anis: aniseed spirit
cerveza: beer (dorada: light, negra: dark)
café con leche: coffee with milk; solo: black; cortado: drop of milk
coñac: cognac
fino: dry sherry
leche: milk
limonada: lemonade
el Manzanilla: wine from Sanlúcar de Barrameda
la Manzanilla: camomile tea
oloroso: sweet sherry
té: tea
vino: wine (blanco: white, tinto: red, rosado: rosé)
zumo: fruit juice

Vocabulary
of drinks

Frontier Crossings

The frontier posts at Irún–Biriatou, Seo de Urgel (to Andorra) and La Jonquera–La Perthus are open throughout the year 24 hours a day.

From France
to Spain

The following frontier posts are open from May or June to September from 7am to midnight or from 8am to 10pm, in winter from 9am to 9pm:

Cerbère–Port-Bou (June 15th to September 30th; 24 hours a day); October 1st to April 30th 7am–midnight
Prats-de-Mollo–Pto d'Ares (June 1st to September 30th; 7am–8pm, winter 8am–8pm)
Bourg-Madame–Puigcerdá
Melles-Pont-del-Rey–Lés (May 1st to September 30th; 24 hours a day)
Bagnères de Luchon–Bosost
Urdos de Bearn–Canfranc (June 16th to September 30th; 24 hours a day)
S. Jean Pied de Port–Valcarlos
St-Etienne-de-Baïgorry–Errazu
Aïnhoa–Dancharinea (in winter 7am–10pm)
Sare–Echalar
Sare–Vera de Bidasoa
Herboure–Vera de Bidasoa
Behobie–Behobia (all year 7am–midnight)

The following customs posts are open from Easter to mid-November from 9am to 7pm but are closed in winter:
Aragnouet–Bielsa; Les Eaux-Chaudes–Sallent de Gállego; Arette–Isaba; Larrau–Ochagavia; Urepel–Eugui

The following frontier crossings are always open:
Badajoz–Caia; Fuentes de Oñoro–Vilar Formoso; Túy–Valença do Minho

From Spain
to Portugal

to Andorra
Seo de Urgel–Andorra

The frontier control point La Línea de la Concepción–Gibraltar is open day and night.

From Spain
to Gibraltar

Passengers from Algeciras to Tangier should have regard to the regulations on entry into Morocco; a passport is essential.

From Spain
to Morocco

Getting to Spain

By Air

Spain is linked with the international network of air services by numerous airports, the most important of which are Madrid–Barajas, Barcelona–El Prat and Palma de Mallorca; the last of these is used mainly by charter flights.

Scheduled services

Iberia, the Spanish national airline, flies regular services to and from very many countries.

From the United Kingdom there are services by British Airways and Iberia and its subsidiaries, Aviaco and Viva Air (see Airlines), either direct or by inter-connecting flights to twenty-nine Spanish airports. The most frequent services (several flights daily) are to Madrid and Barcelona, from which there are connecting flights to other Spanish destinations. Most flights are from London Heathrow, Gatwick and Stansted, with connections from other British airports. Flight time from London to Barcelona or Madrid is just over two hours.

From the United States and Canada there are flights by Iberia from New York, Boston, Los Angeles, Washington, Philadelphia, Miami, Toronto and Montreal. American Airlines fly from Dallas/Fort Worth. Flight time from New York to Madrid is about seven hours.

Reduced fares

Competition between airlines has led them to offer a variety of tariff reductions, with discounts in particular for advance booking, as well as reductions for senior citizens and discounts for children. Iberia's "Moneysaver" fares offer savings for stays that include a Saturday night.

The best plan is to shop around before booking, by finding out from travel agents or the airlines themselves what is on offer.

Charter flights

Charter flights, whether bought on a "seats-only" basis or as part of a package including accommodation as well as transport, are cheaper than scheduled flights, but may involve restrictions on time of travel or the time spent abroad. Again, the best policy is to shop around before booking.

By Car

The cheapest route from Britain to Spain by road is by cross-Channel ferry or through the Channel Tunnel and then down through France. The strain on the driver can be reduced, at considerably greater expense, by using the Motorail (car sleeper) service from Calais to Narbonne or Biarritz, both within easy reach of the Spanish frontier. Still easier, but also more expensive, is to cross from Plymouth to Santander by Brittany Ferries or from Portsmouth to Bilbao by P&O European Ferries (see Car Ferries).

See also Frontier Crossings.

By Train

The train journey to Spain from Britain is not particularly convenient or cheap. It involves a change of trains (and of stations) in Paris. From London to Madrid, for example, it is possible to leave in mid morning, connect with the "Talgo" night train from Paris and arrive in Madrid in time for breakfast. The cost is likely to be greater than for air travel. It is now possible to go via the Channel Tunnel to Paris which takes less time.

Since the Spanish rail system has a wider gauge than the rest of Europe it is necessary to change trains (or change bogies on the rolling-stock) at the Franco–Spanish frontier. It is planned to convert the most important Spanish railway lines to the European standard gauge by the year 2000.

Golf

There are numerous golf courses throughout Spain, particularly on the Mediterranean coast, on the islands and around Madrid.

Nearly all Spanish golf clubs are members of the Royal Spanish Golf Federation (see below).

Information about golf courses in Spain can be obtained from tourist information offices (see Information) or from the Spanish Golf Federation: Information

Real Federación Española de Golf, Calle Capitán Haya 9 (5th floor) E-28020 Madrid; tel. (91) 4 55 26 82

A guide to Spanish golf courses, the "Guía de Golf – España", can be purchased from the Secretaria General de Turismo in Madrid (see Information).

Golf Courses in Spain

1 Club de Golf de La Coruña (18 holes), Apartado 737, E-15080 La Coruña

2 Real Aero Club de Santiago (9), General Pardiñas 34, E-15701 Santiago de Compostela

3 Golf La Toja (9), E-36991 Isla de La Toja

4 Aero Club de Vigo (9), Reconquista 7, E-36201 Vigo

5 Club Deportivo La Barganiza (18), Apartado 277, E-33080 Oviedo

6 Club de Golf de Castiello (18), Apartado 161, E-33080 Gijón

7 Club de Golf Severiano Ballesteros (9), Apartado 760 E-39080 Santander

8 Real Golf de Pederña (18), Apartado 233, E-39080 Santander

9 Real Sociedad de Golf de Neguri (18), Apartado 9, E-48980 Algorta

10 Club de Campo La Bilbaína (18), E-148100 Laucariz-Munguía

11 Real Golf de Zarauz (9), Apartado 82, E-20080 Zarauz

12 Real Golf Club de San Sebastián (18), Apartado 6, E-20080 Fuenterrabía

13 Club de Golf de Ulzama (9), E-31799 Guerendiain

14 Real Club de Golf de Cerdaña (18), Apartado 63, E-17680 Puigcerdá

15 Club de Golf de Pals (18), Playa de Pals, E-17256 Pals

16 Club de Golf Costa Brava (18), La Masía, E-17246 Santa Cristina d'Aro

17 Club Golf Llavaneras (9), E-08392 San Andrés de Llavaneras

18 Club de Golf Vallromanas (18), Apartado 43 E-08080 Montomés del Vallés

19 Club de Golf de San Cugat (18), E-08302 Sant Cugat del Vallés

20 Real Club de Golf El Prat (27), Apartado 10, E-08080 El Prat

21 Club de Golf Terramar (18), Apartado 6, E-08080 Sitges

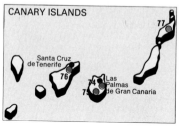

Golf-courses in Spain

9-hole courses ●

18-hole courses ●

27-hole courses ●

36-hole courses ○

22 Club de Golf Costa Dorada (9), Apartado 600, E-43080 Tarragona

23 Real Aero Club de Zaragoza (9), Sección de Golf, Coso 34
E-50004 Zaragoza

24 Club de Golf La Peñaza (18), Apartado 3039, E-50080 Zaragoza

25 Club de Golf Son Parc (9), Plaza Bastio 11, E-07703 Mahón (Minorca)

26 Real Club de Golf de Menorca (9), Apartado 97
E-07780 Mahón (Minorca)

27 Club de Golf Son Servera (9), Urbanización Costa de los Pinos
E-07550 Son Servera (Majorca)

28 Son Vida Club de Golf (18), Urbanización Son Vida
E-07013 Palma de Mallorca

29 Club de Golf de Poniente (18), E-07182 Magalluf–Calvia (Majorca)

30 Club de Golf de Roca Llisa (9), Apartado 200, E-07080 Ibiza

31 Club de Campo del Mediterráneo (18), Urbanización La Coma
E-12190 Borriol

32 Club de Golf Costa de Azahar (9), E-12100 Grao de Castellón

33 Club de Golf Escorpión (18), Apartado 1, E-46180 Bétera

34 Campo de Golf El Saler (18), Parador Nacional, El Saler

35 Club Valdelaguila, Apartado 9, E-28080 Alcalá de Henares

36 Golf La Moraleja (18), Marquesa Viuda de Aldama 50
E-28409 La Moraleja

37 Real Automóvil Club de España (9 and 18), José Abascal 10
E-28003 Madrid, (San Sebastián de los Reyes)

38 Real Club de Puerta de Hierro (36), E-28035 Madrid

39 Club de Campo Villa de Madrid (27), Carretera Castilla, km 2
E-28040 Madrid

40 Nuevo Club de Golf de Madrid (18), N VI Ctra. de la Coruña
E-28290 Las Matas

41 Herrería Club de Golf (18), E-28200 San Lorenzo del Escorial

42 Real Club de Golf Lomas–Bosque (9 and 18), Urbanización El Bosque,
Apartado 51, E-28080 Villaviciosa de Odón

43 Las Encinas de Boadilla (9), E-28660 Boadilla del Monte

44 Centro Deportivo Barberán (9), E-28043 Cuatro Vientos

45 Club de Golf Pozoblanco (9), San Gregorio 2, E-14400 Pozoblanco

46 Club de Golf Los Villares (18), Ronda de los Tejares, E-14080 Córdoba

47 Club de Golf Javea (9), Carretera Javea–Benitachell, km 4.5
E-03730 Javea

48 Club de Golf Ifach (9), Carretera Moraira–Calpe, km 3, E-03720 Benisa

49 Club de Golf Don Cayo (9), Conde de Altea 49, E-03590 Altea

50 Campo de Golf Villamartín (18), Apartado 35, E-03080 Torrevieja

51 La Manga Campo Club de Golf (36), La Manga Club
E-30385 Los Belones

52 Cortijo Grande Club de Golf (9), Cortijo Grande, E-04639 Turre

53 Golf Playa Serena (18), Urbanización Playa Serena
E-04740 Roquetas de Mar

54 Golf Almerimar (18), Golf Hotel Almerimar, E-04700 Ejido

55 Golf Playa Granada (9), Urbanización Playa de Granada, E-18006 Motril

56 Club de Golf Nerja (9), Apartado 154, E-29080 Nerja

57 Club El Candado (9), E-29018 El Palo

58 Club de Campo de Málaga (18), Apartado 324, E-29080 Málaga

59 Golf Torrequebrada (18), Apartado 67, E-29680 Benalmádena

60 Golf Río Real (18), Apartado 82, E-29080 Marbella

61 Club Golf de Mijas (18), Apartado 138, km 3, E-29080 Fuengirola

62 Aloha Golf (18), Nueva Andalucía, E-29600 Marbella

63 Club de Golf Las Brisas (18), Nueva Andalucía, E-29660 Marbella

64 Nueva Andalucía/Los Naranjos (18), Apartado 2, E-29080 Marbella

65 Golf Guadalmina (36), Guadalmina Alta
    E-29670 San Pedro de Alcántara

66 Atalaya Park (18), E-29680 Estepona

67 Golf El Paraíso (18), Carretera Cádiz–Málaga, km 167, E-29080 Estepona

68 Club de Golf Sotogrande (18 and 9), Apartado 14, E-11080 Sotogrande

69 Club de Golf Valderrama (18), Apartado 1, E-11080 Sotogrande

70 Golf San Andrés (9), Ctra. Cadiz–Malaga, E-11130 Chiclana

71 Vista Hermosa Club de Golf (9), Apartado 77
    E-11500 Puerto de Santa María

72 Club Pineda de Sevilla (9), Apartado 796, E-41080 Sevilla

73 Club de Golf Bellavista (9), E-21110 Aljaraque

74 Club de Golf Las Palmas (18), Apartado 183
    E-35080 Las Palmas de Gran Canaria

75 Campo de Golf Maspalomas (18), Avenida de Africa
    E-35100 Playa del Inglés (Gran Canaria)

76 Club de Golf de Tenerife (18), Apartado 125
    E-38080 La Laguna (Tenerife)

77 Club de Golf Costa Deguise (9), Apartado 170
    E-35080 Arrecife (Lanzarote)

Hotels and Paradors

Hoteles Hostales Pensiones	Spanish hotels are officially classified in various categories according to the type and quality of the services they provide: *hoteles* (singular *hotel*; rooms with or without meals, in-house restaurant); *hoteles-apartamentos* (like hotels, but with apartments or chalets); *hostales* (singular *hostal*; more modest establishments, with or without meals); and *pensiones* (singular *pensión*; small guesthouses, offering full board only). *Hoteles, hoteles-apartamentos* and *hostales* may also be run as *residencias* (bed and breakfast only).
Motels	*Moteles* (singular *motel*), usually situated by the roadside, offer limited-stay accommodation.
Fondas	The most modest establishments offering accommodation are *fondas* and *casas de huéspedes*.

Under the official system of classification hotels are divided into five price categories, ranging from the luxury five-star hotel (★★★★★; *de cinco estrellas*) to the modest one-star establishment (★; *de una estrella*).

Categories

This system of classification by stars is not completley accurate; a *hostal* with two stars may be more comfortable than a hotel with two stars. Every establishment, including bars and restaurants, should have a complaints book (*libro de reclamaciones*) available.

The following list of hotels is based on this system of classification. Together with the address and telephone number the number of rooms (r.) is given; the abbreviations are "Ctra." = Carratera (main road), "Avda." = Avenida (avenue). The hotel categories are (H) for hotel, (HS) = *hostal*, (HA) = apartment and (P) = *pension*.

Prices vary widely according to season and region. They are much higher on the Costa del Sol, the Balearic Islands, the Canary Islands and in the cities of Madrid, Barcelona and Seville than in the quieter areas. During festivals (such as the Semana Santa in Seville or the Fiesta de San Fermin in Pamplona) they can almost double. Out of season, however, even expensive hotels offer considerable reductions.

Prices

The prices (in pesetas) in the following table are based on one night's accommodation for two people with breakfast; the price of a single room varies between 60 and 70% of a double room. In some hotels VAT (IVA) at 7% is added. In the Canary Islands, in Ceuta and Melilla a sales tax (IGIC, ITE) of 4% is levied.

Categories for double rooms
★★★★★ 25,000–55,000 Ptas
★★★★ 12,000–25,000 Ptas
★★★ 7000–15,000 Ptas
★★ 4000–10,000 Ptas
★ 2500– 7000 Ptas

Selection of hotels

★★★Valentin (H), Avda. del Generalisimo 21, tel. 12 21 25, 50 r.
★★Pórtico de Castilla (H), Alférez Provisional, tel.12 22 25, 25 r.

Aguilar de Campo

★★★★Los Llanos (H), Avda. España 9, tel. 22 37 50, 102 r.
★★★Gran Hotel (H), Marqué de Molins 1, tel. 21 37 87, 69 r.
★★Eva (P), Carmen 49, tel. 21 03 91, 15 r.

Albacete

★★Alameda (H), Avda. Juan Pablo II, tel. 30 00 31, 34 r.

Alba de Tormes

★★★Bedel (H), San Diego 6, tel. 8 89 37 00, 51 r.
★★Bari (H), Via Complutense 112, tel. 8 88 14 50, 49 r.
★★Torero (HS), Puerta de Madrid 18, tel. 8 89 03 73, 18 r.

Alcalá de Henares

★★★Calpe (H), Ctra. Zaragoza, tel. 83 04 00, 40 r.
★★Meseguer (H), Avda. Maestrazgo 9, tel. 83 10 02, 24 r.

Alcañiz

★Cruz de Alcántara (HS), General Franco 23, tel. 39 00 23, 6 r.

Alcántara

★★★Reconquista (H), Puente San Jorge 1, tel. 5 33 09 00, 77 r.

Alcoy

★★★★Reina Cristina (H), P. de la Conferencia, tel. 60 26 22, 162 r.
★★Anglo Hispano (H), Avda. Villanueva 7, tel. 60 01 00, 30 r.
★★Marina Victoria (H), Avda. La Marina 7, tel. 65 45 01, 49 r.

Algeciras

★★★★★Sidi San Juan (H),, Pda. Cabo la Huerta, tel. 5 16 13 00, 176 r.
★★★Tryp Gran Sol (H), Avda. Méndez Nuñez 3, tel. 5 20 30 00, 148 r.
★★★Estudio Hotel Alicante (HA), Poeta Vila y Blanco 4, tel. 5 21 20 11, 493 r.

Alicante

Hotels and Paradors

★★Alfonso El Sabio (H), Alfonso El Sabio 18, tel. 5 20 31 44, 77 r.
★★Rambla 9 (P), Rambla de Méndez Nuñez 9, tel. 5 14 45 80, 30 r.

Almería
★★★★Gran Hotel Almería (H), Avda. Reina Regente 8, tel. 23 80 11, 117 r.
★★★★Torreluz IV (H), Plaza Flores 5, tel. 23 47 99, 105 r.
★★★Costasol (H), P. de Almería 58, tel. 23 40 11, 55 r.
★★Embajador (H), Calzada de Castro 4, tel. 25 55 11, 67 r.
★★La Perla (H), Plaza del Carmen 7, tel. 23 88 77, 44 r.

Andorra
In Andorra la Vella
★★★★Andorra Park, Roureda Guillemó 3, tel. 82 09 79, 43 r.
★★★Andorra Palace, Carrer de la Roda, tel. 82 10 72, 140 r.
★★★Andorra Center, Doctor Nequi 12, tel. 82 48 00, 140 r.
★★Pyrénees, Av. Príncep Benlloch 20, tel. 86 00 06, 74 r.
★★Cornellá, Av. Meritxell 83, tel. 82 14 80, 90 r.

In Escaldes-
Engordany
★★★★★Roc de Caldes, Crta. d'Engolasters, tel. 86 27 67, 45 r.
★★★★Roc Blanc, Plaça Co-Princeps 5, tel. 82 14 86, 200 r.
★★★Comtes d'Urgell, Av. de las Escoles 29, tel. 82 06 21, 200 r.

In Encamp
★★★Guillem, Els Arinsols, tel. 83 21 33, 74 r.
★★De França, Plaça del Consell 11, tel. 83 12 17, 48 r.

In Ordino
★★★Santa Bàrbara, Plaça, tel. 83 71 00, 23 r.

In Pas de la Casa
★★★Esqui d'Or, Catalunya 9, tel. 85 51 27, 61 r. (Dec.–May)
★★Central, Aballetes, tel. 85 53 75, 52 r.

Aranda de Duero
★★★Los Bronces (H), Carretera N–1 km 160, tel. 50 08 50, 29 r.

Aranjuez
★★★Isabel II (H), Infantas 15, tel. 8 91 09 45, 25 r.
★★Castilla (P), Carrera de Andalucia 98, tel. 8 91 26 27, 17 r.

Arévalo
★★Fray Juan Gil (H), Avda. Deportes 2, tel. 30 08 00, 30 r.

Astorga
★★★Gaudí (H), Eduardo de Castro 6, tel. 61 56 54, 35 r.
★★Galllego (HS), Avda. Ponferrada 78, tel. 61 54 50, 39 r.

Avíla
★★★★Palacio de Valderrábanos (H), Plaza de la Catedral 9, tel. 21 10 23, 73 r.
★★★Cuatro Postes (H), Crta. Salamanca 23, tel. 22 00 00, 78 r.
★★Don Carmelo (H), Paseo D. Carmelo 30, tel. 22 80 50, 60 r.
★★Casa Felipe (HS), Plaza de la Victoria 12, tel. 21 39 24, 11 r.

Avilés
★★★Avilés (H), González Abarca 16, tel. 5 56 26 15, 58 r.
★★San Félix (H), Avda. de Lugo 48, tel. 56 51 46, 18 r.

Badajoz
★★★★Gran Hotel Zurbarán (H), Paseo de Castellar, tel. 22 37 41, 215 r.
★★★Lisboa (H), Avda. Díaz Ambrona 13, tel. 27 29 00, 176 r.
★Niza II (HS), Arcoaguera 16, tel. 22 31 73, 15 r.

Baeza
★★Juanito (H), Avda. Arca del Agua, tel. 74 00 40, 38 r.

Balearic Islands
Mallorca
Palma de Mallorca
★★★★★Meliá Victoria (H), Avda. Joan Miró 21, tel. 73 25 42, 167 r.
★★★★★Son Vida Sheraton (H), Urbanización Son Vida, tel. 79 00 00, 169 r.
★★★★★Valparaíso Palace (H), Francisco Vidal, tel. 40 04 11, 138 r.
★★★★Ciutat de Mallorca (H), Francisco Sureda 24, tel. 70 13 06, 58 r.
★★★★Uto Palma (HA), Avda. Joan Miró 303, tel. 40 12 11, 234 r.
★★★Aparsuit (HA), García Lorca 51, tel. 23 54 47, 160 r.
★★★Majórica (H), Garíta 3, tel. 40 02 61, 153 r.
★★★Saratoga (H), Paseo de Mallorca 6, tel. 72 72 40, 187 r.
★★Sol Horizonte (H), Vista Alegre 1, tel. 40 06 61, 199 r.

★★★★Delta (H), Crta. Cabo Blanco km 6, tel. 74 10 00, 288 r.
★★★★Garonda (H), Ctra. del Arenal, tel. 26 22 00, 112 r.
★★★Acapulco Playa (H), Ctra. del Arenal km 10, tel. 26 18 00, 109 r.
★★★Alexandra (H), Pineda 15, tel. 26 23 50, 164 r.
★★★Bella Playa (H), San Crisóbal 43, tel. 49 06 11, 88 r.
★★★Cactus (H), Acapulco 26, tel. 26 29 32, 110 r.
★★★Copacabana (H), Berlin, tel. 26 16 34, 112 r.
★★★Encant (H), Amilcar 1, tel. 26 05 50, 116 r.
★★★Ipanema Park (H), Antonio María Alcover 11, tel. 26 35 99, 210 r.
★★★Luxor (H), Avda. Son Rigo 21, tel. 26 05 12, 52 r.
★★★Orient (H), Las Lomas, tel. 26 18 50, 273 r.
★★★Venus Playa (H), Vilagarcia de Arosa, tel. 26 02 00, 83 r.
★★Lancaster (H), San Ramón Nonato 16, tel. 26 24 00, 318 r.

Playa de Palma (El Arenal)

★★★Las Arenas (H), Tito Livio 14, tel. 26 07 50, 152 r.
★★★Leo (H), Polacra, tel. 26 44 00, 285 r.
★★★Oleander (H), Playa de Palma, tel. 26 48 50, 264 r.
★★Don Quijote (H), Polacra 3, tel. 26 09 50, 94 r.
★★Isla Azul (H), Plaza Pio IX 3/5, tel. 26 85 62, 51 r.

Playa de Palma

★★★★Playa Cala Mayor (H), Guillem Díaz Plaza 2, tel. 40 32 13, 143 r.
★★★Belvedere Park (H), Can Tapara 3, tel. 40 14 11, 414 r.
★★★Vista Mar (H), Pintor Jaime Juan 17, tel. 40 29 11, 75 r.

Cala Mayor

★★Panoramic (H), More Vermey, tel. 54 54 84, 155 r.
★★More (H), More Vermey, tel. 54 55 05, 115 r.

Alcudia

★★★Borneo (H), Sa Maniga, tel. 58 53 61, 200 r.
★★★Iberotel Flamenco (H), Sa Maniga, tel. 58 53 12, 220 r.
★★★Sumba (H), Sa Maniga, tel. 58 52 12, 280 r.
★★Morito (H), Bonanza 20, tel. 58 56 24, 91 r.

Cala Millor

★★★★Lillot (H), Hernán Cortés 41, tel. 81 82 84, 102 r.
★★★Lago Playa (H), Playa Son Moll, tel. 56 30 58, 95 r.
★★Cala Gat (H), Ctra. del Faro, tel. 56 31 66, 44 r.

Cala Ratjada

★★★★Club Camp de Mar (H), Camp de Mar, tel. 10 52 00, 416 r.
★★Brismar (H), Almirante Riera Alemany 6, tel. 67 16 00, 56 r.

Port d'Andraix

★★★★★Formentor, Playa de Formentor, tel. 86 53 00, 127 r.

Formentor

★★★Castell dels Hams (H), Ctra. Manacor Portocristo, tel. 82 00 07, 191 r.

Portocristo

★★★Capri (H), Anglada Camarasa 69, tel. 53 16 00, 33 r.
★★★Illa d'Or (H), Colón 265, tel. 86 51 00, 119 r.
★★Carotti (H), La Gola, tel. 53 10 96, 30 r.

Port de Pollensa

★★★★Golf Santa Ponsa (H), Santa Ponsa, tel. 69 02 11, 18 r.
★★★Jardin del Sol (H), Es Castellot, tel. 69 13 12, 236 r.
★★Casablanca (H), Via Rey Sancho 6, tel. 69 03 61, 87 r.

Santa Ponça

★★★Edén (H), Es Través, tel. 63 16 00, 152 r.
★★Porto Sollér (H), Costa de la Atalaya, tel. 63 17 00, 127 r.

Sóller

★★★★Port Mahón (H), Avda. Fort de l'Eau 13, tel. 36 26 00, 74 r.
★★★Capri (H), Sant Esteban 8, tel. 36 14 00, 75 r.
★★Noa (HS), Cos De Gracia 157, tel. 36 12 00, 40 r.

Minorca
Mahón/Maó

★★★Cala Blanca (H), Cala Blanca, tel. 38 04 50, 148 r.
★★★Club Hotel Almirante Farragut (H), Cala'N Forcat, tel. 38 28 00, 472 r.
★★Los Delfines (H), Los Delfines, tel. 38 24 50, 92 r.

Ciudadela

Hotels and Paradors

Ibiza
Ibiza Town
and surroundings

★★★★Los Molinos (H), Ramón Muntaner 60, tel. 30 22 50, 147 r.
★★★★Royal Plaza (H), P.-Francés 27–29, tel. 31 37 11, 117 r.
★★★El Corso, Playa de Talamanca, tel. 31 23 12, 179 r.
★★★Simbad (H), Playa Ses Figueres, tel. 31 18 62, 111 r.
★★Cénit (H), Archiduque Luis Salvador, tel. 30 14 04, 62 r.
★★Nautico Ebeso (H), Ramón Muntaner 44, tel. 30 23 00, 113 r.

Formentera
San Francisco
Javier

★★★★Iberotel Club La Mola (H), Playa Mitjorn, tel. 32 80 69, 328 r.
★★Cala Saona (HS), Cala Saona, tel. 32 20 30, 69 r.

Barcelona
Near the Plaza
de Cataluña

★★★★Colón, Avda. Catedral 7, tel. 3 01 14 04, 151 r.
★★★★★Ritz (H), Gran Via 668, tel. 3 18 52 00, 161 r.
★★★★★Glaris (H), Pau Claris 150, tel. 4 87 62 62, 124 r.
★★★★Barcelona (H), Caspe 1–13, tel. 3 02 58 58, 72 r.
★★★★Diplomatic (H), Pau Claris 122, tel. 4 88 02 00, 217 r.
★★★★Regente (H), Rambla de Cataluña 76, tel. 4 87 59 89, 78 r.
★★★Gran Via (H), Gran Via 642, tel. 3 18 19 00, 48 r.
★★★Montecarlo (H), Rambla de los Estudios 124, tel. 3 17 58 00, 73 r.
★★★Regina (H), Vergara 2, tel. 3 01 32 32, 102 r.
★Lloret (H), Rambla Canaletas 125, tel. 3 17 33 66, 52 r.

in and around
the old town

★★★★★Princesa Sofia (H), Plaza Papa Pio XII 4, tel. 3 30 71 11, 505 r.
★★★Gaudí (H), Carrer Nou de la Rambla 12, tel. 3 17 90 32, 73 r.
★★★Oriente (H), Ramblas 45/47, tel. 3 02 25 58, 150 r.
★★España (H), Sant Pau 9/11, tel. 3 18 17 58, 69 r.

other areas

★★★★★Arts de Barcelona (H), Carrer de la Marina 19–21, tel. 2 21 10 10, 397 r.
★★★★★Barcelona Hilton (H), Avda. de la Diagonal 589–591, tel. 4 19 22 33, 276 r.
★★★★★Presidente (H), Avda. de la Diagonal 570, tel. 2 00 21 11, 156 r.
★★★★Balmoral (H), Via Augusta 5, tel. 2 17 87 00, 94 r.
★★★★Majestic (H), Paseo de Gracia 70, tel. 4 88 17 17, 336 r.
★★★Astoria (H), Paris 203, tel. 2 09 83 11, 117 r.
★★★Tres Torres (H), Calatrava 32/34, tel. 4 17 73 00, 56 r.
★★Adagio (H), Fernando 21, tel. 3 18 90 61, 36 r.
★★Antibes (H), Diputación 394, tel. 2 32 62 11, 71 r.

Béjar

★★★Colón (H), Colón 42, tel. 40 06 50, 54 r.
★★Comercio (H), Puerta de Avila 5, tel. 40 02 19, 13 r.

Belmonte

★★La Muralla (P), Isabel I de Castilla, tel. 17 07 79, 7 r.

Benavente

★★Orense (H), Perú 4, tel. 63 01 56, 33 r.

Benidorm

★★★★Gran Hotel Delfin (H), Playa de Poniente, tel. 5 85 34 00, 87 r.
★★★★Costa Blanca Sol (H), Avda. Alcoy, tel. 5 85 54 50, 190 r.
★★★Benilux Park (H), Avda. Panamá, tel. 5 85 28 50, 216 r.
★★★Sol Garzas (H), Avda. Marina Española, tel. 5 85 48 50, 306 r.
★★Bermudas (HA), Estocolmo 17, tel. 5 86 59 24, 108 r.
★★Esmeralda (HS), San Pedro 16, tel. 5 85 13 41, 66 r.

Betanzos

★Los Ángeles (H), Los Ángeles 11, tel. 77 15 11, 36 r.

Bilbao

★★★★★López de Haro (H), Obispo Orueta 2, tel. 4 23 55 00, 53 r.
★★★★★Villa de Bilbao (H), Gran Via 87, tel. 4 41 60 00, 142 r.
★★★★Carlton (H), Plaza de Federico Moyúa 2, tel. 4 16 22 00, 142 r.
★★★Conde Duque (H), Campo de Volantín 22, tel. 4 45 60 00, 67 r.
★★Cantábrico (H), Miravilla 8, tel. 4 15 28 11, 40 r.
★★Maroño (HS), Correo 21, tel. 4 16 58 51, 49 r.

Blanes

★★★Blaumar (H), Avda. Villa de Madrid 31, tel. 35 13 01, 174 r.
★★★Park Hotel (H), Playa S'Abanell, tel. 33 02 50, 127 r.

★★Stella Maris (H), Avda. Villa de Madrid 18, tel. 33 00 92, 90 r.
★San Antonio (H), Paseo Marítimo 63, tel. 33 11 50, 156 r.

★★★Hotel II Virrey (H), Mayor 2–4, tel. 34 13 11, 52 r.   **El Burgo de Osma**

★★★★★Landa Palace (H), Ctra. N–1 km 235, tel. 20 63 43, 42 r.   **Burgos**
★★★★Almirante Bonifaz (H), Vitoria 22, tel. 20 69 43, 79 r.
★★★Condestable (H), Vitoria 8, tel. 26 71 25, 82 r.
★★España (H), Paseo del Espolón 32, tel. 20 63 40, 69 r.
★★Hilton (HS), Vitoria 165, tel. 22 51 16, 11 r.

★★★★Meliá Cáceres (H), Plaza de San Juan, tel. 21 58 00, 86 r.   **Cáceres**
★★★Alcántara (H), Avda. Virgen de Guadalupe 14, tel. 22 89 00, 67 r.
★★Goya (HS), Plaza General Mola, tel. 24 99 50, 15 r.

★★★★Atlántico (H), Avda. Duque de Nájera 9, tel. 22 69 05, 153 r.   **Cádiz**
★★★Francia Y Paris (H), Plaza San Francisco 2, tel. 22 23 48, 69 r.
★★Regio (H), Ana de Villa 11, tel. 27 93 31, 40 r.
★★San Remo (H), Paseo Marítimo 3, tel. 25 22 02, 62 r.

★★★Catalyud (H), N–II km 237, tel. 88 13 23, 63 r.   **Calatayud**
★★Marivella (HS), N–II km 241, tel. 88 12 37, 19 r.

★★★★★Meliá (H), Gomera 6, tel. 26 80 50, 312 r.   **Canary Islands**
★★★★★Reina Isabel (H), Alfredo L. Jones 40, tel. 26 01 00, 234 r.   **Gran Canaria**
★★★★★Santa Catalina (H), Parque Doramas, tel. 24 30 40, 208 r.   Las Palmas
★★★★Concorde (H), Tomás Miller 85, tel. 26 27 50, 127 r.
★★★★Imperial Playa (H), Ferreras 1, tel. 26 48 54, 173 r.
★★★★Sol Iberia (H), Av. Marítima del Norte, tel. 36 11 33, 298 r.
★★★Atlanta (H), Alfredo L. Jones 37, tel. 26 50 62, 64 r.
★★★Fataga (H), Néstor de La Torre 21, tel. 24 04 08, 92 r.
★★★Gran Canaria (H), Paseo de las Canteras 38, tel. 27 17 54, 90 r.
★★Olympia (H), Doctor Grau Bassas 1, tel. 26 17 20, 40 r.
★★Pujol (H), Salvador Cuyas 5, tel. 27 44 33, 48 r.
★Madrid (H), Plaza Cairasco 2, tel. 36 06 64, 39 r.

★★★★★Maspalomas Oasis (H), Playa de Maspalomas, tel. 76 01 70, 334 r.   Maspalomas/
★★★★Apolo (H), Avda. Estados Unidos 28, tel. 76 00 58, 115 r.   Playa del Inglés
★★★★Ifa Faro Maspalomas (H), Playa Maspalomas, tel. 14 22 14, 188 r.
★★★★Las Margaritas (H), Avda. de Gran Canaria 38, tel. 76 11 12, 323 r.
★★★★Maspalomas Palm Beach (H), Avda. del Oasis, tel. 14 08 06, 358 r.
★★★Continental (H), Avda. de Italia 2, tel. 76 00 33, 383 r.
★★★Parque Tropical (H), Avda. de Italia 2, tel. 76 07 12, 235 r.
★★Ifa Regina Mar (H), Avda. de EE.UU 38, tel. 76 76 16, 128 r.

★★★★★Iberotel Tres Islas (H), Playa de Coralejo, tel. 86 60 00, 365 r.   **Fuertaventura**
★★Tamasite (P), León y Castilla 9, Puerto del Rosario, tel. 85 02 80, 18 r.
★Coralejo (H), Playa de Coralejo, tel. 86 61 00, 19 r.

★★★★★Meliá Salinas, Costa Teguise, tel. 59 00 40, 310 r.   **Lanzarote**
★★★Miramar (H), Coll 2, Arrecife, tel. 81 04 38, 90 r.
★★Cardona (P), 18 de Julio 11, Arrecife, tel. 81 10 08, 62 r.

★★★★★Mencey (H), José Naveiras 38, tel. 27 67 00, 298 r.   **Tenerife**
★★★Diplomático (H), Antonio Nebrija 16, tel. 22 39 41, 38 r.   Santa Cruz de
★★Taburiente (H), Dr. Guigou 25, tel. 27 60 00, 90 r.   Tenerife

★★★★★Meliá Botánico (H), Richard J. Yeoward, tel. 38 14 00, 282 r.   Puerto
★★★★★Meliá San Felipe (H), Avda. de Colón 22, tel. 38 33 11, 260 r.   de la Cruz
★★★★★Semiramis (H), Leopoldo Cologán 12, tel. 38 55 51, 275 r.
★★★★Atlantis Playa (H), Playa Martíanez, tel. 38 53 51, 320 r.
★★★★Florida (H), Avda. Blas Pérez González , tel. 38 12 50, 335 r.

Hotels and Paradors

★★★★Orotava Gardens Sol (H), Avda. Aguilar y Quesada 1, tel. 38 52 11, 241 r.
★★★Don Manolito (H), Dr. Madán 6, tel. 38 50 40, 49 r.
★★★Marquesa (H), Quintana 11, tel. 38 31 51, 88 r.
★★Arosa (H), Iriarte 21, tel. 38 42 37, 27 r.

Playa de las Américas
★★★★Colón Guanamani (H), Playa de Fañabre, tel. 79 44 14, 154 r.
★★★★Jardín Tropical (H), San Eugenio, tel. 79 41 11, 376 r.
★★★★La Pinta (H), San Eugenio, tel. 75 58 58, 229 r.
★★★Club Villamar (H), San Eugenio, tel. 75 00 04, 100 r.
★★★Ponderosa (H), Playa de las Américas, tel. 79 02 04, 175 r.

Gomera
★★★★Tecina (H), Playa de Santiago, tel. 89 50 50, 258 r.
★★Garajonay (H), Ruiz de Padrón 15, San Sebastián, tel. 87 05 50, 30 r.

La Palma
★★★San Miguel (H), Avda. El Puente 33, Santa Cruz, tel. 41 12 42, 106 r.
★★★Valle de Ariadne (H), Los Llanos de Ariadne, tel. 46 26 00, 42 r.

Hierro
★★Boomerang (H), Doctor Gost 1, Valverde, tel. 55 02 00, 17 r.
★★Puntagrande (H), Las Puntas-Frontera, tel. 55 90 81, 4 r.

Cartagena
★★★Cartagonova (H), Marcos Redondo 3, tel. 50 42 00, 126 r.
★★Alfonso XIII (H), Paseo de Alfonso XIII 30, tel. 52 00 00, 217 r.
★★Los Habaneros (H), San Diego 60, tel. 50 52 50, 63 r.

Castellón de la Plana
★★★★Mindoro (H), Moyano 4, tel. 22 23 00, 114 r.
★★★Del Golf (H), Playa del Pinar (El Grao), tel. 28 01 80, 127 r.
★★★Turcosa (H), Treballadors de la Mar 1, tel. 28 36 00, 70 r.

Benicarló
★★Marynton (H), Paseo Marítimo, tel. 47 30 11, 26 r.

Benicasim
★★★Intur-Azor (H), Paseo Marítimo, tel. 39 20 00, 88 r.
★★★Orange (H), Gran Avenida, tel. 39 44 00, 415 r.
★★★Trinimar (H), Avda. Ferrándiz Salvador, tel. 30 08 50, 170 r.
★Benicasim (H), Bayer 50, tel. 30 05 58, 80 r.

Ceuta
★★Skol (HS), Avda. Reyes Católicos 6, tel. 50 41 61, 14 r.

Ciudad Real
★★★Santa Cecilia (H), Tinte 3, tel. 22 85 45, 70 r.
★★Almanazor (H), Bernardo Balbuena, tel. 21 43 03, 71 r.

Ciudad Rodrigo
★★★Conde Rodrigo (H), Plaza San Salador 9, tel. 46 14 08, 35 r.
★El Cruce (H), Ctra. de Lisboa 4, tel. 46 04 50, 40 r.

Córdoba
★★★★Adarve (H), Magistral González Francés 15, tel. 48 11 02, 103 r.
★★★★Gran Capitán (H), Avda. de América 3–5, tel. 47 02 50 99, 99 r.
★★★★Las Adelfas (H), Av. Arruzafa s/n, tel. 27 74 20, 101 r.
★★★★Meliá Córdoba (H), Jardines de la Victoria s/n, tel. 29 80 66, 106 r.
★★★El Califa (H), Lope de Hoces 14, tel. 29 94 00, 67 r.
★★★Maimóndes (H), Torrijos 4, tel. 47 15 00, 83 r.
★★Andalucía (H), José Zorilla 3, tel. 47 60 00, 40 r.
★★Colón (H), Alhaken II, 4, tel. 47 00 17, 40 r.

La Coruña
★★★★Atlántico (H), Jardines de Méndez Nuñez 2, tel. 22 65 00, 200 r.
★★★★Finisterre (H), Paseo del Parrote, tel. 20 54 00, 127 r.
★★★Almirante (H), Paseo de Ronda 54, tel. 25 96 00, 20 r.
★★España, Juana de Vega 7, tel. 22 45 06, 84 r.
★Palacio (HS), Plaza de Galicia 2, tel. 22 21 85, 18 r.

Costa Brava Bagur
★★★★Aigua Brava (H), Playa de Fornells, tel. 62 20 58, 85 r.
★★★Bonaigua (H), Playa de Fornells, tel. 62 20 50, 47 r.

★★★Llane Petit (H), Dr. Bartoneus 37, tel. 25 80 50, 35 r.   Cadaques
★★★Rocamar (H), Virgen del Carmen, tel. 25 81 50, 70 r.
★★Port Lligat (H), Port Lligat, tel. 25 81 62, 30 r.

★★★Bonaire (H), Paseo Luis Robert 4, tel. 77 00 68, 45 r.   La Escala
★★Nieves Mar (H), Paseo del Mar 8, tel. 77 03 00, 80 r.

★★★El Paraíso (H), Partatge de Parena 2, tel. 30 04 50, 55 r.   Llafranch
★★★Terramar (H), Paseo de Cipsele 1, tel. 30 02 00, 56 r.

★★★★Monterey (H), Ctra. de Tossa, tel. 36 40 50, 224 r.   Lloret de Mar
★★★★Roger de Flor (H), Turo del Estelat, tel. 36 48 00, 98 r.
★★★Alexis (H), Na Marina 59, tel. 36 46 04, 101 r.
★★★Excelsior (H), Paseo Jacinto Verdaguer 16, tel. 36 41 37, 45 r.
★★Festa Brava (H), Ctra. de Blanes 23–25, tel. 36 45 50, 106 r.
★★Terra Brava (H), Avda. América 41, tel. 36 50 09, 132 r.

★★★Áncora (H), Josep Pla., tel. 31 48 58, 44 r.   Palamós
★★★Trias (H), Paseo del Mar, tel. 31 41 00, 81 r.
★Catalina (HS), Formento 16, tel. 31 43 86, 22 r.

★★★★Colombus (H), Paseo del Mar, tel. 81 71 66, 110 r.   Playa de Aro
★★★Armoar (H), Paseo Marítimo, tel. 81 70 54, 167 r.
★★★Costa Brava (H), Punta D'En Ramis, tel. 81 73 08, 46 r.
★★Bell Repos (H), Virgen del Carmen, tel. 81 71 00, 34 r.
★★Planamar (H), Avda. de la Pau 1, tel. 81 70 92, 86 r.

★★★★Almadabra Park (H), Playa Almadabra, tel. 25 65 50, 66 r.   Rosas
★★★Canyelles Platja (H), Playa Canjelles, tel. 25 60 14, 98 r.
★★★Vistabella (H), D. Pacheco 26–30, tel. 25 60 08, 46 r.

★★★★Caleta Park (H), S'Agaro, tel. 32 00 12, 100 r.   San Feliú
★★★Curhotel Hippocrates (H), Ctra. San Pol, tel. 32 06 62, 87 r.   de Guixols
★★Montecarlo (H), Abad Sunyer 110, tel. 82 23 61, 64 r.
★Mediterráneo (H), Penitencia 8, tel. 32 07 50, 38 r.

★★★★Gran Hotel Reymar (H), Playa Mar Menuda, tel. 34 03 12, 156 r.   Tossa de Mar
★★★Costa Brava (H), Verge de Montserat, tel. 34 01 30, 188 r.
★★★Mar Menuda (H), Playa de Mar Menuda, tel. 34 10 00, 40 r.
★★Diana (H), Plaza de España 6, tel. 34 18 86, 21 r.

★★★★Torremanga (H), San Ignacio de Loyola 9, tel. 22 33 51, 120 r.   **Cuenca**
★★★Cueva del Fraile (H), Ctra. Cuenca-Buenache km 7, tel. 21 15 71, 63 r.
★★Posada de San José (HS), Julián Romero 4, tel. 21 13 00, 25 r.

★★Agiria (HS), Ctra. Sagunto–Burgos km 218, tel. 80 07 31, 30 r.   **Daroca**

★★★Denia (H), Partitda Suertes del Mar, tel. 5 78 12 12, 280 r.   **Denia**
★★★Los Angeles (H), Bovetes Nord A 118, tel. 5 78 04 58, 59 r.

★★Ciudad del Sol (H), Miguel de Cervantes 48, tel. 4 83 03 00, 29 r.   **Ecija**

★★★★Huerto del Cura (H), Porta de la Morera 14, tel. 5 45 80 40, 70 r.   **Elche**
★★Don Jaime (H), Avda. Primo de Rivera 5, tel. 5 45 38 40, 64 r.

★★★★Victoria Palace (H), Juan de Toledo 4, tel. 8 90 15 11, 87 r.   **El Escorial**
★★Miranda Suizo (H), Floridablanca 18, tel. 8 90 47 11, 48 r.   (San Lorenzo
de El Escorial)

★Cristina (HS), Baja Navarra 1–1, tel. 55 07 72, 15 r.   **Estella**

★★★★Iberotel Atalaya Park (H), Ctra. de Cádiz km 168, tel. 78 13 00, 246 r.   **Estepona**
★★★★Stakis Paraíso (H), Ctra. de Cádiz km 167, tel. 78 30 00, 201 r.
★★★Santa Marta (H), Ctra. de Cádiz km 110, tel. 78 07 16, 37 r.

Hotels and Paradors

Figueras
★★★Ampurdán (H), Ctra. de Francia km 763, tel. 50 05 62, 42 r.
★★Ronda (H), Ronda Barcelona, tel. 50 39 11, 45 r.

Fuengirola
★★★★Las Palmeras Sol (H), Paseo Marítimo, tel. 47 27 00, 398 r.
★★★Las Pirámides (H), Miguel Márquez 43, tel. 47 06 00, 320 r.
★★★Angela (H), Paseo Príncipe de España, tel. 47 52 00, 261 r.
★★★Florida (H), Paseo Marítimo, s/n, tel. 47 61 00, 116 r.
★★Cendrillon (H), Ctra. de Cádiz km 212, tel. 47 53 16, 40 r.

Gandia
★★★★Bayren (H), Paseo de Neptuno, tel. 2 84 03 0, 164 r.
★★★Riviera (H), Paseo de Neptuno 29, tel. 2 84 00 66, 72 r.
★★★San Luis (H), Paseo de Neptuno 6, tel. 2 84 08 00, 72 r.
★★Gandía Playa (H), Devesa 17, tel. 2 84 13 00, 126 r.

Gerona
★★★★Sol Girona (H), Barcelona 112, tel. 40 05 00, 114 r.
★★★Utonia (H), Avda. Jaime I 22, tel. 20 33 34, 45 r.
★★Europia (H), Juli Garreta 23, tel. 20 27 50, 26 r.

Gibraltar
★★★★Rock Hotel (H), 3 Europa Road, tel. 7 30 00, 150 r.
★★★★Holiday Inn (H), 2 Governor's Parade, tel. 0 07 27 05 00, 120 r.

Gijón
★★★★Hernán Cortés (H), Fernández Vallin 5, tel. 34 60 00, 109 r.
★★★★Príncipe de Asturias (H), Manso 2, tel. 5 36 71 11, 81 r.
★★★Pasaje (H), Marqués de San Esteban 3, tel. 5 34 49 15, 29 r.
★★Asturias (H), Plaza Mayor 11, tel. 5 35 06 00, 80 r.

Granada
★★★★Alhambra Palace (H), Peña Partida 2, tel. 22 14 68, 132 r.
★★★★Carmen (H), Acera del Darro 62, tel. 25 83 00, 205 r.
★★★★Luz Granada (H), Avda. Constitución 18, tel. 20 40 61, 174 r.
★★★★Meliá Granada (H), Ángel Ganivet 7, tel. 22 74 00, 197 r.
★★★Washington Irving (H), Paseo del Generalife 2, tel. 22 75 50, 68 r.
★★Macía (H), Plaza Nueva 4, tel. 22 75 36, 40 r.
★★Los Tilos (H), Plaza de Bib-Rambla, tel. 26 67 12, 30 r.
★América (H), Real de la Alhambra 53, tel. 22 74 71, 13 r.

Guadalajara
★★★Husa Pax (H), N–II km 57 , tel. 22 18 00, 61 r.
★★España (H), Teniente Figueroa 3, tel. 21 13 03, 33 r.

Guadalupe
★★Hospedería Real Monastério (H), Plaza Juan Carlos I, tel. 36 70 00, 40 r.

Guernica
★★Gernika (H), Carlos Cangoti 11, tel. 6 85 49 48, 24 r.

Haro
★★★★Los Agostinos (H), tel. 31 13 08, 62 r.

Huelva
★★★★Luz Huelva (H), Alameda Sundheim 26, tel. 25 00 11, 106 r.
★★★Tartessos (H), Martín Alonso Pinzón 13 y 15, tel. 24 56 11, 112 r.

Huesca
★★★Pedro I de Aragón (H), Del Parque 34, tel. 22 03 00, 120 r.
★★Montearagón (H), N–240 km 206, tel. 22 23 50, 27 r.
★★Mirasol (HS), Paseo Ramón y Cajal 29, tel. 22 37 60, 13 r.

Jaca
★★★Oroel (H), Avda. de Francia 37, tel. 36 24 11, 124 r.
★★La Paz (H), Mayor 41, tel. 36 07 00, 34 r.

Jaén
★★★Condestable Iranzo (H), Paseo de la Estación 32, tel. 22 28 00, 159 r.
★★★Xauen (H), Plaza de Deán Mazas 3, tel. 26 40 11, 35 r.

Játiva
★★Murta (H), Angel Lacalle 1, tel. 2 27 66 11, 21 r.

Jerez de la Frontera
★★★★Jerez (H), Avda. Alcalde Alvaro Domecq 35, tel. 30 06 00, 120 r.
★★★★Royal Sherry Park (H), Avda. Alvaro Domecq, tel. 30 30 11, 173 r.
★★★Avenida Jerez (H), Avda. Alvaro Domecq 10, tel. 34 74 11, 95 r.

★★★★Conde Luna (H), Independencia 7, tel. 20 65 12, 154 r.   **Léon**
★★★Riosol (H), Avda. de Palencia 3, tel. 2 16 68 50, 141 r.
★★Don Suero (HS), Suero de Quiñones 15, tel. 23 06 00, 106 r.
★Paris (H), Generalisímo 20, tel. 23 86 00, 81 r.

★★★★Condes de Urgel II (H), Avda. de Barcelona 17, tel. 20 23 00, 105 r.   **Lérida**
★★★Sansi Park (H), Alcalde Porqueres 4, tel. 24 40 00, 120 r.
★★Real (H), Blondel 22, tel. 23 94 05, 41 r.

★★★Los Bracos Sol (H), Bretón de Los Herreros 29, tel. 22 66 08, 72 r.   **Logroño**
★★★★Carlton Rioja (H), Gran Vía 5, tel. 24 21 00, 120 r.
★★★Condes de Haro (H), Saturnino Ulargui 6, tel. 20 85 00, 44 r.
★★Marqés de Vallejo (HS), Marqués de Vallejo 8, tel. 24 83 33, 30 r.

★★★Alameda (H), Musso Valiente 8, tel. 46 75 00, 41 r.   **Lorca**
★★La Hoya (H), N–340 km 280, tel. 48 18 06, 36 r.

★★★Gran Hotel Lugo (H), Avda. Ramón Ferreiro, tel. 22 41 52, 168 r.   **Lugo**
★★★Méndez Núñez (H), Reina 1, tel. 23 07 11, 86 r.
★España (H), Villalba 2 bis, tel. 23 15 40, 17 r.

★★★★★Ritz (H), Plaza de la Lealtad 5, tel. 5 21 58 57, 160 r.   **Madrid**
★★★★★Palace (H), Plaza de las Cortes 7, tel. 4 29 75 51, 457 r.   between Plaza de la
★★★★Carlton (H), Paseo de las Delicias 26, tel. 5 39 71 00, 112 r.   Cibeles and Est.
★★★Inglés (H), Echegaray 8, tel. 4 29 656 51, 58 r.   de Atocha
★★★Mercator (H), Atocha 123, tel. 4 29 5 00, 89 r.
★★★Reyes Católicos (H), Ángel 18, tel. 2 65 86 00, 38 r.
★★Mediodía (H), Plaza del Emperador Carlos V 8, tel. 5 27 30 60, 161 r.

★★★★★Eurobuilding (H), Padre Damián 23, tel. 3 45 45 00, 421 r.   between Plaza
★★★★★Husa Princesa (H), Princesa 40, tel. 5 42 35 00, 405 r.   de la Cibeles and
★★★★★Meliá Madrid (H), Princesa 27, tel. 5 71 22 11, 266 r.   Est. del Norte
★★★★Alcalá (H), Alcalá 66, tel. 4 35 10 60, 153 r.
★★★★Emperador (H), Gran Vía 53, tel. 2 47 28 00, 232 r.
★★★★Liabeny (H), Salud 3, tel. 5 32 53 06, 209 r.
★★★Carlos V (H), Maestro Vitoria 5, tel. 5 31 41 00, 67 r.
★★★Gran Vía (H), Gran Vía 25, tel. 5 22 11 21, 174 r.
★★★Moderno (H), Arenal 2, tel. 5 31 09 00, 98 r.
★★Londres (H), Galdó 2, tel. 5 31 41 05, 57 r.
★★Francisco I (H), Arenal 15, tel. 2 48 02 04, 58 r.

★★★★★Villa Magna (H), Paseo de la Castellana 22, tel. 5 76 75 00, 194 r.   in the north
★★★★★Meliá Castilla (H), Capitán Haya 43, tel. 5 71 22 11, 1000 r.
★★★★★Miguel Ángel (H), Miguel Ángel 31, tel. 4 42 81 99, 304 r.
★★★★★Mindanao (H), San Francisco de Sales 15, tel. 5 49 55 00, 281 r.
★★★★★Wellington (H), Velásquez 8, tel. 5 75 44 00, 295 r.
★★★★Aitana (H), Paseo de la Castellana 152, tel. 3 44 11 42, 111 r.
★★★San Antonio de la Florida 13, tel. 5 47 14 00, 100 r.

★★★★Colón (H), Doctor Esquerdo 117–119, tel. 5 73 59 00, 389 r.   Hotels in
★★★★Pintor (H), Goya 59, tel. 4 35 75 45, 176 r.   the east of
★★★Claridge (H), Plaza de Conde de Casal 6, tel. 5 51 94 00, 150 r.   Madrid

★★★★★Tryp Monte Real (H), Arroyo Fresno 17, tel. 3 16 21 40, 77 r.   University
    of Madrid

★★★★Guadalmar (H), Ctra. de Cádiz km 28, Urbanizacion Guadalmar,   **Málaga**
    tel. 2 23 17 03, 352 r.
★★★Bahía Málaga (H), Somera 8, tel. 2 22 43 05, 44 r.
★★★Los Naranjos (H),Paseo Sancha 35, tel. 2 22 43 17, 200 r.
★★Astoria (H), Avda. del Comandante Benítez 3, tel. 2 22 45 00, 61 r.
★★Carlos V (H), Cister 6, tel. 2 21 51 20, 51 r.

Hotels and Paradors

Marbella	★★★★★Meliá Don Pepe (H), Finca Las Merinas, tel. 77 03 00, 202 r.
	★★★★★Los Monteros (H), Ctra. de Cádiz km 187, tel. 77 17 00, 171 r.
	★★★★★Puente Romano (H), Ctra. de Cádiz km 178, tel. 77 01 00, 184 r.
	★★★★★Golf Plaza (H), Nueva Andalucia, tel. 81 17 50, 22 r.
	★★★★Andalucia Plaza (H), Nueva Andalucia, tel. 81 20 00, 424 r.
Medinacelli	★★★Nico Hotel 70 (H), N–II km 151, tel. 32 60 11, 22 r.
Medina del Campo	★★Palacio de las Salinas (H), Ctra. Medina-Velasalvaro km 4, tel. 80 10 54, 64 r.
Melilla	★★★Rusadir San Miguel (H), Pablo Vallesca 5, tel. 68 12 40, 35 r.
	★★Anfora (H), Pablo Vallesca 16, tel. 68 49 40, 145 r.
Mérida	★★★★Las Lomas (H), N–V km 338, tel. 31 10 11, 134 r.
	★★★Emperatriz (H), Plaza de España 19, tel. 31 31 11, 41 r.
	★★Zeus (H), Avda. Princesa Sofia, tel. 31 81 11, 44 r.
Morella	★★Cardenal Ram (H), Cuesta Suñer 1, tel. 16 00 00, 19 r.
Murcia	★★★★Arco de San Juan (H), Plaza de Ceballos 10, tel. 21 04 55, 115 r.
	★★★★Conde de Floridablanca (H), Corbalán 7, tel. 21 46 26, 85 r.
	★★★Fontoria (H), Madre de Dios 4, tel. 21 77 89, 120 r.
	★★★Hispano II (H), Radio Murcia 3, tel. 21 61 52, 35 r.
	★★Casa Emilio (H), Alameda de Colón 9, tel. 22 06 31, 37 r.
	★★Majesti (H), San Pedro 5, tel. 21 47 42, 68 r.
Nerja	★★★★Mónica (H), Playa Torrecilla, tel. 52 11 00, 234 r.
	★★★Balcón de Europa (H), Paseo Balcón de Europa 1, tel. 52 08 00, 102 r.
Olite	★★Carlos III El Noble (H), Rua de Medios 1, tel. 74 06 44, 14 r.
Oña	★★Morales (HS), N–232 km 99, tel. 30 00 73, 6 r.
Orense	★★★Gran Hotel San Martin (H), Curros Enriquez 1, tel. 23 56 90, 90 r.
	★★★Sila (H), Avda. de la Habana 61, tel. 23 63 11, 66 r.
	★Barcelona (H), Avda. de Pontevedra 11, tel. 22 08 00, 40 r.
Orihuela	★★★La Zenia (H), Urbanización la Zenia, tel. 6 76 02 00, 220 r.
	★★★Montepiedra (H), Dehesa de Campomor, tel. 5 32 03 00, 64 r.
Oviedo	★★★★★La Reconquista (H), Gil de Jaz 16, tel. 5 24 11 00, 142 r.
	★★★★Gran Hotel España (H), Jovellanos 2, tel. 5 22 05 96, 89 r.
	★★★★Regente (H), Jovellanos 31, tel. 5 22 23 43, 88 r.
	★★★La Gruta (H), Alto de Buenavista, tel. 5 23 24 50, 105 r.
	★★Barbón (H), Covadonga 7, tel. 22 52 93, 40 r.
Palencia	★★★★Europa Centro (H), Magaz de Pisuerga, tel. 78 40 00, 122 r.
	★★★Castilla la Vieja (H), Casado del Alisal 26, tel. 74 90 44, 87 r.
	★Colón-27 (H), Colón 27, tel. 74 07 00, 22 r.
Pamplona	★★★★Iruña Palace-Tres Reyes (H), Jardines de la Taconera, tel. 22 66 00, 168 r.
	★★★Ciudad de Pamplona (H), Iturrama 21, tel. 26 60 00, 117 r.
	★★★Maisonnave (H), Nueva 20, tel. 22 48 00, 48 r.
	★★★Yoldi (H), Avda. de San Ignacio 11, tel. 22 48 00, 48 r.
	★★Eslava (H), Plaza Virgen de la O 7, tel. 22 22 70, 28 r.
Picos de Europa	★★★Pelayo (H), Covadaonga, tel. 5 84 60 61, 43 r.
	★★El Capitán (H), Cangas de Onis, tel. 5 84 83 57, 28 r.
	★★Ventura (H), Cangas de Onis, tel. 84 82 01, 53 r.

★★★Alfonso VIII (H), Alfonso III 32, tel. 41 02 50, 57 r. —

★★★★Del Temple (H), Avda. Portugal 2, tel. 41 00 58, 114 r. —

★★★★Galicia Palace (H), Avda. de Vigo 3, tel. 86 44 11, 85 r. —
★★★Virgen del Camino 55–57, tel. 85 59 04, 53 r.

★★De Francia (H), Vicaria 8, tel. 75 75 19, 39 r. —

★★Solana del Ter (H), Ctra. Barcelona–Ripoll, tel. 70 10 62, 28 r. —

★★★★Reina Victoria (H), Jerez 25, tel. 87 12 40, 89 r. —
★★★Polo (H), Mariano Soubiron 8, tel. 87 24 47, 33 r.
★★★El Tajo (H), Doctor Cajal 7, tel. 87 62 36, 67 r.

★★Azahar (H), Avda. Pais Valencia 8, tel. 2 66 33 68, 25 r. —

★★★★Gran Hotel (H), Plaza Iglesias 5, tel. 21 35 00, 100 r. —
★★★★Palacio de Castellanos (H), San Pablo 58–64, tel. 26 18 18, 69 r.
★★★Alfonso X (H), Toro 64, tel. 21 44 01, 66 r.
★★★Las Torres (H), Plaza Mayor 26, tel. 21 21 00, 44 r.
★★Condal (H), Santa Eulalia 3–5, tel. 21 84 00, 70 r.
★★Emperatriz (H), Compañia 44, tel. 21 92 00, 61 r.

★★★★Golf Hotel Guadalmina, tel. 78 14 00, 80 r. —
★★★El Cortijo Blanco (H), Ctra. Cádiz-Malaga km 172, tel. 78 09 00, 163 r.

★★★★★Maria Cristina (H), Paseo República Argentina, tel. 42 49 00, 139 r. —
★★★★Costa Vasca (H), Avda. Pío Baroja 15, tel. 21 10 11, 203 r.
★★★★Londres y Inglaterra (H), Zubieta 2, tel. 42 69 89, 145 r.
★★★Gudamendi (H), Barrio de Igueldo, tel. 21 41 11, 20 r.
★★★Niza (H), Zubieta 56, tel. 42 66 63, 41 r.
★★Codina (H), Avda. Zumalacárregui 21, tel. 21 22 00, 77 r.
★★Donastiarra (P), San Martin 6–1, tel. 42 61 67, 15 r.
★★Parma (H), General Jáuregui 11, tel. 42 88 93, 21 r.

★★★★★Real (H), Paseo de Pérez Galdós 28, tel. 27 25 50, 125 r. —
★★★★Santemar (H), Avda. Joaquin Costa 28, tel. 27 29 00, 350 r.
★★★Sardinero (H), Plaza de Italia 1, tel. 27 11 00, 113 r.
★★Liébana (HS), Nicolás Salmerón 9, tel. 22 32 50, 30 r.
★★Rhin (H), Avda. Reina Victoria 155, tel. 27 43 00, 95 r.

★★★★★Araguaney (H), Alfredo Brañas 5, tel. 59 59 00, 64 r. —
★★★★Compostela (H), General Franco 1, tel. 58 567 00, 99 r.
★★★★Peregrino (H), Avda. Rosalia de Castro, tel. 52 18 50, 148 r.
★★★Gelmirez (H), General Franco 92, tel. 56 11 00, 138 r.
★★★Hogar San Francisco (HS), Campillo de San Francisco 3, tel. 58 11 43, 71 r.
★★San Laázaro (HS), Baliño, tel. 58 41 51, 19 r.
★★Santa Lucia (H), Santa Lucia, tel. 54 92 83, 81 r.

★★★Altamira (H), Cantón 1, tel. 81 80 25, 32 r. —
★★★Santillana (H), Avda. Le Dorat 1, tel. 81 80 11, 38 r.
★San Roque (HS), Bo. Castio, tel. 81 82 43, 13 r.

★★★El Corregidor (H), Zumalácarregui 14–16, tel. 34 21 28, 32 r. —

★★★★Los Arcos (H), Paseo Ezequiel González N 24, tel. 43 74 62, 59 r. —
★★★Acueducto (H), Padre Claret 10, tel. 42 48 00, 78 r.
★★★Los Linajes (H), Doctor Velasco 9 II, tel. 43 12 01, 55 r.
★★Las Sirenas (H), Juan Bravo 30, tel. 43 40 11, 39 r.

Hotels and Paradors

Seo de Urgel
★★★★El Castell (H), Ctra. de Puigcerdá km 129, tel. 35 07 04, 40 r.
★★Nice (H), Avda. Pau Claris 4/6, tel. 35 21 00, 56 r.

Seville
★★★★★Alfonso XIII (H), San Fernando 2, tel. 4 22 28 50, 149 r.
★★★★★Colón (H), Canalejas 1, tel. 4 22 29 00, 211 r.
★★★★★Raddison Principe de Asturias (H), Isla de la Cartuja, tel. 4 46 22 22, 303 r.
★★★★Armendáriz (H), Avda. Su Eminencia 15, tel. 4 23 29 60, 90 r.
★★★★Ciudad de Sevilla (H), Manuel Siurot 25, tel. 4 23 05 05, 88 r.
★★★★Gran Hotel Lar (H), Plaza Carmen Benítez 3, tel. 4 41 03 61, 137 r.
★★★★Husa Sevilla (H), Pagés del Corro 90, tel. 4 34 24 12, 128 r.
★★★★Inglaterra (H), Plaza Nueva 7, tel. 4 22 49 70, 116 r.
★★★Alcázar (H), Menéndez Pelayo 10, tel. 4 41 20 11, 116 r.
★★★Casas de la Judería (HA), Callejón de Dos Hermanas 7, tel. 4 41 51 50, 29 r.
★★La Rábida (H), Castelar 24, tel. 4 22 09 60, 87 r.
★Europa (H), Jimios 5, tel. 4 21 43 05, 16 r.
★Simón (H), García de Vinuesa 19, tel. 4 22 66 60, 31 r.

Sierra Nevada
★★★★★Meliá Sierra Nevada (H), Pradollano, tel. 48 04 00, 221 r.
★★★Meliá Sol y Nieve (H), Pradollano, tel. 48 03 00, 178 r.
★★Telecabina (H), Pradollano, tel. 24 91 20, 35 r.

Sigüenza
★★El Doncel (HS), General Mola 1, tel. 39 10 90, 16 r.

Sitges
★★★★★Calípolis (H), Paseo Marítimo, tel. 8 94 15 00, 170 r.
★★★★Mediterráneo (HA), Avda. Sofía 3, tel. 8 94 51 34, 84 r.
★★★★Terramar (H), Paseo Marítimo 30, tel. 8 94 00 50, 209 r.
★★★Galeón (H), San Francisco 44, tel. 8 94 06 12, 47 r.
★★★Platjador (H), Paseo Ribera 35, tel. 8 94 50 54, 59 r.
★★Arcadia (H), Socias 22–24, tel. 8 94 09 00, 38 r.
★★San Francisco (H), Santiago Rusiñol 10–12, tel. 8 94 06 62, 25 r.

Soria
★★★Husa Alfonso VIII (H), Alfonso 10, tel. 22 62 11, 103 r.
★★★Mesón Leonor (H), Paseo del Mirón, tel. 22 02 50, 32 r.

Tafalla
★★Arotza (P), Plaza Navarra 3, tel. 70 07 16, 14 r.

Talavera de la Reina
★★★Beatriz (H), Avda. Madrid 1, tel. 80 76 00, 161 r.

Tarazona
★★★Brujas de Becquer (H), N–122 km 44, tel. 64 04 04, 57 r.

Tarragona
★★★★Imperial Tarraco (H), Passeig Palmeres, tel. 23 30 40, 170 r.
★★★Lauría (H), Rambla Nova 20, tel. 23 67 12, 72 r.
★★★París (H), Maragall 4, tel. 23 60 12, 45 r.
★★Sant Jordi (H), Via Augusta, tel. 20 75 15, 40 r.

Tarrasa
★★★★Don Candido (H), Rambleta Pare Alegre 98, tel. 7 33 33 00, 126 r.

Teruel
★★★Reina Cristina (H), Paseo del Ovalo, tel. 60 68 60, 81 r.
★★Oriente (H), Avda. de Sagunto 5, tel. 60 15 50, 30 r.

Toledo
★★★★Alfonso VI (H), General Moscardó 2, tel. 22 26 00, 88 r.
★★★Cardenal (H), Paseo de Recaredo 24, tel. 22 49 00, 27 r.
★★★María Cristina (H), Marqués de Mendigorria 1, tel. 21 32 02, 65 r.
★★★Real (H), Real de Arrabal 4, tel. 22 93 00, 57 r.
★★Almazara (H), Ctra. Toledo–Arges y Guerva km 3.4, tel. 22 38 66, 21 r.
★★Maravilla (H), Barrio Rey 7, III, tel. 22 33 04, 18 r.

Tolosa
★Oyarbide (HS), Plaza de Gorriti 1, tel. 67 00 17, 19 r.

Tordesillas
★★★El Montico (H), N–620 km 147, tel. 7 77 04 50, 55 r.

★★★Juan II (H), Plaza del Espolón 1, tel. 69 03 00, 42 r.　　Toro

★★★★Al-Andalus (H), Avda. de Montemar, tel. 38 12 00, 164 r.　　Torremolinos
★★★★Don Pablo (H), Paseo Marítimo, tel. 38 38 88, 419 r.
★★★★Meliá Torremolinos (H), Avda. Carlota Alessandri 104, 547 r.
★★★Aguamarina (HA), Camino del Bajondillo, tel. 37 41 42, 130 r.
★★★Cervantes (H), Las Mercedes s/n, tel. 38 40 33, 397 r.
★★Miami (H), Aladino 14, tel. 38 52 55, 26 r.

★★Berenguer IV (H), Cervantes 23, tel. 44 08 16, 48 r.　　Tortosa

★★★Las Cigüeñas (HS), N–V km 253, tel. 32 12 50, 78 r.　　Trujillo
★La Cadena (HS), Plaza Mayor 8, tel. 32 14 63, 8 r.

★★★Tudela (H), Avda. de Zaragoza 56, tel. 41 08 02, 51 r.　　Tudela

★★★Colón Túy (H), Colón 11, tel. 60 02 23, 45 r.　　Túy

★★Consuelo (H), Av. Ramón y Cajal 12, tel. 75 08 41, 39 r.　　Úbeda
★★La Paz (H), Andalucía 1, tel. 75 08 48, 51 r.

★★★★★Sidi Saler Palace (H), Playa del Saler, tel. 1 61 04 11, 272 r.　　Valencia
★★★★Astoria Palace (H), Plaza Rodrigo Botet 5, tel. 3 52 67 37, 208 r.
★★★★Dimar (H), Gran Vía Marqués del Turia 80, tel. 3 95 10 30, 95 r.
★★★★Reina Victoria (H), Barcas 4, tel. 3 52 04 87, 92 r.
★★★Ciudad de Valencia (H), Avda. del Puerto 214, tel. 3 30 75 00, 149 r.
★★★Expo Hotel (H), Avda. Pio XII 4, tel. 3 47 09 09, 396 r.
★★★Londres (HS), Barcelonina 1, tel. 3 51 22 44, 57 r.
★★Bristol (H), Abadia San Martin 3, tel. 3 52 11 76, 40 r.
★★Continental (H), Correos 8, tel. 3 51 09 26, 43 r.
★Internacional (H), Bailén 8, tel. 3 51 94 26, 50 r.

★★★★Felipe IV (H), Gamazo 16, tel. 30 70 00, 131 r.　　Valladolid
★★★★Olid Meliá (H), Plaza de San Miguel 10, tel. 35 72 00, 211 r.
★★★Meliá Parque (H), García Morato 17, tel. 47 01 00, 302 r.
★★★Mozart (H), Meneendez Pelayo 7, tel. 29 78 88, 38 r.
★★Imperial (H), Peso 4, tel. 33 03 00, 81 r.; Roma, Héroes del Alcázar

★★★Can Pamplona (H), N–152, tel. 8 85 36 12, 34 r.　　Vich
★★Ausa (H), Plaza Mayor 4, tel. 8 89 14 47, 26 r.

★★★★Bahía de Vigo (H), Avda. Cánovas del Castillo 5, tel. 22 67 00, 110 r.　　Vigo
★★★★Ciudad de Vigo (H), Concepción Arenal 4, tel. 43 52 33, 101 r.
★★★★Gran Hotel Samil (H), Playa de Samil, tel. 20 52 11, 137 r.
★★★Ensenada (H), Alfonso XIII 7, tel. 22 61 00, 109 r.
★★★México (H), Via Norte 10, tel. 43 16 66, 112 r.
★★Galicia (H), Colón 11, tel. 43 40 22, 53 r.
★★Junquera (H), Uruguay 27, tel. 43 48 88, 42 r.
★Estay (H), Playa de Cánido, tel. 49 01 01, 20 r.

★★★César (H), Isaak Peral 4, tel. 8 15 11 25, 30 r.　　Villanueva
★★Ricard (H), Paseo Marítimo 88, tel. 8 15 71 00, 12 r.　　y Geltrú

★★★★Canciller Ayala (H), Ramón y Cajal 5, tel. 13 00 00, 185 r.　　Vitoria
★★★★Gasteiz (H), Avda. de Gasteiz 45, tel. 22 81 00, 150 r.
★★Dato 28 (H), Dato 28, tel. 23 23 20, 14 r.
★★Desiderio (H), Colegio San Prudencio 2, tel. 25 17 00, 21 r.

★★★Dos Infantas (H), Cortinas de San Miguel 3, tel. 43 01 00, 246 r.　　Zamora
★★★Hostería Real de Zamora (H), Cuesta de Pizarro 7, tel. 53 45 45, 15 r.
★★Trefacio (HS), Alfonso de Castro 7, tel. 51 31 89, 32 r.

Hotels and Paradors

Zaragoza

★★★★★Meliá Corona (H), Avda. César Augusto 13, tel. 43 01 00, 246 r.
★★★★★Palafox (H), Casa Jiménez, tel. 23 77 00, 184 r.
★★★★Gran Hotel (H), Costa 5, tel. 22 19 01, 138 r.
★★★★Don Yo (H), Bruil 4, tel. 22 67 41, 181 r.
★★★Conquistador (H), Hernán Cortes 21, tel. 21 49 88, 44 r.
★★★El Principe (H), Santiago 12, tel. 29 41 01, 45 r.
★★★Ramiro I (H), Coso 123, tel. 29 82 00, 104 r.
★★Avenida (H), Avda. César Augusto 55, tel. 43 93 00, 85 r.
★Paraíso (HS), Plaza Pamplona 23, tel. 21 76 08, 29 r.
★Las Torres (H), Plaza del Pilar 11, tel. 39 42 50, 40 r.

Paradors

The Spanish paradors (*paradores de turismo*, singular *parador*) are a chain of state-run hotels throughout Spain, mostly in historic old castles, palaces and monasteries or convents, with a few which have been purpose built. They are situated in some of the most beautiful parts of Spain and in historic old towns and are comfortably and sometimes luxuriously

Paradors

Castles, Convents, Palaces ●

Modern ●

Buildings typical of the region ●

equipped and excellently run, with high quality cuisine. They are also classified by stars. Often they are more reasonably priced than "normal" hotels with more facilities. Advance reservation is advisable.

Paradores de Turismo de España, S A., Calle Requena 3
E-28013 Madrid; tel (91) 5 59 09 78 and 5 59 00 69 for reservations

Information and reservations

Agent in the United Kingdom:
Keytel International, 402 Edgware Road
London W2 1ED; tel. (0171) 402 8182

P.=Parador

★★★P. de Tuy, Avda. de Portugal, tel. (986) 60 03, 00, 24 r.	**1 Tuy**
★★★★P. Conde de Gondomar, Ctra. de Bayona km 1.6, tel. (986) 35 50 00, 124 r.	**2 Bayona**
★★★P. Casa del Barón, Barón 19, tel. (986) 85 58 00, 47 r.	**3 Pontevedra**
★★★★P. El Albariño, Paseo de Cervantes, tel. (986) 54 22 50, 63 r.	**4 Cambados**
★★★★★P. Hotel Reyes Católicos, Plaza del Obradoira 1, tel. (981) 58 22 00, 136 r.	**5 Santiago de Compostela**
★★★P. de Ferrol, Almirante Fernández Martin, tel. (981) 35 67 20, 38 r.	**6 Ferrol**
★★★P. Condes de Villalba, Valeriano Valdesuso, tel. (982) 51 00 11, 6 r.	**7 Villalba**
★★★P. Parador de Ribadeo, Amador Fernández 7, tel. (982) 10 08 25, 47 r.	**8 Ribadeo**
★★★P. Parador de Villafranca del Bierzo, Avda. Calvo Sotelo, tel. (987) 54 01 75, 40 r.	**9 Villafranca del Bierzo**
★★★P. de Monterrey, tel. (988) 41 00 75, 23 r.	**10 Verín**
★★★P. de Puebla de Sanabria, Ctra. Lago 18, tel. (980) 62 00 01, 44 r.	**11 Puebla de Sanabria**
★★★★P. Molino Viejo, Parque de Isabel la Católica, tel. (98) 5 37 05 11, 40 r.	**12 Gijón**
★★★★★P. Hotel San Marcos, Plaza San Marcos 7, tel. (987) 23 73 00, 200 r.	**13 León**
★★★★P. Rey Fernando II de León, Po. Ramón y Cajal, tel. (980) 63 03 03, 30 r.	**14 Benavente**
★★★P. Rio Deva, tel. (942) 73 66 51, 78 r.	**15 Fuente Dé**
★★★P. Fuentes Carrionas, Ctra. de Resboa km 2.5, tel. (979) 87 00 75, 80 r.	**16 Cervera de Pisuerga**
★★★P. Gil Blas, Plaza Ramón Pelayo 11, tel. (942) 81 80 00, 56 r.	**17 Santillana del Mar**
★★★P. de Argómaniz, Ctra. N–1 km 363, tel. (945) 29 32 00, 53 r.	**18 Argómaniz**
★★★★P. de Sto. Domingo de la Calzada, Plaza del Santo 3, tel. (941) 34 03 00, 61 r.	**19 Santo Domingo de la Calzada**
★★★P. Marco Fabio Quintillano, Paseo Mercadal, tel. (941) 13 03 58, 62 r.	**20 Calahorra**
★★★P. Principe de Viana, Plaza Theobaldos 2, tel. (948) 74 00 00, 43 r.	**21 Olite**

Hotels and Paradors

22 Hondarribia   ★★★P. El Emperador, Plaza de Armas 14, tel. (943) 64 55 00, 36 r.

23 Sos del Rey Católico   ★★★P. Fernando de Aragón, Arq. Sainz de Vicúna 1, tel. (948) 88 80 11, 65 r.

24 Bielsa   ★★★P. Monte Perdido, Valle de Pineta, tel. (947) 50 10 11, 24 r.

25 Artíes   ★★★★P. Don Gaspar de Portolà, Ctra Baquiera Beret, tel. (973) 64 08 01, 40 r.

26 Vielha   ★★★P. Valle de Arán, Ctra. del Tunél, tel. (973) 64 01 00, 135 r.

27 Seo de Urgel   ★★★P. de Seo de Urgel, Sant Domenec, tel. (973) 35 20 00, 78 r.

28 Cardona   ★★★★P. Duques de Cardona, Castillo de Cardona, tel. (93) 8 69 12 75, 57 r.

29 Vic   ★★★★P. de Vic, Paraje el Bac de Sau, tel. (93) 8 12 23 23, 36 r.

30 Aiguablava   ★★★★P. Costa Brava, Platja d'Aiguablava, tel. (972) 62 21 62, 87 r.

31 Tortosa   ★★★★P. Castillo de la Zuda, tel. (977) 44 44 50, 82 r.

32 Alcañiz   ★★★P. de la Concordia, Castillo de Calatravos, tel. (978) 83 04 00, 12 r.

33 Benicarló   ★★★P. Costa del Azahar, Avda. del Papa Luna 5, tel. (964) 47 01 00, 108 r.

34 Soria   ★★★P. Antonio Machado, Parque del Castillo, tel. (975) 21 34 45, 34 r.

35 Sigüenza   ★★★★P. Castillo de Sigüenza, Plaza del Castillo, tel. (949) 39 01 00, 81 r.

36 Tordesillas   ★★★P. de Tordesillas, Ctra. de Salamanca 5, tel. (983) 77 00 51, 71 r.

37 Zamora   ★★★★P. Condes de Alba y Aliste, Plaza de Viriato 5, tel. (980) 51 44 97, 27 r.

38 Segovia   ★★★★P. de Segovia, Avda. Ctra. de Valladolid, tel. (921) 44 37 37, 118 r.

39 Salamanca   ★★★★P. de Salamanca, Teso de la Feria 2, tel. (923) 26 87 00, 108 r.

40 Ciudad Rodrigo   ★★★P. Enrique II, Plaza del Castillo 1, tel. (923) 46 01 50, 27 r.

41 Jarandilla de la Vera   ★★★★P. Carlos V, Adva. García Prieto 1, tel. (927) 56 01 17, 53 r.

42 de Gredos   ★★★P. de Gredos, Ctra. Barraco-Béjar km 43, tel. (920) 34 80 48, 77 r.

43 Ávila   ★★★P. Raimundo de Borgoña, Marqués Canales de Chozas 2, tel. (920) 21 13 40, 61 r.

44 Chinchón   ★★★★P. de Chinchón, Avda. Generalísimo 1, tel. (91) 8 94 08 36, 38 r.

45 Cuenca   ★★★★P. de Cuenca, Paseo Hoz del Huécar, tel. (969) 23 23 20, 62 r.

46 Teruel   ★★★P. de Teruel, Ctra. Sagunto-Burgos N–234, tel. (978) 60 18 00, 60 r.

47 El Saler   ★★★★P. Luis Vives, Avda. Delos Pinares 151, tel. (96) 1 61 11 86, 58 r.

48 Jávea   ★★★★P. Costa Blanca, Playa del Arenal, tel. (96) 5 79 02 00, 65 r.

49 Albacete   ★★★P. de la Mancha, N–301 km 251, tel. (967) 50 93 43, 70 r.

50 Alarcón   ★★★★P. Marqués de Villena, Avda. Amigos de los Castillos 3, tel. (969) 33 03 15, 13 r.

★★★P. de Manzanares, Autovía Andalucía km 174, tel. (926) 61 04 00, 50 r.   **51 Manzanares**

★★★★P. de Almagro, Ronda de San Francisco 31, tel. (926) 86 01 00, 55 r.   **52 Almagro**

★★★★P. Conde de Orgaz, Cerro del Emperador, tel. (925) 22 18 50, 76 r.   **53 Toledo**

★★★★P. Virrey Toledo, Plaza del Palacio 1, tel. (925) 43 00 00, 48 r.   **54 Oropesa**

★★★★P. de Cáceres, Ancha 6, tel. (927) 21 17 59, 31 r.   **55 Cáceres**

★★★★P. de Trujillo, P. de Santa Beatriz de Silva 1, tel. (927) 32 13 50, 46 r.   **56 Trujillo**

★★★★P. de Guadalupe, Marqués de la Romana 10, tel. (927) 36 70 75, 40 r.   **57 Guadalupe**

★★★★P. Via de la Plata, Plaza de la Constitución 3, tel. (924) 31 38 00, 82 r.   **58 Mérida**

★★★★P. Hernán Cortés, Plaza Corazón María 7, tel. (924) 55 45 40, 45 r.   **59 Zafra**

★★★P. Costa de la Luz, El Castillito, tel. (959) 32 07 00, 54 r.   **60 Ayamonte**

★★★P. Cristóbal Colón, Playa de Mazagón, tel. (959) 53 63 00, 43 r.   **61 Mazagón**

★★★★P. Alcázar del Rey Don Pedro, Alcázar, tel. (95) 4 14 10 10, 63 r.   **62 Carmona**

★★★★P. La Arruzafa, Avda. de la Arruzafa, tel. (957) 27 59 00, 94 r.   **63 Córdoba**

★★★★P. Castillo de Santa Catalina, tel. (953) 23 00 00, 45 r.   **64 Jaén**

★★★★P. Condestable Dávalos, Plaza de Vásquez Molina, tel. (953) 75 03 45, 31 r.   **65 Úbeda**

★★★P. el Adelantado, Sierra de Cazorla, tel. (953) 72 70 75, 33 r.   **66 Cazoria**

★★★★P. de Mojácar, Playa de Mojácar, tel. (950) 47 82 50, 98 r.   **67 Mojácar**

★★★P. de Puerto Lumbreras, Avda. de Juan Carlos I 177, tel. (968) 40 20 25, 60 r.   **68 Puerto Lumbreras**

★★★★P. San Francisco, Real de la Alhambra, tel. (958) 22 14 40, 36 r.   **69 Granada**

★★★★P. de Nerja, Almuñécar 8, tel. (95) 2 52 00 50, 73 r.   **70 Nerja**

★★★★P. del Golf, Apartado de Correos 324, tel. (95) 2 38 12 55, 60 r.   **71 Málaga**

★★★P. Castillo de Gibralfaro, tel. (95) 2 22 19 02, 38 r.   **72**

P. de Ronda, Plaza de España, tel. (95) 2 87 75 00, 78 r.   **73 Ronda**

★★★P. de Antequara, Paseo Garcia del Olmo, tel. (95) 2 84 09 01, 55 r.   **74 Antequara**

★★★P. Casa del Corregidor, Plaza del Cabildo, tel. (956) 70 05 00, 24 r.   **75 Arcos de la Frontera**

★★★★P. Hotel Atlántico, Avda. Duque de Nájera 9, tel. (956) 22 69 05, 97 r.   **76 Cádiz**

★★★★P. La Muralla, Plaza Ntra. Sra. de Africa 15, tel. (956) 51 49 40, 106 r.   **77 Ceuta**

★★★P. de Melilla, Avda. Cándido Lobera, tel. (95) 2 68 49 40, 40 r.   **78 Melilla**

★★★P. Santa Cruz de la Palma, Avda. Marítima 34, tel. (922) 41 23 40, 32 r.   **79 La Palma**

★★★★P. Conde de la Gomera, San Sebastián de la Gomera, tel. (922) 87 11 00, 42 r.   **80 Gomera**

Information

81 El Hierro	★★★P. La Isla de Hierro, Las Playas, tel. (922) 55 80 36, 47 r.
82 Tenerife	★★P. Parador Las Cañadas del Tiede, tel. (922) 38 64 15, 23 r.
83 Fuenteventura	★★★P. de Fuenteventura, Playa Blanca 45, tel. (928) 85 11 50, 50 r.

Information (Información turística)

In the United Kingdom

London	Spanish Tourist Office 57–58 St James's Street, London SW1A 1LD; tel. (0171) 499 0901

In the United States

New York	Tourist Office of Spain 665 Fifth Avenue, New York NY 10022; tel. (212) 759 8822
Los Angeles	Tourist Office of Spain 8383 Wilshire Boulevard, Suite 960, Beverly Hills CA 90211 tel. (213) 658 7188
Miami	Tourist Office of Spain 1221 Brickell Avenue, Miami FL 33131; tel. (305) 358 1992

In Canada

Toronto	Tourist Office of Spain 102 Bloor Street West (14th floor) Toronto, Ontario M5S 1M8; tel. (416) 961 3131

Information within Spain

Central Departments

General Directorate for Tourism (National)	Dirección General de Turismo Príncipe de Vergara 132, E-28000 Madrid tel. (91) 5 80 24 41
Institute of Tourism for Spain	Secretaria General de Turismo Instituto de Turismo de España (Turespaña) Calle de María de Molina 50, E-28006 Madrid tel. (91) 4 11 60 11 and 4 11 40 14

Provincial offices

Andalucía	Dirección General de Turismo de la Junta de Andalucía Avda. República Argentina, 31 B; E-41011 Sevilla, tel. (95) 4 27 77 22
Aragon	Dirección General de Turismo de la Diputación General de Aragon Paseo María Agustin 36; E-50004 Zaragoza, tel. (976) 22 43 00
Asturia	Plaza de España; E-33007 Oviedo, tel. (985) 5 24 25 27
Balearic Islands	Consejería de Turismo de la Comunidad Autónoma de las Baleares, Montenegro 5; E-07012 Palma de Mallorca, tel. (971) 71 20 22

Departamento de Comercio, Consumo y Turismo del Gobierno Vasco **Basque Country**
Adriano VI 14–16; E-01008 Vitoria-Gasteiz, tel. (945) 18 99 84

Consejería de Turismo del Gobierno Canario, Arrieta **Canary Islands**
E-35003 Las Palmas de Gran Canaria, tel. (928) 36 16 00

Dirección General de Turismo de la Diputacíon Regional de Cantabria **Cantabria**
Plaza Velarde; E-39001 Santander, tel. (942) 21 24 25

Dirección General de Turismo de la Junta de Comunidades **Castille-**
de Castilla-La Mancha, Cuesta del Alcázar 5 **La Mancha**
E-45001 Toledo, tel. (925) 25 21 99

Dirección General de Turismo de la Junta de Castilla y León **Castille-León**
Monasterio N. Sra. de Prado; E-47071 Valladolid, tel. (983) 41 15 00

Dirección General de Turismo de la Generalidad de Cataluña **Catalonia**
Paseo de Gracía 105
E-08008 Barcelona, tel. (93) 2 37 90 45

Consejería de Industría y Turismo de la Junta de Extramadura **Estremadura**
Cárdenas 11; E-06800 Mérida, tel. (924) 38 13 00

Secretaría General para el Turismo de la Xunta de Galicia **Galicia**
Plaza de Mazarelos 15; E-15703 Santiago de Compostela, tel. (981) 56 28 44

Dirección General de Turismo de la Comunidad de Madrid **Madrid**
Principe de Vergara 132; E-28002 Madrid, tel. (91) 5 80 22 00

Dirección General de Turismo de la Comunidad Murciana **Murcia**
Isidoro de la Cierva 10; E-30071 Murcia, tel. (968) 36 20 00

Dirección General de Comercio y Turismo de la Comunidad Foral **Navarra**
de Navarra, Avenida Carlos III 36
E-31004 Pamplona, tel. (948) 10 77 30

Secretaría General de Turismo de la Comunidad de la Rioja **La Rioja**
Villamediana 17; E-26071 Logroño, tel. (941) 29 11 00

Dirección General de Turismo de la Generalidad Valenciana **Valencia**
Isabel la Católica 8; E-46071 Valencia, tel. (96) 3 86 68 00

Local Tourist Information Offices

Within Spain tourist information can be obtained from Oficinas de Turismo and Oficinas Municipales de Turismo (usually in the Town Hall), or Centros de Iniciativas Turísticas, or Patronatos Provinciales de Turismo, or, in provincial capitals, from Direcciónes (or Delegaciónes, etc.) Provinciales de Turismo.

Centro de Iniciativas Turísticas, Plaza de España 32 **Aguilar**
E-34800 Aguilar de Campóo, tel. (988) 12 20 24 **de Campóo**

Oficina de Turismo, Virrey Morcillo 1 **Albacete**
E-02005 Albacete, tel. (967) 21 56 11

See Salamanca **Alba de Tormes**

Oficina de Turismo, Callejón de Santa María 1 **Alcalá**
E-28801 Alcalá de Henares, tel. (91) 8 89 26 94 **de Henares**

Oficina de Turismo, Avenida de Mérida 21 **Alcántara**
E-10980 Alcántara, tel. (927) 39 08 63

Information

Alcañiz

Officina de Turismo, Plaza España 1
E-44600 Alcañiz, tel. (974) 83 02 00

Alcoy

Centro de Iniciativas Turisticas, Puente de San Jorge I
E-03803 Alcoy, tel. (965) 33 28 57

Algeciras

Oficina de Turismo, Avenida de la Marina
E-11201 Algeciras, tel. (956) 57 04 45

Alicante

Oficina de Turismo, Portugal 17; E-03003 Alicante, tel. (96) 5 92 98 02

Almería

Oficina de Turismo, Hermanos Machado 4, Edificio Servicos Múltiples
E-04002 Almería, tel. (950) 23 08 58

Altamira

See Santander

Andorra

Sindicat d'Iniciativa de les Valls d'Andorra/Oficina de Turismo, Carrer Dr
Vilanova, Andorra la Vella, Principat d'Andorra, tel. 82 02 14 (dialling code
from UK 00 376)

**Aranda
de Duero**

Oficina de Turismo, Jardines de Don Diego 3
E-09400 Aranda de Duero, tel. (947) 50 01 00

Aranjuez

Oficina de Turismo, Puente de Baracas
E-28300 Aranjuez, tel. (91) 8 91 04 27

Astorga

Oficina de Turismo, Plaza Arquitecto Gaudí
E-24700 Astorga, tel. (987) 61 68 38 (temporary)

Ávila

Oficina de Turismo, Plaza de la Catedral 4; E-05001 Ávila, tel. (920) 21 13 87

Avilés

Oficina de Turismo, Ruiz Gómez 21; E-33400 Avilés, tel. (985) 5 54 43 25

Badajoz

Oficina de Turismo, Pasaje de San Juan 1
E-06001 Badajoz, tel. (924) 22 27 63

Baeza

Oficina de Turismo, Casa del Pópulo
E-23440 Baeza, tel. (953) 74 04 44

Balearics

For all Balearic Islands: see Provincial Offices
For Majorca:
Conell Insular de Mallorca, Palau Reial I
E-07001 Palma de Mallorca, tel. (971) 17 35 00
For Minorca:
Consell Insular de Menorca, Plaza de la Explanada 40
E-07703 Mahón, tel. (971) 36 37 90
For Ibiza:
Paseo Vara del Rey 13; E-07800 Ibiza, tel. (971) 30 19 00
For Formentera:
Oficina de Información Turística Municipal, Port de la Sabina
E-07608 San Francisco Javier, tel. (971) 32 20 57

Barcelona

Oficina de Turismo, Plaza de Sants
E-08003 Barcelona, tel. (93) 4 90 91 71

Béjar

Oficina de Turismo, Paseo Cervantes 6; E-37700 Béjar, tel. (923) 40 30 05

Belmonte

See Cuenca

Benavente

Oficina de Turismo, Plaza Encomienda
E-49600 Benavente, tel. (988) 63 33 22

Oficina de Turismo, Avenida Martínez Alejos 16
E-03500 Benidorm, tel. (96) 5 85 32 24

See La Coruña

Centro de Iniciativas Turisticas, Alameda de Mazarredo
E-48001 Bilbao, tel. (94) 4 24 48 19

Oficina de Turismo, Plaza Cataluña; E-17300 Blanes, tel. (972) 33 03 48

Centro de Iniciativas Turisticas, San Carlos
E-09003 Burgos, tel. (947) 20 89 60

Oficina de Turismo, Plaza Mayor 37; E-10003 Cáceres, tel. (927) 24 63 47

Oficina de Turismo, Calderón de la Barca 1
E-11003 Cádiz, tel. (956) 21 13 13

Oficina de Turismo, Plaza El Fuerte
E-50300 Calatayud, tel. (976) 83 13 14

On Fuerteventura:
Oficina de Turismo, Avenida Primero de Mayo 39
E-35600 Puerto del Rosario, tel. (928) 85 10 24
On Gomera:
Oficina de Turismo, Calle del Médio 20
E-38800 San Sebastián de la Gomera, tel. (922) 87 01 55
On Gran Canaria:
Casa del Turismo, Parque de Santa Catalina
E-35007 Las Palmas de Gran Canaria, tel. (928) 26 46 23
Centro de Iniciativas Turísticas, Pueblo Canario
E-35003 Las Palmas de Gran Canaria, tel. (928) 24 35 93
On Hierro:
Oficina de Turismo, Licenciado Bueno 3
E-38900 Valverde de el Hierro, tel. (922) 55 03 02
On Lanzarote:
Oficina Turismo, Parque Municipal
E-35500 Arrecife, tel. (928) 81 18 60
On La Palma:
Oficina de Turismo, Calle O'Daly 8
E-38700 Santa Cruz de la Palma, tel. (922) 41 21 06
On Tenerife:
Oficina de Turismo, Plaza de España, Bajos del Palacio Insular
E-38003 Santa Cruz de Tenerife, tel. (922) 60 55 92

Oficina de Turismo, Plaza del Ayuntamiento
E-30201 Cartagena, tel. (968) 50 64 83

Oficina de Turismo, Complejo Penyeta Rotja
E-12003 Castellón de la Plana, tel. (964) 33 98 83

Oficina de Turismo, Muelle Cañonero Dato 1
E-11701 Ceuta, tel. (956) 51 13 79

Oficina de Turismo, Avenida Alarcos 31
E-13001 Ciudad Real, tel. (926) 21 29 25

Oficina de Turismo, Puerta de las Amayuelas 5
E-37500 Ciudad Rodrigo, tel. (923) 46 05 61

Oficina de Turismo, Palacio de Congresos, Torrijos 10
E-14003 Córdoba, tel. (957) 47 12 35

Information

Cuenca	Oficina de Turismo, Glorieta Gonzalez Palencia 2 E-16002 Cuenca, tel. (969) 17 88 00
Daroca	Oficina de Turismo, Plaza de España 7 E-50360 Daroca, tel. (976) 80 01 29
Denia	Oficina de Turismo, Plaza Oculista Duilgues 3 E-03700 Denia, tel. (96) 5 78 07 24
Ecija	Oficina de Turismo, Avenida de Andalucía E-41400 Ecija, tel. (95) 4 83 30 62
Elche	Oficina de Turismo, Parque Municipal, Paseo de la Estación E-03203 Elche, tel. (96) 5 45 27 47
El Escorial (San Lorenzo de)	Oficina de Turismo, Floridablanca 10 E-28280 San Lorenzo de el Escorial, tel. (91) 8 90 15 54
Estella	Oficina de Turismo, San Nicolás 2; E-31200 Estella, tel. (948) 55 40 11
Estepona	Oficina de Turismo, Paseo Marítimo, Pedro Manrique E-29680 Estepona, tel. (95) 47 95 00
Figueras	Oficina de Turismo, Plaza del Sol E-17600 Gugueras/Figueres, tel. (972) 50 31 55
Fuengirola	Oficina de Turismo, Plaza de España E-29640 Fuengirola, tel. (952) 47 95 00
Gandía	Tourist-Info Gandía, Marqués de Campo E-46700 Gandía, tel. (96) 2 87 77 88
Gerona	Oficina de Turismo, Estación RENFE E-17007 Gerona/Girona, tel. (972) 21 62 96
Gibraltar	Gibraltar Tourist Office, Plaza John Macintosh GB-Gibraltar, tel. (0 03 50) 4 24 00
Gijón	Oficina de Turismo, Marqués de San Esteban 1 E-33206 Gijón, tel. (98) 5 34 60 46
Granada	Oficina de Turismo, Plaza de la Mariana Pineda 10 E-18001 Granada, tel. (958) 22 66 88
Guadalajara	Oficina de Turismo, Plaza Mayor 7 E-19001 Guadalajara, tel. (949) 22 06 98
Guadalupe	Oficina de Turismo, Plaza Mayor; E-10140 Guadalupe, tel. (927) 15 41 28
Guernica	Oficina de Turismo, Artekale 5; E-48300 Guernica, tel. (94) 6 25 58 92
Haro	Oficina de Turismo, Plaza San Agustín 2 E-26200 Haro, tel. (941) 31 27 26
Huelva	Oficina de Turismo, Avenida de Alemania 1 E-21001 Huelva, tel. (959) 25 74 03
Huesca	Oficina de Turismo, Coso Alto 23, Bajos E-22022 Huesca, tel. (974) 22 57 78
Jaca	Oficina de Turismo, Regimiento de Galicia 2 E-22700 Jaca, tel. (974) 36 00 98
Jaén	Oficina de Turismo, Arquitecto Berges 1 E-23007 Jaén, tel. (953) 22 27 37

Oficina de Turismo, Noguera 1
E-46800 Játiva, tel. (96) 2 27 33 46
Játiva

Oficina de Turismo, Alameda Cristina 7
E-11403 Jerez de la Frontera, tel. (956) 33 11 50
**Jerez
de la Frontera**

Oficina de Turismo, Dársena de la Marina
E-15001 La Coruña, tel. (981) 22 18 22
La Coruña

Oficina de Turismo, Plaza de Regla 4
E-24003 León, tel. (987) 23 70 82
León
(Town)

Oficina de Turismo, Plaza de la Paheria 11
E-25007 Lérida, tel. (973) 24 81 20
Lérida

Oficina de Turismo, Miguel Villanueva 10
E-26001 Logroño, tel. (941) 29 12 60
Logroño

Oficina de Turismo, Palacio de Guevara, López Gisbert 12
E-30800 Lorca, tel. (968) 46 61 57
Lorca

Oficina de Turismo, Plaza de España 28
E-27001 Lugo, tel. (982) 23 13 61
Lugo

Oficina de Información Turística de la Comunidad de Madrid:
Duque de Medinaceli 2, E-28014 Madrid, tel. (91) 4 29 49 51
Oficina Municipal de Turismo, Plaza Mayor 3
E-28012 Madrid, tel. (91) 2 66 48 74
Madrid

Oficina de Turismo, Pasaje de Chinitas 4
E-29016 Málaga, tel. (95) 2 21 34 45
Málaga

Oficina de Turismo, Avenida Miguel Cano 1
E-29600 Marbella, tel. (95) 77 46 93
Marbella

Centro de Iniciativas Turísticas, Plaza Mayor 1
E-42240 Medinaceli, tel. (975) 32 60 73
Medinaceli

Oficina de Turismo, Plaza Mayor 1
E-47400 Medina del Campo, tel. (983) 80 48 17
**Medina
del Campo**

Oficina de Turismo, Avenida General Aizpuru 20
E-29804 Melilla, tel. (95) 2 68 40 13
Melilla

Oficina de Turismo, Pedro María Plano
E-06800 Mérida, tel. (924) 31 53 53
Mérida

Oficina de Turismo, Torre de San Miguel
E-12300 Morellá, tel. (964) 17 30 32
Morellá

Oficina de Turismo, Alejandro Seiquer 4
E-30001 Murcia, tel. (968) 21 37 16
Murcia
(Town)

Oficina de Turismo, Puerta del Mar 2
E-29780 Nerja, tel. (95) 2 52 15 31
Nerja

Oficina de Turismo, Plaza del Ayuntamiento
E-31390 Olite, tel. (948) 74 00 35
Olite

Oficina de Turismo, Curros Enríquez 1, Edificio Torre de Orense
E-32003 Orense, tel. (988) 23 47 17
Orense

Oficina de Turismo, Francisco Díe 25
E-03300 Orihuela, tel. (96) 5 30 27 47
Orihuela

Information

Oviedo
Oficina de Turismo, Plaza de Alfonso II, El Casto 6
E-3303 Oviedo, tel. (98) 5 21 33 35

Palencia
Oficina de Turismo, Conde De Vallellano 1–4
E-34002 Palencia, tel. (988) 72 35 57

Pamplona
Oficina de Turismo, Duque de Ahumada 3
E-31020 Pamplona, tel. (948) 22 07 41

Picos de Europa
Federación Asturiana de Montaña, Melquiades Alvarez (Asturian Mountaineering Association); E-33003 Oviedo, tel. (985) 21 10 99

Plasencia
Oficina de Turismo, El Rey 8; E-10600 Plasencia, tel. (927) 42 21 59

Ponferrada
Oficina de Turismo, Gil y Carrasco 4
E-24400 Ponferrada, tel. (987) 42 42 36

Pontevedra
Oficina de Turismo, General Mola 2
E-36001 Pontevedra, tel. (986) 85 08 14

Reus
Oficina de Turismo, Plaza de la Libertad
E-43201 Reus, tel. (977) 75 96 32

Ripoll
Oficina de Turismo, Plaça de l'Abat Oliba 3
E-17500 Ripoll, tel. (972) 70 23 51

Ronda
Oficina de Turismo, Plaza de España 1
E-29400 Ronda, tel. (95) 2 87 12 72

Sagunto
Oficina de Turismo, Plaza Cronista Chabret
E-46500 Sagunto, tel. (96) 2 66 22 13

Salamanca
Oficina de Turismo, Calle España 39
E-37001 Salamanca, tel. (923) 26 85 71

San Sebastián
Oficina de Turismo, Reina Regente
E-20003 San Sebastián, tel. (943) 42 10 02

Santander
Oficina de Turismo, Plaza Velarde
E-39001 Santander, tel. (942) 31 07 08

Santiago de Compostela
Oficina de Turismo, Rúa del Villar 43
E-15705 Santiago de Compostela, tel. (981) 58 40 81

Santillana del Mar
Oficina de Turismo, Plaza Roman Pelayo
E-39330 Santillana del Mar, tel. (942) 81 82 51

Santo Domingo de la Calzada
Oficina de Turismo, Zumalacárregui 70
E-26250 Santo Domingo de Calzada, tel. (941) 34 22 34

Segovia
Oficina de Turismo, Plaza Mayor 10
E-40001 Segovia, tel. (921) 46 03 34

Seo de Urgel
Oficina de Turismo, Avenida Valira
E-25700 Seo de Urgel, tel. (973) 35 15 11

Seville
Oficina de Turismo, Avenida de la Constitución 21
E-41004 Sevilla, tel. (95) 4 22 14 04

Sierra Nevada
Agencio de Medio Ambiente, Gran Via de Colón 48
E-18001, tel. (951) 28 00 62

Sigüenza
Oficina de Turismo, Cardenal Mendoza 2
E-19250 Sigüenza, tel. (911) 39 12 62

Sitges
Oficina de Turismo, Plaza Villafranca
E-08170 Sitges, tel. (93) 8 94 12 30

Oficina de Turismo, Plaza Ramón y Cajal
E-42003 Soria, tel. (975) 21 20 52 — **Soria**

Ayuntamiento, Plaza Navarra 7; E-31300 Tafalla, tel. (948) 70 00 92 — **Tafalla**

Oficina de Turismo, Paseo de los Arqueros
E-45600 Talavera de la Reina, tel. (925) 80 53 00 — **Talavera de la Reina**

Oficina de Turismo, Iglesias 5; E-50500 Tarazona, tel. (976) 64 00 74 — **Tarazona**

Oficina de Turismo, Calle Mayor 39; E-43001 Tarragona, tel. (977) 29 62 24 — **Tarragona**

Oficina de Turismo, Tomás Nogués 1; E-44001 Teruel, tel. (978) 60 22 79 — **Teruel**

Oficina de Turismo, Puerta de Bisagra; E-45003 Toledo, tel. (925) 22 08 43 — **Toledo**

Centro de Iniciativas Turísticas, Calle San Juan
E-20400 Tolosa, tel. (943) 65 04 14 — **Tolosa**

Centro de Iniciativas Turísticas, San Antón 5
E-47100 Tordesillas, tel. (983) 77 03 27 — **Tordesillas**

Oficina de Turismo, Ayuntamiento
E-49800 Toro, tel. (988) 69 18 63 — **Toro**

Oficina de Turismo, Rafael Quintana
E-29620 Torremolinos, tel. (95) 2 38 15 78 — **Torremolinos**

Patronato Municipal de Turismo, Plaza del Bimilenario
E-43500 Tortosa, tel. (977) 44 25 67 — **Tortosa**

Oficina de Turismo, Plaza Mayor
E-10200 Trujillo, tel. (927) 32 06 53 — **Trujillo**

Oficina de Turismo, La Carrera 4
E-31500 Tudela, tel. (948) 82 15 39 — **Tudela**

Oficina de Turismo, Puente de Tripes, Avenida Portugal
E-36700 Túy, tel. (986) 60 17 89 — **Túy**

Oficina de Turismo, Plaza de los Caídos
E-23400 Úbeda, tel. (953) 75 08 97 — **Úbeda**

Oficina de Turismo, Plaza Ayuntamiento 1
E-46002 Valencia, tel. (96) 3 51 04 17 — **Valencia** (Town)

Patronato de Turismo, Angustias 48
E-47003 Valladolid, tel. (983) 42 71 00 — **Valladolid**

Oficina de Turismo, Plaza Mayor 1, E-08500 Vich, tel. (93) 8 86 20 91 — **Vich**

Oficina de Turismo, Jardines de las Avenidas
E-36201 Vigo, tel. (986) 43 05 77 — **Vigo**

Oficina de Turismo, Plaza de la Vila 8
E-08800 Villanueva y Geltrú, tel. (93) 8 93 00 00 — **Villanueva y Geltrú**

Oficina de Turismo, Avenida de Gasteiz 81
E-010085 Vitoria, tel. (945) 16 15 98 — **Vitoria**

Oficina de Turismo, Calle Santa Clara 20
E-49002 Zamora, tel. (980) 53 18 45 — **Zamora**

Oficina de Turismo, Torreón de la Zuda, Glorieta Pío XII
E-50003 Zaragoza, tel. (976) 39 35 37 — **Zaragoza**

As the mother tongue of over 220 million people Spanish is the most widely spoken of the Romance languages and, after English, the world's most important commercial language. Since it originated in the Castilian dialect, Spanish (*español*) is also referred to as *lengua castellana*. It incorporates many words of Arabic origin.

Side by side with Spanish, which is spoken throughout the country, Catalan (*català*) is spoken in Catalonia, Basque (*vasco, euskara*) in the Basque country and Galician (*gallego*) in Galicia.

It adds greatly to the pleasure of a visit to Spain, and may avoid some problems, to have at least some acquaintance with the language. In the larger hotels and shops and in the popular tourist centres English is widely understood, but visitors travelling on their own who want to get off the beaten track of tourism will find it a great help to have some idea of the pronunciation of Spanish, the basic rules of grammar and a few everyday expressions.

The Language

Pronunciation

Vowels are pronounced in the "continental" fashion, without the diphthongisation normal in English. The consonants *f, k, l, m, n, p, t* and *x* are normally pronounced much as in English; *b* has a softer pronunciation than in English, often approximating to *v* when it occurs between vowels; *c* before *e* or *i* is pronounced like *th* in "thin", otherwise like *k; ch* as in English; *d* at the end of a word or between vowels is softened into the sound of *th* in "that"; *g* before *e* or *i* is like the Scottish *ch* in "loch", otherwise hard as in "go"; *h* is silent; *j* is the Scottish *ch; ll* is pronounced like *l* followed by consonantal *y*, i.e. like *lli* in "million" (in many areas like *y* without the *ll); ñ* like *n* followed by consonantal *y*, i.e. like *ni* in "onion"; *qu* like *k; r* is strongly rolled; *z* is like *th* in "thin".

Stress

The general rule is that words ending in a vowel or in *n* or *s* have the stress on the second-last syllable; words ending in any other consonant have the stress on the last syllable. Any departure from this rule is indicated by an acute accent on the stressed vowel. Thus Granada and Esteban, with the stress on the second-last syllable, and Santander and Jerez, with the stress on the last syllable, are spelt without the acute accent: contrast Málaga, Alcalá, Sebastián, Alcázar, Cádiz, etc. For this purpose the vowel combinations *ae, ao, eo, oa* and *oe* are regarded as constituting two syllables, all other combinations as monosyllabic: thus *paseo* has the stress on *e*, *patio* on *a*, without the need of an acute accent to indicate this. The accent is, however, required when the first vowel in the combinations *ia, ie, io, iu, ua, ue, ui, uo* and *uy* is to be stressed (e.g. *sillería, río*), and when the second vowel in the combinations *ai, au, ay, ei, eu, ey, oi, ou* and *oy* is to be stressed (e.g. *paraíso, baúl*).

Numbers
Cardinal numbers

0	cero	11	once
1	uno, una	12	doce
2	dos	13	trece
3	tres	14	catorce
4	cuatro	15	quince
5	cinco	16	dieciséis
6	seis	17	diecisiete
7	siete	18	dieciocho
8	ocho	19	diecinueve
9	nueve	20	veinte
10	diez	21	veintiuno

22	veintidós	153	ciento cincuenta y tres	
30	treinta	200	doscientos	
31	treinta y uno	300	trescientos	
40	cuarenta	400	cuatrocientos	
50	cincuenta	500	quinientos	
60	sesenta	600	seiscientos	
70	setenta	700	setecientos	
80	ochenta	800	ochocientos	
90	noventa	900	novecientos	
100	ciento (cien)	1000	mil	
101	ciento uno	1,000,000	un millón	

1st	primero (primera)	7th	sétimo/séptimo	Ordinal numbers
2nd	segundo	8th	octavo	
3rd	tercero	9th	nono/noveno	
4th	cuarto	10th	décimo	
5th	quinto	20th	vigésimo	
6th	sexto	100th	centésimo	

½	medio (media)	¼	un cuarto	Fractions
⅓	un tercio	⅒	un décimo	

January	enero	**Months**
February	febrero	
March	marzo	
April	abril	
May	mayo	
June	junio	
July	julio	
August	agosto	
September	setiembre	
October	octubre	
November	noviembre	
December	diciembre	

Sunday	domingo	**Days of the Week**
Monday	lunes	
Tuesday	martes	
Wednesday	miércoles	
Thursday	jueves	
Friday	viernes	
Saturday	sábado	

Morning	mañana	**Times of Day**
Midday	mediodía	
Evening	tarde	
Night	noche	

Good morning!	¡Buenos días!	**Everyday Expressions**
Good afternoon!	¡Buenas tardes!	
Good evening, good night!	¡Buenas noches!	
Goodbye!	¡Adios!	
¡Hasta luego!		
Yes, no	Sí, no (señor, señora, etc.)	
Please	Por favor	
Thank you (very much)	(Muchas) gracias	
Not at all! (You're welcome!)	¡De nada!	
¡No hay de qué!		
Excuse me! (*e.g. for a mistake*)	¡Perdón!	
Excuse me! (*e.g. when passing in*	*front of someone*)	
¡Con permiso!		

Language

Do you speak English?	¿Habla Usted inglés?
A little, not much	Un poco, no mucho
I do not understand	No entiendo
What is the Spanish for . . .?	¿Cómo se dice en español . . .?
What is the name of this church?	¿Cómo se llama esta iglesia?
The Cathedral (of St John)	La catedral (San Juan)
Where is Calle . . .?	¿Dónde está la calle . . .?
Where is the road to . . .?	Dónde está el camino para . . .?
To the right, left	A la derecha, izquierda
Straight ahead	Siempre derecho
Above, up	Arriba
Below, down	Abajo
When is it open?	¿A qué horas está abierto?
How far?	¿Qué distancia?
Today	Hoy
Yesterday	Ayer
The day before yesterday	Anteayer
Tomorrow	Mañana
Have you any rooms?	¿Hay habitaciones libres?
I should like . . .	Quisiera . . .
A room with private bath	Una habitación con baño
With full board	Con pensión completa
What does it cost?	¿Cuánto vale?
Everything included	Todo incluído
That is too dear	Es demasiado caro
Bill, please! (*to a waiter*)	¡Camarero, la cuenta, por favor!
Where is the lavatory?	¿Donde está el retrete?
Wake me at six	Llámeme Usted a las seis
Where is there a doctor?	¿Dónde hay un médico?
a dentist	un dentista?
a chemist?	una farmacia?
Help!	¡Socorro!
I have a pain here	Siento dolores aquí
I am suffering from . . .	Padezco de . . .
I need medicine for . . .	Necesito un medicamento contra . . .
How often must I take it?	¿Cuántas veces tengo que tomar esta medicina?

Road Signs	Aduana	Customs
	¡Alto!	Halt
	¡Atención!	Caution
	Aparcamiento	Car park
	Autopista	Motorway
	Bifurcación	Road-fork
	Cañada	Track for livestock
	¡Ceda el paso!	Give way
	¡Cuidado!	Caution
	Desvío	Diversion
	Dirección única	One way only
	Grúa	Tow-away area
	¡Lleva la derecha, la izquierda!	Keep to the right/left
	Niebla	Fog
	¡Obras!	Road works
	¡Al paso!	Dead slow
	Paso a nivel	Level crossing
	Paso prohibido	No entry
	Peaje	Toll (*on motorway, etc.*)
	Peatones	Pedestrians
	¡Peligro!	Danger
	Playa	Beach
	Prohibido el adelantamiento	No overtaking

Prohibido aparcar	No parking	
Sentido único	One-way street	
Viraje peligroso	Dangerous bend	
All aboard!	¡Viajeros al tren!	**Travelling by Train**
All change!	¡Cambiar de tren!	
Arrival	Llegada	
Departure	Salida	
Fare	Precio, importe	
Halt	Apeadero	
Junction	Empalme	
Luggage, baggage	Equipaje	
Non-smoking compartment	No fumadores	
Platform	Andén	
Smoking compartment	Fumadores	
Station	Estación	
Stop	Parada	
Ticket	Billete	
Ticket-collector, conductor	Revisor	
Ticket-window	Taquilla de billetes	
Timetable	Horario de trenos	
Waiting room	Sala de espera	
Address	Dirección	**At the Post Office**
Air mail	Por avión	
Express	Por correo urgente	
Letter	Carta	
Letter-box, post-box	Buzón	
Postage	Porte, franqueo	
Postcard	Tarjeta postal	
Poste restante	Lista de correos	
Postman	Cartero	
Post office	Correo	
Printed matter	Impreso	
Registered letter	Carta certificada	
Stamp	Sello	
Telegram	Telegrama	
Telephone	Teléfono	
Alcazaba, alcázar	Moorish castle	**Geographical, Architectural, etc., Terms**
Arco	Arch	
Arrabal	Outlying district of a town	
Artesonado	Coffered (ceiling)	
Audiencia	Court of appeal	
Ayuntamiento	Town hall	
Azulejos	Glazed tiles (originally blue - *azul*)	
Bahía	Bay	
Barrio	District, quarter (of a town)	
Cabo	Cape	
Calina	Heat-haze (in southern Spain)	
Calle	Street	
Camino	Road, track, path	
Campiña	Flat stretch of cultivated land	
Capilla	Chapel	
Capilla mayor	Principal chapel, containing the high altar	
Carretera	(Main) road	
Cartuja	Charterhouse, Carthusian monastery	
Casa	House	
Casa consistorial	Town hall	
Castillo	Castle	
Cementerio	Cemetery, churchyard	

Cimborio	Dome
Ciudad	City, town
Claustro	Cloister
Colegio	College, seminary
Convento	Monastery, convent
Coro	Choir
Costa	Coast
Coto	(Nature) reserve
Cuesta	Slope, hill
Cueva	Cave
Cumbre	Summit
Custodia	Monstrance
Diputación provincial	Provincial council (offices)
Embalsae	Reservoir, artificial lake
Ermita	Chapel, small church
Estrella	Rose window
Faro	Lighthouse
Fonda	Inn, small restaurant
Fuente	Fountain, spring
Glorieta	Roundabout, street intersection
Hostal	Inn, hostelry
Huerta	Fertile irrigated area
Iglesia	Church
Jardín	Garden
Llano	Plain
Loma	Hillock
Lonja	(Stock) exchange
Mar	Sea
Mezquita	Mosque
Mihrab	Prayer niche in a mosque (indicating the direction of Mecca)
Mirador	Viewpoint
Monasterio	Monastery, convent
Montaña, monte	Mountain, hill
Mudéjar	See p. 59
Paisaje	Landscape
Palacio	Palace
Palacio Arzobispal	Archbishop's Palace
Palacio Episcopal	Bishop's Palace
Pantano	Reservoir, artificial lake
Parque	Park
Parroquia	Parish church
Paseo	Avenue, promenade
Paso	Figure, group of saints, etc., carried in Easter procession
Patio	Courtyard
Peña	Crag, cliff
Pico	Peak, summit
Picota	Pillory
Playa	Beach
Plateresque	See p. 61
Playa	Beach
Plaza	Square
Portillo	Side gate; narrow pass
Pueblo	Village
Puente	Bridge
Puerta	Door(way)
Puerto	Port, harbour; pass
Punta	Point, headland
Quinta	Country house
Rambla	Watercourse (which dries up during the summer); avenue, boulevard

Reja	Grille, grating
Retablo	Retable, reredos, altarpiece
Ría	Tidal estuary of a river
Río	River
Roque	Rock
Sagrario	Sacristy, chapel
Sala capitular	Chapterhouse
Seo	Cathedral
Serrania	Range of hills
Sierra	Mountain range
Sillería	Choir-stalls
Taberna	Bar, tavern
Teleférico	Cableway
Torre	Tower
Torrente	Mountain stream
Trascoro	Retrochoir
Trassagrario	Rear side of high altar
Urbanización	Housing development
Valle	Valley
Vega	Fertile irrigated plain
Venta	Country inn

Language Courses

Information on courses in Spain or Spanish courses in Britain can be obtained from the Instituto Cervantes, 102 Eaton Square, London SW1 9AN, tel. (0171) 235 1485.

Medical Care (Asistencia médica)

British citizens, like nationals of other European Union countries, are entit-led to obtain medical care under the Spanish health services on the same basis as Spaniards (i.e. free hospital and medical treatment, with a partial charge for prescribed medicines, but free to pensioners, and usually the full cost of dental treatment). Before leaving home they should apply to their local post office for the booklet "Health Advice For Travellers" containing form E 111, which certifies their entitlement to insurance cover. **Health insurance**

In most holiday resorts only a limited service is available. To get free treatment the instructions issued with the E 111 must be followed: show the original form E 111 to the doctor and also hand over a photocopy, otherwise you will be charged. If you have to pay for a consultation or a hospital stay the costs will rarely be refunded.

It is nevertheless advisable, even for EU nationals, to take out some form of short-term health insurance (available, for example, under the AA's 5-Star Service if you intend taking your car) providing full cover and pos-sibly avoiding bureaucratic delays. Nationals of non-EU countries should certainly have insurance cover.

In tourist areas and the larger towns in Spain medical services are excellent. In both towns and country areas there are public hospitals, and in the larger tourist centres there are private clinics. In a case of medical emergency help can be obtained through the hotel reception desk, the nearest police station or, in the case of minor disorders, the local first aid station (*casa de socorro*).

Motoring

Spain has more than 317,000km/197,000 miles of roads, including over 2172km/1350 miles of motorway, and more are projected. A considerable **Roads** development programme has been under way in recent years, the most important improvements being on the Madrid–Alicante, Alicante–Murcia and Málaga–Algeciras roads.

Motorways (Autopistas)

Tolls are payable on most Spanish motorways (*autopistas*), identified by the word *peaje*, however there is a growing number of non-paying *autovías*.

One of the busiest Spanish motorways is the Autopista del Mediterráneo, which runs down the Mediterranean coast from the French frontier to Alicante. Other important motorways are the one linking the Cantabrian coast with Catalonia and the one between Cádiz and Seville.

Emergency telephones

There are emergency telephones at intervals along the motorways and main roads through which help can be summoned in case of accident or breakdown. See also Emergencies.

National highways (Carreteras nacionales)

The national highways (*carreteras nacionales*), numbered with the prefix N, are mostly good modern roads. On hills there are crawler lanes for heavy goods vehicles to permit overtaking. The best of the national highways are the six main roads radiating from Madrid, identified by Roman numbers on red and white kilometre stones: N I to Irún (near the Spanish–French border), N II to Barcelona, N III to Valencia, N IV to Cádiz, N V to Badajoz and N VI to La Coruña.

Secondary roads (Carreteras Comarcales)

Secondary roads or regional highways (*carreteras comarcales*), numbered with the prefix C, are also, for the most part, reasonably good. Un-numbered minor roads may sometimes be in poor condition.

Road conditions

Road improvements are constantly in progress, though frequently little warning is given of road works (*obras*) or diversions (*desvíos*). Similarly stretches of particularly bad road or potholes are usually not signposted. Care is therefore always necessary, particularly after dark. Railway level crossings are sometimes inadequately guarded or signposted.

Driving in Spain

In Spain, as in the rest of continental Europe, traffic travels on the right, with overtaking on the left.

Documentation

See Travel Documents

Priority

At junctions and roundabouts traffic coming from the right has priority. This applies even to side streets in towns; exceptions are signposted.

Turning

For left-hand turns off a main road there is often a specially marked filter lane to the right which then turns to cross the main road at right angles.

Spanish cyclists and motorcyclists often indicate a change of direction by waving an arm up and down, but this does not always make their intention clear: the right arm may be used to give warning of a left turn, or vice versa.

Overtaking

When overtaking the left-hand indicator must be kept on during the whole process and the right-hand one used when pulling back to the right. Drivers about to be overtaken must operate their right-hand indicator to acknowledge the following driver's intention to overtake. The horn must be sounded (or, after dark, the headlights flashed) before overtaking or before a bend. A good lookout should be kept for overtaking lorries.

Overtaking is prohibited within 100m/110yd of a blind hill and on roads where visibility is less than 200m/220yd.

Lights

On well lighted roads (other than expressways or motorways) sidelights alone may be used. Beware of unlighted vehicles!

Motorists in Spain are obliged to carry a spare set of light bulbs.

Parking

Parking is permitted in one-way streets only on the side with even numbers on even-numbered days and on the side with odd numbers on odd-numbered days.

Care is necessary in towns, particularly when the streets are busy in the evening, to avoid pedestrians, who are sometimes reluctant to give way to cars on the roadway. Caution is also required on country roads with relatively little traffic, since country people often pay little heed to the rules of the road.

Pedestrians

Farm and other animals are often a hazard on country roads. In Extremadura, and also in other parts of Spain, there is often a strip of grazing land alongside the road (even at intersections – a drove road (*cañada*) for travelling flocks of sheep). A powerful horn is therefore very desirable.

Animals

Foreign motorists in particular should observe strict driving discipline for the sake of their national reputation as well as for their own safety. The directions of the Policia Municipal in towns and the Guardia Civil de Tráfico (traffic police) should be immediately complied with: if a driver fails to stop when signalled to do so the police may well make use of their revolvers, since they are not infrequently on the alert for terrorists. Fines for traffic offences must be paid on the spot, and are high.

Driving discipline

To call the police dial 091 (throughout Spain, including the Balearics and Canaries).

Accidents

An accident in Spain can have very serious consequences, including the impounding of the car until any legal proceedings have been completed and the detention of the driver pending bail. It is very desirable, therefore, to have a bail bond (see Travel Documents).

An accident should be reported at once to your insurance company in accordance with the instructions on your green card or other insurance document.

See below Spanish Motoring Organisations

Breakdown services

The towing of broken-down vehicles by private cars is prohibited.

Towing

Speed limits are 120km p.h./74½ m.p.h. on motorways, 100km p.h./62 m.p.h on dual carriageways, 90km p.h./56 m.p.h. on other roads and 60km p.h./37 m.p.h. in built-up areas. Cars towing a caravan or trailer are restricted to 80km p.h./50 m.p.h. on motorways, 80km p.h./50 m.p.h. on dual carriageways and 70km p.h./43½ m.p.h. on other roads.

Speed limits

The wearing of seat belts both in front and in rear seats is obligatory.

Safety belts

The blood alcohol limit is 0.8 per 1000 (8 milligrams per millilitre).

Alcohol

Standard grade petrol (*gasolina normal*): 92 octane (not recommended)
    Premium grade (*gasolina súper*): 97 octane
    Lead-free (*gasolina sin plomo*): 95 octane
    Diesel fuel (*gasoleo*) is also available.

Fuel

The number of garages selling lead-free petrol is steadily increasing but may still be scarce in some remote parts.

A spare can containing up to 10 litres can be taken into Spain without payment of duty.

Spanish Motoring Organisations

Real Automóvil Club de España (RACE)
Head office: Calle José Abascal 10
E-28003 Madrid; tel. (91) 4 45 62 05

RACE

Reial Automobil Club de Catalunya (RACC), Santaló 8
E-08021 Barcelona; tel. (93) 2 00 33 11

Real Automóvil Club de España (RACE), Marqués de Cénia 37
E-07014 Palma de Mallorca; tel. (971) 23 73 46/47

Breakdown
services

RACE runs a breakdown service:

in Madrid (24-hour English-speaking service all year round):
tel. (91) 5 93 33 33

in Barcelona: tel. (93) 2 00 07 55

in Valencia: tel. (96) 3 33 94 05

Other areas (over 600 service points throughout Spain): see local telephone directory

Information

RACE operates a "Help on the Road" service (tel. (91) 7 42 12 13).

Nature Parks and National Parks

Nature Parks

Nature parks are areas dedicated to the preservation of the landscape and the natural flora and fauna which also offer recreation for visitors.

Visitors to nature reserves should respect certain codes of behaviour and not interfere with the flora and fauna in their enjoyment of the tranquillity provided by the parks.

Do not stray from the marked footpaths and cross hedges, walls and fences as these are often private property in Spain.

It is forbidden to pick wild flowers or plants, catch animals or birds or disturb their breeding by approaching too close and climbing rocks or trees to take photographs.

No litter should be thrown away but disposed of in the containers provided, if this is not the case litter should be taken home. Wild camping and lighting fires is also forbidden unless it is otherwise stated. Cigarette ends must not be thrown away especially in areas endangered by fire.

1 Dunas de
Liencres

Province: Cantabria. Area: 194.5 hectares/480 acres
This area of dunes on the Cantabrian coast, with its pines and euphorbias, is the haunt of seabirds like gulls and cormorants.

2 Cadi-Moixeroi

Provinces: Lérida, Gerona, Barcelona. Area: 41,324 hectares/102,070 acres
This great tract of hill country, extending over three provinces, is a region of high mountain ridges and jagged peaks. In the predominantly coniferous forests live chamois, wild pigs and capercaillies.

3 Montseny

Provinces: Gerona, Barcelona. Area: 13,255 hectares/32,740 acres
This park lies in the eastern Sierra Montseny, the highest part of the Catalonian coastal range. In this hilly region, traversed by numerous mountain streams, holm oaks and Aleppo pines grow up to 800m/2600ft, with firs and junipers higher up.

4 Islas de Cies

Province: Pontevedra. Area: 433 hectares/1070 acres
Off the mouth of the Ría de Vigo lie the three islands of San Martín, Monte Faro and Monte Agudo, a nature reserve which is the nesting-place of herring gulls, the lesser black-backed gull, green cormorants and some twenty pairs of guillemots.

5 Monte Alhoya

Province: Pontevedra. Area: 746 hectares/1843 acres
This small nature park lies in a gentle upland region watered by a tributary of the Miño. The forests consist mainly of Corsican pines.

6 Lago de
Sanabria

Province: Zamora. Area: 5027 hectares/12,417 acres
In the centre of this nature park, which lies at heights of between 800m/2625ft and 2100m/6900ft, is the Lago de Sanabria. Among the trees that grow here are Turkey oaks, chestnuts and holly. The fauna includes roe deer and partridges, and the numerous mountain streams are well stocked with trout.

National Parks

Mountain parks	○
Water parks	○
Island parks	●

Nature parks

Mountain parks	▣
Water parks	▣
Island parks	▣
Karst regions	▢
Dunes	▣
Woodland and bush	▣
Canyons	▣

Provinces: Burgos, Soria. Area: 9530 hectares/23,539 acres	**7 Cañon del Río Lobos**

This 3km/2 mile long canyon has been cut through the limestone rocks in the north-west of Soria province by the Río Lobos on its way to join the Duero. In addition to roe deer, foxes and wild pigs visitors may be lucky enough to see birds of prey like the griffon vulture, the golden eagle and the kestrel.

Province: Zaragoza. Area: 1388 hectares/3428 acres	**8 Dehesa del Moncayo**

This richly wooded mountain region, lying between 800m/2625ft and 2300m/7500ft, is the home of many species of birds – larks, cuckoos, coal tits, great tits and various birds of prey, including golden eagles, hawks and a colony of griffon vultures.

Province: Tarragona. Area: 32,000 hectares/79,000 acres	**9 Delta del Ebro**

South of Tarragona is the Ebro delta, one of the largest wetland areas in Europe. Rice is grown in this area, and it is the haunt of many birds: in addition to large numbers of migrants there is a permanent population of ducks, herons, coots and flamingos in the marshland.

Nature Parks and National Parks

10 Tejera Negra

Province: Guadalajara. Area: 1391 hectares/3436 acres
Characteristic of this hilly region, in which the Río Lillas rises, are the dense beech forests, sometimes interspersed with oaks and yews, in which roe deer and wild pigs live. It is also the home of golden eagles, red kites and hawks.

11 Cuenca Alta del Manzanares

Province: Madrid. Area: 5025 hectares/12,412 acres
The southern slopes of the Sierra de Guadarrama, near Madrid, occupy the upper basin of the Manzanares, a mountain region rising to 2380m/7810ft in which pine forests predominate, giving place at higher altitudes to scrub and grass. The forest is the habitat of roe deer and wild pigs.

12 Monfragüe

Province: Cáceres. Area: 17,852 hectares/44,094 acres
The Tagus traverses the whole length of this nature reserve, in which Mediterranean flora flourishes. The predominant trees are cork-oaks, arbutus, wild olives, holm oaks and, in reafforested areas, eucalyptuses.

There are more species of birds of prey to be found here than anywhere else in Spain, including some 46 pairs of black vultures and six pairs of imperial eagles which have found a safe refuge here. Lynxes are occasionally to be seen in the forest.

13 Lagunas de Ruidera

Provinces: Ciudad Real, Albacete. Area: 3780 hectares/9337 acres
These terraced lagoons, fed by the Río Guadiana, are well stocked with freshwater fish like barbel and pike. The commonest bird of prey in this marshy region is the marsh harrier.

14 Sierras de Cazorla y Segura

Province: Granada. Area: 214,336 hectares/529,410 acres
This park in the north of Granada province is Spain's largest nature reserve. In this karstic region is the source of the Guadalquivir. The extensive forests consist mainly of larches, holm oaks, arbutus, Corsican pines and Aleppo pines. The Cazorla violet, found only in this region, grows in crevices in the rock. As well as red deer, roe deer and wild pigs the fauna includes ibexes, moufflons and fallow deer, which have been successfully introduced here. Of over a hundred species of birds found here the rarest is the bearded vulture or lammergeier.

15 Sierra de Espuña

Province: Murcia. Area: 9961 hectares/24,604 acres
This park, rising to 1580m/5184ft, is a region of pine forests and dense scrub. The most important animal species are the arruis, an African species of moufflon, and the black vulture.

16 Monte el Valle

Province: Murcia. Area: 1900 hectares/4700 acres
In this region of moderate height (100–600m/330–2000ft) the forests consist mainly of Aleppo and stone pines. The fauna includes foxes, hares, screech owls and sparrowhawks.

17 Torcal de Antequera

Province: Málaga. Area: 1170 hectares/2890 acres
The name of the park comes from the *torcas,* the depressions and dolines characteristic of this karstic landscape. The vegetation cover consists mainly of bushes and scrub.

18 Sierra de Grazalema

Provinces: Cádiz, Málaga. Area: 47,120 hectares/116,386 acres
Forests of cork-oak, holm oak and durmast oak cover large areas of this hilly karstic region. The Spanish fir (*Abies pinsapo),* found nowhere else, also grows here.

19 Dunas de Corralejo/ Isla de Lobos

Province: Las Palmas
The trade winds have created in northern Lanzarote and the offshore island of Lobos a landscape of dunes in which euphorbias, gorse and lilies flourish. The Atlantic lizard (*Lacerta atlantica*) or *lagarto de haria* is found only on Fuerteventura and Lanzarote. The osprey is occasionally seen.

20 Islotes del Norte de Lanzarote/ Riscos de Famara

Province: Las Palmas
The north of Lanzarote and the offshore islets of Alegranza, Graciosa, Montaña Clara, Roque del Este and Roque del Oeste form a nature reserve whose greatest attraction is the Famara cliffs, up to 600m/2000ft high, the

nesting-place of large numbers of seabirds, as well as ospreys and a species of falcon which is found only here.

Spain's nine national parks have a total area of 123,000ha/303,933 acres. Six more parks are to be added over the next few years: the Sierra Nevada in Andalusia, the woods of Cabañeros in the province of Ciudad Real, Montagüe in the province of Cáceres, the Picos de Europa in Cantabria, the steppes of Los Monegros in the province of Aragón and the Roque Nublo on Gran Canaria. In the following list of National Parks the date of establishment of the park is given in brackets after its name.

National Parks

National Parks in Mainland Spain

Province: Asturias. Area: 17,000 hectares/42,000 acres
The Covadonga National Park lies in the western part of the Picos de Europa between Asturias and León. The most important rivers are the Río Cares and Río Dobra. The park contains two of Spain's few natural lakes, the picturesque Lagos de Covadonga – Lago de Enol (alt. 1070m/3511ft; area 121,500 sq.m/145,300 sq.yd) and Lago de Ercina (alt. 1108m/3635ft; area 121,000 sq.m/144,700 sq.yd).

In this area grow holly (*Ilex aquifolium* L.), here threatened with extinction, and ivy (*Hedera helix* L.). Among the birds found here are the golden eagle (*Aquila chrysaetos*), Bonelli's eagle (*Hieraaetus fasciatus*), the eagle owl (*Bubo bubo*) and the capercaillie (*Tetro unogallus*).

A: Parque Nacional de la Montaña de Covadonga o de Peña Santa (1918)

Province: Huesca. Area: 16,000 hectares/39,500 acres
The Valle de Ordesa is a U-shaped valley in the Aragonese Pyrenees with a maximum width of 3km/2 miles. Unusually, it extends not from north to south but from east to west, from the cirque of Cotatuero (Soaso; about 1000m/3300ft) to the Puente de los Navarros on the Pico de Diazas (2237m/7340ft). The park includes some 15km/9 miles of the course of the Río Araza, which rises at 1787m/5863ft and flows into the Río Ara at 1090m/3576ft. There are numerous waterfalls.

The flora includes lilies (*Lilium pyrenaicum* Gonan.) and edelweiss (*Leontopodium alpinum* Cass.). Of the birds found here the most notable are the bearded vulture and the ptarmigan. Among the reptiles and amphibians the most interesting are the asp (*Vipera aspis*) and the midwife toad (*Alytes obstetricans*). In this area, too, lives the only surviving group of Pyrenean mountain goats.

B: Parque Nacional del Valle de Ordesa (1918)

Province: Lérida. Area: 22,396 hectares/55,318 acres
This national park lies in the Sierra de los Encantos, to the south of the National Game Reserve of Alto Pallars–Arán (Pico Pinato, 2653m/8704ft), which is a kind of buffer zone protecting the park. The whole area is a "glacier garden", with numerous moraines. The characteristic land-form is the cirque, and there are many waterfalls.

The flora includes lilies (*Lilium martagon* L., *L. pyrenaicum* Gonan.), gentians (*Gentiana nivalis* L. and *G. burseri* Lapeyr.), saxifrages (*Saxifraga oppositifolia* L., *S. aizoides* L.), aconites (*Aconitum anthora* L., *A. napellus* L.), and numerous species of fungi, lichens and algae. One unusual animal to be found in the rivers is the western desman (*Galemys pyrenaicus*), a rare mole-like creature which is an excellent swimmer and can even make its way up rapids. Among the amphibians are the interesting Pyrenean mountain salamander (*Euproctus asper*) and the dark green racer (*Coluber viridiflavus*). Among the birds are the red kite (*Milvus milvus*) and the ptarmigan.

C: Parque Nacional de Aigües Tortes y Lago de San Mauricio (1957)

Province: Ciudad Real. Area: 1975 hectares/4878 acres
This unusual national park lies in the La Mancha area of New Castile. The *tablas* are the shallow lagoons formed by rivers flooding out beyond their normal beds. Now overgrown by dense vegetation, they are linked by a network of channels which can be negotiated only in flat-bottomed punts. Scattered about in the water are numerous islands.

D: Parque Nacional de las Tablas de Daimiel (1973)

The water is covered with a dense mat of aquatic plants known as *ovas*. A curious feature of the area is that the Río Cigüela brings in brackish water from the salt Parameras de Cabrejas, while the water of the Río Guadiana is fresh. Reeds (*Phragmites communis* Trin.) flourish in the fresh water, fen sedge (*Cladium mariscus* L. – the largest stand in western Europe) in the salt water. Since the canalisation of the Guadiana has reduced the inflow of fresh water the salt content is increasing, and it is feared that this may lead to changes in the ecosystem. It is now proposed to pump in additional fresh water. The only species of tree or shrub in the area is the tamarisk (*Tamarix gallica* L.), which grows on the islands.

Over 200 species of birds nest in this area, and it was to protect them that the national park was established. Resident species include the kingfisher (*Alcedo atthis*). Of the migrants which frequent the *tablas* the most notable are the purple heron (*Ardea purpurea*), the little egret (*Egretta garzetta*), the night heron (*Nycticorax nycticorax*) and the hobby (*Falco subbuteo*). The marshy banks and shores are the haunt of the avocet (*Recurvirostra avosetta*) and the ruff (*Philomachus pugnax*), while the reeds provide nesting-places for the fan-tailed warbler (*Cisticola jundicis*), Savi's warbler (*Locustella luscinoides*) and the bearded reedling (*Panurus biarmicus*).

E: Parque Nacional de Doñana (1969)

Provinces: Seville, Huelva. Area: 75,765 hectares/187,140 acres
This is the largest of the Spanish national parks, and perhaps the most interesting, with a fauna which incudes many African species. It lies in the delta at the mouth of the Guadalquivir, on the very edge of Europe and on the route followed by migratory birds on their way to Africa.

There are two different ecosystems in the park – the wetlands (Doñana húmedo), consisting of the *marisma* or fenland in the river delta and the lagoons (only a few hundred hectares of which are within the national park), and the dry area (Doñana seco). The areas which are under water for most of the year (*almajales*) consist of the abandoned channels of the Guadalquivir (*caños*), the *ojos* (springs) and of *lucios* ("pikes" – long shallow lagoons); between these are the *paciles* (small circular hummocks) and the *vetas* or *vetonas* (higher and longer expanses of dry land).

Fenland (marisma)

There are sharp differences in water level over the year. During the dry season (July to September, with the water at its lowest point in August) the area is arid and deserted; then at the end of September the first migrants (wild geese and ducks) make their appearance. The usual way of getting about is in flat-bottomed boats (*cajones*), which are either punted or drawn by horses. The commonest plants are sedges – bulrushes (*Scirpus maritimus* and *S. Lacustris* L.) and the broad-leaved reed-mace (*Typha latifolia* L.). Many migratory birds spend the winter here or rest on their way to Africa – wigeon (*Anas penelope*), pintail (*A. acuta*), teal (*A. crecca*), shoveler (*A. clypeata*), pochard (*Arytha ferina*), etc. Among birds which nest here in spring are the coot (*Fulica atra*), the mallard (*Anas platyrhyncos*), the gadwall (*A. strepera*), the great crested grebe (*Podiceps cristatus*), the little grebe (*P. ruficollis*), the purple heron (*Ardea purpurea*), the gull-billed tern (*Gelochelidon nilotica*), the whiskered tern (*Chelidonias hybrida*) and the black tern (*C. niger*).

Lagoons

These are distributed widely throughout the area, the largest ones lying parallel to the coast (Laguna de Santa Olalla, Laguna Dulce, Laguna del Taraje), the smaller ones farther inland (Laguna del Moral, de Navaza del Toro, del Sapo, del Brezo, del Caballo, del Pino, etc.). The lagoons are fringed by clumps of trees – cork-oaks (*Quercus suber* L.) and pines (*Pinus pinea* L.) – and by tree heaths (*Erica scoparia* L.), dwarf gorse (*Ulex minor* Roth.) and bracken (*Pteridium aquilinum* L.). The principal water-dwelling species of fauna are marsh frogs (*Rana ridibunda*), the European pond terrapin (*Emys orbicularis*) and the Caspian turtle (*Clemmys caspica leprosa*). All the species of duck mentioned above frequent the lagoons, which are also the last European refuge of an endangered species, the crested coot (*Fulica cristata*). Their shores are also visited by fallow deer, red deer and wild pigs, while otters (*Lutra lutra*) live in the water.

This biotope has become rare in many parts of the national park, but there is a swathe between the marisma and the Monte de Doñana. In these cork-oak forests are the famous nesting-places (*pajareras*) which whole colonies of birds during the breeding season. Among birds which nest here are the grey heron (*Ardea cinerea*), the little egret (*Egretta garzetta*), the cattle egret (*Ardeola ibis*), the spoonbill (*Platalea leucorodia*) and a few white storks (*Ciconia ciconia*). Some birds of prey also visit the colonies or nest there – the buzzard (*Buteo buteo*), the red kite (*Milvus milvus*), the kestrel (*Falco tinnunculus*) and many jackdaws (*Corvus monedula*), which are great nest-robbers. Wild pigs (*Sus scrofa*) often come here, and the poisonous Lataste's viper (*Vipera latasti*) is commonly found.

Cork-oak forest (alcornocal)

Monte here means not hill but woodland or scrub. This biotope consists of Mediterranean-type macchia with scattered cork-oaks. The flora includes *Halimium halimifolium* L., *Phyllirea angustifolia* L., heather (*Calluna vulgaris* L.) and rosemary (*Rosmarinus officinalis* L.), and at higher altitudes juniper (*Juniperus phoenicia* L.), *Halimium commutatum* Pan., French lavender (*Lavandula stoechas* L.) and white thyme (*Thymus mastichina* L.). Among reptiles and amphibians there are the spur-thighed tortoise (*Testudo graeca*), the ladder snake (*Elaphe scalaris*), the Montpellier snake (*Malpolon monspessulanus*) and the small but very poisonous Lataste's viper (*Vipera latasti*). In addition to the birds of prey mentioned above there are the magpie (*Pica pica*), the great shrike (*Lanius excubitor*), the red-necked nightjar (*Caprimulgus ruficollis*) and large numbers of red-legged partridges (*Alectoris rufa*). The commonest mammals are red deer (*Cervus elaphus*), fallow deer (*Dama dama*), and wild pigs (*Sus scrofa;* others include the weasel (*Mustela nivalis*), the polecat (*Putorius putorius*), the wild cat (*Felis sylvestris*), foxes (*Vulpes vulpes*) and, more rarely, the genet (*Genetta genetta*). Badgers (*Meles meles*) are very common, and there are large numbers of rabbits (*Oryctolagus cuniculus*), which provide an abundant food supply for the larger predators.

Monte de Doñana

This biotope is found mainly in the southern part of the park. Between the pines (*Pinus pinea* L.) is an undergrowth consisting mainly of tree heaths, cistuses, the broom-like *Osyris alba* L. and the mastic tree (*Pistacia lentiscus* L.). Wood pigeons (*Columba palumbus*), turtle-doves (*Streptopelia turtur*), blackbirds (*Turdus merula*), mistle thrushes (*Turdus viscivorus*), buzzards (*Buteo buteo*), red kites (*Milvus milvus*) and kestrels (*Falco tinnunculus*) are residents; annual visitors are the hobby (*Falco subbuteo*) and the short-toed eagle (*Circaetus gallicus*). A very rare bird, found here but hardly anywhere else, is the azure-winged magpie (*Cyanopica cyanus*).

Pine forests (pinares)

Along the coast extend long travelling dunes, which as they move inland enclose little islands (*corrales*) of pines. The trees eventually die, leaving groups of dried-up and contorted trunks which are known as *campos de cruces.* The flora is very sparse, consisting mainly of lyme grass (*Ammophila arenaria* L.) and a shrub called *camarina (Corema album* Don.), with a sweet-tasting fruit which is eaten by birds. A common species of lizard is *Acanthodactylus erythrurus,* the spiny-footed lizard; common snakes are Lataste's viper (*Vipera latasti*) and the Montpellier snake (*Malpolon monspessulanus*). These reptiles provide food for the short-toed eagle (*Circaetus gallicus*) and the barn owl (*Tyto alba*).

Dunes (dunas)

Rare species found only in the Coto de Doñana are the pardel lynx (*Lynx pardinus*), which is spotted and smaller than the European lynx, and the snake-eating true ichneumon (*Herpestes ichneumon*), the only European representative of the ichneumon family, groups of which can frequently be seen trotting through the park in Indian file. Other species very rare in Europe are the imperial eagle (*Aquila heliaca*) and the greater flamingo (*Phoenicopterus ruber*). Here too is the only nesting colony in Europe of the purple gallinule (*Porphyrio porphyrio*). Rare species of duck which are protected here are the ferruginous duck (*Aythya nyroca*) and two species which winter in the park, the ruddy shelduck (*Tadorna ferruginea*) and the white-headed duck (*Oxyura leucocephala*).

National Parks in the Canaries

The national parks in the Canary Islands are notable for their interesting volcanic formations, but even more for their unique vegetation, including species which can be traced back to the Tertiary era and have been preserved here because the effects of the Ice Age on these islands were much less severe than in mainland Europe.

F: Parque Nacional de la Caldera de Taburiente (1954)

Province: Santa Cruz de Tenerife. Area: 4690 hectares/11,584 acres
Within this park, on the island of La Palma, is the Caldera de Taburiente, one of the largest volcanic craters in the world (circumference 28km/17 miles, greatest diameter 9km/6 miles). The highest point on the rim of the crater (near which is an observatory) is the Roque de los Muchachos (2426m/7960ft), and the floor of the crater has an average altitude of 800m/2625ft. The area is well supplied with water and accordingly has suffered severe erosion. The natural outlet for water from the springs, which forms numerous waterfalls up to 50m/165ft in height, is a gorge called the Barranco de las Angustias.

The most important tree is the Canary pine (*Pinus canariensis* DC). On the higher slopes are the so-called Canary cedars (*Juniperus cedrus* Webb-Berth.), growing in bizarre forms. Also found at high altitudes are a species of forget-me-not (*Viola palmensis* Webb-Berth.) and cistus (*Cistus vaginatus* Ait.). On the crater floor there are holly (*Ilex canariensis* Poir.) and clumps of laurels (*Laurus canariensis* Webb-Berth.). There are also many succulents, like *bejeques* (genus *Aeonium*), *tabaibas* (genus *Euphorbia*) and *verodes* (genus *Kleinia*). The fauna includes the blackcap (*Sylvia atricapilla*) and the Canary lizard (*Lacerta galloti*).

G: Parque Nacional de Garajonay (1979)

Province: Santa Cruz de Tenerife. Area: 3974 hectares/9820 acres
The Garajonay National Park, on the island of Gomera, takes its name from Mt Garajonay, which lies within its bounds. More than half the park's area, made up of mountain ridges, chains of hills and gorges, is covered by forest. A country road leads from the little town of San Sebastián to the park, which offers pleasant walks on a network of footpaths.

The vegetation consists predominantly of holly, heaths, laurels, bay trees and other shrubs. The trunks and branches of the trees are often covered with moss and lichen. There are large numbers of birds.

H: Parque Nacional del Teide (1954)

Province: Santa Cruz de Tenerife. Area: 13,500 hectares/33,350 acres
The Teide National Park (visitor centre), in the centre of Tenerife, is a gigantic lunar landscape. The whole park lies at more than 2000m/6500ft above sea level. It is bounded on the north by Mt Teide (3178m/10,427ft) and on the south, east and west by the steep rock walls of the Caldera de las Cañadas. In winter the summit of Teide is snow-capped and the rocks and bushes in the caldera are covered in the morning by a layer of crystalline ice up to 10cm/4 in. thick which sparkles in the sun (*cencellada*). A road runs up Mt Teide from Santa Cruz, and a cableway takes visitors almost to the summit.

In spite of its altitude and its poor soil the national park is covered in spring and summer with a rich growth of vegetation, producing flowers which stand out against the dark volcanic rock. On the steep rock faces there are bizarrely shaped "Canary cedars" (*Juniperus cedrus*) and occasional Canary pines (*Pinus canariensis* DC). The most characteristic species, however, is the Teide broom (*Spartocytisus nubigenus* Webb-Berth.), the flowers of which are much sought after by bees. Other common species are two types of bugloss, *tajinaste roio* (*Echium wildpretii* Pears.), with flower stems up to 2m/6½ft high, and *tajinaste azul* (*Echium auberanium* Webb-Berth.).

Flowers found on the lava fields are the *hierba del Teide* (*Nepeta teydea* Webb-Berth.), the *alhelí de las Cañadas* (*Cheiranthus scoparius* Bro.), resembling a gillyflower, and the *hierba pajonera* (*Descurainia bourgaeana* Webb). The Cañada de Diego Hernández is notable for its many rare species like the "Teide daisy" (*Chrysanthemum anethifolium* Brouss.), the *hierba de la cumbre* (*Scrophularia glabratra* Ait.), rare mosses (*Polycarpea tenuis* Webb-Berth.) and the *verode barbudo* (*Aeonium smithii* Webb-Berth.). Two species rarely seen are the "Guanche rose" (*Bencomia stipulata* Svent.) and the Teide violet discovered by Alexander von Humboldt (*Viola cheiranthyfolia* H.B. and K.). Apart from goats and cats which have gone wild and rabbits the fauna consists almost entirely of birds – the red kite (*Milvus milvus*), the kestrel (*Falco tinnunculus*), the sparrowhawk (*Accipiter nisus*), the carrion-eating Egyptian vulture (*Neophron percnopterus*), the rock dove (*Columba livia*), the Barbary partridge (*Alectoris barbara*), crows (*Corvus tinginatus*) and the endemic blue Canary finch (*Fringilla teydea*). The Canary lizard (*Lacerta galloti*) lives on the lava fields.

Province: Gran Canaria. Area: 5170 hectares/12,770 acres
The Timanfaya National Park, in north-western Lanzarote, is a centre of volcanic activity. The lower part of the park consists of a large lava field out of which rise a series of cones and craters, like the Caldera Roja, near which is the only spring in this very hot and dry area, the Fuente de los Miraderos. These higher points, covered with volcanic ash, lapilli and "bombs", are a striking sight with their varied hues of black, yellow and red. Visitors can follow the Ruta de los Volcanes (14km/9 miles) through the park.

I: Parque Nacional de Timanfaya (1974)

The inhospitable volcanic terrain is slow to recover a mantle of vegetation. The most resistant plants are the lichens, of which there are more than a dozen species. They are usually followed by succulents like *Aeonium lancerotense* Prager and various euphorbias (*E. balsamifera* Ait., *E. obtusifolia* Poir.); also common is *aulaga maiorera* (*Zollikoferia spinosa* Boiss.), which the local people set on fire for the benefit of tourists. A curious feature to be seen on the coast, where the lava has formed natural bridges, is the growth of rushes (*Juncus acutus* L.) in regular rows on the porous subsoil which stores up water. The only vertebrates are reptiles, the commonest and most interesting of which is the Atlantic lizard (*Lacerta atlantica*) or *lagarto de haria,* a species endemic in the Canaries.

Newspapers and Periodicals (Periódicos, revistas)

British and other foreign newspapers (including European editions of U.S. papers) are usually on sale in the main tourist centres during the holiday season on the evening of the day of publication or the following day.

Foreign newspapers, magazines, etc.

ABC
Serrano 61, E-28006 Madrid
tel. (91) 4 35 84 45, 4 35 60 25 and 4 35 31 00
(Branch office in Seville)

National dailies
(a selection)

Diario 16
San Romualdo 26, E-28037 Madrid
tel. (91) 7 54 40 66

El País
Miguel Yuste 40, E-28037 Madrid
tel. (91) 7 54 38 00

La Vanguardia
Pelayo 28, E-08001 Barcelona
tel. (93) 3 01 54 54

Among well known periodicals published in Madrid and sold throughout the country are El Globo, El Tiempo and Epoca.

Periodicals

Paradors

See Hotels and Paradors

Photography

Many of the well-known brands of film are on sale in Spain, but since they are dearer than in Britain it is advisable to take a supply of films from home. Ten films for each of two cameras and a cinecamera can be taken into Spain duty-free.

Photographers should bear in mind, when selecting aperture and exposure, that the light in Spain, particularly in the south of the country in the middle of the day, is much stronger than in more northern latitudes.

Post, Telegrams, Telephone

Post (Correos), Telegrams (Telégrafos)

Most letters and postcards sent abroad go by air mail, this can take up to a week.

Spain has more than 6000 post offices (including offices at railway stations, airports and ports), which deal with postal services, money orders and telegrams. The larger hotels also provide these services.

Stamps
Stamps (*sellos*) can be bought not only at post offices but also in tobacconists (*estancos:* identified by a sign with a stylised tobacco leaf and the letter T), which are open until late at night (and which also sell phone cards and bus tickets). Postcard shops do not sell stamps.

Post-boxes
Post-boxes are yellow. Foreign mail should be posted in boxes marked "Extranjero".

Opening times
Post offices are generally open from 9am–2pm Monday to Saturday but head post offices in Barcelona, Bilbao and Madrid and post offices at international airports are open round the clock. Telephone calls cannot be made from post offices and telegraph offices in Spain.

Telegrams
Telegrams can be dispatched from post and telegraph offices and also by telephone.

Postal rates
Postcards: 45 ptas.
Letters (up to 20 grams): to EU countries 45 ptas, other countries 50 ptas.

Poste restante
Mail, including parcels and money orders, can be sent poste restante to any post office, addressed "Lista de Correos". Mail will be given out on production of the addressee's passport.

Telephone (Teléfono)

International
dialling codes
From Britain to Spain: 00 34
From the United States or Canada to Spain: 011 34
From Spain to Britain: 07 44
From Spain to the United States or Canada: 07 1

In dialling an international call the 0 (in Spain the 9) in the local dialling code must be omitted.

Some Spanish exchanges have not yet been connected to the subscriber trunk dialling network, and calls must still be booked through the operator.

There are coin-operated payphones all over Spain (in most cities there are telephone offices which are open round the clock), with instructions in several languages. Put the money in the slot **before** lifting the receiver and do **not** push the button to the left of the dial or you may lose your money. Phones take 5 peseta pieces (for calls within Spain only; a minimum of two 5 peseta coins required) and 10, 25, 50, 100, 200 and 500 peseta pieces. There are also public telephones taking phone cards which are purchased from tobacconists (*estancos*).

Payphones

General: dial 098. Europe: dial 008. Outside Europe: dial 005. Spain: dial 009. Madrid: dial 003.

Information

Public Holidays (Días de fiesta, Días feriados)

January 1st	Año Nuevo (New Year's Day)	Statutory
January 6th	Reyes Magos (Three Kings, Epiphany)	public
May 1st	Día del Trabajo (Labour Day)	holidays
August 15th	Asunción (Assumption)	
October 12th	Día de la Hispanidad (commemorating the discovery of America)	
November 1st	Todos los Santos (All Saints)	
December 6th	Día de la Constitución (Constitution Day)	
December 8th	Inmaculada Concepción (Immaculate Conception)	
December 25th	Navidad (Christmas)	

In some places the following are also observed as public holidays:

March 19th	San José (St Joseph's Day)
June 24th	San Juan (St John's Day: the king's name-day)
June 29th	San Pedro y San Pablo (SS. Peter and Paul)
July 25th	Santiago (St James's Day)

Jueves Santo (Maundy Thursday)
Viernes Santo (Good Friday)
Corpus Christi
Ascension

Movable feasts

Railways (Ferrocarriles)

Most routes are operated by the Spanish State Railways RENFE (Red Nacional de los Ferrocarriles Españoles) which has its own travel agencies in all the larger towns. In addition there are various private companies on the mainland and the islands. A total of 13,000km/8078 miles of track link the important cities of Spain to each other but the network is not as developed as in other countries of Central Europe. However, a modernisation programme is underway; in the south EXPO '92 resulted in improvements being made. The opening of the Madrid–Seville route for the high-speed AVE train reduced the journey time to three hours. Another AVE route is planned between Madrid and Barcelona.

General

Since the main lines are on a wider gauge than in the rest of Europe it is necessary to change trains at the Franco–Spanish frontier except on certain international trains which change bogies at the frontier.

Railways

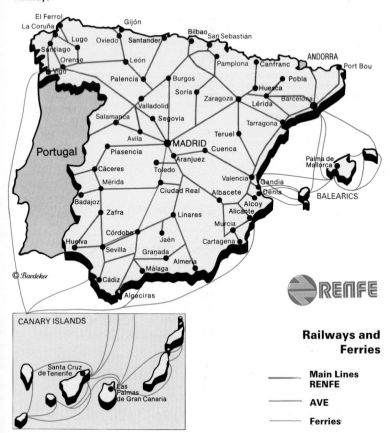

Smoking is prohibited in sleeping cars and couchettes and in all local trains, except in corridors. On long-distance trains there are 1st and 2nd class smoking compartments.

Smoking is permitted on platforms. Stations have waiting rooms for smokers and non-smokers.

Information	Red Nacional de los Ferrocarriles Españoles (RENFE) European headquarters: 1–3 Avenue Marceau, F-75116 Paris tel. (010 331) 47 23 52 01
Types of train	AVE: high-speed train (Spanish: Tren de **A**lta **VE**locidad Talgo/Electrotrén: air-conditioned, well equipped long distance trains (diesel/electric, supplement) TAE/TER: express (diesel/electric, supplement) Exprés/Rápido: semi-fast (with restaurant/buffet) Semidirecto: fast stopping train Rápido Automotor: fast railcar Tranvia: local stopping train

RENFE operates the lowest tariff for rail travel in Western Europe. Children under 3 travel free, 3–7 year olds on national routes and 4–12 year olds on international routes travel at half fare. Early booking is necessary for international trains, sleepers and couchettes. Tickets can be purchased at a RENFE office or railway station where the ticket windows are separate for different routes.

Prices and reductions

On the so-called "blue days", which usually do not coincide with festivals, the day before a festival or holidays, tickets are half price.

Dias Azules

People living outside Spain are eligible to purchase a Tourist Card (*Tarjeta Turística*) which is valid for unlimited travel on all RENFE long distance trains, with the exception of the high speed AVE and Talgo 200. There are no supplements to pay other than sleeping facilities on overnight services. They can be bought for travel between 3 and 10 days within a two month period (first or second class; children under 12 half price). The card may be obtained at major railway stations in Spain on production of a passport.

Tourist Card

Special Tourist Trains

This luxuriously equipped train (with discothèque, video shows, bars, etc.) operates three three-day tours. The first runs from Seville to Córdoba, Granada and Málaga. The second trip, runs from Barcelona to Santiago de Compostela via Pamplona or Logrono, Burgos, Léon and Ponferrada, and the third takes in cities around Madrid – Avila, Salamanca, Toledo and Segovia. The fare for each of the three-day trips includes sightseeing tours and lunches, participation in fiestas and other events, and dinner, bed and breakfast.
Information about these trains can be obtained from RENFE offices.

Al-Andaluz

On Majorca railway enthusiasts will enjoy a trip on the old-world train which runs from Palma to Sóller, from which an equally nostalgic tram runs through orange and lemon groves to Puerto de Sóller.
Information from the station in Palma or from a Majorcan tourist office (see Information).

"Red Lightning"

Another nostalgic journey is from Madrid (Puerta de Atocha) to Aranjuez. Between May and October the "Tren de la Fresa", a locomotive from the Madrid railway museum pulls carriages dating from 1914 three times daily to Aranjuez.

"Strawberry train"

The Auto-Expreso service operates from Madrid to La Coruña, Bilbao, San Sebastian, Barcelona, Valencia, Alicante, Málaga, Algeciras and Cádiz.

Motorail

Restaurants

Restaurants serve lunch between about 1.30 and 3.30pm and dinner usually from 9 to 11 or 11.30pm. For a quick meal there are cafeterias, which are open throughout the day, often until 1am. For those who prefer something light in the evening there are the *tascas* – bars which serve a variety of appetising titbits (*tapas*) with drinks (see Food and Drink).
In the tourist resorts and larger towns there is a vast array of restaurants serving international cuisine. Original Spanish dishes are often found in simpler establishments away from the tourist hotels. The restaurants of the paradors can usually be recommended for typical regional cooking (see Hotels and Paradors).

Mealtimes

Selection of restaurants

The following list of restaurants have been recently mentioned in all the renowned food guides and, with the exception of the larger cities and tourist centres, are not excessively expensive.

Note

559

Restaurants

Aguilár de Campo El Cortes, El Puente, tel. 12 30 55

Albacete Nuestro Bar, Alcalde Conangla 102, tel. 22 72 15

Alcañiz Calpe, Ctra. de Zaragoza, tel. 83 07 32
Meseguer, Avda. Maestrazgo, tel. 83 10 02

Alcoy L'Escaleta, Avda. País Valencia, tel. 5 59 24 17
La Venta del Pilar, Valencia 118, Concentaina, tel. 5 59 23 25

Algeciras Pepe Moreno, Murillo, tel. 65 28 03

Alicante Dársena, Muelle del Puerto, tel. 5 20 75 89
El Delfín, Esplanada de España 12, tel. 5 21 49 11
Jumanillo, César Elguezábal 62, tel. 5 21 49 11
Nou Manolin, Villegas 4, tel. 5 20 03 68

Almería Bellavista, Urb. Bellavista, tel. 22 71 56

Andorra 1900, Unió 11, Las Escaldas, tel. 82 67 16
Casa Canut, Carlemany 107, Encamp, tel. 82 13 42
Celler d'En Toni, Verge del Pilar 4, Andorra la Vella, tel. 82 12 52
El Rusc, Ctra. d'Arinsal, Escaldaes-Engordany, tel. 83 82 00

Aranda de Duero Méson de la Villa, Plaza Mayor 3, tel. 50 10 25

Aranjuez Casa Pablo, Almibar 42, tel. 8 91 14 51

Arévalo La Pinalla, Teniente Garcia Fanjul 1, tel. 30 00 63

Astorga La Peseta, Plaza San Bartolomé 3, tel. 61 72 75

Ávila La Cochera, Avda. Portugal 47, tel. 21 37 89
Mesón del Rastro, Plaza del Rastro 1

Avilés La Serrana, La Fusta 9, tel. 56 58 40

Badajoz La Toja, Avda. Elvas, tel. 23 74 77

Baeza Juanito, Paseo Arca del Agua, tel. 27 09 09

Balearics Mallorca Bahía Maditerráneo, Paseo Marítimo 33, Palma de Mallorca, tel. 26 10 45
Koldo Royo, Paseo Marítimo 3, Palma de Mallorca, tel. 45 70 21
Porto Pí, Joan Miró 174, Palma de Mallorca, tel. 40 00 87
Xoriguer, Fábrica 60, Palma de Mallorca, tel. 28 83 32

Menorca Pilar, Forn 61, Máhon, tel. 36 68 17
Rocamar, Fonduco 32, Máhon, tel. 36 56 01

Ibiza I Ama-Lur, Ctra. de San Miguel km 2.3, Ciudad de Ibiza, tel. 31 45 54
Grill San Rafael, Ctra. de San Antonio km 6, Ciudad de Ibiza, tel. 31 44 75

Formentera Es Moll de Sal, Playa Illetas

Barcelona Beltxena, Mallorca 275, tel. 2 15 38 48
Botafumeiro, Gran de Gràcia 81, tel. 2 18 42 30
Casa Isidoro, Las Flores 12, tel. 2 41 11 39
El Dorado Petit, Dolors Monserdá, tel. 2 04 55 06
Finisterre, Avda. Diagonal 469, tel. 2 39 75 76
Florian, Bertrand i Serra 20, tel. 2 12 46 27
Neichel, Avda. de Pedralbes 16, tel. 2 03 84 08

La Odisea, Copons 7, tel. 3 02 36 92
Reno, Tuset 27, tel. 2 00 91 29
Vía Veneto, Ganduxer 10, tel. 2 00 70 24

Nietos de Martin Fierro, Ctra. de Salamanca km 68, tel. 40 40 08   **Béjar**

Don Luis, Avda. Dr. Orts Llorca (EDif. Zeus), tel. 5 85 46 73   **Benidorm**
Tiffany's, Avda. del Mediterráneo 11, tel. 5 85 44 68

Casanova, Plaza García Hermanos 15, tel. 77 06 03   **Betanzos**

Berneo, Ercilla 37, tel. 4 43 88 00   **Bilbao**
Goizeko Kabi, Particular de Estraunza 4, tel. 4 42 11 29
Gorrotxa, Alameda Urkijo 30 (Galerías Urkija), tel. 4 43 49 37
Guría, Gran Vía de López de Haro 66, tel. 4 41 05 43
Jolastoky, Avda. Leidako, tel. 4 69 30 31

Patacano, Paseo del Mar, tel. 33 00 02   **Blanes**

Virrey Palafox, Universidad 7, tel. 34 02 92   **El Burgo de Osma**

Fernán González, Calera 19, tel. 20 940 41   **Burgos**
Mesón del Cid, Plaza Santa Marma 8, tel. 20 87 15
Ojeda, Vitoria 5/Plaza de Calvo Sotelo, tel. 20 90 52

Atrio, Avda. de España 30, tel. 24 29 28   **Cáceres**
El Figón de Eustaquio, Plaza San Juan 12, tel. 2 4 81 94

1800, Paseo Marítimo 3, tel. 26 02 03   **Cádiz**
El Faro, San Félix 15, tel. 21 25 01
Mesón del Duque, Paseo Marítimo 12, tel. 28 10 87

Churchill, Léon y Castillo, Las Palmas de Gran Canaria, tel. 24 85 87   **Canary Islands**
Julio, La Naval 132, Las Palmas de Gran Canaria, tel. 27 10 39   Gran Canaria
Mesón La Paella, José María Durán 47, Las Palmas de Gran Canaria,
  tel. 27 16 40
Orangerie, Hotel Palm Beach, Maspalomas, tel. 76 29 20
El Pote, Pasaje José María Durán 4, Las Palmas de Gran Canaria,
  tel. 27 80 58
San Agustin Beach Club, Plaza Cocoteros, San Agustin, tel. 76 04 00

Méson El Reducto, Fred Olsen 1, Arrecife, tel. 81 63 69   Lanzarote
Picasso, José Betancourt 33, Arrecife, tel. 81 24 16

Amos, Poseta Tomás Morales, Santa Cruz de Tenerife, tel. 28 74 73   Tenerife
Coto de Antonio, Grl. Goded 13, Santa Cruz de Tenerife, tel. 27 21 05
La Magnolia, Ctra. de Botánico 5, Puerto de la Cruz
My Vaca y Yo, Cruz Verde 3, Puerto de la Cruz, tel. 38 52 47
Régulo, San Félipe 10, Puerto de la Cruz, tel. 38 45 06
La Riviera, Rambla Grl. Franco 155, Santa Cruz de Tenerife, tel. 27 58 12

Casa del Mar, frd Olsen 2, San Sebastián, tel. 87 12 19   Gomera

Chipi-Chipi, Ctra. de Velhoco, Santa Cruz de la Palma, tel. 41 10 24   La Palma

Noche y día parilla, San Francisco, Valverde, tel. 55 07 65   Hierro

Barlovento, Cuatro Santos 33, tel. 50 66 41   **Cartagena**
Los Habaneros, San Diego 60, tel. 50 25 50

Nina y Angelo, Paseo Buenavista 32, El Grao, tel. 23 92 92   **Castellón de la Plana**
Rafael, Churruca 26, El Grao, tel. 22 20 88

Restaurants

Ceuta
Casa Silva, Almirante Lobo 3, tel. 51 37 15

Ciudad Real
Miami Park, Ronda Ciruela 48, tel. 22 20 43

Ciudad Rodrigo
Estoril, Travesia Talavera 1, tel. 46 05 50

Córdoba
El Caballo Rojo, Cardenal Herrero 28, tel. 47 53 75
El Churrasco, Romero 16, tel. 29 08 19
Ciros, Paseo de la Victoria, tel. 29 04 64
Oscar, Plaza de Chirinos 8, tel. 47 75 17

La Coruña
Casa Pardo, Novoa Santos 15, tel. 28 71 78
Gallo de Oro, Arteixo, tel. 60 04 92
La Viña, Puente del Pasaje, tel. 28 08 54

Costa Brava
Bahía, Paseo del Mar 17, San Feliú de Guixols, tel. 32 02 19
Can Toni, Garrofers 54, San Feliú de Guixols, tel. 32 10 26
La Galiota, Narciso Monturiol 9, Cadaqués, tel. 25 81 87
La Gamba, Plaza San Pedro 1, Palamós, tel. 31 46 33
Hacienda El Bulli, Cala Montjoi, Rosas, tel. 25 76 51
Hispania, Real 54, Arenys de Mar, tel. 7 91 03 06
La Ilar, Ctra. Rosas–Figueras km 40, tel. 25 53 68
Portinyol, Puerto de Arenys de Mar, tel. 7 92 13 31
Santa Marta, Playa de Santa Cristina, tel. 36 49 04
Sa Punta, Bagur, tel. 63 64 10
Trias, Paseo del Mar, Palamós, tel. 31 41 00
El Trull, Cala Canyelles, Lloret de Mar, tel. 36 49 28

Cuenca
Casas Colgadas, Canónigos, tel. 22 08 76
Figón de Pedro, Cervantes 15, tel. 22 68 21

Denia
El Poblet, El Poblet, tel. 5 78 41 79
Mesón Troya, Abu Zeynán 3, tel. 5 78 14 31

Elche
La Finca, Ctra. Perleta km 1.7, tel. 5 45 60 07
Mesón El Granaino, José M. Buch 40, tel. 5 46 01 47

El Escorial
(San Lorenzo de El Escorial)
Charoles, Floridablanca 24, tel. 8 90 59 75
Parilla Príncipe, Floridablanca 6, tel. 8 90 16 11

Estella
La Cepa, Plaza de los Fueros 18, tel. 55 00 32

Estepona
La Alcaría de Ramos, Urb. El Paraiso, tel. 78 61 78

Figueras
Ampurdan, Antigua Ctra. de Francia, tel. 50 05 62
Duran, Lasauca 5, tel. 50 12 50

Fuengirola
Los Marinos I, Paseo Marítimo, Carvajal, tel. 47 62 91

Gandía
La Gamba, Ctra. Nazaret–Olivia, tel. 2 84 13 10

Gibraltar
El Patio, 4 Irish Town

Gijón
Casa Gerardo, N–632 km 79.5, Prendes, tel. 87 02 29
Casa Victor, Carmen 11, tel. 35 00 93
El Retiro, Begoña, tel. 35 00 30

Granada
La Alacena de las Monjas, Plaza Padre Suárez, tel. 22 40 28
Carmen de San Miguel, Plaza de Torres Bermejas, tel. 22 67 23
Horno de Santiago, Plaza de los Campos 8, tel. 22 34 76
Mirador de Morayma, Callejón de las Vascas, tel. 22 82 90
Ruta del Veleta, Ctra. de la Sierra 50, tel. 48 61 34

Casa Victor, Bardales 6, tel. 21 22 47
Horche, in Horche, tel. 29 01 96

Mesón del Cordero, Convento 11, tel. 36 71 31

Faisán de Oro, Adolfo Urioste 4, tel. 6 85 10 01
Baserri Maitea, Ctra. Guernica–Bermeo, Forua, tel. 6 85 34 08

Beethoven II, Santo Tomás 6, tel. 31 11 81

Las Candelas, Ctra. Punta Umbria, tel. 31 83 01
La Muralla, San Salvador 17, tel. 25 50 77

Navas, San Lorenzo 15, tel. 22 47 38
Las Torres, Maria Auxiliadora 3, tel. 22 82 13
Venta del Sotón, Ctra. de Pamplona, Esquedas, tel. 27 02 41

La Cocina Aragonesa, Cervantes 5, tel. 36 10 50
Gaston, Avda. Primo de Rivera 14, tel. 36 29 09

Mesón Vicente, Arco del Consuelo 1, tel. 26 28 16

El Bosque, Avda. Alcalde Alvaro Domecq 26, tel. 30 70 30
La Mesa Redonda, Manuel de la Quintana 3, tel. 34 00 69

Adonias Pozo, Santa Nonia 16, tel. 20 67 68
Casa Pozo, Plaza San Marcelo 15, tel. 22 30 39
Independencia, Independencia 4, tel. 25 47 52

Fonda del Nastasi, Ctra. de Huesca km 2.5, tel. 24 92 22
Forn del Nastasi, Salmerón 10, tel. 23 45 10
Moli de la Nora, Viallanueva de la Barca, tel. 19 00 17

Cachetero, Laurel 3, tel. 22 84 63
La Merced, Mayor 109, tel. 22 11 66
Mesón Lorenzo, Mayor 135, tel. 25 91 40

El Teatro, Plaza Colón 12, tel. 46 99 09

Alberto Cruz 4, tel. 22 83 10
La Barra, San Marcos 27, tel. 24 20 36

El Amparo, Puigcerdá 8, tel. 4 31 64 65
El Bodegón, Pinar 15, tel. 2 62 31 37
Casa Ciriaco, Mayor 84, tel. 2 48 50 66
El Cenador del Prado, Prado 4, tel. 4 29 15 61
Combarro, Reina Mercedes 12, tel. 2 54 78 15
Fortuny, Fortuny 34, tel. 3 08 32 67
Jaun de Alzate, Princesa 18, tel. 2 47 10 00
Jockey, Armador de los Ríos 6, tel. 4 19 10 03
Lúculo, Génova 19, tel. 4 19 40 29
O'Pazo, Reina Mercedes 20, tel. 2 53 23 23 33
Principe de Viana, Manuel de Falla 5, tel. 2 59 14 48
Zalacaín, Alvarez de Baena 4, tel. 2 61 48 40
   (top-class restaurant of international renown)

Antonio Martin, Paseo Marítimo 4, tel. 22 21 13
El Figeon, Cervantes, Ed. Horizonte, tel. 22 32 23
Refectorium I, Juan Sebastián Elcano 146, tel. 29 45 93

La Fonda, Santo Cristo 9, tel. 77 25 12
La Hacienda, Urb. Las Chapas, tel. 83 11 16
La Meridiana, Camino de la Cruz, tel. 77 61 90

Restaurants

Medinacelli
Duque de Medinaceli, N–II km 150, tel. 32 61 11

Medina del Campo
Madrid, Claudio Moyano 2, tel. 80 01 34

Melilla
Duala, Ctra. Alfonso XIII 63, tel. 68 36 29
Los Salazones, Conde Alcaudete 15, tel. 68 79 12

Mérida
Parador Via de la Plata, Plaza de la Constitución 3, tel. 31 38 00

Morella
Mesón del Pastor, Cuesta Jovani 5, tel. 16 02 49

Murcia
Hispano, Lucas 7, tel. 21 61 52
La Huertancia, Infantes 5, tel. 21 74 77
Rincón de Pepe, Apóstoles 34, tel. 21 22 49

Nerja
Casa Luque, Plaza Cavana 2, tel. 52 10 04
Rey Alfonso, Paseo Balcón de Europa, tel. 52 01 95

Orense
San Miguel, San Miguel 12, tel. 22 12 45
Martín Fierbo, Sáenz Díez 65, tel. 23 48 20

Oviedo
Casa Conrado, Argüelles 1, tel. 22 39 19
Casa Fermín, San Francisco 8, tel. 21 64 52
La Goleta, Covadonga 32, tel. 21 38 47

Palencia
Casa Damián, Martínez de Azcolitia 9, tel. 74 46 28
Gran San Bernardo, Avda. República Argentina 14, tel. 72 58 99

Pamplona
Hartza, Juan de Labrit 19, tel. 22 45 68
Josetxo, Plaza Príncipe de Viana 1, tel. 22 20 97
Sarasate, García Castañon 12, tel. 22 51 02

Plascencia
Alfonso VIII, Alfonso VIII 32, tel. 41 02 50

Ponferrada
Virgen de la Peña, in Congosto, tel. 46 71 02

Pontevedra
Doña Antonia, Soportales de la Herrería 9, tel. 84 72 74
Gallego, Gagos de Mendoza 2, tel. 86 10 28

Reus
Prim, Paseo Prim 3, tel. 31 57 52
On the Tarragona road, 1km/½mile south-east: Masia Típica Crusells

Ronda
Don Miguel, Villanueva 4, tel. 87 10 90
Pedro Romero, Virgen de la Paz 18, tel. 87 10 61

Sagunto
L'Armeler, Subida Castillo 44, tel. 2 66 43 82

Salamanca
El Candil II, Plaza de la Reina 1, tel. 21 90 87
Chez Victor, Espoz y Mina 26, tel. 21 31 23 (French cuisine)
Río Chico, Plaza de Ejército 4, tel. 24 18 78
Río de la Plata, Plaza del Peso 1, tel. 21 90 05

San Sebastián
Akelarre, Barrio de Igueldo, tel. 21 20 52
Arzak, Alto de Miracruz 21, tel. 27 84 65 (exclusive)
Chomin, Avda. Infanta Beatriz, tel. 21 07 05
Nicolasa, Aldamar 4, tel. 42 17 62
Patxiku Kintana, San Jerónimo 22, tel. 42 63 99

Santander
Bar del Puerto, Hernán Cortes 63, tel. 21 30 01
Cañada, Gomez Oreña 15, tel. 31 49 25
Rhin, Plaza Italia, tel. 27 30 34
La Sardina, Doctor Fleming 3, tel. 27 10 35

Anexo Vilas, Avda. Villagarcía 21, tel. 59 83 87
Don Gaiferos, Rúa nova 23, tel. 58 38 94
Vilas, Rosalía de Castro 88, tel. 59 10 00

Altamira, Cantón 1, tel. 81 80 25

Mesón El Peregrino, Zumalacárregui 18, tel. 34 02 02

La Cocina de Segovia, Paseo Ezéquiel González 24, tel. 43 64 62
Mesón de Cándido, Plaza Azoguejo 5, tel. 42 81 02
Mesón Duque, Cervantes 12, tel. 43 05 37

El Castell, Ctra. Lérida–Puigcerdá km 129, tel. 35 07 04

Florencia, Avenida Eduardo Dato 49–51, tel. 4 57 00 40
San Marco, Cuna 6, tel. 4 21 24 40
La Dorada, Virgen del Aguasantas, tel. 4 45 51 00
Bailén 14, Bailén 34, tel. 4 22 52 81
Don Raimundo, Argote de Molina 26, tel. 4 22 33 55

El Motor, Calvo Sotelo 12, tel. 39 03 43

La Masa, Paseo Vilanova, tel. 8 94 10 76

Maroto, Paseo del Espolón 20, tel. 22 40 86

Tubal, Plaza de Navarra 2, tel. 70 08 52

Sol Ric, Via Augusta 227, tel. 23 20 32
Verdaguer, San Agustin 19, tel. 23 44 33

El Celler, Gaudi 2, Matadepera, tel. 7 87 08 57

Kalanchoe, Avda. de Sagunto 39, tel. 60 01 03
La Menta, Bartolomé Estaban 10, tel. 60 75 32

Asador Adolfo, La Granada 6, tel. 22 73 21
Casa Aurelio, Singoga 6, tel. 22 20 97
Hostal del Cardenal, Paseo Recaredo, tel. 22 08 62

Julian, Santa Clara 6, tel. 67 14 17

El Torreón, Dimas Rodriguez 11, tel. 77 15 12

Casa Guaquin, Carmen 37, La Carihuela, tel. 38 45 30
María, Eurosol 25, tel. 38 95 25

Hostal Pizarro, Plaza Mayor 13, tel. 32 02 55

Morase, Paseo de Invierno 2, tel. 82 17 00

Galicia, Avda. González Besada 8, tel. 60 00 01

Pintor Orbaneja, Virgen de Guadalupe, tel. 75 90 98

Eladio, Chiva 40, tel. 3 26 22 44
El Estimat, Avda. Neptuno 16–18, tel. 3 71 10 18
El Gourmet, Tapuígrafo Martí 3, tel. 3 74 50 71
La Hacienda, Navarro Reverter 12, tel. 3 73 18 59
Marísquería Civera, Lérida 11, tel. 3 47 59 11
El Timonel, Felix Pizcueta 13, tel. 3 52 63 00

Shopping, Souvenirs

Valladolid	La Fragua, Paseo de Zorrilla 10, tel. 33 71 02 Mesón Cervantes, Del Rastro 6, tel. 30 61 38 Mesón Panero, Marina Escobar 1, tel. 30 16 73
Vich	La Taula, Plaza Don Miguel de Clariana 4, tel. 8 86 32 29
Vigo	La Oca, Purificación Saavedra 8, tel. 37 12 55 Puesto Piloto Alcabre, Avda. Atlántico 194, tel. 29 79 75 Sibaris, Garcia Barbón 168, tel. 22 15 26
Vilanueva y Geltrú	Peixerot, Passeig Maritim 56, tel. 8 15 06 25 Bernard et Marguerite, Ramón Llull 4, tel. 8 15 56 04 (French cuisine)
Vitoria	Dos Hermanas, Madre Vedruna 10, tel. 13 48 33 Ikea, Castilla 27, tel. 14 47 47 El Portalón, Correría 151, tel. 14 27 55
Zamora	Paris, Avda. de Portugal 14, tel. 51 43 25 Rey Don Sancho II, Plaza de la Marina Española, tel. 52 60 54
Zaragoza	Asador Goyesco, Manuel Lasala 44, tel. 35 68 71 Los Borrachos, Paseo Sagasta 64, tel. 27 50 36 Gayarre, Ctra. del Aeropuerto km 4.3, tel. 34 43 86 Txalupa, Fernando el Católico 62, tel. 56 61 70

Bars

Most bars provide *tapas* (see Food and Drink) as an alternative to a substantial meal late in the evening. The bar is one of the focal points of life in Spain and there are several to be found in every village. People meet here for breakfast, during the lunchbreak, to play dominoes and drink a coffee, beer, *fino* or anise in the afternoon, and in the evening it is the custom to visit different bars sampling the tapas. *Bocadillos*, long rolls filled with ham, cheese or sausage, and sandwiches are also available.

Shopping, Souvenirs

Spanish handicrafts have a long tradition, and many articles are still produced following old models, as well as new designs.

Markets	Visitors will find plenty to interest them in a stroll through the various antique and flea markets (for times, enquire at local tourist office) and in the market halls to be found in all towns of any size.
Carpets	Hand-woven carpets in beautiful colours are made particularly in Cáceres, Granada and Murcia.
Copperware	Copper jugs come mainly from Guadalupe and Granada.
Discs, books, posters, postcards	Records or tapes of Spanish folk music and illustrated books on Spain make attractive souvenirs. The Mercado San Antonio in Barcelona is a mine of treasure trove in the form of old books, posters and postcards.
Esparto grass	Attractive articles in esparto grass are produced in Murcia.
Fabrics	Also very attractive are articles of clothing, designed by local couturiers and mostly hand-made, from the island of Ibiza.
Glass	There are numerous glassworks, where visitors can see glass-blowers at work, on Majorca and elsewhere in Spain.

The jewellery produced in Barcelona's municipal centre of arts and crafts, the Escola Massana, has an international reputation. The materials used include plastics, copper and steel, matt-finished silver and gold, thin wire and much else.	Jewellery

Toledo is famed for its gold inlay work.

The artificial pearls produced in the factories of Manacor on Majorca can scarcely be distinguished from real ones.

The main lace-making centres are Camariñas (pillow lace), Seville (mantillas), Granada, Almagro and the Canaries (the lace of Vilaflor being particularly fine). The Canaries also produce attractive articles (tablecloths, place mats and items of clothing) decorated with drawn-thread embroidery.   Lace, embroidery

Good modern leather goods are found mainly in Andalusia, Catalonia and the Balearics (e.g. large leather and shoe factories at Inca on Majorca; shoes particularly on Minorca), traditional products in Córdoba ("cordovan leather").   Leather goods

Pottery (tableware, decorative plates) can be bought all over Spain, and almost every region has its own distinctive style. Talavera de la Reina still holds mainly to traditional forms (including particularly tiles), while Sargadelos in Galicia is the leading place for avantgarde designs. Majorca is famed for its majolica, Manises in Valencia province for ware with a metallic glaze.   Pottery

Spanish sweets are a popular buy – the pastries (*ensaimadas*) and candied fruit of Majorca, the *turrón* (nougat) of Alicante, confections from Pamplona and Logroño, the truffle chocolates of Vitoria and the *yemas de Santa Teresa* (candied yolk of egg) of Ávila.   Sweets

Wines and spirits are also good buys – not only the native Spanish products but international brands produced in Spain.   Wines and spirits

Traditional Spanish furniture is still made, particularly in Valencia. Castile and León have developed their own styles.   Wood furniture

Wrought-iron work is produced in Castile, and also in Seville and Logroño, damascene steel articles in Toledo ("Toledo blades") and Eibar, small metal articles (knives, daggers) in Albacete.   Wrought-iron work, weapons

Taxis

Taxis can either be hailed in the street or picked up at a taxi rank.

Fares vary from place to place, but are lower than in most other European countries. Most taxis have meters. If a taxi has no meter, ask the driver what the fare is or – particularly for a journey across country – negotiate the fare before getting in.   Fares

There are additional charges for trips at night, weekends and public holidays, waiting time, journeys to the airport, seaport or station, luggage and domestic pets (ask for receipt).

Time

From October to March mainland Spain and the Balearics are on Central European Time, one hour ahead of GMT. In summer (last Sunday of March to last Sunday of September) Summer Time is in force, and Spain is then two hours ahead of GMT.   Mainland and the Balearics

Canaries · From October to March the Canaries are on Western European Time (i.e. GMT). From the last Sunday of March to the last Sunday of September Summer Time is in force (GMT + 1).

Tipping

Although hotel and restaurant bills include a charge for service (*servicio*), it is customary to leave waiters (*camareros*) an additional 5–10% of the bill, and to give chambermaids (*camareras* or *muchachas*), porters and hotel pages (*mozos*) a suitable tip (*propina*).

Guides, ushers or usherettes in cinemas, theatres and bullrings and taxi-drivers also expect a small tip.

Travel Documents

Personal papers · Visitors from the United Kingdom, the Commonwealth and the United States require only a valid passport for entry to Spain; no visa is required for a stay of up to 90 days provided that they are not taking up any employment. An extension of stay can be granted by the police authorities in Spain. Children under 16 may be entered on a parent's passport. Visitors may be requested to show visible means of support for their stay in Spain; a minimum of 5,000 pesetas per day or a total of 50,000 pesetas.

Car papers · The pink EU-type driving licence (as currently issued in Britain) is acceptable in Spain, otherwise a national driving licence (accompanied by a translation) or an international driving permit is required. The car's registration document is also obligatory.

Cars must display an oval nationality plate.

An international insurance certificate ("green card") is required, and a bail bond (issued by a motoring organisation or an insurance company along with the green card) should also be taken out, since in the event of an accident the car involved may be impounded pending payment of bail.

See also Motoring.

When to Go

The best times of year for a visit to Spain are spring and autumn, from about mid March to the beginning of June and from the beginning of September to the beginning of November (in northern Spain to the beginning of October).

Summer · Summer is the best time to go to the Atlantic coastal regions of northern and north-western Spain, since at other times of year there may be a good deal of rain. The seaside resorts on the south-eastern coast and in the Balearics and the hill resorts in the Pyrenees, the Sierra de Guadarrama and the Sierra Nevada are much frequented in summer; and the coastal resorts, with sea breezes mitigating the heat of summer, tend to be particularly busy during the school holidays (July–August). The months of July and August are almost unbearably hot in the interior of the country.

Autumn · In the interior of the Iberian peninsula the weather in autumn is usually settled, but much of the land is parched after the summer heat.

Winter · For winter sports and winter holidays on the south and south-east coasts the best months are December, January and February. In recent years the Balearics and the Mediterranean coast have become popular with people able to take a long winter holiday of several weeks or even months.

The Canaries, with their mild and equable climate, can be visited at any time of year. Canaries

Many hotels offer attractive cheap rates outside the main holiday season.

In mountain areas and on the Atlantic coast, even in summer, visitors should take stout footwear, protection from rain and a thick pullover or other warm clothing.

See Facts and Figures, Climate Climate

Wine

Although Spain, with 1.6 million ha/4 million acres has more land under vines than any other country in the world, it has not enjoyed an international reputation compared with French or Italian wines. More than two thirds of the wines produced are table wines (*vino de mesa*) with a shelf life of only two years. Only about a third of Spanish wines are quality wines (*domación de origen, D.O.*). Andalusian sherry, however, is in a class of its own.

See also Food and Drink

The Language of the Wine Label

White	Blanco
A cellar in which wine is made, stored and sometimes drunk	Bodega
Wine-making cooperative	Bodega cooperativa
Type of vine or grape	Cepa
Light red wine	Clarete
Harvest; (with year) vintage	Cosecha
Grown and bottled by . . .	Criado y embotellado por . . .
Sweet	Dulce
Made and aged by . . .	Elaborado y añejado por . . .
Estate bottled	Embotellado/ Engarrafado
Sparkling	Espumoso
Fine (a term applied to the driest sherry)	Fino
Mature quality wine	Reserva
Rosé	Rosado
Dry	Seco
Red	Tinto
Grape harvest; (with year) vintage	Vendimia

Wine

Viña, viñedo	Vineyard
Vino corriente	Wine for everyday drinking (usually not bottled)
Vino de cosecha propria	A wine made by the owner of the vineyard
Vino de mesa	Table wine

Wine-Producing Areas in Spain

Galicia

Ribeiro: centre of the Galician wine-growing region on the Río Miña around Ribadavia; light acidy white wines and vigorous red wines.

Monterrey: on the Río Támega in the south of Orense province; heavy red and white wines (14% alcohol).

Valdeorras: on the Río Sil in the eastern part of Orense province; dry white wines and fruity red wines which need to be drunk young.

Old Castille and León

Ribera del Duero: on the Río Duero in the province of Valladolid and Burgos;
mainly red and rosé wines to be laid down.

Rueda: in the south of Valladolid province; almost exclusively white table and dessert wines.

La Rioja

The best known Spanish wine after sherry, it can be white, red or rosé.

Rioja alavesa: north of the Río Ebro, mainly excellent fruity full-bodied red wines.

Wine-producing Areas in Spain

Rioja alta: around Haro; these wines are considered by connoisseurs to be even better than the rioja alavesas.

Rioja baja: powerful wines but not of the same quality as the other two regions with which they are often blended.

Navarra

Powerful red and white wines are produced in the areas of Valdizarbe, Tierra Estella, Baja Montaña, Ribera Alta and Ribera Baja. A speciality is the young, piquant Txacoliñ.

Aragón

Campo de Borja: west of Zaragoza; heavy red and rosé wines (15–16% alcohol).

Cariñera: in the south of Zaragoza province; deep dark red wines, dry rosé and white wines, dessert wines.

Somontaño: Huesca province; light red wines.

Catalonia

Alella: very small valley north of Barcelona; chiefly white wines.

Ampurdán-Costa Brava: at the foot of the Pyrenees; sparkling and rosé wines.

Conca de Barberá: west of Vilafranca de Penedes; sparkling wines

Penedés: south-west of Barcelona; 90% of all Spanish sparkling wines come from here, as well as strong red wines from the Bajo Penedés on the Mediterranean coast and white table wines.

Priorato: west of Tarragona; very strong deep red wines, fortified sherry-like white wines

Tarragona: red and white mass-produced wines.

Terra alta: in the south-west of Catalonia; average full-bodied red and white wines.

Castille-La Mancha

The largest wine region in Spain producing a third of all Spanish wines.

Almansa: in the south-west of Albacete province; dark, strong red wines.

La Mancha: the largest single wine-growing region, mainly in the province of Ciudad Real; nondescript white wines (13–14% alcohol) which are mostly blended or distilled.

Manchuela: mass-produced wines without any distinguishing characteristics.

Méntrida: south-west of Madrid; medium dry red and rosé wines with a high alcohol content (13–14%).

Valdepeñas: in the south of Ciudad Real province; mainly white wines to be drunk young.

Extramadura

Tierra de Barros: around Almendralejo in the province of Badajoz; dry, powerful white wines, aromatic red wines from Salvatierra de los Barros.

Huelva

Dessert and aperitif wines resembling sherry, but not of the same standard; everyday wines.

Jerez

In the triangle between Jerez de la Frontera, Sanlúcar de Barrameda and El Puerto de Santa Maria the world-famous sherry is produced by the Solera method. Sherries are not vintage wines but blends of wines from different vintages but of similar character. After harvesting, the grapes are dried in the sun for several days, depending on the variety, before pressing. The young wine is fortified with brandy to an alcohol level of 15–18% and drawn off into oak casks which are filled only four-fifths full. After the first fermentation the wines are distributed among the so-called *soleras* according to their type. These consist usually of five rows of barrels lying on top of each other of wines of the same quality. The oldest wine is on the bottom row, the youngest wine is on the top row. Wine is only drawn off from the bottom row and this is replaced with wine from the next row which is in turn replaced by wine from the third row and so on. This process ensures that the quality and character of the wine remains the same over several years.

Wine

Sherry is drunk from *copitas*, small glasses which taper towards the brim, allowing the aroma to develop fully. Finos and amontillados are served ice cold; only the sweet wines are served at room temperature. A small glass of fino can be drunk on any occasion and not just as an aperitif.

Fino is a pale yellow, extremely dry, slightly acidy and lively wine with an alcohol content of 15–17%; it is the most typical of sherries and is drunk the most. Amontillado, named after wine from Montilla, is a more mature fino, amber in colour and softer but still with an alcohol content of 16–18%. Manzanilla is an excellent, very light, dry fino from the bodeagas of Sanlúcar de Barrameda.

Oloroso is a dark golden colour. It can be slightly dry to slightly sweet and has a distinctive nutty aroma. The alcohol content is 18–20% Varieties include Raya, not a particularly good quality and Palo Cortado, which is difficult to find.

Cream sherries are the sweetest and heaviest sherries made by blending oloroso and a sweet wine (often Muscatel). They contain up to 20% alcohol.

Malaga

On the Costa del Sol around Malaga and Estepona: classical dessert wines. Malaga wines are also produced by the Solera method; in order to increase their sweetness grape juice is added.

The most famous is the Dulce Color, of a dark amber colour and an alcohol content of 15–23%. Equally popular is the dark, fruity Muscatel with 15–20% alcohol. The light red Pedro Ximénez (16–20% alcohol) comes from just one grape variety. The palest and rarest Málaga is the Blanco Seco, drier and lower in alcohol content than the usual málagas. Lágrima, a golden-coloured wine, is the most expensive. The grapes are not pressed, the grape juice is extracted by the weight of the grapes alone.

Montilla-Moriles

In the south of the province of Córdoba: excellent aperitif and dessert wines which are blended by the Solera method but in large clay jugs, *tijanas*, instead of oak barrels. The wine-growers from Montilla-Moriles produce the same wines as their colleageus from Jerez.

Index

Index

Imprint

158 colour photographs
26 general maps, 50 town plans, 9 ground plans, 1 large map of Spain

Text: Rosemarie Arnold, Birgit Borowski, Rainer Eisenschmid, Prof. Hans-Dieter Haas, Prof. Wolfgang Hassenpflug, Peter M. Nahm, Christine Wessely and Vera Beck

Editorial work: Baedeker Stuttgart (Rainer Eisenschmid)

English language edition: Alec Court

Design and layout: Creativ GmbH Ulrich Kolb, Leutenbach; Baedeker Redaktion

General direction: Dr Peter Baumgarten, Baedeker Stuttgart

Cartography: Gert Oberländer, Munich; Christoph Gallus, Hohberg; Mairs Geographischer Verlag, Ostfildern-Kemnat (large map of Spain)

English translation: James Hogarth

Revision and additional translation: Julie Waller

Source of illustrations: Bader, Baedeker-Archiv, Bavaria, Bohnacker, Borowski, Brödel, Cabos, dpa, Dieterich, Eisenschmid, FOAT, Historia-Photo, Klu, Kruska-Bludszat, Ludwig, Miguel-Peribáñez, Nahm, Pfaffinger, Rudolph, SEAT Deutschland, Seitz, Sindicat d'Iniciativa Andorra la Vella, Spanish National Tourist Office, Sperber, Stetter, Szerelmy, Ullstein, Würth, ZEFA.

2nd English edition 1996

©Baedeker Stuttgart
Original German edition 1994

©1996 Jarrold and Sons Limited
English language edition worldwide

©1996 The Automobile Association
United Kingdom and Ireland

Published in the United States by:
Macmillan Travel
A Simon & Schuster Macmillan Company
1633 Broadway
New York, NY 10019–6785

Macmillan is a registered trademark of Macmillan, Inc.

Distributed in the United Kingdom by the Publishing Division of the Automobile Association, Fanum House, Basingstoke, Hampshire RG21 2EA

The name *Baedeker* is a registered trade mark

A CIP catalogue record of this book is available from the British Library

Licensed user:
Mairs Geographischer Verlag GmbH & Co.,
Ostfildern-Kemnat bei Stuttgart

Printed in Italy by G. Canale & C.S.p.A – Borgaro T.se –Turin

ISBN 0–02–860683–3 USA and Canada
       0 7495 1241 5 UK